REFERENCE
DO NOT REMOVE
FROM LIBRARY

WITHDRAWN FROM
TSC LIBRARY

LIBRARY
COMMUNITY COLLEGE

C0-ARR-013

EXTREMIST GROUPS

Information
for Students

EXTREMIST GROUPS

Information
for Students

VOLUME 2: L-Z

THOMSON
GALE

Detroit • New York • San Francisco • San Diego • New Haven, Conn. • Waterville, Maine • London • Munich

EXTREMIST GROUPS: INFORMATION FOR STUDENTS: VOLUME 2

Produced by Thomson Gale Editorial and Production Staff

© 2006 by Thomson Gale, a part of The Thomson Corporation.

Thomson and Star Logo are trademarks and Gale is a registered trademark used herein under license.

For more information, contact
Thomson Gale
27500 Drake Rd.
Farmington Hills, MI 48331-3535
Or you can visit our internet site at
http://www.gale.com

ALL RIGHTS RESERVED
No part of this work covered by the copyright herein may be reproduced or used in any form or by any means—graphic, electronic, or mechanical, including photocopying, recording, taping, Web distribution, or information storage retrieval systems—without the written permission of the publisher.

This publication is a creative work fully protected by all applicable copyright laws, as well as by misappropriation, trade secret, unfair competition, and other applicable laws. The authors and editors of this work have added value to the underlying factual material herein through one or more of the following: unique and original selection, coordination, expression, arrangement, and classification of the information.

For permission to use material from the product, submit your request via the Web at http://www.gale-edit.com/permissions, or you may download our Permissions Request form and submit your request by fax or mail to:

Permissions Department
Thomson Gale
27500 Drake Rd.
Farmington Hills, MI 48331-3535
Permissions Hotline:
248-699-8006 or 800-877-4253, ext. 8006
Fax 248-699-8074 or 800-762-4058

Since this page cannot legibly accommodate all copyright notices, the acknowledgments constitute an extension of the copyright notice.

While every effort has been made to secure permission to reprint material and to ensure the reliability of the information presented in this publication, Thomson Gale neither guarantees the accuracy of the data contained herein nor assumes any responsibility for errors, omissions or discrepancies. Thomson Gale accepts no payment for listing; and inclusion in the publication of any organization, agency, institution, publication, service, or individual does not imply endorsement of the editors or publisher. Errors brought to the attention of the publisher and verified to the satisfaction of the publisher will be corrected in future editions.

LIBRARY OF CONGRESS CATALOGING-IN-PUBLICATION DATA

Extremist groups : information for students.
   p. cm.
   Includes bibliographical references and index.
   ISBN 1-4144-0345-3 (hardcover : alk. paper)
   1. Radicals–Encyclopedias. 2. Radicalism–Encyclopedias. 3. Terrorists–Encyclopedias.
4. Terrorism–Encyclopedias.

   HN90.R3.E975 2006
   322.4'203–dc22
                                          2005035599

British Library Cataloguing-in-Publication Data
A catalogue record for this book is available from the British Library.
ISBN 1-4144-1120-0 (vol. 2)

This title is also available as an e-book.
ISBN 1414404832
Contact your Thomson Gale sales representative for ordering information.

Printed in the United States of America
10 9 8 7 6 5 4 3 2 1

Table of Contents

VOLUME 1

A

VOLUME 2

Introduction

Extremist Groups: Information for Students is designed to provide key facts and insight into the history, philosophy, and motivations driving 150 extremist organizations. Although some groups are included for historical perspective, the vast majority are active in some form today. The groups profiled range from local political activist and special-interest groups to international terrorist organizations.

What constitutes extremism is usually contentious and often a matter of cultural or political perspective. Some groups actually admit and embrace their extremism as justifiable toward accomplishment of their agenda or goals. Others work hard to present themselves as more mainstream or "activist" groups. Although many extremist attitudes and acts are seemingly indefensible to a large segment of society, it is also fair to note that the charge of "extremism" is an often-used label applied by opponents in order to marginalize or dismiss an organization's philosophical goals.

Consider the similarities and differences in the use of the word "extremists" in the following quotes:

> What is objectionable, what is dangerous about extremists, is not that they are extreme, but that they are intolerant. The evil is not what they say about their cause, but what they say about their opponents. *Robert F. Kennedy*

> The question is not whether we will be extremists, but what kind of extremists we will be ... The nation and the world are in dire need of creative extremists. *Martin Luther King, Jr.*

Clearly these contrasting uses show that the problems of defining extremism dwarf those encountered with other problematic definitions related to "terrorism" or "hate groups," and can at times mimic those encountered for "activist" or "radical groups". For example, all terrorist groups are extremist groups, but the reverse is certainly not true. The vast majority of extremist groups are not terrorist groups. Even if some members engage in violence, most groups can not be easily categorized as terrorist groups because the violent actions associated with them are often those of a disturbed individual or smaller subgroup working under the same philosophical umbrella.

Accordingly, without an accepted scholarly or even popular definition of "extremism" the editors faced difficult choices. Violence or advocacy of violence was always qualifying, but another criteria applied to the selection of non-terrorist, nonviolent groups was whether the group's tactics were not those generally endorsed or used by the majority of groups with similar goals. Some groups operate so far outside the pale of generally accepted morality, ethics, and historical fact that their inclusion as extremist groups was warranted simply based upon rhetoric. Groups that engaged in the loftier types of positive change extremism, were not, conversely, included.

With literally thousands of potential candidate groups, the editorial focus narrowed to including those groups that could best represent the broad spectrum and global diversity of agendas and tactics. The editors, additionally, sought to provide an overview of the variety of responses to extremist groups and the efforts of government and civilian efforts to quash or counter these groups.

Extremist Groups: Information for Students seeks to give readers the basic tools and information to form their own judgments regarding the groups and philosophies examined herein. In an era where news, fact, "spin," and opinion often too easily commingle, *Extremist Groups: Information for Students* should provide a foundation for further critical reading. By offering global perspectives from an international staff of researchers, we intend that *Extremist Groups: Information for Students* will challenge readers—not necessarily to agree with all the definitions, labels, and assertions contained herein, but rather to form their own opinions about what constitutes extremism.

ADVISORS AND CONTRIBUTORS

While compiling this volume, the editors relied upon the expertise and contributions of an experienced and internationally distributed research staff composed of multilingual scholars, researchers, journalists, and writers. In the vast majority of cases, researchers, writers, and advisors were based in the countries or regions in which the extremist groups listed in this book principally operate.

The editors gratefully acknowledge and extend deep thanks to the editors, imaging, and permissions teams at Thomson Gale for their patience and counsel in handling both content and publishing issues related to this project.

The Editors
Paris
December, 2005

About the Book

Each entry in *Extremist Groups: Information For Students* contains the following six elements:

Overview: Provides a brief overview of the subject of the entry.

History: Provides the background and history of the group, including its origins and the individuals associated with the development and organization of the group.

Philosophy and Tactics: Provides an overview of the philosophy of the group and how that philosophy is implemented by the group to bring about change.

Other Perspectives: Provides an overview of reactions to the group by governments, individuals, or other groups.

Summary: Provides a brief summary of the groups' leaders, governing philosophy, and actions.

Sources: Provides a list of sources consulted or cited within the entry.

The first page of each entry includes quick "at a glance" information about the basics of the organization, such as its leaders, the year it was established, and the estimated size of the group. In addition, most entries feature sidebars with supplemental information, including short biographies of the group's leadership, key events in the history of the group, and primary source excerpts about the group and its activities. Photographs showing members of the group or the results of the group's activities are found in most entries.

When the only verifiable or attributable source of information for an entry comes from documents or information provided by a governmental organization (e.g., the U.S. Department of State), the editors endeavored to carefully note when the language used and perspective offered was that of a governmental organization.

Acknowledgements

The editors wish to thank the copyright holders of the excerpted criticism included in this volume and the permissions managers of many book and magazine publishing companies for assisting us in securing reproduction rights. We are also grateful to the staffs of the Detroit Public Library, the Library of Congress, the University of Detroit Mercy Library, Wayne State University Purdy/Kresge Library Complex, and the University of Michigan Libraries for making their resources available to us. Following is a list of the copyright holders who have granted us permission to reproduce material in this volume of EGIS. Every effort has been made to trace copyright, but if omissions have been made, please let us know.

Copyrighted excerpts were reproduced from the following periodicals:

BBC News, October 30, 1998; April 23, 1999; May 2, 2000; March 31, 2001; May 7, 2002; June 22, 2002; December 8, 2002; December 18, 2002; December 8, 2003; June 11, 2004; August 13, 2004; December 27, 2004; January 4, 2005; June 18, 2005; July 7, 2005; September 16, 2005; September 26, 2005. © BBC MMV. All reproduced by permission from BBC News at bbcnews.com.-*New York Times,* September 25, 2005. Copyright 2005 The Associated Press. All rights reserved. Reprinted with permission of the Associated Press./ March 11, 1986; November 29, 1987; December 8, 1988; June 27, 1993; December 17, 1993; June 16, 2002; February 5, 2004; March 11, 2005; September 2, 2005. Copyright © 1986, 1987, 1988, 1993, 2002, 2004, 2005 by The New York Times Co. All reprinted by permission.-Southern Poverty Law Center, summer, 1998; fall, 1998; summer, 1999; fall, 2000; summer, 2001; fall, 2001; winter, 2002; fall, 2002; winter, 2003; fall, 2003; spring, 2004; summer, 2004; summer, 2005. © Copyright 1998, 1999, 2000, 2001, 2002, 2003, 2004, 2005 Southern Poverty Law Center. All reproduced by permission.

Photographs and illustrations were received from the following sources:

Activists from both sides of the abortion issue on the steps of the federal courthouse, New York, New York, July 16, 1992, photograph. AP/Wide World Photos.-African National Congress supporter takes cover from gunfire alongside South African National Defense Force members, Umlazi township, South Africa, February 25, 1996, photograph by Joao Silva. AP/Wide World Photos.-Afrikaner Resistance Movement members lie dead in Mafikeng street, Mmabatho, South Africa, March 11, 1994, photograph by David Brauchli. AP/Wide World Photos.-Afrikaner Resistance Movement protestors and police in a chaotic clash, Ventersdorp, Transvaal, South

Africa, 1991, photograph. © Ian Berry/Magnum Photos.-Akhil Bharatiya Vidyarthi Parishad members during a rally opposing Sonia Gandhi becoming India's first foreign-born prime minister, Bombay, India, May 17, 2004, photograph. AP/Wide World Photos.-Al Aqsa Martyrs Brigades shoot in the air during a rally, Nablus, August 5, 2004, photograph by Nasser Ishtayeh. AP/Wide World Photos.-Al Jamaa Islamiye members demonstrate in support of Osama bin Laden, Tripoli, Lebanon, October 12, 2001, photograph. Courtney Kealy/Getty Images.-Al-Gamaa al-Islamiyya's twelve leaders, Cairo, June 21, 2002, photograph. AP/Wide World Photos.-Al-Ghozi, Fathur Rohman, suspected Indonesian terrorist, Mainla, Philippines, January 19, 2002, photograph by Ed Wray. AP/Wide World Photos.-Al-Masri, Sheikh Abu Hamza, speaks at the 2nd Conference of the Islamic Revival Movement, London, February 26, 1999, photograph. Gerry Penny/AFP/Getty Images.-Animal rights protester is held down by Arkansas police during a demonstration, October 29, 2001, photograph by Danny Johnston. AP/Wide World Photos.-Animal rights protestor outside the gates of a Huntingdon Life Sciences laboratory, Eye, Suffolk, UK, photograph. Philippe Hays/Peter Arnold, Inc.-Anti-abortion activists demonstration, Washington, D. C., January 22, 2003, photograph. AP/Wide World Photos.-Anti-fur activists graffiti, photograph. Robert Gumpert/Alamy.-Arafat, Yasser, mural liberating his people, Jericho, 1995, photograph. © Abbas/Magnum Photos.-Armed Palestinians kneel in prayer, Gaza City, 2004, photograph. © Abbas/Magnum Photos.-Aryan Nation march, Idaho, 1998, photograph. © Donovan Wylie/Magnum Photos.-Aryan National Alliance members, Coeur d'Alene, Idaho, October 23, 2000, photograph by Tom Davenport. AP/Wide World Photos.-Aryan Nations members with Christian Identity Minister Johnathan Williams, Alabama, September 18, 2004, photograph. David S. Holloway/Getty Images.-Aryan Republican Army, photograph. AP/Wide World Photos.-Assad, Bashar, Syrian President meets with the leaders of ten Damascus-based Palestinian radical organizations, September 10, 2005, photograph. Sana/EPA/Landov.-Azhar, Maulana Massod, leader of the Pakistani Jaish-e-Mohammad terrorist group, Islamabad, Pakistan, August 26, 2001, photograph. Mian Khursheed/Reuters/Landov.-Barboza, Esteban, a rondero, Huantam, Ayacucho, Peru, July 25, 2003, photograph by Martin Mejia. AP/Wide World Photos.-Bari, Judi, photograph by Paul Sakuma. AP/Wide World Photos.-Begin, Menahem, leader of the Irgun Party, Tel-Aviv, Israel, November, 1950, photograph. © Robert Capa © 2001 Cornell Capa/Magnum Photos.-bin Laden, Osama, Al-Qaida leader, with his deputy Ayman al-Zawahri, September 10, 2003, photograph. AP/Wide World Photos.-Black, Don, Ku Klux Klan grand wizard, New Orleans, Louisiana, May 14, 1981, photograph. AP/Wide World Photos.-Bo Gritz, James, Randy Weaver, and William Goehler, Freemen organization supporters, Brussett, Montana, April, 1996, photograph by James Woodcock. AP/Wide World Photos.-Bodies of policemen killed in an ambush by Shining Path guerrillas, Huallaga valley, Tingo Maria, Peru, February 20, 2005, photograph by EPENSA. AP/Wide World Photos.-British National Party street rally, Bethnal Green, London, photograph. David Hoffman Photo Library/Alamy.-Carabinieri police officer patrols Venice courthouse, near Rialto bridge where a bomb exploded, August 9, 2001, photograph by Francesco Proietti. AP/Wide World Photos.-Carette, Pierre, leader of the Combatant Communist Cells, Leuven, Belgium, February 25, 2003, photograph. Oliver Hoslet/AFP/Getty Images.-Civilian patriots patrol their village to protect it against the extremist Armed Islamic Group, Oran, Algeria, 2001, photograph. © Paolo Pellegrin/Magnum Photos.-Communist rebels march during a meeting between government officials and New People's Army, Surigao del Sur, Philippines, January 6, 2004, photograph by Froilan Gallardo. AP/Wide World Photos.

Commuter train, after a bomb exploded near the town of El Affroune, February 24, 1998, photograph. AP/Wide World Photos.-Convicted Palestinian terrorist awaiting an interview with the press, 1969, photograph. © Micha Bar Am/Magnum Photos.-Cow being sacrificed as part of an Ashura ritual, Tehran, Iran, 1997, photograph. © Abbas/Magnum Photos.-Czech riot policemen clash with drunken skinheads, Kozolupy, photograph by Jiri Bervida/CTK. AP/Wide World Photos.-Department store goes up in flames from a bomb planted by the Irish Republican Army, Londonderry, Northern Ireland, January 4, 1972, photograph. AP/Wide World Photos.-Duke,

David, Ku Klux Klan leader, London, 1978, photograph. AP/Wide World Photos.-Duke, David, president of the National Association for the Advancement of White People, August 19, 1980, photograph. © Bettman/Corbis.-Earth First protester, California, 1989, photograph. Jeremy Hogan/Alamy.-East Timorese listen to a speech during the first day of the Revolutionary Front for an Independent East Timor National Congress, Dili, East Timor, May 15, 2000, photograph by Joel Rubin. AP/Wide World Photos.-East Timorese militia patrol with their weapons, Liquica, April, 1999, photograph. AP/Wide World Photos.-Edward Street, after a massive car bomb exploded, Portadown, Northern Ireland, February 24, 1998, photograph by Paul McErlane. AP/Wide World Photos.-Egyptian movie poster defaced by Islamic fundamentalist extremists, 1984, photograph. © Micha Bar Am/Magnum Photos.-Egyptian soldiers tend to wounded after members of the Al Jihad movement opened fire during a military parade, Cairo, Egypt, October 6, 1981, photograph. AP/Wide World Photos.-Etzion, Yehuda head of the Jewish terrorist underground movement, photograph. © Gueorgui Pinkhassov/Magnum Photos.-Fatah Hawks, the military wing of Yasser Arafat's PLO faction, march through the occupied Gaza Strip, Gaza City, Palestine, March 14, 1994, photograph by Jerome Delay. AP/Wide World Photos.-Fatah movement gunman, with a gunman from the Islamic group Hamas face Israeli forces, Bethlehem, October 20, 2001, photograph by Lefteris Pitarakis. AP/Wide World Photos.-Fatah Revolutionary Council training camp run by the Abu Nidal Organization, photograph. © Alain Nogues/Corbis Sygma.-Fatah Youth Organization, Gaza City, January 1, 2001, photograph by Murad Sezer. AP/Wide World Photos.-FBI agents sift through debris of burned down home of Robert J. Matthew, the founder of the neo-Nazi group known as The Order, Whidbey Island, Washington, December, 1984, photograph by Tim Klass. AP/Wide World Photos.-Female guerrillas display traditional Kurdish garb and deadly accessories, Northern Iraq, August 1, 1991, photograph by Burhan Ozbilisi. AP/Wide World Photos.-Filipino Muslim peers through a window prior to a mass funeral of alleged Abu Sayyaf detainees, March 16, 2005, Taguig, Philippines, photograph by Bullit Marquez. AP/Wide World Photos.-Filipino Muslims lower one of the bodies of alleged Abu Sayyaf detainees into a common grave, Taguig, Philippines, March 16, 2005, photograph by Bullit Marquez. AP/Wide World Photos.-Fire fighters emerge after cleaning toxic gas-contaminated train cars, Tokyo, March 21, 1995, photograph. AP/Wide World Photos.-Fire inspectors examine damage to McDonald's restaurant, after a suspected arson attack from the Animal Liberation Front, Merksem, Belgium, August 12, 1999, photograph by Yves Logghe. AP/Wide World Photos.-Firefighters and police pull an Earth First protester to safety, Missoula, Montana, June 19, 2002, photograph by Tom Bauer. AP/Wide World Photos.-Firemen examine the wreckage of a Civil Guard patrol vehicle, after an ETA bomb exploded, Spain, August 20, 2000, photograph by EFE, Javier Belver. AP/Wide World Photos.-Firey cross at a Ku Klux Klan meeting, photograph. © Hulton-Deutsch Collection/Corbis.-Fiumicino Airport, after Palestinian guerrillas engaged in a gunfight with police before hijacking a jetliner, Rome, December 17, 1973, photograph. AP/Wide World Photos. -Fujimori, Alberto, then Peruvian President, passing the bodies of two Tupac Amaru rebels who were killed in the storming of Japanese ambassador's residence, Lima, April 23, 1997, photograph. AP/Wide World Photos.-Funeral of an 18 year old Catholic girl, Ulster, Northern Ireland, 1997, photograph. © Abbas/Magnum Photos.-Funeral of Bobby Sands, Belfast, Northern Ireland, 1981, photograph. © Peter Marlow/Magnum Photos.-Funeral of the Israeli athletes who were taken hostage by Palestinian terrorists during the 1972 Munich Olympics, photograph. © Micha Bar Am/Magnum Photos.-German neo-Nazis pass by the Brandenburg Gate, Berlin, March 12, 2000, photograph by Herbert Knosowski. AP/Wide World Photos.-Goehler, Bill, Freemen supporter, Jordan, Montana, April 19, 1996, photograph by Bob Zellar. AP/Wide World Photos.-Gonzales, Dan, vice chairman of the League of the South, during the controversy over the fate of Terry Schiavo, Florida, March 22, 2005, photograph. © Winston Luzier/Reuters/Corbis.-Greenpeace activists sail alongside other boats, photograph by Joerg Sarbach. AP/Wide World Photos.-Guynan, Dave, British National Party candidate, Sunderland, England, April 29, 2003, photograph by Will Walker. AP/Wide World Photos.-Hakim, Abu Haris Abdul, photograph by B. K. Bangash. AP/Wide World

Photos.-Hale, Rev. Matthew, leader of the World Church of the Creator with members of the Ku Klux Klan, October 26, 2002, Fayetteville, West Virginia, photograph. AP/Wide World Photos.-HAMAS suicide bomb attack in downtown Jerusalem, March 3, 1996, photograph by Eyal Warshavsky. AP/Wide World Photos.

Hannan, Mufti Mohammad Abdul, believed key leader of the Harkat-ul-Jihad-al-Islam/Bangladesh organization, October 1, 2005, photograph. Abir Abdullah/EPA/Landov.-Haradinaj, Ramush, former leader in the Kosovo Liberation Army, March 9, 2005, photograph. Reuters/Landov.-Harkat-Ul-Jehadi Islami suspected militants jump out of a police truck, Lakhanpur, India, June 30, 2003, photograph by Channi Anand. AP/Wide World Photos.-Harshman, Greg, of the Spokane Regional Intelligence Unit, uses the internet to track and monitor Web sites, like that of Rev. Matthew Hale, founder of the World Church of the Creator, December 9, 1999, photograph by Jeff T. Green. AP/Wide World Photos.-Hekmatyar, Gulbuddin, Afghan warlord, confers with Ustad Abdul Rab Rasul Sayaf an Afghan guerrilla leader, Peshawar, January 17, 1987, photograph. Dimitri Kochko/AFP/Getty Images.-Hertford College boat house, after fire bombed by The Animal Liberation Front, Oxford, England, August 25, 2005, photograph by Kirsty Wigglesworth. AP/Wide World Photos.-Hezbollah guerrillas, Chebaa Farms region, Lebanon, April 10, 2002, photograph by Hezbollah Military Media/HO. AP/Wide World Photos.-Hezbollah militia member, Lebanon, April 14, 1996, photograph. AP/Wide World Photos.-Hideouts of Al-Qaida-linked militants along the Afghan border, South Waziristan, Pakistan, photograph. AP/Wide World Photos.-Hill, Paul, photograph by Mark Foley. AP/Wide World Photos.-Hooded man reads the IRA's Easter Message at a rally, Crossmaglen, Northern Ireland, April 7, 1996, photograph. AP/Wide World Photos.-Horien, Adrian, one of four demonstrators from the militant Army of God anti-abortion group, photograph by David Duprey. AP/Wide World Photos.-Indian Border Security Force personnel escort Sajad Bhat suspected district leader of the Jaish-e-Mohammed, Srinagar, January 3, 2005, photograph. Fayaz Kabli/Reuters/Landov.-Indian man prepares to jump to his death as Hindu extremists demand that the Babu Jammid mosque be destroyed, 1990, photograph. Network Photographers/Alamy.-Indonesian anti-riot troops beat a student protester during an anti-government protest, Jakarta, August 23, 1999, photograph by Ramli. AP/Wide World Photos.-Indonesian boy wearing a t-shirt featuring a portrait of Osama bin Laden, 2004, photograph. © Abbas/Magnum Photos.-Iranian women demonstrate in support of the Mujahedin-e Khalq Organization, Tehran, Iran, October 28, 2002, photograph. Reuters/Landov.-Irish Republican Army graffiti, West Belfast, Northern Ireland, March 5, 2001, photograph by Peter Morrison. AP/Wide World Photos.-Islamic Jihad member holds up a Holy Koran and a grenade during a rally, Gaza City, Gaza Strip, February 21, 2003, photograph by Brennan Linsley. AP/Wide World Photos. -Islamic Jihad members display weapons during prayers, photograph. Spencer Platt/Getty Images.-Islamic Jihad militant during the funeral processions of Hazem Rahim, a local Islamic Jihad commander and Abdulraof Abu Asse, Gaza City, July 23, 2004, photograph by Adel Hana. AP/Wide World Photos.-Israeli soldiers try to stop young Jewish settler extremists from entering the Kfar Darom settlement, Gush Katif, Gaza Strip, photograph. © Paolo Pellegin/Magnum Photos.-Izzedine Al-Qassam Brigades fighter, Jebaliya, Gaza Strip, October 11, 1994, photograph by Jerome Delay. AP/Wide World Photos.-Janjalani, Khaddafi, and Radulan Sahiron sit with fellow Abu Sayyaf rebels inside their jungle hideout in the Sulu province, Philippines, July 16, 2000, photograph. AP/Wide World Photos.-Jewish Defensive League hate graffiti on an Arab home, Hebron, West Bank, 2003, photograph. © Larry Towell/Magnum Photos.-Jewish settler fires on a crowd of Palestinians, Hebron, December 3, 1993, photograph by Jerome Delay. AP/Wide World Photos.-Jewish settler hate graffiti in a Muslim cemetery, Hebron, West Bank, 2003, photograph. © Larry Towell/Magnum Photos.-Kach Party symbol with graffiti in a burned-out Palestinian home, Hebron, 2003, photograph. © Larry Towell/Magnum Photos.-Kahane, Rabbi Meir, at a Jewish Defense League protest, photograph. © Bettmann/Corbis.-Khaled, Leila, a member of the Popular Front for the Liberation of Palestine, Amman, Jordan, 1970, photograph by Hagop Toranian. AP/Wide World Photos.-King Fahd Mosque, target of a bombing plot by the chairman and another member of the militant Jewish Defense League, Culver City, California, December 12, 2001, photograph by Damian Dovarganes. AP/Wide World Photos.-Kosovar Albanians march, Malisevo, Kosovo, March 16, 2004, photograph. Valdrin Xhemaj/EPA/Landov.-Ku Klux Klan female members, North Carolina, 1964, photograph. Charles Moore/Black Star/Alamy.-Ku Klux Klan member, Greensburg, Pennsylvania, August 16, 1997, photograph by Gary Tramontina. AP/Wide World Photos.-Lebron, Lolita, with three other women shortly after they opened fire from the visitors gallery of the U.S. House of Representatives, Washington, D. C., March 1, 1954, photograph. AP/Wide World Photos.-Leonardo da Vinci Airport, after a terrorist attack by seven Abu Nidal gunmen, Rome, Italy, December 27, 1985, photograph. AP/Wide World Photos.-Londonderry riots, Northern Ireland, 1985, photograph. © Stuart Franklin/Magnum Photos.-Loyalist Volunteer Force announcing their ceasefire in Portadown, Belfast, Northern Ireland, May 15, 1998, photograph. AP/Wide World Photos.-Maaroufi, Tarek ben Habib, co-founder of the Tunisian Combatant Group, Brussels, Belgium, September 13, 2004, photograph. Thierry Roge/Reuters/Landov.-Mahameed, Khaled, Israeli Arab lawyer, Nazareth, May 24, 2005, photograph by Eitan Hess-Ashkenazi. AP/Wide World Photos.-Malcolm X, photograph. © Corbis-Bettmann.-Man training for the Kosovo Liberation Army, Drenica, 1999, photograph. © Corbis Sygma.-McDermott, Bill, white supremacist, with two friends, Dubuque, Iowa, 1991, photograph. William F. Campbell/Time Life Pictures/Getty Images.-McLaren, Richard, self-styled ambassador of the Republic of Texas group, Texas, March 6, 1997, photograph by Ron Heflin. AP/Wide World Photos.-Means, Russell, 1970, photograph. AP/Wide World Photos.

Metzger, Tom, leader of the White Aryan Resistance group, Coeur d' Alene, Idaho, September 5, 2000, photograph. AP/Wide World Photos.-Michigan Militia members set fire to a United Nations flag, Lansing, Michigan, October, 24, 1995, photograph. AP/Wide World Photos.-Morales, William, bomb maker for the terrorist group FALN, 1983, photograph. AP/Wide World Photos.-Moro, Aldo, Italian Premier, body found 55 days after he was kidnapped in a Red Brigade ambush, May 9, 1978, photograph. AP/Wide World Photos.-Mother Teresa, on a tour of Trilokpuri, a Sikh section of Delhi, photograph. AP/Wide World Photos.-Mourners carry the coffin of Israeli Arab George Khoury, March 21, 2004, photograph. Menahem Kahana/AFP/Getty.-Movimento dos Sem Terra group camp out in front of the INCRA Agrarian Reform Government Agency, Rio de Janeiro Plaza, March 20, 1998, photograph by Renzo Gostoli. AP/Wide World Photos.-Muhammed, Elijah, leader of the Nation of Islam, Chicago, Illinois, February 26, 1966, photograph. AP/Wide World Photos.-Mujahedin-e Kahlq members pass through a U. S. checkpoint, Dayala, Iraq, May 12, 2003, photograph. Roberto Schmidt/AFP/Getty Images.-National Alliance members demonstrate against U. S. support for Israel, Washington, D.C., August 24, 2002, photograph. AP/Wide World Photos.-National Bolshevik Party militants march in front of St. Basil Church, Moscow, 1998, photograph. © Abbas/Magnum Photos.-National Liberation Army, Santa Ana, November 1, 1997, photograph. AP/Wide World Photos.-Nazi storm troopers, Luitpold Arena, Nuremberg, Germany, September 20, 1936, photograph. AP/Wide World Photos.-Neo-Nazis and white supremacists celebrate at NordicFest, Kentucky, 2001, photograph. © Jonas Bendiksen/Magnum Photos.-Neo-Nazis and white supremacists watch a burning swastika at NordicFest, Kentucky, 2001, photograph. © Jonas Bendiksen/Magnum Photos.-Neo-Nazis, Skinheads and Ku Klux Klansmen march in Pulaski, Tennessee, 1989, photograph. © Leonard Freed/Magnum Photos.-New Black Panther members and white-hooded Ku Klux Klansmen, Jasper, Texas, June 27, 1998, photograph by Pat Sullivan. AP/Wide World Photos.-Nicholls, Karen, abortion-rights activist shields herself from anti-abortion leader Rev. Flip Benham, Wichita, Kansas, July 14, 2001, photograph. AP/Wide World Photos.-Ocalan, Abdullah, Beirut, 1998, photograph by Jamal Saidi. Archive Photos/Getty Images.-Ocean Warrior flagship of marine conservation group Sea Shepherd, Port of Miami, July 11, 2001, photograph. AP/Wide World Photos.-Officers clear the scene after a bomb exploded under a police car, Sanguesa, Spain, May 30, 2003, photograph. © Reuters/Corbis.-Okamoto, Kozo, member of the Japanese Red Army group, photograph. © Micha Bar Am/Magnum Photos.-Palestinian gunman wears a slogan that reads, "martyr Abu Ali Mustafa brigade, Popular Front for the Liberation of Palestine," photograph by Rick Bowmer. AP/Wide World Photos.-Palestinian militant during a march of the al-Aqsa Martyrs Brigades, Gaza City, August 14, 2002, photograph. © Reuters/ Corbis.-Palestinian militant fires at an Israeli armored helicopter, Gaza, photograph. © Abbas/Magnum Photos.-Peace Wall that separates Catholics from Protestants, Ulster, Belfast, 1997, photograph. © Abbas/Magnum Photos.-People Against Gangsterism And Drugs lead members to return fire during clashes with the police, Hannover Park, Cape Town, South Africa, August 11, 1996, photograph by Sasa Kralj. AP/Wide World Photos.-People for the Ethical Treatment of Animals protest the Canadian governments go-ahead for a seal hunt, Washington, April 6, 2005, photograph by Stephen J. Boitano. AP/Wide World Photos.-Philippines National Police Regional Mobile Group patrol the outskirts of a petroleum company, Manila, Philippines, March 16, 2000, photograph. Luis Liwanag/Getty Images.- Plainclothes police officers carry the dead body of a businessman believed kidnapped by the Turkish Hezbollah, Istanbul, Turkey, January 19, 2000, photograph. AP/Wide World Photos.-Police officer looks at the damage after the Shiv Sena party allegedly set fire to the hospital, Thane, India, August 27, 2001, photograph. AP/Wide World Photos.-Police officer reads graffiti in a Lashkar-e-Jhangvi hideout, Quetta, Pakistan, February 18, 2005, photograph. AP/Wide World Photos.-Police officers cordon off the McDonald's restaurant, after a bomb exploded, Brittany, France, April 19, 2000, photograph by Franck Prevel. AP/Wide World Photos.-Police officers examine a hole in the wall, after a bomb explosion, Madrid, Spain, March 13, 1998, photograph by Paul White. AP/ Wide World Photos.-Police officers hold back photographers following a bomb blast at the Marriott Hotel linked to the Jemaah Islamiyah terror group, Jakarta, Indonesia, August 5, 2003, photograph by Achmad Ibrahim. AP/ Wide World Photos.-Police officers remove the bodies of victims of a shooting, which includes Maulana Azam Tariq, the one-time leader of Sipah-e-Sahaba, Islamabad, Pakistan, October 6, 2003, photograph. AP/Wide World Photos.- Policeman guard members of the Russian National Union, Moscow, May 12, 1998, photograph. AP/Wide World Photos.-Policeman

inspects a guitar during a search operation, Gauhati, India, April 2, 2005, photograph. AP/ Wide World Photos.-Popular Front for the Liberation of Palestine members during a demonstration, Nablus, October 13, 2001, photograph by Nasser Isstayeh. AP/Wide World Photos.-Poster against imprisonment of militant members of the Red Army Faction, photograph. © Raymond Depardon/Magnum Photos.-Posters of religious leaders and martyrs in Beirut, Lebanon, photograph. © Paolo Pellegrin/Magnum Photos.-Pro-choice demonstrators, photograph. Leonard Lessin/Peter Arnold, Inc.-Protest against the Neo-Nazi party, West Germany, 1965, photograph. © Leonard Freed/Magnum Photos.-Provisional Irish Republican Army mural, West Belfast, Northern Ireland, March 8, 2001, photograph by Peter Morrison. AP/Wide World Photos.- Pulver, Bruce, climbs a fire ladder to photograph newly-constructed homes destroyed by ELF arsonists, photograph. AP/Wide World Photos.- Rahman, Sheikh Omar Abdel, spiritual leader of Jamaa Islamiyya, New York, June, 1993, photograph. Mark D. Phillips/AFP/Getty Images.-Railway workers and police examine debris of a destroyed train at Atocha railway station, Madrid, Spain, March 11, 2004, photograph by Anja Niedringhaus. AP/Wide World Photos.-Raviv, Avishai, leader of the militant right-wing group Eyal, Tel Aviv Magistrates Court, November 8, 1995, photograph by Nati Harnik. AP/Wide World Photos.-Rayen, Nizar, one of the leaders of HAMAS, Gaza City, photograph. © Abbas/Magnum Photos.-Rebel soldiers look over lime covered bodies believed to be victims of the Interahamwe during recent battles, Goma, Congo, September 15, 1998, photograph by Jean-Marc Bouju. AP/Wide World Photos.-Regener, Michael, and his lawyer wait for the sentence of the German Federal Supreme Court, Karlsruhe, Germany, March 10, 2005, photograph by Thomas Kienzle. AP/ Wide World Photos.-Republic of Texas members, Robert "White Eagle" Otto, Gregg Paulson, and their leader Richard McLaren, Fort Davis, Texas, July 10, 1997, photograph. AP/Wide World Photos.-Rescue worker helps a casualty to an ambulance after an explosion ripped through the Admiral Duncan Pub, Soho, London, April 30, 1999, photograph by David Thomson. AP/Wide World Photos.- Restaurant damaged by a blast inside two movie theaters, New Delhi, India, May 22,

2005, photograph by Press Trust of India. AP/ Wide World Photos.

Revolutionary Armed Forces of Colombia march during a military practice, La Macarena, Colombia, August 6, 2001, photograph by Zoe Selsky. AP/Wide World Photos.-Revolutionary Armed Forces of Colombia, San Vicente Del Caguan, Colombia, photograph by Ariana Cubillos. AP/Wide World Photos.- Revolutionary Peoples Liberation Party-Front members demonstrate in Istanbul, Turkey, May 1996, photograph. Mustafa Ozer/AFP/Getty Images.-Revolutionary Peoples Liberation Party-Front members march during May Day celebrations, Ankara, Turkey, May 1, 2004, photograph by Burhan Ozbilici. AP/Wide World Photos.-Revolutionary United Front soldier lies dead after a clash with Nigerian peace-keeping soldiers, Sierra Leone, June 11, 1997, photograph by Enric Marti. AP/Wide World Photos.-Reward handout for the capture of leaders of the Abu Sayyaf Islamist extremist group, circulated by the U.S. embassy, Manila, May, 2000, photograph. AP/Wide World Photos.- Right-wing militants fight with anti-fascists during a demonstration, Lyon, France, November 14, 2004, photograph. Jean Philippe-Ksiazek/ AFP/Getty Images.-Rockwell, George Lincoln, leader of the American Nazi Party, Montgomery, Alabama, May 23, 1961, photograph. AP/Wide World Photos.-Royal Ulster Constabulary officers examine the Mahon Hotel after Sunday nights bomb attack, believed to have been planted by an Irish Republican Army splinter group, the Continuity IRA, Irvinestown, Northern Ireland, February 7, 2000, photograph by Peter Morrison. AP/Wide World Photos.-Saichi, Amari, No. 2 leader of the Salafist Group for Call and Combat, photograph. AP/Wide World Photos.-Saifi, Amari, the No. 2 of the Salafist Group for Call and Combat group, photograph. AP/Wide World Photos.-Sakar, Anwar, member of the Islamic Jihad movement who became a suicide bomber, photograph. © Abbas/Magnum Photos.- Sankoh, Foday, leader of the Revolutionary United Front, visits troops at camp in Port Loko, Sierra Leone, December, 1999, photograph by Teun Voeten. © Teun Voeten. Reproduced by permission.-Shigenobu, Fusako, founder of the Lebanon-based faction of Japanese Red Army, Tokyo station, Tokyo, Japan, photograph. © AFP/Corbis.-Singh, Danilo, and Rolando Marcello suspected leaders of the Alex Boncayao Brigade, July 17, 2001, photograph. Joel Nito/AFP/Getty Images.-Skinhead supporter of the rightwing German National Democratic Party, NPD, Verden, Germany, April 2, 2005, photograph by Joerg Sarbach. AP/Wide World Photos.-South Carolina Council of Conservative Citizens protest state Senate Bill 61, Columbia, South Carolina, January 30, 1999, photograph by Kim Truett. AP/Wide World Photos.-Spanish fireman, Madrid, January 21, 2000, photograph by Dani Duch/La Vanguardia. AP/Wide World Photos.- Supporter of Puerto Rican nationalist leader Filiberto Ojeda Rios, photograph by Andres Leighton. AP/Wide World Photos.-Supporter of Rabbi Meir Kahane demonstrates on the anniversary of his death, 1995, photograph. © Abbas/Magnum Photos.-Taliban supporters protest during the Pakistani Independence Day Parade, Manhattan, New York City, August 25, 2002, photograph. © Thomas Dworzak/ Magnum Photos.-Tamil Tigers march on the road to Thopigila Camp, Sri Lanka, March 4, 2004, photograph by Julia Drapkin. AP/Wide World Photos.-Tamil Tigers women suicide squad members join in the celebration of "Heroes Day," Mullathivu, Sri Lanka, November 27, 2002, photograph by Gemunu Amarasinghe. AP/Wide World Photos.-Tareq, Abu, brother of Abdel Karim As-Saadi, leader of Asbat al-Ansar, Ain el-Helweh refugee camp, Lebanon, photograph. Mahmoud Zayat/AFP/ Getty Images.-Tavistock Square, damage from bus bombing, London, August 7, 2005, photograph. Dominic Burke/Alamy.-Teenaged skinheads walk through the gates of Auschwitz, the former Nazi death camp, April 6, 1996, photograph. AP/Wide World Photos.-Terreblanche, Eugene, leader of the Afrikaner Resistance Movement, Western Transvaal, South Africa, 1994, photograph. © Ian Berry/Magnum Photos.-Terry, Randall, founder of Operation Rescue, during a demonstration in Lafayette Park, August 1, 2001, photograph by Stephen J. Boitano. AP/Wide World Photos.-Three Afghan Mujahidin, "holy warriors" stand on a mountain in Pakistan near the Afghan border, photograph. © Steve McCurry/Magnum Photos.-Tokyo Subway passengers affected by sarin gas planted by the Aum Shinri Kyo cults, 1995, photograph by Chikumo Chiaki. AP/ Wide World Photos.-Truck burned by rebels of the Revolutionary Armed Forces of Colombia, Los Chorros, January 19, 2004, photograph.

AP/Wide World Photos.-Truck with a hand-painted portrait of Osama bin Laden, Indonesia, 2004, photograph. © Abbas/Magnum Photos.-Tupac Amaru rebels show victory sign from roof top of the Japanese ambassador's residence, Lima, Peru, photograph by Kiyohiro Oku-Sankei Shimbum. AP/Wide World Photos.-U. S. flag flies upside down outside a church occupied by members of the American Indian Movement, on the site of the 1890 massacre at Wounded Knee, South Dakota, March 3, 1973, photograph by Jim Mone. AP/Wide World Photos.

Ugandan soldier walks past a charred body after a massacre believed to be committed by the Lord's Resistance Army, Barlonyo camp, Uganda, February 23, 2004, photograph by Karel Prinsloo. AP/Wide World Photos.-Ulster Freedom Fighters, Belfast, Northern Ireland, December 8, 1999, photograph by Peter Morrison. AP/Wide World Photos.-Ulster Volunteer Force marching band, Crumlin Road, Belfast, July 12, 2002, photograph. AP/Wide World Photos.-United Nuwaubian Nation of Moors compound, Eatonton, Georgia, January 22, 2003, photograph by Mark Niesse. AP/Wide World Photos.-Vishwa Hindu Parishad and Shiv Sena activists obstruct train tracks, Bombay, India, September 26, 2002, photograph. AP/Wide World Photos.-Voice of Citizens Together member asking that pre-natal care be denied to illegal immigrants, June 11, 1996, photograph by Damian Dovarganes.

AP/Wide World Photos.-Watson, Captain Paul, Sea Shepherd Conservation Society founder, with Makah Indian Elder Jeff Ides, Monaco, October 20, 1997, photograph. AP/Wide World Photos.-Weapons and paraphernalia seized from the terrorist group November 17, photograph. AP/Wide World Photos.-White separatist demonstrator is sprayed with mace by a counter-protestor during a National Alliance rally, Washington, D. C., August 24, 2002, photograph. AP/Wide World Photos.-Wilson, Eddie, Mississippi police lieutenant examines a hunting rifle found in the home of accused sniper Larry Shoemake, photograph. AP/Wide World Photos.-Woman shouts during a protest against the Basque separatist group, Madrid, February 23, 2000, photograph. AP/Wide World Photos.-World Trade Center, hijacked airplane preparing to crash into the south tower, photograph by Carmen Taylor. AP/Wide World Photos. -Yagan, Bedri, Dursun Karatas, and Sinan Kukul, founders of Turkeys Revolutionary Peoples Liberation Party-Front, photograph. AFP/Getty Images.-Zapatista National Liberation Army, Subcomandante Marcos, during an exclusive interview in La Realidad, Chiapas, May 18, 1999, photograph by Eduardo Verdugo. AP/Wide World Photos.-Zapatista supporters being searched by Mexican Army soldiers at a checkpoint near, La Realidad, Chiapas, May 7, 1999, photograph by John Moore. AP/Wide World Photos.

Lashkar-e-Jhangvi (LeJ)

OVERVIEW

Lashkar-e-Jhangvi (LeJ), or Army of Jhangvi, is an extremist organization active in Pakistan. It allegedly has an agenda of liberation and communism. Lashhar-e-Jhangvi believes that the entire nation of Pakistan should only be comprised of a Sunni Muslim population, thus making the group a part of the overall Sunni *deobandi* movement. In pursuit of this goal LeJ is believed to have engaged in a variety of violent activities directed against Sh'ite Muslims in Pakistan. The U.S. Department of State designated Lashkar-e-Jhangvi as a Foreign Terrorist Organization in 2003.

Lashkar-e-Jhangvi is also known by other names such as Lashkar-i-Jhangvi, Lashkar-e-Jhangvie, Laskar-e-Jhangvi, Lashkare Jhangvi, Lashkar-e-Jhangwi, Lashkar-i-Jhangwi, Jhangvi Army, Lashkar-e Jhangvi, Lashkar Jhangvi, Lashkar-e-Jhanvi (LeJ), Lashkar-i-Jangvi, Lashkar e Jhangvi, Lashkar Jangvi, and Laskar e Jahangvi.

LEADER: Riaz Basar
YEAR ESTABLISHED OR BECAME ACTIVE: 1996
USUAL AREA OF OPERATION: Pakistan

HISTORY

Lashkar-e-Jhangvi (LeJ) is an off-shoot of another Islamic extremist group known as Sipah-e-Sahaba (SSP) and is reported to have formed during the mid 1990s. Even though LeJ's history is reportedly only a few years old,

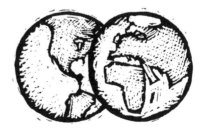

A Pakistani police officer reads anti-Shiite Muslim propaganda in a militants' hideout on February 18, 2005 in Quetta, Pakistan. The name of their group, Lashkar-e-Jhangvi, is written in bold print in the middle of the wall. AP/Wide World Photos

the impact of events staged by this group has pushed it into the limelight. The parent group of LeJ, Sipah-e-Sahaba, was allegedly cofounded by *Maulana* (a term used to address scholarly Islamic people) Haq Nawaz Jhangvi. LeJ was named in honor of him.

LeJ is believed to have been formed by SSP members who felt that the group had deviated from its primary focus, which led to dissatisfaction and disagreements among its supporters and prominent group members. Some of these members reportedly decided to form their own organization, and named it Lashkar-e-Jhangvi in honor of Maulana Haq Nawaz Jhangvi. The initial movement of LeJ allegedly began under the leadership of Akram Lahori and Riaz Basra, who later came to be known as the founders of this group.

PHILOSOPHY AND TACTICS

LeJ allegedly seeks annihilation of Shi'ite Muslims within Pakistan and the establishment

of complete Sunni control of the country. LeJ seeks to achieve its mission by violent means. LeJ has publicly admitted and assumed the responsibility for the killing of numerous Sh'ite Muslims and is thought to be responsible for many other attacks. In an effort to drive off the Shi'ite community, LeJ's agenda also includes attacks on Iranian citizens residing in Pakistan.

Reports suggest that Lashkar-e-Jhangvi primarily employs *Jehadis* (warriors against those who do not believe in Islamic fundamentalism) with a history of fighting the Afghan Soviet war. A majority of these jehadi activists have allegedly emerged from Sunni Madrassas, where they have been taught that Sunnis are superior to other Muslims.

In order to spread terror among the Shi'ite community, LeJ targets Shi'ite religious leaders, kills people in Shi'ite mosques, and attacks high-profile Shi'ite political leaders. In 1999, after an unsuccessful attempt on the life of the former prime minister of Pakistan, Nawaz Sharif

LEADERSHIP

RIAZ BASAR

Media reports suggest that the initial movements of the LeJ were triggered by Riaz Basra, who claimed the leadership of this off-shoot group in 1996. Reports also claim that Basra was a firm believer in the Sunni sect and was highly motivated to achieve the goal of the group. As a young boy, Basra reportedly quit his primary school to learn religion from *Madrassas* (Islamic religious schools).

It has been alleged by counter-terrorism experts that the popularity of Riaz Basra rose to new heights when he participated in the provincial assembly elections in Lahore under the JUI (F) ticket in year 1988. He is also reported to be an Afghan war veteran. According to media reports, Riaz Basra had a stronghold on Pakistan politics and was considered to be a dreaded terrorist even by prominent politicians and lawmakers. One of the reports claims that Basra sent a threatening note compelling the then-president of Pakistan, Nawaz Sharief, to stop attending the open courts.

Riaz Basra was accompanied by three other members of LeJ on May 14, 2002, when they were reportedly shot and killed by Pakistani law officials.

KEY EVENTS

1996: Allama Mureed Abbas Yazdani, Shi'ite leader was assassinated in September 1996, in Islamabad, Pakistan, triggering the LeJ movement.

1998: Another Shi'ite leader was killed in Peshawar, Pakistan.

1998: Five people were shot just outside a Pakistani mosque by activists reportedly belonging to LeJ group.

1999: A prominent Pakistan Television (PTV) official was killed in Rawalpindi, Pakistan, allegedly by LeJ terrorists.

2000: Two lawyers were killed in Khanewal, while 17 people were shot at a mosque in Malohwali. LeJ is thought to be responsible.

2001: Several businesspersons, political leaders, religious leaders, and many others of the Shi'ite community were massacred, allegedly by LeJ terrorists.

2002: *Wall Street Journal* reporter Daniel Pearl is murdered by a group of terrorists, allegedly including some LeJ members. LeJ is also thought responsible for the killing of several teachers, doctors, and political leaders.

(a Shi'ite), media reports claimed that he was a chief target of the LeJ. It has been frequently reported by the media that the LeJ's activities are not limited only to Pakistan and that the group is reportedly actively involved in several acts of terror against non-Shi'ite Muslims belonging to other countries, including Iran and Afghanistan. Several LeJ operatives were allegedly involved in the kidnapping and murder of *Wall Street Journal* reporter Daniel Pearl in 2002. Eventually, the members of Jaish-e-Mohammad, another Pakistan-based extremist group, were implicated for masterminding Pearl's kidnap and subsequent murder. However, authorities

did not rule out the involvement of LeJ in the Daniel Pearl case.

Both SSP and LeJ are known to have links with the Taliban in Afghanistan. As of 2005, LeJ has reportedly confirmed its association with other Sunni extremist groups: Harkat-al Mujahideen and Jaish-e-Mohammed. All three groups combined are known to represent the Pakistan wing of al-Qaeda, making them a part of the most dreaded terrorist group in the world.

News reports claim that the LeJ split in October 2000 as a result of two separate opinions emerging within the group. It has been further reported that the split occurred partly because of the ideological differences arising

PRIMARY SOURCE

Lashkar i Jhangvi (LJ)

DESCRIPTION

Lashkar i Jhangvi (LJ) is the militant off-shoot of the Sunni sectarian group Sipah-i-Sahaba Pakistan. LJ focuses primarily on anti-Shia attacks and was banned by Pakistani President Musharraf in August 2001 as part of an effort to rein in sectarian violence. Many of its members then sought refuge in Afghanistan with the Taliban, with whom they had existing ties. After the collapse of the Taliban, LJ members became active in aiding other terrorists with safe houses, false identities, and protection in Pakistani cities, including Karachi, Peshawar, and Rawalpindi. In January 2003, the United States added LJ to the list of Foreign Terrorist Organizations.

ACTIVITIES

LJ specializes in armed attacks and bombings. The group attempted to assassinate former Prime Minister Nawaz Sharif and his brother Shabaz Sharif, Chief Minister of Punjab Province, in January 1999. Pakistani authorities have publicly linked LJ members to the kidnap and murder of US journalist Daniel Pearl in early 2002. Police officials initially suspected LJ members were involved in the two suicide car bombings in Karachi in 2002 against a French shuttle bus in May and the US Consulate in June, but their subsequent investigations have not led to any LJ members being charged in the attacks. Similarly, press reports have linked LJ to attacks on Christian targets in Pakistan, including a grenade assault on the Protestant International Church in Islamabad in March 2002 that killed two US citizens, but no formal charges have been filed against the group. Pakistani authorities believe LJ was responsible for the bombing in July 2003 of a Shiite mosque in Quetta, Pakistan. Authorities have also implicated LJ in several sectarian incidents in 2004, including the May and June bombings of two Shiite mosques in Karachi that killed over 40 people.

STRENGTH

Probably fewer than 100.

LOCATION/AREA OF OPERATION

LJ is active primarily in Punjab and Karachi. Some members travel between Pakistan and Afghanistan.

EXTERNAL AID

Unknown.

Source: U.S. Department of State. *Country Reports on Terrorism.* Washington, D.C., 2004.

within the prominent member of LeJ after the military coup in Pakistan in October 1999. In 2001, Pakistan's President Parvez Musharraf banned the activities of the organization.

OTHER PERSPECTIVES

In a 2003 statement released by the United States Treasury Department regarding the designation of LeJ, it was mentioned that "LJ is responsible for the January 2002 kidnapping and killing of U.S. journalist Daniel Pearl. LJ is also responsible for a March 2002 bus bombing that killed 15 people, including 11 French technicians." The statement further mentioned that, "LJ also has ties to al Qa'ida and the Taliban. In addition to receiving sanctuary from the Taliban in Afghanistan for their activity in Pakistan, LJ members also fought alongside Taliban fighters. Pakistani government investigations in 2002 revealed that al Qa'ida has been involved with training of LJ, and that LJ fighters also fought alongside the Taliban against the Northern Alliance. The Pakistan Interior Minister, speaking of LJ members, stated that "They have been sleeping and eating together, receiving training together, and fighting against the Northern Alliance together in Afghanistan."

SUMMARY

The government of Pakistan banned the activities of LeJ in 2001, and in 2003 the U.S. Department of State declared LeJ as a Foreign Terrorist Organization. In spite of that, the LeJ has reportedly maintained the intensity of its activities as of 2005. In May 2005, media reports have claimed the involvement of LeJ in suicide bombings at the Bari Inam shrine in Pakistan.

Experts are of the opinion that the law enforcement agencies of Pakistan will succeed in curbing the activities of LeJ only after the activities of Sipah-e-Sahaba (the parent organization of LeJ) have been controlled. SSP and also LeJ allegedly receive patronage from the government of Saudi Arabia, which makes it more difficult for the Pakistan government to restrain its violent activities.

SOURCES

Web sites

MIPT Terrorism Knowledge Base. "Group Profile: Lashkar-e-Jhangvi (LEJ)." < http://www.tkb.org/Group.jsp?groupID = 65 > (accessed October 19, 2005).

South Asian Terrorism Portal. "Lashkar-e-Jhangvi." < http://www.satp.org/satporgtp/countries/pakistan/terroristoutfits/LeJ.htm > (accessed October 19, 2005).

U.S. Treasury Department. "Treasury Department Statement Regarding the Designation of Lashkar i Jhangvi." < http://www.ustreas.gov/press/releases/kd3814.htm > (accessed October 19, 2005).

U.S. Department of State. "Designation of Lashkar I Jhangvi as a Foreign Terrorist Organization." < http://www.state.gov/secretary/former/powell/remarks/2003/17063.htm > (accessed October 19, 2005).

SEE ALSO

Sipah-e-Sahaba (SSP)

Lashkar-e-Tayyiba (LT)

ALTERNATE NAME: Army of the Righteous
LEADER: Hafeez Mohammed Saeed
YEAR ESTABLISHED OR BECAME ACTIVE: 1989
USUAL AREA OF OPERATION: Kashmir (India)

OVERVIEW

Lashkar-e-Tayyiba (LT) is considered by most terrorism analysts to be the largest militant organization operating in the Jammu & Kashmir (state of India) region. LT claims that it was formed in 1989, in Pakistan, as a military faction of Markaz-ud-Dawa-wal-Irshad (MDI), an Islamic extremist organization. LT is also known as Army of the Righteous, Lashkar-e-Toiba, Lashkar-e-Taiba (LeT), al Monsooreen, al-Mansoorian, Army of the Pure, as well as Army of the Pure and Righteous.

After the September 11, 2001, attacks in the United States, LT was categorized as a Foreign Terrorist Organization by the U.S. Department of State for its alleged involvement with al-Qaeda (the group that claimed responsibility for the attacks). The Pakistan government subsequently froze all LT assets and banned the group.

HISTORY

In 1989, Zafar Iqbal, Hafiz Mohammed Saeed, and Abdullah Azam, leaders of Markaz-ud-Dawa-wal-Irshad (MDI), an Islamic fundamentalist organization headquartered in the town of Muridke outside Lahore, Pakistan, created an army wing known as Lashkar-e-Tayyiba. The

LEADERSHIP

HAFIZ MOHAMMED SAEED

In 1987, three scholarly individuals, Hafiz Mohammad Saeed, Zafar Iqbal, and Abdullah Azzam, collaborated to form the Markaz Dawat-ul Irshad (MDI, Center for Religious Learning and Social Welfare). Lashkar-e-Tayyiba, a faction of MDI, represents the armed forces of this organization. The organization was reportedly founded with the seed money provided by the al-Qaeda group, due to the alleged links between its leader, Hafiz Mohammed Saeed, and Osama bin Laden.

After graduating from the Government College at Sargodha, Pakistan, Saeed took off to Saudi Arabia and earned his Masters in Islamic Studies and in Arabic Lexicon, from King Saud University, Riyadh. Subsequently, he served as a Professor of Islamic Studies at the University of Engineering and Technology in Lahore, Pakistan, for many years.

After forming the Lashkar-e-Tayyiba, Saeed is thought to be the mastermind behind several acts of terrorism. Several of Saeed's family members allegedly hold high-ranking positions at LT.

In 2001, in a revelation to the Pakistani media, Saeed mentioned that the LT would undergo changes and will emerge stronger than ever. This was after it was designated a terrorist organization by the United States. Towards the end of 2001, he was arrested by the Pakistani police, but was freed in November 2002, in absence of charges against him.

Saeed has frequently expressed vehement disregard for India and the United States (especially in the aftermath of September 11). Analysts argue that Saeed believes that prospective peace talks between India and Pakistan are fraudulent, and that India and the United States are trying to coerce President Musharraf (of Pakistan) to restrict the activities of LT.

---

main objective was to support the Afghan *mujahideens* (a term represented as "Muslim warriors fighting for a religious cause" against those who do not believe in Islamic fundamentalism) fighting against the Soviet Union. At that time the Soviets were protecting the communist regime in Afghanistan. After the Afghan war ended, the LT shifted its focus on the *jihad* (holy war) against India for the liberation of Kashmir. The LT is reportedly one of the three most prominent and highly skilled terrorist organizations operating in Kashmir.

LT has claimed responsibility for a large number of terrorist activities conducted against the Indian security forces, as well as civilians in Jammu and Kashmir (J&K), since 1993. The Indian authorities have also blamed LT for several terrorist attacks conducted in other parts of India. As alleged by the Indian government, Lashkar e-Tayyiba has been receiving financial and operational support from the Pakistani Inter-Services Intelligence agency (ISI) since 1996. News reports within the media have also

suggested that the involvement of ISI increased after the U.S. government declared another Pakistan-based militant group, Harakat ul-Ansar (HUA), a terrorist organization in 1997.

Reportedly, LT and its parent organization MDI were also supported by the ISI and the U.S. Central Intelligence Agency (CIA) during the Afghan war. However, Indian authorities argue that after the war was over, the CIA withdrew its support but the ISI continued to help LT—only now its focus was on J&K and other parts of India.

Apart from the ISI, the LT is thought to have obtained significant funding from Osama bin Laden (of al-Qaeda) as well as Islamic charities, and Pakistani and Pakistan-occupied Kashmir's (PoK) businesspeople. Reports suggest that Osama bin Laden provided significant funding for the vast campus of MDI in Muridke, Pakistan. There have also been reports in the Indian media that the LT has, in the past, received financial and other support from the government of Pakistan.

KEY EVENTS

2000: LT members allegedly massacre 35 Sikhs at Chattisinghpora, Anantnag, J&K, on the eve of then-U.S. President Bill Clinton's official visit to India.

2001: LT reportedly behind the attack on the Indian army barracks in the Red Fort in New Delhi.

2001: An attack on India's Parliament is blamed on the LT by India.

2002: The Pakistani police force arrest Saeed. However, he is released after a few months as the Lahore High Court cites that the arrest was unlawful.

2002: The Indian government names LT as the group behind the attack on Akshardham, a Hindu temple in Gandhinagar, India. The attack killed around 30 people and injured many more.

2003: Lashkar-e-Tayyiba works together with militant groups fighting against United States led coalition forces in Afghanistan and Iraq.

2005: The United Nations bans the group, freezing its assets.

2005: Islamic Inquilabi Mahaz, Islamic revolutionary group also known as or linked to Lashkar-e-Tayyiba (Lashkar-e-Taiba) claims responsibility for a bombing in New Delhi that kills fifty-nine people.

Lashkar e-Tayyiba, over the years, has allegedly conducted numerous terrorist operations in J&K. Thousands of civilians (belonging to non-Islamic religions such as Hinduism and Sikhism) and Indian security force personnel have been killed as a result of these operations. After 1997, there was a significant rise in terror activities in the J&K region, particularly in the districts of Poonch and Doda that have allegedly been repeated targets of the group. Indian officials claimed that most of the terror activities

during this period were carried out by the Lashkar-e-Tayyiba. Prominent among them is the attack at Srinagar airport, killing five Indians; the attack on a police station in Srinagar that took the lives of at least eight officers and caused injuries to many more; attacks on Hindu temples in the state; as well as several attacks on the security forces stationed along the Indian border.

Indian authorities suspect members of LT to be the masterminds behind various other terrorist acts in other states of India. One of the most prominent incidents includes the attack in December 2001 on the Indian Parliament in New Delhi. The government of India claims that this attack was organized by the LT and another Pakistan-based terrorist organization—Jaish e-Mohammed (JEM). The LT has also been held responsible for attacks on a temple in Gujarat, India, (in 2002), and the site of the temple of Ram in Ayodhya, India.

The attack on India's parliament is just one example of cooperation between the LT and other terrorist organizations. Indian intelligence agencies and monitor groups blame the Chattisinghpora massacre of 2000 on a combined operation between the LT and the Kashmir-based faction of Hizb-ul-Mujahideen. That attack left 35 people dead in the Anantang district of J&K.

In 1998, the LT reportedly joined Osama bin Laden's International Islamic Front for Jihad against Crusaders and Jews. Indian intelligence officials allege that in 2001, the outfit relocated to Muzaffarabad, capital of Pakistan-occupied Kashmir (PoK). This move, as reported by the officials, was made after the Pakistani government clamped down the operations of the group due to mounting international pressure, as a result of the September 11 attacks in the United States. At this time, Maulana Abdul Wahid Kashmiri was appointed leader of the operations in Kashmir, and Zaki ur-Rehman took over as Supreme Commander (replacing Hafeez Mohammed Saeed).

PHILOSOPHY AND TACTICS

Lashkar-e-Tayyiba aims at establishing Islamic rule in India and other Asian countries. Its immediate objective is to liberate Jammu & Kashmir, and eventually other Muslim dominated regions of India such as Junagadh (in western India), and the city of Hyderabad (eastern India). The group has declared that jihad is the obligatory right of every religious Muslim. The group, like many other militant outfits, is reported to be inspired by the ideology of Osama bin Laden, and al-Qaeda. It allegedly denounces all non-Islamic religions and also condemns those Islamic nations that oppose its philosophy.

The MDI (parent organization) and LT belong to the Ahle Hadith school of Islam of the Wahabi orientation (a sect of Islam) and are considered by most to be extremely conservative and religious minded. Several terrorism experts consider them to be religious fanatics. The LT reportedly has the largest, most efficient, and highly independent jihad network among all other militant Islamic organizations based in Pakistan.

Reports indicate that the organization was initially not a part of the United Jihad Council (a council of numerous militant organizations allegedly organized by the ISI of Pakistan), and had its own specific methods of operation. However, it is speculated by terrorism experts that the tactics employed by the group's fedayeen fighters (an Arabic word meaning "one who is ready to sacrifice his life for the cause,"—more commonly known as suicide fighters) against the Indian military earned them great respect among other Islamic extremist groups, and it was eventually made part of the Jihad Council.

The Indian government is of the opinion that Lashkar-e-Tayyiba has in the past adopted violent tactics to achieve its objectives. This includes killing people who follow religions other than Islam. LT has reportedly killed several infants, children, women, and other civilians. The main strategy that is adopted for such purposes is suicide bombing. Suicide units, or fedayeen, have been involved in many of its terrorist activities. Additionally, its members have also used traditional means of combat with the use of guns, grenades, and explosives. Analysts state that the members of LT believe that they would attain martyrdom when they die in combat in the name of religion.

In 2002, it was reported in the Indian news media that several LT members, disguised as Hindu holy men, duped innocent civilians and murdered 27 people, including 13 women and one child. Mass murders in the disputed Kashmir valley region are not uncommon, and are usually attributed to Lashkar-e-Tayyiba.

The majority of the outfit's members have a Punjabi background (one of the common sects in both India and Pakistan) and speak the local language. This makes it difficult for the Indian authorities to trace them. Besides, Indian terrorism experts state that common language and cultural traits help members of LT establish rapport among the young minds of Kashmir.

Most of LT's recruits are non-Kashmiri Pakistanis trained in *madrassas* (Islamic schools). However, the LT reportedly has thousands of followers in the disputed Kashmir valley region in India and the Pakistan-occupied region of Azad Kashmir. Analysts argue that although most of the jihad organizations recruit local men and women with additional help from nationals of other Islamic countries, LT does the complete opposite. Also, Indian intelligence agencies and monitor groups state that LT and its founder organization MDI are extremely secretive and do not reveal much about their internal workings.

Many reports have suggested that at its command centers based in Pakistan and PoK, the group members teach young new recruits their own interpretation of militant Islam. The group has reportedly set up numerous training camps throughout Pakistan and also along the "Line of Control" (an unmarked border between J&K and PoK). It is thought by intelligence agencies that many of these training camps are comparable with the most advanced military training centers around the world.

The group, reportedly, also runs various religious schools, prints religious publications, and runs social welfare organizations to attract new members. Analysts claim that members and leaders of the Lashkar-e-Tayyiba also use the Internet to propagate their ideology, and appeal for donations and funding.

It has often been reported that LT has developed close associations with various Islamic terrorist outfits operating in India such as Student's Islamic Movement of India (SIMI). As reported in the January 2001 edition of *The Hindu Business Line*, a national news publication in India, the leader of LT, Hafeez Mohammed Saeed, in an interview to the Lahore Press Club in 1996 stated that, "The jehad in Kashmir would soon spread to entire India. Our Mujahideen would create three Pakistans in India."

Although, in the early 2000s, the group reportedly underwent structural and leadership changes, including the induction of Maulana

PRIMARY SOURCE

Lashkar e-Tayyiba (LT) a.k.a. Army of the Righteous

DESCRIPTION

LT is the armed wing of the Pakistan-based religious organization, Markaz-ud-Dawa-wal-Irshad (MDI), an anti-US Sunni missionary organization formed in 1989. LT is led by Hafiz Muhammad Saeed and is one of the three largest and best trained groups fighting in Kashmir against India. It is not connected to any political party. The Pakistani Government banned the group and froze its assets in January 2002. Elements of LT and Jaish-e-Mohammed combined with other groups to mount attacks as "The Save Kashmir Movement."

ACTIVITIES

LT has conducted a number of operations against Indian troops and civilian targets in Jammu and Kashmir since 1993. LT claimed responsibility for numerous attacks in 2001, including an attack in January on Srinagar airport that killed five Indians; an attack on a police station in Srinagar that killed at least eight officers and wounded several others; and an attack in April against Indian border security forces that left at least four dead. The Indian Government publicly implicated LT, along with JEM, for the attack on December 13, 2001, on the Indian Parliament building, although concrete evidence is lacking. LT is also suspected of involvement in the attack on May 14, 2002, on an Indian Army base in Kaluchak that left 36 dead. Senior al-Qa'ida lieutenant Abu Zubaydah was captured at an LT safe house in Faisalabad in March 2002, suggesting some members are facilitating the movement of al-Qa'ida members in Pakistan.

STRENGTH

Has several thousand members in Azad Kashmir, Pakistan, in the southern Jammu and Kashmir and Doda regions, and in the Kashmir valley. Almost all LT members are Pakistanis from madrassas across Pakistan or Afghan veterans of the Afghan wars.

LOCATION/AREA OF OPERATION

Based in Muridke (near Lahore) and Muzaffarabad.

EXTERNAL AID

Collects donations from the Pakistani community in the Persian Gulf and United Kingdom, Islamic NGOs, and Pakistani and other Kashmiri business people. LT also maintains a Web site (under the name Jamaat ud-Daawa), through which it solicits funds and provides information on the group's activities. The amount of LT funding is unknown. LT maintains ties to religious/militant groups around the world, ranging from the Philippines to the Middle East and Chechnya through the fraternal network of its parent organization Jamaat ud-Dawa (formerly Markaz Dawa ul-Irshad). In anticipation of asset seizures by the Pakistani Government, the LT withdrew funds from bank accounts and invested in legal businesses, such as commodity trading, real estate, and production of consumer goods.

Source: U.S. Department of State. *Country Reports on Terrorism.* Washington, D.C., 2004.

Abdul Wahid Kashmiri as the head of the Kashmir faction (in place of Hafeez Mohammed Saeed), monitor groups and analysts allege that Saeed is still the supreme leader of Lashkar-e-Tayyiba. Experts and Indian intelligence agency officials also argue that such changes are merely cosmetic moves to avoid ramifications of the ban placed on the group.

As of 2005, Western and Indian intelligence/security sources state that Lashkar-e-Tayyiba members have been actively participating in terrorist activities in Chechnya, the Middle East, and Bosnia, and allegedly have strong links with al-Qaeda. In 2005, the United Nations banned Lashkar-e-Tayyiba, categorically stating it to be a terrorist organization. According to published

U.S. State Department reports, as of 2005, Lashkar-e-Tayyiba has an estimated strength of several hundred trained members.

OTHER PERSPECTIVES

Since 2001, internal clashes and external pressures have turned the Lashkar-e-Tayyiba against the United States and Israel, besides its traditional target: India. Addressing the Pakistan Ulema Convention at Lahore in 2004, Hafeez Mohammed Saeed stated, "We do not fear America. We can defeat it through Jihad very easily, but General Musharraf is holding us up. He has become the biggest enemy of jihad, and if we can get him out of the picture, we can take care of the infidels." This was after Pakistani President Musharraf started clamping down on the operations of the LT as a result of sustained international pressure. Leaders of the group have reportedly stated that "there is no all-Islamic government in any country," and that the former "Taliban regime in Afghanistan was almost an Islamic government."

After the September 11, 2001, attacks on the United States, President Bush ordered a freeze on the assets of Lashkar-e-Tayyiba. President Bush stated that "Lashkar-e-Tayyiba is an extremist group based in Kashmir. LeT is a stateless sponsor of terrorism, and it hopes to destroy relations between Pakistan and India. To achieve its purpose, LT has committed acts of terrorism inside both India and Pakistan. LeT is a terrorist organization that presents a global threat. And I look forward to working with the governments of both India and Pakistan in a common effort to shut it down and to bring the killers to justice." Subsequently, President Musharraf froze the assets of Lashkar-e-Tayyiba and banned the organization. This move of President Musharraf was well received in the international community and among the leaders of the world, including that of the United States and India.

SUMMARY

According to the Indian government, Lashkar-e-Tayyiba has worked around many of the restrictions that have been imposed on its operations by Pakistan and the United Nations. After September 11, news sources have reported that the group has collected close to $1.75 million through anonymous donations and gifts by charitable organizations. The training camps run by the outfit in undisclosed places in Pakistan and northern India, particularly in Kashmir, are considered by military experts to be state of the art and well equipped. According to several media reports, LT leader Saeed openly declared in 2004 that the group had recruited more than 7,000 youths to fight in the Kashmir Jihad. It was also reported that he boasted that more than 800 of these had already attained martyrdom. The Indian government and media has reported that more than 50,000 people, including innocent civilians, have been murdered in Kashmir, and many more continue to die in this constant tug of war between India and terrorist organizations. Additionally, it has been alleged by Indian intelligence that most of these militant outfits are backed by Pakistani authorities.

LT is believed to have strong ties with other terrorist organizations, including al-Qaeda. Intelligence reports indicate that the group has also expanded its range of activities in Chechnya, the Philippines, and the Middle East, and may have set up sleeper cells in the United States and Australia. In 2004, 11 individuals suspected to be working for LT were detained in Virginia, United States, and were later charged with conspiracy and weapons charges. Authorities speculated that some of them had been to Pakistan to train at LT camps. Earlier that year, the Australian authorities arrested a terrorist who was alleged to be the leader of LT operations in Australia.

Lashkar-e-Tayyiba is considered by counter-terrorism analysts and intelligence experts to be powerful and influential militant organization. Authorities also fear that efforts by India and Pakistan and other countries to establish peace in this region might encourage LT to take drastic measures to thwart the peace proceedings. Experts warn that the threat of LT to strike at other targets besides the Indian subcontinent is imminent as LT allegedly possesses the potential to execute its threats.

SOURCES

Web sites

BBC News. "Profile: Lashkar-e-Toiba." < http://news.-bbc.co.uk/1/hi/world/south_asia/3181925.stm > (accessed October 20, 2005).

MIPT Terrorism Knowledge Base. "Lashkar-e-Taiba (LET)." < http://www.tkb.org/ Group.jsp?groupID = 66 > (accessed October 20, 2005).

South Asian Terrorism Portal. "Lashkar-e-Toiba." < http://www.satp.org/satporgtp/countries/india/states/ jandk/terrorist_outfits/lashkar_e_toiba.htm > (accessed October 20, 2005).

Overseas Security Advisory Council. "Lashkar-e-Tayyiba (LT) (Army of the Righteous)." < http://www.ds-osa-c.org/Groups/group.cfm?contentID = 1286 > (accessed October 20, 2005).

SEE ALSO

Jaish-e-Mohammed (JEM)

League of the South

LEADER: J. Michael Hill

YEAR ESTABLISHED OR BECAME ACTIVE: 1994

ESTIMATED SIZE: 10,000

USUAL AREA OF OPERATION: United States

OVERVIEW

Founded in 1994 by a group of southern academics led by Michael Hill, the League of the South is a self-described southern nationalist organization dedicated to the establishment of an independent republic somewhere within the current boundaries of the southern United States. Membership is estimated at 10,000, with chapters in 20 states. Recognizing that southern secession is very unlikely to become a viable political movement in the foreseeable future, the current focus of the group is in the defense of southern culture against what is perceived as a concerted attack from "cultural elites" in Washington, Hollywood, and the Ivy League.

HISTORY

The League of the South was founded in Tuskaloosa, Alabama, in 1994 by Michael Hill, then a professor of British history at Stillman College, a historically black institution. Other founding members included academics and journalists from throughout the southern United States. The group considers this focus on leadership by intellectuals and academics as its major strength.

The impetus for the group's founding was what Hill perceived as the denigration and

Dan Gonzales addresses a crowd in front of Florida's Pinellas County Justice Center on March 22, 2005. Gonzales, vice chairman of the Florida chapter of the League of the South, is reading a letter from the League to the state House of Representatives, calling for Terry Schiavo's feeding tube be reinserted. © Winston Luzier/Reuters/Corbis

rejection of southern heritage and values by the larger, majority U.S. culture. The League's manifesto gives voice to this theme, noting that in a time when all cultures are celebrated and protected and considerable social pressure is brought to bear on anything that resembles racism, southerners are still routinely portrayed as "rednecks" or "crackers" in movies and on television, and it is still socially acceptable to refer to them as such.

The group originally called itself the Southern League, but in 1997 changed its name to the League of the South in order to avoid legal conflict with a minor league baseball association with an established prior claim to the same name.

The League of the South quickly came to the forefront of the larger so-called southern heritage movement, growing from its initial membership of about 40 in 1994 to 4,000 in 1998, to an estimated 10,000 today. Its stated purpose is to "advance the cultural, social, economic, and political well being and independence of the southern people by all honorable means." By all accounts, these means have been limited to the political and intellectual spheres, and no violent actions have ever been attributed to the group's members. Nevertheless, the Southern Poverty Law Center, a civil rights group that has itself been the subject of controversy, denounced the League of the South as a hate group in its quarterly publication, *The Intelligence Report.*

Unquestionably, the League of the South does stake out a number of philosophical positions that place it well outside the cultural mainstream. It is intensely critical of the U.S. federal government, which it refers to as the American Empire. In Hill's view, the southern secession of 1860–1861 was a legal termination of a voluntary contract between the states and Lincoln's maniacal determination to preserve the union by force created a tyrannical, illegitimate federal government that would have appalled the framers of the constitution.

The group aims to reclaim the symbols of the Confederacy from their current negative associations with bigotry and racial violence, and to restore Christianity as a dominant force in society. Hill urges his followers to "de-legitimate" all institutions controlled by the federal government, including public schools. He calls on members to secede from American popular culture, eschew its institutions, and replace them with what he considers uniquely southern cultural inventions, such as home schooling.

In the twenty-first century the League of the South continues to expand, with local chapters springing up throughout the southern United States. The group has established an educational arm, the League of the South Institute for the Study of Southern Culture and History, which has its own operating budget and board of directors. The group hosts an annual conference, which is attended by hundreds of core members and large donors.

Despite the fact that Hill continually reminds members that cultural revival must precede political efforts, the League of the South has become increasingly politically active. It has worked to defeat candidates who are deemed disloyal to the South, usually because they

LEADERSHIP

J. Michael Hill

Before founding the largest and most influential southern heritage organization in the United States, Michael Hill was a professor of British history at Stillman College, a historically black institution. One biographer alleges that he was always an oddity at the school, with his openly pro-Confederate views and affectations, though his career lasted for decades there.

Hill began developing his views about southern sovereignty and the Celtic nature of the Old South in the 1970s, studying under Grady McWhiney. In the early 1990s, Hill published two books on Celtic history, expounding on his mentor's views. In 1994, he and 40 others established the League of the South. Hill left his position at Stillman in 1998 to focus full time on League activities.

---

supported the removal of the Confederate battle flag from state facilities. The group claims responsibility, for example, for helping defeat then South Carolina Governor David Beasely in 1996, after he went on record as supporting the removal of the battle flag from the state-house. In 2004, the group called for an economic boycott of Georgia after voters elected to remove all traces of the Confederate emblem from the state flag. That same year, the group campaigned heavily for Tom Parker, who was ultimately elected to the Alabama supreme court.

The League of the South has had a profound impact on other southern heritage movements. Groups like the Council of Conservative Citizens have adopted much of the League's "unreconstructed" southern history as doctrine. One such doctrine is the idea of the Celtic nature of the South, reflected in the League's insistence on Oxford rather than U.S. spelling conventions in all its publications.

PHILOSOPHY AND TACTICS

At the center of the League of the South is a small group of academics who teach at major universities like Emory and the University of Virginia. They are historians and philosophers and teachers of religion whose views have been progressively abandoned by the mainstream since feminism and multiculturalism took root and became the dominant forces in academia, transforming the liberal arts curriculum.

The founders of the League of the South are unhappy because they feel that the culture and heritage of the South has been unfairly marginalized, ridiculed, and condemned within U.S. culture as a whole. From their perspective, *Huckleberry Finn* has been removed from the lists of great books, Thomas Jefferson knocked from his lofty perch in the American pantheon, and the history of the Civil War refocused on the suffering caused by the South's economic dependence on slave labor. The League of the South was created to fight against this trend, and takes this war of words and ideas very seriously. As Clyde Wilson (University of South Carolina professor of history and editor of the papers of the great antebellum leader John C. Calhoun) put it at League seminar in April 2005: "Those who want to wipe out our memories want to wipe us out as well."

As *de facto* President for life, Hill has been very clear about the organization's objectives. These are to defend and promote the culture of the old South though educational efforts and political activism; to establish a chapter in every county of every southern state; and to eventually lead the South to secession from the United States and the establishment of an independent southern republic.

The leaders of the League seem to be modeling their strategy after more developed, successful secessionist movements in other countries. A connection to the Northern League of Italy is tacitly acknowledged in the League of the South's foundational documents. The politically successful Quebec sovereignty movement no doubt provides some inspiration as well.

Applying these models to their own cause, Hill and the other leaders have chosen to focus first and foremost on cultural revitalization and recruitment. Detailed instructions for forming country chapters are found on the group's web site, along with a voluminous listing of activities

KEY EVENTS

1996: The League campaigns vigorously against South Carolina Governor David Beasely, who is defeated.

1998: Hill leaves his position at Stillman College.

2003: Hill and others establish the Southern Party as a national third political party.

2004: The League campaigns successfully for the election of Tom Parker to the Alabama supreme court.

that new members should engage in. These include the display of the Confederate flag, support for locally owned businesses, involvement in local politics, and pamphleteering and otherwise actively promoting the League at the grassroots level. Members are encouraged to run for local office, and particularly the office of county sheriff. Networking and cross-membership with other southern heritage organizations like the Council of Conservative Citizens is encouraged as well, as is involvement in conservative causes like the anti-abortion movement.

Members are urged to withdraw their children from the public school system to protect them from assimilating to the majority U.S. culture. Home schooling or, for those that can afford it, private Christian education are the prescribed alternatives. The League's Institute provides recommendations for instructional materials, speakers for local conferences and seminars, and is in the process of developing a home schooling curriculum.

On a personal level, the group calls on its members to attend their local churches, live Christian lives, care for their local needy families, and to be good stewards of their own private property.

At the state level, the group has claimed some success in helping to defeat unsympathetic gubernatorial candidates and campaigning for politicians who support their causes. The most

prominent examples are the defeat of South Carolina governor David Beasely in 1996, and the successful campaign to elect Tom Parker to the Alabama supreme court in 2004.

On a national level, the group seems to be fighting a losing battle in well publicized campaigns to keep the Confederate flag flying on public property. Despite the efforts of the League and other heritage groups, only Mississippi still incorporates the Confederate emblem in its state flag. An extended series of protests by the NAACP and others in South Carolina resulted in the removal of the Confederate battle flag from atop the statehouse to a monument on the Capitol lawn, a solution that has proven to be unsatisfactory to both sides of the debate. Today, the NAACP continues its economic boycott of South Carolina.

For candidates running for national office, personal association with any southern heritage or neo-Confederate group remains tantamount to political suicide. This was dramatically illustrated in December 2002 when Senate Majority Leader Trent Lott was forced to step down after it was revealed he had a longtime association with the Council of Conservative Citizens.

OTHER PERSPECTIVES

The Southern Poverty Law Center (SPLC), a Montgomery, Alabama, civil rights group, has been consistent in its vocal opposition to the League of the South, first naming the latter as a hate group in the summer, 2000 edition of its quarterly *Intelligence Report*. As evidence for this charge, the SPLC quotes semi-anonymous postings on various neo-Confederate web sites by former and current League of the South members, along with excerpts from a few of Hill's speeches that the SPLC sees as thinly veiled racism. Most of the quotes attributed to Hill are taken from speeches in which he attempts to defend slavery in the old South.

Other watchdog groups like the Anti-Defamation League (ADL) have not included the League of the South in their lists of hate groups, though the ADL does list the annual League of the South conference on their calendar of extremist events.

Supporters of the League dispute the claim that they are a racist or hate group. They point to the fact that the group's official materials are rife with statements denouncing racism—although they are marked by defensive complaints about "anti-southern bigotry." No articles denigrating any other culture or race can be found on the group's web site. No member of the group has ever been accused of violent or illegal activities, and the group's materials stress that members should conduct themselves in an honorable, law-abiding manner.

With that said, it may be inevitable that a group that so proudly trumpets the glories of the white antebellum South and that has defended slavery as being a relatively benign—more like the portrayal in *Gone with the Wind* than in *Uncle Tom's Cabin*—would be charged with promoting racist ideas, and might indeed attract some racists among its 10,000 members.

SUMMARY

Founded by a group of southern academics led by Michael Hill, the League of the South has grown from forty members at its inception in 1994 to an estimated 10,000 members in 2005. Despite the unrealistical nature of its goals (which include secession from the United States), and the eccentric views of its leaders, the League of the South is the fastest growing, most influential group in the larger southern heritage movement.

To spearhead its educational efforts, the group has established the League of the South Institute for the Study of Southern Culture and History in Killen, Alabama. The Institute has its own operating budget and board of directors. The Institute hosts an annual national conference, provides speakers for state chapter events, and provides recommendations for home schooling.

Members are encouraged to be active in local politics and conservative causes, while living civically responsible lives. At the same time, members are urged to withdraw from the majority U.S. culture and its institutions, including the public school system. Recruitment and promoting southern culture are the primary focus of the group's activities.

SOURCES

Books

Ignatieff, Michael. *Blood and Belonging : Journeys into the New Nationalism.* New York: Farrar, Straus and Giroux, 1995.

Periodicals

Southern Poverty Law Center. "A League of Their Own." *Intelligence Report.* Summer 2000.

Web sites

Boston.com. "Last of the Confederates." < http:// www.boston.com/news/globe/editorial_opinion/oped/ articles/2005/02/21/last_of_the_confederates/ > (accessed October 18, 2005).

TIME.com. "Loathing Abe Lincoln." < http://www. time.com/time/nation/article/0,8599,1077193,00.html > (accessed October 18, 2005).

Lord's Resistance Army

LEADER: Joseph Kony

USUAL AREA OF OPERATION: Uganda

OVERVIEW

The Lord's Resistance Army (LRA) is a rebel group fighting the Ugandan government in northern Uganda. The group routinely targets civilians, primarily of the Acholi ethnic group.

HISTORY

The Lord's Resistance Army (LRA) has been in operation in northern Uganda since 1986, when current Uganda President Yoweri Museveni came into power. The group is known for killing unsuspecting men, women, and children, on buses, in their village homes, and out in the fields while farming. Often, victims are burned, or hacked to death by machetes.

In 2002, the Ugandan government began forcing villagers in northern Uganda to move into protective camps called displaced persons' camps (IDPs). There are normally several thousand people in very condensed camps, with people living in small clay huts. The government claims that IDP camps are the only way it can protect the citizens from the LRA.

Fearing LRA attacks, residents in the area stopped going into the fields, and must rely on food rations and supplies provided by the United Nations World Food Programme and other aid organizations. The LRA has also

At least 200 people were killed in a massacre in northern Uganda on February 23, 2004. It was believed to have been carried out by the Lord's Resistance Army. AP/Wide World Photos. Reproduced by permission

attacked and killed aid workers, who now are only able to reach the IDP camps safely under military protection. This means less-frequent trips to the unsanitary camps, which are fraught with high levels of disease and malnutrition.

The LRA began its operations while a power vacuum existed in northern Uganda in the mid-1980s. Remnants of forces loyal to former presidents Milton Obote and Tito Okello fled to the north after they were defeated when Museveni's forces fought their way into power. Eventually, the LRA emerged as a force claiming to fight for the rights of the Acholi ethnic group. Joseph Kony, the group's founder and leader, is an Acholi.

The Acholi people have claimed that the government in Kampala often neglects them, but there has been little public support among the Acholi for the LRA. It is in the Acholi villages where most of the LRA violence occurs.

The LRA attacks do not only target the Acholi people in northern Uganda. There are pockets of Sudanese Acholi living in southern Sudan who have experienced some of the same brutality from the LRA as their Ugandan neighbors. Other ethnic groups in northern and northeastern Uganda, like the Langi, have also experienced LRA violence.

There was an escalation of attacks on the Langi, near the town of Lira in northern Uganda in 2004. The people in Lira held violent protests in which they placed blame on the Acholi people for their LRA-related sufferings.

The LRA is a weak threat to the toppling of the Ugandan government in Kampala. They have not been active south of the Nile River, where Kampala is located. The LRA soldiers move on foot, and live in the bush.

The LRA has base camps hidden across the border in southern Sudan, where the group occasionally creates havoc among Sudanese villagers,

LEADERSHIP

JOSEPH KONY

The Acholi leader and founder of the LRA, Joseph Kony, has been an elusive target for the Ugandan government. Kony is thought to be in his 40s, with as many as sixty wives and many more sex slaves. He is a self-proclaimed mystic prophet who likes to give long sermons. Kony says he communicates directly with the Holy Spirit. He was born in northern Uganda, and is a former Catholic altar boy. Kony was educated as a social worker. He is the nephew of a voodoo priestess, and it is said that Kony is obsessed with supernatural intervention on the battlefield. The Ugandan military has offered an $11,000 reward for any information that leads to Kony's capture.

---

to replenish supplies. The Ugandan government claims that the Sudanese government in Khartoum provides arms to the LRA, in retaliation for the Ugandan government's support of the Southern People's Liberation Army (SPLA), who were fighting the Sudanese government.

The Ugandan government has been largely unsuccessful in stopping the LRA, even though it has captured or killed several high-ranking LRA officials. Although denied by the Ugandan government, it is claimed by the international community of donor countries (namely, the United States, Europe, and Japan) that the Ugandan military is not active enough in the northern region.

In 2002, under urgings from the U.S. government, Uganda and Sudan signed an agreement to contain the LRA in the border areas. After several air strikes on LRA positions in Uganda, there was an increase in LRA attacks.

The United States has given millions of dollars to Uganda in food aid for northern Uganda, and to support former child soldiers and others who had once been abducted by the LRA. The U.S. Congress passed the Northern Uganda

Crisis Response Act in May 2004. The Act urges Uganda to do more to peacefully solve the conflict with the LRA, which the United States calls a terrorist organization.

PHILOSOPHY AND TACTICS

The often-hidden leader of the LRA, Joseph Kony, has made statements that the group wants to implement a theocratic government in Uganda based on the biblical Ten Commandments. At other times, the LRA has stated that they want to fight for the rights of the Acholi people, who have been the primary victims of LRA attacks. Some claims have been made that the LRA wants to replace the existing Acholi people with an Acholi ethnic group that shares the LRA values.

Former LRA soldiers have said that Kony uses Bible references to explain why it is necessary to kill his own people. It is also reported that the LRA wants to kill the Acholi for not fully supporting Kony's causes.

The LRA uses indiscriminate guerilla tactics, roaming around Uganda's countryside in small units. This has helped them avoid final defeat by the Ugandan military. As the LRA burns and destroys villages and takes victims, they also take food and other bits of property they might need.

Religious superstitions and witchcraft are used to manipulate and scare the LRA soldiers. There are claims that water and other substances are used to protect the LRA soldiers from the bullets of the Ugandan military. A high-ranking LRA captive claimed that water was sprinkled on him, and that he was marked with crosses made of clay and nut oil. This was said to remove his sins, and ensure that the Holy Spirit would look after him.

It is said that at the camps, the LRA has been fairly self-sustaining. They grow their own food, and attend religious services often led by Kony. Although they claim to be a Christian-oriented group, many of the prayer services take on a more Muslim form.

The LRA is known for using children to advance their cause. Estimates are that between 8,000 and 20,000 children have been abducted by the LRA over the years. Typically, the abducted children are forced to be soldiers. Many of the

KEY EVENTS

1980s: Lack of leadership existed in northern Uganda, creating a power vaccum.

1986: The Lord's Resistance Army (LRA) was formed in northern Uganda.

2002: The Ugandan government began forcing villagers in northern Uganda to move into protective camps called displaced persons' camps (IDPs).

2002: Uganda and Sudan signed an agreement to contain the LRA in the border areas.

2004: The U.S. Congress passed the Northern Uganda Crisis Response Act in May 2004.

The LRA has operated in a way that has created fear and chaos in northern Uganda. The people are imprisoned within the camps in their own villages. They are unable to go into the fields to produce their own food for fear of being killed or kidnapped. A bus ride between towns has become a dangerous event, as buses are often attacked.

The LRA has made some peace agreements with the Ugandan government. These agreements are typically violated, or completely ignored by the LRA. In 2000, the Ugandan government offered amnesty to all LRA members. Some of the LRA members did take this offer, although Kony ignored it.

Much of the LRA's communication to the outside world has been through priests who claim neutrality between the LRA and the Uganda military. Regardless, religious institutes and people have been targeted by the LRA. Many of their abductions have taken place at religious boarding schools or orphanages.

girls are taken back to LRA camps in Sudan to serve as sex slaves and wives for the group's commanders. The children born within the camp are used to increase the LRA population.

Children who are abducted are often required to kill their parents and other people in their villages, so that they will have nowhere to return. These children are often forced to fight as soldiers for the LRA. Other children are used as porters to carry LRA supplies. If the children become too weak, they are killed or left to die. It is not uncommon for captives to have their lips or ears cut off if they do not behave as LRA leaders would like. Boys are put on the frontlines as unarmed decoys when the Ugandan military engages the LRA.

In many areas where the LRA is active, children have resorted to sleeping on the streets of the major trading centers of towns such as Gulu, Lira, and Kitgum, which are generally better protected from the LRA than the rural areas. These children will walk up to seven miles a night, while their parents stay back in their rural homes to protect the home's property. It is not uncommon for several thousand children to be found sleeping on the verandas of shops, or in schoolyards.

OTHER PERSPECTIVES

Over the years, the LRA has not made their motivations clear. The media, the Ugandan government, the citizens of northern Uganda, and the international community have all failed to truly understand the objectives of the LRA. It is agreed that the roots of the issue are complicated.

The LRA war may have started out like Kony has said, to topple the Ugandan government. However, the practical reasons that the fighting has persisted likely go beyond the initial motivations.

Many agree that this struggle could not have been maintained without the backing of Sudan. The motivations of Sudan may have been to damage the Ugandan government for its support of the SPLA. There have been thoughts that the LRA would weaken as the peace process moves forward in Sudan. So far, this correlation is not apparent.

It is also likely that the leadership of the LRA wants to continue the struggle to maintain their comfortable lifestyle with many wives.

It is generally agreed that Uganda's diversity of ethnic groups, and the tensions between them, have created the situation that allows a group

PRIMARY SOURCE

Lord's Resistance Army (LRA)

DESCRIPTION

The LRA was formally established in 1994, succeeding the ethnic Acholi-dominated Holy Spirit Movement and other insurgent groups. LRA leader Joseph Kony has called for the overthrow of the Ugandan Government and its replacement with a regime run on the basis of the Ten Commandments. More frequently, however, he has spoken of the liberation and honor of the Acholi people, whom he sees as oppressed by the "foreign" Government of Ugandan President Museveni. Kony is the LRA's undisputed leader. He claims to have supernatural powers and to receive messages from spirits, which he uses to formulate the LRA's strategy.

ACTIVITIES

The Acholi people, whom Kony claims to be fighting to liberate, are the ones who suffer most from his actions. Since the early 1990s, the LRA has kidnapped some 20,000 Ugandan children, mostly ethnic Acholi, to replenish its ranks. Kony despises Acholi elders for having given up the fight against Museveni and relies on abducted children who can be brutally indoctrinated to fight for the LRA. The LRA forces kidnapped children and adult civilians to become soldiers, porters, and "wives" for LRA leaders. The LRA prefers to attack camps for internally displaced persons and other civilian targets, avoiding direct engagement with the Ugandan military. Victims of LRA attacks sometimes have their hands, fingers, ears, noses, or other extremities cut off. The LRA stepped up its activities from 2002 to 2004 after the Ugandan army, with the Sudanese Government's permission, attacked LRA positions inside Sudan. By late 2003, the number of internally displaced had doubled to 1.4 million, and the LRA had pushed deep into non-Acholi areas where it had never previously operated. During 2004, a combination of military pressure, offers of amnesty, and several rounds of negotiation markedly degraded LRA capabilities due to death, desertion, and defection of senior commanders.

STRENGTH

Estimated in early 2004 at between 500 and 1,000 fighters, eighty-five percent of whom are abducted children and civilians, but numbers have since declined significantly.

LOCATION/AREA OF OPERATION

Northern Uganda and southern Sudan.

EXTERNAL AID

Although the LRA has been supported by the Government of Sudan in the past, the Sudanese now appear to be cooperating with the Government of Uganda in a campaign to eliminate LRA sanctuaries in Sudan.

Source: U.S. Department of State. *Country Reports on Terrorism.* Washington, D.C., 2004.

---

like the LRA to exist. The country has been independent for forty years, and because of colonialism, many ethnic groups that may not have naturally coexisted peacefully, were put within the borders of one state. There are many stereotypes and deep-rooted feelings that ethnic groups have about each other.

A theory among the people in northern Uganda is that Museveni and his government have no real desire to stop the chaos in the north. A retired Anglican bishop told *Time* magazine that the current leaders of Uganda are of the Banyankole ethnic group, who used to be hired by the Acholi people to be servants or to watch after their cattle. With the Acholi people in such a weakened state, they pose no threat to the current power seat of the Ugandan government.

Regardless, the Ugandan government says it is doing what it can to stop the LRA. Museveni, the former army general, believes the group must be stopped with military power. The Religious Leaders Peace Initiative in Uganda has pushed for a non-military solution to dealing with the LRA. The UN and other aid workers have spoken out against a military solution in Uganda, saying the risk of women and children caught in the crossfire is too high.

SUMMARY

The LRA continues to be active, causing civilian deaths, even as Ugandan government reports say that the LRA structure is weakening. The Government claims that numbers of high-ranking LRA officers have been killed, captured, or resigned. The group's leader, Kony, is not among these.

Children and villagers continue to be the primary victims of LRA activity. The UN's Under Secretary General for Humanitarian Affairs, Jan Egeland, held a press conference in October 2004, stating that ninety percent of the population is displaced. The UN's World Food Programme director said there were 1.6 million displaced people in approximately 135 camps at the end of 2003. This number was up from 465,000 in April 2002.

In December 2004, there were renewed talks between Ugandan government officials and the LRA. This included the Minister of Internal Affairs, Ruhakana Rugunda. The talks took place in the bush, after Museveni declared a temporary ceasefire in the area.

SOURCES

Books

Anderson, Sean, and Stephen Sloan. *Historical Dictionary of Terrorism, 2nd Edition.* Lanham, Md.: Scarecrow Press, 2002.

Periodicals

"In Search of Uganda's Lost Youth." *Time International.* July 28, 2003: vol. 162, i. 4, p. 42.

"Uganda the Horror." *Smithsonian.* February 2005: vol. 35, i. 11, p. 90.

"UGANDA: Museveni offers to Negotiate with LRA Rebels, Kampala." *IRIN News.* April 16, 2004.

Web sites

BBC News World Edition. "Profile: Uganda's LRA Rebels." < http://news.bbc.co.uk/1/hi/world/africa/3462901.stm > (accessed October 20, 2005).

BBC News World Edition. "Q&A: Uganda's NorthernRebellion." < http://news.bbc.co.uk/2/hi/africa/3514473.stm > (accessed October 20, 2005).

Interaction. "Out of Harm's Way." < http://www.interaction.org/library/detail.php?id = 2744 > (accessed October 20, 2005).

North Carolina Wesleyan College. "Religious Terrorism." < http://faculty.ncwc.edu/toconnor/429/429lect13.htm > (accessed October 20, 2005).

Loyalist Volunteer Force (LVF)

YEAR ESTABLISHED OR BECAME ACTIVE: 1996

ESTIMATED SIZE: 150

USUAL AREA OF OPERATION: Northern Ireland;
Scotland

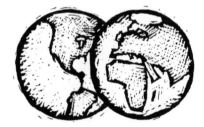

OVERVIEW

The Loyalist Volunteer Force (LVF) is a
Protestant paramilitary organization based in
Northern Ireland. It was formed in 1996 by dissident Ulster Volunteer Force (UVF) members
led by Billy "King Rat" Wright and soon became
notorious for its attacks on civilians and rival
loyalist paramilitaries, as well as targeting
prominent lawyers and journalists.

HISTORY

The Loyalist Volunteer Force was formed in the
summer of 1996 by dissident Ulster Volunteer
Force members following the expulsion from its
ranks of Billy Wright, its renegade mid-Ulster
Brigade Commander.

Wright, dubbed King Rat, is one of the most
controversial, charismatic, and violent individuals associated with Northern Ireland's thirty-
year-long troubles. He was linked with the
murders of more than forty Catholics in the
Portadown area of Ulster, most of who were
civilians without connection to paramilitary
activity. His notoriety brought him minor fame
and a loyal backing, and he sought a greater role
within the UVF leadership, ambitions, which,
when stunted, would bring him into conflict
with its hierarchy. Moreover, during a UVF

Members of the Loyalist Volunteer Army declare their ceasefire in Portadown, Northern Ireland, in a televised annoucement on May 15, 1998. AP/Wide World Photos. Reproduced by permission

ceasefire in the mid 1990s, he increasingly disagreed with their politics.

A particular point of contention was his support for the Orange Order marches in Drumcree, a particular hot point in Ulster's controversial marching season. At the height of the 1996 Orange Order stand-off, Wright sanctioned the murder of a Catholic taxi driver, Michael McGoldrick, an intentionally incendiary action designed to sink Drumcree into a state of insurrection.

Incensed by his potentially calamitous action, the UVF ordered Wright's unit to disband. When Wright refused, the UVF gave him seventy-two hours to leave Northern Ireland or face summary execution. Wright stayed and formed the LVF from the remnants of the mid-Ulster Brigade. "I'll either be shot dead, framed or I'll disappear," he said in the autumn of 1996. "But I'm scared of no one. I've just celebrated my 36th birthday and I fully intend to be around for my 37th."

The LVF quickly set out its stall as an organization that would bring terror to Northern Ireland's Catholic community—and to any Protestants who dared mingle with them. The murder, in July 1997, of an eighteen-year-old Catholic woman near Portadown was typical; likewise the shooting, in March 1998, of a Catholic and his Protestant friend as they sat drinking at a bar.

Religious hatred seemed to be the principle motivation of the LVF—particularly its leader, Wright. Yet, it was his violent sectarianism that brought his downfall, in December 1997. Incarcerated at the Maze Prison for threatening to kill a woman, Wright was killed in a daring attack carried out by prisoners who were members of the Irish National Liberation Army (INLA), who had smuggled a gun into the prison.

LEADERSHIP

BILLY "KING RAT" WRIGHT

In the violent history of Northern Ireland's recent past, Billy Wright, stands apart as arguably the most notorious loyalist paramilitary of the Troubles. Born in Wolverhampton, England to an Irish Protestant family in 1960, Wright was brought up in South Armagh, Northern Ireland. Involved in paramilitary activity from the age of fifteen, he was soon arrested for arms offences and hijacking in 1977 and sentenced to six years imprisonment.

After serving forty-two months, he returned to frontline activity and quickly earned himself a reputation as a brutal and ruthless killer of Catholics in the Portadown area. Despite repeated arrests and the attentions of the IRA and INLA, that tried on many occasions to kill him (and succeeded in murdering his uncle, father-in-law, and brother-in-law), Wright—dubbed King Rat by the press—was undeterred and went on to serve as a Commander of the Ulster Volunteer Force's mid-Ulster Brigade.

Wright seemed to be a man of many contradictions. At once a cold-blooded murderer and closely associated to the drugs trade, he was also renowned for exerting a strong moral force on paramilitaries serving under him and had even served as a lay preacher. Famously, while serving a prison sentence, he banned pornography from fellow paramilitaries.

His rising influence and cult following among parts of Northern Ireland's loyalist community inevitably brought him into conflict with the UVF leadership. By 1996, Wright wanted to exert more influence in the UVF's running, but was snubbed by its leaders. He also wanted to lead attacks on Catholics at the Orange Order's march at Drumcree. Again, he was refused on account of a ceasefire in place but went ahead anyway and murdered a Catholic taxi driver. The UVF ordered his brigade to disband, but Wright refused. He was then ordered out of Northern Ireland within seventy-two hours or face summary execution, but Wright stayed. From the remnants of his mid-Ulster Brigade, he formed the Loyalist Volunteer Force and installed himself as its leader.

An iconic figure, Wright was only able to lead his nascent organization for a matter of months. He was jailed in March 1997 for eight years for threatening to kill a woman and sent to Maghaberry Prison and then the Maze. It was there, on December 27, 1997, that Wright was murdered by a three-man unit from INLA, while waiting in a van for a visit. INLA claimed that his execution was in reprisal for Wright's sectarianism and the catalogue of deaths linked to his name.

Yet, his name is synonymous with the organization he created, and in some minds he remains a legendary figure, his image bearing down from dozens of loyalist murals across Northern Ireland and in parts of Scotland, too. If Bobby Sands was the IRA's Che Guevara, Wright probably emerged as his loyalist equivalent.

In death, Wright was instantly deified, made an iconic figure in the loyalist community. Yet, just five months after his killing, his successors called a ceasefire—a possibility he had vigorously opposed—in the run up to a referendum on the Good Friday Agreement. The LVF urged its supporters to vote no, but when the vote passed in favor, the LVF reaped its benefits anyway, as its prisoners were eligible for release under the treaty's early release scheme.

Despite its ceasefire, the sectarian attacks continued, although they were carried out under guise of the "Red Hand Defenders"—a badge of convenience also used by another loyalist paramilitary group, the Ulster Defense Association. The most notorious of the murders carried out in this period was of the prominent human rights lawyer, Rosemary Nelson, in March 1999. Nelson had previously represented Catholic residents opposed to Orange Order marches in Portadown. (The Royal Ulster Constabulary, whom she also stood against in a number of high-profile cases and who reportedly threatened her, was also accused of complicity in her killing.)

KEY EVENTS

1996: UVF ordered disbandment of Wright's mid-Ulster Brigade after renegade action at the Orange Order march in Drumcree. From its remnants, Wright forms the LVF.

1997: Wright jailed for eight years for threatening a woman.

1997: LVF linked to murder of an eighteen-year-old Catholic woman.

1997: Wright murdered by three INLA members while incarcerated at the Maze Prison.

1998: LVF declare a ceasefire.

1999: Murder of nationalist human rights lawyer, Rosemary Nelson.

2001: Murder of journalist Martin O'Hagan; British government says it no longer recognizes the LVF ceasefire.

Yet, the LVF became as noted for its fratricidal war with the UVF as it did for violence against Catholics. They were accused of murdering the alleged UVF leader, Richard Jameson, in January 2000. Yet this inter-Loyalist conflict was increasingly based as much on fighting for the spoils of organized crime in Northern Ireland as on long-standing political differences. In particular, LVF members became notorious for their involvement in drug smuggling, even to the extent that they allegedly cooperated with their Catholic enemies.

So valuable was the drugs trade to the LVF and so ruthless were they in their methods that, in September 2001, LVF paramilitaries killed Martin O'Hagan, an investigative journalist who wrote for the *Dublin Sunday World*. O'Hagan had, over a number of years, built a reputation as a fearless exposer of the LVF's crimes and follies, and his killing provoked outrage across Ireland. In the wake of his murder, the British Northern Ireland secretary, Paul Murphy, declared that his government no longer recognized the LVF's ceasefire.

In June 2002, Wright's successor as LVF leader, Mark "Swinger" Fulton, was found hanged in Maghaberry Prison of an apparent suicide. Fulton had been Wright's notorious partner in crime since their days with the UVF's mid-Ulster Brigade and his death marked, in many ways, the end of a notorious era for the organization. Since then, the feud with the UVF has continued, but with the LVF's position waning, further killings have been accompanied by suggestions that the UVF is intent on eradicating its dissident offspring for good.

PHILOSOPHY AND TACTICS

The core aim of the Loyalist Volunteer Force is the maintenance of Northern Ireland's ties with Great Britain. It resists any efforts to weaken such links, particularly perceived threats posed by closer integration with the Republic of Ireland.

Shortly after the double murder of a Protestant and his Catholic friend at a bar in Poyntzpass in 1998, the LVF issued a ten-page policy document threatening politicians, Church, and industry leaders and paramilitaries who it claimed were colluding in a "peace surrender process designed to break the Union [i.e., the United Kingdom] and establish the dynamic for Irish unity, within an all-Ireland Roman Catholic, Gaelic Celtic state." Later, in a *Sunday Times* interview, an LVF representative said his organization supported the views of the Reverend Ian Paisley, the controversial leader of the Democratic Unionist Party.

The LVF has sought to prevent a political settlement with Irish nationalists in Northern Ireland by attacking those Catholic politicians, civilians, and even Protestant politicians who endorse the Northern Ireland peace process. In reality, however, since the Good Friday Agreement passed, many of their energies have been focused on their long-running feud with the UVF; as well as maintaining their preeminence in aspects of organized crime throughout the province, particularly drug dealing. This should not detract, however, from the sectarian killings it has carried out on both Catholic civilians and Protestants who associate with them.

PRIMARY SOURCE
Loyalist Volunteer Force (LVF)

DESCRIPTION

An extreme Loyalist group formed in 1996 as a faction of the Ulster Volunteer Force (UVF), the LVF did not emerge publicly until 1997. Composed largely of UVF hardliners who have sought to prevent a political settlement with Irish nationalists in Northern Ireland by attacking Catholic politicians, civilians, and Protestant politicians who endorse the Northern Ireland peace process. LVF occasionally uses the Red Hand Defenders as a cover name for its actions but has also called for the group's disbandment. In October 2001, the British Government ruled that the LVF had broken the cease-fire it declared in 1998 after linking the group to the murder of a journalist. According to the Independent International Commission on Decommissioning, the LVF decommissioned a small amount of weapons in December 1998, but it has not repeated this gesture. Designated under EO 13224 in December 2001.

ACTIVITIES

Bombings, kidnappings, and close-quarter shooting attacks. Finances its activities with drug money and other criminal activities. LVF attacks have been particularly vicious; the group has murdered numerous Catholic civilians with no political or paramilitary affiliations, including an eighteen-year-old Catholic girl in July 1997 because she had a Protestant boyfriend. The terrorists also have conducted successful attacks against Irish targets in Irish border towns. From 2000 to 2004, the LVF has been engaged in a violent feud with other Loyalists, which has left several men dead.

STRENGTH

Small, perhaps dozens of active members.

LOCATION/AREA OF OPERATION

Northern Ireland and Ireland.

EXTERNAL AID

None.

Source: U.S. Department of State. *Country Reports on Terrorism.* Washington, D.C., 2004.

OTHER PERSPECTIVES

"What terror groups do well is to exert a grip on their own communities, one that demands loyalty to their self-proclaimed mission to speak for that community," wrote the journalist, John Lloyd, in the *New Statesman* in 2003. "This loyalty is bought in part by playing on, and magnifying the oppression felt by, that same community, but more by using the instruments of terror on that community itself.

"This is what Northern Ireland has now come to: a state of affairs in which substantial sections of the working-class areas, almost wholly 'pure' Catholic—nationalist/republican or Protestant—unionist/loyalist, live in communities where the fear of one or other version of terrorist republicanism, or terrorist loyalism, rules. These are now networks of organised crime, especially on the loyalist side, where drug-dealing is a major source of income and wealth. To describe this in the abstract cannot convey the fear, the stuntedness of life, the glamour of the terrorist—crime bosses for the young men on the housing estates, the struggle, especially for women, of trying to keep families decent and optimistic, and the arbitrariness of punishment and of injury or death."

"Wright was one of the most brutal terrorist killers of the Troubles," said the *Daily Telegraph* on his death in December 1997. They marked his murder by running a previously unpublished interview with the terrorist, reporting: "He was believed to have been [directly] responsible for the murders of more than a dozen innocent Roman Catholics in the 'murder triangle' of

Mid Ulster. There were the 'dial-a-Catholic' murders whereby the UVF's Mid Ulster brigade, commanded by Wright, would telephone a taxi or food-delivery firm. The randomly summoned victim—religion the only criterion—would then be lured to a place where his killers lay in wait... 'I am seen as a soldier,' he said... 'The Protestant people and their culture are under attack and they have a right to be defended.'... As the evening light faded, Wright was silent for more than a minute when asked how he would like to be remembered after his death. 'As a Loyalist, firm and true,' he said finally. 'And as someone who finally helped to secure peace for his people.'"

SUMMARY

Still beset by the same feud with the UVF that marked its birth in 1996, the LVF is alternatively perceived as an organization on the brink of destruction, or one that is merely going through the latest of its periodic crises. Indeed, if nothing else, it is an indefatigable force, and it should not be forgotten that it has already survived all number of challenges to its existence. These have included death warrants issued against its members; the murder of one of its leaders and suicide of another; countless arrests; a potentially ruinous turf war with the UVF; plus, all the usual attentions of republican rivals and the British and Irish security forces. Its role in Northern Irish organized crime ensures a regular income, and its grip over important loyalist strongholds, notably Portadown, suggest that those who announce the LVF's imminent demise may well be premature.

Nevertheless, the LVF's refusal to engage in the post-Good Friday Agreement political process has marginalized it, and, without a leader of charisma like the late Billy Wright or the Ulster Freedom Fighters' Johnny Adair, it has struggled to assert its identity in the maze of Northern Irish politics. This, along with its notorious input into Northern Ireland's ganglands, has left it with something of an identity crisis: it is potentially still a violent and deeply sectarian terrorist organization, or it is merely a Protestant crime gang?

SOURCES

Books

Anderson, Chris. *The Billy Boy: The Life and Times of Billy Wright*. Edinburgh: Mainsteam, 2003.

Web sites

BBC.co.uk "Paramilitaries: Loyalist Volunteer Force." < http://www.bbc.co.uk/history/war/troubles/factfiles/ lvf.shtml > (accessed October 14, 2005).

Macheteros

ALTERNATE NAME: Popular Army of Boricua

LEADER: Filiberto Ojeda-Rios

USUAL AREA OF OPERATION: Puerto Rico

OVERVIEW

The Puerto Rican organization *Macheteros* (Cane Cutters) derives its name from an insurgency group that appeared in Puerto Rico in 1898, as Spain ceded Puerto Rico to the United States at the end of the Spanish-American War. The modern-day group, *Ejercito Popular de Boricua* (EPB, Popular Army of Boricua), is committed to an armed struggle for complete autonomy and independence from the United States.

Beginning in 1978, the EPB has claimed responsibility for numerous attacks on U.S. government and military installations. In 1992, several members of EPB were tried and convicted for their involvement in a 1983 bank robbery. As a result, much of EPB activities came to a halt. However, the founder and leader of EPB, Filiberto Ojeda-Rios, has evaded capture. Also evading capture is Victor Gerena, who remains on the U.S. Federal Bureau of Investigation (FBI) top ten most wanted list.

HISTORY

The present-day organization, Macheteros, or EPB, derives its name from Puerto Rican history. In a 2002 declaration of the origins of the EPB, founder Filiberto Ojeda-Rios recalled a

A supporter of Puerto Rico nationalist leader Filiberto Ojeda Rios holds a poster that says in Spanish, "Wake up, Puerto Ricans, defend what's yours." The demonstration in San Juan on September 23, 2005, followed the death of Ojeda Rios during an attempt by the FBI to capture him earlier in that day. AP/Wide World Photos.

pact between Spain and Puerto Rico, declaring the island's independence from the European power. However, in 1898, at the close of the Spanish-American War, Spain ceded Puerto Rico and other Caribbean territories to the United States as a provision of the Treaty of Paris. As a result, a group of insurgents launched a campaign against the United States; this group called itself Macheteros.

By 1948, Puerto Rico was ruled under a popularly elected governor. In 1952, voters in Puerto Rico adopted a constitution that enacted internal self-governing mechanisms. The island voted to become a commonwealth of the United States, allowing it exemption from paying federal income tax and providing no representation in the U.S. Congress.

In 1978, the modern-day Macheteros embarked on its first operation. Believing that the FBI maintained files on 150,000 Puerto Ricans and embarked on daily political assassinations, the EPB launched a campaign to force the United States off of the island. On August 24, 1978, the EPB issued its first communiqué which claimed responsibility for the death of Puerto Rican police officer, Julio Roman Rodriguez. The communiqué cited the action as retaliation for the death of two EPB members, Carlos Satto Arrivi and Arnoldo Dario Rosado. The group then began to target U.S. government facilities and U.S. military installations on Puerto Rico.

Believing they were at war with a colonial power, the EPB targeted U.S. military bases and personnel. In 1978, two bombs were found and detonated at a Reserve Officer Training Corps (ROTC) building in San Juan. In addition, the EPB claimed responsibility for an attack on a bus carrying off-duty U.S. sailors. The gunmen opened fire on the bus, killing two and injuring eight. The attack was cited as retaliation for the death of Angel Rodriguez Cristobel, who was serving time in a Tallahassee, Florida, prison. Cristobel was found hanged in his cell and the death was ruled a suicide, but the EPB called it an assassination. In 1981, the most costly of the EPB attacks on U.S. military interests on the island occurred. In January, members from the EPB infiltrated the National Guard base and blew up 11 planes, causing $45 million in damage.

However, the group's most notorious activity occurred in 1983. The EPB launched an operation called "White Eagle." One of its operatives, Victor Gerena, who was working as a driver for Wells Fargo, held two of his coworkers at gunpoint and injected them with a sedative. Along with other members of the EPB, the group robbed Wells Fargo of $7.2 million, only $80,000 of which has been recovered. Jorge Masetti, a former spy for Cuba, claimed that the Cuban government helped to fund and to plan the heist. Masetti explained that $4 million was shipped to Cuba via diplomatic pouch. Victor Gerena was also smuggled to Cuba, where he is believed to still reside.

No immediate connection was made between the robbery and the EPB. It was six weeks later when the EPB launched rockets into an FBI office in San Juan that the

LEADERSHIP

FILBERTO OJEDA-RIOS

Filiberto Ojeda-Rios is the founder of EPB. Although Ojeda-Rios cited his occupation as that of musician, he began his political career in 1967 as he formed the Independent Armed Revolutionary Movement (MIRA). Ojeda-Rios, along with other members of the MIRA, were trained and funded by the Cuban government and engaged in activities in the continental United States, mainly in and around New York City. He was arrested for his participation in MIRA activities, but jumped bail. He then returned to Puerto Rico and participated in the Armed Forces of the National Liberation before creating the EPB. In September 1990, he was arrested once again for his involvement in the Wells Fargo robbery of 1983. However, he once again escaped. In 1992, he was tried in abstentia and sentenced to fifty-five years as well as fined $600,000. On September 23, 2005, Ojeda-Rios was shot and killed by FBI agents as they attempted to arrest him at his home outside Hormigueros, Puerto Rico.

connection was made. The EPB claimed responsibility for the rocket attack, citing it as retaliation for the U.S. invasion of Grenada. The FBI increased its surveillance of the group. While executing a search warrant, agents discovered detailed recordkeeping that spelled out ties to the Wells Fargo robbery. In 1990, Ojeda-Rios and other EPB members were arrested for their involvement in the robbery. However, before he could stand trial, Ojeda-Rios escaped. He, along with the other members of the group, including Gerena, was convicted of the robbery by 1992. As a result, the activities of the EPB slowed.

However, in 1998, the EPB began activities again after the announcement that the Puerto Rican government was to sell its telephone company to GTE. As a result, the EPB claimed responsibility for two explosions, occurring at branches of Banco Popular in San Juan.

In 1999, after pressure from human rights organizations, President Clinton granted clemency to 16 of the EPB members convicted of the Wells Fargo robbery. Despite widespread criticism of the action, Clinton offered three reasons for the clemency: the crimes did not cause bodily injury; he believed that the sentences were unduly harsh; and all the members were required to renounce violence. Ojeda-Rios and Gerena were not among those offered clemency. Gerena remains in hiding and is currently sought by the U.S. government. Ojeda-Rios was killed during a 2005 arrest attempt.

PHILOSOPHY AND TACTICS

The philosophy of the EPB is based in the belief that the island of Puerto Rico gained independence from Spain and therefore the Treaty of Paris that ceded the island to the United States is void. Prior to the group's formation, many of its members believed that the island had been infiltrated by U.S. agents and military personnel whose goal was the eradication of the Puerto Rican identity. Members of the EPB believe that the U.S. government has exploited the resources and people of the island under a colonial rule. It was a result of this "aggression" that caused groups like EPB to form. In his explanation of the origins of the EPB, Ojeda-Rios states, "The defense of the culture has constituted a bastion of tireless struggle. The defense of our language, our traditions, our folklore, and our patriotic values has become central to the efforts of the people to ensure their own survival. Armed struggle has been indispensable because it represents in itself the right of any colonized country to struggle for its independence."

The armed struggle that Ojeda-Rios undertook with the EPB became its prevailing tactic in seeking complete independence from the United States. As a result, the group engaged in a series of bombings throughout the late 1970s and early 1980s. Beginning in 1979, the group raised the stakes by targeting U.S. military personnel. In addition to killing two U.S. sailors, the group also began a campaign to destroy military property. As a result, the EPB attacked the National Guard base, causing damage to the property. In order to fund its activities, the EPB planned and executed the largest bank robbery in U.S.

KEY EVENTS

1978: Communiqué is issued claiming responsibility for the death of Puerto Rican police officer, Julio Roman Rodriguez, as retaliation for the death of two members.

1978: Two bombs are found and detonated at an ROTC building in San Juan.

1979: Members of EPB open fire on off-duty U.S. sailors, killing two and injuring eight.

1981: Commandos infiltrate the national guard base in San Juan and destroy eleven planes, causing $45 million in damages.

1983: Members of EPB engaged in operation White Eagle, a robbery of $7.2 million from the Wells Fargo depot.

1990: Ojeda-Rios and other members of EPB were arrested on charges surrounding the Wells Fargo robbery; Ojeda-Rios escapes back to Puerto Rico.

1992: Ojeda-Rios and others members of EPB are convicted of robbery.

1998: After sale of state-owned phone company to GTE, EPB set off two explosions at Banco Popular branches in San Juan.

1999: Sixteen members of EPB serving sentences in relation to the Wells Fargo robbery are granted clemency by President Clinton.

2005: Ojeda-Rios killed during an FBI arrest attempt.

history, at the time. Proceeds from this robbery helped to fund other activities of the group.

OTHER PERSPECTIVES

In 1988, a federal report on terrorism cited that the EPB had "declared war" on the U.S. government. This notion was seconded nearly a decade later when Attorney General Janet Reno identified the EPB as a terrorist organization.

The connection of the group to Cuba is of concern to the U.S. government. Two former Cuban spies claimed that Cuba financed, trained, and organized activities of the EPB. Jorge Masetti, who testified before the House Committee on Government Reform, claimed that he helped to smuggle $4 million from the Wells Fargo robbery, as well as Victor Gerena, to Cuba. In addition, Garcia Beilsa, Chief of the American Department of the Cuban Communist Party Central Committee claimed that he oversaw funding and direction of the EPB.

Although the EPB appears to have ties to Cuba and is cited as a terrorist organization by the U.S. government, the group remains an active force on Puerto Rico. However, the movement for independence on the island is minimal. Since the 1952 adoption of the constitution, in referendums in 1967, 1993, and 1998, voters have chosen to remain a commonwealth. Polls show that the voters' preference toward statehood and commonwealth status are divided evenly but that independence is largely not even considered. Ojeda-Rios states, "Their apparent indifference to the patriotic project is a product of a multiplicity of factors." He cites one of these factors as "massive campaigns of destructive ideological transculturation that have created enormous disruptions and disorientation."

SUMMARY

In his 2002 article, Ojeda-Rios states that the EPB is, and has always been, on a "war footing." As a result, the group is dedicated to armed conflict with the United States in order to gain its independence. The EPB, who cite their historical reference to an original independence organization, has operated for the last twenty-seven years. The group has targeted both U.S. military and government offices, as well as individuals they felt are sympathetic to the United States.

Since 1992 and the convictions of many of its members for participation in the 1983 Wells Fargo robbery, the majority of the activities of the EPB came to a halt. However, its leader, Filiberto Ojeda-Rios, and most notorious operative, Victor Gerena, evaded capture for many years. Ojeda-Rios continued to make statements to the press and publish his doctrines for independence until his death in 2005, and stated that the Macheteros have been renamed the Boricua-Macheteros Popular Army.

SOURCES

Periodicals

Mahoney, Edmund. "A Rocket Attack, an FBI Revelation." *Hartford Courant.* November 12, 1999.

Ojeda-Rios, Filberto. "The Boricua-Macheteros Popular Army, Origins, Program, and Struggle." *Latin American Perspectives.*2002: i. 127, vol. 29, no. 6, pp. 104–116.

Suarez, Manny. "Possible Macheteros Office Contained FBI Information." *The San Juan Star.* April 5, 1984.

Tamayo, Juan O. "Attacks Put Puerto Rican Separatists Back in the Limelight." *The Miami Herald.* August 28, 1998.

Turner, Harry. "Macheteros Suspects May Face '79, '81 Raps." *The San Juan Star.* October 8, 1987.

Web sites

MIPT Terrorism Knowledge Base. "Macheteros." < http://www.tkb.org/Group.jsp?groupID = 3227 > (accessed October 14, 2005).

FAS Intelligence Resource Program. "Macheteros." < http://www.fas.org/irp/world/para/faln.htm > (accessed October 14, 2005).

Latin American Studies. "Los Macheteros." < http:// www.latinamericanstudies.org/epb-macheteros.htm > (accessed October 14, 2005).

MSNBC. "Former Spy to Testify about Cuban Support for Los Macheteros." < http://www.cubanet.org/CNews/ y99/dec99/30e3.htm > (accessed October 14, 2005).

Audio and Visual Media

"U.S. Senator Orrin Hatch (R-UT) holds hearing on Judiciary and FALN." *Wire Transcription Service* October 10, 1999.

Manchester Education Committee (MEC)

YEAR ESTABLISHED OR BECAME ACTIVE: 2004

USUAL AREA OF OPERATION: United Kingdom

OVERVIEW

The Manchester Education Committee (MEC) is a group of militant Manchester United soccer fans opposed to the takeover of their club by the American businessman, Malcolm Glazer. Their emergence in 2004–2005 represented a new brand of soccer hooliganism, a blight that has long marred the English game.

HISTORY

In 2004, the U.S.-based businessman and owner of the NFL franchise, Tampa Bay Buccaneers, upped moves to buy the English soccer club, Manchester United. United is the richest club in the world, and by some margin, best-supported club in Britain. An outstanding run of success in the 1990s also made its trophy room among the most glittering on the planet. Glazer had long held a significant shareholding in United, but through 2004 and early 2005, he increased it until it reached a level at which he could make a formal takeover bid. He succeeded in this in February 2005.

Glazer's bid to buy Manchester United was treated with universal derision by its famously passionate fans. At the root of many complaints was the way the deal had been structured: Glazer possessed only around one-third of the

LEADERSHIP

NICK TOWLE

The leader of the Manchester Education Committee is unknown, but it is widely assumed that the organization operates as a militant splinter of the more mainstream group, Shareholders United. Nick Towle is Shareholders United's chairman and has acted as one of the leading opponents to the Glazer family's takeover of Manchester United. He has not advocated violence or extremism under his watch, although Shareholders United have in the past pledged that they are willing to "get dirty" with the Glazer family.

£800 million (US $1.3 billion) needed to buy the club and intended to saddle United with the shortfall, which would be paid off by United's profits over a number of years. Fans feared that it was they who would end up picking up Glazer's tab through increased ticket prices and that the squad would suffer through lack of investment.

Different Manchester United fans reacted in different ways to the impending takeover of their club. One group, believing that the essence of United had been sold, formed a breakaway side, named FC United, which they entered into a minor league the following summer with the intention of it rising through the football pyramid. Other fans took a more direct approach, organizing protests before, after, and even during games.

A more shadowy group also emerged—calling itself the Manchester Education Committee (MEC)—which took a more extremist approach to defending the future of United. From 2004, it threatened and intimidated individuals that had sold shares to Glazer (this included vandalizing a United director's car) and bombarded both Glazer and those even tentatively associated with the family with telephone calls, emails, and faxes. On one occasion, around thirty MEC members wearing

balaclavas invaded the pitch during a reserve team match and unfurled anti-Glazer banners.

As the takeover neared and the American made a formal takeover offer for the club, the MEC issued a statement in the sort of language that seemed more rooted in the parlance of a Northern Irish paramilitary than that of a fan club. Warning of "consequences" if Glazer's latest offer was approved, it stated: "Any failure to maintain a rejectionist position in the face of Glazer's overtures will be regarded as an act of treachery—treachery that will place board members in an extremely vulnerable position for years to come... We trust that this is clear enough: offering either due diligence or a bid-recommendation to Glazer will be punished."

Ultimately, Glazer's takeover went through without much of the violence threatened by the MEC materializing, although the group now regard Manchester United's Old Trafford home as "occupied territory."

MEC exemplified the fierce passion aroused by English football, ardor that could quickly teeter over into extremism. Although they were not a conventional hooligan group and did not wage indiscriminate violence, in many ways they represented an age when the sport was beset by fan-instigated violence.

Indeed, football and violence seemed to be intrinsically linked. Even when it assumed its most basic form in the Middle Ages, the game had attracted trouble and was infamously banned outright by James II of Scotland. Even after a proper set of rules was formulated in the 1860s, it did little to improve things. In 1884, a match between Preston and Bolton Wanderers at Deepdale saw the visitors win, which irked the locals: "Orange peel and cinders were thrown at the goalkeeper," noted one eyewitness. "Stones, kicks and blows aimed at players and away spectators at the end of the game, hardly a member of the Wanderers party, i.e. players and spectators got to the station intact." At Everton, there was a riot in 1895 when a match was abandoned; a year later, there was serious trouble at a Scotland v. England match, and so it went on. From 1895–1915, the FA closed grounds on eight occasions and issued seventeen cautions to clubs as to the future conduct of their fans. Between 1921 and 1939, there were eight closures again, but this time sixty-four cautions.

It was only in the 1950s and 1960s that the crowd violence increasingly associated with

English football crept upon the national consciousness. Trains were wrecked by traveling fans, bottles thrown onto pitches, fighting broke out on the terraces, opposing supporters were ambushed and terrorized, and pubs ransacked. By the 1970s and early 1980s, football hooliganism was all pervasive and largely responsible for a drop in attendances that plunged the game into recession. During this period, the wrong-colored scarf worn in the wrong place would make almost any fan a target, sometimes with appalling consequences. As one fan put it: "If you ran you got caught and were given a good hiding and if you stayed and fought the local police would try and arrest you."

English fans following their clubs overseas in European competition or watching the England national team abroad reinforced the perception that they were the black sheep of world football. A riot in Turin in 1980 while England was playing a European championship match against Belgium led Italian police to fire tear gas at supporters, which then drifted over to the field of play and affected the players. In 1982, England fans fought pitched battles with Denmark supporters in the streets of Copenhagen. The horrific denouement of English football hooliganism came in May 1985 at the Heysel Stadium in Brussels, when a combination of drunken Liverpool fans charging at Juventus supporters and a dilapidated stadium caused a wall to collapse, killing thirty-nine people. Three years later, at the European Championships in West Germany, German and Dutch fans seeking to topple England supporters from their position as the "worst of the worst" provoked large-scale running battles through the streets of Stuttgart and Düsseldorf, which caused £500,000 worth of damage. The events prompted the British Minister for Sport, Colin Moynihan, who had been trying to implement draconian legislation to deal with football fans, to describe England's supporters as "the effluent tendency."

Ironically for Margaret Thatcher's Conservative government, football hooliganism was a guaranteed vote winner. Although crowd violence could be horrific, the problem was exaggerated by the British news media, causing what has been described as a "moral panic." The government gleefully sought to clamp down on the problem with a raft of measures that largely misunderstood the phenomena, but which earned it unstinting support from those sections of the population concerned about the violence.

On April 16, 1989, at an FA Cup semi-final between Liverpool and Nottingham Forest at the Hillsborough stadium in Sheffield, a crush of Liverpool supporters against the high metal fencing designed to keep the hooligans away from the pitch killed ninety-six people. The crush had been due to the failings of the police force in charge rather than hooliganism, but there was only one reason why the fence had been there. The subsequent inquiry into the Hillsborough Disaster by Lord Justice Taylor led to a massive investment in English football stadia, which kick-started the game's return to respectability. Policing improved also.

Violence returned periodically during the 1990s and beyond—for example, an Ireland v. England match in Dublin was abandoned in 1995 because of a riot; fighting between Millwall and Liverpool fans in 2004 saw several prison sentences handed out—but far from being the norm, they proved to be the exception. One of the reasons the MEC attracted so much attention was because they emerged during such a comparatively peaceful stage in English football's history.

PHILOSOPHY AND TACTICS

What prompts football-related violence is the perennial question pondered by a succession of sociologists who have studied the problem. As with the MEC, the motivation boils down to tribalism and the sense that fans are defending the honor and integrity of their team. Some football supporters—arguably a majority—are more ready to identify with their team than their city, nationality, or religion. Minor violence between Everton and Liverpool fans is not uncommon, despite the teams being separated less than a mile geographically, and some families within the city of Liverpool being split along blue and red lines (the respective colors of the two clubs).

At the height of football hooliganism in the 1970s and 1980s, violence was often indiscriminately waged against rival fans. Like soldiers in battle, hooligans would pick off scarves, rosettes, and other souvenirs denoting the allegiance of their victims. Although most clubs had at least one gang whose notoriety was well

KEY EVENTS

1950s–1960s: Emergence of football hooliganism as an acknowledged social problem. Trains wrecked, bottles thrown on pitches, fighting between rival fans.

1970s: English football becomes slowly dominated by a hooliganism problem.

1980: Rioting between England and Belgian fans in Turin leads to tear gas fired by Italian police.

1984: In a widely publicized incident, some England "fans" refuse to recognize John Barnes' goal v. Brazil on account of the color of his skin.

1985: Heysel Stadium disaster: rioting Liverpool fans murder thirty-nine Juventus supporters.

1989: Hillsborough Disaster: Ninety-six Liverpool supporters crushed to death; the recommendations made by the subsequent report into the disaster by Lord Justice Taylor revolutionize English football and virtually eradicate domestic hooliganism.

1998: England fans involved in serious clashes with Algerian youths in Marseilles.

2004: Emergence of Manchester Education Committee in wake of Malcolm Glazer's proposed takeover of Manchester United.

---

known—the Chelsea Headhunters; the Inter City Firm (West Ham), the Soul Crew (Cardiff City), and so on—these tended to be comparatively small and loosely affiliated groups of like-minded individuals, who might instigate violence, but would not be responsible for it on a larger scale. Arranging ambushes of rival fans was often the extent of their organized activity.

Usually football hooliganism was spontaneous and indiscriminate, never more so than at the Heysel Stadium disaster in 1985, when drunken Liverpool supporters took advantage of a poorly segregated and dilapidated stadium

to attack Juventus fans of Turin, Italy. Thirty-nine people were crushed to death when a wall collapsed under the weight of fleeing supporters—something none of the instigators could have envisaged or intended.

Violence has almost never been directed at players. One exception was when the Manchester United midfielder, Nobby Stiles, had a dart thrown at him by a Liverpool supporter in the late 1960s. That incident virtually stands alone in the history of the English game.

Unlike Italian Ultras or South American Barras Barras, English football hooliganism has seldom had an overtly political side. Sometimes it bubbled over into racist chanting, although this was often spontaneous. The supporters of some clubs, particularly London-based sides like Chelsea, West Ham, and Millwall, have had links to the British far right, most notoriously Combat 18. It has been alleged that Combat 18 instigated the riot at an Ireland v. England match in Dublin in February 1995, which caused the game's abandonment. Previously, the National Front would occasionally use football grounds to pass out leaflets and recruit members. It has also been suggested that they infiltrated supporters groups to spread their racist invective. In 1984, England's Jamaican born winger, John Barnes, scored what is commonly credited as one of the greatest goals of all time, as England recorded an unlikely 2-0 victory over Brazil in the Maracana Stadium in Rio de Janeiro. A section of the England support refused to recognize the 2-0 victory because a black man had scored one of the goals and at the airport they berated Football Association officials for picking Barnes. As the social commentator, James Walvin, put the widely reported attack: "A political organisation which could never expect more than a minimal coverage by the media at home—and a mere handful of votes at national elections—had secured massive, albeit notorious, coverage by the simple tactic of racial abuse."

Since the Hillsborough Disaster, improved policing and better-equipped stadia have led to an inexorable decline in English football hooliganism. That which still occurs is usually carried out away from the grounds and is less indiscriminate, instigated as it often is by small, highly organized hardcore groups that arrange to meet like-minded groups from other teams. When it does occur on a larger scale, it tends to be overseas where the reputation gained in the 1970s and 1980s precedes English fans. Often, this is instigated by locals seeking to prove something against the so-called "kings" of football hooliganism and is usually responded to in kind. Most notably, this occurred in Marseilles at the 1998 World Cup when local Algerian youths attacked England supporters, leading to running battles throughout the city. It also occurs on a smaller scale in Eastern Europe, where football faces hooliganism problems of the kind experienced in England a generation ago.

Groups like the MEC, which proffer intimidation toward executives involved in the running of the sport, are generally exceptional. MEC's campaign came as part of a wider initiative to stop Malcolm Glazer from taking over Manchester United. Tactics included fans buying up shares, "flash" protests, and symbolic gestures, such as wearing black at a match to commemorate the "death" of United. Elsewhere, there have been reports of other club chairpersons and directors being targeted by disgruntled fans, although seldom on a basis that could be described as organized.

OTHER PERSPECTIVES

The Heysel Stadium disaster of 1985, when rioting Liverpool fans were responsible for the deaths of thirty-nine Juventus supporters, marked the nadir of English football hooliganism. Andrew Hussey, Contributing Editor of the *Observer Sports Monthly* and a Liverpool supporter, has spent twenty years trying to make sense of what happened that evening. In 2005, he wrote: "Since the early 1970s English fans had been wreaking havoc in Europe and, at home, on each other. Their behaviour was received with platitudes and inertia from the media and the government. Those who ran the game, those who could do something about the bad grounds, the lousy security, the climate of hate and the racism, invariably looked away. Everybody who attended a match during this period knew that something was deeply wrong. Heysel changed everything about the culture of English football, much of it ultimately for the better...

"For a variety of reasons, it has not been quite expunged from memory. Perhaps it never will be. The hard line of Uefa has had far-reaching consequences for the game in England and there

are still those who talk regretfully about lost opportunities and a lost generation of English players... The truth is that the collapsed wall at Heysel was a deadly metaphor for the gathering destructive forces that brought English football culture to its knees. Most significantly, Heysel marked the culmination of a long trajectory of violence and neglect in England's football culture, which, despite the success of its clubs in Europe, was heading inexorably for self-destruction. Looking back, it is a miracle that anyone has made it out of the wreckage."

Writing in the *Daily Telegraph*, Harry Mount noted how well simple crowd-control methods—"all-seater stadiums, body searches, tight stewarding, no alcohol or bottles on the terraces"—had worked in the twenty years since Heysel, but also how football authorities in other countries could learn from the English example. "England was once the world-beater when it came to football violence," he wrote. "Violence has now, to all intents and purposes, been wiped out in this country... The violence has gone because the violent people who are still drawn to football have been effectively penned into the little square foot marked out by their plastic, moulded bucket seats.

"While the violent English are reined in on the terraces, if not on the pitch or the dance floor, violent Italians can go on behaving as appallingly as they did last week... [At] the badly designed Stadio delle Alpi, Juventus supporters were able to rain bottles down on the heads of Liverpool supporters conveniently gathered beneath them in a low tier. Meanwhile, in Milan, where AC Milan were playing Inter Milan, there was mayhem. It was hard to spot the ball for all the flares, bottles and keys thrown at the pitch. One flare hit the AC Milan goalkeeper, and the match was abandoned. So, twenty years after the pariahs of Europe—the English clubs—were banned from European competitions for five years (and Liverpool for seven years), the English are the choirboys, and their erstwhile Italian victims are allowed to run wild.

"And not because the Italians are naturally any more violent than English fans. Quite the opposite. When I went to Fiorentina games in Florence a decade ago, the elegant, trim fans wore green, padded husky jackets and sipped espresso rather than lager before the game. The banners around the stadium, overlooking the Duomo, advertised a Salvador Dali exhibition in the centre of town. But even these civilised men had a taste for violence, a taste that has been allowed to remain unchecked. The pockets of the padded jackets were openly stuffed with flares. It is time for a rare thing: for the English to teach the Italians how to behave."

SUMMARY

Football-related violence in England has gone into a dramatic decline in the last fifteen years. Although it still resurfaces from time to time—primarily at matches played overseas—improved policing, all-seater stadia, and a shift in mentality post-Heysel and post-Hillsborough have seen hooliganism confined to all but a small and closely knit minority, who tend to keep their violence among themselves. The emer-gence of the Manchester Education Committee represented a new breed of football "extremists," although their brand of intimidation and minor violence shared few of the characteristics commonly associated with football hooliganism.

SOURCES

Books

Corbett, James. *England Expects*. London: Aurum, 2006.

Walvin, James. *Football and the Decline of Britain*. London and New York: Macmillan, 1986.

Murphy, Patrick, et al. *Football on Trial: Spectator Violence and Development in the Football World*. Oxford: Routledge, 1990.

Web sites

Observer Sports Monthly. "Lost Lives That Saved A Sport." < http://football.guardian.co.uk/News_Story/ 0,1563,1448505,00.html > (accessed October 20, 2005).

Minuteman Civil Defense Corps

OVERVIEW

The Minuteman Civil Defense Corps, also called the Minuteman Project, is an organization concerned with border security that invokes the image of Revolutionary War militiamen, ready at a moment's notice to fight for America's freedom. Although the majority of the group's members are white, some Mexican Americans work to patrol the borders as well, deeply invested in the organization's call for legal immigration as a measure to protect American society and American resources.

In January 2003, Chris Simcox, an Arizona newspaper publisher, was arrested by federal park rangers on a stretch along the Arizona-Mexico border. Simcox was armed with a single pistol, police scanner radios, and was charged with a misdemeanor, subsequently serving a year on probation. His goal: to stop illegal Mexican border crossings.

On April 1, 2005, Simcox led a group of 900 volunteers in an effort to patrol a twenty-three-mile stretch of the U.S.-Mexico border in Arizona, preaching the goal of informing border patrol officials of violations. Simcox's efforts have spread to other border states, including Vermont and New York. Simcox dubbed the movement the Minuteman Civil Defense Corps (also known as the Minuteman Project). Although Simcox himself advocates law-abiding

ALTERNATE NAME: The Minuteman Project

LEADER: Chris Simcox

YEAR ESTABLISHED OR BECAME ACTIVE: 2005

USUAL AREA OF OPERATION: United States

LEADERSHIP

CHRIS SIMCOX

Chris Simcox, the forty-three-year-old leader of the Minutemen Civil Defense Corps (also known as the Minuteman Project), is the former publisher of the Tombstone, Arizona, *Tombstone Tumbleweed* newspaper. After teaching at a private school in California for thirteen years, he turned to publishing shortly after the terrorist attacks on U.S. soil on September 11, 2001. He drained his savings to buy the newspaper and used it to disseminate his ideas about illegal immigration, border crossings, and political issues.

activity on the part of the volunteers—using "standard operating procedure," and simply verbally informing federal border patrol guards of illegal border crossings—his movement has spawned copycat vigilante groups and allegations of intimidation and violence on the part of border patrol volunteers.

HISTORY

Chris Simcox, the leader of the Minuteman Civil Defense Corps, traces his "awakening" on the issue of protecting American borders to the September 11, 2001, attacks on the World Trade Center, the Pentagon, and in Pennsylvania. In 2002, he founded the Civil Homeland Defense Corps, the precursor to the Minuteman Civil Defense Corps. By 2003, his ideas had evolved into a desire for vigilantism, patrolling the borders to prevent illegal immigration. It was his belief that the federal border patrol officers were too lax in their work; after watching a convoy of trucks from Mexico flanked by men carrying AK-47s and seeing the border patrol fail to act, Simcox decided to patrol borders on his own, which led to his arrest and misdemeanor conviction.

Over the next two years, he reshaped his image; his efforts evolved into the Minuteman Civil Defense Corps, also called the Minuteman Project.

On April 1, 2005, the organization gained national attention when 900 volunteers gathered to patrol twenty-three miles of border between Arizona and Mexico. Simcox claimed that the volunteers' efforts decreased illegal border crossings by 98%, but federal officials dispute these numbers. The group was hailed by California Governor Arnold Schwarzenegger, and Simcox used his web site to promote the group's experiences to expand Minuteman to as many as sixteen states.

PHILOSOPHY AND TACTICS

The group's slogans include "Americans doing the jobs Congress won't do," and "Operating within the law to support enforcement of the law." Most Minutemen do not vilify the illegal immigrants themselves; in fact, Simcox and others publicly state that they believe the illegal immigrants are victims of problems in their own society and of American corporations eager for cheap labor to boost profits.

Simcox addresses potential Minuteman recruits on his web site by appealing to their sense of law, order, and justice: "You are considering joining the Minuteman HQ not because of bias towards people from another country, but rather because you feel your government owes the citizens of the United States protection from people who wish to take advantage of a free society. We demand that President Bush, members of Congress and the Senate maintain an orderly queue of entry into our country. We are three years post September 11, 2001, and still our government is more concerned with securing the borders of foreign lands than securing the borders of the United States. Enough is enough."

The group's rhetoric appeals to white American men from lower socio-economic classes, many of whom are displaced from manufacturing jobs that pay a family wage by Mexican immigrants—both legal and illegal— who are willing to work for less than half of the standard American wages. Simcox's appeal to these men is simple: by patrolling the borders as citizen "militias" and bringing attention to

KEY EVENTS

2002: Chris Simcox founds the Civil Homeland Defense organization, to patrol borders.

2003: Leader Chris Simcox arrested on the Arizona border; charged with misdemeanor for carrying a loaded pistol, sentenced to one year of probation.

2005: Renaming the group the Minuteman Civil Defense Corps (also known as The Minuteman Project), 900 volunteers patrol a twenty-three-mile section of the Arizona-Mexico border.

the cause of illegal border crossings, Americans can make a difference through action.

Ranch Rescue, a different vigilante group that aims to stop illegal border crossings, uses a more violent approach and is often confused with the Minutemen. The Minutemen do not advocate violence. Simcox advises volunteers to bring video cameras to document illegal border crossings and to give the tapes to federal officials. Minutemen have been accused of racial profiling, however, approaching persons of color, asking whether they speak English, asking where they live, and questioning them while not quizzing Caucasians in the same areas.

The Minuteman Civil Defense Corps web site spells out a "standard operating procedure" for Minutemen, which includes directives such as "Minutemen are courteous to everyone with whom they come into contact, and never discriminate against anyone for any reason."

The group holds up an American ideal as part of its appeal for volunteers; illegal immigration is portrayed as the reason for the loss of high-paying manufacturing jobs, health care crises in emergency rooms on the borders, edu-

cation problems in border state districts, and other socio-economic problems.

OTHER PERSPECTIVES

The American Civil Liberties Union (ACLU) is strongly opposed to the actions of the Minuteman Project. The Executive Director for the ACLU of Arizona, Eleanor Eisenberg, states that: "We recognize the right of a country to defend its borders but it must be done by the proper authorities and in a humane way. Too many migrants, coming to this country for the jobs we offer, have died in the desert from heat, dehydration and exhaustion. It would be even more tragic to have migrants die as a result of violence." Eisenberg accuses the Minutemen of using harassment and threats in the course of their patrols. The ACLU was present during the April 2005 Minuteman campaign, and arguments frequently broke out between the opposing sides.

SUMMARY

Using the Internet, weblogs, and word of mouth, The Minuteman Project has drawn interest from over 15,000 volunteers thus far, responding to Simcox's call to act. Members of Congress, such as U.S. Senator Diane Feinstein have expressed concern about the group's intent, calling for the addition of 2,000 new border patrol agents, rather than the possible vigilantism of hundreds or thousands of untrained, unregulated volunteers.

SOURCES

Books

Ellingwood, Ken. *Hard Line: Life and Death on the U.S.-Mexican.* New York: Pantheon, 2004.

Web sites

Salon.com. "The Angry Patriot" < http://www.salon.com/news/feature/2005/05/11/minuteman/ > (accessed October 23, 2005).

Movimento dos Sem Terra (Landless Movement)

LEADERS: Egydio Brunetto; Jose Rainha Jr.; Joao Pedro Stedile

USUAL AREA OF OPERATION: Brazil

OVERVIEW

Movimento dos Sem Terra (MST; Portuguese for Landless Movement) is a Leninist-Marxist Brazilian revolutionary movement, inspired and supported by the Catholic clergy, including several bishops. Their "Theology of Liberation," developed in the mid 1960s, provided the doctrinaire base for a christianized version of Communist theories as a political recipe for Latin American countries. In spite of the official condemnations by the late Pope John Paul II and his successor of this Marxist Catholicism, some Brazilian clergy continued to fully support, preach, and organize several revolutionary social movements in Brazil. Among some prominent clergy figures directly involved in the organization of MST since 1985 is the Dominican Friar Beto, one of the founders and mentors of PT, the Workers' Party, and of MST, who keeps close ties with Egydio Brunetto, Jose Rainha Jr., and Joao Pedro Stedile, the main leaders of MST.

HISTORY

Before MST was officially formed, several Catholic priests were already encouraging the population, in the mid 1970s and early 1980s, to invade rural properties "in the name of Christ," especially in the Brazilian states of Acre, Rondonia, Mato Grosso, Para, and

Rural members of the Movimiento de Sin Tierras/ Landless Movement (MST) group camp out in front of the INCRA agrarian reform government agency on March 20, 1998. The MST demanded that the government set aside more funds for its agrarian reform program. AP/Wide World Photos. *Reproduced by permission.*

Amazonas. Churches all over Brazil started regular meetings to divulge the Theology of Liberation, with religious radio programs, and local daily TV shows as their main propaganda tools, along with parochial pamphlets.

INCRA (National Institute for Agrarian Reform) was already applying a federal program of agrarian reform and colonization in the Amazonian regions and allocating federal land for rural workers, along with subsidized financial loans from the Bank of Amazon, providing agricultural implements and technical assistance to the new settlers. Most of those settlers originated from the more traditional rural areas of the south of the country, such as the states of Santa Catarina, Parana, and Sao Paulo, and

some from the center of Brazil, such as the Mato Grosso, Minas Gerais, and Goias states. However, Catholic priests incited their congregations to invade these same new farms, especially those showing successful results; these actions often resulted in violence and deaths.

MST is the more recent result of KGB-backed infiltrations. In 1959, Mikhail Suslov ordered KGB agents abroad to infiltrate the Christian and Islamic religious organizations. The Soviet 631 Institute, written by Suslov, reads: "It is essential to increase the infiltration into churches and other religious organizations. We have already received protests from our comrades who believe to be a waste of time such work inside the Churches, and this is a deplorable attitude that cannot be tolerated. The Churches are influent and are involved in every step of life. Once installed inside the religious organizations, our men can deliver a valuable service to the Party."

The consequence of such methodic infiltration in the Catholic Church of Latin America led to the Theology of Liberation in 1968, officially approved by the CELAM (Latin American Episcopal Commission) in 1972. Pope John Paul II opened the III Latin American Episcopal Conference in Puebla City, Mexico in 1979, criticizing the adoption by the clergy of the Theology of Liberation as a tool aiming to replace the Christian faith with Marxism, therefore leading to the destruction of the Church.

With the end of the military dictatorship in Brazil in 1985, the MST was finally organized under the initial leadership of Rainha Jr. and Stedile, with Friar Beto's support and guidance. An extensive and well-coordinated offensive against farms and ranches took place immediately and rapidly spread from Para (on the north) to the state of Rio Grande do Sul (in the extreme south of Brazil). Between 1985 and 1989, armed clashes between MST activists, police, and farmers caused 640 deaths in the countryside.

The 1995 Forum of SaoPaulo, a Cuban-oriented meeting of the International Communist Movement annually held to discuss strategies for power taking in Latin America, took place in Montevideo, Uruguay. Representatives of the Brazilian political party known as PT (Workers' Party), MST leaders, and other Brazilian left-wing parties attended the meeting as well as the leaders of *Fuerzas Armadas Revolucionarias de Colombia*

KEY EVENTS

2002: MST helps Jose Ignacio Lula da Silva (PT Party) be elected for the Presidency of Brazil.

2003: MST launched 110 invasions throughout Brazil.

2004: MST militias invaded 271 properties.

2005: At least forty MST-related incidents were reported between January and July, including new invasions, occupation of public buildings, and hostage takings.

(Colombian Revolutionary Armed Forces; FARC) and of Peru's *Sendero Luminoso* (Shining Path; SL). FARC and Sendero Luminoso, besides being terrorist organizations, are known to be the largest operators of drug trafficking in South America. PT and MST leaders, after confiding with the FARC and Sendero Luminoso leaders, declared at the occasion that MST would act as the PT's armed branch in Brazil in order to create the necessary social upheaval to facilitate power-taking by the left. While PT political activism would try to ascend to power through democratic elections as representatives of the labor unions in the industrialized centers, MST would incite the rural population to start an armed revolution in the countryside. In spite of the gravity of such an announcement, the major sectors of the Brazilian press failed to take notice or to mention this fact to the public at that time.

In 1996, during a court-ordered eviction operation of MST activists from a farm in Eldorado dos Carajas, Para, police were met with resistance, and the outcome was nineteen deaths and fifty-one injured people. By the first months of 1998, more then 50,000 MST militants had already occupied, by force, more than 29,000 square miles of rural lands. Under the pretext of pressing authorities to speed up agrarian reform, MST also invaded and destroyed several police precincts, public buildings, banks, and even government offices. In April

2002, MST invaded the farm of the son of Fernando Henrique Cardoso, the then-President of Brazil, looted the entire property, destroyed tractors and other implements, and killing the farm animals in the process. In mid 2003, the death toll of clashes between farmers and MST amounted to another 200 deaths, as well as the destruction of plantations, herds, public and private buildings, houses, and tractors, with several cases of abductions of farmers and public servants, murders, looting, extortions, and blackmail.

MST violence, and the mild and sluggish response on the part of judges and law enforcement authorities to its crimes, has led many farmers to buy weapons and to hire security guards to prevent invasions. Many farmers complain that they are forced to pay MST a toll in order to be allowed to transport their production out of their properties.

PHILOSOPHY AND TACTICS

The main strategic force behind MST is the Brazilian Catholic Church, today virtually dominated by the Marxist wing of the clergy and their followers, including teachers and intellectuals. They act as the main force inside schools, universities, and the media, directing public opinion toward a sympathetic attitude to MST, shown as a social movement trying to help the poor improve their standard of living through the access to land.

The clergy uses the Theology of Liberation to encourage awareness among the poorest social segments, comprised of rural and blue-collar workers, regarding the social-economic forces responsible for their predicaments. The document recommends, among other tactics, that the religiosity of the masses should be used as a tool to revolutionize the fundaments of the Catholic Church through the formation of Ecclesiastical Base Communities and other parochial activities. The Theology of Liberation, officially born in 1968, should be taught to the masses, thereby changing the religious focus from salvation of the soul to the salvation of men from social injustice and inequalities. Social movements should be organized and implemented to fight against capitalism and the economic elites, blamed as the main oppressors of the poor.

The Theology of Liberation shifted the focus of religious preaching from metaphysical concern with the inner life of the individual and his relationship with God to that of political, economical, and social demands of the masses. Jesus, Mary, Moses, and other biblical personalities are presented by the Theology of Liberation as social revolutionaries and precursors of Communist ideologues such as Karl Marx, Mao, and Antonio Gramsci. Therefore, the real meaning of religious life should be the search for social justice and the promotion of social well-being through the redistribution of income and the destruction of privileged minorities. The "elites" are the enemy to be fought against by the masses, as well as the International Monetary Fund (IMF), transnational companies, the United States, etc. Two sectors crucial to such a revolution are the labor unions in the industrialized urban centers and the rural population in the countryside. In Brazil, the Theology of Liberation led priests to inspire and organize the founding of the PT Party and the "social movement" of MST.

The Marxist-Leninist approach adopted by MST and the Theology of Liberation preaches a radical socio-political change and power shift. In order to promote social justice and income distribution, a combination of armed conflict and social rioting is used to achieve political power. Therefore, its main objective is to take power through revolution. Its leadership is not comprised of true rural workers but by professional militants instructed by Marxist priests. MST alignment with FARC, Sendero Luminoso, and Fidel Castro's policies aiming to create a communist block in Latin America is openly stated. The propaganda power of the Catholic Church in the manipulation of the masses is well illustrated by Jorge Baptista Ribeiro, a former adept of Theology of Liberation, in his article of December 1988, published in the newspaper *Ombro a Ombro*. Ribeiro cited a comrade of the Marxist Catholicism who commented on how fun it was to manipulate the masses: "We laughed a lot after we preached, transmitting to the stupid masses the messages in favor of our cause, which like parrots they repeated.... Good examples of our smartness you can find in the biographies of Lula and many others."

The most effective propaganda tool used by MST is the association of clearly perceived real facts (poverty, illiteracy) with false or unilaterally selected factors in order to promote hatred against specific institutions and segments of society. In short, prejudice, mistrust, and hatred is fomented between social classes. This tactic consists of the perpetual victimization of one social segment while demonizing another, as well as the systematic denial in acknowledging the positive actions in favor of the first segment while accusing the second of being against social justice.

OTHER PERSPECTIVES

The growing number of rural property invasions incited by the Marxist clergy during the 1980s led farmers to organize their own union, the UDR, to defend their lands and rights, and to provide legal assistance to those affected. Therefore, UDR is systematically vilified by MST leadership and the clergy, as dangerous elitists eager to commit murder and intimidate MST militants.

Even sectors of the Catholic Church are presently discretely criticizing MST and comparing the agrarian reform in Brazil with that of President Mugabe's in Zimbabwe. In April 2005, the magazine *Catolicismo* reported that the MST leadership is embezzling money allocated by the federal government and by private donors to the settlements in Pernambuco and elsewhere. According to the same source, approximately $9 million were allocated by the government to two cooperatives (CONCRAB and ANCA) between 2003 and 2004, both administered by the MST leadership. A Congressional Investigation Committee has heard several witnesses among settlers, agriculture technicians, and members of MST who testified that their leadership is using these two cooperatives to funnel the money to other MST activities alien to their original goals.

In October 2004, Jose A. F. Rodrigues Neto, General of the Brazilian Army in Porto Alegre, Rio Grande do Sul, alerted in an article that the MST has a great number of guerrilla training camps throughout Brazil, where militias are trained in terrorist techniques developed by FARC and Sendero Luminoso. He is not alone in his concerns about this issue. Several journalists and political scientists all agree that MST keeps a close relationship with the network of drug traffickers organized and commanded by

FARC to finance communist movements in Latin America.

SUMMARY

In the first half of 2005, the MST inaugurated a new school, built with $1.3 million donated by the Friends of MST from several countries. Egydio Brunetto, the national leader of MST said in the inauguration speech that: "The main objective of the school is to teach how to invade rural properties—whether productive or not—since the main goal of this school is to form trained contingent to occupy land." Stedile, also present at the ceremony, added: "This school is to take the power for the working class, so our comrades will be able to transform

scientific knowledge in tools of liberation and not of exploitation."

SOURCES

Books

Hutton, Joseph B. *The Subverters*. New York: Arlington House, 1972.

SEE ALSO

Revolutionary Armed Forces of Colombia (FARC)

Sendero Luminoso (Shining Path)

Muhammed's Army

LEADERS: Abu al-Hassan; Khaled Abdennabi

USUAL AREA OF OPERATION: Yemen

OVERVIEW

In 1998, the Muhammad's Army, also called the Islamic Army of Aden-Abyan, issued its first in a series of communiqués expressing its desired goals and objectives for Yemen and the rest of the world. The group sought foremost the removal of the members of the ruling Yemeni regime, to be tried under *shari'a* (Islamic) law and supplanted by a government that would rigorously adhere to the principles of Islamic law. In the communiqués, the army articulated its support for Osama bin Laden and called for operations against U.S. and other Western interests that would force those "infidels" to withdraw from the region. Since 1998, the Muhammad's Army has utilized both bombings and kidnappings to achieve their goals. As a result, they have been listed for sanctions as terrorists under United Nations Security Council Resolution #1333. In Arabic, the group is known as Jaysh Adan-Abiyan al-Islami. The army has also been called the Aden Islamic Army, the Army of Mohammed, the Jaish Adan al Islami, the Islamic Aden Army, and Jaysh Adan.

Yemen possesses geographic importance due to the strategic value of the Gulf of Aden. Osama bin Laden expressed the strategic value of the Gulf of Aden in his "Declarations of War." Within the gulf, the port functions as a refueling station and manages the westward flow

LEADERSHIP

KHALED ABDENNABI (KHALID ABD AL-NABI AL-YAZIDI)

Khaled Abdennabi is the current leader of Muhammed's Army. In 2003, he was detained by Yemeni forces in connection to the attack on the medical convoy that wounded seven people. However, he was quickly pardoned and released.

ZEIN AL-ABIDI ABU BAKR AL-MEHDAR (ABU AL-HASSAN)

Zein al-Abidi Abu Bakr al-Mehdar (Abu al-Hassan) was the founder of Muhammed's Army and a member of the salafi sect of the Sunni Muslim tradition. He was trained in guerilla warfare tactics in preparation for fighting the Soviet forces in Afghanistan. In 1994, he aided the Yemeni government in the suppression of the civil war caused by the socialists in South Yemen who had declared their intent to become independent from the Republic of Yemen. Al-Hassan was offered an appointment within the ruling party, but rejected it as he believed that the government was not being run under strict adherence to Islamic law. In October 1999, al-Hassan was convicted of his role in the December 1998 kidnapping of sixteen Western tourists, which led to the death of four tourists. He was sentenced to death and executed by firing squad on October 17, 1999.

of maritime traffic out of the Persian Gulf. All ships that travel from the Red Sea through the Suez Canal make use of Aden.

HISTORY

The roots of the Muhammed's Army has much to do with modern Yemeni history. The Republic of Yemen emerged in 1990 when Northern Yemen, known as the Yemen Arab Republic (YAR), and the Southern People's Democratic Republic of Yemen decided to unite. Northern Yemen had functioned under Turkish rule until 1918, after which it was controlled by Imam Yahya, and later his son, Ahmad, until 1962. With the assistance of Egyptian President Nasser, the Imam was deposed and the revolutionary forces declared the Yemen Arab Republic in 1970.

To the south, Southern Yemen functioned under a British mandate until 1965 when two rival groups sought to conquer British rule. Two violent years of conflict resulted in the British pulling out of the region. By 1969, the Soviet Union assisted the radical wing of the Marxist movement in Yemen to assume control and declare the People's Democratic Republic of Yemen (PDRY). Through the 1970s, the government of the PDRY maintained a close alliance with the Soviet Union and China and provided safe haven for Palestinian extremists. The state was considered a haven for terrorists by the international community. Exiles from the PDRY received military training in Pakistan and fought as *mujahideen* (fighters) in the Afghan-Soviet war.

In 1972, the governments of the YAR and the PDRY acknowledged a desire to unify. However, only minimal steps forward were initially made toward that goal. To also slow the process, beginning in 1979, the PDRY initiated a sponsored insurgency against the YAR. Nevertheless, by 1989, after intercession by the Arab League, the regimes of the YAR and the PDRY agreed to unite under the terms originally agreed upon in 1981. On May 22, 1990, the Republic of Yemen (ROY) declared itself as a state and was quickly recognized by the international community. Acceptance of the agreement to unify was ratified by Yemenis by May 1991. The celebration of unification was quickly tempered. By 1994, a faction located in the southern region declared the south's withdrawal from the ROY. Fighting from the civil war occurred mainly in the southern region and was suppressed by July of that same year.

Although the Muhammad's Army did not officially emerge until 1998, its formation is tangled with these aspects of Yemeni history. In 1998, Muhammad's Army issued its first communiqué stating its objectives. However the group existed long before then. The leadership of Muhammad's Army is made up of those individuals sent to Saudi Arabia and Pakistan for religious and military training in preparation to battle the Soviet Union in Afghanistan. In 1984, between 5,000 and 7,000 Yemenis volunteered to fight against the USSR. These mujahideen were trained in guerilla warfare tactics and many adopted the fundamentalist salafi sect of Sunni Islam. The salafi sect calls for a puritan interpretation of Islam.

After returning to Yemen, these mujahideen formed Jamiat al-Jihad and formed an alliance with the opposition to the ruling party. During the 1994 civil war, these war veterans were used to suppress those residing in the south seeking to secede from the ROY and carried out over 150 assassinations of Socialist Party members. As a reward for their assistance in subduing the insurrection during the civil war, many of these religious fundamentalists were granted ranking positions in the Education and Judicial branches of the Yemeni government. Many of the mujahideen saw this as an attempt by the government to incorporate and have power over their religious movement. Individuals such as Zein al-Abidi Abu Bakr al-Mehdar, known as al-Hassan, were disheartened by the government's choice to not rigorously follow traditional Islamic law. Led by al-Hassan, like-minded salafi began to depart from Yemeni government circles in 1996.

The Yemeni government denied the existence of Muhammed's Army until the organization issued its first communiqué. The communiqué was delivered in response to the U.S. strikes on Osama bin Laden's training camps in Afghanistan, which were in retaliation for the embassy bombings in Kenya and Tanzania. Muhammad's Army expressed its allegiance to Osama bin Laden and commended the embassy bombings. The communiqué called for the overthrow of the Yemeni government, which, they believed, should be tried under shari'a law. The new government in Yemen would then be created with leadership that austerely adhered to the fundamental interpretation of Islamic law. The group also called for armed opposition targeting U.S. and Western interests that would force the withdrawal of this influence on Yemen. In a subsequent communiqué, Muhammed's Army demanded the resignation of the ruling Yemeni government.

In December 1998, the group commenced its operations against Western influences with the kidnapping of sixteen British, American, and Australian tourists, the largest kidnapping incident in Yemen. The travelers were stopped at a roadblock in Mawdiyah. Operatives then took the hostages to a Muhammed's Army safe-house where the captors demanded the release of several comrades. Yemeni security forces discovered the location where the tourists were being held and surrounded the house. After an attempt at negotiations failed, a firefight commenced. The Muhammed's Army members used several of the hostages as human shields, resulting in the deaths of four tourists. Three of the Muhammed's Army kidnappers were also killed.

In October 1999, the leader of the operation and of Muhammed's Army, al-Hassan, was convicted of the crime and sentenced to death by execution. Two other Muhammed's Army members were sentenced to death and one was sentenced to twenty years in prison. Ten other operatives were tried, yet acquitted. Al-Hassan was executed by firing squad on October 17, 1999, within days of his conviction even in spite of threats that the members of Muhammed's army would retaliate.

Muhammed's Army continued to operate after al-Hassan's death. On October 12, 2000, the U.S.S. Cole, a U.S. Naval vessel was refueling in the port of Aden. A dinghy filled with explosives smashed into the vessel, killing seventeen U.S. sailors and injuring thirty-nine. Although the U.S. and Australian intelligence services believe that the bombings were organized and carried out by al-Qaeda, many believe that the bombing were only arranged and funded by al-Qaeda. The operatives came from Muhammed's Army. In September 2001, the IAA was designated for sanctions as a terrorist organization under U.S. presidential Executive Order 13224. In that same month, the group was again designated for sanctions under the United Nations Security Council Resolution 1333. Nevertheless, the group continued to function. On October 6, 2002, Muhammed's Army claimed responsibility for the bombing of a French refueling tank, the Limburg. The group asserted that its target had actually been a U.S. Navy vessel. On the third anniversary of al-Hassan's execution, the spiritual leader of Muhammed's Army, Abu-Hamzah al-Masri, declared that the group had joined the al-Qaeda organization.

The most recent activity by Muhammed's Army occurred on June 21, 2003, with an attack on a military medical convoy, which wounded seven people. During investigation of suspects

KEY EVENTS

2002: Mohammed's Army claims responsibility for the attack on the French tanker, The Limburg.

2002: Three Yemenis connected to Muhammed's Army were convicted of bombings at the Port of Aden.

2003: Mohammed's Army launches attack on military medical convoy, which injures seven people.

2003: Yemeni security forces take on members of Muhammed's Army at a base in Harat. During arrests for the attack on the medical convoy, security forces find cache of weapons.

2003: Car bomb attacks planned by Muhammed's Army for the U.S., British, and German embassies in capital of Sana'a are disrupted.

Soviet Union in Afghanistan. The salafi philosophy is founded in the struggle to expel external influences from the Middle East.

The strategic importance of Aden is religious as well as geographic. Al-Hassan held a literal interpretation of the teaching of Muhammad, specifically that 12,000 holy warriors would emerge from Aden-Abyan to restore Islam. Osama bin Laden also voices this belief in his "Declarations of War," as he asserts the strategic importance of the Yemen.

As a result, Muhammed's Army has employed tactics such as bombings and kidnappings to force the expulsion of U.S. and Western influences on Yemen. The highest profile kidnapping in Yemen's history took place in December 1998, as sixteen tourists were kidnapped from a roadblock. After a failed attempt at negotiations, four of the tourists were killed in a shoot-out. In addition to kidnappings, Muhammed's Army has carried out bombings. Although the group claims responsibility for the bombing of the U.S.S. Cole, blame is generally placed on the larger Islamic organization, al-Qaeda. In addition, Muhammed's Army claimed responsibility for the bombing of the French oil tanker, The Limburg, in 2003.

for the attack, Yemeni security forces seized a cache of weapons, including cars packed with explosives, hand grenades, and rocket-propelled grenades.

Western intelligence services estimate that there are 100 core members in Muhammed's Army, who are both Yemeni and Saudi. These operatives are located in the United Kingdom, Sudan, Pakistan, Jordan, and Eritrea. The current leader is Khaled Abdennabi, or Khalid Abd al-Nabi al-Yazidi.

PHILOSOPHY AND TACTICS

The philosophy of Muhammed's Army is rooted in the salafi sect of Sunni Islam and the belief that the Yemeni government should function under rigorous adherence to Islamic law. Many of the members of Muhammed's Army were influenced toward salafi while in Saudi Arabia and gaining guerilla warfare training to fight the

OTHER PERSPECTIVES

The Yemeni government denied the existence of Muhammed's Army until 1998 and the release of communiqués. The Yemeni government currently asserts that the group has been disbanded. Australian and U.S. intelligence agencies, however, estimate that there are approximately 100 core members of Muhammed's Army residing in the United Kingdom, Sudan, Pakistan, Jordan, and Eritrea. The attempt early on by the Yemeni government to incorporate the salafi into its ranks demonstrates the government's belief that those within Muhammed's Army are of little threat.

Before his execution, al-Hassan spoke of his participation with the hostage-taking in 1998 saying, "Dialogue between civilizations is useless. The only dialogue should be with bullets." As a result of comments like this and ties to the al-Qaeda network, the IAA has been renewed on both the U.S. and Australian terrorist watch-lists.

PRIMARY SOURCE

Islamic Army of Aden (IAA) a.k.a. Aden-Abyan Islamic Army (AAIA)

DESCRIPTION

The Islamic Army of Aden (IAA) emerged publicly in mid-1998 when the group released a series of communiqués that expressed support for Usama Bin Ladin, appealed for the overthrow of the Yemeni Government, and called for operations against U.S. and other Western interests in Yemen. IAA was first designated under EO 13224 in September 2001.

ACTIVITIES

IAA has engaged in small-scale operations such as bombings, kidnappings, and small arms attacks to promote its goals. The group reportedly was behind an attack in June 2003 against a medical assistance convoy in the Abyan Governorate. Yemeni authorities responded with a raid on a suspected IAA facility, killing several individuals and capturing others, including Khalid al-Nabi al-Yazidi, the group's leader. Before that attack, the group had not conducted operations since the bombing of the British Embassy in Sanaa in October 2000. In 2001, Yemeni authorities found an IAA member and three associates responsible for that attack. In December 1998, the group kidnapped sixteen British, American, and Australian tourists near Mudiyah in southern Yemen. Although Yemeni officials previously have claimed that the group is operationally defunct, their recent attribution of the attack in 2003 against the medical convoy and reports that al-Yazidi was released from prison in mid-October 2003 suggest that the IAA, or at least elements of the group, have resumed activity. Speculation after the attack on the USS Cole pointed to the involvement of the IAA, and the group later claimed responsibility for the attack. The IAA has been affiliated with al-Qa'ida. IAA members are known to have trained and served in Afghanistan under the leadership of seasoned mujahedin.

STRENGTH

Not known.

LOCATION/AREA OF OPERATION

Operates in the southern governorates of Yemen—primarily Aden and Abyan.

EXTERNAL AID

Not known.

Source: U.S. Department of State. *Country Reports on Terrorism.* Washington, D.C., 2004.

SUMMARY

In 1998, Muhammed's Army emerged with clear objectives. It declared support of the international Islamic *jihad* (holy war) led by Osama bin Laden, and asserted the need for the removal and replacement of current Yemeni government to one based on strict adherence to Islamic law. The group also sought the expulsion of external influence on Yemen and the Middle East. These goals originated in the struggle of its leaders when they fought as mujahideen against the Soviet Union in Afghanistan. During their military training, many adopted salafi, a fundamentalist sect of Sunni Islam and expressed the desire to create governments based on that religious fundamentalism. As a result, upon return from the Afghan war, some mujahideen were disillusioned by what they perceived to be a lack of adherence to Islamic law on the part of the Yemeni government. Consequently, Muhammed's Army began in 1998 to move toward achieving those goals. Since 1998, the group has employed the tactics of bombings and kidnappings. The most famous kidnapping occurred in December 1998 and resulted in the death of four hostages. Following the hostage crisis, Muhammed's Army leader, al-Hassan, was arrested and subsequently executed. Several years after his death, Muhammed's Army officially announced its alliance with al-Qaeda. The last known activity of the group occurred in 2003, but U.S. and Australian intelligence agencies approximate that the group still has 100 core members.

SOURCES

Periodicals

Karmon, Ely. "The Bombing of the U.S.S. Cole: An Analysis of the Principle Suspects." *International Policy Institute for Counter Terrorism.* October 24, 2000.

Kerr, Simon. "Yemen Cracks Down on Militants." *Middle East Journal.* December 1, 1999.

McGregor, Andrew. "Strike First." *The World Today.* December 1, 2002.

Web sites

Center for Defense Information. "In the Spotlight: Islamic Army of Aden." < http://www.cdi.org/program/document.cfm?DocumentID = 2679/index.cfm > (accessed October 16, 2005).

National Security Australia. "Islamic Army of Aden." < http://www.nationalsecurity.gov.au/agd/WWW/nationalsecurityHome.nsf/Page/Listing_of_Terrorist_Organisations_terrorist_listing_Islamic_Army_of_Aden_-_Listed_11_April_2003 > (accessed October 16, 2005).

MIPT Terrorism Knowledge Database. "Aden Abyan Islamic Army." < http://www.tkb.org/Group.jsp?groupID = 4 > (accessed October 16, 2005).

FAS Intelligence Resource Program. "Islamic Army of Aden." < http://www.fas.org/irp/world/para/iaa.htm > (accessed October 16, 2005).

SEE ALSO

Al-Qaeda

Mujahedin-e Khalq Organization

OVERVIEW

The Mujahedine-e Khalq Organization (MEK) was established in the 1960s in Iran. The group, which was founded by college-educated children of Iranian merchants, sought to overthrow the Shah's regime in the country. Created initially as an Islamic student organization, the MEK originally wanted democratic reform in the nation. Over the decades, the group has experienced a variety of changes in ideology and organization and has been identified by both the U.S. government and the European Union as a terrorist organization.

Mujahedine-e Khalq (translation, People's Holy Warriors) has operated under different names. The National Council of Resistance, the political front of the group, operates in various nations' capitals, even though the MEK has been labeled a terrorist organization. In addition, the Muslim Iranian Student's Society served as a front to generate fundraising from Iranians living abroad. The group's militant wing was developed in 1987 and named The National Liberation Army. Another name connected to the group is the People's Mujahedine of Iran. Largely known as the MEK, the group has developed into the largest and most militant organization that opposes the Islamic Republic of Iran.

LEADERS: Maryam Rajavi; Massoud Rajavi
USUAL AREA OF OPERATION: Iran; Iraq

Members of the Mujahedin-e Kahlq pass through a U.S. checkpoint in Dayala, Iraq, on May 12, 2003.
Roberto Schmidt/AFP/Getty Images.

HISTORY

The MEK was founded in Iran in the 1960s. Its founding members were the college-educated children of Iranian merchants. In the beginning, the group, which started as an Islamic student organization, was founded under an ideology that fused Marxism with Islam. The group's primary objective, however, was the overthrow of the Shah's regime. The MEK began operating in public in 1971 and were then oppressed by Shah Mohammad Reza. Top leaders of the MEK were executed and members were imprisoned.

Later in the 1970s, the massive public unrest in Iran led to the Shah releasing prisoners, including members of the MEK, in an effort to gain public support and retain power. The MEK, however, began its support of the revolutionary movement sweeping Iran. During this period, the MEK was blamed for the death of several U.S. military and civilian personnel working in Iran. In addition, the MEK supported the 1979 takeover of the U.S. Embassy in Tehran.

Although the MEK supported the 1979 Iranian revolution, once the regime of Ayatollah Khomeini came into power, the group became the target of a violent crackdown on dissidents. In 1981, the MEK fought against the actions by detonating bombs at the Islamic Republic Party and the Premier's office, killing seventy high-ranking Iranian officials. Also in 1981, and as a result of its increasing activities, the membership of the MEK, including its top leaders, fled Iran and settled in a compound outside of Paris. The group remained in France until 1987 when the militant faction of the group, The National Liberation Army, began to form camps scattered in Iraq, along the border with Iran. The MEK was invited and welcomed into Iraq by the regime of Saddam Hussein, which armed and funded many of the MEK's cross-border insurgence into Iran, in an effort to weaken Iran during the Iran-Iraq war.

In the 1990s, the group expanded its operations in Iraq and the rest of the world. The MEK

Iranian women stand outside the Tehran United Nations office holding pictures of relatives who are members of the Mujahedin-e Khalq Organization on October 28, 2002. The Iraq-based organization opposes the Iranian government, and its members are being held by Iraqi federal authorities. Reuters/Landov

assisted the Iraqi regime in suppressing two uprisings that occurred in 1991: The Shi'ite and Kurdish uprising in southern Iraq, and the Kurdish uprising in northern Iraq. In 1992, the group engaged in its largest overseas operation by conducting simultaneous attacks on Iranian embassies and installations in thirteen various countries.

With its political leadership exiled in France and its military leadership operating out of Iraq, the MEK continued to expand its operations. In 1999, the group assassinated the deputy Chief of the Iranian Armed Forces General Staff. The next year, the group failed in its next assassination attempt, targeting the Commander of the Nasr Headquarters—Tehran's interagency board in charge of directing policies on Iraq. Later in 2000, the group initiated "Operation Great Bahman" by launching dozens of attacks against targets in Iran and Iranian interests abroad. Between the years 2000 and 2001, the MEK engaged in mortar and hit-and-run attacks on Iranian military, law enforcement, and government buildings near the Iran-Iraq border. However, as 2001 came to a close, the group's operations slowed.

In May 2003, coalition forces bombed MEK bases at the onset of Operation Iraqi Freedom. The leadership of the MEK ordered its members to not resist. A ceasefire was reached, and 3,000 of its members were confined to Camp Ashraf, north of Baghdad. The group is protected under the Geneva Convention and has relinquished its weapons.

PHILOSOPHY AND TACTICS

The MEK began in Iran as a liberal nationalistic party supporting regime change against the Shah and the Western influences. The group created an eclectic ideology that combines its own interpretation of Shi'ite Islamism with Marxist principles. The group seeks to overthrow the current regime in Iran and to create a democratic, socialist Islamic republic. The group believes that this Islamic socialism can only be accomplished through the destruction of the ruling regime and the removal of Western influence, referred to as "Westoxication." If necessary, to achieve this Islamic ideology, the group is willing to use physical force, armed struggle, or *jihad* (holy war).

The goals of the group have been laid out in a sixteen-point plan following the 1995 conference of the NCR. These goals include the removal of the Islamic fundamentalist regime in power in Iran and replacing it with the NCR. In addition, the group seeks the freedom of belief, expression, and the press, without government or religious censorship; guaranteed freedom for political parties, and unions, with the exception of those loyal to either the Shah or Ayatollah Khomeini, provided the groups' activities stay within the law; democratically elected government; adoption of the United Nations Universal Declaration of Human Rights; eliminating the courts, tribunals, security departments introduced by the Khomeini regime; granting equal rights to women and religious minorities; the abolishing of privileges

PRIMARY SOURCE

Mujahedin-e Khalq Organization (MEK) a.k.a. The National Liberation Army of Iran, The People's Mujahedin Organization of Iran (PMOI), National Council of Resistance (NCR), The National Council of Resistance of Iran (NCRI), Muslim Iranian Students' Society

DESCRIPTION

The MEK philosophy mixes Marxism and Islam. Formed in the 1960s, the organization was expelled from Iran after the Islamic Revolution in 1979, and its primary support came from the former Iraqi regime of Saddam Hussein starting in the late 1980s. The MEK conducted anti-Western attacks prior to the Islamic Revolution. Since then, it has conducted terrorist attacks against the interests of the clerical regime in Iran and abroad. The MEK advocates the overthrow of the Iranian regime and its replacement with the group's own leadership.

ACTIVITIES

The group's worldwide campaign against the Iranian Government stresses propaganda and occasionally uses terrorism. During the 1970s, the MEK killed US military personnel and US civilians working on defense projects in Tehran and supported the takeover in 1979 of the U.S. Embassy in Tehran. In 1981, the MEK detonated bombs in the head office of the Islamic Republic Party and the Premier's office, killing some

seventy high-ranking Iranian officials, including Chief Justice Ayatollah Mohammad Beheshti, President Mohammad-Ali Rajaei, and Premier Mohammad-Javad Bahonar. Near the end of the 1980–1988 war with Iran, Baghdad armed the MEK with military equipment and sent it into action against Iranian forces. In 1991, the MEK assisted the Government of Iraq in suppressing the Shia and Kurdish uprisings in southern Iraq and the Kurdish uprisings in the north. In April 1992, the MEK conducted near-simultaneous attacks on Iranian embassies and installations in thirteen countries, demonstrating the group's ability to mount large-scale operations overseas. In April 1999, the MEK targeted key military officers and assassinated the deputy chief of the Iranian Armed Forces General Staff. In April 2000, the MEK attempted to assassinate the commander of the Nasr Headquarters, Tehran's interagency board responsible for coordinating policies on Iraq. The normal pace of anti-Iranian operations increased during "Operation Great Bahman" in February 2000, when the group launched a dozen attacks against Iran. One of

those attacks included a mortar attack against the leadership complex in Tehran that housed the offices of the Supreme Leader and the President. In 2000 and 2001, the MEK was involved regularly in mortar attacks and hit-and-run raids on Iranian military and law enforcement units and Government buildings near the Iran-Iraq border, although MEK terrorism in Iran declined toward the end of 2001. After Coalition aircraft bombed MEK bases at the outset of Operation Iraqi Freedom, the MEK leadership ordered its members not to resist Coalition forces, and a formal cease-fire arrangement was reached in May 2003.

STRENGTH

Over 3,000 MEK members are currently confined to Camp Ashraf, the MEK's main compound north of Baghdad, where they remain under the Geneva Convention's "protected person" status and Coalition control. As a condition of the cease-fire agreement, the group relinquished its weapons, including tanks, armored vehicles, and heavy artillery. A significant number of MEK personnel have "defected" from the Ashraf group, and several dozen of them have been voluntarily repatriated to Iran.

LOCATION/AREA OF OPERATION

In the 1980s, the MEK's leaders were forced by Iranian security forces to flee to France. On resettling in Iraq in 1987, almost all of its armed units were stationed in fortified bases near the border with Iran. Since Operation Iraqi Freedom, the bulk of the group is limited to Camp Ashraf, although an overseas support structure remains with associates and supporters scattered throughout Europe and North America.

EXTERNAL AID

Before Operation Iraqi Freedom, the group received all of its military assistance and most of its financial support, from the former Iraqi regime. The MEK also has used front organizations to solicit contributions from expatriate Iranian communities.

Source: U.S. Department of State. *Country Reports on Terrorism*. Washington, D.C., 2004.

LEADERSHIP

MARYAM RAJAVI

Maryam Rajavi is the principle leader of the MEK and elected by the group in 1993 as the "future president of Iran." Rajavi was born to an upper-middle-class family in Iran in 1953. She was introduced to the anti-shah movement in 1970 when she entered Sharif University of Technology in Tehran to pursue her education. While at the university, she began to participate in the student movements and joined the MEK. In 1980, she was a candidate for parliamentary elections in Tehran and received more than a quarter of a million votes.

Rajavi participated in the organizing of two major peaceful demonstrations in Tehran in April and June 1981 against the Khomeini regime. As a result, Rajavi experienced the scrutiny of the government as the Pasdaran, the Revolutionary Guards Corps, raided her places of residence.

In 1982, along with the other MEK members, Rajavi moved the political headquarters of the movement to Paris. In 1985, she was elected as the MEK joint leader and four years later, in 1989, became the Secretary General of the organization. In 1987, she was appointed the National Liberation Army's (NLA) Deputy Commander-in-Chief. In August 1993, the National Council of Resistance, the Iranian Resistance's Parliament, elected Rajavi as Iran's future president for the transitional period following the mullahs' overthrow. In June 2003, Rajavi was arrested after the French government raided the MEK compound under suspicion of terrorist activities. She was released on bail and confined to the MEK compound, but $8 million was confiscated.

MASSOUD RAJAVI

Massoud Rajavi is the leader of the military forces of the MEK and the husband of Maryam Rajavi. Massoud led the operations of the NLA in Iraq until the May 2003 ceasefire established with coalition forces. The location of Massoud has been in question since the start of Operation Iraqi Freedom.

based on gender, religion, or ethnic group; ending enforced religious practice; recognizing the right of Iranian Kurdistan to autonomy; protection of social, cultural, and political rights for ethnic minorities; repealing laws determined to be anti-labor and anti-peasant; repatriation of exiled Iranians living abroad after fleeing either the Shah or Khomeini regime; the creation a free marked economy based on national capitalism and private ownership; developing welfare to assist the poor; living in peaceful co-existence with its neighbors; and fostering new alliances.

OTHER PERSPECTIVES

According to the Council on Foreign Relations, "experts say the MEK resembles a cult, devoted to Massoud Rajavi's secular interpretation of the Koran." This view of the MEK is seconded by Professor Ervand Abrahamian as transitioning from a "mass movement" toward possessing "all the main attributes of a cult." However, Maryam Rajavi asserts that, "the MEK is the answer to American prayers as Tehran continues to dabble defiantly in both terrorism and nuclear arms." Many in the U.S. Congress agree with Rajavi's assertion and have pushed to have the organization removed from the terrorist watch list. Supporters of the group cite the MEK's 2002 revelation and producing of evidence that Iran was operating a secret nuclear facility in Natanz. However, some disagree with the effectiveness of the MEK. In his testimony to the Senate Foreign Relations Committee, Abbas William Samii, the Regional Analysis Coordinator, Southwest Asia, stated that "the association with [the MEK] will discredit the U.S. in the Iranian eyes." In addition, an article in the *New York Time* magazine quotes exiled Iranians as

KEY EVENTS

1960s: The MEK is founded as an Islamic Student organization.

1971: The group begins public protests of the Shah's government resulting in the execution of some of its leadership and the imprisonment of some of its members.

1970s: U.S. military and civilian personnel are killed in Iran. Iranian and U.S. governments believe the MEK was responsible for these deaths.

1979: The MEK supports the takeover of the U.S. Embassy, and the revolution that overthrows the Shah's regime.

1981: The MEK organizes peaceful demonstrations against the Khomeini government. This results in massive crackdowns by the regime on dissidents and the MEK's departure from Iran.

1981: The MEK detonates bombs at the offices of the Islamic Republic Party and Premier, causing the deaths of 79 high-ranking officials.

1982: The MEK resettles in France.

1987: The National Liberation Army, the militant faction of the MEK, is founded by Massoud Rajavi and settles in Iraq.

1991: The MEK participates in suppressing the Shi'ite and Kurdish uprising the southern Iraq and the Kurdish uprising in northern Iraq.

1992: The MEK conducts its largest overseas operation by simultaneously attacking Iranian embassies and installations in 13 countries.

1993: Maryam Rajavi is elected the "future president of Iran" by the National Council of Resistance, the political front to the MEK.

1997: The MEK is listed as a terrorist organization by the U.S. government.

1999: The MEK assassinates the Deputy Chief of the Iranian Armed Forces General Staff.

2000: The MEK launches "Operation Great Bahman," unleashing dozens of attacks on Iranian targets. The group also fails in its attempt to assassinate the commander of the Nasr Headquarters.

2001: The MEK targets Iranian military, law enforcement, and government buildings near the Iran-Iraq border for mortar or hit-and-run attacks.

2002: The European Union designates the MEK as a terrorist organization.

2003: Coalition forces bomb MEK bases in Iraq at the beginning of Operation Iraqi Freedom. After a formal ceasefire is reached, the MEK operatives are granted protected status under the Geneva Convention.

2003: The National Council of Resistance is added to the U.S. terrorism watch list.

considering the MEK, "as toxic, if not more so, than the ruling clerics."

SUMMARY

In the 1960s, the MEK was established as an Islamic student organization that opposed the excesses of the Shah's regime and the influence of Western powers in Iran. As a result, the group supported the 1979 revolution that toppled the Shah's government and set in place the current system of ruling clerics. The group, however, sought democratic changes and continued to protest the Khomeini government. As a result, the group was forced to flee Iran and set up its organization in France. In 1987, the group established its military faction called the National Liberation Army. The NLA was invited to set up camp in Iraq along the Iranian border. Saddam Hussein offered military and financial support to the group, which in turn aided Iraq in the Iran-Iraq war. Eventually, the group assisted the Iraqi government in suppressing the uprisings that occurred in 1991. The group then expanded its operations to attacks on overseas Iranian interest and installations, assassinations, and mortar and hit-and-run attacks. When Operation Iraqi Freedom began, the MEK leadership ordered its members to not resist coalition forces, and a formal ceasefire was reached, which granted protected status to the operatives.

The group's political leader, Maryam Rajavi, was arrested at her compound outside of France. She was later released on bail but confined to the compound. The group's military leader, Massoud Rajavi, was last seen in Iraq, but his whereabouts are unknown. Most of the group's membership is confined to Camp Ashraf in Iraq. As a result, the group's operations have ended.

SOURCES

Periodicals

Dickey, Christopher, Mark Hosenball, and Michael Hirsh. "Looking for a Few Good Spies." *Newsweek*. February 14, 2005.

Hosenball, Mark. "Mixed Signals on MEK." *Newsweek*. April 11, 2005.

Web sites

Canadian National Security. "Mujahedine-e Khalq Organization." < http://www.psepc-sppcc.gc.ca/national_security/counter-terrorism/Entities_e.asp#38 > (accessed October 14, 2005).

Council on Foreign Relations. "Terrorism: Questions and Answers: Mujahedine-e Khalq Organization." < http://cfrterrorism.org/groups/mujahedeen.html > (accessed October 14, 2005).

MIPT Terrorism Knowledge Base. "Mujahedine-e Khalq Organization." < http://tkb.org/Group.jsp?groupID= 3632 > (accessed October 14, 2005).

U.S. Department of State. "Country Reports on Terrorism, 2004." < http://library.nps.navy.mil/home/tgp/mek.htm > (accessed October 14, 2005).

Audio and Visual Media

Congressional Testimony. "Iran: Weapons Proliferations, Terrorism and Democracy." May 19, 2005.

Nation of Islam

LEADER: Louis Farrakhan

USUAL AREA OF OPERATION: United States

OVERVIEW

Based in Chicago, Illinois, the Nation of Islam acts as a religious and social organization with a goal of representing the interests of black men and women, both in the United States and around the world, through an ideology that is linked to Islam. The group ascribes divinity to its founder, Wallace Fard Muhammad, who founded the movement in 1930 and is referred to by adherents of the movement as "the Master."

The stated goals of the movement are to enhance the spiritual, mental, social, and economic positions of the black race. Positions attributed to the group have been perceived as defamatory speech against Caucasians and claims that the Nation of Islam is an anti-white and anti-Semitic organization. The group openly suggests that the original race was black and that whites are a historical and social aberration.

HISTORY

Wallace Fard Muhammad founded the Nation of Islam in 1930 as a loose gathering of African Americans who were suffering the effects of the Depression in Detroit, Michigan. Fard Muhammad taught that a war between the races was imminent and that the black people had to find their sense of purpose, which had

Elijah Muhammed, leader of the Nation of Islam from 1932 until 1975, addresses a crowd. AP/Wide World Photos

been robbed from them by the Caucasians. Espousing the belief that Christianity was a religion of the slave owners, which had been forced upon the blacks, Fard Muhammad taught that Islam was the true religion of the black race.

In 1934, Muhammad disappeared from Detroit under mysterious circumstances and was never seen again. One of Muhammad's first students was Elijah Poole, who had had his name changed by his teacher to Elijah Muhammad. Upon the disappearance of Fard Muhammad, Elijah assumed the head of the Nation of Islam movement and taught that Fard Muhammad was a divine figure who has been since accepted as a holy figure within the movement, with his birthday celebrated as "Savior's Day."

Elijah Muhammad traveled across the United States spreading the messages of the Nation of Islam and setting up mosques. His teachings would become increasingly widespread over time, with his followers continuing the outreach. The messages were spreading from inner city streets to larger conference halls and having a strong impact in prisons all over the United States.

It was in prison while he was serving a sentence for robbery that one of the movement's most well-known followers, Malcolm Little, was introduced to the Nation of Islam in 1952. Renamed Malcolm X, he would become one of the most vocal spokespeople for the Nation of Islam until the time of his assassination in 1965.

In 1955, Louis Farrakhan, who would assume the role of leader of the organization, was introduced to the teachings of Elijah Muhammad. Following the assassination of Malcolm X, Farrakhan would assume the role of spokesperson for the Nation of Islam and has become one of the strong advocates for black nationalism.

In February 1975, Elijah Muhammad died and the leadership of the Nation of Islam placed his son W.D. Wallace Muhammad in the position of Supreme Minister. W.D., much to the objection of many members of the group,

Malcom X, a Nation of Islam member and leader.
© Corbis/Bettmann

advocated a more moderate approach in regard to their relationship with other ethnic groups and tried to move the Nation of Islam closer to the teachings of mainstream Islam. He renamed the group the Muslim American Society and was publicly involved in reaching out to whites and other Muslim groups and opposed many of his father's views on religion and the need for black separatism.

Farrakhan, who was one of the fiercest opponents to the new stream of thought being advocated by W.D., made the decision in 1976 to distance himself from, rather than create a complete break within, the organization. In 1978, after viewing the continued changes brought on by W.D., Farrakhan decided to recreate the original Nation of Islam movement as it was taught by Elijah Muhammad. In 1979, the movement established its newspaper, *The Final Call*, which continues to be produced today.

The public influence of the Nation of Islam continued to grow with one of the movement's greatest accomplishments coming in 1995 with the Million Man March to Washington D.C., which was designed to be a public display of black influence in American society and which organizers claimed was the biggest public activist gathering in American history.

In October 2005, the Nation of Islam marked the anniversary of the Million Man March with another gathering in Washington D.C., entitled the Millions More Movement, to further strengthen the role of black identity in the greater society.

PHILOSOPHY AND TACTICS

The modern-day ideological beliefs followed by adherents of the Nation of Islam have been handed down from the original teachings of Wallace Fard Muhammad and Elijah Muhammad. The basic approach of these teachings in regard to world society is that the world can be divided into three primary groups. The first group, made up by 85% of the world's population, are those ignorant masses being misled by the second group, comprising 10% of the world's population, defined as "the rich slave makers," who rely on manipulation and the ignorance of the masses to control society. The third group is the remaining 5%, the "righteous teachers," who are always at war with the 10% of manipulators in an effort to advance a proper vision for society.

The Nation of Islam approaches slavery as a period of history inflicted upon blacks that caused them to lose independence over their lives. The movement further believes that slavery was in fulfillment of a biblical prophecy that has led adherents of Nation of Islam to recognize themselves as the children of Abraham.

According to the beliefs of the movement, the world was created seventy-eight trillion years ago at which point God was created. God was manifested in man who then died, but the essence of God remains for all time with men with divinity who would live and die, but they have all been black men, with the latest godly figure being Wallace Fard Muhammad.

The teachings of the Nation of Islam are spread through an intricate network of sermons,

LEADERSHIP

WALLACE FARD MUHAMMAD

A great deal of mystery surrounds the life of the founder of the Nation of Islam movement, Wallace Fard Muhammad. According to adherents of the movement, Fard Muhammad was born in 1877 in Mecca and made his way to the United States. However, according to the FBI, he is believed to have been born in either New Zealand or Portland, Oregon, in 1891 or 1893. He spent several years in prison, allegedly for drug offenses; believers in his "divinity" say he committed no crimes but was imprisoned for preaching about the black race. When he was ordered to leave his home base of Detroit, Michigan, in 1934 for alleged involvement in a murder, he left without a trace and was never heard from again, although rumors existed that he remained alive in New Zealand into the 1960s.

ELIJAH MUHAMMAD

Prior to his departure, Fard Muhammad had assigned the position of leader of the Nation of Islam to a native of Georgia by the name of Eli Poole, later known as Elijah Muhammad, who would act as the head of the Nation of Islam until his death in 1975. Elijah Muhammad preached that Fard Muhammad has been God in the form of a person and that he had handed over his teachings to Elijah in 1931. For the remainder of his life, Elijah Muhammad was involved in spreading the ideologies of the group throughout the United States and succeeded in building numerous mosques (or temples as they are referred to within the movement).

LOUIS FARRAKHAN

With Elijah Muhammad's death in 1975, his son, W.D. Muhammad, became the leader of the movement, but because of his departure from the separatist views of his father, the control over the Nation of Islam would fall into the hands of Louis Farrakhan. Farrakhan was an accomplished singer and violinist when he was introduced to the Nation of Islam in the early 1950s. He quickly rose through the ranks of the organization to become the head of major temples—first in Boston and then in Harlem in New York. Because of the active and vocal role that he has assumed in his position as spokesman for black separatism and purism, he has become a controversial public image in American society.

lectures, and publications, including a highly circulated newspaper called *The Final Call* and has adapted to modern communication with a high reliance on the Internet. Critics of the movement say that the theologies and teachings of the Nation of Islam are rarely based in any historical fact but rather are myths developed out of excerpts from the scriptures, which are manipulated in ways to allow the religious leaders of the Nation of Islam to attract followers.

In addition to its religious activities, the Nation of Islam is actively involved in the commercial and business sectors of black society in an effort to provide blacks with their own sources of employment, which fits in with the philosophy that the movement has developed about what blacks need to fend for themselves in society. The organization owns food service companies, bakeries, and restaurants, as well as large plots of farmland in the state of Georgia. The group also works on social programs on behalf of the black communities, with drug prevention and rehabilitation programs and anti-gang efforts. The group makes a concerted effort to work with former convicts to rehabilitate them and keep them from returning to prison.

OTHER PERSPECTIVES

As popular as the Nation of Islam has become within much of mainstream African-American society, as a result of its outspoken approach to non-blacks, it is often characterized as a hate

KEY EVENTS

1930: Nation of Islam founded by Wallace Fard Muhammad.

1934: Fard Muhammad disappears, and Elijah Muhammad takes over leadership of Nation of Islam.

1975: Louis Farrakhan takes over leadership of the group, and continues in that position as of 2005.

1995: One of Nation of Islam's greatest accomplishments, the Million Man March to Washington D.C.

group. Its leaders have been identified for making statements specifically negating the rights of existence of other ethnicities.

Both the Anti-Defamation League and the Southern Poverty Law Center, which are working against hatred in society, have described the Nation of Islam as a hate group. The Nation of Islam, while maintaining strong working relationships with some leading black Christian leaders, including Rev. Jesse Jackson and Rev. Al Sharpton, has been openly critical of Christianity, claiming that it was involved in enslaving and subjugating blacks. Many of the black Christian leaders have advanced a position that the advancement of brotherhood of the black race by the Nation of Islam is reason enough to put aside the differences that exist so that they could work towards that common goal.

The more controversial comments that have emerged from leaders of the Nation of Islam have come in regard to their perceptions of Jews. Jewish groups have fiercely criticized a statement by Louis Farrakhan in which he said that Adolf Hitler was a great man. The Nation of Islam has also publicly suggested that wealthy Jews were involved in financing Nazi Germany. Jews who work in black communities have been described by the Nation of Islam as "blood suckers" for profiting without investing in the welfare of black communities. In a book published by the Nation of Islam in 1991, the group said that Jews were responsible for anti-Semitism and had been racist toward blacks. The book, which was presented as a history of the relationship between Jews and blacks, was accepted as a factual representation of that history by followers of the Nation of Islam.

SUMMARY

The Nation of Islam movement, while not adhered to by many blacks in the United States, has a strong influence on many African Americans and has stood at the center of some of the black community's largest public events—most notably the Million Man March in 1995.

Even as it has continued to exert influence, the group has adhered to a position of separatism for blacks from white society. Through the leadership of Louis Farrakhan, it has been criticized as a group that promotes an agenda of hatred toward Caucasians, who are blamed by the movement for the problems faced by blacks in society. The group has played a major role in advancing their particular form of Islam within the African-American community.

SOURCES

Books

Tsoukalas, Steven Malcolm. *The Nation of Islam; Understanding the Black Muslims.* Phillipsburg, New Jersey: P&R Publishing, 2001.

X, Malcolm. *The Autobiography of Malcolm X (As Told to Alex Haley).* New York: Balantine Publishing Group, 1964.

National Alliance

LEADER: William Pierce

YEAR ESTABLISHED OR BECAME ACTIVE: 1974

USUAL AREA OF OPERATION: United States

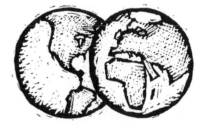

The National Alliance emerged from an earlier group, the National Youth Alliance, which had been led by Willis Carto. A faction composed of former members of the defunct American Nazi Party led by William Pierce became dissatisfied with Carto's leadership and formed the National Alliance. In a few short years, it would become the most influential white supremacist organization in the United States and perhaps in the world.

Due in large part to Pierce's intelligence and ambition, the National Alliance grew to over 1,500 active members, with cells in thirty states. Financially solid, with a working business model that brought in over $1 million a year in profit, the group published a magazine, a newsletter, a successful record label, and a weekly radio address.

The group's fortunes rapidly declined after Pierce's death in 2002. Today, the group remains a weakened shell of its former self and is believed to be in its death throes.

HISTORY

The National Alliance had its beginnings in the Youth for Wallace campaign of 1968. Established by Willis Carto after George Wallace's failed presidential bid, the National Youth Alliance focused

A counter-protester sprays mace at a white separatist demonstrator during a National Alliance rally in Washington, D.C., on April 24, 2002. AP/Wide World Photos

on recruiting college students to its cause. In 1970, Carto's recruiting efforts were successful in attracting William Pierce. Pierce was already a veteran of the white supremacy movement, having been a member of the American Nazi Party (ANP) and its successor, the National Socialist White People's Party. Other former American Nazi Party activists soon joined Pierce in the National Youth Alliance. By 1974, the former ANP contingent had become disaffected with Carto's leadership and left the group to form the National Alliance.

Pierce proved to be a remarkably savvy leader and businessman. A former physics professor, he held weekly meetings near Washington D.C. to recruit new members. He wrote a novel, *The Turner Diaries*, which went on to become the undisputed bible for right-wing survivalists worldwide. In the book, white revolutionaries

overthrow the federal government and begin the systematic killing of non-whites and Jews to create an Aryan nation. The book has been the acknowledged inspiration behind many violent acts in recent history, including Timothy McVeigh's bombing of the federal building in Oklahoma City. The popularity of the novel among white extremists across the world increased Pierce's notoriety and helped the National Alliance become a powerhouse among white supremacy groups. In 1985, Pierce purchased a 346-acre farm in Millpoint, West Virginia, as a new base.

Pierce ran the National Alliance with an iron hand, controlling both its message and its growing business interests. He produced a weekly radio address, *American Dissident Voices*, and a publishing firm for his racist materials, National Vanguard Books. By 1998, he could claim 1,000

National Alliance members protest U.S. support for Israel on August 24, 2002, in Washington, D.C.
AP/Wide World Photos

paying members. In 1999, he moved into a new venture, one that had the potential to extend the movement beyond most observers' wildest imagining, and one that would consume his interest until his dying days. He purchased a racist, "white-power" music company called Resistance Records from a Canadian group that had been operating out of Detroit to evade Canada's stringent laws against hate speech. Resistance Records had made a name for itself in the skinhead movement, featuring heavy metal rock music paired with racist lyrics. Pierce soon moved to purchase another white-power music label, Nordland Records out of Switzerland, essentially doubling his publishing holdings and cementing Resistance Records as the preeminent outlet for the new emerging genre of "hate-core" music. By this time, the National Alliance boasted over 1,500 dues paying members and annual revenues in excess of $1 million.

To cement his position as the undisputed impresario of hate-core, Pierce took in and championed the cause of Hendrik Möbus, an East German musician who had been convicted of murdering a fourteen-year-old youth. Appearing on Pierce's radio show in 2000, Möbus discussed plans to join forces with Pierce to extend their mutual racist message to more of the European audience. At the same time as he was developing this inroad to the young skinhead culture, Pierce was busy forging alliances with racist groups in Britain, Germany, as well as with other U.S. power players in the white supremacy movement, such as Matt Hale.

Then, in 2002, Pierce succumbed to cancer, and the group lurched into almost immediate decline. Erich Gliebe, Pierce's successor, has shown none of his mentor's organizational and management genius; he has succeeded only in permanently alienating core members of the group. Senior membership ultimately banded together to demand his resignation, only to find themselves purged from the group's rolls. These banished activists wasted no time in forming a new group, the National Vanguard.

Today, the National Alliance is a shadow of its former self, with Gliebe appointing one of his

KEY EVENTS

1974: Former American Nazi Party contingent forms National Alliance.

1985: Pierce purchased a 346-acre farm in Millpoint, West Virginia, as a new base for National Alliance.

2002: Pierce succumbed to cancer, and the group goes into decline.

few remaining loyalists, Shaun Walker, as Chief Operating Officer in a belated response to the overwhelming demand that he step down. As long as Gliebe and Walker remain in control, the group that Pierce brought from obscurity to an international force seems destined to be overshadowed and absorbed by the National Vanguard.

PHILOSOPHY AND TACTICS

Pierce developed a philosophy he called "Cosmotheism," a system of beliefs that inform the activities of the group. Simply put, Cosmotheism states that humans are part of nature, the white race is the highest form of humanity, and nature is intrinsically hierarchical and non-egalitarian. Pierce contrasts his philosophy with the major Western religions, which espouse a "Semitic" point of view that sets humanity apart from nature and binds them to service to a man-like supreme being. Multiculturalism and feminism are seen as sicknesses infecting society and threatening its downfall. Allowing women and non-whites to vote was the first big mistake that led to this downward spiral towards a "darker world." Allowing the Jews to control the American media establishment was the second mistake. The result is that the non-white population is exploding throughout the world and white populations are at best static. The National Alliance wants to reverse this trend, in order to ensure the survival of the Aryan race.

The goal of the National Alliance is to establish a "White Living Space": all of Europe, the "temperate zones of the Americas," Australia, and South Africa. All non-whites and Jews are to be purged from the living space, in order to stop and reverse the trend toward a "darker" world that the disastrous multicultural policies of the last century have helped create.

There are specific acknowledgements that this purging process will be violent, systematic, and messy. A white government must arise, halt non-white immigration, deport all non-whites, and halt all forms of foreign aid to the non-white governments in the world. The larger urban areas within the United States are largely written off, and their hopelessly multicultural degenerate masses left to perish "in the chaos preceding the final cleansing." With this accomplished, nature would reassert itself and the white race would thrive. Non-whites would soon become if not extinct, at least returned to their naturally weakened pre-colonial state, due to their inherent inability to provide for themselves. The societies that evolve in the White Living Space must be purged not only of undesirable races but of all Semitic and non-white influences. Jazz and rock and roll will be forbidden, but the polka will be encouraged.

To this end, a reformed Aryan educational structure must be put in place, such that the education provided is gender specific and aimed at reinforcing Aryan character at least as much as it is imparting knowledge. Permissiveness is the reason for the failure of the current educational system, and discipline is the answer.

Pierce was vague about the kinds of government that would evolve in the Aryan world. In certain contexts, he seemed to be calling for a strong centralized government ruling over the entire White Living Space. In others, he specifically envisioned a variety of white governments that were endemic to their locales: a Baltic state, a Celtic state, a Germanic state. Somehow, these Aryan governments would avoid the evils of both unchecked capitalism and innovation-crushing Marxism by subordinating all economic policy to "racial progress."

The structure of the group itself evidenced this same vagueness. Dues-paying members could join local "units" that were run like chapters and led by unit coordinators; they could affiliate in small groups, or "proto-units"; or they could remain independent. Whatever level

PRIMARY SOURCE

Against the Wall: Beset by internal battles, plunging revenues and membership, and attacks from without, America's leading hate group is in serious trouble

The most important hate group in America is sinking. The National Alliance, the neo-Nazi organization that has produced and influenced more violent criminals in the last three decades than any other, may soon be facing irrelevancy.

In the last year, membership has plunged from around 1,400 to fewer than 800 who still pay their dues. The staff, once the largest of any hate group in decades, has been cut by nearly half. Income from selling white power music and paraphernalia, which with dues was said to be bringing in more than $1 million last year, has dropped to the point where the Alliance spends more than it takes in.

Alliance chapters in Boston, Dallas, Georgia, Maryland, Memphis, Phoenix and Southern California are falling apart or have been reduced to a few staunch holdouts. And a pitched battle for control of the National Alliance and its 423-acre West Virginia compound is under way.

"[T]he National Alliance appears to be well on its way to dissolution," wrote Wayne Sims, who was a key editor at the Alliance's National Vanguard Books until running afoul of the Alliance's current leadership this summer. "[G]rand as it was until July 2002, [the Alliance] has been stripped of its spirit and will, I think, soon lose its solvency. I recommend that its members find or create another group."

The group's fortunes have fallen fast. When Alliance founder and long-time leader William Pierce died on July 23, 2002, the organization was doing better than at any time since its founding in 1974. It had developed a successful business model, and was regularly adding staff to Resistance Records and National Vanguard Books, the chief income-earners for the group.

Its prestige, maintained by Pierce's essays, commentaries on current events and broadcasts over the Internet and shortwave radio, reached all the way to the European radical right. The Alliance was in the streets and in the news, and its members were never more optimistic.

Today, all of that seems little more than a distant memory. Since former boxer Erich Gliebe (see profile Führer of the Titanic) was named chairman six days after Pierce's death, the Alliance has been plagued by vicious internal battles and almost daily attacks from outside right-wing radicals. It now seems possible the Alliance could completely founder.

THE DESCENT INTO DARKNESS

The trouble began with Gliebe. Although he had earned Pierce's respect, bringing Resistance Records to profitability in a couple of years and making his Cleveland unit the most active in the country, Gliebe was no Pierce.

of organization a member belongs to, the primary activity was recruiting. Members typically meet once a month to discuss ideology, upcoming events, and methods of recruiting, typically involving the dissemination of National Alliance literature purchased from Vanguard Books. The group's leaders have been quite inventive in developing methods for getting their message heard. Members have leased billboards, distributed flyers, and published racist comic books to target the young where they live and go to school. Recruiters have found fertile ground on college and high school campuses, in suburbia, in prisons, and within the ranks of the armed forces.

Throughout his life, Pierce exercised tight control over the message, requiring members to get his approval before speaking publicly in the group's name or creating new materials for distribution. While he lived, there was very little of the dissension and infighting that runs rampant in other racist movements. He made alliances with all types of racists, from young skinheads to middle-aged ex-Klansmen. No one dared oppose the racist genius who wrote *The Turner Diaries* and inspired racists the world over to organize resistance against the forces that opposed them. In the end, it seems obvious that Pierce's intelligence, organizational abilities, and drive were the chief assets of the group he founded.

Where Pierce was a former university physics professor and an intellectual capable of bringing in recruits through his writings, Gliebe was a one-time tool-and-die maker who was hard-edged, humorless and remarkably clumsy in his dealings with other members.

WHITHER THE NATIONAL ALLIANCE?

A remarkable series of events seems to have coalesced that may ultimately wreck what has for years been the most important hate group in America. The unexpected death of William Pierce; the naming of a man to replace him who had none of Pierce's intellectual qualities and few people skills; financial woes almost certainly due to poor management; the appearance of several Internet sites that aired all kinds of movement criticism of the Alliance; and the failure of Gliebe to raise money for a member in trouble—have all contributed to the present situation.

Hundreds of members have left the Alliance and key units are coming close to collapse. Although Gliebe claims to have added new chapters since Pierce's death, the reality is that these units are generally far smaller than the six-member minimum that Pierce insisted on, and they often consist of people who are brand new.

At press time, Gliebe had actually managed to fire or alienate everyone on staff who understood how to access the Alliance's membership database, which is protected by a sophisticated system of passwords at various levels. Presumably, he will regain access to the database, but even the temporary loss is telling.

Many former and present Alliance members think that various units of the organization will spin off and become independent groups. There has even been talk of "growing a new head"—that is, spinning off a new national group from units of the present Alliance and then choosing an entirely new leadership to head it.

Gliebe may yet pull the Alliance back from the brink. But with the huge amount of animosity he has created, with many of his former key activists now in leading roles of other groups, and with his own finances flagging, it seems almost impossible that the Alliance can regain the influence it once wielded.

Today, what seems more likely is that the struggle over the Alliance will eventually devolve into a simple battle over the substantial commercial assets the group still controls.

Mark Potok

Source: Southern Poverty Law Center, 2003

OTHER PERSPECTIVES

In the years since Pierce's death in 2002, civil rights watchdog groups such as the Anti-Defamation League and the Southern Poverty Law Center have all but pronounced the National Alliance dead. While it is true that the group is no longer on the growth trajectory it enjoyed under Pierce's leadership, many local units are still active.

In August 2005, homes in Belmont, Massachusetts were leafleted by NA members, prompting the local Human Rights Commission to hold a town meeting in an attempt to combat the spread of racism in the community.

In September 2005, an NA member was forced to take down presumably bogus Hurricane Katrina charity web sites when the Missouri Attorney General initiated legal proceedings against him.

In October, local civil rights activists in Vermont and Utah accused the anti-immigration group, the Minuteman Civil Defense Corps, of being affiliated and/or infiltrated by members of the National Alliance.

In the meantime, most of the former leadership of the National Alliance has formed a new organization, the National Vanguard, that has pledged to continue Pierce's legacy. In

April 2005, the activists delivered a petition to the National Alliance headquarters, demanding Gliebe and Walker step aside, that the Executive Committee assume the function of Board of Directors, and that all future decisions and leadership functions come from the Board. When the deadline passed, the activists formed the National Vanguard. While only time will tell if the National Vanguard can live up to Pierce's vision and example, for the time being the group is intent on recruiting activities, having already established very active cells in Virginia, Florida, Nevada, and New Jersey.

In Nevada, members are trying to enter politics under the name of the White People's Party. In their first attempt at national action, members have organized a boycott of Home Depot, for their alleged pro-immigration stance. After Hurricane Katrina, members organized a National Vanguard First Response Team to offer aid to Caucasian families in Alabama and Mississippi. Based in Charlottesville, Virginia, the group has no formally designated leader, but former National Alliance Executive Committee member Kevin Alfred Strom is their spokesmen and apparent first among equals.

1995 Oklahoma City bombing of the Alfred P. Murrah Federal Building.

Pierce established an array of businesses, and built a financial model that brought in more than $1 million annually. He published a magazine, a newsletter, a successful record label, and a weekly radio address. The record label, Resistance Records, established Pierce as the acknowledged impresario of the emerging racist "hate-core" genre. Hate-core, which combines heavy metal music with violently racist lyrics, afforded him new inroads with youth, particularly in Europe. By the time of his death in 2002, the National Alliance was the most important white supremacist group in the United States, and perhaps the world, with 1,500 registered, dues-paying members and important alliances with racist groups worldwide.

After Pierce's death, Erich Gliebe took over leadership of the group, and promptly became embroiled in a power struggle with senior members. Several of the leadership came together to demand his resignation, which Gliebe failed to acknowledge. The dissident members eventually formed a rival organization, The National Vanguard, which claims to represent the true legacy of William Pierce.

SUMMARY

The National Alliance was founded in 1974 by Dr.William Pierce, a former physics professor and veteran of several white supremacist organizations, including the American Nazi Party and the National Youth Alliance. Pierce articulated an unabashed philosophy of white supremacy he called Cosmotheism, and called for the establishment of a White Living Space encompassing all of Europe, the United States, Australia, and South Africa. An organizational and financial genius, Pierce exercised tight control over the groups message, membership, and financial interests His novel, *The Turner Diaries*, became the undisputed bible of right-wing fanatics worldwide, and is reported to have inspired the

SOURCES

Periodicals

"As He Lay Dying." *The Village Voice*. September 4–10, 2002.

Southern Poverty Law Center. "Against the Wall." *Intelligence Report*. Fall 2003.

Web sites

ADL.org. "National Alliance." < http://www.adl.org/learn/ext_us/N_Alliance.asp > (accessed October 15, 2005).

SEE ALSO

American Nazi Party

National Association for the Advancement of White People

LEADER: David Duke

USUAL AREA OF OPERATION: United States

OVERVIEW

The National Association for the Advancement of White People (NAAWP) was founded in 1980 by David Duke. According to its web site, it is a "not for profit, non-violent, civil rights educational organization." Its focus lies in providing a source of pride and unification for the white population as well as ensuring that minority populations do not receive special rights or treatment. The organization is concerned about the future of the United States and does not want it to become a third-world nation due to the massive incorporation of diversity. Although the organization does not consider itself a hate group or racist, many other sources view it as so, and it has gained publicity through not only its views, but also through its founder and his extremist actions.

HISTORY

The NAAWP was created in 1980 by David Duke, after he left the Knights of the Ku Klux Klan. Duke claims that he created the NAAWP with basically the same beliefs as the Knights of the KKK. He was supposedly involved in a money scandal involving his attempt at selling the Knights of the KKK, so this is perhaps why he went on to found an organization with a

David Duke, shortly after announcing the creation of a group called the National Association for the Advancement of White People on August 19, 1980. © *Bettman/Corbis*

similar ideology. Duke eventually left the NAAWP. Currently the organization's National President is Reno Wolfe. The organization's ideology does not seem to have significantly shifted over time through the exit of Duke and the continuation of the group.

PHILOSOPHY AND TACTICS

The NAAWP hopes to achieve all that is laid out in their Mission and Vision Statements. In a section on their web site titled "Why should I join?" it is explained that the group's goal is not to hate others but rather to build "a new, better society. A homogeneous community where everyone contributes, everyone benefits, and all share a common set of values and moral beliefs, without the continual attacks on culture." The web site also shares the views that the quality of America has declined from the time of the founding of the nation, and the NAAWP

would like to ensure that no further decay follows.

The group is also dedicated to a project called Operation Appalachian, launched in 2000, claimed to be a grassroots effort that focuses on helping the population of poor European Americans that live in Appalachia. The web site requests donations of either money or supplies to this cause.

The group's web site implies that the NAAWP's strategy is to create a respectable group that will hold influence in the actions of the government, so that they can truly focus on ensuring that whites will not be subject to unequal rights. However, reports from other sources seem to focus on the group's methodology of providing school supplies to Appalachia. One particular article from the Southern Poverty Law Center's Intelligence Report explains that the NAAWP brought school supplies to a church in West Virginia but also brought their own propaganda along. The church had not been previously aware of the group's

LEADERSHIP

DAVID DUKE

David Duke, born in 1950, has had a long history of association with white supremacy/ extremist groups. He joined the Ku Klux Klan (KKK) as a teenager. When he attended Louisiana State University in the 1970s, he led the White Youth Alliance, which was a white supremacist organization on campus. In 1974, he became the leader of the Knights of the KKK in Louisiana. During his time with this group, he focused on making the group more presentable to the public, through changing some of the group's terminology and rituals so that they did not seem as extremist or extraordinary in comparison to other organizations. In 1980, Duke left the Knights of the KKK, supposedly when he tried to secretly sell the group to the head of a different KKK group in a meeting that he did not know was being taped. Although Duke denies that this occurred, in any case, he left the organization and founded the NAAWP. He eventually left the NAAWP after setting down the groundwork, although he is still involved and is known to give speeches at their events. Since then, he has delved into politics, winning a spot in the Louisiana State Legislature in 1989. Otherwise, he has not been very successful, as in his running for President of the United States in both 1988 and 1992. He has also formed a new group, The National Organization for European American Rights, in order to focus on promoting the rights of European Americans. On their web site, the Anti-Defamation League refers to Duke as possibly America's best-known racist.

background and appreciated the supplies, but they were not converted into NAAWP members. The article even indicated that the NAAWP would not be invited back to the church. In this case, their tactic was to present these free items while also promoting their own beliefs. There was another report of similar activity from *The*

Charleston Gazette, in which the group provided supplies to a church in Charleston, and although it was acknowledged that the supplies were a nice gesture by the group, the church was not aware of the NAAWP's philosophy and also did not request a return visit. This tactic of the group seems to be effective in being able to donate but not in establishing a relationship with any of these churches because of the goals and beliefs of the group.

OTHER PERSPECTIVES

The Charleston Gazette speaks out against the organization in at least two articles, one focused on the inaccuracy of the group's take on the white population being oppressed and the other expressing amazement that the group is still allowed to operate, with its bigotry and racism. The newspaper is not afraid to speak out openly against the group and refers to its philosophy as "crackpot gibberish." The newspaper's attitude seems to be triggered by the group's donation of school supplies to a church in the local community. The newspaper obviously suspects the group's motives.

The web site, Stormfront.org, with a logo stating "White Pride World Wide," is in support of the NAAWP. On the web site, it has a posting for an NAAWP Heritage Rally, with a discussion by members of the group about the rally and possible attendees. Stormfront.org claims itself to be a white nationalist community, so its views seem to incorporate well with those of the NAAWP. The site also features a web radio show with David Duke, no doubt strengthening the association between this web site and the organization.

SUMMARY

The NAAWP remains an active organization, as of 2005. Its web site provides abundant information about the group, although it does not provide any statistics about membership. The group still aims toward creating a group that whites can be proud of, as well as improving society so that no particular minority group receives special attention. It continues to depend on the freedom of speech to allow its views to be projected to the nation.

KEY EVENTS

1980: David Duke founds NAAWP.

1989: Duke wins a spot in the Louisiana State Legislature.

SOURCES

Periodicals

Bridges, T. "Duke Brewed Hatred in a Potion of Lies." *Times-Picayune*. March 16, 2003: 7.

Radmacher, D. "Most Whites in U.S. Not Exactly Oppressed, Earn More than Minorities." *The Charleston Gazette*. August 25, 2000: 4A.

Staff writer. "Bigotry Racism Lingers." *The Charleston Gazette*. August 26, 2000: p. 4A

Web sites

Anti-Defamation League. "NAAWP." < http://www. adl.org/hate_symbols/groups_naawp.asp > (accessed October 18, 2005).

Southern Poverty Law Center Intelligence Report. "Mainstreaming Hate: Racists Offer Poor Whites School Supplies and Hate." < http://www.splcenter.org/intel/intelreport/article.jsp?aid = 220 > (accessed October 18, 2005).

SEE ALSO

Ku Klux Klan

Stormfront.org

National Bolshevik Party

LEADER: Eduard Limonov

YEAR ESTABLISHED OR BECAME ACTIVE: 1994

ESTIMATED SIZE: 7,000

USUAL AREA OF OPERATION: Russia; United States; Canada; Sweden; Israel; Spain; Venezuela

OVERVIEW

The National Bolshevik Party (NBP), set up in 1994, is known to be headed by a radical Russian writer, Eduard Limonov. The NBP, although a political party, has been repeatedly denied any official status by the Russian government because of its disrepute. Though active mostly in Russia, it reportedly has branches in the United States, Canada, Sweden, Israel, Spain, and Venezuela.

The Nationalist Bolshevik Party, since it was formed, has been making strong efforts to form clandestine armed units by taking young men into their fold and collecting weapons illegally. It has also been accused of planning terrorist attacks in Russia and other countries and of vehemently demanding changes in the borders of the Russian Federation, including an armed invasion of Kazakhstan.

HISTORY

The National Bolshevik Party was reportedly formed in 1994 by Russian scholars Eduard Limonov and Aleksandr Dugin and musicians Yegor Letov and Sergei Kurikhin. Aleksandr Dugin is thought to have left the party soon after its formation. According to published reports, the party formation process actually

Young members of the National Bolshevik Party march by St. Bastile Church in Moscow, 1998. The group combines the tenets of Nazism and Communism. © Abbas | Magnum Photos

started in 1992 but was announced during the launch of its paper, *Limonoka*, two years later. Though the party was registered as an inter-regional organization in early 1997 and then re-registered on February 9, 1998, it has failed to get national registration in Russia. *Bolshevik* (Russian for majority) is a reference to the Bolshevik party that overthrew the Russian government in 1917 and established communist rule. The party has been headquartered in Moscow.

Before forming the National Bolshevik Party, Eduard Limonov was reportedly the head of the National Radical Party. In the early 1990s, this party suffered a split. According to analysts, it was divided into the Right-Radical Party and the Limonov Party, even as the Limonov faction retained the National-Radical title. In 1994, it was renamed as Nationalist Bolshevik Party.

Party leaders have often tried to contest elections in Russia but were unsuccessful in winning. According to news reports, in the Duma (state assembly) elections of 1995, Eduard Limonov and Alexander Dugin's attempts to get seats through a single mandate constituency were unsuccessful.

Throughout the 1990s and the early 2000s, members of the NBP have been accused of planning aggressive protests as well as terrorist acts in Russia, with the aim of dethroning President Vladimir Putin's government. Members of the NBP have often disrupted political rallies by throwing eggs, mayonnaise, and tomatoes at politicians of opposing parties.

In 2005, police officers raided the Bolsheviks' headquarters in Moscow where they reportedly arrested forty-eight members. Soon after, in June 2005, the National Bolshevik Party was banned by a Moscow court. However, in August 2005, the Russian Supreme Court overturned the ban.

The Nationalist Bolshevik Party, as of 2005, is said to have over 7,000 members in fifty-one regions of the country. Most of these members are reportedly between the ages of twenty and twenty-two.

LEADERSHIP

EDUARD LIMONOV

Founder of the Nationalist Bolshevik Party, Eduard Limonov is known to be a rebellious writer. Limonov was a member of the Soviet Literary Underground Group in the 1960s. In 1974, he went to the United States and started writing novels. In 1982, Limonov flew to France and came in close contact with European political radicals, including Jean-Marie Le Pen. In 1994, soon after returning to Russia, Limonov started a radical newspaper, *Limonaka*. At this time, Limonov and other Russian scholars formed the National Bolshevik Party.

Analysts state that Limonov's tactics have been aimed at Russian and the U.S government policies. He is thought to be behind many of the aggressive strategies implemented by the NBP.

In April 2001, Limonov and some followers were arrested at Altai (a mountain range in Siberia) on the charge of terrorism and preparing an armed rebellion in Kazakhstan. Limonov was imprisoned for two and a half years. While in prison, Limonov wrote a book, *The Other Russia*, in which he branded President Vladimir Putin's Russia as a "police state."

PHILOSOPHY AND TACTICS

The Nationalist Bolshevik Party is a leftist revolutionary organization, whose philosophies are based on communism. Party leader Eduard Limonov is known for undertaking rebellious activities against the Russian government. The NBP was reportedly formed with the aim of creating a Russian-dominated "Eurasia" that consists of Europe and Russia. Analysts and monitor groups state the NBP is also anti-American.

The party is also known to be extremely critical of the Vladimir Putin government in Russia. Party members have often publicly criticized the policies of Putin. Over the years, NBP has employed several anti-government strategies, including disrupting political rallies by throwing eggs and tomatoes at political leaders.

According to news reports, the party is also known to have recommended aggressive measures for forming Eurasia. In a project titled "Second Russia," the party recommended specific actions against countries with sizable Russian-speaking minorities—Kazakhstan, Ukraine, and Latvia. The group wanted the aggressive takeover of the land of these countries. "The initial spark should be kindled outside Russia. It should be understood that the emergence of a conflict is not the ultimate goal, but only an indispensable first stage of an armed revolt to replace the powers in Moscow," the party newspaper *Limonaka* stated.

The National Bolshevik Party's ideologies are based on what is commonly known as National Bolshevism. According to proclamations made by the party, it considers foreign enemies such as the United States as well as the Russian government to be "Satan."

The NBP also claims that if it comes to power, it will "transform" Russia by uniting all Russians (and Russian-speaking countries) into one state.

Leaders of the NBP have publicly rejected friendship ties with the United States, while at the same time maintaining that ties with other countries such as Germany, Iran, India, and Japan should be built.

Analysts suggest that NBP members, because of their anti-West stance, are also known to have recommended dissolving all contracts with Western countries, especially the United States. NBP proclamations claim that the Russian economy should be based on the principle of communism.

OTHER PERSPECTIVES

The activities and philosophies of NBP have received criticism as well as support in Russia. Talking about the activities of the Nationalist Bolshevik Party in 1990s, Ilya Ponamarev, leader of the Communist Party-controlled Young Left Front said that the "organization never was or is a youth movement at all. It is a postmodernist aesthetic project of intellectual provocateurs (in the positive meaning of the word) in

KEY EVENTS

2003: Two Nationalist Bolshevik Party members detained for throwing mayonnaise at Alexander Veshnyakov, chairman of the Central Election Committee of Russia.

2003: Nationalist Bolshevik Party members attack Communist Party leader Gennady Zyuganov.

2003: Natalia Tchernova of NBP hurls an egg at Prime Minister Mikhail Kasyanov.

2003: Fourteen members of National Bolsheviks Party seize roof of Ministry of Justice and display "Liberty or Death!"

2003: NBP central committee announces boycott of Presidential elections of March 14, 2004.

2004: Tula's National Bolshevik Party activists seize roof of the Department of Justice building.

2004: Moscow Special Police raid the office of NBP paper *General Line*.

which many bright and nontrivial personalities like Eduard Limonov, Aleksandr Dugin, Sergei Kurikhin and (analyst) Stanislav Belkovsky were involved. It was an effort, and, a quite successful one, to mobilize the most passionate and intellectually dissatisfied part of society (in contrast to the Communist Party, which utilized the social and economic protests of the leftist

electorate). For this mobilization, the NBP used a bizarre mixture of totalitarian and fascist symbols, geopolitical dogma, leftist ideas, and national-patriotic demagoguery."

While banning the National Bolshevik Party in June 2005, the Moscow Regional Court noted that the NBP's actions were "targeted at forced constitutional change, breaking the integrity of the Russian Federation, establishing armed units."

SUMMARY

The Nationalist Bolshevik Party (NBP) was founded by rebel writer Eduard Limonov. The party has failed to get national registration as it reportedly indulges in illegal activities. As of 2005, the party is still active. A Russian court banned the party in June 2005, an action that was later overturned by the Russian Supreme Court in August 2005. According to analysts, as of 2005, the party, with over 7,000 members and branches in fifty-one regions of Russia, aims at creating a unified Russian nation with all Russian-speaking countries.

SOURCES

Web sites

MosNews.com. "Moscow Court Bans Russia's Radical National Bolshevik Party." < http://www.mosnews.com/news/2005/06/29/nbpliquidated.shtml > (accessed October 15, 2005).

The St. Petersburg Times. "Ban on National Bolshevik Party Overturned by Court." < http://www.sptimes.ru/story/483 > (accessed October 15, 2005).

The Seattle Times. "Reincarnated Bolsheviks Rattle Russia's Leaders." < http://seattletimes.nwsource.com/html/nationworld/2002486682_bolsheviks11.html?syndication = rss > (accessed October 15, 2005).

National Liberation Army (ELN)

LEADERS: Fabio Vásquez Castaño; Felipe Torres

USUAL AREA OF OPERATION: Colombia

OVERVIEW

The National Liberation Army (ELN, its Spanish acronym for Ejército de Liberación Nacional), was founded between 1963 and 1965 by Marxist urban intellectuals inspired by Fidel Castro's success in Cuba. The group views themselves as the champion of the poor and also seeks to end foreign influence in Colombia. Priests from the Catholic Church, following the ideas of "liberation theology"—which argues that the church needs to play a major role in promoting human rights and social justice—joined with the group in the latter part of the 1960s. The group's ideology became a mixture of Marxist and Christianity, with a mission to overthrow the existing national government and create a popular, leftist government that gave more power to the people.

The National Liberation Army uses kidnapping, ransoming, and extortion of oil executives as its primary method for funding. Other activities include attacking the infrastructure, armed conflict, and bombings. At times, the group has joined with Revolutionary Armed Forces of Colombia (known by its Spanish acronym, FARC), a fellow insurgent group in Colombia that also uses violence to attain its goals. At other times, the two groups clash, leading to a two-front battle.

Members of Colombia's second largest guerrilla group, the 5,000-member National Liberation Army, in Santa Ana on November 1, 1997. AP/Wide World Photos. Reproduced by permission.

HISTORY

It is estimated that more than 200,000 people have been killed in Colombia since 1964, when the National Liberation Army began what it called a "civil war" in Colombia. The group, founded by a liberal university student named Fabio Vásquez Castaño, was formed as a Marxist organization. In the wake of Fidel Castro's Cuban Revolution, a coalition of university students, urban workers, and disenchanted peasants—*Movimiento de Obreros, Estudiantes, y Campesinos* (MOEC, or Movement for Workers, Students, and Peasants)—formed in Bogota as an initial response to the Cuban Revolution. The group organized labor strikes, protests, and other political actions designed to force the national government to pay attention to their cause.

Vásquez , a member of MOEC, went on to form the National Liberation Army, whose goal was to use Marxist approaches in creating a government structure that would combat Colombia's poverty, governmental corruption, and unequal political participation and access to the political process. After receiving training in Havana from Fidel Castro, Vásquez returned to Colombia and began his "people's war."

In 1966, he was joined by Father Camilo Torres, a Catholic priest who believed in the principle of "liberation theology," the belief that the Catholic Church and its priests needed to play a public role in politics where necessary, if it leads to social justice, better protection of human rights, and better outcomes for the poor and disenfranchised. Within a short time, the ELN blended Christian ideas into its philosophy; devout peasants and urban workers were

LEADERSHIP

FABIO VÁSQUEZ CASTAÑO

Fabio Vásquez Castaño, a Colombia rebel trained by Fidel Castro in the early 1960s, is the founder of the National Liberation Army. Vásquez was a university student with middle-class, liberal roots when he became part of a *fidelista* (follower of Fidel Castro) movement. Vásquez' father had been killed by Conservative party militias. In the early 1960s, a group called Movement for Workers, Students, and Peasants (MOEC) formed in Bogota, the first of such fidelista organizations. Vásquez and others went on from MOEC to form the National Liberation Army.

---

generally more open to the group's message when it appeared to be approved by priests and the Catholic Church. By combining the Marxist goal of a communist revolution like Fidel Castro's with Christian teachings about improving the lives of the poor and stemming human rights abuses, the group stands out from other leftist organizations that do not include Catholic priests among their members.

ELN has two distinct types of work: military/political insurgency, and social work in reaching out to the peasants, urban workers, and the poor. In 1965, after organizing members of ELN into a military unit, they experienced their first instance of armed conflict in the town of Simacota. Declaring themselves the victors, ELN issued the "Simacota Manifesto," which outlined the National Liberation Army's mission, ideals, and plans for Colombia. By starting a Cuban-style revolution, the leaders determined that they needed the support of large numbers of farmers in the countryside and the rural poor.

For the first eight to ten years of ELN's operations, the focus was on armed conflict, disrupting power supplies, targeted bombings, protesting against government officials, and gaining supporters to provide supplies, funding,

and support throughout rural areas. The group received funding and training from Cuba, the Soviet Union, and El Salvador. Father Torres was killed in one of the first armed conflicts; in 1970, Father Manuel Pérez Martinez, a defrocked Spanish priest, became the group's political and philosophical leader. Under his leadership, the group grew from some 100 members to more than 3,000. He continued to lead the group until his death in 1998. Pérez kept ELN from engaging in narco-trafficking on moral grounds; some experts believe that this refusal to engage in the drug trade held back ELN's growth compared to FARC, although after his death, ELN was reported to have become engaged in some aspects of the drug trade.

By the early 1970s, the Colombia government began cracking down on insurgent groups like ELN and Revolutionary Armed Forces of Colombia (FARC), a larger leftist organization in Colombia that began operations at roughly the same time that ELN formed. The military succeeded in preventing these groups from establishing a stronghold in urban areas, but the groups did gain influence in the countryside. Reports of inhumane prison conditions and torture of captured FARC and ELN insurgents received widespread press coverage in the late 1960s and early 1970s but did not stop the Colombian military from their efforts to eliminate these leftist groups.

At the same time that the national government instituted these crackdown policies, the National Liberation Army began to use kidnappings as a political tool. By kidnapping oil company executives and holding them for ransom, ELN acquired needed funds while gaining press attention for their actions. Over time, the National Liberation Army targeted foreign oil company executives, as part of a campaign against foreign investment and influence in Colombia. From 1973–1974, the Colombian military carried out the "Anorí operation," during which the ELN was nearly eliminated. President Alfonso López Michelsen tried to broker a peace agreement with the National Liberation Army leaders; this gave the group time to escape and regroup to rebuild the organization.

Over the next twenty-five years, the National Liberation Army became well known for the kidnapping of oil executives and other wealthy foreign nationals. In 1998, it is estimated

KEY EVENTS

1964: The National Liberation Army began what it called a "civil war" in Colombia.

1966: Father Camilo Torres, a Catholic priest who believed in the principle of "liberation theology," joins ELN.

1999: The Colombian government gave FARC control over a section of the country, but refused to do so for ELN.

---

that ELN raised more than $84 million from ransoms and $255 million from extortion alone.

Clashes with FARC have been a major source of conflict for ELN as well. FARC and ELN, while championing similar beliefs and goals, are structured very differently and follow different lines of communist thought (FARC aligns with Soviet theory, while ELN aligns with Cuban theory). FARC's membership far exceeds that of ELN (estimates give FARC as many as 18,000 members), and these conflicts have significantly hurt the National Liberation Army as well as civilian supporters of each group, who are often targeted by the opposing organization. In 1999, the Colombian government gave FARC control over a section of the country but refused to do so for ELN. In response, the National Liberation Army stepped up attacks on the oil pipelines owned by foreign companies, a step that U.S. President George W. Bush later condemned, requesting that Colombian military forces be used to protect the pipelines.

In the late 1970s and early 1980s, a new form of insurgent group emerged in direct response to FARC and ELN: a right-wing paramilitary militia movement. Referred to as the United Self-Defense Forces of Colombia (AUC, an acronym for their Spanish name *Autodefensas Unidas de Colombia*), the group numbers approximately 8,000, and is growing steadily. Organized in loose vigilante groups initially, this reaction movement developed in response to fears from

national and foreign corporations and the elites. These vigilante groups formed to protect landowners and often drug-traffickers, and grew as a result of their support. By the 1980s, the Colombian government viewed these groups as a viable response to FARC and ELN and began supplying the vigilante groups with arms. By 1989, however, the paramilitary militias had become increasingly aggressive and faced accusations of attacking civilian villages without provocation. The Colombian government outlawed the groups, but they continued to receive unofficial financial support, training from retired military members and increased membership from former military soldiers.

In 1997, one of the strongest groups, under the leadership of Carlos Castano, formed to create the AUC officially—until this time, the groups had operated as a very decentralized whole. AUC has been accused of destroying entire villages solely because they were suspected supporters of FARC or ELN. Approximately 3,500 civilians die in Colombia each year as a result of FARC, ELN, AUC, and Colombian military actions. In recent years, FARC and ELN combined are considered to be responsible for 15% of those deaths; experts believe AUC is responsible for 75%.

Since 1997, ELN and FARC have been listed as terrorist organizations on the Foreign Terrorist Organizations roster from the U.S. Department of State. On October 15, 2001, the United States listed the National Liberation Army as a serious terrorist threat, claiming that the area of Colombia controlled by ELN and FARC was a training ground for terrorists.

PHILOSOPHY AND TACTICS

The National Liberation Army's original goal was a popular democracy that would permit more involvement in the political process for the average Colombian. Over time, that goal shifted to the creation of a Marxist state, one with equality for poor and rich alike, with income and land redistribution part of the economic plan. In recent years, as ELN's power has waned, the organization has stated that they wish to create a "popular democracy" that permits the rural poor a greater say in national and local government.

In 2000, ELN was allegedly responsible for more than 750 kidnappings throughout Colombia. Most of the targets are foreign employees of large corporations, whom the group holds for large ransom payments. One common tactic is the creation of a roadblock on roads where wealthier citizens and foreign nationals are known to travel. ELN causes traffic jams frequently, as it accesses computer databases on the persons stopped in cars. A background check is run on each person; if they are determined to be insufficiently wealthy, the person is permitted to pass. Those who have enough to make a kidnapping worthwhile, in the eyes of the insurgent, are captured on the spot and held for ransom.

The National Liberation Army conducts frequent assaults on oil production infrastructure and has inflicted major damage on pipelines. In addition, the group bombs electrical lines, to protest the privatization of utilities. Between these two actions, the ELN's message is made clear: foreign corporate interests and privatization of energy needed by Colombian citizens are both unacceptable in the ELN's eyes.

The National Liberation Army often employs extortion and bombings as tools against U.S. corporations and other foreign businesses, especially the petroleum industry. In the year 2001 alone, pipeline bombings cost corporations more than $500 million. Since the 1980s, FARC and the National Liberation Army have bombed oil pipelines a combined total of more than 850 times. Colombia is the third largest recipient of foreign aid from the United States, behind Israel and Egypt, and the insurgents frequently target U.S. companies. Since Perez' death, the group has been reported to force coca and opium poppy cultivators to pay protection money and to attack the government's efforts to eradicate these crops.

In addition, on April 10, 2002, a communiqué from the group stated that: "From this moment, all property or goods of these [petroleum] companies will be military targets of our organization and whoever works for them is doing so at their own risk." Kidnappings increased, both from the National Liberation Army and from AUC. AUC began kidnapping oil company employees and executives, claiming their targets were ELN sympathizers. In response, oil companies experienced employee strikes and protests concerning the abductions and killings.

Negotiations with the national government opened up when Mexican President Vicente Fox offered Mexico's services as a mediator in May 2004. Experts contend that ELN has three options at this point: to surrender or lose outright, to blend with FARC, or to negotiate with the national government. ELN's experience with the kidnappings of European and Israeli ecotourists in 2003 led to a loss of European tolerance for ELN; the Colombian government's ability to negotiate a safe return of the hostages signaled to Europe that ELN was weaker than FARC.

On June 2, 2004, the Colombian government let the National Liberation Army's current leader, Francisco Galán, out of prison for one day, to meet with the Colombian Vice President and to address Congress with his group's demands. In the end, the demands—a cessation of all hostilities and the release of all ELN prisoners—were not met, but the negotiation gesture has led to an opening for future mediation and discussion.

OTHER PERSPECTIVES

In an article published by *Colombia Report*, a private publication dedicated to Colombian events, author Garry Leech commented on the U.S. Department of State's actions that placed ELN and FARC on a terrorist organization list, but put AUC on a lesser list: "... the inclusion of the AUC finally acknowledges what human rights organizations and even the State Department's own annual human rights reports have stated for years: the AUC is responsible for the majority of civilian massacres and human rights abuses in Colombia. The AUC was also included in the report for its involvement in kidnapping and the drug trade.

"These are the same activities that have repeatedly landed the FARC and the ELN on the FTO list, which forbids providing funds or material support to FTO groups, denies their members visas to enter the United States, and requires U.S. financial institutions to block the funds of FTO organizations and their members. And yet, despite their engagement in the same terrorist activities, the AUC's inclusion on the secondary list means these State Department

PRIMARY SOURCE

National Liberation Army (ELN)

DESCRIPTION

The ELN is a Colombian Marxist insurgent group formed in 1965 by urban intellectuals inspired by Fidel Castro and Che Guevara. It is primarily rural-based, although it possesses several urban units. In May 2004, Colombian President Uribe proposed a renewal of peace talks but by the end of the year talks had not commenced.

ACTIVITIES

Kidnapping, hijacking, bombing, and extortion. Minimal conventional military capability. Annually conducts hundreds of kidnappings for ransom, often targeting foreign employees of large corporations, especially in the petroleum industry. Derives some revenue from taxation of the illegal narcotics industry. Frequently assaults energy infrastructure and has inflicted major damage on pipelines and the electric distribution network.

STRENGTH

Approximately 3,000 armed combatants and an unknown number of active supporters.

LOCATION/AREA OF OPERATION

Mostly in rural and mountainous areas of northern, northeastern, and southwestern Colombia, and Venezuelan border regions.

EXTERNAL AID

Cuba provides some medical care and political consultation. Venezuela continues to provide a hospitable environment.

Source: U.S. Department of State. *Country Reports on Terrorism.* Washington, D.C., 2004.

---

sanctions do not apply to the organization or its members."

The political left, in the United States, has argued against the increasing role of the U.S. military in Colombia, stating that the "war on drugs" and the use of U.S. resources to protect oil interests are unacceptable.

SUMMARY

In 2005, Colombian President Alvaro Uribe signed an order granting limited immunity to right-wing AUC insurgents—but the order does not grant the same rights to members of the ELN and FARC, a fact that has generated considerable protest among leftists worldwide. Critics charge that President Uribe, a close U.S ally, is using the agreement to increase foreign aid and investment. They also charge that the AUC is, in many instances, the only buffer between the government and ELN or FARC, and by disengaging the AUC, he opens the door for an increase in leftist political violence.

In recent years, the ELN has suffered losses in fighting against AUC and is considered to be a far weaker force than FARC. FARC has entered into various negotiations with the Colombian national government, negotiations that ELN has chosen not to join. The National Liberation Army continues to stage kidnappings. On July 24, 2004, they kidnapped Misael Vacca Ramírez, the Catholic Bishop of Yopal. The group claimed that they would send a message with his release but when the bishop was handed over just three days later, ELN did not make a public statement.

SOURCES

Books

Murillo, Mario Alfonso, and Jesus Rey Avirama. *Colombia and the United States : War, Terrorism, and Destabilization.* New York: Seven Stories Press, 2003.

Pearce, Jenny. *Inside Colombia: Drugs, Democracy, and War* New Brunswick, NJ: Rutgers University Press, 2004.

Safford, Frank, and Marco Palacios. *Colombia: Fragmented Land, Divided Society*. England: Oxford University Press, 2001.

Web sites

Amnesty International. "Colombia, A Laboratory of War: Repression and Violence in Arauca." < http://web.amnesty.org/library/index/engamr230042004 > (accessed October 21, 2005).

Amnesty International. "Colombia: Report 2005." < http://web.amnesty.org/report2005/col-summary-eng > (accessed October 21, 2005).

Colombia Report. "Good Terrorists, Bad Terrorists: How Washington Decides Who's Who." < http://www.colombiajournal.org/colombia62.htm > (accessed Octo 21, 2005).

Foreign Policy Research Institute. "E-Notes: Terrorism in Colombia." < http://www.fpri.org/enotes/latin.20020121. posada.terrorismincolombia.html > (accessed October 21, 2005).

Human Rights Watch. "War without Quarter: Colombia and International Humanitarian Law." < http://www.hrw.org/reports98/colombia/ > (accessed October 21, 2005).

Human Rights Watch. "Colombia and the "War." on Terror: Rhetoric and Reality." < http://hrw.org/english/docs/2004/03/04/colomb7932.htm > (accessed October 21, 2005).

SEE ALSO

Revolutionary Armed Forces of Colombia (FARC)

National Socialist German Workers Party

LEADER: Adolf Hitler

YEAR ESTABLISHED OR BECAME ACTIVE: 1920

USUAL AREA OF OPERATION: Primarily in Germany, but during World War II (1939–1945), in most of Europe and northern Africa

OVERVIEW

The National Socialist German Workers Party (NSDAP, best known as the Nazi Party) was a political party that Adolf Hitler led in Germany beginning in 1921. The NSDAP made anti-Semitism the basis of its policies and propaganda. Using the power of the NSDAP to build his own military regime in Germany, Hitler intended to control the world. Convinced that the German race was superior to all other races, Hitler felt that purification/extermination was essential to accomplish his plans of domination.

Hitler and his NSDAP members killed millions of Jews, gypsies, Poles and other Slavs, blacks, people with physical and mental disabilities, homosexuals, Jehovah's Witnesses, Communists, Socialists, political and religious dissidents, and many other perceived dangerous and inferior persons. Hitler used NSDAP members to strengthen his dictatorial rule during World War II, gaining control of most of Europe and northern Africa. In the end, the Allied Forces (England, United States, and the Soviet Union) defeated Hitler and his Axis Forces (Germany, Italy, and Japan) in 1945. That same year, the NSDAP was declared illegal and its leaders arrested and later convicted of war crimes. Hitler committed suicide.

A skinhead supporter of the rightwing German National Party joins a neo-Nazi march in Verden, northern Germany on April 2, 2005. AP/Wide World *Photos. Reproduced by permission.*

HISTORY

The German Workers' Party was formed in 1919. While a member of the German army, Adolf Hitler was ordered to observe the suspected left-wing revolutionary group. Hitler ended up joining the group, eventually becoming a member of its executive committee and its propaganda manager.

The group was renamed the National Socialist German Workers Party (NSDAP) on February 24, 1920. The NSDAP soon organized its Twenty-Five Points Plan—rejecting the Versailles Treaty, calling for reunification of all German people, and that equal rights were acceptable only to German citizens. At this time, NSDAP possessed about 2,000 members.

On July 29, 1921, after realizing that party growth was due primarily to his oratory/recruitment/fundraising skills, Hitler challenged and defeated the incumbent to become NSDAP chairman. Hitler quickly converted the NSDAP's already radical principles to ones that used violent means such as intimidation to achieve his goals.

Through the NSDAP, Hitler began forming many subgroups to carry out his agenda, such as the Storm Troopers, who expanded the new agenda of fear, protected Hitler from harm, and disrupted meetings held by opponents.

From 1923–1925, the NSDAP was dissolved when Hitler and several leaders were convicted of treason after trying to overthrow Bavaria in what came to be known as the Beer Hall Revolt (Putsch).

The NSDAP was reestablished in 1925 with Hitler again elected its leader. At this time, NSDAP leaders were determined to control the German government, among them Hermann Goring, Rudolf Hess, Joseph Goebbels, Heinrich Himmler, Gottfried Feder, Rudolf Jung, and Max Amann. To accomplish this goal, the leaders formed the SS (or *Schutzstaffel*) to enforce their actions and developed another economic Twenty-Five Points Plan, a foreign policy, and a set of anti-Semitic opinions. The NSDAP began to expand throughout Germany, gaining power as it went.

In the 1925 and 1929 elections, the NSDAP performed poorly. However, the world depression that began in 1929 helped to increase its popularity. In 1932, Hitler and other NSDAP leaders campaigned throughout the country, declaring that the liberal democratic government in power was not effective and only the NSDAP could produce a strong government. By this time, many citizens were blaming the Weimar Republic for its defeat in World War I, the Versailles treaty that imposed punishments, the 1930s depression, and the spread of communism.

In spite of strong rival political parties, the Nazi Party proved popular as it promoted an authoritarian organization that emphasized stability for the struggling economy. Its promises of national resurgence, opposition toward France, Jews, and other non-German races, and defeat of the German Weimar Republic were popular with German citizens. The NADAP received 37% of the votes in the 1932 election.

On January 30, 1933, Hitler was appointed chancellor of the coalition government. A month later, on February 27, the Reichstag parliament caught fire. The Nazi Party accused the Communist Party of Germany of starting the blaze when the fire was "almost certainly due to the Nazis." Because of Hitler's power, he banned the Communist Party, eliminated most German civil liberties in order to stop perceived national threats, and placed loyal Nazis in important positions. Then, in March, the Nazi Party, with a membership of about 2.5 million, held a special election with the intent to gain total control. Victorious in the result, Hitler passed the Enabling Act—

Third Reich Fuehrer Adolf Hitler delivers a speech at Luitpold area on "Brown Shirt Day" to an audience of nearly 100,000 Nazi storm troopers in Nuremberg, Germany, on September 20, 1936. AP/Wide World Photos. Reproduced by permission.

allowing him to enact legislation, change the constitution, control state and local governments, negotiate treaties, and perform other government duties—all without legislative approval.

In August 1934, Hitler's government merged the office of president and chancellor. In effect, Hitler became the head of government, head of state, and NSDAP chairman—all under the title of *Fuehrer* and Reich Chancellor. With virtual control of Germany, Hitler banned all political parties, except the NSDAP, and replaced all labor unions with the Nazi-dominated German Labor Front. Hitler forced all citizens to be dependent on the loyalty of his dictatorship. When perceived to be against Nazi authority, citizens were sent to concentration camps, subjected to harsh consequences, or simply killed.

In 1935, Hitler began to increase the size of the military in preparation for war and his plan

of world domination. Three years later, on November 9, 1938, what is now called the Night of Broken Glass, over 7,000 Jewish businesses were destroyed, almost all synagogues were set on fire, many homes were damaged, thousands of Jews sent to concentration camps, and dozens of others killed.

By 1939, Hitler had converted Germany into an anti-Semitic, fully militarized regime, and the NSDAP into a mass movement. That same year, Hitler started World War II.

Germany had already gained control over Austria and Czechoslovakia. Its armies soon spread Nazi dominance over Europe by conguering Poland, France, Denmark, Norway, Holland, Belgium, Romania and other countries as Hitler expanded his dominance through fallen governments.

The defeat of Hitler came on May 8, 1945, when the Allied Powers defeated the Axis

LEADERSHIP

ADOLF HITLER

After his mother died in 1908, Hitler (at the age of nineteen) lived on inherited money, refusing to find employment. When his money ran out, Hitler was forced into a homeless shelter. There, he was introduced to the writings of Lanz von Liebenfels, a radical who promoted the master German race and the inferiority of other races (especially Jewish).

Hitler lived in near-poverty until 1914 when he volunteered for a Bavarian unit in the German army during World War I. While recovering from injuries at war's end, Hitler decided that Jews had caused his country's defeat—vowing he would enter politics in order to return Germany to its former greatness.

While still in the military, German Army Intelligence gave Hitler the job of monitoring a racist group. Hitler found the political agenda of the German Workers' Party similar to his own: nationalism, anti-communist, anti-Semitism, and anti-Weimar Republic. He joined the party in 1919—finding that he possessed talents as a political agitator, public speaker, and party organizer/recruiter.

In the summer of 1920, Hitler was elevated to the party's spokesman, in a group with 100–200 members. Steadily gaining power, on July 29, 1921, Hitler was elected absolute leader. Hitler changed the group's name to the National Socialist German Workers' Party.

Both Hitler and NSDAP members despised the role that Jews played in the Weimar Republic and vowed to eliminate their power. Hitler's book, *Mein Kampf* (*My Struggle*), which was published in 1926, contained his basic ideas of ruling a racially pure Germany and eventually the world. Hitler steadily became more powerful, ultimately becoming the leader of Germany. He started World War II in 1939 in an attempt to control the world but lost the war in 1945.

Hitler is considered by many historians as one of the twentieth century's most powerful and ruthless dictators. Hitler committed suicide on April 30, 1945.

Powers to end World War II. The NSDAP was soon declared illegal and forced to disband. At this time, its membership rolls were listed at about 8.5 million members.

PHILOSOPHY AND TACTICS

The NSDAP was converted into a violent radical organization and eventually a mass movement due to the actions of Adolf Hitler. Anti-Semitism was the basis of its propaganda philosophy. The NSDAP believed that Jews were responsible for the degradation of German society after its defeat in World War I. Hitler, in particular, stressed an ideology that emphasized destruction of inferior races. The NSDAP, which also despised Bolshevism (based on a Karl Marx doctrine), felt that the communists were conspiring with the Jews to destroy Germany. Hitler also saw liberal democracy, especially within the Weimar Republic, as a destructive force. Thus, the NSDAP based its theories on the belief that the world needed to be saved from communism, capitalism/democracy, and the Jewish race.

Starting in 1919, the NSDAP was led by its new spokesman, Adolf Hitler. He recruited new members by appealing to the many beleaguered soldiers and former soldiers who rejected the liberal democratic republic that was formed following World War I. Hitler also linked the people's hatred for communism with a hatred of Jews. The NSDAP was perceived to be the only political party that had viable yet simple answers to the German societal problems.

Hitler outlined his Twenty-Five Points political platform in a February 4, 1920 speech. Its many features included the union of all Germans around the world into an empire called the Third Reich; refutation of the Treaty of Versailles;

KEY EVENTS

1919: German Workers' Party is formed.

1920: German Workers' Party is renamed National Socialist German Workers Party.

1921: Hitler becomes NSDAP chairman.

1923–1925: NSDAP is dissolved when Hitler and leaders are convicted of treason.

1925: NSDAP is reestablished with Hitler as leader.

1932: NSDAP receives 37% of the vote in national elections.

1933: Hitler is appointed chancellor of German coalition government.

1933: NSDAP bans most German human rights.

1939: Hitler starts World War II.

1945: World War II ends with defeat of Hitler's Germany.

1945: NSDAP is declared illegal and forced to disband.

1945: Hitler commits suicide.

---

acquisition of more German territories; adoption of various anti-capitalist measures; acceptance of citizenship based on race, with Jews not to be considered; confiscation of all income not earned by work; reorganization of the German educational system; freedom of religion, except those that threatened the German race; and execution of strong legislation through a dictatorial government. In the summer of 1920, Hitler adopted the swastika as the Nazi flag—what many historians consider one of the most infamous symbols ever conceived.

During the 1930s depression, Hitler and other Nazi leaders exploited grievances by German citizens by promising whatever would convince their particular audiences. They promised price controls and tax decreases to farmers in rural areas and spoke in favor of redistribution of wealth and against high corporate profits in working-class areas. They spoke of reducing

union power and destroying communism to corporate leaders and said that Germany's economic problems were due to the Treaty of Versailles and the Weimar Republic.

NSDAP goals—in essence, Hitler's dictatorial goals—were to conquer the entire world so Hitler could enforce his idea of racial purity among German people. In order to accomplish its goals, the NSDAP used violent tactics such as sterilization and euthanasia upon people he considered inferior. By 1945, over 400,000 people had been sterilized to prevent the potential that they might produce physically or mentally defective children. Early on, Hitler forced schools to teach Nazi ideology, along with indoctrinating young boys into the Hitler Youth and young girls into the League of German Girls so that new generations were already controlled by adulthood.

Early on during Hitler's reign, Jews were denied government employment and restricted from attending universities. Later, they were denied citizenship, excluded from many jobs, forbidden to own automobiles, and denied the right to own property. In all, thousands of German Jews were sent to concentration camps by the Nazis and hundreds of thousands of others fled for their lives from Germany. About one-third of the estimated eighteen million Jews around the world were killed because of Hitler's actions—in what would later be called the Holocaust.

OTHER PERSPECTIVES

As stated in an article by Spartacus Education, the following three quotes, deemed as commonly held opinions in their day, were directed to Adolf Hitler and his Nazi Party.

In August 1923, Morgan Philips Price of the *Daily Herald* said, "Herr Hitler has built up a force estimated at about 30,000 armed men, but he is keeping them in the background and is for the moment concentrating on trying to convert some of the less stable elements of the working classes in the Bavarian towns to his National Socialist programmes."

In August 19, 1934, Frederick T. Birchall of *The New York Times* wrote the following upon Hitler's takeover of Germany: "The endorsement gives Chancellor Hitler, who four years ago was not even a German citizen, dictatorial powers unequaled in any other country, and probably unequaled in history since the days of Genghis Khan."

Less than six years later, in a May 1940 speech before the British House of Commons, Clement Attlee said, "It is essential to remember that civilization takes long to build and is easily destroyed. Brutality is infectious. However, there is something more than these outward expressions of the return to barbarism in the Nazi regime. There is a denial of the value of the individual. Christianity affirms the value of each individual soul. Nazism denies it. The individual is sacrificed to the idol of the German Leader, German State or the German race. The ordinary citizen is allowed to hear and think only as the rulers decree."

SUMMARY

Over sixty million people are estimated by historians to have died worldwide due to World War II, and tens of millions of other people lost their health, livelihoods, and homes. Hitler was considered directly responsible for more than half of those deaths—over thirty million people, mostly between 1939 and 1945.

Since the NADAP was dissolved and made illegal in 1945, an extremist movement called neo-Nazism has evolved in Germany and around the world. Several groups have claimed to have succeeded the NSDAP, but only one— the National Democratic Party of Germany (NPD)—was actually declared by German and Allied officials (at one point in time) to be NSDAP's successor. As of 2005, the NPD is still a presence in German politics.

The American Nazi Party, whose strength declined after the 1960s, was also noted as an extremely dangerous group by U.S. government officials. As stated by the Anti-Defamation League (ADL), such groups still use the flag of the NSDAP: a swastika on a red background.

Since the end of World War II, according to the ADL, an anti-Semitic propaganda movement has developed to lessen or (even) contradict the historical significance of Nazi genocide against the Jewish people (the Holocaust).

As of the beginning of the twenty-first century, no organizations are considered successors to Hitler's NSDAP. According to the ADL, most Nazi-like groups are in reality hate groups that promote white supremacy, anti-Semitism, and other similar ideas. Members of such hate groups are primarily discontented young males who ridicule and sometimes violently target blacks, Jews, homosexuals, and members of other minority groups.

SOURCES

Books

Hitler's Apologists: The Anti-Semitic Propaganda of Holocaust Revisionism. New York: Anti-Defamation League, 1993.

McDonough, Frank. *Hitler and the Rise of the NSDAP.* London and New York: Pearson/Longman, 2003.

Spielvogel, Jackson J. *Hitler and Nazi Germany.* Upper Saddle River, NJ: Prentice-Hall, 2001.

Web sites

The Avalon Project, Yale University. "Program of the National Socialist German Workers' Party." < http://www.yale.edu/lawweb/avalon/imt/nsdappro.htm > (assessed October 20, 2005).

BBC.co.uk. "Adolf Hitler (1889–1945)." < http://www.bbc.co.uk/history/historic_figures/hitler_adolf.shtml > (assessed October 20, 2005).

Florida Center for Instructional Technology, University of South Florida. "Victims." < http://www.spartacus.schoolnet.co.uk/GERnazi.htm > (assessed October 20, 2005).

Jewish Virtual Library, The American-Israeli Cooperative Enterprise. "Holocaust Denial." < http://www.jewishvirtuallibrary.org/jsource/Holocaust/denial.html > (assessed October 20, 2005).

The Open University, British Broadcasting Corporation (BBC). "Adolf Hitler Timeline." < http://www.open2.net/oulecture2005/hitler_timeline.html > (assessed October 20, 2005).

Spartacus Educational. "Nazi Party (NSDAP)" < http://www.spartacus.schoolnet.co.uk/GERnazi.htm > (assessed October 20, 2005).

The Time 100 (The Most Important People of the Century), Time, Inc. "Adolf Hitler." < http://www.time.com/time/time100/leaders/profile/hitler.htm > (assessed October 20, 2005).

SEE ALSO

American Nazi Party

Neo-Nazis

USUAL AREA OF OPERATION: Worldwide

OVERVIEW

Neo-Nazis, literally meaning "new" Nazis, is a general term referring to all social or political movements that work to reintroduce concepts of the Nazi period of 1933–to 1945 in Europe and are based upon the racial policies of fascism. By definition, all manifestations of neo-Nazism need to have emerged after the fall of the original Nazi regime, which was brought to an end by the allied victory in Europe, sealed in May 1945 with the German surrender. Neo-Nazi groups can be found internationally, including in modern-day Germany, despite aggressive governmental attempts to limit their influence on society.

Neo-Nazi groups are largely defined by their philosophies, which are based upon an allegiance to Adolf Hitler and usually include a dedication to anti-Semitism and racism. These groups can be militaristic and, on occasion, violent. Neo-Nazi groups, particularly in the United States, are linked with other hate groups, particularly the white power movement whose goal it is to create a white racist state.

HISTORY

The original Nazi regime that the neo-Nazi movement is designed to recreate came to power in 1933 through the legal rise of Adolf

A scene from NordicFest, an annual gathering of neo-Nazis, white supremecists, and other racist groups in Kentucky, 2001. © *Jonas Bendiksen / Magnum Photos*

Hitler to power in Germany. From 1933 until 1939, Hitler and his National Socialist Party, known as the Nazi party, instituted harsh racial policies aimed predominantly against the Jewish population of Germany. Policies included random deportations and arrests of Jews and extreme restrictions on the roles that Jews would be allowed to play in the Aryan, or white, segments of German society.

With the German invasion of Poland in 1939 and the eventual annexation of countries all across Europe, these racial policies were extended into all countries under Nazi control. Under the Nazi rule, the "Final Solution" was instituted in 1942, calling for the mass extermination of Jews, eventually leading to the deaths of 6 million Jews by 1945; this period is generally referred to as the Holocaust. The allied forces were able to defeat the Nazis between the winter of 1944 and May of 1945; on May 8, 1945, the Nazi regime offered their unconditional surrender.

In the wake of the Nazi period, the new democratic government of Germany, together with the allied forces that remained in the region,

attempted to stop the renewal of Nazi ideology through a policy of "denazification." This policy called for tight restrictions on any Nazi imagery or production of materials bearing the swastika, the predominant symbol of the Nazi regime. Materials of this nature found in Germany today are largely smuggled in from the United States and northern Europe countries with more liberal positions on the freedom of speech.

In the years immediately following the fall of Nazism, neo-Nazi activity was limited to the outer fringes of German society, as was the case in most of Europe. Beginning in the 1960s, some former Nazis began to once again embrace the ideologies as well as encourage the younger generation to support it. The fall of the Berlin Wall in 1990 and the subsequent reunification of East and West Germany allowed for the considerable growth of neo-Nazism in the area. The largest population for neo-Nazis in Germany of the 1990s were teenagers from the areas that formerly made up East Germany, who had been the victims of economic uncertainty and high unemployment during the period of communist rule.

A smiling Adolf Hitler impersonator reaches out to the camera at a protest against the neo-Nazi party in West Germany, 1965. © *Leonard Freed | Magnum Photos*

The 1990s saw the neo-Nazis in Germany becoming increasingly organized and violent, with the primary target of their activities being foreigners who had moved into Germany. The period saw numerous attempts at arson against homes of people seeking refuge from foreign countries. In 1992 and in 1993, several Turkish immigrants were killed in arson attacks.

The general population largely responded with outrage at the actions and the rise of the neo-Nazi movement. Large demonstrations brought hundreds of thousands of people out in the large German cities to protest against the new influence of extremist groups. The neo-Nazis responded with counter demonstrations, a situation that continues today. The two opposing demonstrators have erupted into violence on numerous occasions.

The National Democratic Party (NPD) today is considered to be the political party that best represents the interests of the neo-Nazis in Germany. In 2004, the party received 9.1% of the vote in the region of Saxony and was thus given a presence in the national parliament. Following the election, all other national parties refused to enter into any political negotiations with the NPD.

In the United States, the growth of neo-Nazism has been aided by the country's more lenient stance, as compared to Germany, on issues of freedoms of speech and expression. Racial and anti-Semitic speech, which is the primary tool of the neo-Nazis, is protected under the First Amendment of the U.S. constitution and has facilitated the ability of the groups to organize themselves, often within the confines of the law. Anti-Semitic groups existed in the United States even before the rise of national socialism in Germany. While they were extremely unpopular during the World War II period, support for Nazi racial policies continued to exist and, following the war, new organizations would emerge.

In the United States, the groups that do exist that are defined as neo-Nazi are very small in number, and any public demonstrations they hold are usually met with far larger counterdemonstrations. The United States groups often enjoy most of their support and recruitment through alliances with other racist hate groups that include neo-Nazi ideas in their philosophies, such as the Aryan Nations and other white power groups. The largest such organization, the Ku Klux Klan, while founded in the nineteenth century well before the rise of Nazism, is not considered a neo-Nazi group but shares many of the views of non-white races and Jews; relationships do exist between the Klan and Neo-Nazi groups.

While the right for the neo-Nazi groups to exist and to demonstrate remains protected in the United States, state and federal laws have made it easier to prosecute criminals within the organizations. Specifically, the United States Congress has passed legislation that provides additional penalties for crimes defined as hate crimes, where it is proven that the motive of the criminal was inspired by an ideology of hatred. Accordingly, such crimes as vandalizing a synagogue or a Jewish cemetery with swastikas will carry heavier penalties than crimes with no such motive.

Internationally, neo-Nazi groups exist in Britain, as well as a strong presence in the former

Skinheads, neo-Nazis, and Ku Klux Klansmen carry Confederate paraphernalia through Pulaski, Tennessee, in 1989. © *Leonard Freed | Magnum Photos*

Soviet Union, where despite the nation's bitter history with the Nazis, the rise of extreme nationalism has aided in the growth of neo-fascist groups that have declared a willingness to overthrow the ruling government. With the numerous social and economic problems that emerged following the fall of the Soviet regime in the early 1990s, there is a large number of people have turned to extremist paramilitary organizations like the neo-Nazis. The largest base in Russia is the youth, who have been most affected by the end of the Soviet period; many of them have embraced neo-Nazism as an outlet for their frustrations.

PHILOSOPHY AND TACTICS

The movement finds its ideological base in fascism, which is the political philosophy that Hitler based the Nazi party on in his rise to power. Fascism is based upon a notion that the government should be allowed to control all aspects of

the lives of the people living in that society. Fascism distinguishes itself from other political ideologies by placing the needs of the state or nation over the needs of the individual and that the citizens should be loyal to a single leader.

Within the fascist model and within the understanding that has been adopted by neo-Nazism, adherents to the government should be willing to use violence and all tools of propaganda or censorship to deal with social or political opposition. The state is entitled to exercise economic or social restraints on the citizenry and retains the right to police people living within the system as it sees fit in the best interests of the future of the state.

In deference to their positions on Jews, neo-Nazis regularly subscribe to Holocaust denial or revisionism, which claims that the murder of six million Jews at the hands of the Nazis is a myth that has been greatly exaggerated.

While Holocaust revisionism is a regular practice of neo-Nazis, it is often believed that this aspect of their ideology is not actually

LEADERSHIP

In an effort to avoid dealing with law enforcement agencies, Neo Nazi groups have made considerable efforts to construct their organizations in a manner that places the ideological leaders of the organization at a distance from the more violent and criminal daily activities of the group. These activities are placed in the hands of younger members so that there will be no direct linkage to the leadership and the leaders.

Even with this structure in place, certain names have emerged as the more prominent leaders in the neo-Nazi world. Matthew F. Hale, who is the head of the World Church of the Creator, is recognized as one of the public leaders of the neo-Nazi movement in the United States. Hale was recently convicted for soliciting the murder of a federal judge, which has virtually brought to a halt his activities.

The founder of the American Nazi Party in 1959 was George Lincoln Rockwell who, after reading Adolf Hitler's book *Mein Kampf* (My Struggle), became an adherent of the Nazi ideology. In 1967, Rockwell was shot and killed by John Patler, who had been an editor of the American Nazi Party newspaper, *The Stormtrooper*. Following Rockwell's death, William Pierce who also founded the National Alliance white supremacist movement, assumed the leadership position of the American Nazi Party. Pierce was the author of a novel entitled *The Turner Diaries*, a book that details a future race war in the United States and was said to have been an inspiration for Timothy McVeigh, the man behind the bombing of the Oklahoma City Federal Building in 1995 that killed 168 people.

believed by members of their organization, but it is rather out of a desire to personally distance them from the genocide carried out by the Nazis. On other occasions, neo-Nazis attempt to rationalize the Nazi actions by saying that it was in response to acts of Jewish sabotage or terrorism or that the Germans' actions in World War II were no worse than the fire bombings of German cities that were carried out by the allies.

Neo-Nazi organizations often believe that they belong outside of the law and the political process and advocate the overthrow of the ruling government. Particularly in the international arena, neo-Nazis allege that the world's nations are increasingly being taken over by Jews and non-whites. The neo-Nazi position advocates killing or expelling non-natives with the belief that such action would be the best way to deal with any social, political, or economic problems that exist in their nation. In Russia the neo-Nazi movement supports a slogan of "Russia for the Russians," which has been adopted by other extremist organizations.

Neo-Nazi groups have actively been involved in discovering ways to put their vision of overthrowing the state into practice. Often organizing as paramilitary groups, neo-Nazi branches are involved in physical training as well as training in explosives and the handling of weapons. They generally operate outside of the realm of the central political arena but can often find allies with far-right politicians as has been the case in Russia, Germany, and Austria.

A primary outlet for strength for neo-Nazi organizations is through establishing alliances both with similarly minded organizations in their countries as well as with other groups around the world. The Internet is an increasingly important tool for these groups with innovative web sites that are used for both propaganda and recruitment. For those nations with more stringent speech laws like Germany, groups base their web sites out of countries like the United States or northern European nations to avoid limitations.

OTHER PERSPECTIVES

The primary opponents of neo-Nazis are private groups such as the Anti-Defamation League (ADL) and the Southern Poverty Law Center. While the actions of neo-Nazi groups are understood to represent far less danger in terms of its impact upon society than in the way the German Nazis did, these advocates against hate organizations recognize that neo-Nazis have expressed their commitment to violence and crime. They are therefore involved with exposing the activities of neo-Nazis and proposing ways to limit their influence on society.

KEY EVENTS

1945: The Nazi regime under the leadership of Adolf Hitler falls to the allies bringing an end to World War II and the Holocaust.

1960s: The neo-Nazi groups began to gain power with the reintroduction of the ideologies by former Nazis.

1990: The fall of the Berlin Wall and German reunification; the influence of German neo-Nazi groups began to swell.

1990s: Neo-Nazis in Germany carried out numerous violent attacks primarily against foreigners living in the country.

2004: The German right-wing party that most closely identifies with the neo-Nazism, the National Democratic Party (NPD), gained a presence in the German parliament.

The ADL, which is based in the United States, is dedicated to fight the defamation of Jewish people all over the globe and to lobby national governments to take action to defeat neo-Nazism. The ADL has defined neo-Nazis as representing a danger to society.

One of the principal complaints lodged by the ADL against the work of neo-Nazis was in reference to their use of the Internet. Describing the work of the neo-Nazis as poisoning the web, a report issued by the ADL says that these hate groups are the "Storm troopers of the web," and that "the symbols associated with Hitler's Nazis are attractive to bigots on the Web because they suggest anti-Semitism in an immediate, forceful way to the general public."

The American Civil Liberties Union (ACLU), which is one of the United States' most vocal advocates for the rights of free speech, has defended the position of the neo-Nazis to meet and demonstrate. One of the most famous cases involving the rights of the neo-Nazis to demonstrate in public came in 1977 in Skokie, Illinois. In this suburb of Chicago, where one of every six Jewish residents at the time was a survivor of the Holocaust, a neo-Nazi group submitted a request for a permit to host a parade through the town. When the town refused the permit on grounds that it represented a threat to public safety by offending the sensibilities of the local residents, the ACLU sued the city and forced their decision to be overturned, which has become known as one of the most famous free speech cases in U.S. history.

Many of the nations of Western Europe have outlawed neo-Nazi groups, Holocaust denial, and the display or sale of Nazi propaganda.

SUMMARY

While clearly not impacting upon societies in the exact way the original Nazis did, the emergence of neo-Nazi groups in increasing numbers displays the impact that extremist groups can have, as well as the fact that hatred and intolerance continues to attract a considerable following around the globe. The neo-Nazis have been proven to be successful in publicizing their efforts, not because of the size of their organization but largely as a result of the dangerous nature of their message.

The constantly changing global political and social environments of recent decades have contributed greatly to the ability of the neo-Nazi movement to grow. With the breakdown of the Soviet Union and the communist control over Eastern Europe, large populations of young people facing desperate economic and social conditions have been turning to neo-Nazism. With the increased passage of time since the end of World War II, those nations that were most negatively impacted by the war, like Germany and Russia, are becoming less traumatized by the events of that period, leading to the slow reemergence of hate groups like the neo-Nazis. An ever-global world has brought about the increased flood of foreign immigration into countries like Germany, which has served to provide the neo-Nazis with a target for their hatred. The Internet has served as a critical resource for hate groups that rely on the borderless nature of the world wide web to reach populations all over the globe and are able to spread their message, often without concern for the legality of their sites.

At the same time, with much of the world voicing considerable opposition to the messages being advocated by groups like neo-Nazis, they have limited impacts upon the overall population and operate on the outskirts of society. In the United States, where free speech allows neo-Nazi groups to get their message out, concerted efforts both by private organizations and by government have worked to limit the activities of hate groups and to ensure that their crimes be prosecuted.

SOURCES

Books

Strum, Philippa. *When the Nazis Came to Skokie; Freedom for Speech We Hate.* Lawrence, Kansas: University Press of Kansas, 2000.

Web sites

The Southern Poverty Law Center. "Intelligence Project; Monitoring Hate and Extremist Activity." < http://www.splcenter.org/intel/intpro.jsp > (accessed October 13, 2005).

The Anti-Defamation League. "Fighting Anti-Semitism, Bigotry and Extremism." < http://www.adl.org/ > (accessed October 13, 2005).

SEE ALSO

Aryan Nations

Ku Klux Klan

American Nazi Party

New Black Panther Party

OVERVIEW

The New Black Panther party, which members of the original Black Panthers are quick to point out is in no way associated with them, is a radical, black nationalist, anti-Semitic, anti-white, extremist group that is an outgrowth of the Nation of Islam. The original Black Panthers have publicly stated that the New Black Panther Party should not have the right to use their name or image and that they are not in any way philosophically or politically similar.

The group is also called the New Black Panther Party for Self-Defense. It was founded in 1990 by Aaron Michaels, is headquartered in Washington, D.C., and is currently led by attorney Malik Zulu Shabazz. The previous leader of the group, Khalid Muhammad, died of a brain aneurysm in February 2001. The group's philosophical and ideological orientation is described as a mix of radical black Nationalism, pan-Africanism, racism, black separatism, and anti-Semitism. The New Black Panther Party claims to have been influenced by the original Black Panthers, the Nation of Islam, and the Black Panther Militia. The primary activities of the group consist of organizing (purportedly peaceful) demonstrations across the country that call for civil rights and the empowerment of black people in America. According to the media, the demonstrations are also replete with examples of racist and anti-Semitic bigotry.

LEADERS: Aaron Michaels; Khalid Muhammad; Malik Zulu Shabazz

YEAR ESTABLISHED OR BECAME ACTIVE: 1990

USUAL AREA OF OPERATION: United States

New Black Panther members carry rifles as they march through Jasper, Texas on June 27, 1998. Ku Klux Klansmen, wearing hoods and waving Confederate flags, also marched in the Texas town. Police monitored the proceedings and kept the two sides apart. AP/Wide World Photos. Reproduced by permission.

HISTORY

Huey Newton and Bobby Seale organized the original Black Panther Party in 1966 in Oakland, California. The group was an ideological mix of Marxism and militant Black Nationalism, designed to empower black people across America to fight for and obtain civil rights. They advocated confrontation and self-defense, but did not explicitly encourage overt acts of terrorism or wanton violence. By the end of the 1960s, the Black Panthers had an estimated 5,000 members, and had chapters in more than twenty areas across the country. By the mid 1970s, the group had lost most of its momentum as a result of internal strife and violent confrontations with law enforcement agencies. Although the group ceased to be publicly active, the ideological and philosophical

constructs continued to be studied and adopted by various radical groups through the years.

In 1984, Michael McGee, a former member of the original Black Panthers, was elected to the Milwaukee (Wisconsin) City Council. In 1987, he became quite concerned about the poverty and high unemployment rates among the inner city's black population and threatened to disrupt the city's Summerfest events unless more jobs were created for black people. Ultimately, he opted to pursue another avenue for garnering attention: he helped to mobilize the inner city communities to engage in demonstrations to force the public to acknowledge their plight.

By 1990, McGee had become a city alderman, and he used the forum of a city hall press conference to officially state his threat to create a group called the Black Panther Militia unless the problems of the inner city black population were instrumentally attended to. His plan was to encourage members of local gangs to join the Militia, as they would already have some street-fighting and gun usage experience. He planned to provide them with more sophisticated weapons and ideological training and to prepare them for acts of violent terrorism against big business, the wealthy, and the local government. At public meetings designed to recruit members for the Militia, McGee stated that their mission would be to engage in violence, armed combat, and urban guerilla warfare.

By 1992, McGee had organized a chapter of the Black Panther Militia in Indianapolis whose leader was a black Muslim named Mmoja Ajabu and one in Dallas that was led by Aaron Michaels. The latter evolved into the first chapter of the New Black Panther Party.

Dallas County Commissioner John Wiley Price had a nightly talk radio show called *Talkback*, which hired Aaron Michaels as producer in 1990. Michaels was strongly influenced by Price, who was the organizer of several confrontational protests and who introduced him to the concepts inherent in Black Nationalism. Michael McGee was an on-air guest in 1990, and Price encouraged his listening audience to make financial contributions to the Black Panther Militia.

Shortly thereafter, Michaels organized a group of supporters into a radical group he named the New Black Panther Party (NBPP), in tribute to the original Black Panthers; he officially registered the name of the group in 1991. Although he ignored the original Black Panthers "Core Principles, and commitment to community service," he did adopt their confrontational style and militarist manner. Over the next several years, the group broadened its base of operations across the United States.

The Dallas chapter of the New Black Panther Party hosted a National Black Power Summit and Youth Rally on May 29, 1993, which was attended by less than 250 people. One of the Rally's speakers was Michael McGee, who asserted that the new Black Panthers had chapters in more than twenty cities across the country at that time. As part of the effort to advance the notion of racial separatism, the White Aryan Resistance (WAR) was asked to provide a speaker. Tom Metzger, a WAR member not only appeared and spoke at the Rally, he tacitly encouraged the use of violent acts as a means of achieving the stated goals of the group.

Over time, McGee became a more peripheral figure in the NBPP, and Aaron Michaels assumed leadership. Under Michaels, the group became progressively more radical. Khalid Abdul Muhammad, Louis Farrakhan's national spokesman for the Nation of Islam (NOI), was ascending on a fast track through the NOI hierarchy from his place as one of Farrakhan's earliest followers. He joined the group in 1967, and moved with Farrakhan to the more radical separatist group in 1978. In November 1993, Muhammad spoke at Kean College in New Jersey, where he delivered a speech widely criticized as bigoted, anti-Catholic, anti-Semitic, and homophobic. He called followers of Judaism "bloodsuckers," made crude remarks about Pope John Paul II, made anti-homosexual slurs, and encouraged genocide against the white races. The remarks engendered enormous media attention, and Muhammad was reprimanded by a large number of religious and political leaders. In 1994, the United States Congress issued a statement condemning the speech as "the most vicious and vile kind of hatemongering."

Farrakhan's response to Muhammad's actions was to remove him from NOI leadership. Despite (or perhaps as a result of) the enormously controversial and inflammatory nature of his remarks and his underlying belief system, Muhammad remained a public speaker who was very much in high demand by colleges and universities.

A former NOI member, James Bess, attempted to assassinate Muhammad after he (Muhammad) concluded a speech at the University of California in Riverside on May 29, 1994. He was shot in the leg; four bodyguards and a bystander were wounded before the gunman was apprehended. Bess was convicted for the shootings and received a prison sentence of life, plus twenty-two years. Bess stated that he shot Muhammad because of his negative influence on black youth, as well as the divisive nature of his extremist views.

Khalid Muhammad went to Dallas to recuperate from his gunshot wounds; once there, he began to form an alliance with Aaron Michaels, as well as an interest in the New Black

Panther Party. Muhammad joined the leadership of the NBPP and set about increasing the public visibility of the group.

In 1996, Michaels requested assistance from Muhammad in the movement of a group of armed NBPP members from Dallas to Greenville, Texas, in response to the burning of two local area black churches. Muhammad agreed to do so and issued public statements calling for armed patrols to protect black churches across the country, extolling extreme or lethal violence against any whites who might consider doing damage to a black church or to any property owned or used by black people. Ultimately, a black teenager was arrested and indicted in connection with the two church arsons.

By the summer of 1998, Muhammad had seized control of the NBPP from Michaels and had become the new leader of the group. Michaels was relegated to the position of New Black Panther Party Minister of Defense. In June of that year, Muhammad took a group of about fifty NBPP members, some of whom were armed with rifles and shotguns, to Jasper, Texas, to provide visible protection in the aftermath of the murder of James Byrd Junior by three white supremacists. The Ku Klux Klan staged a rally in the area a couple of weeks after the murder, and Muhammad staged a counter-protest by the NBPP, dressed in militant garb evocative of the original Black Panthers.

Muhammad's next plan for increased visibility was to organize the Million Youth March, which was to occur in Harlem, New York, in 2000. The purported purpose of the march was to bring together black youth from all over the United States in an effort to create a sense of solidarity among them, in celebration of Black Power in the Year 2000. Muhammad also hoped to show the black youth of America that there were other groups (the NBPP) than the NOI that were capable of providing them with support and mentorship. The march was intentionally scheduled so as to compete with the NOI-sponsored Million Youth Movement, occurring in Atlanta. The goal of the NOI Movement was to gather black youth and expose them to the tutelage of mainstream black leaders, including the Reverend Jesse Jackson.

Muhammad traveled across the nation in an effort to gather support for the march. He was aided by the Brooklyn-based anti-racism advocacy group called the December 12 Movement. He was able to obtain the support of a number of prominent black leaders, including the Reverend Al Sharpton, who agreed to be a speaker at the event.

Initially, New York Mayor Rudolph Giuliani refused to grant the NBPP a permit for the Million Youth March to occur in Harlem, citing Muhammad's hate-based rhetoric as a safety concern. A federal judge overruled Mayor Giuliani, the permit was obtained, and the march took place in Harlem, New York, on September 5, 1998. Those in attendance heard a series of speeches laden with racist and anti-Semitic overtones; the day ended when a skirmish occurred as the New York City police attempted to end the march at the appointed time. Muhammad had told the crowd to do battle with the police, telling them to beat the police with rails or clubs and use their (the police's) own guns to shoot them. Roughly 6,000 people attended the march, and Muhammad's popularity continued to increase. He was elected the National Chairman of the New Black Panther Party not long after the event.

Muhammad created an institutional hierarchy within the NBPP and staffed it with many former members of the Nation of Islam and other Black Muslim factions. By the start of the twenty-first century, NBPP leadership claimed thirty-five national chapters and a membership of several thousand.

Khalid Muhammad died of a brain aneurysm quite suddenly on February 17, 2002. He was fifty-three years old. Under his leadership, the NBPP had become the largest and the most vocal racist and anti-Semitic black group in the United States. His second in command, Malik Zulu Shabazz, was his successor.

Shabazz was an attorney, as well as Muhammad's second in command. He had a lengthy history of outspoken extremism, racial separatism, and anti-Semitism, starting from his student days at Howard University. In 1988, Shabazz founded a group called Unity Nation, comprised of NOI supporters. Shabazz used the forum of his leadership as a means of publicly denigrating whites and Jewish people, in the guise of promoting black pride and raising the group's consciousness.

In 1998, Muhammad appointed Shabazz National Youth Director for the Million

KEY EVENTS

1966: The original Black Panther Party is founded by Huey Newton and Bobby Seale in Oakland, California.

1984: Michael McGee, former member of the original Black Panthers, was elected to the Milwaukee City Council.

1987: McGee chooses to lead demonstrations around the issue of black employment, rather than causing overt violence.

1990: McGee publicly states his intention to create the Black Panther Militia.

1990: Aaron Michaels organized a group of black nationalists to form the New Black Panther Party.

1993: McGee stated that the New Black Panther Party had chapters in twenty cities.

1998: Michaels steps down from leadership of the NBPP, and Khalid Muhammad ascended to power.

2001: Muhammad dies of a brain aneurysm, and Malik Zulu Shabazz assumes leadership of the group.

Youth March and charged him with conveying the NBPP rhetoric to the mainstream media. During the course of a radio interview prior to the march, Shabazz stated that his difficulties with the Jewish people lay in the existence of the State of Israel; he went on to state his beliefs that the Jewish people were involved in the African holocaust and the African slave trade; he also expressed a belief that the Zionists were causing worldwide problems for people of color. Throughout the march, Shabazz continued to espouse anti-Semitic rhetoric.

In the year 2000, Shabazz created a Washington, D.C. chapter of the NBPP, which would eventually house their national headquarters. After Muhammad's death in

2001, Shabazz worked to increase the NBPP's media visibility by organizing and staging protests across the country. He tended to target black communities that were experiencing high-profile racial difficulties. The style of protest organized by Shabazz appeared to lack clear motivation—the group would travel to an area, be sufficiently loud and visible as to attract media attention, and then leave. There was no social change occurring. It appeared that Shabazz's strengths were more organizational than public-welfare oriented. He has been credited with the production and implementation of the *Official National NBPP Black Power Manual*, containing a ten-point action plan advocating full employment, safe and fair housing, equal and quality education, improved living and working conditions for black people, and tax exemption. It also demands that black women and men be exempt from military service and that black people and other people of color be released from penal institutions due to the increased likelihood that they did not receive fair or impartial trials. The manual lists membership requirements for the NBPP, specifies the dress code, and suggests that members of the NBPP should own a weapon, which they are skilled at using.

PHILOSOPHY AND TACTICS

Although the New Black Panther Party claims philosophical and ideological roots in the original Black Panther Party, it has evolved into a far more extremist and violent faction than its purported predecessor. Since the earliest days with Michael McGee, the group has espoused violence, racism, and anti-Semitism. It has put forth an agenda of racial separatism for the United States, while demanding equal opportunity and equal rights with the white communities. Both Muhammad and Shabazz have embraced a platform involving a belief in an anti-Jewish conspiracy theory, homophobia, racism, and black separatism. Since the terrorist attacks in the United States on September 11, 2001, Shabazz has increased the volume and intensity of his Jewish conspiracy propaganda. On October 31, 2001, Shabazz co-chaired a meeting with a group of American Muslim leaders, who referred to themselves as the Muslims for Truth and Justice at the National Press

Club. The meeting was publicly broadcast on C-SPAN. Shabazz stated his belief that the Jewish people were directly responsible for the terrorist attacks and named the United States and Israel as the two most significant terrorist factions in the world. He thoroughly denigrated Zionism and expressed the opinion that the Jewish people are the underlying reason for the high death tolls on September 11, 2001. He did not provide a specific explanation for his beliefs. Other members of the NBPP echoed his beliefs and purported that several thousand Jewish businesspeople did not go to work at the Pentagon and the World Trade Towers on the day of the attacks, thereby escaping harm. They also put forth the NBPP theory that Israel masterminded and implemented the September 11 attacks in retaliation for the United States' failure to quell the Intifada.

In April 2002, Shabazz spoke out at an NBPP demonstration in front of the B'nai Brith offices in Washington, D.C. He led chants in which he advocated the decimation of the State of Israel, demonized the white races, and called for the death of every Zionist in Israel, regardless of age or infirmity.

Shabazz's leadership of the NBPP has become progressively more separatist, gradually developing into an exclusively racist ideology. He advocates extreme violence and terrorist activities and fails to state a clear agenda for social change or for betterment of the living conditions of black people in America.

OTHER PERSPECTIVES

Shabazz has raised the ire of the original Black Panthers to the point that they have issued a public statement disavowing any relationship with the group and condemning the NBPP's tactics of racial and anti-Semitic bigotry. David Hilliard, a member of the original Black Panthers and the Executive Director of the Dr. Huey P. Newton Foundation, has said that the New Black Panther Party has "totally abandoned our survival programs. The racism that the group espouse(s) flies directly in the face of the Black Panthers' multicultural ideology and purpose." Bobby Seale, one of the founders of the original Black Panthers, has

said of the New Black Panthers that they have "hijacked our name and are hijacking our history."

SUMMARY

The New Black Panther Party has garnered much attention from the media and the public because of its name: many people initially believe it to be related in some significant way to the original Black Panther Party. There has emerged no underlying ideology aimed at social change; no positive programs have been initiated. Shabazz has come to focus exclusively on promoting a platform of violence, racism, and anti-Semitism. He states, "our position is the Panther exclusively belongs to no one. It belongs to the people." Of the original Black Panthers, he goes on to say that they "are really working with the Zionists. I think their lawyer is one. I think they are being used by outside forces to keep alive the counterintelligence program of the F.B.I. and the U.S. government, creating divisions and factions among black organizations." Although it has been successfully able to capture the attention of the black community and to attract a significant membership, the New Black Panther Party does not appear to state any commitment to move beyond the rhetoric of hate to affect significant positive change in the quality of life in the black communities of America.

SOURCES

Web sites

Anti-Defamation League: Anti-Semitism U.S.A.. "Farrakhan Reaches Out to Anti-Semitic Black Panther Party." < http://www.adl.org/main_Anti_Semitism_Domestic/farrakhan_black_panther_party.htm > (accessed October 18, 2005).

Black Press USA. "Blacks and Jews Split—again—over Farrakhan (New Black Panther Party Will Attend MMM)." < http://freerepublic.com/focus/f-news/1404429/posts > (accessed October 18, 2005).

Bobby Seale's Homepage, Black Panther Party Founder. "From the Sixties ... to the Future." < http://publicenemy-seale.com/ > (accessed October 18, 2005).

Camera One Public Interest News and Culture. "Inaugural Protests Biggest Since Vietnam." < http://www.camerao-ne.org/inaguration.html > (accessed October 18, 2005).

Frontpagemag.com. "New Black Panther Mouthpiece." < http://www.frontpagemag.com/Articles/Read Article.asp?ID = 12053 > (accessed October 18, 2005).

The Dr. Huey P. Newton Foundation. "There is No New Black Panther Party: An Open Letter from the Dr. Huey P. Newton Foundation." < http://www.blackpanther. org/newsalert.htm > (accessed October 18, 2005).

NBC5i.com. "New Black Panther Party Emerges, Voices Demands." < http://www.nbc5i.com/news/3277640/detail. html > (accessed October 18, 2005).

SEE ALSO

Nation of Islam

New People's Army (NPA)

LEADER: Jose Maria Sison

YEAR ESTABLISHED OR BECAME ACTIVE: 1969

ESTIMATED SIZE: 16,000

USUAL AREA OF OPERATION: Philippines

U.S. TERRORIST EXCLUSION LIST DESIGNEE: The U.S. Department of State declared the New People's Army a terrorist organization in 2005

OVERVIEW

The New People's Army (NPA) is a left-wing, communist-based, revolutionary organization that operates under the direction of the Communist Party of the Philippines (CPP). It was formed on March 29, 1969, primarily as the military fighting section of the CPP, but also with secondary duties in organizing and propaganda. The objective of the NPA is to reverse injustices dealt to the Filipino people by the Philippine government and the capitalist class such as the large landlord/property owners. The three perceived injustices it is primarily fighting against are bureaucrat-capitalism, imperialism, and semi-feudal landlordism.

To accomplish these objectives, the NPA carries out an agrarian revolution for the express purpose of overthrowing the Philippine government through the actions of extended guerrilla warfare. Specifically, NPA leaders counter the abuses to the Filipino people with respect to the land tenancy system and, specifically, the peasant desire for farm/rural reform; the economic and unemployment conditions including unfair income distribution; and the corrupt systems and abusiveness within the government and the military. In the end, the NPA hopes to establish its own communistic/socialistic system of government in the Philippines.

Communist rebels in the Philippines march on January 6, 2004, during a meeting between government officials and New People's Army, a group engaged in a longstanding communist insurgency in Asia. AP/Wide World Photos. Reproduced by permission.

HISTORY

In the 1930s, conflicts between rural property owners and tenants resulted in poverty conditions for most peasant farmers living near Manila in central Luzon. Many farmers, who had earlier participated in agrarian protest movements, joined the pro-land reform Communist Party.

When the Japanese occupied the Philippines during World War II (1939–1945), the Communist Party joined with the People's Anti-Japanese Army to fight the intruders. The new resistance group was called the Hukbalahaps, or the Huks. By early 1943, the Huks—consisting of about 10,000 members—was effectively battling the Japanese using remote mountain bases and operating out of fields and paddies.

After the war, the Philippine government began to perceive the Huks, who took up the cause of land reform, as a threat to its power. By 1949, the Huks possessed an army of between 12,000 and 13,000 guerrilla soldiers, along with the support of about 100,000 peasants. At this time, the Huks began to organize farmers into unions, which further perturbed the government. In 1950, the Huks nearly defeated the Philippine government with about 15,000 guerrillas. However, in 1954, the Philippine government crushed the revolution with assistance from the United States.

Fifteen years later, on March 29, 1969, the New People's Army was formed when the newly established CPP, under the leadership of Jose Maria Sison, joined with the remaining members of the Huks. Under the guidance of Bernabe Buscayno (alias, Commander Dante), the Huks gave the CPP—whose members were mostly students, teachers, and other intellectuals—what it lacked: guerrilla warfare experience.

The NPA was comprised of approximately 400 guerrilla soldiers, 500 support troops, and between 3,000 and 4,000 support personnel. The

LEADERSHIP

JOSE MARIA SISON

Jose Maria Sison (alias, JoMa Sison) is the founder and chairman of the CPP Central Committee and the founder of the NPA. Originally, in the 1960s, a movement on Philippine college campuses rallied many people against U.S. imperialism. Sison, an English literature instructor at the University of the Philippines, became the leader of a coalition of radial groups brought together to oppose the Philippine government for the benefit of peasants. Sison formally established the CPP on December 26, 1968. He modeled its revolutionary approach to the model provided by Mao Tse-tung of China. From 1977 to 1986, Sison was a prisoner of the Philippine military. As of 2005, Sison leads the CPP and the NPA from the Netherlands where he remains due to his exile after being released from prison.

---

members acted primarily within the regions of Pampanga and Tarlac in central Luzon.

By 1970, the NPA had grown to several thousand soldiers. It also relocated most of its bases and activities to Quezon in southeastern Luzon, and Isabela in northeastern Luzon. The group made agrarian reform its primary focus, especially publicizing the broken campaign promises of re-elected President Ferdinand Marcos.

In 1971, the Philippine government fought its first unified attack against the group near a major NPA base in the Cagayan Valley of northeastern Luzon. Then, in 1972, Philippine military forces launched a counter-military effort—complete with martial law—that resulted in heavy NPA losses. That year, the NPA consisted of 1,000–2,000 soldiers, 7,000–8,000 trainees, and an estimated 100,000 supporters.

Between 1973 and 1974, government forces steadily drove NPA soldiers out of the villages and into remote mountain regions, killing many

in the process. As a result, Sison formed small guerrilla groups among the islands to provide flexibility of movements. Each group was self-supporting and able to develop its own agenda based on its specific needs.

With few police present, the NPA was able to help peasants with land reform conflicts involving the Philippine government and private corporations, disputes against landlords, and abuses by the military. For example, in 1976, NPA leaders helped Kalingas tribal members who were being forced off their sacred lands by the government's Chico River Dam project. Because of these actions, the NPA became popular with the citizenry.

Between 1976 and 1977, CPP leader Sison and NPA leader Buscayno were captured. Other leaders were also captured or killed. After these victories, the Philippine government stopped pursuing the NPA. As a result, the remaining NPA leaders used this time to strengthen its political and organizational activities.

By 1978, the NPA began to use military methods that were more conventional, rather than its earlier-used ambush techniques. By 1979, recruitment drives had increased NPA membership to around 3,000 soldiers.

In 1980, the CPP newspaper declared that the NPA would resume its full-time military operations with twenty-six guerrilla fronts in Luzon, Mindanao, and the Viayas. The increased military activity was due primarily to economic difficulties, government corruption, military abuses, martial law, and unemployment, At this time, the NPA had units in forty-six of the seventy-four provinces.

Although still using small fighting units and avoiding conflicts with large military forces, by late 1982 the NPA was organizing units that numbered 200–300 soldiers. By 1983, it declared that approximately 20% of the villages were under its control and that it had support from about 180,000 citizens. Various foreign analysts estimated that the NPA possessed 5,000–10,000 guerrillas. On September 29, 1983, the largest number of deaths to government personnel since 1969 occurred when about seventy NPA soldiers attacked a government patrol. Thirty-nine soldiers and seven civilians died on Mindanao. At the end of 1983, government leaders admitted that its military forces had been attacked by NPA cells almost every day during the year.

By the end of 1984, according to CPP figures and most Asian terrorist experts, the NPA was operating in sixty-two of the seventy-four provinces with around 20,000 full-time and part-time soldiers and with forty-five guerrilla fronts.

As of 1986, the NPA was considered a serious threat to national security. At this time, the NPA had expanded into nearly all of the country's regions, while the CPP-NPA organization was operating at its most efficient level to date.

The NPA leaders moved toward tactics that were more aggressive when the government seemed ready to collapse in the late 1980s. Three of the more violent attacks included, on October 29, 1987, the bombing of a Pepsi Cola bottling plant and two Del Monte pineapple facilities; on November 14, 1987, the bombing of the Manila Garden Hotel (owned by Japan Air Lines), which injured ten people; and on April 1, 1988, the killing in Davao of two security guards of a Japanese businessman, who was an employee of the Takeda Chemical Corporation and the manager of the Davao Central Chemical Corporation.

In 1992, the CPP launched a campaign to strengthen its revolutionary strategy, solidify its peasant contacts, and broaden its ideological knowledge. As a result, frequent attacks were made. Two of the more violent attacks were, on July 16, 1992, the killing of a Philippine-Chinese businessman and the wounding of his wife when their automobile was attacked in Manila, and on June 4, 1996, the attack on a helicopter owned by the Arimco Mining Corporation, which resulted in the death of a Canadian geologist near Didipio in Nueva Viscaya.

In 1992, the United States closed its Philippine bases. Before that time, the NPA had regularly targeted U.S. military facilities, equipment, and personnel because it opposed any type of U.S. presence in the country. The NPA claimed it had previously killed several U.S. personnel. In 1999, however, the Philippine and U.S. governments signed the Visiting Forces Agreement (VFA), which allowed for joint military training exercises. Because NPA leaders claimed the VFA compromised the country's independence, the CPP ended its peace talks with the government and the NPA resumed its violent actions against the U.S. military.

Between 1999 and late 2001, while the United States conducted its VFA exercises, the NPA claimed it would target U.S. military interests and personnel at the U.S. Embassy. However, no attacks were made. The NPA did claim responsibility for attacks on Philippine security forces in 1999, including several ambushes and kidnappings against Philippine military and police members. In January 2002, NPA leaders made public statements declaring that it would target any U.S. personnel found within its regions of operations.

During the 2000s, the NPA claimed responsibility for several major attacks. Some of these attacks included, in May 2001, the killing of a Philippine congressman from Quezon; in June 2001, the killing of a Philippine congressman from Cagayan; on November 5, 2004, the attacking of the headquarters of Petron Corporation and Caltex Philippines; on January 18, 2005, the killing of an alleged spy in Gaboc, Baay Village, Labo, Camarines Norte who was working for the military and police; on February 6, 2005, the killing of a public market administrator of Malabon who was (allegedly) abusing his authority and torturing children; on March 31, 2005, the abducting of two farmers in Recto Village, General Luna, Quezon; and on May 10, 2005, the killing of Leon Aracillas, the Santa Rosa mayor, and his bodyguard.

PHILOSOPHY AND TACTICS

The NPA is founded under a Maoist-based revolutionary philosophy, with its model being the Chinese People's Liberation Army. Its philosophy is based on Marxism, Leninism, Confucianism, and the ideas promoted by Mao Tse-tung. The NPA specifically adapted communist doctrines into its Maoist philosophy based on its "people's democratic" revolution of land reform.

The mission of the NPA is to overthrow the Philippine government. The primary functions of the NPA are to: conduct a people's war against the government; build a national united front; organize revolutionary committees; circulate propaganda to attract members and supporters; serve the citizens in ways other than militarily; support local party organizations; carry out projects that help itself, the CPP, and the citizens; assist in maintaining public order; conduct training, communications, medical care, intelligence, and logistics seminars; and

KEY EVENTS

1969: NPA is formed.

1971: First unified government attack against NPA occurs.

1972: Philippine government launches a counterattack that results in heavy NPA losses.

1973–1974: Government forces expel NPA into mountainous regions.

1976: NPA leaders help Kalingas tribal members who are being forced off sacred lands by Chico River Dam project.

1976–1977: CPP leader Sison is captured and imprisoned.

1978: NPA emphasizes political and organizational activities over violent ones.

1980: CPP declares that NPA will resume military operations.

1983: NPA soldiers attack government patrol on Mindanao, with a loss of government personnel totaling forty-six.

1999: NPA restarts its violence against U.S. military in the country after the Visiting Forces Agreement.

1999: NPA claims responsible for attacks, ambushes, and abductions on Philippine security forces.

2001: NPA claims responsibility for killing one Philippine Congressman from Quezon (May) and another Congressman from Cagayan (June).

2004–2005: NPA steps up its number of violent acts.

---

recuperate and indoctrinate during inactivity periods.

In order to carry out its mission, the NPA initially began to establish and consolidate a front of rural bases in remote areas that were relatively free from police enforcement. With an established rural base, the NPA began its next step of building up around the cities. During this time, NPA members targeted for assassination (especially those considered corrupt or voicing opinions criticizing its goals and tactics) such public and private figures as judges, politicians, police and law enforcement officials, security personnel, government informers, Philippine military personnel, U.S. soldiers, former-NPA members, rival extremist groups, news media members, drug traffickers, and alleged criminals. The NPA also targeted foreign investors and foreign-owned companies to force them to leave the country.

The group also used hit-and-run ambushes and raids for many of its attacks. Such attacks helped to replenish its arms, ammunition, and equipment. The NPA also targeted government installations and projects. NPA leaders were always conscious to protect innocent bystanders by only conducting attacks on verified enemies.

The NPA opposed U.S. imperialism (especially its control over the Philippines) and domestic feudalism. From 1969–1986, the NPA contended with the corrupt government of President-Dictator Ferdinand Marcos. During most of this time, NPA leaders gained public support from perceived dishonesty within Marcos' administration. The NPA wanted all foreign investors to leave the country; thus, rejected the Marcos administration that gave preferential treatment to foreign investors.

Tactically, the NPA is organized in areas called guerrilla bases. Zones around guerrilla bases are called fronts and more distance areas that are less secured are called preparation zones. NPA leaders divide its units into two broad categories: regular forces and local forces, with regular force units containing better trained and equipped soldiers. The majority of NPA members are not armed soldiers but simply Philippine citizens whose work is coordinated by NPA leaders.

Over the years, NPA leaders employ sabotage in their tactics. They have displayed an exceptional sense of urban and rural guerrilla warfare. For instance, units generally remain in their local area to defend those areas. The NPA encourages peasants to begin farming without the aid of landlords in order to be able to purchase food directly from the farmers. This system helped the NPA to feed its troops and further its support from the rural citizenry. NPA leaders are well versed in selecting the correct strategy about discipline, operations, tactics, and training.

Most NPA members come from workers, students, and professionals such as teachers. In many rural areas, members of the police force are often members of the NPA. According to the CPP, membership is open to all people who are 18 years of age and older and mentally and physically able and willing to fight.

Although the organization carries out most of its acts in rural parts of the Philippines, the NPA possesses cells within urban areas such as Manila and other metropolitan centers. Such cells are called assassination squads (or sparrow units) that usually consist of less than five soldiers.

In areas where guerrilla fronts are well established, the NDF functions, essentially, as the government of that area as it provides public works and schools, implements land reform programs, collects taxes, and enforces laws. NPA leaders often issue warnings to anyone accused of crimes, which if left unheeded often results in executions at the discretion of the NPA.

From 1969–1975, the NPA was supported partially by the People's Republic of China, that provided material support. For the next five years, the NPA was weakened financially by the loss of China's support. Later, funds and materials were obtained primarily through the levying of taxes, robberies, confiscations, intimidations, and extortions. Today, it also obtains funds through various other means such as local mining and logging firms, local businesses, and rural communities. Most of the businesses that are taxed and extorted by the NPA are remote plantations.

During the 1980s, the NPA established a more comprehensive organizational plan in order to integrate diverse groups (such as students, labor unions, and religious groups) into its membership. It employs sophisticated methods of obtaining funds. As a result, the group possesses a large arsenal of weapons, along with well-developed communications systems. The NPA is believed to be involved in smuggling, especially in the sale of illegal drugs.

OTHER PERSPECTIVES

In 2004, according to Ernie B. Esconde, a reporter for *The Manila Times*, the NPA had maintained a steady presence in the town of Samal in Bataan. NPA soldiers had been accepted by the townspeople. Esconde stated that the NPA effectively controlled problems such as robberies, addictions, abusive police officers and local officials, and marital disagreements. However, after many years of a NPA-controlled town, the citizens saw no advancement for land reform by the NPA and turned against the group. After leaving, rumors spread that the NPA had extorted money from rich families, businesses, and farmers. One farmer claimed, however, that he and his neighboring farmers had never been approached by NPA members for food or money.

According to Benjie Oliveros of the Philippine newspaper *Bulatlat*, the Manila Overseas Press Club in July 2004 stated that the NPA continues to be the primary threat to "peace and security" in the country. The threat continues because of the NPA presence throughout the Philippines and its continuing ability to launch attacks against government forces in its continuing attempt to take over from the present government.

SUMMARY

The NPA maintains part of its funding through contributions from supporters primarily in the Philippines and Europe but also in various other regions of the world. The other part of its funding comes from local businesses and politicians who are forced to pay what is locally called "revolutionary taxes": in other words, extortion money.

The Philippine Communist Party, acting through its New People's Army, has fought a decades-long guerrilla insurgency against the national government. During the 1990s, the NPA conducted several unsuccessful peace talks with the Philippine government. As of 2005—after over thirty-five years of attacks—the NPA has yet to overthrow the Philippine government. With the U.S. military presence gone from the Philippines, the NPA has lost one of its primary targets. Today, it engages primarily in urban warfare and terrorist activities against (alleged) corrupt politicians, police, and drug traffickers. The group is considered a significant threat to the Philippine government.

According to newspaper reporter Benjie Oliveros, the highest number of reported casualties to governmental military forces from NPA attacks since 1999 occurred in 2004. Oliveros considers that confrontations between the NPA soldiers and government forces will likely increase in the near future based on reported trends and expansions of the NPA's guerrillas fronts. Oliveros considers the conflict to be far from being resolved.

SOURCES

Books

Chapman, William. *Inside the Philippine Revolution.* New York: W.W. Norton, 1987.

Corpus, Victor N. *Silent War.* Zuezon City, Philippines: VNC Enterprises, 1989.

Sison, Jose Maria. *The Philippine Revolution: The Leader's View.* New York: Crane Russak, 1989.

Web sites

Benjie Oliveros, Bulatlat. "AFP-NPA Armed Clashes Increased in 2004." < http://bulatlat.com/news/4-46/4-46-clashes_printer.html > (accessed Ocot21, 2005).

Embassy of the Philippines. "History of the Philippines." < http://www.philembassy.au.com/phi-hist.htm > (accessed October 21, 2005).

Ernie B. Esconde, The Manila Times. "A Former Rebel Town: A Case in Perspective." < http://www.manilatimes.net/national/2004/aug/11/yehey/prov/20040811pro12.html > (accessed October 21, 2005).

Major Rodney S. Azama, GlobalSecurity.org. "The Huks and the New People's Army: Comparing Two Postwar Filipino Insurgencies." < http://www.globalsecurity.org/military/library/report/1985/ARS.htm > (accessed October 21, 2005).

MIPT Terrorism Knowledge Base, National Memorial Institute for the Prevention of Terrorism. "Group Profile: New People's Army (NPA)." < http://www.tkb.org/Group.jsp?groupID = 203 > (accessed October 21, 2005).

Tribung Pinoy. "A Brief History of the Philippines from a Filipino Perspective." < http://www.tribo.org/history/history3.html > (accessed October 21, 2005).

Operation Rescue

ALTERNATE NAME: Operation Save America
LEADERS: Randall Terry; Philip (Flip) Benham
YEAR ESTABLISHED OR BECAME ACTIVE: 1982
USUAL AREA OF OPERATION: United States

OVERVIEW

Operation Rescue was among the best known and most aggressive anti-abortion groups in the United States during the 1980s and 1990s. The group's members were frequently arrested for protesting outside women's clinics and were suspected of inciting violence against the doctors who worked there. Following a series of lawsuits and new legislation restricting their tactics, the organization became less visible during the 1990s. The original group exists today in the form of several autonomous offshoots, which continue to fight against abortion using a variety of tactics.

HISTORY

Operation Rescue was one of a series of groups formed during the 1970s and 1980s for the purpose of ending abortion in the United States. In the years following the 1972 Supreme Court decision (now known simply as *Roe vs. Wade*), abortion quickly became one of the most emotionally charged and highly polarized issues on the American political landscape. Both supporters and opponents of abortion rights lobbied vigorously, often heatedly, for their respective positions. Supporters of abortion rights cited individual freedoms, arguing that the

Anti-abortion activist Randall Terry, the founder of Operation Rescue, speaks to reporters about his opposition to stem cell research during a demonstration in Lafayette Park across from the White House on August 1, 2001. AP/Wide World Photos.

Constitution provides an implicit right to individual privacy, which precludes the government from interfering in an individual's reproductive choices. They also took the position that an unborn child is not yet a human being and hence is not afforded the protection of constitutional rights. Finally, supporters of abortion rights claimed that legalized abortion is a more equitable arrangement, since it guarantees this right to poor women who might not otherwise have access to it.

Opponents of abortion rights based their position primarily on ethical and moral grounds. In broad terms, abortion opponents cited a belief in the sanctity of all human life, arguing that human life is inherently valuable. They also took the position that human life begins at the moment of conception, making a developing child as fully human as its mother. Further, they saw abortion as a cheapening of human worth, potentially leading to practices such as euthanasia and assisted suicide, which they opposed on similar grounds.

In the years following the court ruling, abortion opponents employed a variety of tactics. In addition to educational campaigns, political efforts were also launched, leading to the passage of state laws tightening limitations on abortions. The pro-life, or right-to-life, movement actually originated in the 1960s and simply gained strength following *Roe vs. Wade*. To many within this movement, abortion was not a simple, amoral medical procedure, but rather the willful destruction of a human life, or murder. For this reason, the steady increase in the number of abortions during the 1970s created frustration and anger within this camp. While many tactics were used in the fight, nonviolence remained the norm during the 1970s.

Around 1980, a young activist named Randall Terry, along with his wife Cindy, joined the anti-abortion movement. Terry publicly proclaimed himself to be a Christian in 1976, and he and Cindy soon joined a local anti-abortion group. This group, like most others at the time,

Abortion-rights activist Karen Nicholls shields herself from anti-abortion leader Rev. Flip Benham, who attempts to pray for Nicholls during a 2001 demonstration by the two groups outside a clinic in Wichita, Kansas. AP/Wide World Photos

focused most of its efforts on the facilities where abortions were being performed, as well as the women who went there for services.

In a typical action, group members would gather near a clinic before it opened. As employees arrive, the protesters harass them, calling them names and urging them to leave their jobs. After the employees were inside, attention turned to women who were arriving for abortions and other medical treatment. Group members typically tried to convince women not to enter the clinic; in some cases, they displayed large photos of fetuses or physically tried to block the clinic entrance. In general, the intent was to make the trip to the clinic so intimidating that potential clients would leave, rather than carrying out the planned abortion.

Despite these and other efforts, abortion numbers continued to climb. In 1972, the first year of legalized abortion, 585,000 procedures were performed in the United States. By 1980, according to the Centers for Disease Control, that number had more than doubled to 1,297,000, and it continued to climb until its eventual peak in 1990. Activists within the anti-abortion movement were well aware of these figures, and some concluded that the non-violent approach was failing to achieve its objectives.

In 1986, Randall Terry launched Operation Rescue, a nominally Christian organization committed to ending abortion in the United States. Operation Rescue would soon distinguish itself from most existing anti-abortion groups with its willingness to employ violence

LEADERSHIP

RANDALL TERRY

Following a 1976 conversion experience, Randall Terry made plans to become a Pentecostal missionary. Instead, he and his wife Cindy remained in the United States, where they first became involved in anti-abortion efforts around 1980. In 1983, the Terrys began picketing a women's services clinic in Binghamton, New York. Their tactics were aggressive, but largely non-violent, including such acts as physically blocking the entrance, displaying photos of fetuses, and harassing clinic workers.

In 1986, Terry launched Operation Rescue, a militant group dedicated to ending abortion in America. Despite his first arrest that year, Terry continued his work with Operation Rescue, leading the group's first "rescue mission" in 1986 and numerous others in later years. In 1992, he was sentenced to a year in jail for violating a restraining order against approaching abortion clinics.

In 1995, the National Organization for Women (NOW) filed suit against Operation Rescue and Randall Terry under federal anti-racketeering laws. Terry reached a settlement, but immediately filed for bankruptcy to avoid payment of the judgment. He later began fundraising efforts to secure a new home in Florida.

In 1998, Terry ran for Congress but was soundly defeated. In 2003, the parents of brain-damaged Florida resident Terri Schiavo asked him to coordinate their fight to keep the woman alive. Following her eventual death in 2005, Terry conducted the family's private memorial service.

PHILIP (FLIP) BENHAM

Like Randall Terry, Flip Benham turned to Christianity in 1976. Following his conversion, he returned to school and earned his Master of Divinity degree, founding and leading the Garland Free Methodist Church from 1980–1992. In 1988, he launched Operation Rescue Dallas/Fort Worth, and four years later, he left his pulpit to become the local group's full-time director.

In 1994, Benham assumed the position of National Director for Operation Rescue. In the years that followed, he traveled the country, protesting and being arrested in numerous cities; photos of several of his arrests decorated his office wall. As of 2005, Benham's group is devoid of assets, due largely to numerous lawsuits. Benham is supported by income from speaking and writing articles, and from personal donations.

---

in pursuit of its objectives. While the majority of Christian groups oppose violence, anti-abortion violence is justified by some extremist groups as an attempt to prevent murder, much as a father might kill an intruder in his home in order to protect his family. This rationale of "rescuing" unborn children would form the basis of Operation Rescue's actions for the following decade.

Operation Rescue's first "rescue" was staged in 1986 at a Binghamton, New York, clinic. Randall Terry and seven followers barricaded themselves inside the clinic to protest the practice of abortion there. Following their arrest, they were jailed for several days. The group also continued its sidewalk work outside other clinics, though the tactics gradually became

more extreme and threatening. Combined with numerous massive protests around the country, these "rescues" increased the group's influence within the anti-abortion movement.

As the public face of Operation Rescue, Randall Terry led protests and often served jail time with his followers (as of 2005, he claims to have been arrested forty times). As Operation Rescue expanded, Terry gradually stretched the group's objectives beyond ending abortion, eventually leading his followers to oppose homosexuals and others he perceived as anti-Christian. In 1993, he was quoted in the Fort Wayne, Indiana, *News-Sentinel*: "I want you to just let a wave of intolerance wash over you. I want you to let a wave of hatred wash over you. Yes, hate is good . . . Our goal is a Christian nation. We have a Biblical duty; we are called by God, to conquer this country. We don't want equal time. We don't want pluralism."

Randall Terry left the Operation Rescue in 1994. His website claims that, during his tenure (1987–1994), the group's civil disobedience and rescues resulted in 70,000 arrests, more than ten times the number of arrests during the civil rights protests of 1958–1968. Many of the group's protests were now met by equally aggressive counter-protestors and workers trained to help women into clinics. President Clinton also signed the Federal Access to Clinic Entrances Act of 1994, which imposed fines and jail terms for many of the tactics used by Operation Rescue and similar groups, severely limiting their options.

Following Terry's departure, the group's leadership was assumed by Philip "Flip" Benham, a former saloon owner turned Methodist pastor. Benham had been serving as head of Operation Rescue's Dallas chapter before taking over as director of the national organization. Benham inherited an organization facing major decisions. While the group had successfully used what they called "sidewalk counseling" throughout its history, the 1994 access law sharply limited this tactic. And whereas group members had previously been able to protest at clinics and risk only a small fine or a night in jail, the new law's penalties specified stiff penalties for violations, making protests far more costly for Operation Rescue members.

Organizationally, the group faced an identity crisis. Randall Terry and his associates had originally intended Operation Rescue to be a cause, rather than an organization. For this reason, the name Operation Rescue had never been copyrighted, and anti-abortion groups throughout the country had started to use it. While this practice lent credibility to the local organizations and raised the profile of the national group, it also meant that each was blamed for the actions of the other. In some cases, local leaders found themselves attempting to excuse offensive statements by national leaders, while in other cases, the national organization was forced to distance itself from extremist actions at the local level. While the abortion battle continued to rage, Flip Benham inherited a movement that appeared to be past its prime.

The year 1995 brought a public relations coup for Operation Rescue. While working in Dallas, Flip Benham met and became friends with Norma McCorvey, the young pregnant woman referred to as "Jane Roe" in the landmark Supreme Court case. Some time later, Benham baptized McCorvey, who later announced her new anti-abortion position. Throughout the following years, Operation Rescue continued a full slate of activities, including ongoing protests at abortion clinics. In 1998, Benham was indicted for trespassing and served six months in jail; he and several associates had allegedly refused to leave a Lynchburg, Virginia, high school where they were distributing anti-abortion literature.

Also in 1995, the National Organization for Women (NOW) filed suit to procure a nationwide injunction against the Pro-Life Action League, Operation Rescue, and their leaders, including former leader Randall Terry. The suit was unusual because it attempted to prosecute abortion rights leaders under federal racketeering laws. These laws, which were originally passed to fight organized crime, allow the leaders of a criminal organization to be prosecuted for the actions of group members. NOW eventually won the case and the verdict was upheld on appeal. Terry reached an out-of-court settlement with NOW and filed for bankruptcy to protect his assets. The following year, Flip Benham formally changed the organization's name to Operation Save America; the national organization continues to use both the old and new names, while numerous local groups retain the Operation Rescue moniker.

In 2003, James E. Kopp, one of Randall Terry's most ardent followers, was charged with the 1998 killing of a Buffalo, New York, physician. In an unusual trial, the prosecution and defense jointly submitted a thirty-five-page list of agreed-on facts, including an admission of guilt by Kopp. Attorneys then argued the case briefly before the judge, with Kopp's counsel stating that Kopp only meant to injure the doctor in order to end his work. Kopp had hidden outside the doctor's home and shot him through a kitchen window.

Following the shooting, Kopp fled the country and was placed on the FBI's most wanted list before his apprehension in France in 2001. The judge in the case found Kopp guilty of second-degree murder and sentenced him to twenty-five years to life in prison, the maximum allowed.

In 2005, a highly publicized event reunited many of the players in the Operation Rescue

KEY EVENTS

1972: *Roe vs. Wade* decision legalizes abortion in the United States; 585,000 procedures are performed during the first year.

1986: Randall Terry launches Operation Rescue in Binghamton, New York. In the following decade, the group's activities lead to more than 70,000 arrests.

1993: Randall Terry proclaims in a widely publicized speech that "hate is good."

1994: President Clinton signs the Federal Access to Clinic Entrances Act, increasing legal penalties for blocking clinic entrances.

1994: Randall Terry leaves Operation Rescue; Flip Benham assumes the role of National Director.

1995: The National Organization for Women (NOW) files federal racketeering charges against Operation Rescue and other anti-abortion organizations, as well as Randall Terry. Terry settles with the group, which eventually wins the suit.

1998: James E. Kopp, one of Terry's associates, murders a doctor. He is sentenced to twenty-five years to life. Kopp admits the shooting, but claims he only intended to injure the man.

1998: Benham changes the group's name to Operation Save America. The original name, Operation Rescue, continues to be used by his and other groups.

2005: Randall Terry, Operation Rescue, and Operation Save America converge on Florida to oppose the court decision removing Terri Schiavo from life support.

saga. While the world looked on, a heated battle took place as relatives of Terri Schiavo, in a coma for years, battled over her future. Following a protracted legal process, Schiavo's husband was granted the right to end her life support, while her parents pressed for it to

continue. In response, Operation Rescue West, headed by Troy Newman, promised to risk arrest in order to feed Mrs. Schiavo. Randall Terry, who had been working with Schiavo's parents on the case since 2003, also appeared in Florida to support the parents' efforts. Flip Benham was sentenced to ten days in a Florida jail when he and others tried to take water to Mrs. Schiavo; the judge in the case labeled Benham a habitual offender. Later that year, Randall Terry announced his plan to run for the Florida State Senate.

PHILOSOPHY AND TACTICS

The philosophy behind the work of Operation Rescue and similar anti-abortion groups is based on several key principles. Abortion opponents believe that murder is morally indefensible and that the unjustified killing of another human being should be prohibited and punished by law.

Anti-abortion activists also believe that human life begins at the moment of conception, a perspective that makes a fertilized egg, an eight-month-old fetus, and a forty-five-year-old adult equally valuable and equally worthy of protection. For this reason, most anti-abortion groups believe that any abortion, regardless of the time or circumstance, is equivalent to murder. By extension, they also believe that the doctors and other personnel that perform the procedure are guilty of a criminal act.

As professed followers of Christianity, most anti-abortion activists believe that human law frequently conflicts with divine law, and in such cases, they are compelled to abide by divine teaching, even at the risk of criminal penalties. The nature of the response to this conflict is what sets Operation Rescue and other violent groups apart from more mainstream Christians. While a majority of Christians oppose abortion on demand, they differ widely in their enactment of this belief. Only a tiny fraction find moral justification for using violence against doctors and women who are involved in the practice of abortion.

Operation Rescue was created, at least in part, in response to the perception that existing anti-abortion groups were not aggressive enough. In response, Operation Rescue employed a full gamut of techniques, ranging from local prayer vigils to massive rallies to political action. While numerous anti-abortion groups were active during the 1980s, Operation Rescue was the most successful in rallying large numbers of demonstrators.

From 1986–1991, Operation Rescue rose to the forefront of the movement. Its members, led by Randall Terry and others, staged sit-ins and blockades at hundreds of abortion clinics throughout the United States. During these events, members taunted workers, attempted to block entrances, and harassed women entering the clinics. In response to police orders to disperse, members often fell limp to the ground and had to be carried away one by one.

During the summer of 1988, Operation Rescue launched a series of anti-abortion protests in Atlanta. Calling the event the "Siege of Atlanta," group members converged on the city's abortion clinics, where Terry was arrested on the first day of the protest. More than 100 other group members were also arrested in Atlanta; many followed Terry's instructions in refusing to provide their real names to the police.

In 1989, the group organized a massive protest in Los Angeles. Naming the event a "Holy Week of Rescue," activists managed to shut down a local clinic for several days. Numerous protestors were arrested and attempted to base their court case on the "necessity defense," which states that human law can be broken when a higher good is involved. The judge in the case refused to allow the defense.

In 1991, the group organized a massive anti-abortion event in Wichita, Kansas called "Summer of Mercy." Lasting more than six weeks, the campaign shut down local abortion clinics for the duration of the event. More than 2,700 protesters were arrested as a result, and the campaign culminated in a massive stadium rally with than 30,000 in attendance.

Operation Rescue's earliest efforts attracted support from mainstream Christian leaders. Pat Robertson, founder of the Christian Broadcasting Network, spoke at the concluding rally during the Summer of Mercy campaign. Well-known evangelist Jerry Falwell also threw his support behind the group, donating $10,000 and holding a press conference in support of the group and its tactics during a 1987 protest.

Operation Rescue, like most similar groups, was not openly violent, nor did it openly promote violence. However, the strident language and confrontational tactics endorsed by Terry and others clearly held the potential to encourage violence among the movement's more extreme members. In truth, many of the group's techniques, including physically blocking entrances, falling down in front of car doors to block them, and forcing police to carry their limp bodies away, were profoundly physical in nature. By painting the battle against abortion as a sort of holy war and personally leading them to protests and jail, Terry appears to have justified extreme measures in the minds of his followers. In 1992, Terry arranged for a dead fetus to be delivered to Bill Clinton, who was attending the Democratic National Convention as he prepared to accept the party's nomination for President. Terry was subsequently arrested and sentenced to five months in prison for the stunt.

One of Terry's more extreme followers was James E. Kopp. From the earliest days of Operation Rescue, Kopp was a close confidante of Terry's. In 1998, Kopp stalked a Buffalo, New York, abortion doctor to his home, shooting the man through a window as he stood in his kitchen. Kopp fled the country and was placed on the FBI's most wanted list. He was arrested in France and extradited to the United States, where he was convicted and sentenced to twenty-five years to life in prison.

The 1998 killing brought to an end a string of similar shootings dating back to 1994. Each of these attacks occurred in late October or early November, and all were carried out in northern New York state and Canada. In each case, an abortion provider was shot through a window or glass door at his home, prompting Canadian authorities to offer more than $300,000 in rewards. Kopp was not charged with the other attacks, despite the similarities.

OTHER PERSPECTIVES

Operation Rescue has enjoyed long-standing support from numerous religious organizations. However, some supporters have grown increasingly critical of Operation Rescue's tactics. The group claims that its display of graphic materials depicting abortion and pornography is essential to its mission. Critics assert the material is inappropriate for public viewing, especially among children and teens. Many anti-abortion supporters claim that Operation Rescue's increasing extremism has pushed the group out of the mainstream, non-violent anti-abortion movement.

One of Operation Rescue's key tactics, holding demonstrations in close proximity to health care facilities that provide abortion services, has come under repeated fire. Planned Parenthood claims that some anti-abortion protestors violate legal protest boundaries by harassing patients and trespassing on clinic property. In 2001, the National Organization of Women (NOW) successfully brought charges in the Court of Appeals against Operation Rescue under the Racketeer-Influenced and Corrupt Organizations (RICO) Act. The court found that Operation Rescue used extortion, violence, and intimidation to harass women seeking abortions and abortion providers.

SUMMARY

Operation Rescue was in the vanguard of the early anti-abortion movement. Because of its willingness to employ tactics deemed too aggressive by other groups, it attracted a large following. The group's members were frequently arrested for their actions, which included marches at abortion clinics and staging public rallies. The group's tactics appear to have moderated somewhat following the departure of its founder. The group's heirs today remain active in the fight against abortion, though as a more fragmented, less visible movement.

SOURCES

Books

Baird, Robert M., and Stuart E. Rosenbau, eds. *The Ethics of Abortion: Pro-Life vs. Pro-Choice.* Amhurst, NY: Prometheus Books, 2001.

Solinger, Rick (ed). *Abortion Wars: A Half Century of Struggle, 1950–2000.* Berkeley, CA: University of California Press, 2001.

Web sites

Abortion facts.com. "U.S. Statistics." < http://www.abortionfacts.com/statistics/us_stats_abortion.asp > (accessed Octo 16, 2005).

Media Matters for America.org. "Who is Randall Terry?" < http://mediamatters.org/items/200503220001 > (accessed October 16, 2005).

Religious Tolerance.org. "How Christians View Non-Christian Religions." < http://www.religioustolerance.org/chr_othe2.htm > (accessed October 16, 2005).

Orange Volunteers (OV)

LEADER: Bob Marno

USUAL AREA OF OPERATION: Ireland

OVERVIEW

The Orange Volunteers are a loyalist paramilitary group in Northern Ireland. They support Northern Ireland remaining part of the United Kingdom, with their goal being to keep the Protestant-majority province known as Ulster under British rule, while preventing the Republic of Ireland and Northern Ireland from becoming unified. The Irish Republican Army (IRA) and Sinn Fein seek the unification of Ireland, putting them in opposition to the Orange Volunteers.

The Orange Volunteers began acts of violence in Northern Ireland during the peace process, with their actions intended to destabilize the peace process, encourage acts of retaliation by groups such as the IRA and Sinn Fein, and prevent the unification of Ireland.

HISTORY

In 1993, the Northern Ireland peace process began, with the process an attempt to create a unified Ireland. On December 15, 1993, the Joint Declaration on Peace was released on behalf of the British and Irish governments. The statement included that the British government would allow the people of Northern Ireland to decide between remaining part of the United

LEADERSHIP

BOB MARNO

Bob Marno was the leader of the Orange Volunteers. Marno was a soldier in the Royal Irish Regiment and a senior member of the Orange Order in the county of Antrim.

In November 1999, the Royal Ulster Constabulary discovered around 300 military intelligence files in an Orange Hall in the county of Antrim. The files were leaked from the British Army and contained details of republicans in the Belfast and Armagh areas and were considered as being used to identify Catholics to target in bomb attacks. Marno was a key-holder of the Orange Hall where the documents were found, suggesting that the documents were for the use of the Orange Volunteers.

In November 1999, Marno was arrested near his home. He escaped custody but gave himself up to police ten days later. After being questioned by police, he was released without charge.

━━━━━━━━━━━

Kingdom or becoming part of a unified Ireland, while the Irish government showed their intention of forming a unified Ireland. This led to a series of negotiations that continued until 1998.

On Good Friday, April 10, 1998, the Irish government, the British government, and the political parties of Northern Ireland reached agreement. The Good Friday Agreement, or Belfast Agreement, stated that the future of Northern Ireland would be decided by a referendum. The Good Friday Agreement also included that all paramilitary prisoners who belonged to organizations observing a ceasefire would be released from prison within two years and that paramilitary groups would decommission their weapons.

One of the groups involved in the peace process was the Ulster Freedom Fighters, also known as the Ulster Defense Association. The group is a loyalist group in Northern Ireland that has been operating since 1971. It is against the unification of Ireland and has been involved in various attacks on Catholic civilians. During the peace process negotiations, the group announced ceasefires in 1993 and 1998. The Loyalist Volunteer Force was another loyalist group in Northern Ireland that was against unification and was involved in the negotiations. In 1998, the Loyalist Volunteer Force issued a ceasefire and later handed back weapons for destruction. However, the Loyalist Volunteer Force remained against unification and urged the people of Northern Ireland to vote no in the referendum.

The Orange Volunteers is thought to be made of up former members of the Ulster Freedom Fighters and the Loyalist Volunteer Force, with these members against the ceasefires. The Council on Foreign Relations also states that authorities suspect that the Orange Volunteers may be a cover name used by members of the Ulster Freedom Fighters and the Loyalist Volunteer Force. This view takes into account that acts of violence by the Ulster Freedom Fighters or the Loyalist Volunteer Force would prevent imprisoned members from being released, since the terms of the Good Friday Agreement states that only members of paramilitary groups observing ceasefires will be guaranteed prison release.

On May 22, 1998, the referendum was held. The Good Friday Agreement was passed, with a 71% yes vote in Northern Ireland and a 94% yes vote in the Republic of Ireland. The passing of the Good Friday Agreement was followed by the beginning stages of its implementation. According to the MIPT Terrorism Knowledge Base, the Orange Volunteers formed in 1998 in direct response to the successful peace process in Northern Ireland, with their intent being to destabilize the peace process.

The Orange Volunteers first emerged in the news in 1998 as they threatened to launch a campaign of violence against the IRA, Sinn Fein, and other enemies of Ulster. These threats emerged as part of conflicts over the Drumcree marches, a known flashpoint within Northern Ireland occurring because the Protestant group known as the Orangemen march down nationalist streets. In June 1998, the Parade Commission banned the Protestant Orangemen from marching down Garvaghy Road in Portadown, a Nationalist Road that had been the site of

KEY EVENTS

1998: The Irish government, the British government, and the political parties of Northern Ireland signed the Good Friday Agreement. The agreement described how a referendum would be used to determine the future of Northern Ireland.

1998: The referendum was held; the Good Friday Agreement was passed by a majority yes vote in both the Republic of Ireland and Northern Ireland.

1998: The Orange Volunteers emerged as part of conflict over the Orangemen's march in Drumcree.

1998: Members of the Orange Volunteers kidnapped a television journalist as a means of communicating their message to the public. The Orange Volunteers described how they plan to attack IRA members being released from prison under the terms of the Good Friday Agreement.

2001: The Orange Volunteers issued a back to war statement, warning that they may soon end their ceasefire and take action again to protect their people, their faith, and their country.

violence and standoffs in previous years. The Orangemen responded by stating that they would march their traditional route and would stand their ground if prevented from doing so.

On July 5, 1998, the Orangemen attempted to march down Garvaghy Road but were prevented from doing so by security forces. Thousands of loyalists joined the group and violent sieges followed and continued for several nights. *The Guardian* reported that members of the Orange Volunteers were present at the protest.

In November 1998, members of the Orange Volunteers kidnapped a television journalist and his crew and took him to an unknown location.

The journalist was present at a meeting of the Orange Volunteers, where they revealed that they would launch attacks on republicans and IRA members who were being released from prison as part of the Good Friday Agreement. A prepared statement by the Orange Volunteers also described their belief that the IRA ceasefire was a ploy to get the British troops and the British people out of Ulster, with the Orange Volunteers stating that they would not allow the IRA to succeed in this mission. The statement also expressed their dissatisfaction with the peace process.

During late 1998 and 1999, the Orange Volunteers claimed responsibility for attacks on various Catholic businesses. In February 2001, the Orange Volunteers released a statement describing their mission as being to protect their people, their faith, and their country.

PHILOSOPHY AND TACTICS

The Orange Volunteers emerged during the Northern Ireland peace process, with bombings beginning after the Good Friday Agreement was made and continuing as the Good Friday Agreement was implemented. Their actions were considered to be part of their plans to undermine the Good Friday Agreement and prevent Northern Ireland from becoming part of a unified Ireland.

On December 17, 1998, the Orange Volunteers claimed responsibility for a bomb explosion in a bar in the county of Armagh, Northern Ireland. The group claimed that the target of the attack was a senior IRA commander. Another loyalist group named the Red Hand Defenders also claimed responsibility for the bombing, increasing speculation that both groups might be cover names used by members of the Loyalist Volunteer Force or the Ulster Defense Association. There was also speculation that the two groups could have some of the same members. The Red Hand Defenders are a loyalist group that appeared around the same time as the Orange Volunteers. They claimed responsibility for various bomb attacks. These included a bomb blast in Portadown, Northern Ireland, that killed a policeman, the murder of a Catholic man in Belfast, and the murder of human rights lawyer Rosemary Nelson in a car bomb attack. Both the Orange Volunteers and the Red Hand Defenders share the same purpose, though the Red Hand Defenders are known for more violent attacks than the Orange Volunteers.

On January 6, 1999, the Orange Volunteers claimed responsibility for a bomb explosion in the Gaelic Sports Club in Magherafelt, Northern Ireland. The Orange Volunteers warned in a statement that nationalists had everything to fear and stated that they would continue defending the Protestant people.

On January 19, 1999, the Orange Volunteers claimed responsibility for a bomb explosion in the home of a Catholic family in Loughinisland, Northern Ireland. The explosion caused minor injuries to the homeowner.

On February 8, 1999, the Orange Volunteers claimed responsibility for a grenade attack on a pub in Castledawson, Northern Ireland. The incident had no casualties. The pub was owned by Sinn Fein lawyer Francis McNally, with the Orange Volunteers warning that there would be more attacks on individuals they considered as enemies of Ulster. RUC Chief constable Ronnie Flanagan told BBC News that the attack was aimed at provoking retaliation from Republicans and stated that the loyalists were targeting the Good Friday Agreement and trying to undermine the peace process.

The ongoing attacks on Catholic business targets, IRA individuals, and Sinn Fein individuals had two purposes. One was to undermine and destabilize the peace process in Northern Ireland. This included that the attacks were completed for the purpose of provoking the IRA to retaliate. Any act of retaliation would then anger the Protestant population of Northern Ireland, potentially influencing people to reject the peace process. At the same time, any act of retaliation would raise questions about the IRA's commitment to the ceasefire. In turn, this would support the Orange Volunteer's wish for Northern Ireland to remain part of the United Kingdom, rather than to become unified with the Republic of Ireland.

Another purpose of the ongoing attack was to make it difficult for IRA and Sinn Fein members to decommission weapons, as was required as part of the Good Friday Agreement. With IRA members and Sinn Fein members the target of attacks, a need was created for the groups to maintain weapons to defend themselves. This put a strain on the process of decommissioning weapons. The decommissioning of weapons remained a public issue throughout 1999, with the process still not complete by the end of 1999. In the Christmas message given by Northern Ireland secretary Peter Mandelson, he stressed the importance of decommissioning all weapons, called it an essential part of the Good Friday Agreement. The actions of the Orange Volunteers were considered to be part of the reason that the IRA had not decommissioned their weapons earlier. This was considered to be the intention of the Orange Volunteers, with the IRA's failure to decommission weapons creating concerns about the legitimacy of the Good Friday Agreement and the willingness of groups such as the IRA and Sinn Fein to abide by the terms of the agreement.

In June 1999, the Orange Order was again banned from marching down Garvaghy Road in Portadown. *The Guardian* reported that the Orange Volunteers and another Northern Ireland loyalist group known as the Red Hand Defenders, issued a joint statement describing how they would put all service units on standby, warning that the politicians and the religious leaders would suffer the consequences of selling out Northern Ireland. The Orange Volunteers referred to the need for the culture and history of the Protestants to be protected.

In September 2000, the Orange Volunteers issued a ceasefire. They have not since claimed responsibility for any attacks. In 2001, they issued what they called a "back to war" statement, where they claimed that the ceasefire was under review and stated that they may return to war soon. In this statement, they described Sinn Fein and the IRA as winning at the moment, stating that terrorism was being rewarded. They also stated that they did not want to use violence but would do so in defense of democracy. They warned that if they returned to war, their targets would be the tourist industry of Southern Ireland. This included mentioning the possibility of planting a dozen bombs in bins in Dublin. Despite this claim of possibly returning to war, there were no known incidents involving the group between 2001 until 2005.

OTHER PERSPECTIVES

In his book titled *Loyalists: War and Peace in Northern Ireland*, Peter Taylor offers an inside look at the loyalist groups of Northern Ireland.

The book shows that the loyalists believe that they are protecting their country of Ulster. With this perspective, the loyalists consider themselves acting as part of a war against what they consider terrorists groups of the Republic of Ireland, including the IRA, Sinn Fein, and the Provisional IRA. This shows that the loyalists consider their actions as justified political actions, rather than criminal actions. Statements made by the Orange Volunteers where they refer to protecting their country support that this is their perspective. In Peter Taylor's book, the history of Northern Ireland is presented, which shows a long history of conflict between Northern Ireland and groups within the Republic of Ireland. This provides background to the current conflict and helps to explain the perspectives of members of the Orange Volunteers.

Other sources refer to the Orange Volunteers as a threat to peace in Northern Ireland. In an article titled "Loyalist Splinter Threat," BBC News described paramilitary groups, including the Orange Volunteers, as a major threat to lasting peace in Northern Ireland. The article also describes the groups as a threat to loyalist groups maintaining ceasefires and quotes Progressive Unionist Party spokesperson David Ervine stating his concerns that the major aim of the active loyalist groups is to force the Provisional IRA to end their ceasefire. This could lead to loyalist groups within Northern Ireland being forced off their own ceasefires, potentially returning Northern Ireland to a state of violence. This concern is shared by Sir Ronnie Flanagan, chief constable of the RUC. In a BBC News article titled "Loyalists 'Aim to Create Peace Crisis,'" Flanagan described the Orange Volunteers as acting specifically to provoke reactions from other groups as a means of destabilizing the peace process.

SUMMARY

While the actions of the Orange Volunteers strained the peace process, the Good Friday Agreement has continued to be implemented. In October 2001, the IRA began decommissioning their weapons, suggesting that the peace process is moving forward.

The Orange Volunteers have not been known to be active since the spate of incidents in 1998 and 1999. The 2001 statement warning of future attacks was not followed by any known incidents. However, the Orange Volunteers remain on the lists of illegal terrorist organization for the United Kingdom and the United States of America.

SOURCES

Books

Taylor, Peter. *Loyalists: War and Peace in Northern Ireland*. New York: TV Books, 2004.

Tonge, Jonathan. *Northern Ireland: Conflict & Change*. New York: Longman, 2002.

Web sites

BBC News. "Loyalist Splinter Threat." < http://news.bbc.co.uk/hi/english/static/northern_ireland/understanding/themes/loyalist_splinter.stm/ > (accessed October 19, 2005).

BBC News. "Loyalists 'Aim to Create Peace Crisis.'" < http://news.bbc.co.uk/1/hi/events/northern_ireland/latest_news/276539.stm > (accessed October 19, 2005).

Council on Foreign Relations. "Irish Loyalist Paramilitary Groups." < http://cfrterrorism.org/groups/uvf_print.html > (accessed October 19, 2005).

The Guardian. "Ulster Braced for Week of Orange Unrest." < http://www.guardian.co.uk/uk_news/story/0,,339130,00.html > (accessed October 19, 2005).

MIPT Terrorism Knowledge Base. "Terrorist Group Profile: Orange Volunteers (OV)." < http://www.tkb.org/Group.jsp?groupID = 79 > (accessed October 19, 2005).

SEE ALSO

Irish Republican Army

Provisional IRA

The Order

ALTERNATE NAME: Silent Brotherhood (*Bruder Schweigen*)

LEADER: Robert Jay Matthews

YEAR ESTABLISHED OR BECAME ACTIVE: 1982

ESTIMATED SIZE: More than fifty

USUAL AREA OF OPERATION: United States

OVERVIEW

Robert Jay Matthews founded The Order, an ultra-conservative right wing, neo-Nazi, white supremacist, anti-Semitic, racist extremist group in 1982. The group was coalesced as a result of the 1983 meeting of the Aryan Nations Congress: the most violent members of the organizations present at the Congress were recruited to form this group. The mission of The Order was to garner sufficient financial resources to support the revolution planned by the Aryan Nations Congress—in which the American government would be overthrown and a separatist Aryan Nation would be created.

The Order performed its original mission by counterfeiting money and by committing a series of robberies. Between December 1983 and July 1984, The Order's robberies netted the group in excess of $4 million.

The Order was active for a brief period, between 1982 and 1984, but has continued to be lauded by the white supremacist movement more than twenty years later, largely because it was an extremely successful criminal organization.

HISTORY

The Order, or *Bruder Schweigen*, was founded by Robert Jay Matthews, who had been previously active in the John Birch Society and the National

Robert J. Matthews, founder of the neo-Nazi group known as The Order, died when illumination flares ignited a fire on his waterfront cottage following a thirty-five-hour standoff with the FBI in December 1984. AP/Wide World Photos. Reproduced by permission.

Alliance. The National Alliance, a white supremacist group, was founded by William Pierce, a former physics professor and publicist for the American Nazi Party who became famous for authoring a book called *The Turner Diaries*. Pierce's book is a fictional account of a right-wing ultra-conservative group that catalyzes a white supremacist revolution; the group is called The Order.

Matthews was talking to his friend and fellow white supremacist Bruce Pierce (a member of the Christian Identity Aryan Nations group) about *The Turner Diaries* in late 1982 and suggested that they form a radical revolutionary group similar to The Order.

The 1983 meeting of the Aryan Nations Congress further fueled the group, and a number of the most violent members of the organizations present at the Congress were recruited into The Order. The primary mission of The Order was to gather the necessary financial resources to be able to fund the revolution planned by the

Aryan Nations Congress—in which the American government would be overthrown and a separatist Aryan Nation would be created.

Initially, The Order set about securing legal funding for the revolution: they successfully bid on, and contracted for, a large trail-clearing contract—but the group found the intense physical labor both too difficult and too time-consuming. They quickly turned to robbery and counterfeiting in order to acquire financial resources.

In April 1983, the group committed its first criminal act by robbing a porn shop in Spokane and netting $369. They tried counterfeiting next and printed bills at the Aryan Nations' compound. Bruce Pierce was arrested for attempting to pass the bills. Rather than giving up, the group studied the process more carefully and adopted more sophisticated and more successful methods. They continued to hone their robbery skills as well. In December 1983, Robert Jay Matthews used a note in order to rob a

LEADERSHIP

ROBERT JAY MATTHEWS

Robert Jay Matthews was a member of the John Birch Society and a leader of the white supremacist group called the National Alliance before founding The Order in 1982. Prior to being drawn to racist extremist groups, Matthews was an active part of the tax protest movement and had been arrested for tax fraud.

Matthews had been inspired by the racist novel entitled *The Turner Diaries* and had suggested to his friend Bruce Pierce (a member of the Christian Identity white supremacist Aryan Nations) that they found a radical group based on the fictional white supremacist faction that directed the race war in *The Turner Diaries*, called The Order.

Matthews, and those he and others recruited from such white supremacist organizations as the Covenant, Sword, and Arm of the Lord, the Aryan Nations, and the National Alliance, used *The Turner Diaries* as the framework upon which they created and built The Order.

The Order declared war on the U.S. government and created a document stating this as well as its plan to create an all-white homeland within the eventually government-less country.

In December 1984, Robert Jay Matthews was killed in a fire during a gun battle with law enforcement authorities at his cabin. Members of present-day white supremacist organizations consider Matthews a hero and a martyr to their cause.

BRUCE PIERCE

Bruce Carroll Pierce, the friend and fellow white supremacist with whom Robert Jay Matthews founded The Order, is currently serving the longest sentence received by any member of the group: 255 years. In the early days of the organization, his specialty was the creation and dissemination of counterfeit money, for which he was arrested. He successfully jumped bond and remained underground until the FBI arrested the large group. He was also interested in explosives and was involved in the bombing of a synagogue in Boise, Idaho, as well as a Seattle theater. He is credited, by other members of the organization, with the death of Aryan Nations member Walter West. He was convicted of all of these crimes, as well as the murder of Jewish talk radio host Alan Berg.

Citibank branch and walked away with $29, 500. In March 1984, The Order began to hold up armored cars. A Brinks employee who was a white supremacist supporter gave the group some inside information regarding a route, and they held up a Brinks truck in a California redwood forest on July 19, 1984. That robbery was by far their most successful, and they garnered $3.6 million.

In addition to their financial dealings, The Order also engaged in violent terrorist activities. Bruce Pierce bombed a synagogue in Boise, Idaho; the group murdered Order member Walter West on the suspicion that West had been talking to "outsiders" about the group. In June 1984, Bruce Pierce and David Lane assassinated Jewish radio talk show host Alan Berg outside of his home in Denver, Colorado.

Members of The Order had previously phoned in to his talk show and had reportedly gotten into an argument with Berg, who was deemed by listeners (and members of The Order themselves) to have had the upper hand in the debate.

The FBI had the group under surveillance and killed Robert Jay Matthews during an attempted capture on Whidbey Island in Oregon. The group continued; David Tate murdered a state trooper during a routine traffic stop in Arkansas. He was captured at the CSA compound a week later and was sentenced to life in prison.

Throughout most of its active phase, The Order was under FBI surveillance. During a robbery, Robert Jay Matthews dropped the gun that was in his pants; it was traced to Order member Tom Martinez, who opted to become a police informant.

KEY EVENTS

1982: Robert Jay Matthews, inspired by the *Turner Diaries*, asks Bruce Pierce to help him found a white supremacist group based on the book; they decide to call the group The Order.

1983: Aryan Nations Congress recruits members into The Order, and charges them with the mission of acquiring the financial means to fund the impending revolution and overthrow of the American government.

1984: David Lane and Bruce Pierce assassinate Jewish radio talk show host Alan Berg outside of his home in Denver, Colorado.

1984: The Order ambushes a Brinks armored truck and robs it of $3.6 million.

1984: Robert Jay Matthews is killed in a shootout and fire with FBI during his attempted capture.

1984—1988: The Order members are captured, tried, convicted, and imprisoned. Several act as informants for an unsuccessful sedition trial of white supremacists in 1988.

The group was finally intercepted and halted by the FBI while in the final phases of planning to rob an armored car in St. Louis; assassinate the founder of the Southern Poverty Law Center; poison a water reservoir; rob a bank; rob and murder a wealthy homosexual male; execute a person who had publicly denigrated the Aryan Nations; bomb the Simon D. Weisenthal Center; assassinate an African-American radio talk show host; and attack the New York office of the B'nai Brith, among other things.

Twenty-four members of the group were arrested and thirteen of those pled guilty and testified against other members. All were convicted of racketeering, some were convicted of murder. All received lengthy prison sentences, ranging from forty to several hundred

(essentially, life without parole) years. The convictions signaled the effective end of The Order, although several members are still active in prison.

PHILOSOPHY AND TACTICS

The Order was formed for several reasons: first, it was the goal of Robert Jay Matthews to create an ultra-conservative, right-wing, anti-Semitic, white supremacist group that would be capable of either fomenting or assisting in the overthrow of the U.S. government and the establishment of a separatist Aryan Nation within the northwest region of the United States. He had read, and been inspired by, William Pierce's novel, *The Turner Diaries*, so he decided to name his group The Order after the protagonist group in the book. Many of the terrorist acts committed by the group bear a striking similarity to those delineated in the book.

In addition, The Order was catalyzed by the 1983 Aryan Nations Congress, which added significantly to its membership and tasked the group with raising funds for their planned revolution.

The group began by attempting to earn money by fulfilling a trail-clearing contract, but soon found the lengthy and arduous physical labor both exasperating and too difficult—so the group turned to illegal means of money acquisition. One track chosen by the group was the manufacture of counterfeit money, which was carried out at the Aryan Nations' compound. Initial efforts were met with little success, and Bruce Pierce was arrested for trying to pass the poorly made bills. Over time, however, the operation became much more sophisticated and was fairly successful. In addition, the group engaged in bank and armored car robberies. This was quite a triumphant endeavor, and The Order garnered more than $4 million in total. Much of the largesse (several hundred thousand dollars) was shared among various white supremacist and anti-Semitic groups across the United States and, more than thirty years later, $2 million of the stolen money remains unaccounted for.

The group also killed a number of individuals who were either deemed enemies or opponents to the white supremacist cause. Among the most notable was the Jewish radio talk show host Alan Berg, who was gunned down outside his home in Denver, Colorado, as a result of engaging in an on-air verbal sparring match with members of The Order who had called in to his show.

When twenty-four members of the group were arrested, they were reported to be in the final stages of planning to carry out a number of robberies and terrorist acts.

OTHER PERSPECTIVES

The Anti-Defamation League says the following about the founder of The Order: "We think that Robert Jay Matthews was a criminal of the worst kind. Not only was he guilty of bank and armored car robberies as well as complicity in murder, he was guilty of attempting to overthrow our government and building a paramilitary organization to that end. As to the reverence with which others of his ilk embrace him, we simply consider the source and watch them carefully."

Citizens Against Hate, in a review of the membership and actions of The Order, stated "... when the essence of being human becomes threatened within the person it becomes imperative to justify ones actions if only to oneself, and to legitimize ones very existence. Thus, the crisis of race extinction and the fantasy of a racial holy war thereby rendering them both necessary and just in their own minds ... No man convicted of such abhorrent behaviors as those evidenced by the members of The Order should ever be allowed to recruit or to indoctrinate others within our society."

SUMMARY

The Order, a white supremacist, ultra conservative, right-wing, anti-Semitic extremist group was active for a brief moment, historically speaking—the founding member, Robert Jay Matthews, has been dead for more than twenty years, and most of the group lives in the penal system and will do so for the rest of their lives. That being said, The Order continues to have a profound impact on the white supremacist movement in the United States. Matthews is lauded as a hero and a martyr, and the incarcerated members of the group are referred to by other racial extremists as "P.O.W.s (prisoners of war)." They have continued to write and publish separatist and anti-Semitic rhetoric under the guise of the *14 Words Press*.

SOURCES

Web sites

Anti-Defamation League Law Enforcement Agency Resource Network. "Hate Symbols: The Order." < http://www.adl.org/hate_symbols/groups_order.-asp > (accessed October 5, 2005).

Anti-Defamation League. "The Order and Phineas Priesthood." < http://www.adl.org/backgrounders/an_phineas.asp > (accessed October 5, 2005).

Eye on Hate, Seeking a Kinder and Gentler World. "Martyrs, Heroes, & Prisoners of War: The Order." < http://eyeonhate.com/pows/pows2.html > (accessed October 5, 2005).

Eye on Hate, Seeking a Kinder and Gentler World. "Martyrs, Heroes, & Prisoners of War: The Order." < http://eyeonhate.com/pows/pows3.html > (accessed October 5, 2005).

Eye on Hate, Seeking a Kinder and Gentler World. "Martyrs, Heroes, & Prisoners of War: The Order." < http://eyeonhate.com/pows/pows4.html > (accessed October 5, 2005).

MILNET Domestic Terrorist Group Profiles. "The Order." < http://www.milnet.com/domestic/data/order.htm > (accessed October 5, 2005).

SEE ALSO

Aryan Nations

Covenant, The

National Alliance

Palestine Islamic Jihad (PIJ)

OVERVIEW

Harakat al-Jihad al-Islami fi-Filastini, better known as the Palestinian Islamic Jihad (PIJ) or Palestinian Islamic Jihad-Shaqaqi/Shiqaqi faction, is a militant Palestinian group, headquartered in Damascus, Syria. It calls upon the doctrine of *jihad* (a term interpreted by Islamist extremists as a holy war against those who do not believe in Islamist fundamentalism) in its efforts towards destroying Israel. PIJ is also referred to as the Islamic Jihad Movement in Palestine, or the Islamic Jihad. The Palestinian Islamic Jihad allegedly carries out various targeted acts of violence against Israeli people and aims at disrupting communal harmony in Israel. The fundamentals of the jihad movement in Egypt form the basis of the PIJ ideology. Analysts opposing the PIJ state that the group believes in complete violence and the only goal of its members is to create an Islamic Palestinian state.

PIJ propagates its ideology through violence and opposes the peace processes between Israel and Palestine. Unlike other Palestinian resistance groups, such as the Democratic Front for the Liberation of Palestine (DFLP), HAMAS, and Hezbollah that also focus on social and educational reforms, PIJ's mission reportedly is extreme violence and absolute acceptance of Islam, along with total termination of the state of Israel and its inhabitants. PIJ considers the United States as its enemy, allegedly due to the

LEADERS: Fathi Abd al-Aziz Shaqaqi; Dr. Ramadan Abdullah al-Shallah

YEAR ESTABLISHED OR BECAME ACTIVE: 1979

USUAL AREA OF OPERATION: Israel, the West Bank, and Gaza Strip

A Palestinian member of Islamic Jihad holds up a Koran in one hand and a grenade in the other as a crowd looks on during an Islamic Jihad rally in Gaza City on February 21, 2003. AP/Wide World Photos. Reproduced by permission.

friendly relations between Israel and the United States.

HISTORY

The Palestinian Islamic Jihad claims to be formed in 1979 by a group of Palestinian Islamic students who were previously part of the Palestinian Muslim Brotherhood in the Gaza Strip. These extremist individuals, Fathi Abd al-Aziz Shaqaqi, Sheikh Abd al-Aziz Odeh, and Bashir Musa, were of the opinion that the Brotherhood had become too lenient and had neglected the cause of Palestine. They decided to form their own organization with radical ideology of removing Israel and establishing the Islamic state of Palestine.

These radicals were reportedly also closely associated with the terrorist organization of Islamic students in Egypt that had allegedly murdered the Egyptian President in 1981. Following the furor, the radicals escaped Egypt and settled in the Gaza Strip, where they commenced their terrorist operations. The PIJ is allegedly responsible for various terrorist activities during the 1980s. Eventually, in the late 1980s, two of PIJ's prominent members, Shaqaqi and Odeh were sent to exile in Lebanon. However, analysts argue that the organization became stronger and more politically influential during this period.

Reports suggest that the Israeli-Palestinian Oslo Agreement signed by Yasser Arafat (chairman of the Palestine Liberation Organization) was a disappointment for PIJ, and subsequently they instigated targeted acts of violence meant to disrupt the peace and communal harmony in the region during the mid 1990s. Eventually, Shaqaqi was assassinated in 1995 on Malta, allegedly by the Israeli intelligence agency Mossad. Ramadan Abdullah al-Shallah took over the leadership of PIJ following Shaqaqi's death.

A Palestinian Islamic Jihad militant raises a rocket-propelled grenade in Gaza City on July 23, 2004, during the funeral processions of Islamic Jihad militants Hazem Rahim, a local Islamic Jihad commander, and Abdulraof Abu Asse. AP/Wide World Photos. Reproduced by permission.

The PIJ is thought to be responsible for several instances of suicide bombings, killing innocent civilians as well as members of the military in Israel. It fervently opposes all talks of peace and uses underhanded tactics in derailing peace processes initiated by either Israel or Palestine. The PIJ also does not accept the authority of the Palestinian government, which experts and monitor groups argue became evident when it did not participate in the 1996 elections (and thereafter). The government has since reportedly arrested several lower-ranked members of the PIJ.

It is thought by Western and Israeli intelligence officials that the Palestinian Islamic Jihad, though a small movement, is garnering popularity as an ever-increasing number of Palestinians have started to consider that jihad is their only way to attain Islamic supremacy. According to published U.S. State Department reports, as of 2005, PIJ has a number of splinter groups such as Islamic Jihad Squad, Islamic

Jihad Temple, Islamic Jihad- al-Aqsa Battalions, and al-Quds Brigades.

PHILOSOPHY AND TACTICS

The PIJ is thought to be influenced by the Shi'ite Islamic revolution in Iran and has vehemently opposed the Arab regime. Members and leaders of the group claim that Islamic unity would be achieved only after the dissolution of Israel and the establishment of Islamic Palestine.

The ideology of the PIJ is reportedly derived from three main sources: the Islamic revolution in Iran, the jihad movement in Egypt, and the staunch belief in militant Islamic supremacy. PIJ followers claim that Quran (the holy book of Islam) advocates that Palestine is the core of constant battle between the Muslims and Jews. The group aims at making Palestine a launch pad for expanding the rule of Islam globally.

LEADERSHIP

FATHI ABD AL-AZIZ SHAQAQI

After completing his bachelor's degree (mathematics major) at West Bank in the late 1960s, Shaqaqi went on to study medicine in Egypt. During this period, he allegedly became involved in the Muslim Brotherhood that was operating in Egypt. However, he left the organization in 1974, owing to ideological differences.

The Iranian revolution led by Ayatollah Khomeini (religious leader of Iran) is thought to have influenced the beliefs of Shaqaqi to a great extent. Later on, he publicly started propagating Khomeini's principles. The Egyptian authorities arrested Shaqaqi for publishing a radical pamphlet praising Khomeini's stance. Shaqaqi eventually returned to Gaza in the early 1980s, where he reportedly formed the Palestinian Islamic Jihad organization. Subsequently, Shaqaqi was exiled to Lebanon. Egyptian and Israeli intelligence officials assert that during his stay there, he worked toward strengthening the organization by bringing in influential members and associating the organization with other terrorist outfits.

RAMADAN ABDULLAH AL-SHALLAH

Dr. Ramadan Abdullah al-Shallah, one of the prominent members of PIJ, and a close aide of Shaqaqi, took over leadership responsibilities after Shaqaqi's death. As a student, he met Shaqaqi and fellow Islamic extremists in Egypt. Upon his return to Gaza Strip, he became a speaker at the Islamic University at Gaza. He went on to England to pursue his doctorate degree in Islamic Economics. Simultaneously, he was also allegedly responsible for handling various overseas operations of the PIJ. In the early 1990s, he moved to the United States, where he taught at the University of South Florida in Tampa. He also served as the executive director of the World and Islam Studies Enterprise (WISE), an organization thought by Western intelligence to be closely associated with the PIJ.

Members of the PIJ reportedly assert that jihad is the only way through which Palestine can be liberated. According to the group, all acts of violence committed in the name of jihad are validated and supported by their Holy Scriptures and religious leaders.

The PIJ group leaders are thought to have tremendous respect for Ayatollah Khomeini, a key operative in the Iranian revolution. In spite of following the Sunni sect, they have accepted the Shi'ite beliefs of Iranian revolution, as a model for their jihad. (Sunni and Shi'ite are two distinct sects of Islam that considerably differ in ideology.) Analysts argue that the PIJ's philosophy has always been to follow the principle that "the men of religion shall lead"—originally a Shi'ite concept. In fact, while a student in Egypt, Shaqaqi authored a controversial book praising the efforts of Khomeini. The book was subsequently banned by the Egyptian authorities because of its volatile nature. Those opposing the group state that the PIJ believes in advocating Islamic rule by religious leaders so strongly that it has also allegedly conducted targeted acts of violence against the Arab authorities of Jordan, Lebanon, and Egypt.

During the period of its leaders' exile in Lebanon, the group reportedly intensified its association with other terrorist organizations, including HAMAS and Hezbollah. Although PIJ had a history of rivalry with HAMAS, the common militant Islamic beliefs and the Middle East peace processes brought them together. Eventually, the group also became a prominent member of the Rejection Front (a faction of the Palestine Liberation Organization) and allegedly carried out aggressive acts of terrorism against Israel. Following the 1993 Oslo Peace Agreement between Israel and Palestine that was opposed by various terrorist organizations in Palestine, including PIJ, there were several incidents of suicide bombings all over Israel. Many of these thought to be orchestrated by the PIJ.

KEY EVENTS

1988: Islamic Jihad Movement leaders Shaqaqi and Abd al-Aziz Odeh exiled to Lebanon.

1995: Israeli authorities claim PIJ is responsible for Beit Lid junction bombing that killed 20 soldiers and one civilian.

1995: Shaqaqi assassinated in Malta, allegedly by Mossad agents. Dr. Ramadan Abdallah Shallah becomes the new PIJ chief.

2002: Members of PIJ are the reported masterminds behind the suicide bombing at Megiddo Junction, Israel, that kills seventeen people and injures more than thirty-five.

2003: PIJ reportedly organizes a suicide bombing in Maxim restaurant, Haifa, Israel, killing twenty-one people and injuring sixty.

2005: Israeli authorities claim that PIJ is responsible for various instances of suicide bombings at public places in Jerusalem, Netanya, West Bank, and Tel Aviv, including the suicide bombing outside Hasharon Mall in Netanya, which leaves three dead and more than ninety injured.

Influenced by the terrorism tactics used by HAMAS and Hezbollah, the PIJ has also used suicide and car bombings extensively to spread terror. Shoot-outs and assassinating Israeli civilians and military personnel are other tactics reportedly employed by the group. Experts assert that the philosophy of the PIJ is depicted in the emblem of the PIJ. The emblem displays the full map of Palestine in red, allegedly to portray its prominence and to reestablish their belief that Israel should be replaced by Palestine. The controversial Al-Aqsa mosque in Jerusalem is displayed above the Palestine map. A pair of fists and two crossed rifles, along with the inscription "Allah is the Greatest," also forms a part of the emblem.

PIJ receives its funding from various sources. Western and Israeli intelligence authorities claim that the biggest financial backing for terrorist activities carried out by the PIJ comes from the government of Iran. The group is also affiliated with several Islamic jihad groups—these, allegedly, also provide funding.

The PIJ is a relatively smaller organization with lower political influence as compared with HAMAS or Hezbollah. According to many published reports, the primary places for recruiting new members and supporters for this group are religious schools, mosques, and universities. Like many other terrorist organizations, the PIJ often recruits very young Islamic students and inducts in them their Islamic militant ideology. Consequently, as thought by intelligence officials, most of these end up joining the PIJ in their war against Israel and other countries, especially the United States. Although, the PIJ has never directly attacked the United States, it has often threatened to attack the U.S. Embassy in Israel, whenever there are indications of shifting the embassy from Tel Aviv to Jerusalem. The group is reported to have bases in Lebanon, Syria, and some Palestinian territories. The PIJ has refused to get involved in Palestinian legislative elections since 1996. However, experts argue that the group does not endorse shunning the elections and is open to its members participating in them.

The death of Shaqaqi and the repercussion of September 11 attacks in the United States have acted as a set back in the organization's activities. Also, according to monitor groups, the new group leader, Ramadan Shallah, is not as dynamic and resourceful as Shaqaqi and has not been able to garner as much support as his predecessor.

OTHER PERSPECTIVES

"True peace means Israel does not exist." These were the strong words of Fathi Al-Shaqaqi, founder and former secretary-general of the Islamic Jihad Movement in Palestine. Other leaders have always endorsed this belief, even when there were signs that other extremist organizations were reportedly softening their approach.

After HAMAS declared that it would stop using suicide bombings against Israel, Abu Imad Al Rifai, a representative of the PIJ refused to succumb to the pressure and insisted that the PIJ continue using suicide bombings in its war against Israel. Al Rifai, in an interview, told *Reuters* that, "Our position is to continue. We have no other choice. We are not willing to compromise."

PRIMARY SOURCE

Palestinian Islamic Jihad (PIJ) a.k.a. Islamic Jihad of Palestine, Al-Quds Brigades

DESCRIPTION

Formed by militant Palestinians in the Gaza Strip during the 1970s, the Palestinian Islamic Jihad (PIJ) is committed to the creation of an Islamic Palestinian state and the destruction of Israel through attacks against Israeli military and civilian targets inside Israel and the Palestinian territories.

ACTIVITIES

PIJ militants have conducted many attacks, including large-scale suicide bombings, against Israeli civilian and military targets. The group maintained operational activity in 2004, claiming numerous attacks against Israeli interests. PIJ has not yet directly targeted US interests; it continues to direct attacks against Israelis inside Israel and the territories, although US citizens have died in attacks mounted by the PIJ.

STRENGTH

Unknown.

LOCATION/AREA OF OPERATION

Primarily Israel, the West Bank, and the Gaza Strip. The group's primary leadership resides in Syria, though other leadership elements reside in Lebanon, as well as other parts of the Middle East.

EXTERNAL AID

Receives financial assistance from Iran and limited logistical assistance from Syria.

Source: U.S. Department of State. *Country Reports on Terrorism.* Washington, D.C., 2004.

Most of the countries in the world have condemned the tactics employed by the PIJ. In the aftermath of the September 11 attacks, President Bush, while issuing a strong warning against all countries harboring terrorism, explicitly called upon Syria to "choose the right side in the war on terror by closing terrorist camps and expelling terrorist organizations;" it was concluded by experts that he was referring to the Palestinian Islamic Jihad, as it is the most prominent terrorist group operating out of Syria. At the Rose Garden speech (in June 2002) in which President Bush called for a new Palestinian leadership, he mentioned that, "Every nation actually committed to peace will stop the flow of money, equipment and recruits to terrorist groups seeking the destruction of Israel—including Hamas, Islamic Jihad [PIJ], and Hezbollah."

provides operation support and facilitates terrorist activities, and Iran provides financial backing. The PIJ continues with suicide bombings and car bomb blasts at public places aimed at disrupting the peace proceedings in the Middle East. In the past, the PIJ has reportedly tried to end the ceasefire agreement between Israel and Palestine, and has continuously called upon Islamic extremists to support their mission of eradicating Israel. Israeli intelligence officials state that consistent attacks on Israeli targets have demonstrated efforts by the PIJ followers to enhance their significance among other Palestinian Islamic Extremist organizations.

Palestinian Islamic Jihad has carried out numerous activities using adult men, women, and even teens as suicide bombers. Most of these attacks are targeted at the general public.

SUMMARY

The Palestinian Islamic Jihad organization is allegedly dependent primarily on three countries to execute its operations. Damascus in Syria houses the headquarters of the outfit, Lebanon

SOURCES

Periodicals

Barsky, Yehudit. "Terrorism Briefing Islamic Jihad Movement in Palestine." *American Jewish Committee.* July 18, 2002.

Web sites

Center for Defense Information. "Palestine Islamic Jihad." < http://www.cdi.org/program/document.cfm/ > (accessed October 20, 2005).

Intelligence and Terrorism Information Center at the Center for Special Studies (C.S.S). "Profile of the Palestinian Islamic Jihad, Perpetrator of a Suicide Bombing Attack in Tel Aviv, February 25, 2005." < http://www.intelligence. org.il/eng/sib/3_05/pji.htm > (accessed October 20, 2005).

MIPT Terrorism Knowledge Base. "Palestinian Islamic Jihad." < http://www.tkb.org/Group.jsp?groupID = 82 > (accessed October 20, 2005).

Office of the Press Secretary, The White House. "President Bush Calls for New Palestinian Leadership." < http://www.whitehouse.gov/news/releases/2002/06/ 20020624-3.html > (accessed October 20, 2005).

SEE ALSO

HAMAS

Hezbollah

Palestine Liberation Organization (PLO)

LEADER: Mahmoud Abbas

USUAL AREA OF OPERATION: Israeli-occupied
    territories

OVERVIEW

The Palestine Liberation Organization (PLO) is
the representative body of the Palestinian people.
It comprises an umbrella group of various
Palestinian organizations, many of which have
paramilitary connections, that makes up the
689-member Palestinian National Council,
although most political power rests with the
fifteen-man PLO Executive. The PLO also holds
permanent observer status at the UN General
Assembly. Despite its status as a political organization, the PLO's critics, particularly Israel,
say that this is nominal and they have accused it
of carrying out a vast number of terrorist and
extremist acts.

HISTORY

The PLO was founded at a Palestinian Congress
held in East Jerusalem (then under Jordanian
control) in May 1964. It marked the culmination
of several years of efforts to create a formal representative body for the Palestinian Diaspora, refugees, and Israeli-Arabs by Ahmad al-Shuqeiri,
representative of the Palestinian Arabs in the
Arab League, and the Egyptian President, Gamal
Abdul Nasser. In 1959, Nasser had suggested the
creation of a "Palestinian Entity" to further the
cause of the Palestinian people internationally
but also to advance his own interests within

A 1995 Jericho mural depicts Yasser Arafat bursting out of the ground and pulling apart a barbed wire fence to liberate his people. © Abbas / Magnum Photos

inter-Arab politics and to maintain a decisive say across Egypt's northeastern border. At the Arab Summit in January 1964, Nasser had further argued the case for this Palestinian Entity and talked a reluctant King Hussein of Jordan around to the creation of what would, four months later, become the PLO. This comprised the Palestinian National Council, a kind of Palestinian Parliament, topped by an Executive Committee, that would, in practice, hold much of the power.

The PLO's first Executive Committee was formed on August 9, with Ahmad al-Shuqeiri nominated chairman. At the second Arab Summit in September 1964, it established what was intended as a regular army—the Palestine Liberation Army (PLA)—to fall under PLO control, although in practice its units (comprised of Palestinian battalions already set up by the Egyptian, Syrian, Jordanian, and Iraqi regimes) would remain under the control of their host nations. The only PLA force that ever came under PLO command was the Ein Jalut Brigade, which participated in the Yom Kippur War and later served in the Lebanese Civil War until the evacuation of Palestinians from Beirut in September 1982. (The Syrian brigades were also used in the same conflict, though for Syria's purposes and under Damascus' orders).

The early life of the PLO was dogged by accusations that al-Shuqeri was merely a Nasserite puppet and that the organization was an extension of Egyptian foreign policy. The catastrophic Six Day War of 1967 and the growing number of guerilla attacks carried out by increasingly popular groups such as Yasser Arafat's Fatah Revolutionary Council, quickly shook away these vestiges of complacency. The Battle of Karameh, of March 1968, when Fatah destroyed the myth of Israeli invincibility by reaping a limited victory after an Israel Defense Force (IDF) border raid, gave Arafat an inexorable momentum. That July, at the Fourth Session of the Palestine National Council (PNC) in Cairo, Fatah joined the PLO along with several other militant groups, whose leaders were elected to key positions within the organization. Arafat became the

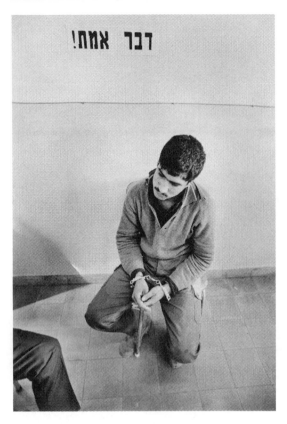

A convicted Palestinian terrorist awaits an interview with the press in 1969 as he squats in Bet Dagan Police Station's "interrogation room." The text on the wall behind him reads "Speak the truth." © *Micha Bar Am | Magnum Photos*

PLO's spokesman and was elected chairman the following February.

The Fourth Session of the PNC transformed the PLO from the talking shop, political sop envisaged and encouraged by Nasser, to a radical umbrella organization for various Palestinian interests, be they the guerilla groups—that now formed its core—civilians, or the large-scale Palestinian Diaspora. Fatah dominated the new movement, a factor that brought it into conflict with the likes of George Habash's Popular Front For The Liberation of Palestine (PFLP), which were unwilling to accept the political discipline demanded by Arafat. The PLO also claimed to speak as the sole representative of the Palestinian people, centering attention on Arafat, which quickly made him one of the most famous men on earth—a completely unparalleled position for a guerilla leader still to carry out his "revolution."

The essence of what the newly radicalized PLO stood for was encompassed in its charter, to which it had made sweeping changes at the Fourth Session of the NPC. When it had been constituted four years earlier, the charter had included clauses denying PLO sovereignty over parts of Palestine occupied by Jordan and Egypt and been circumscribed by the demands of other Arab states. These were ripped up and replaced by clear demands that the "Palestinian Arab people [Arab citizens living permanently in Palestine until 1947 and their descendents; also Jews living permanently in Palestine until the invasion were 'considered Palestinians'] possess the right to a homeland." It declared "the claim of a historical or spiritual tie between Jews and Palestine" to be "null and void" and that "Judaism . . . is not a nationality . . . the Jews are not one people."

It also contained a call to arms: "The liberation of Palestine . . . is a national duty to repulse the Zionist, imperialist invasion . . . and to purge the Zionist presence from Palestine . . . The Palestinian people . . . through the armed Palestinian revolution, reject any solution that would be a substitute for the complete liberation of Palestine . . . Armed struggle [defined as 'a strategy not a tactic'] is the only way to liberate Palestine . . . [guerilla] action forms the nucleus of the popular Palestinian War of Liberation."

The revised charter attracted much criticism in the West, particularly Israel, for its extreme language and was usually referred back to as evidence of PLO complicity whenever one of the growing number of Palestinian international terror attacks were carried out.

This was one of the principal problems facing the PLO. Despite Arafat's calls for moderation and his attempts to rein in the extremists, the PLO would be repeatedly singled out by Israel for responsibility whenever there was a hijacking or shooting by one of its member groups. According to the Israeli government, as self-appointed representatives of the Palestinian people, the PLO bore responsibility for whatever excess were carried out in the name of Palestinian liberation. Indeed, for many years, the Israelis would make no distinction between the PLO, groups within it, or even groups—like the PFLP—opposed to it. It was a situation akin to blaming the Arab League in it entirety for an act carried out by just one of its member states. This did much to discredit the PLO in the eyes of a world usually unable to distinguish

LEADERSHIP

KEY EVENTS

MAHMOUD ABBAS (OR ABU MAZEN)

Dr. Mahmoud Abbas (or Abu Mazen) became leader of the PLO on November 11, 2004, following the death of Yasser Arafat. One of the founding members of Fatah in 1957, he had accompanied Arafat for the majority of his five-decade-long political career, through exile in Jordan, Lebanon, Tunisia, and finally back in the occupied territories in the 1990s.

For most of this time, he was known more as a backroom operator than political ideologue and has been credited with engaging in secret talks with Israeli "doves" in the late 1980s, discussions that directly led to the peace agreements of the early 1990s. He was also instrumental in repairing damage done in the PLO's relationship with Gulf States, after it had backed Iraq in the first Gulf War.

As Arafat's credibility crumbled during the al-Aqsa intifada, both Israel and the United States refused to deal with him, forcing him to appoint Abbas as Prime Minister in March 2003. He resigned six months later after Arafat repeatedly undermined his position.

As the preeminent Fatah politician (the other candidate, Marwan Barghouti, was in an Israeli jail) following Arafat's death, Abbas was the natural candidate to take over as Chairman of the PLO and followed this up with election as President of the Palestinian Authority the following January. This was greeted with renewed optimism that the peace process would resume, and even the Israeli Prime Minister, Ariel Sharon, called Abbas to congratulate "him on his personal achievement and his victory in the elections and [to] wish him luck."

---

between rival Palestinian factions and discredited Arafat's attempts to be seen as a legitimate political leader. The reality was, however, that the PLO itself had no specific means to carry out military raids, despite Arafat's Fatah movement frequently being identified with them.

1964: PLO formed in Jerusalem.

1968: Fourth Congress of the PNC: PLO Charter rewritten; militants elected to key positions.

1969: Yasser Arafat elected chairman of the PLO.

1973: Arab Summit recognizes PLO as "legitimate" representative of the Palestinian people.

1976–1982: PLO involvement in Lebanese Civil War; this eventually prompts a full-scale Israeli invasion and PLO exile into Tunisia.

1988: Arafat renounces terrorism.

1991: Madrid Talks.

1993: Oslo Peace Agreement between PLO and Israel.

1994: Formation of Palestinian Authority.

2000–2005: Al-Aqsa intifada.

2004: Death of Arafat and accession of Mahmoud Abbas.

The Arab Summit of November 1973 recognized the PLO as "legitimate" representatives of the Palestinian people. Subsequently, at the twelfth PNC session in Cairo in June 1974, the PLO moderated some of its demands and accepted the strategy of building a Palestinian state in stages. With hindsight, this acknowledgement can be seen as the first step towards the creation of the modern Palestinian Authority in Gaza and the West Bank.

The PLO also received generous funding from other Arab states (the Israelis claimed that this was diverted into the bank accounts of militant groups) with which they set up the apparatus of a government in exile, and social, health, and educational institutions in the refugee camps. In November 1974, Yasser Arafat's appearance before the UN—the first representative of a liberation movement and not a

---

During the second session of the 107th Congress House, in 2002, Resolution 4693 (H.R. 4693) was sponsored or cosponsored by eighty representatives and resulted in nothing more than subcommittee hearings. The bill was designed to "hold accountable" the Palestine Liberation Organization and the Palestinian Authority, and for other purposes.

SECTION 1. SHORT TITLE.

This Act may be cited as the 'Arafat Accountability Act".

SEC. 2. FINDINGS.

Congress makes the following findings:

(1) The Palestine Liberation Organization (PLO), under the leadership of Chairman Yasser Arafat, has failed to abide by its promises, enumerated in the Oslo Accords, to commit itself to "a peaceful resolution of the conflict between the two sides', that "all outstanding issues relating to permanent status will be resolved through negotiations', and that the PLO "renounces the use of terrorism and other acts of violence and will assume responsibility over all PLO elements and personnel in order to assure their compliance, prevent violence, and discipline violators".

(2) Yasser Arafat failed to exercise his authority and responsibility to maintain law and order in the West Bank and Gaza, which has resulted in ongoing acts of terrorism against Israeli and American civilians in the State of Israel.

(3) Yasser Arafat has failed, through words and deeds, to offer credible security guarantees to the Palestinian and Israeli peoples, and has once again violated his commitment to peace through the recent purchase of 50 tons of offensive weaponry from Iran.

(4) Yasser Arafat and the forces directly under his control are responsible for the murder of hundreds of innocent Israelis and the wounding of thousands more since October 2000.

(5) Yasser Arafat has been directly implicated in funding and supporting terrorists who

government to do so—and the PLO's subsequent invitation to join the UN as an "observer" gave the PLO an additional vestige of political credibility.

The confusion about PLO's identity—was it an extremist organization or a political force?—grew with the onset of the Lebanese Civil War in 1975. After King Hussein had removed the Palestinians from Jordan in 1970, groups under its umbrella had regrouped in Lebanon, particularly in the south and in parts of Beirut. This led to accusations that Arafat had effectively formed a "state within a state." Maronite Christian militias massacred twenty-seven Palestinians on a bus in April 1975, and reprisal killings bubbled over into all-out civil war.

The subsequent fifteen-year-long conflict became muddled by the input of external forces, but what of the PLO's role? Certainly, there was collusion between individual Palestinian

guerilla groups acting under the umbrella of the PLO; the PLA also fought in the conflict. However, Israeli and Maronite forces accused the PLO of virtually every attack carried out by Palestinians—accusations that betrayed the actual capability of the PLO. Moreover, many Palestinian groups, such as the PFLP-GC, were fighting not under PLO orders, but those of external powers, such as Syria or Iran. At several stages within the conflict, anti-Arafat Palestinians even turned on PLO forces.

On most occasions, Israeli reprisals or attacks were far in excess of what the PLO could muster. For instance, in July 1981, Israeli artillery bombarded the West Beirut suburb where Fatah's headquarters were based, killing 200 and wounding 600, most of whom were civilians. Arafat then ordered rocket attacks on northern Israel. This killed six people and wounded fifty-nine. In 1996, the World

have claimed responsibility for homicide bombings in Israel.

Under the present circumstances, Yasser Arafat's failure to adequately respond to end the homicide bombings further complicates the prospects for a resolution of the conflict in that region.

SEC. 3. STATEMENT OF CONGRESS.

(a) SENSE OF CONGRESS- It is the sense of the Congress that—

(1) the United States should continue to urge an immediate and unconditional cessation of all terrorist activities and the commencement of a cease-fire between Israel and the Palestinians;

(2) the Palestine Liberation Organization and the Palestinian Authority should immediately surrender to Israel for detention and prosecution those Palestinian extremists wanted by the Government of Israel for the assassination of Israeli Minister of Tourism Rehavam Zeevi; and

(3) PLO Chairman Yasser Arafat and the Palestine Liberation Organization must take immediate and concrete action to—

(A) publicly condemn all acts of terrorism, including and especially homicide bombings, which murdered over 125 Israeli men, women, and children during the month of March 2002 alone, and injured hundreds more;

(B) confiscate and destroy the infrastructures of terrorism, including weapons, bomb factories, and other offensive materials;

(C) end all financial support for terrorism; and

(D) urge all Arab nations and individuals to immediately cease funding for terrorist operations and payments to the families of terrorists.

SUPPORT FOR PEACE EFFORTS - The Congress supports the President's efforts, in conjunction with Israel, the Arab states, and members of the international community, to achieve a comprehensive peace in the region, and encourages continued efforts by all parties.

Source: H.R. 4693 U.S. Congress *Congressional Record* Washington, D.C., 2002.

Maronite Union accused the PLO of genocide and the deaths of 100,000 Lebanese civilians, entirely spurious claims that exaggerated the PLO's role in the civil war beyond recognition (the U.S. State Department puts the number of dead for the "entire" conflict at 100,000).

In June 1982, Israel accused the PLO of attempting to murder its London ambassador, Shlomo Argov, and used it as a pretext to launch a full-scale invasion of Lebanon. The accusation was entirely false; it was actually the PLO's avowed enemy, Abu Nidal, who had been responsible for the attempt. In the ensuing conflict, approximately 17,000 people died, including 2,000 Palestinian refugees at the refugee camps of Sabra and Shatila. Within months, Israel fulfilled its intention of driving the PLO out when a peace deal saw 15,000 PLO members leave Lebanon into exile, mostly to Tunisia.

Despite being demonized by Israel, Arafat continued to preach—if not always practice—moderation among the PLO. His case had weakened following Israel's peace deal with Egypt in 1978, which removed one of the PLO's more moderate backers and allowed countries like Iraq, Libya, and Syria to exert a greater influence on the more radical elements within the PLO. Likewise, the Lebanese experience had had a negative impact on the PLO and physically removed the organization to the fringes.

Arafat was not averse to launching terrorist raids, however. He had his own personal guard as Fatah leader, Force 17, which began launching seaborne attacks against Israeli targets in 1985. After it killed three Israeli civilians aboard a yacht in Cyprus in September, Israeli Prime Minister Yitzhak Rabin ordered a bombing raid on the PLO headquarters in Tunisia, killing fifty-six Palestinians and fifteen Tunisians. Israel's difficulty in recognizing the difference between the PLO and one of its member groups (even if it did share the same leader) was never more apparent.

But the slow path to peace picked up again when, in December 1988, Arafat publicly renounced terrorism. Talks with Israel opened at Madrid in 1991, but were tentative; more progress was made at secret talks staged in Oslo in 1993, which resulted in a Declaration of Principles (DOP) between Israel and the PLO. The PLO reaffirmed its commitment to the peace process, and Israel and the United States formally recognized it as the legal representative of the Palestinian people. In 1994, Palestinians, including Arafat, began returning from exile into the occupied territories, and in 1995, the Palestinian Authority (PA) was formed. However, Arafat was poor at day-to-day government and administration, but also stubbornly unwilling to delegate. Life in the PA quickly deteriorated.

Arguably, this was not helped by the Israeli government, which—despite recognizing the PLO as a partner for peace—continued to list it as a "terrorist organization."

Nevertheless, when the peace process ground to a halt in 2000 and the al-Aqsa *intifada* (uprising) broke out, there was less of a readiness to tar the PLO with the crimes of some of its constituent members. Even if Yasser Arafat was again singled out for culpability, that was more in relation to the activities of various Fatah offshoots and the failings of his government, than the suggestion that the PLO was operating as a homogenous terrorist organization.

PHILOSOPHY AND TACTICS

The PLO is an umbrella organization comprising a number of Palestinian liberation organizations that are committed to the creation of a Palestinian homeland. In the pre-Oslo Accords era, it served to bring attention to the plight of the Palestinian people and to serve as a kind of government-in-exile. Since the creation of the Palestinian Authority in 1995, many of these functions have been duplicated between the two bodies. It publicly renounced violence in 1988, although the involvement of organizations that

still use extremism mean that this commitment is often treated with skepticism.

It does not propagate any sort of political philosophy, although it is a secular organization. It nevertheless continues to campaign about political issues relevant to the Palestinian people. According to its Department of Negotiation Affairs, these include the right of return for refugees, either in Palestine or resettlement in a third country; an equitable share of water supply from the Jordan River; full control of its economic borders and policies; compensation for Palestinian property stolen or destroyed by Israel; the removal of Israeli settlements from the occupied territories; and control of East Jerusalem in conformity with the Oslo DOP and international law.

OTHER PERSPECTIVES

Ghada Karmi, assessing the impact of the PLO in the *Guardian* in 2003, believed that its achievements are monumental. She recalled: "In 1969, Israel's prime minister Golda Meir astonished the world with this: 'It was not as if there was a Palestinian people in Palestine and we came and threw them out and took their country away from them,' she said. 'They did not exist.' Such a statement would be unimaginable today, thanks mainly to a tireless Palestinian struggle for recognition and legitimacy. Today's Middle East road map would seem to be an important landmark in this struggle. It establishes some significant benchmarks: it explicitly acknowledges the need for Palestinian statehood and underlines the role of territory as fundamental to a settlement of the conflict.

"It is hard to believe that in the 1960s, the very word 'Palestine' had slipped out of the lexicon. Growing up in England, I remember people thinking I meant 'Pakistan' when I said where I was born. The 1948 exodus, tragic though it was, created a new category—'Arab refugees'—but no one remembered where they came from. It took the PLO's establishment in 1964, an armed campaign against Israel and several terrorist attacks in the 1970s to force the Palestine question on to the international agenda. Political maneuvering thereafter, led by the much disparaged Yasser Arafat, kept it there. The eruption of Palestinian resistance to Israeli occupation in the 1987 intifada forced

Israel to negotiate the Oslo Accords with the PLO. Failed though these were, they helped establish the structures of Palestinian statehood and make it broadly acceptable."

In *Time* magazine, at the outbreak of the al-Aqsa intifada, Tony Karon and Jamil Hamad argued that, while the PLO had been effective negotiators and had succeeded in raising global awareness of the Palestinian problem, the long years in exile had seen it lose the Palestinian street (a term used to denote popular opinon). "Many of those who led the last intifada believe it was their efforts that saved Arafat and the PLO and made the peace process possible, and yet there's widespread resentment in their ranks at being sidelined politically once the exiled leaders arrived home," they argued. "To be sure, it's unlikely that Chairman Arafat's headquarters would have moved from Tunis to the West Bank without the intifada. The PLO's efforts to launch guerrilla warfare against Israel from neighboring Arab states had been singularly unsuccessful. Arafat's headquarters had been in Jordan in the late '60s and Lebanon in the '70s and early '80s, but by 1987 he was billeted in far-off Tunisia with few instruments to pursue his nationalist struggle. Then came the uprising in the West Bank and Gaza. The young men of the territories occupied by Israel in 1967 may have suffered heavy casualties as they hurled stones and gasoline bombs at a well-armed adversary with little patience for their protests, but they also created a political crisis for Israel. It was the intifada more than anything that forced Israel to abandon efforts to foster an alternative leadership in territories under their control, to acknowledge the PLO as the legitimate representative of Palestinian aspirations and to open negotiations."

SUMMARY

Mahmoud Abbas's takeover of the leadership of the PLO and PA in 2004 has done much to restore the diminishing credibility of both organizations. Although closely associated to Yasser Arafat for the majority of his political life, he does not carry the hint of extremism his predecessor—right or wrongly—once did. His acknowledgement of the problems caused by Palestinian violence and readiness to tackle insurgency head on have been welcomed by Israelis, while his steadfast adherence of the PLO's historic principles have won him plaudits among the Palestinian population. Nothing can be foretold with any great accuracy in the uncertainty of the Arab-Israeli conflict, but Abbas has already progressed the cause of the PLO from the state of stagnation in which he inherited it.

SOURCES

Books

Aburish, Said. *Arafat: From Defender to Dictator.* London and New York: Bloomsbury, 1998.

Cleveland, William L. *A History of the Modern Middle East.* New York: Westview, 2000.

Fisk, Robert. *Pity the Nation.* England: Oxford, 2001.

Wallach, Janet. *Arafat: In the Eyes of the Beholder.* Amsterdam: Citadel, 2001.

SEE ALSO

Fatah Revolutionary Council

Popular Front For The Liberation of Palestine (PFLP)

Palestine Liberation Front (PLF)

LEADER: Abu Ahmed Halab Shibli (Omar Shibli)
USUAL AREA OF OPERATION: Lebanon

OVERVIEW

The Palestine Liberation Front (PLF) is a leftist nationalist Palestinian organization dedicated to the creation of a Palestinian homeland. In its four-decade-long history, it has taken the form of many incarnations as a result of splits, mergers, further splits, and reorganization. It has nevertheless undertaken a handful of notorious terrorist attacks, most notably the hijacking of the Italian cruise ship, Achille Lauro, in 1985.

HISTORY

The Palestine Liberation Front (PLF) has seen many guises in its long history. It was originally formed by Ahmad Jibril, a former captain in the Syrian army, in Damascus in 1961. It had the backing of the Syrian government, but besides launching several unsuccessful raids from south Lebanon into northern Israel, remained a minor force. With Syrian support, the PLF merged with two other groups—George Habash's Youth of Revenge (the military wing of the Arab National Movement) and the Lebanese-based Heroes of Return—in 1967 to form the Marxist-Leninist Popular Front for the Liberation of Palestine (PFLP). However, this coalition lasted only months, when Jibril's PLF followers seceded after an argument over Syria's

A Palestinian militant shoots at an armored Israeli aircraft hovering over Gaza. © *Abbas | Magnum Photos*

KEY EVENTS

1961: Formation of the original PLF by Ahmed Jibril.

1967: PLF merges with two other Palestinian militant groups to form Popular Front for the Liberation of Palestine (PFLP), led by George Habash.

1968: Jibril leads his pro-Syrian faction out of the PFLP after disagreements with Habash and forms a new organization, the PLFP-General Command.

1977: Following Syria's "Black June" support of Maronite forces against Palestinian guerillas in the Lebanese Civil War, Abu Abbas leads a faction away to form a new PLF.

1983–1984: PLF splits yet again, this time three ways as members go to Lebanon, Syria, and Tunisia.

1985: Achille Lauro hijacking.

1991: Abu Abbas leaves the PLO to live in semi-retirement in Iraq, he later backs the Oslo Accords.

2004: Abu Abbas dies in U.S. custody.

sponsorship of the organization and formed the Popular Front for the Liberation of Palestine-General Command (PFLP-GC).

Jibril's continued kowtowing to Damascene demands would be a continued theme in the PFLP-GC's history. It carried out a number of attacks in the early 1970s in the name of a socialist-inspired liberation of Palestine, but by the middle of the decade the PFLP-GC was increasingly becoming just an instrument of the Damascus government and carrying out intimidation acts in the interests of Syria rather than the Palestinian people. This culminated in "Black June" of 1976 when Syria invaded Lebanon, which had just broken out into civil war, and supported a Maronite Christian force attacking Palestine guerillas within the country. PFLP-GC gave its unequivocal support to its Syrian hosts.

Following this act of Arab heresy, PLFP-GC split, with Muhammad Zaiden (Abu Abbas)

and Tal'at Ya'akub leading the breakaway faction, which they named the Palestine Liberation Front (PLF). They moved to Lebanon where the PLF fought alongside PLO forces in the incipient civil war. Essentially, it operated as a militia in south Lebanon, carrying out border raids against Israeli targets, also trying to take hostages during its operations. The attacks it carried out, however, such as a mission in April 1981 to capture hostages by crossing the Israeli border in a hot air balloon, were less notorious than those carried out by other Palestinian militant groups, both in terms of savagery and ubiquity.

In 1983–1984, after the expulsion of the PLO from Lebanon, the PLF split again, though this time three ways. One faction, headed by Abd al-Fatah Ghanim, returned to Syria and based itself in Damascus. It would continue staging

Armed Palestinians pray at the dedication of a new mosque in Gaza City. © *Abbas | Magnum Photos*

terrorist attacks against Israel from the south Lebanese border, which continued to be controlled by Syria through Hezbollah. The second faction was headed by Abu Abbas, and followed Yasser Arafat and the PLO to Tunisia. A final faction was headed by Tal'at Ya'akub, the PLF's General Secretary, which remained in Lebanon. When Ya'akub died of a heart attack in November 1988, the remnants of his disintegrating faction merged with Abbas's forces. Confusingly, each side described themselves as the PLF, although it was Abbas's faction that was to emerge as the most infamous.

By the time of this latest split, the PLF was still struggling to make a name for itself in the maze of Palestinian liberation politics. This changed in October 1985, almost by accident. The Abbas faction, which numbered not more than 100 individuals, attracted instant worldwide notoriety after it hijacked the Italian cruise liner, Achille Lauro. The aim had been for stowaway militants to enter Israel under its cover, but they were detected before the ship entered Israel, and they took control of the ship. In almost farcical circumstances, they attracted the attention of the world as the hijackers sailed around the Mediterranean with a small number of the Lauro's passengers (the majority had been on a sightseeing trip of Alexandria when the hijackers took control), not quite knowing what to do. The PLF made some vague demands for the release of fifty Palestinian terrorists and murdered one passenger, a New Yorker named Leon Klinghoffer, before the situation was diffused after Arafat led negotiations. (This bungled adventure would surely have been forgotten but for a controversial opera, "The Death of Klinghoffer," produced in New York in 1991 and subsequently staged elsewhere in the world.)

The incident was the cause of intense embarrassment for the PLO given that Abbas was part of its ten-man executive. His role had been exaggerated because the U.S. authorities had tried to use the hijacking as a pretext to secure his arrest and extradition, but they subsequently bungled the operation to arrest him as badly as the PLF had done the hijacking. In turn, this led to a transcontinental manhunt for Abbas after he slipped out of Italian custody while awaiting extradition. The PLO, for its part, temporarily

LEADERSHIP

ABU AHMED HALAB SHIBLI (OMAR SHIBLI)

Abu Ahmed Halab Shibli (known as Omar Shibli) was elected leader of the PLF following the death in U.S. custody of Abu Abbas. He was born in the Shibli Haifa village in Mandate Palestine in 1943 and served in a variety of positions within the Palestinian Resistance, including as Abbas' deputy.

Little is known about his plans for the leadership of the PLF, and his public outpourings—in the Western media at least—have consisted almost wholly of accusations that his predecessor's death was the result of a U.S./Israeli conspiracy. "Continuous interrogation by agents from the Mossad and the CIA led to his [Abbas'] tragic death," he said in March 2004. "Since his apprehension last April, Abu Abbas has been the target of a slow assassination plot conducted by the Americans. We all expected him to die in detention as a result of the inhumane conditions he was going through."

Shibili's apparent lack of vision for the PLF is seemingly an indication of the group's present weakness. He is closely allied to the PLO and is a member of the Palestinian National Council and the PLO's Higher Political Council.

Abbas backed the Oslo peace accords and condemned terrorism, following which Israel allowed him to return to Gaza. In 1996, he admitted that seizing the Achille Lauro was "a mistake," and apologized for killing Klinghoffer. Israeli courts confirmed his immunity in 1999.

Abbas later castigated the September 11, 2001, attacks on New York and Washington and publicly denounced al-Qaeda. He was still doubted, however, with the reports that PLF units were planning more attacks in the al-Aqsa *intifada* (uprising). It has also been alleged that Iraq used the PLF as a conduit to fund the families of suicide bombers, and that PLF forces were sent to Iraq to train under Saddam Hussein's forces. Neither of these accusations have ever been backed up with firm evidence, and as of 2005, the PLF has apparently claimed no part in any attack during the al-Aqsa intifada.

Following the U.S. invasion of Iraq in 2003, Abu Abbas was arrested by U.S. forces, despite apparent assurances to the Palestinian Authority that he would be immune from prosecution, and Washington dropping an earlier arrest warrant. The U.S. detained him for eleven months without charge, and he died while in custody in March 2004 in what the Pentagon described as "apparently... natural circumstances." Nevertheless, Abbas' family called for international human rights organizations to conduct an investigation into the causes of his death.

expelled Abbas, although they were later reconciled and he retook his place on the executive.

In many ways, this marked the highpoint for the PLF in terms of the influence and notoriety it exerted, but it was also the onset of its decline. Over subsequent years, it increasingly became a mere offshoot of Fatah. The PLF initiated an abortive raid on Israel in 1990, but with moves toward peace between the PLO and Israel being discussed, Abbas, and as a consequence, his movement, were increasingly forced to take a back seat. In 1991, he left the PLO Executive and went into semiretirement in Iraq, where he was joined by many of his remaining supporters.

PHILOSOPHY AND TACTICS

The PLF is a secular nationalist Palestinian liberation organization, with Marxist-Leninist origins that have eroded since the fall of the USSR (although it maintains a red star on its emblem). It holds pan-Arab convictions too, which probably earned it the sympathy of the Ba'athist regime of Saddam Hussein, who, for years, provided sanctuary to Abu Abbas.

In many ways, the botched hijacking of the Achille Lauro has distorted the PLF's place in the history of Palestinian liberation groups. Almost by accident, the group attracted worldwide attention through its "shambolic" attack and the United States' equally calamitous attempts to capture Abu Abbas. Though

PRIMARY SOURCE

Palestine Liberation Front (PLF)

A.K.A. PLF-ABU ABBAS FACTION

DESCRIPTION

The Palestine Liberation Front (PLF) broke away from the PFLP-GC in the late 1970s and later split again into pro-PLO, pro-Syrian, and pro-Libyan factions. The pro-PLO faction was led by Muhammad Abbas (a.k.a. Abu Abbas) and was based in Baghdad prior to Operation Iraqi Freedom.

ACTIVITIES

Abbas' group was responsible for the attack in 1985 on the Italian cruise ship Achille Lauro and the murder of U.S. citizen Leon Klinghoffer. Abu Abbas died of natural causes in April 2004 while in US custody in Iraq. Current leadership and membership of the relatively small PLF appears to be based in Lebanon and the Palestinian territories. The PLF has become more active since the start of the al-Aqsa intifadah and several PLF members have been arrested by Israeli authorities for planning attacks in Israel and the West Bank.

STRENGTH

Unknown.

LOCATION/AREA OF OPERATION

Based in Iraq since 1990, has a presence in Lebanon and the West Bank.

EXTERNAL AID

Received support mainly from Iraq; has received support from Libya in the past.

Source: U.S. Department of State. *Country Reports on Terrorism.* Washington, D.C., 2004.

Abbas held a senior position within the PLO, his identification with the attack meant it was later politically expedient for Arafat to sideline him when making moves toward peace.

Prior to Achille Lauro, the PLF had been involved in small-scale border raids from south Lebanon. Because it has never had any presence in the occupied territories, however, the sort of guerilla attacks—shootings, suicide bombings, ambushes, etc.—carried out by other Palestinian groups have been conspicuous by their absence.

OTHER PERSPECTIVES

Almost by accident, the shambolic Achille Lauro hijacking in 1985 and murder of Leon Klinghoffer, thrust the PLF into the limelight. *Time* magazine characterized Abbas—possibly with a hint of sarcasm—as "a would-be Palestinian Rambo" when profiling the accidental villain. "He goes by a variety of names: Abul Abbas, Mohammed Abbas, Mohammed Abul Abbas Zaidan, Abu Khaled," they reported. "He has been an ally and enemy of Syria's, a colleague and critic—simultaneously—of Palestine Liberation Organization Chairman Yasser Arafat's. Until a few weeks ago he was one of the more obscure leaders within the fragmented P.L.O., a member of its ten-man executive committee but directly in charge of only a splinter of a splinter, with perhaps fewer than 100 hard-core followers. His supposed allies openly deride Washington's characterization of him as a terrorist mastermind. Said one P.L.O. official in Tunis: "Abbas is a would-be Palestinian Rambo, big on brawn with some cunning. The problem is he has no brains."

The Egyptian government allegedly "abetted" the escape of Abbas and the Achille Lauro hijackers. This was not through any great sympathy for their actions, believed David Bar Illan, editor of the right-wing *Jerusalem Post*. He cited the "blind eye" as the latest symptom of the rampant anti-Semitism that plagued Egyptian society. By aiding Klinghoffer's murderers, this was also the latest violation of Egypt's 1978 peace agreement with Israel, he believed:

"Some 40-odd agreements undertaken by Israel and Egypt under the terms of their peace treaty have not been implemented because of Egyptian intransigence," he complained. "These range from trade, tourism, agricultural projects, transportation, and telecommunication to cultural relations, the exchange of youth delegations, and the cessation of anti-Israel propaganda. But that is hardly all. More than forty Israelis have been murdered by terrorists and Egyptian soldiers on Egyptian soil, to total official indifference. The Protocols of the Elders of Zion is still widely printed and distributed in Egypt, and Nazi-style propaganda against Israelis and Jews is rampant in the semi-official press. Polls in Egypt show that most members of the intelligentsia oppose peace with Israel, and the few Egyptian scientists and journalists who have dared to visit the country have been ostracized and boycotted by their professional guilds on their return. Israeli tourists and diplomats have been accused of importing every imaginable scourge, from hoof-and-mouth disease to AIDS. And Israel has been charged with perpetrating virtually every terrorist act which the rest of the world associates with Muslim extremists, from Pan Am 103 to the World Trade Center bombing."

SUMMARY

The notorious murder of Leon Klinghoffer in 1985 marked the high point of PLF activity, and the onset of its decline. Because its leader,

Abu Abbas, was so inexorably linked to the hijacking in American minds, it made him a political liability for Yasser Arafat and saw his influence as a member of the PLO Executive decline. Having lived through a series of splits, his group was down to barely 100 members by 1985, and the PLO negotiating table was seemingly the best way for him to exert PLF influence.

His semiretirement to Baghdad in 1991 further moved the PLF from the heart of the action, although it had never had any presence in the occupied territories anyway. Abbas was succeeded in 2004 by Omar Shibly following Abbas' death while in U.S. custody.

SOURCES

Books

Cleveland, William L. *A History of the Modern Middle East.* New York: Westview, 2000.

Savigh, Yezid. *Armed Struggle and the Search for State: The Palestinian National Movement, 1949—1993.* England: Oxford University Press, 1999.

Web sites

CBC Archives. "The Hijacking of Achille Lauro." < http://archives.cbc.ca/IDC-1-71-1153-6340-11/that_was_then/conflict_war/achille_lauro > (accessed October 22, 2005).

Audio and Video Media

CNN. "The Death of Richard Klinghoffer." < http://www.cnn.com/resources/video.almanac/1985/achille.lauro/klinghoffer.dead.45.mov > (accessed October 22, 2005).

People's War Group

LEADER: Muppala Laxman Rao

USUAL AREA OF OPERATION: India

OVERVIEW

In 1980, the People's War Group (PWG) was founded in Andhra Pradesh, a southern state in India. The group considers themselves to be champions of the peasants and landless and adheres to the ideology of Mao Tse Tung's organized peasant rebellion. Since its founding, the group has participated in an armed struggle against the Indian government, landowners, and those the group believes to conspire with the government. The group has been known under the names the People's Guerilla Army, the Naxalites, and the Communist Party of India–Marxist-Leninist. The group spent much of the last twenty-five years combating other communist groups as well as the government and landowners. However, in 2004, the PWG announced a merger with a former competitor for power of the Naxalite movement, the Maoist Communist Centre of India (MCC). The group declared a joining of forces to become the Communist Party of India-Maoist.

HISTORY

On April 22, 1980, Kondapalli Seetharamaiah, one of the most influential Naxalite leaders in the Andhra Pradesh state founded the

LEADERSHIP

KONDAPALLI SEETHARAMAIAH

Kondapalli Seetharamaiah was the founder of the People's War Group. In 1981, he presided over the first meeting geared at unifying the various Naxalite groups such as the MCC and the Communist Party of India (Marxist-Leninist). In 1982, Seetharamaiah was arrested in a conspiracy case and later expelled from the PWG. He died in April 2002.

MUPPALA LAXMAN RAO

Muppala Laxman Rao is also known as Ganapathi. He served as the state secretary of the PWG. Upon presiding over the merger between the MCC and the PWG, Ganapathi assumed the role of general secretary of the CPI-M.

People's War Group. (The name, Naxalite, refers to the 1967 Marxist uprising in Naxalbari, West Bengal, which targeted only the feudal landlords.) Seetharamaiah and the other Naxalites within the PWG based their goals on the theories of Chinese leader, Mao Tse Tung, which promote an organized peasant insurgency. The group rejected the ideas of democracy and parliamentary process in India and professed that an armed struggle is the only way to capture power and redistribute land and wealth. As a result, the PWG has spent the last twenty years sponsoring a series of assassinations, bombings, and attacks on upper-caste members.

The caste system in India is explained in the centuries-old Laws of Manu, in which a system for the distribution of wealth, land, and education is created. However, the 1950's constitution, passed shortly after India gained its independence, pledged a democratic government, universal adult suffrage, and the abolishment of the caste system. Yet, the remnants of the caste system can be seen in many aspects of Indian culture. A person's caste can still determine the

level of education one will receive. As a result, India possesses a low 64% literacy rate, which has created further disparity between the castes and fueled political movements such as the PWG. Since its inception in 1980, the PWG has professed its goal as "uplifting the downtrodden tribal people who are considered the lowest rungs of Indian society." In addition to providing the lower castes the promise of land reform, the PWG provides services such as medical care to the rural areas it controls, thereby attracting membership and support.

At its formation, the PWG was not the only Naxalite group seeking a peasant revolution in India. The Maoist Communist Centre of India (MCC) shared some of the ideology of the PWG, and the leadership of the groups sought to merge. However, the effort to merge the groups in the 1980s failed, resulting in decades of strife and conflict between the ideological allies.

The PWG, however, led the armed struggle against the Indian government and the expansion of capitalism in India. The group targeted the states of Andhra Pradesh, Orissa, and Bihar. By 1987, the PWG began to aim its violence at the police, believed to be an oppressive force and corrupt agency. The groups spent much of the 1980s striking police officers, border security forces, and their offices. In 1987, six police personnel were killed by members of the PWG. Later that year, members of the PWG abducted six state government officials. This started a pattern of killings and kidnappings that characterized the PWG's activities.

By 1998, the PWG again sought to expand its power by merging with the Communist Party of India (Marxist-Leninist). This absorption created conflict between the MCC and the PWG. The two groups began to engage in territorial and leadership clashes. The two groups struggled for power and, as a result, hundreds of the groups' respective supporters and members were killed. Nevertheless, the PWG continued its campaign of violence against its stated enemies—landowners, police, and other symbols of authority.

In spite of a ban of the PWG by the government in 2001, the group continued its activities and expanded the violence to include development projects and businesses. An example of the escalation in violence occurred in June 2003 when the PWG launched a series of assassinations and attacks. Beginning June 5, 2003,

KEY EVENTS

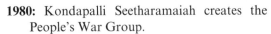

1980: Kondapalli Seetharamaiah creates the People's War Group.

1981: Initial talks for unifying the PWG and the MCC fail, leading to clashes between the groups.

1987: The PWG claims responsibility for the deaths of six police officers and abducts six government officials.

1989: Seven police officers are killed by PWG activities.

1991: A landmine blast detonated by PWG members kills 10 police officers and injures thirteen additional officers.

1992: The PWG targets and kills thirteen personnel from the Border Security Force.

1993: In activities throughout the year, twenty police officers and government officials are killed. Nine are killed by a landmine blast.

1997: Members of the PWG storm a police station and kill sixteen officers and personnel.

1998: A merger between the PWG and the Communist Party of India (Marxist-Leninist) intensifies the clashes with the MCC.

1999: Attacks by the PWG target and kill the state transportation minister, the Assistant Inspector General.

2001: An unprecedented wave of violence striking police, government officials, development projects, and businesses, precursors a governmental ban on the PWG.

2002: Continued violence occurs, including landmine blasts, assassinations, and the destruction of development projects. The government extends the ban on the PWG, while seeking to establish peace talks with the group.

2003: Widespread violence by the PWG continues, including a series of assassinations in the month of June.

2004: Government declares a three-month ceasefire with the PWG as peace talks begin. However, in October, the PWG announces its merger with the MCC to form the CPI-M.

members of the PWG tied up an inspector and constable at a police station and detonated a landmine at the station. In subsequent assassinations that month, PWG members raided the homes of village and political leaders and then shot them to death. In addition to assassinations that month, the PWG also blew up several motor boats at the tourism division office to protest the promotion of tourism in the region. The government extended the ban in 2002, while at the same time seeking to create peace talks with the group. These peace talks would not occur until 2004, when the two entities declared a ceasefire. However, by this time, the PWG had entered into a dialogue with the MCC, resulting in a merger of the once-contentious groups. In October 2004, the PWG announced that as a result of its merger with the MCC, the PWG would begin to operate under the name of the Communist Party of India-Maoist (CPI-M).

PHILOSOPHY AND TACTICS

The driving philosophy of the PWG is the Maoist theory of peasant insurrection. This theory asserts that those with power whose interests run counter to the masses must be overtaken. As such, the PWG sees itself as a champion of the weak and oppressed. Its goal is to gain control of the land and wealth so that it may be redistributed to better serve the masses. Its eventual objective is a "new democratic revolution," resulting from a true people's government, and thereby creating a communist state. The PWG believes that an armed struggle is the only way to capture the power needed to create this government.

The armed struggle consists of initially creating guerilla zones in rural areas. Once the PWG establishes control of these zones, the area is deemed a "liberated zone" where the land and wealth can be distributed. As a result, the PWG targets and kills those it determines as class enemies. These include landowners, police, symbols of authority, and informants.

The group capitalizes on the disparity of wealth and education—a system deeply rooted in India's centuries-old caste system. The PWG provides medical services to many who would otherwise go without. In addition, the group operates "people's courts," where police and other perceived oppressors are tried and sentenced for their alleged crimes. The group encourages government neglect of the regions controlled by them by attacking development projects, such as power dams, and threatening any intruders in their territories, such as teachers, missionaries, and tourists.

According to a government report, the PWG funds its activities through extortion. The group seeks payments from various individuals, including government officials, contractors, traders, businessmen, doctors, lawyers, and other professionals.

In December 2000, the PWG divided its military and political branches into separate entities. The military group was called the People's Guerilla Army. It consisted of platoons of twenty-five–thirty trained guerillas, sixty mobile squads, 1,000 underground cadres and 5,000 overt activists. The political structure was directed by a central committee consisting of twenty-one permanent members and six alternating members. The People's Guerilla Army began to operate under the leadership of the CPI-M when the MCC and the PWG merged in 2004.

OTHER PERSPECTIVES

India's economy has experienced unprecedented growth in the last years. However, this growth has not changed the lives of the majority of the county's citizens. The economic upturn has provided the emergence of an urban middle class, but the poorly educated and historically lower-caste regions remain the same. In a *Time* magazine Asia Edition article, one village tailor is quoted as saying, "Once the elections are over, the politicians forget us. Only the Naxalites are solving our problems." The government's perceived ignoring of their problems is only compounded by a belief that the officials in the government are corrupt. The *Economist* writes, "The main reason the government does not stop the carnage is that the

state's politicians and administrators are creatures of the conflict that give rise to it. As a result, the PWG's people's courts that pass judgment on allegedly corrupt officials are widely supported among the populace. One PWG supporter stated, '[If]the government does not' take care of the police, the PWG will."

The disparity in economic growth between the regions, the belief that the government ignores the rural regions, and the rampant corruption has provided the PWG with a wide base of potential membership and supporters. As a result, the New Delhi-based Institute of Conflict Management stated that the PWG, and subsequent CPI-M, are "the largest single internal security challenge in the country after terrorism in Kashmir."

SUMMARY

In India in 1980, the educational and economic disparity between the castes remained a contentious element in Indian culture in spite of the promise of the 1950 constitution to abolish the caste system. This disparity as well as the perception of corruption within the government led to a rise in the communist movement. Those adhering to the ideology of communism and the redistribution of wealth called themselves Naxalites, paying homage to the 1967 Marxist uprising in Naxalbari, West Bengal, which targeted only the feudal landlords. The Naxalites, however, were not in agreement as to their leadership and tactics. As a result, several groups emerged and struggled among themselves for leadership of the movement.

The People's War Group, established in 1980, was at the forefront of the armed struggle laid out by the Naxalites. This armed struggle invokes the Maoist theory of peasant insurrection. Therefore, the group spent the last twenty years targeting those it considered class enemies. The PWG stated its goal as "uplifting the downtrodden tribal people who are considered the lowest rungs of Indian society." As the champion of the weak and the masses, the PWG called for the destruction of the government which should be replaced with a new democratic revolution and the installment of a "people's government." As such, the group has claimed responsibility for much of the violence, which is a tactical movement. According to the tactics, the violence initially creates a guerilla zone. Once the PWG gained complete control over the area, it would be deemed a liberated zone and the wealth and land would then be redistributed.

In 2004, the PWG entered into a ceasefire with the government. However, at the same time, the group engaged in negotiations with its strongest competition, the MCC. By October 2004, the two groups had merged to create the Communist Party of India–Maoist and the assets of both organizations were absorbed into the new group.

SOURCES

Periodicals

Desmond, Edward, W. "The Spirit of the Age Is in Favor of Equality, through Practice." *Time International.* April 13, 1992.

"India: Untouchable Bihar." *The Economist.* June 24, 2000.

"India: The Politics of Extremism." *The Economist.* October 2, 1999.

Turbiville, Graham H. Jr. "Naxalite Insurgency Draws Indian Concerns." *J.F.K. Special Warfare Center and School.* February 21, 2005.

Web sites

Christian Science Monitor. "A Band of Maoist Rebels Terrorizes an Indian Region." < http://www.csmonitor.com/2002/0813/p07s02-wosc.html > (accessed October 11, 2005).

FAS Intelligence Resource Program. "People's War Group (PWG)." < http://www.fas.org/irp/world/para/pwg.htm > (accessed October 11, 2005).

MIPT Terrorism Knowledge Base. "The People's War Group (PWG)." < http://www.tkb.org/Group.jsp?groupID = 3658 > (accessed October 11, 2005).

South Asia Terrorism Portal. "The People's War Group (PWG)." < http://www.satp.org/satporgtp/countries/india/terroristoutfits/pwg.htm > (accessed October 11, 2005).

People Against Gangsterism and Drugs (PAGAD)

YEAR ESTABLISHED OR BECAME ACTIVE: 1995

USUAL AREA OF OPERATION: South Africa

OVERVIEW

People Against Gangsterism and Drugs (PAGAD) is a group operating in and around Cape Town, South Africa. The group initially formed as a community-based anti-crime organization in 1995, with their intention being to help eliminate drug dealing and gang behavior from local neighborhoods.

During the period from 1995–2000, PAGAD became increasingly violent, both as a response to retaliation from gangs and as a result of the group adopting a view in which they considered themselves at war with the government. This led to a series of bombings on various targets, including Planet Hollywood in Cape Town.

PAGAD has maintained that they were not responsible for the bombings. This has led to speculation that an extremist section of PAGAD broke away from the main group and is responsible for the bombings. In 2000, PAGAD was also considered by South African authorities as having formed links with the extremist Islamic group Qibla. This led to the group being viewed as anti-Western and anti-American.

HISTORY

People Against Gangsterism and Drugs (PAGAD) originally formed in December

Members of People Against Gangsterism And Drugs (PAGAD) clash with police at Hannover park in Cape Town, on August 11, 1996. AP/Wide World Photos. Reproduced by permission.

1995 in Cape Town, South Africa. The group was initially formed to act as a community-based anti-crime organization, with the specific purpose of reducing gang-related behavior and drug deals from occurring in the neighborhood. In the forming stages, the group had a majority of Muslim members, but was not exclusively Muslim. Drug dealing in the neighborhood was an ongoing problem for residents. Residents found it particularly difficult to take action because the drug dealers were supported both by criminal gangs and by some corrupt police officers.

PAGAD's initial intention was for members of the community group to patrol the streets, with this patrolling meant to discourage drug dealers from operating in the area. In a report on PAGAD, Bill Dixon and Lisa-Marie Johns note that PAGAD members were initially open

to working with other anti-crime groups and with the police.

After its initial formation, PAGAD grew quickly, gaining new members and expanding to new areas of the community. In these early days of expansion, PAGAD positioned itself as an organization devoted to helping people help themselves. This focus appealed especially to Muslim communities in Cape Town, due to the Muslim focus on acting as a united community. With this new membership, PAGAD gradually became a mainly Muslim organization.

In the early days of the PAGAD patrolling, the group achieved reasonable success in limiting drug deals in the area. At this point, PAGAD had a reasonable amount of public support and even support from the area police.

In May 1996, PAGAD marched to parliament and called on the government to address the problems of gangsterism and drug dealing. PAGAD gave the government sixty days to respond. After sixty days, PAGAD had not received a response they considered satisfactory. Considering that they had given the government the opportunity to address the problem and been denied, PAGAD developed their own plan of action for preventing drug dealing.

This led to PAGAD's system of protest, where they marched on the houses of known drug dealers and demanded that they stop drug dealing.

During 1996, the drug dealers began to respond to PAGAD's actions in increasingly violent ways. PAGAD also became increasingly frustrated with the failure of the government to take any action in response to drug dealing or gang behavior. These issues caused a gradual change in PAGAD: from a loosely organized community group to a well-organized group willing, and seeing it as necessary, to employ more violent tactics.

In August 1996, Rashaad Staggie was murdered after a PAGAD protest march in Salt River. Rashaad Staggie was the twin brother of Rashied Staggie and co-leader of one of the most powerful gangs in Western Cape, the Hard Livings. Ali Parker, a member of PAGAD, called for a holy war, or jihad, against drug dealers and gang members. The group later stated that is was not exclusively Muslim or a militant group, suggesting that Parker's calls for a jihad represented the desire of one member and not of the group as a whole. In August 1996, PAGAD issued an ultimatum to gangs demanding that they stop drug dealing. Later in the same month, a member of PAGAD was murdered in what was considered as being a revenge attack by the gangsters.

In December 1996, PAGAD members protested near the Cape Town International Airport. The protest was intended to raise concerns about the lack of control preventing drugs from entering the country. The government declared that the protest was illegal and arrested several PAGAD members.

During 1997, conflict in the Cape Town area increased. This included conflict between PAGAD and gangs. Specific incidents included a drug dealer's home being burned down, as well as several retaliation attacks on mosques and Muslim individuals. In 1997, speculation also grew about a possible split within PAGAD. This split was thought to involve some members of PAGAD operating independently from the mainstream group, possibly with the support of the extremist Islamic group, Qibla.

In early 1998, a number of gang members were killed in drive-by shootings. These included Moeneeb Abrahams, Leonard Achilles, and Ivan Oliver, who were all members of the Hard Livings. This was the same group that Rashaad Staggie was a member of.

In 1998, PAGAD's role changed as their actions grew more violent and expanded to include bomb attacks. This change in strategy resulted in PAGAD being viewed as a violent terrorist organization. In August 1998, a bomb explosion at Planet Hollywood in Capetown killed two people and injured twenty-six.

Bombings continued throughout 1999. These included a car bomb at the V & A Waterfront and three bomb explosions outside police stations. PAGAD was accused of the bombings, though it denied responsibility.

In February 1999, one of the senior investigators of the V & A Waterfront was assassinated on the Cape Flats. Another senior detective investigating urban terror was killed at Cape Town International Airport. PAGAD was suspected of being involved but denied responsibility for both attacks. PAGAD was also suspected of being involved in a bombing on a gay bar and a bombing of a pizza store. PAGAD also denied responsibility for these attacks.

In 2000, PAGAD was suspected of being involved in more bombings. These included a bombing outside a New York Bagel restaurant, a bombing at Cape Town International Airport, and a bombing outside a coffee shop. PAGAD denied responsibility for these attacks.

In 2000, a number of PAGAD members were arrested for various crimes. A magistrate residing over several of the trials was murdered in September 2000, increasing speculation that PAGAD was responsible for the Cape Town bombings.

In late 2000, a number of PAGAD members were found guilty of various crimes, including acts of terrorism, and were sentenced to imprisonment.

In September 2000, Steve Tshwete, the Safety and Security Minister, and Penuell Maduna, the Justice Minister, stated that PAGAD was responsible for the bombings in Cape Town. Tshwete also declared war on PAGAD.

KEY EVENTS

1995: PAGAD forms as a community-based anti-crime organization.

1996: PAGAD marched on the parliament, calling on the government to address the problems of gangsterism and drug dealing.

1996: PAGAD considered that the government was not going to deal with the problems of gangsterism and drug dealing satisfactorily and started their own plan of attack, which involved marching on the houses of known drug dealers.

1996: Co-leader of the gang the Hard Livings, Rashaad Staggie, was murdered after a PAGAD protest march in Salt River. Later in the month, a member of PAGAD was murdered in what was considered a revenge attack.

1996: PAGAD members protested near the Cape Town International Airport. The government declared that the protest was illegal and arrested several PAGAD members.

1998: A bomb explosion at Planet Hollywood in Cape Town killed two people and injured twenty-six. PAGAD was attributed to the bombing, but denied responsibility.

1999–2000: PAGAD was accused of several bombings, including attacks on American targets. PAGAD denied responsibility for the attacks.

2000: PAGAD was suspected of forming alliances with extremist Islamic group, Qibla. Incidents attributed to PAGAD included attacks on tourist attractions and Westerners. PAGAD denied responsibility for the attacks.

This led to the next stage in PAGAD's evolution as the group expanded its interests beyond just local communities. The focus became on fighting gangsterism and drugs on a larger scale. This included that PAGAD now considered the South African government as a threat to the Muslim communities of Cape Town and adopted an anti-Western philosophy. PAGAD formed an alliance with the extremist Islamic group Qibla, and two groups were established to carry out violent actions. These were named Muslims Against Global Oppression (MAGO) and Muslims Against Illegitimate Leaders.

This led to a series of bombings on targets, including South African authorities, tourist attractions, and businesses in South Africa owned by Westerners.

PHILOSOPHY AND TACTICS

Information on PAGAD suggests that they initially started only with the intention of eliminating gangsterism and drug dealing from their communities. One of their first actions was a march on the government, where they demanded that the government take action against gangsters and drug dealers. At this point in their history, there was no suggestion that their intentions were violent. Instead, their intentions seemed to be to raise awareness about the issue and to push the government into taking action. When the government showed no sign that they would eliminate the problems, PAGAD then started their own system of action designed to limit gangsterism and drug dealing.

Even when these actions started, there were no initial signs that PAGAD intended to be a violent group. Instead, their tactic of marching on the homes of drug dealers and demanding that they stop dealing was a non-violent attempt at influencing the drug dealers. PAGAD's tactics at this point involved rallying in numbers and did not include any acts of violence.

This history of PAGAD suggests that the group began to change as the gangsters began to retaliate. This is especially related to the death of gangster Rashaad Staggie on August 4, 1996. At this point in PAGAD's history, it was a loosely aligned group with no formal leadership. It is also suggested that while the group was not considered as being a terrorist group, there may have been overlap in that some members may have also been affiliated with the extremist Islamic group, Qibla. While it is not known for certain who was responsible for the death of Rashaad Staggie, it must be noted that even if it was a member of PAGAD or a group of members from PAGAD, this does not mean that the entire PAGAD organization supported the murder. Despite these unanswered questions, the murder sparked retaliation from gangsters and led to an ongoing rivalry.

During these early formation years, members of PAGAD were also increasingly frustrated with the government. Initially, the frustration was based on the government's inability or unwillingness to deal with gangsterism and drug dealing issues. As PAGAD continued its actions, the group became frustrated with the treatment of its members. This included three members of PAGAD being charged with sedition, the government putting up road blocks to prevent PAGAD from marching on a drug dealer's house, and a statement made by the government during PAGAD's march on the Cape Town International Airport that referred to PAGAD as having become gangsters themselves. This led to a situation where PAGAD was considering itself as having to fight against the gangsters, the drug dealers, and the government.

This led to a major change in tactics, with PAGAD becoming increasingly violent in 1997 and 1998. While there was increased violence, PAGAD continue to deny their involvement in attacks on innocent people. However, the years did involve the deaths of thirteen gangsters and drug dealers, as well as attacks on Muslim targets. This suggests that the period involved a war between PAGAD members and gang members.

Speculation also continued about whether all PAGAD members were involved in the violence, or whether some members of PAGAD formed independent extremist units and carried out acts of violence without the knowledge or support of the main group.

This may extend to the various bombings in Cape Town, for which PAGAD continues to deny responsibility. In a report on PAGAD, Bill Dixon and Lisa-Marie Johns interviewed a senior PAGAD member and asked him if PAGAD was involved in the bombing of Planet Hollywood or the bombing at St Elmo's pizzeria. The PAGAD member replied that the group did not do such things, order such things, and that such attacks were not part of the group's agenda. The PAGAD member went on to say that he could not guarantee that the individual or individuals who organized the bombings were not members of PAGAD, since he could not control every member of PAGAD. This response highlights that, while individuals

might be members of PAGAD, they do not act only based on their membership of the organization. Individuals may have other affiliations, other agendas, and may be part of attacks not agreed on by the group as a whole.

This suggests that PAGAD as a whole may have maintained its primary mission of eradicating drug dealing and gangsterism in Cape Town. At the same time, some members of PAGAD may have redirected their mission and considered themselves in a war against both the gangsters and the government. Some sources suggest that there has been a split in PAGAD with an extremist offshoot of the main group responsible for the most violent actions.

Speculation also continues about the links between PAGAD and the extremist Islamic group, Qibla. Some sources suggest that PAGAD only claims to exist to fight gangsterism and drugs as a cover for its real purpose, which is to undermine the government and install a Muslim state. It is not known whether PAGAD as a whole has links to Qibla or whether some members have links to Qibla. It is also not known whether it is the members linked to Qibla that are responsible for the bombings.

The Muslims Against Global Oppression (MAGO) is generally accepted as being responsible for the Planet Hollywood bombing, although the group has never claimed responsibility. MAGO has links to PAGAD, though the exact links are unknown. It is speculated that MAGO may be a cover name used by PAGAD or that extremist members of PAGAD may have formed the MAGO group. However, the bombings are thought to have occurred in retaliation for the United States bombing al-Qaeda targets in Afghanistan. This purpose does not link well with PAGAD's usual purpose, adding to speculation that MAGO is a separate group with an entirely different purpose. As noted though, it is possible that there is some overlap in the membership of the two groups.

OTHER PERSPECTIVES

On December 11, 1996, Sydney Mufamadi, the Minister for Safety and Security, issued a statement where he described PAGAD as a drain on police resources. Mufamadi referred to the resources needed to police ongoing marches. Mufamadi also referred to PAGAD members

PRIMARY SOURCE
People Against Gangsterism and Drugs (PAGAD)

DESCRIPTION

People Against Gangsterism and Drugs (PAGAD) and its ally Qibla (an Islamic fundamentalist group that favors political Islam and takes an anti-US and anti-Israel stance) view the South African Government as a threat to Islamic values. The two groups work to promote a greater political voice for South African Muslims. PAGAD has used front names such as Muslims Against Global Oppression and Muslims Against Illegitimate Leaders when launching anti-Western protests and campaigns.

ACTIVITIES

PAGAD formed in November 1995 as a vigilante group in reaction to crime in some neighborhoods of Cape Town. In September 1996, a change in the group's leadership resulted in a change in the group's goal, and it began to support a violent jihad to establish an Islamic state. Between 1996 and 2000, PAGAD conducted a total of 189 bomb attacks, including nine bombings in the Western Cape that caused serious injuries. PAGAD's targets included South African authorities, moderate Muslims, synagogues, gay nightclubs, tourist attractions, and West-ern-associated restaurants. PAGAD is believed to have masterminded the bombing on August 25, 1998, of the Cape Town Planet Hollywood. Since 2001, PAGAD's violent activities have been severely curtailed by law enforcement and prosecutorial efforts against leading members of the organization. Qibla leadership has organized demonstrations against visiting U.S. dignitaries and other protests, but the extent of PAGAD's involvement is uncertain.

STRENGTH

Early estimates were several hundred members. Current operational strength is unknown, but probably vastly diminished.

LOCATION/AREA OF OPERATION

Operates mainly in the Cape Town area.

EXTERNAL AID

May have ties to international Islamic extremists.

Source: U.S. Department of State. *Country Reports on Terrorism.* Washington, D.C., 2004.

---

being investigated for crimes, including murder, attempted murder, arson, and unlawful possession of an explosive device. Mufamadi also stated that PAGAD has undermined the ability of the police to deal with drugs and related crime. This statement suggests that PAGAD is indirectly responsible for increasing gang and drug behavior, rather than preventing it.

In a report on PAGAD, Bill Dixon and Lisa-Marie Johns note that it is not clear whether PAGAD are responsible for a series of bombings in Cape Town. According to Bill Dixon and Lisa-Marie Johns, the group has not shown great concern about the death of gang leaders but has repeatedly condemned attacks on civilian targets. Bill Dixon and Lisa-Marie Johns also describe government ministers as being quick to blame PAGAD for various attacks, while noting that it is not possible to prove that they were involved. This suggests that the authors' view that PAGAD may have continued its operations only for the purpose of targeting drug dealers.

An article on BBC News on September 13, 2000, questions whether PAGAD is a vigilante group or a terrorist group. The article notes that PAGAD started with good intentions, with residents taking peaceful actions aimed at discouraging drug dealers. The article then describes the attack on Planet Hollywood, stating that the attack was blamed on Muslim fundamentalist groups with links to PAGAD. This statement suggests that the groups having links to PAGAD does not necessarily mean that the attack was asked for or condoned by PAGAD. The article finished by stating that PAGAD has denied responsibility for the attacks and said that it does not condone violence. While no final answer is given as to whether PAGAD is a terrorist group, the article does raise questions about the legitimacy of claims that PAGAD is responsible for terrorist bombings.

SUMMARY

In a report on PAGAD and violence in the Cape Town area, Bill Dixon and Lisa-Marie Johns state that the prospects for breaking the cycle of violence are bleak. They also note that the distrust and sour relations between groups, including PAGAD, the government, and gang members, are likely to continue.

In 2000, many members of PAGAD were convicted of crimes and imprisoned. This reduced the strength of the group and it has not been involved in major acts of violence since. However, PAGAD is still classified as a terrorist organization by the governments of South Africa and by the United States of America.

SOURCES

Books

Africa, C., J. Christie, R. Mattes, M. Roefs, and H. Taylor. *Crime and Community Action: Pagad and the Cape Flats, 1996–1997.* Cape Town: Public Opinion Service, Institute for Democracy in South Africa, 1998.

Dixon, B. and L. Johns. *Gangs, PAGAD & the State: Vigilantism and Revenge Violence in the Western Cape.* Cape Town: Center for the Study of Violence and Reconciliation, 2001.

Web sites

BBC News. "PAGAD: Vigilantes or Terrorists?" < http://news.bbc.co.uk/1/hi/world/africa/923701.stm > (accessed October 19, 2005).

Ministry for Safety and Security, South African Government. "Media Statement by Mr. Sydney Mufamadi, Minister for Safety and Security, Pretoria, 11 December 1996." < http://www.info.gov.za/speeches/ 1996/12170x86496.htm > (accessed October 19, 2005).

People for the Ethical Treatment of Animals (PETA)

LEADERS: Ingrid Newkirk, Alex Pacheco
YEAR ESTABLISHED OR BECAME ACTIVE: 1980
ESTIMATED SIZE: 700,000
USUAL AREA OF OPERATION: Worldwide

OVERVIEW

People for the Ethical Treatment of Animals, often referred to simply as PETA, is the largest animal rights organization in the world, claiming more than 700,000 members. Founded in 1980 by Ingrid Newkirk and Alex Pacheco, the group supports "total animal liberation," opposing the use of animals for food, research, entertainment, and even as assistance dogs for the physically disabled. The group is well known for its outrageous publicity stunts, controversial advertisements, and an ongoing string of inflammatory public statements from its leaders. It has frequently been criticized for its use of heavy-handed tactics and has been linked to several acts of animal rights violence. PETA currently has offices in North America, Europe, and Asia.

HISTORY

The animal rights movement emerged during the 1970s, partly in response to the publication of *Animal Liberation* by Peter Singer in 1975. This volume, while not fully consistent with the modern animal rights movement, proposed the concept of "speciesism," defined as discrimination against a particular being based solely on the species to which it belongs. As a philosopher, Singer took the position that human suffering

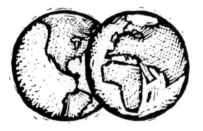

PETA members Brandi Valladolid, center, and Erin Edwards, left, demonstrate outside the U.S. Canadian Embassy on April 6, 2005 to protest Canada's condonement of a seal-hunt in Newfoundland. They say they are recreating scenes of bloodied seal carcasses in that province.

AP/Wide World Photos. Reproduced by permission.

and animal suffering are equal evils and that the use of animals for human food cannot be justified, since it requires animal suffering. Singer's overall perspective was actually rather pragmatic, proposing veganism as a lifestyle, but acknowledging the necessity of some animal experiments for medical purposes.

The year after the book's appearance, the Animal Liberation Front (ALF) was formed. The group's roots actually ran back to the 1960s, when opponents of fox hunting in England would sabotage hunts in an effort to bring about their abolition. By the early 1970s, these efforts became progressively more violent, employing such tactics as slashing hunters' tires and smashing their car windows. In 1975,

members of these groups formed ALF, which was registered in the United States as a 501(c)3 non-profit organization in 1979. Among the group's alleged members was Alex Pacheco, an animal rights activist whose previous work included a tour of duty on the Sea Shepherd, an anti-whaling ship specially designed to ram and sink whaling vessels.

In 1980, Pacheco joined forces with Ingrid Newkirk. Newkirk had worked as a Maryland law enforcement officer, winning numerous convictions against animal abusers, as well as in various other animal protection positions. While working at an animal shelter, she met Alex Pacheco, who gave her a copy of Peter Singer's book. After reading it, she and Pacheco founded PETA, which launched its efforts by picketing a poultry house in Washington, followed by the National Institutes of Health.

In 1981, PETA quickly rose to national prominence with what came to be known as the Silver Spring Monkeys incident. Dr. Edward Taub was a highly respected behavioral scientist working in Silver Spring, Maryland. At the time, Taub was studying an unusual neurological condition in which humans mysteriously lose the use of a limb; Taub's research involved inducing this condition in monkeys, then studying how to correct it.

Pacheco was able to secure employment in Taub's lab by posing as a student worker. He soon gained Taub's confidence and was given keys to the lab when he volunteered to work at night; Pacheco used this access to take photos of the lab animals, which later appeared in PETA ads.

During a vacation by Dr. Taub, two of the lab's student assistants called in with excuses and did not come to work. Because of these absences, the lab was not adequately staffed and the animal cages were not properly cleaned. Pacheco, taking advantage of the conditions, took additional photos. He also began inviting animal rights activists and members of the Humane Society to tour the facility at night.

After the tours, Pacheco's guests provided written statements that accused the lab of housing animals in inappropriate conditions. Armed with his photos and these statements, Pacheco was able to initiate a police investigation of the lab. A search warrant was issued, and seventeen monkeys were seized from the facility; Dr. Taub was served with a seventeen-count indictment.

PETA is against animal sacrifices, such as this one in Tehran, Iran, in 1997. © *Abbas | Magnum Photos*

Following a trial and an appeal, Dr. Taub was acquitted on all seventeen counts; four independent scientific groups also conducted independent investigations and found him innocent. PETA, however, immediately began raising funds for the legal battle, a practice the group continued even after Dr. Taub was acquitted. PETA also marketed a videotape describing the case as the first police raid of a research facility and the first conviction of a researcher on animal rights charges.

In 1982, the Animal Liberation Front made its first known break-in at a medical lab, burglarizing the University of Pennsylvania Head Injury Clinic. The break-in netted videotapes of researchers treating baboons inhumanely; PETA supported ALF's efforts by distributing ALF news releases and staging a sit-in at the National Institutes of Health in Washington, D.C. The university was eventually cited for failing to comply with animal care guidelines and lost federal funding for the project; the Head Injury Clinic ultimately closed. PETA's involvement and support suggested that PETA might be

serving as the legal, public face of a partnership with the outlaw group ALF.

This possibility was further supported in 1983, when Ingrid Newkirk left her position at the D.C. Animal Control Division. A Washington Post article dated November 13, 1983, noted that while working there, Newkirk had repeatedly endorsed, and at times served as an intermediary for, the Animal Liberation Front. A fact sheet on the PETA web site likens ALF to the Underground Railroad of the Civil War; PETA also solicits donations to provide legal aid to activists arrested while trying to liberate animals.

In 1989, ALF members burglarized a medical research lab at Texas Tech University, stealing records, freeing animals, and destroying more than $50,000 worth of equipment being used by Dr. John Orem. PETA immediately began publicizing the raid as part of fundraising efforts and published interviews with two of the ALF members responsible. However, the group also published Dr. Orem's home address, ostensibly so members could write him polite letters, but also opening him up to harassment and

Street graffiti painted by anti-fur activists in San Francisco. © Robert Gumpert / Alamy

threats. In the years that followed, ALF continued their illegal activities, and PETA continued to support and publicize them. The FBI has classified ALF as a domestic terrorist organization and blames it for more than 100 crimes. Alex Pacheco of PETA has stated simply, "Damaging the enemy is fair game."

In one of the lighter incidents in the group's history, Michael Doughney, a Maryland resident, registered PETA's web address; from late 1995 to early 1996, Doughney used the address as the home of a fictitious group known as People Eating Tasty Animals, which offered resources for "those who enjoy eating meat, wearing fur and leather, hunting, and the fruits of scientific research . . ." Following legal action, the website was removed, but the domain name remained in dispute until June 2000, when a federal court ordered Doughney to surrender the domain name.

PHILOSOPHY AND TACTICS

Since its founding, PETA has taken the position that animals and human beings are equally valuable, thus criminalizing any human activity that takes advantage of, or creates "suffering" for, an animal. In advancing this radical viewpoint, PETA has employed a variety of tactics, many designed to elicit shock and attract maximum attention. PETA's earliest tactics included protests, picketing, and throwing blood on fur coat owners. In the years since, PETA has been linked to far more extreme tactics.

The troubling implications of PETA's position are perhaps best demonstrated by PETA's frequent public statements. PETA leaders may initially appear to be using hyperbole to make a point, such as when one leader likened hunters and fishermen to death-camp guards and slave owners. However, PETA's top officials have been so consistent in these statements that it has become apparent the leaders are not exaggerating simply to make a point but actually believe what they are saying. For example, at a 2001 Animal Rights conference, PETA vegan campaign coordinator Bruce Friedrich stated that if the group truly believed in animal rights, it would naturally be blowing things up and smashing windows. And Tom Vernelli, while serving as coordinator of PETA in Europe, classified serving children hamburgers as child abuse, similar to serving them weed killer.

PETA President Ingrid Newkirk, in particular, has a well-earned reputation for radical invective, offering a seemingly endless stream of startling sound-bites. In 1988, she told *Harpers Magazine* that she did not believe in pets; rather humans and animals should live separately. In 1989, she told *Vogue* magazine that even if animal research produced a cure for AIDS, PETA would oppose it. In a 1990 *Readers' Digest* interview, she likened mankind to a cancer, blighting the planet. Perhaps the most famous of Newkirk's statements came after Palestinians loaded a donkey with explosives and sent it into Jerusalem on a suicide mission. No humans died in the explosion, but Newkirk posted a letter to Yasser Arafat, asking that his group "leave the animals out of this conflict." When asked later if she would petition Arafat to stop killing human beings, Newkirk responded, "It's not my business to inject myself into human wars."

While PETA has used a remarkable variety of tactics, it has garnered the most media attention for its major ad campaigns, many aimed at large corporations. PETA offended many Christians with its "Jesus was a Vegetarian"

LEADERSHIP

INGRID NEWKIRK

Ingrid Newkirk was born in England in 1949. During the 1970s, she held a variety of jobs related to animal protection, including law enforcement work in Maryland, where she prosecuted animal abuse cases. She eventually went to work in the District of Columbia as an animal protection officer and in 1978 became Chief of Animal Disease Control for the Commission on Public Health in the District of Columbia. In 1980, she co-founded People for the Ethical Treatment of Animals.

During the years since PETA's founding, Newkirk has continued to play an integral role in the group's work. She also sits on the advisory boards of several other activist groups, including EarthSave International and United Poultry Concerns. She is the author of numerous books related to animal rights and currently serves as PETA's president, as well as its most vocal spokesperson. Her frequent inflammatory statements provide the group an ongoing source of publicity.

campaign, which included an ad showing a hog and the words, "He Died for Your Sins." Numerous Christian leaders questioned both the taste and the accuracy of the campaign, with most mainstream theologians rejecting the vegetarian claim. PETA also attracted both positive and negative attention with its so-called "Lettuce Ladies," attractive women who appear in public wearing bikinis apparently made of lettuce and distributing information on vegan eating.

The response was overwhelmingly negative, however, when PETA launched its "Holocaust on Your Plate" campaign, featuring photos of Holocaust victims next to photos of dead animals, equating the butchering of animals with the Holocaust. Jewish groups were outraged at the campaign, although PETA claimed the ads were not attempting to equate the two situations.

PETA has frequently singled out specific corporations to bear the brunt of its efforts. McDonald's, as the nation's largest fast food chain, has attracted the group's attention. Calling its campaign "McCruelty," PETA repeatedly targeted McDonald's and attempted to bring about changes in its animal husbandry techniques. Using such eye-catching graphics as a so-called "Unhappy Meal" featuring an axe-wielding clown, the group's efforts eventually led to changes in the company's animal raising and slaughtering practices.

Burger King has also been targeted by PETA, which launched its "Murder King" campaign following the group's settlement with McDonald's in 2000. The Burger King effort included support from Alec Baldwin and other celebrities, as well as more than 800 protests at local Burger King outlets. In 2001, Burger King announced that it would agree to PETA's demands by allowing more space for chickens, increasing inspections at poultry plants, and instituting other changes in its meat-packing process. In response, PETA ended its action against the firm.

The "Wicked Wendy's" campaign against the Wendy's chain also ended in a claim of victory for PETA in 2001. For this campaign, PETA used graphics that depicted Wendy's founder Dave Thomas with his head inserted in his posterior and the company's trademark "Wendy" character holding a large bloody knife. These ads, along with protests at Wendy's restaurants, led the company to agree to the same standards adopted at the other two burger chains.

Following two years of discussions, PETA announced a campaign against KFC in 2003. Supported by celebrities such as Pamela Anderson and Sir Paul McCartney, the "Kentucky Fried Cruelty" campaign employed traditional tactics such as protests at local restaurants. In 2003, KFC President Cheryl Bachelder met with PETA's Ingrid Newkirk, promising reforms; Ms. Bachelder left KFC shortly thereafter. In 2005, PETA once again met with KFC executives, however little progress was made. As of mid 2005, the campaign remains active. PETA has also discussed possible future campaigns against targets, including Chick-Fil-a, Churches Chicken, and Wal-Mart.

KEY EVENTS

1975: Peter Singer writes *Animal Liberation*, setting the stage for the animal rights movement.

1979: Animal Liberation Front (ALF) registers as a 501(c)3 non-profit entity.

1980: Ingrid Newkirk and Alex Pacheco organize PETA.

1981: PETA targets Dr. Edward Taub in the Silver Spring Monkey incident; Dr. Taub is later cleared of all charges.

1982: Animal Liberation Front breaks into the University of Pennsylvania Head Injury Clinic, exposing animal abuses; the clinic is eventually closed.

1983: A Washington Post article links Ingrid Newkirk to the Animal Liberation Front, which PETA documents liken to the Underground Railroad.

1989: The FBI classifies ALF as a domestic terrorism group. PETA continues its financial support of the group.

2002: PETA organizes the "Running of the Nudes" through the streets of Spain to protest the famous Running of the Bulls held two days later. The run becomes an annual event.

2003: PETA targets children with its "Your Mommy Kills Animals" campaign.

PETA has not limited its efforts to food industry firms. PETA has repeatedly targeted Ringling Brothers circuses for its alleged mistreatment of animals. The group has also set its sights on the Pro Rodeo Cowboys Association in an attempt to end rodeos. Other PETA efforts have been aimed at the use of monkeys in the film and commercial industries, and operators of animal theme parks.

In trying to rid the world of fur coats and similar clothing, PETA has taken a two-pronged approach. The group's long-running and popular "I'd rather go naked than wear fur" campaign features celebrities in various states of undress and puts an attractive face on the anti-fur effort. In sharp contrast, in 2003 the group launched a campaign targeting children of parents who wear fur. This campaign stationed PETA workers outside performances of "The Nutcracker" ballet. When the activists observed a woman wearing fur, they would hand the woman's child a flier which featured a photo of a woman stabbing a rabbit with a knife, along with the words "Your Mommy Kills Animals." Child psychologists criticized the tactics as manipulative.

In recent years, PETA activists also appeared to be adopting even more intrusive tactics in dealing with corporate executives. In one case, the group's efforts to influence a fast-food executive went beyond traditional tactics such as letter-writing and picketing. Instead, members met with the CEO's church pastor and went to his country club. Activists also protested outside the man's church during Sunday services, with one of the protestors wearing a chicken suit. PETA has also begun to buy shares in restaurant and food corporations, allowing the group to introduce shareholder resolutions in an attempt to change restaurant practices regarding meat and poultry. *Fortune* magazine described the group's tactics against corporations as resembling the way in which a speeding locomotive impacts a stalled automobile.

In 2005, two PETA members were arrested on sixty-two counts of animal cruelty in North Carolina. Police had observed the two throwing animal carcasses into commercial dumpsters over a period of several weeks. The dead animals were determined to have come from animal shelters, whose operators were told that PETA would find homes for the animals. The two PETA members were also in possession of restricted-use narcotics, which might have been used to kill the animals.

Tax records from PETA also confirm that the group continues to offer financial support to the Animal Liberation Front and Earth Liberation Front; the FBI estimates that these two groups have combined since 1996 to commit more than 600 crimes and inflict more than $43 million in damage, making them, in the FBI's words, the country's "most serious domestic terrorism threat."

OTHER PERSPECTIVES

As a not-for-profit organization, PETA is required to follow specific regulations. In several cases, outside observers have claimed that PETA does not qualify for this tax designation or that it is not a properly administered charitable organization. A 1992 report by the National Charities Information Board cited shortcomings in PETA's operations, including its use of 42% of total income for fund-raising purposes. Activist watchdog groups claim that PETA's actual expenditures for animal relief total only 1% of its income, and that in 2003 alone the group killed more than 1,900 animals at its facilities. However, following a lengthy investigation, the IRS in May 2005 allowed PETA to retain its tax-exempt status.

SUMMARY

People for the Ethical Treatment of Animals (PETA) remains one of the nation's most visible and active extremist groups. Well-funded and highly organized, it has managed to keep public attention on its cause since its earliest days of existence. Critics of the group say that its openly confrontational tactics, its financial support for recognized extremist organizations, and its leaders' often outrageous statements all raise questions about the group's legitimacy. Supporters of the group justify its actions in the name of protecting animals and argue that such in-your-face tactics are necessary to attract attention and advance the group's cause.

SOURCES

Books

Singer, Peter. *Animal Liberation, (3rd Edition)*. New York: Harper Collins, 2002.

Best, Steven, and Anthony J. Nocella (eds.). *Terrorists or Freed Fighters: Reflections on the Liberation of Animals*. New York: Lantern Books, 2004.

Web sites

Activist Cash.com. "People for the Ethical Treatment of Animals." < http://www.activistcash.com/organization_overview.cfm/oid/21 > (accessed October 19, 2005).

Mike Doughney's Page. "People Eating Tasty Animals." < http://mtd.com/tasty/ > (accessed October 19, 2005).

The Center for Consumer Freedom. "GRRR . . . PETA Pitches Violence to Kids." < http://www.consumerfreedom.com/news_detail.cfm/headline/1904 > (accessed October 19, 2005).

SEE ALSO

Animal Liberation Front (ALF)

Sea Shepherd Conservation Society

Popular Front for the Liberation of Palestine-General Command (PFLP-GC)

OVERVIEW

The Popular Front for the Liberation of Palestine-General Command (PFLP-GC) is a secular, Marxist-Leninist group that stands for the armed liberation of Palestine, destruction of Israel, and global socialist revolution. It formed the Syrian-backed faction of the original PFLP, breaking ranks in 1968, barely a year after the coalition's inception. It has been heavily backed over the years by both Syria and Iran, although its activities, which have declined inexorably since 1990, and its commitment to the Palestinian cause—as opposed to Syrian interests—has been under question since the 1980s.

LEADER: Ahmad Jibril

USUAL AREA OF OPERATION: Syria; Lebanon; Israel

U.S. TERRORIST EXCLUSION LIST DESIGNEE: The U.S. Department of State first declared the PFLP-GC a terrorist organization in October 1997

HISTORY

The Popular Front for the Liberation of Palestine-General Command (PFLP-GC) can trace its origins back to the creation, in 1959, of the Palestine Liberation Front (PLF) by Ahmad Jibril. Jibril had been born in Palestine but moved to Syria in his teens. Later, he became a captain in the Syrian Army's engineering corps, where he cultivated ties with emergent military figures that would later wield considerable power in Damascus and provide military and logistical assistance to his political ambitions.

The president of Syria, Bashar Assad, center, meets with ten leaders of radical Palestinian organizations on September 10, 2005. The groups Hamas, Fatah, the PFLP-GC, Struggle Front, the DFLP, the PFLP, Al-Saiqa, the Communist Party, and Islamic Jihad are represented. Sana/EPA/Landov

In 1967, the Syrian Government backed the PLF's merger with two other groups, the paramilitary wing of George Habash's Arab National Movement, Youth for Revenge (or Youth Avengers), and the Heroes of the Return, a paramilitary group set up in Lebanon in 1966. This new movement, the Popular Front for the Liberation of Palestine (PFLP), fell under the leadership of Habash.

The coalition was, however, an uneasy one, and a power struggle between Jibril and Habash bubbled over less than a year after its inception. At the core of their disagreement was the principle of state sponsorship, with Jibril believing that the Palestinian struggle could not succeed without outside intervention, and Habash fearing Syrian domination and believing his own position against a Damascus-backed rival, backing an independent line. At one stage in 1968, Habash was imprisoned in Damascus, following which the two rival factions went their separate ways. Jibril founded the Popular

Front for the Liberation of Palestine-General Command (PFLP-GC) with his followers in December 1968, leading it from Damascus; while Habash went to Lebanon leading a diminished PFLP.

Outside backing aside, both groups had much in common, maintaining a resolutely hard line against moves towards a political settlement with Israel. They were also mostly at odds with the PLO. Nevertheless, despite greater financial and political backing, it was Habash's faction that exerted and continued to exert most power and infamy.

Two terror attacks carried out by the PFLP-GC stand out, however. In February 1970, it used a barometric pressure device to blow Swissair Flight 330 out of the sky. All forty-seven passengers on the flight bound for Israel died, including, the group boasted, senior Israeli officials, information that turned out to be incorrect. In April 1974, three PFLP-GC members massacred eighteen Israeli civilians, including nine children, in

LEADERSHIP

AHMAD JIBRIL

The PFLP-GC's founder and leader, Ahmad Jibril, was born in Jaffa, Palestine (now Israel) in 1928 but was raised in Syria, later becoming an army captain in the country's engineering corps. He founded the Palestine Liberation Front with the backing of military allies he had cultivated, forming the PFLP with George Habash in 1967, before going his own way with PFLP-GC a year later.

An utterly uncompromising individual, Jibril, despite sharing many of the leftist, secular aims of other Palestinian liberation groups, has always trod his own path with seemingly unstinting loyalty to Damascus. From the early 1980s, his group succumbed to every intrigue and underhand action of his adopted country, even when it ran counter to the interests of Palestinian liberation. Such intransigence and betrayal, combined with his refusal to accept the Oslo Accords of 1993, left Jibril a marginalized figure, a man who could only attract attention by claiming responsibility for illicit acts his group was seemingly no longer capable of.

the town of Kiryat Shmona, near the Lebanese border.

From holding outright opposition to the PLO, the PFLP-GC went on to hold a seat on the PLO's Executive Committee and Central Council in 1974. The intention, however, was entirely to do the bidding of its Syrian hosts, that at the time were holding out for a peace agreement with Israel. When such prospects faded, Jibril abandoned all pretence at moderation, vehemently rejecting any political solution to the Arab-Israeli conflict.

In 1976, Syrian troops invaded Lebanon and attacked not the Israeli-backed Maronite Christians, but the Palestinian guerrillas operating from refugee camps across the country. This was an act of pan-Arab heresy akin to King Hussein's Black September purge five years

earlier, but the PLFP-GC openly endorsed the intervention—a sure indication of its confused priorities. At this stage, a faction led by Mahmoud Zeidan (Abu Abbas), left the group and established the Palestine Liberation Front.

From this point, the PLFP-GC can be viewed almost entirely as a tool that, like the Abu Nidal Organization, operated in the interests of whichever government gave it military and financial backing. In 1983, after Yasser Arafat had intimated that he was willing to negotiate with Israel, the PFLP-GC and a pro-Syrian Fatah breakaway, Fatah Uprising, backed by Syrian artillery, drove remaining Arafat supporters out of northern Lebanon. When King Hussein of Jordan reached an agreement with Arafat in February 1985 about the future involvement of Jordan in the West Bank, Jibril's men were sent on a number of anti-Jordanian guerilla missions on Syrian instructions.

Syrian backing, however, steadily decreased as the country became plagued with economic problems in the late 1980s, and the PFLP-GC started flirtations with other regimes. Libya provided training camps, funding, and military aid, for instance, providing a hang glider used to stage an attack in November 1987 on an Israeli military base near Kiryat Shmona, which killed six soldiers. It was also linked to the bombing of Pan Am Flight 103 over Lockerbie, Scotland, an atrocity blamed on Libyan intelligence agents, but which implicated a number of groups by association. At the Lockerbie trial in 2001, the defense claimed that the attack was the responsibility of PFLP-GC, a claim which was rejected by the court. Lockerbie, nevertheless, saw Libya renounce terrorism in 1989, shortly after the PFLP-GC began receiving Iranian funds.

The PFLP-GC resolutely opposed the Oslo Accords, and in the early 1990s, assassinated a number of Arafat allies in south Lebanon. In April 1995, it was reported that a PFLP-GC agent had infiltrated Arafat's security detail with the intention of killing him but was uncovered following an Egyptian intelligence tip.

Nevertheless, the attacks and militancy of PFLP-GC seemed to be on the wane throughout the 1990s, with the organization lacking the physical presence in the Occupied Territories enjoyed by those groups that had returned post-Oslo Accord. This changed with the onset of the second intifada in October 2000 and the election of Bashar al-Assad following his father's death in June that year.

KEY EVENTS

1968: Ahmad Jibril leads a his Syrian—backed faction away from George Habash's PFLP and forms the PFLP-GC.

1970: Bombs Swissair Flight 330, killing all forty-seven passengers.

1974: Massacres eighteen Israeli civilians in the town of Kiryat Shmona.

1974: PFLP-GC joins the PLO for the first time.

1976: Syria invades Lebanon to attack Palestinian guerillas. After PFLP-GC leadership offers its support, a faction led by Abu Abbas leaves the group and establishes the Palestine Liberation Front.

1984: PFLP-GC leaves the PLO.

2000: Death of Syrian leader, Hafez al-Assad, and the election of his son Bashar, who increases support for PFLP-GP during the al-Aqsa intifada that year.

Bashar upped PFLP-GC's funding, seeking to increase his influence in the Occupied Territories under the cover of the uprising. Its attacks included border raids from south Lebanon into Israel and rocket attacks on Israeli settlements. Jibril also claimed that a huge arms shipment uncovered by the Israelis was destined for its forces, although this was almost certainly untrue and merely a boast to increase his organization's prestige.

PFLP-GC were also implicated in a plot to blow up the Azrieli Center in Tel Aviv in 2001, a fifty-story twin-towered building modeled on the World Trade Center in New York. Whether PFLP-GC was behind the attack remains to be seen: different sources have also linked the PFLP and Hamas to the attack.

PHILOSOPHY AND TACTICS

Like the preeminent PFLP, the PLFP-GC is a Marxist-Leninist organization committed to the liberation of Palestine and creation of a new world order based on socialism. It seeks the destruction of Israel as a way of creating a Palestinian homeland and has spent much of its existence at odds with the PLO, a feud that occasionally assumed murderous proportions. It opposed the Oslo Accords of 1993.

Since at least the early 1980s, however, these ideals have fitted in with Syrian political interests. Indeed, the actions of the PFLP-GC, far from serving the Palestinian people, because of its subordination to Damascus have, in practice, often worked against them.

Its actions have included shootings, guerilla raids into Israel, Jordan, and Lebanon (in which it has almost killed more Arab than Israeli targets), and rocket attacks. It was also responsible for the bombing of a Swiss jet in 1970 and implicated in the Lockerbie bombing in 1988.

OTHER PERSPECTIVES

In April 2003, U.S. President George W. Bush, added Syria to his so-called Axis of Evil, for, among other things, sponsoring terrorism. Charles Cato, Director of Defense Policy Studies at the Cato Institute, said that these accusations were probably true, but they ought not to be exaggerated. "The current rhetoric about Syria is déjà vu," he wrote. "It's almost like an instant replay of what was said about Iraq. Syria has weapons of mass destruction. Syria supports and harbors terrorists. Add to this the claims that Syria supplied the Iraqi military with night vision goggles and allowed Islamic fighters to cross the border to fight against U.S. forces, and that Syria has allowed Iraqi leaders (perhaps even Saddam Hussein himself) to flee across its border."

"...The truth is—much like Iraq—that Syria's weapons of mass destruction and support for terrorism do not represent a direct threat to the United States. And rather than trying to beat Syria into submission and increasing the U.S. military presence in the region, the administration needs to develop an exit strategy to remove U.S. troops from Kuwait, Saudi Arabia, and Iraq. That will do more to lessen the threat of terrorism against America than regime change in Damascus."

The "Axis of Evil" accusation begged Sir Andrew Green, the former British Ambassador

PRIMARY SOURCE

Popular Front for the Liberation of Palestine-General Command (PFLP-GC)

DESCRIPTION

The PFLP-GC split from the PFLP in 1968, claiming it wanted to focus more on fighting and less on politics. Originally it was violently opposed to the Arafat-led PLO. The group is led by Ahmad Jabril, a former captain in the Syrian Army, whose son Jihad was killed by a car bomb in May 2002. The PFLP-GC is closely tied to both Syria and Iran.

ACTIVITIES

Carried out dozens of attacks in Europe and the Middle East during the 1970s and 1980s. Known for cross-border terrorist attacks into Israel using unusual means, such as hot-air balloons and motorized hang gliders. Primary focus is now on guerrilla operations in southern Lebanon and small-scale attacks in Israel, the West Bank, and the Gaza Strip.

STRENGTH

Several hundred.

LOCATION/AREA OF OPERATION

Headquartered in Damascus with bases in Lebanon.

EXTERNAL AID

Receives logistical and military support from Syria and financial support from Iran.

Source: U.S. Department of State. *Country Reports on Terrorism.* Washington, D.C., 2004.

---

to Syria (1991–1994), to reassess Syria's credentials as a rogue nation. With specific regard to its support of Palestinian militants, he wrote: "The Syrians have long given hospitality to the political wing of Palestinian rejectionist movements. They permit the Iranians to channel through Damascus airport the arms required by Hezbollah in south Lebanon. These are regarded as potential levers in negotiations with Israel for return of the occupied Golan Heights. They also give Syria some measure of influence over the Palestinian and Hezbollah resistance. This is tough diplomacy, Middle East style; it hardly amounts to being a rogue state."

SUMMARY

It could be said that the PFLP-GC threw away what support it had as far back as 1976 when it backed the Syrians in the Black June attacks against Palestinian guerillas in Lebanon. The increase in funding from Bashar al-Assad has done little to change this situation during the al-Aqsa intifada, nor the idle boasts of its founder-leader, Ahmad Jibril. Nevertheless, the organization was still regarded a serious enough threat for someone to murder Jibril's son and heir apparent, Jihad, in a car bomb attack in 2002. Jibril immediately pointed the finger at Israel, but it could equally have been from the other side of the Arab-Israeli divide.

SOURCES

Books

Cummings, Bruce. *Inventing the Axis: The Truth about North Korea, Syria and Iran.* New York: New Press, 2004.

Deeb, Marius (ed.). *Syria's Terrorist War on Lebanon and the Peace Process.* New York: Macmillan, 2004.

Seale, Patrick. *Assad of Syria: The Struggle for the Middle East.* Berkeley, CA: University of California Press, 1989.

SEE ALSO

Abu Nidal Organization

Popular Front for the Liberation of Palestine (PFLP)

Popular Front for the Liberation of Palestine (PFLP)

LEADER: Ahmed Sadaat

ESTIMATED SIZE: 800

USUAL AREA OF OPERATION: Syria; Lebanon; Israel; West Bank; Gaza Strip

U.S. TERRORIST EXCLUSION LIST DESIGNEE: The U.S. Department of State first designated the PFLP a terrorist organization in October 1997

OVERVIEW

The Marxist-Leninist PFLP emerged from the Arab Nationalist Movement in 1967. It viewed the Arab-Israeli conflict not as a religious struggle nor even particularly nationalistic but as part of a broader revolution against Western imperialism. During the so-called heyday of Palestinian terrorism in the early 1970s, the PFLP gained a reputation for spectacular attacks, particularly aircraft hijackings. In the recent past, its most notorious act was the assassination of the Israeli Tourism Minister, Rehavam Ze'evi, in October 2001.

HISTORY

The roots of the Popular Front for the Liberation of Palestine (PFLP) lie as far back as 1953 with the formation of the Arab Nationalist Movement (ANM) by the Palestinian-Christian, Dr. George Habash in Beirut. Habash identified the Palestinian fight for independence as part of a wider struggle within the Arab world against Western imperialism. He saw that the Arab people were inherently weak because of a lack of education and unity when compared to their Western "enemy," and in order to progress and shake off its colonial shackles, Arab society had to be rebuilt and a new breed of man emerge.

A Palestinian militant from the Popular Front for the Liberation of Palestine (PFLP) wears a slogan that translates as, "martyr Abu Ali Mustafa brigade, Popular Front for the Liberation of Palestine." AP/Wide World Photos. Reproduced by permission.

Habash's ideas were similar to those of Egyptian President Gamal Abdel Nasser and his emergent Ba'ath movement, in that they both propagated a kind of anti-imperialist, secular pan-Arabism. However, Habash was a Marxist-Leninist doctrinaire and his worldview was framed by socialism. Later, he liked to compare himself to the Cuban revolutionaries.

The ANM formed underground branches throughout the Middle East, including Libya, Saudi Arabia, Lebanon and several Gulf States. It also formed a commando group, Youth for Revenge (or Youth Avengers) in 1964, which began carrying out attacks in Israel that year. In 1967, shortly after the devastating Six Day War, Youth for Revenge merged with two other groups, the Syrian-backed Palestine Liberation Front, and Heroes of the Return, a paramilitary group set up in Lebanon in 1966, which already had strong links to the ANM. This new coalition was named the Popular Front for the Liberation of Palestine (PFLP) and would retain strong links to the ANM.

Like the ANM, the PFLP combined militant nationalism and violence, explained and justified in Marxist rhetoric. For instance, it considered itself "a progressive vanguard organization of the Palestinian working class [dedicated] to liberating all of Palestine and establishing a democratic socialist Palestinian state." Essentially, like all Palestinian liberation groups, it was committed to the elimination of Israel, but only as part of a global communist revolution.

Habash, a particularly uncompromising individual, was, from the outset, in conflict with Yasser Arafat's Fatah movement over various issues of principle but also power and representation in the PLO. He refused to join the PLO in 1968, a position he maintained until 1972, although following Jordan's "Black September" crackdown on Palestinian groups in 1970, the PFLP agreed to take part in the Palestinian National Council and some other PLO institutions.

Nor was it just Arafat that Habash fell out with. A power struggle between Ahmad Jibril, the leader of the Palestine Liberation Front element of the PFLP coalition, and Habash bubbled over in spring 1968. The two disagreed on the principle of state sponsorship, with Jibril believing that the Palestinian struggle could not succeed without outside sponsorship. Habash, fearing Syrian domination and for his own position against a Damascus-backed rival, disagreed, and the two rival factions went their separate ways. Jibril founded the Popular Front for the Liberation of Palestine-General Command (PFLP-GC) with his followers in December 1968, leading it from Damascus. Habash returned to Lebanon, leading a diminished PFLP.

Nevertheless, Habash's faction quickly made a name for itself with a series of spectacular terrorist attacks. In July 1968, PFLP terrorists forced an El Al plane flying from Rome to Tel Aviv to land in Algeria. The flight had been targeted because the PFLP incorrectly believed the Israeli general, Ariel Sharon, to be on board. At Algiers, twenty-one passengers and eleven crew members were held hostage for thirty-nine days. This marked the first in a series of plane hijackings orchestrated by the organization (and the only time an El Al flight has been successfully hijacked).

Like the Abu Nidal Organization after it, the PFLP showed a remarkable ability to conduct terrorist attacks from a variety of locations. Gunmen opened fire on an El Al flight leaving

Leila Khaled, a member of the radical Palestinian faction Popular Front for the Liberation of Palestine (PFLP), reads a magazine in Amman, Jordan, in 1970. AP/Wide World Photos. Reproduced by permission.

Athens for New York in December 1968, killing one passenger. (In accordance with a policy of holding Arab governments responsible for fedayeen terrorism, Israel responded with a commando mission on Beirut Airport, which destroyed thirteen Lebanese passenger jets valued at $100 million and nearly plunged the region into war.) In a repeat attack at the Zurich airport, on February 18, 1969, PFLP opened fire on an El Al passenger jet taxiing for take off. In August that year, a PFLP cell, led by Leila Khaled (who would emerge as the PFLP's most glamorous and iconic member), hijacked a TWA flight from Los Angeles to Damascus and held two Israeli passengers hostage for forty-four days. In September, it simultaneously carried out grenade attacks on the Israeli embassies in The Hague, Bonn, and El Al's Brussels office.

Yet, the PFLP saved its most notorious attack for the following year. On September 6, 1970, the PFLP simultaneously hijacked three passenger jets: a TWA flight from Frankfurt; a Swissair flight traveling between Zurich and New York; and a Pan Am flight from Amsterdam. A fourth attempt to hijack an El Al flight led by Leila Khaled was thwarted, and the plane took an emergency landing at London. The TWA and Swissair flights were taken to Dawson's Field in Jordan; the Pan Am flight, which had been more spontaneous and carried out by two PFLP members denied passage on Khaled's flight, was taken to Cario via Beirut. There, it was blown up as a sign of the PFLP's disgust at Nasser for agreeing to Middle East peace negotiations.

Concerned that they might not have enough British nationals to trade for Khaled's release, four days later a PFLP team hijacked a London-bound BOAC flight shortly after its takeoff from Bahrain. The VC-10, carrying 105 passengers and a crew of ten, was ordered by two gunmen to land at Dawson's Field (renamed by the terrorists as "Revolution Airstrip") beside the two other hijacked aircraft.

Meanwhile, the PLFP, with worldwide attention focused on them and their cause, held regular press conferences at which they extolled their demands for the release of Palestinian prisoners from Europe and Israel, also giving publicity to the cause of Palestinian liberation. The hostage takers draped banners on the airliners' open doors and even painted the Popular Front's name in large Arabic letters across the fuselage of two of the crafts. They also provided ambulance rides for child hostages, helped older passengers climb down onto the tarmac for daily exercise, and brought in a doctor to attend to medical problems. Hostages would later joke of the congenial atmosphere that predominated, with one stewardess likening it to a "six day pajama party."

Concerns, however, that U.S. or Israeli commandos were preparing a raid on the hostage takers led them to evacuate the jets and blow them up, thus bringing an end to the dramatic hostage crisis.

King Hussein of Jordan, however, disliked the global attention the crisis had brought on his country, and, fearing an uprising from the 25,000 Palestinian fedayeen in his country, used it as a pretext to crackdown on militants. These events became known as "Black September," and forced the Palestinians out of Jordan at a cost of thousands of lives.

In turn, Black September was to have a unifying effect on the PLO, which would lessen the PFLP's violence. Moves towards membership of the PLO were instigated immediately after Black

Palestinians of the Popular Front for the Liberation of Palestine (PFLP) demonstrate in the northern West Bank town of Nablus on October 13, 2001. AP/Wide World Photos. Reproduced by permissions.

September, with full membership following in 1972. Throughout the 1970s, the PFLP would exist as the second largest group within the PLO, although it rejected Arafat's attempts to engineer a settlement with Israel, and in September 1976 left the PLO Executive in protest at such attempts.

Moves towards politicization were not, however, always without internal conflicts. Habash came to have little faith in the pursuit of terrorism and did not believe that it would further the Palestinian cause. Wadi Haddad, the mastermind behind the PFLP's litany of attacks, by contrast, was a staunch supporter in taking the armed struggle to the world.

At the Third Congress of the PFLP in March 1972, Habash persuaded the majority of delegates to reject "operations outside Palestine," but Haddad refused to accept the decision. In May 1972, he used PFLP allies from the Japanese Red Army (a left wing Japanese terror group) to stage what became known as the "Deir Yassin Operation." Posing as tourists, the Red Army operatives bypassed Israeli security officials at Lod Airport, before opening fire with automatic weapons: twenty-five Israelis were killed and seventy-eight wounded.

Haddad continued to utilize overseas contacts to engage in terror. On June 27, 1976, two Haddad operatives, along with two members of the West German Baader-Meinhof Gang posing as German tourists, hijacked an Air France jet in Athens and took it to Entebbe in Uganda, via Libya, where it held the passengers and crew hostage. Israeli commandos ended the crisis with a daring raid, which killed all the terrorists and liberated all but one of the hostages. The following October, another PFLP/Baader-Meinhof team hijacked a Lufthansa plane to Mogadishu, where West German paramilitaries eventually freed the aircraft.

The outbreak of the Lebanese civil war in 1975 saw the PFLP return to Syria, where the Syrian President Assad sought to curtail its extremism. From thereon, the militancy of the PLFP was severely limited, and it followed a Fatah pledge in 1988 not to engage in terrorism outside Gaza and the West Bank. The decline and fall of the USSR, on which it was reliant for financial,

LEADERSHIP

AHMED SADAAT

The PFLP's Secretary-General, Ahmed Sadaat, currently languishes in a jail in the West Bank City of Jericho, having been the highest ranked Palestinian arrested by the Palestinian Authority, in January 2002. This followed Israeli pressure in the wake of the assassination of its tourism minister, Rehavam Ze'evi, three months earlier.

Originally trained as a mathematics teacher, Sadaat became a well-known militant, coming to prominence during the first Palestinian intifada. He was known as one of the PFLP's insiders, having chosen to stay in the occupied territories rather than take exile abroad, spending a total of ten years in Israeli jails on eight separate occasions.

When he was elected as General-Secretary of the PFLP in October 2001, following the assassination of Abu Ali Mustafa, Sadaat was seen as a more radical leader and more loyal to the "original" principles of George Habash. At his inaugural press conference, he demanded, "Our right of return, and our independence, with Jerusalem as the capital." He also vowed to avenge the assassination of Abu Ali.

His arrest in January 2002 polarized his supporters and the PLO, with PFLP members accusing the PLO of "Zionist capitulation."

---

military, moral, and political support, also weakened the organization. Its opposition to the Oslo Accords in 1993 also precluded it from returning to the Occupied Territories and playing a part in the Palestinian Authority, until it accepted an invitation from the PA to join it in 1999.

George Habash's retirement in 2000 and the onset of the al-Aqsa intifada later on that year saw a shift in strategy. Israel accused the PFLP of carrying out several bomb attacks in Jerusalem, and in August 2001 assassinated Habash's successor Abu Ali Mustafa, a killing that prompted worldwide outrage. In reprisal,

the PLFP killed Israel's hard-line Tourist Minister Ramavah Ze'evi two months later.

Under pressure from Israel, the Palestinian Authority subsequently arrested a number of PFLP leaders, including its new leader, Ahmed Sadaat. Nevertheless, the organization has continued to show glimpses of its deadly potential. For instance, in April 2002, Israeli officials claimed to have foiled an attempt to blow up a Tel Aviv skyscraper (this has also been linked to the PFLP-GC), and it has been linked to a number of subsequent suicide bombings in Israel.

PHILOSOPHY AND TACTICS

The Popular Front for the Liberation of Palestine is a Marxist-Leninist organization committed to the liberation of Palestine and creation of a new world order based on socialism. Its founder and long-term leader, George Habash, often compared the Palestinian struggle to that of the Cuban revolutionaries, and its central tenet is a commitment to socialism as opposed to nationalism (like Fatah) or religion (like Hamas). It is committed to the destruction of Israel as a way of creating a Palestinian homeland, and it opposed the PLO's efforts to reach a political settlement in the 1970s and 1980s, likewise the Oslo Accords of 1993.

In its early stages, Habash sought to model the PFLP on the Cuban revolutionaries, building up a small, highly educated and ideologically motivated organization. Given its physical limitations, it used international terrorism as a way of bringing world attention to the Palestinian problem, particularly through the use of aircraft hijackings. Casualties in these attacks and waged frequent press conferences to publicize their cause. In particular, Leila Khaled, became an iconic figure through such publicity.

From the late 1970s, the PFLP was hamstrung by its Syrian hosts and was thus limited in its extremist activities. Its return to Palestine in 1999 and the retirement of Habash a year later has seen attempts to switch the PFLP's focus to being a mainstream secular alternative to Fatah, although only with limited success. Terrorist activities since then have consisted of attacks on Israeli civilians, as well as accusations of suicide bombings and the assassination of a senior Israeli politician.

KEY EVENTS

1967: PLFP forms as an amalgamation of three paramilitary organizations: Palestine Liberation Front, Heroes of the Return, and Youth for Revenge. It splits with the PLF element that forms the PFLP-GC.

1968: PLFP hijack an El Al fight between Rome and Tel Aviv, forcing it to land in Algiers.

1970: Swissair flight 330 is blown up, killing forty-seven on board.

1970: PFLP simultaneously hijacks four planes (one unsuccessfully) and later captures a fifth; the crisis prompts Black September.

1972: Habash renounces violence; although Wadi Haddad vows to continue armed struggle.

1976: Joint PFLP/Baader-Meinhof hijacking of Air France jet.

1993: PFLP reject Oslo Accords.

1999: PFLP accept invitation to join Palestinian Authority.

2000: Habash steps down as PFLP leader.

2001: Israeli special forces assassinate Habash's successor Abu Ali Mustafa.

2001: PFLP murders Israeli Tourism Minister Rehavam Ze'evi.

2002: Arrest of PFLP leader Ahmed Sadaat.

OTHER PERSPECTIVES

In the wake of the PFLP's quadruple hijacking in September 1970, *Time* magazine hinted at some of the global outrage caused by such audacity. "Skyjackers are the greatest threat to travel since bandits roamed the Old West, " it asserted. "With astonishing impunity, the pirates of the skies are able to take over the swift vehicles that represent the most advanced developments of modern technological civilization. Less and less often are the culprits misfits and former mental patients seeking psychic as well as physical

escape. Increasingly, they are dedicated, vicious political fanatics, who have discovered that one of the most vulnerable points of the developed world is a jetliner at an altitude of 30,000 ft."

Time then went on to suggest that such acts did little to further the Palestinian cause. "If the world has become a global village . . . the Palestinians have become its most troubled ghetto minority," it stated. "Evicted from their ancient homeland by the influx of Jews after World War II, the Palestinians were driven into the squalid misery of refugee camps on the Jordanian desert. The Arab governments, which could have helped them, preferred to allow the refugees to remain in the camps as living symbols of the Israeli usurpation. The Israelis were unwilling to accept large numbers of Palestinians inside their own borders and thus risk becoming a minority within their own state. Gradually, the Palestinians honed their hostility. From the sons and daughters of the original refugees have sprung thousands of guerrilla fighters whose fury intimidates even the Arab governments."

In a 1974 essay on guerilla warfare, Walter Lacquer traced back two centuries of guerilla movements all the way through to the Palestinians. While hijackings and suchlike might provoke outrage and consternation, it kept the Palestinian cause alive. "Despite all their setbacks, the Palestinian terrorist organizations have succeeded in their main aim, which is to keep the Palestinian issue alive," he wrote. "Their failure to establish an effective resistance movement inside Israel was regarded by the Israelis as a decisive defeat, but with guerrilla warfare in the generally accepted meaning of the term impossible inside Israel, the Palestinians found by trial and error that there were other ways of carrying on the struggle, and that publicity was the decisive weapon in this particular fight. Hence the decision to hijack planes, the attacks against foreign ambassadors in Khartoum, the Munich massacre, and similar operations.

"These actions were widely condemned, but what was infinitely more important, they were given a great deal of publicity. The Israelis, it was said, had driven the Arab refugees to these acts of despair, and there would be no peace in the Middle East unless justice were done to the Palestinian cause. It remains doubtful whether this strategy would have succeeded but for the growing dependence of the industrialized countries on Arab oil, but there was an auspicious

PRIMARY SOURCE

Popular Front for the Liberation of Palestine (PFLP)

DESCRIPTION

Formerly a part of the PLO, the Marxist-Leninist PFLP was founded by George Habash when it broke away from the Arab Nationalist Movement in 1967. The PFLP does not view the Palestinian struggle as religious, seeing it instead as a broader revolution against Western imperialism. The group earned a reputation for spectacular international attacks, including airline hijackings, that have killed at least twenty US citizens.

ACTIVITIES

The PFLP committed numerous international terrorist attacks during the 1970s. Since 1978, the group has conducted attacks against Israeli or moderate Arab targets, including killing a settler and her son in December 1996. The PFLP has stepped up its operational activity since the start of the current intifadah, highlighted by at least two suicide bombings since 2003, multiple joint operations with other Palestinian terrorist groups, and assassination of the Israeli Tourism Minster in 2001 to avenge Israel's killing of the PFLP Secretary General earlier that year.

STRENGTH

Unknown.

LOCATION/AREA OF OPERATION

Syria, Lebanon, Israel, the West Bank, and the Gaza Strip.

EXTERNAL AID

Receives safe haven and some logistical assistance from Syria.

Source: U.S. Department of State. *Country Reports on Terrorism.* Washington, D.C., 2004.

international constellation and the Palestinians made the most of it. Confidence has risen dramatically in recent months. The Zionist state, as the Palestinian terrorists see it, is in a condition of advanced decay; a few more determined pushes and it will collapse altogether. 'We believed the struggle would last a hundred years, now we think it will last only ten,' one of the Palestinian leaders in Beirut was quoted as saying the other day."

SUMMARY

Following the retirement of a charismatic leader, PFLP has struggled to carve a niche in the post-Oslo political era, created by a peace deal that it steadfastly rejected. Attacks linked to it in the al-Aqsa intifada at best seem to be exaggerated attempts to grab some of the limelight, and it looks as if the PFLP's heyday passed with its last skyjacking nearly three decades ago.

SOURCES

Books

Khaled, Leila. *My People Shall Live: The Autobiography of a Revolutionary.* London: Hodder and Stoughton, 1973.

Savigh, Yezid. *Armed Struggle and the Search for State: The Palestinian National Movement, 1949–1993.* England: Oxford University Press, 1999.

Web sites

Red Pepper Magazine. "Interview with Leila Khaled." < http://www.redpepper.org.uk/intarch/x-khaled.html > (accessed October 19, 2005).

Time Magazine. "Habash: 'Israel Will Fall.'" < http://www.time.com/time/archive/preview/0,10987,945844,00.html > (accessed October 19, 2005).

SEE ALSO

Popular Front for the Liberation of Palestine-General Command (PFLP-GC)

Abu Nidal Organization

Posse Comitatus

LEADERS: William Potter Gale; James Wickstrom
YEAR ESTABLISHED OR BECAME ACTIVE: 1969

OVERVIEW

The Posse Comitatus was a loosely organized collection of racist anti-government organizations that developed through the 1970s, garnered media attention during the 1980s, and had largely disappeared by the end of the 1990s. The group believed that the federal government's authority is illegitimate and that any citizen can declare himself sovereign, or free of government control; its members also espoused radical racist positions, claiming that the U.S. government had come under the control of a Jewish conspiracy. The group's leaders advocated violence and the use of financial fraud in order to achieve their objectives. By the turn of the twenty-first century, Posse Comitatus' members and leaders had been largely absorbed into various other white supremacist groups.

HISTORY

White supremacist organizations have a long history in North America. Among the earliest of these groups was the Silver Shirts, a pro-Nazi group dating to the 1930s. This anti-Semitic organization attracted as many as 15,000 followers at its peak in 1934, though its numbers quickly dwindled in the years that followed; its members drifted away or moved to other white supremacist groups.

Among the members of the original Silver Shirts was a retiree named Henry Beach, a resident

Michigan Militia members torch a United Nations flag outside the State Capitol Building in Lansing, Michigan, on October 24, 1995, to protest United Nations Day. AP/Wide World Photos

of Portland, Oregon. Although the Silver Shirts had long since dissolved, Beach retained his racist views, and in 1969 launched an organization he named the Sheriff's Posse Comitatus. Beach's group professed a blend of racist and anti-government beliefs. At roughly the same time in California, William Potter Gale launched a similar organization called the United States Christian Posse Association. Gale was a long-time racist, and his organization had much in common with Beach's, including anti-Semitic beliefs and a belief in local, rather than federal rule. Little is known about how or even if the two groups coordinated their efforts, however, their beginning forms the genesis of the broader Posse Comitatus movement. From Beach and Gale's groups, similar Posses formed through-out the country, particularly in the Midwest and in agricultural regions. By 1975, approximately eighty such groups existed across the nation.

Posse Comitatus organizations existed with-out any formal hierarchy or authority, cooperating as they saw fit and operating autonomously. Despite this independence, several basic beliefs united the movement and fueled its efforts. Foremost among their beliefs is an unwillingness to submit to federal or state government authority.

The term "Posse Comitatus" is taken from a common law term meaning "power of the county," though it is often interpreted more loosely to mean simply the power of citizens to rule themselves. In practical use, the term refers to the local sheriff's authority to gather a group of men and force them to assist him in administering justice; many classic Western movies include a scene in which the sheriff leads a posse to arrest fleeing criminals.

The term also refers to legislation passed in the United States following the Civil War, the Posse Comitatus Act of 1878. This law gen-erally forbids the use of federal troops for law enforcement actions within the United States, except as authorized by the Constitution, Congress, or Presidential order. The original

LEADERSHIP

JAMES WICKSTROM

James Wickstrom was first introduced to the Posse Comitatus by Thomas Stockheimer, the founder of the Wisconsin Posse Comitatus. While initially unsure about the group's beliefs that whites are the modern-day descendents of God's chosen people, Wickstrom soon became a convert, due in part to the influence of sermon tapes from group founder, William Potter Gale. Following Stockheimer's imprisonment on assault charges in 1976, Wickstrom moved to Missouri, where he soon started his own church. After a falling out with another white supremacist preacher in 1978, he moved to Wisconsin to join a fledgling community called Constitutional Township of Tigerton Dells. Wickstrom opened a church there and declared himself the community's head of counterinsurgency.

Wickstrom traveled extensively, preying on distraught farmers by telling them that they were victims of a Jewish plot and that the federal government was illegitimate; he advocated lynching as a simple solution to these problems. In later years, Wickstrom ran unsuccessfully for U.S. Senator and governor of Wisconsin. He later served jail time for various charges. In 2004, he was named the World Chaplain for the Aryan Nations, a white supremacist group that reportedly adopted the motto, "No Jew left alive in 2005."

WILLIAM POTTER GALE

William Gale co-founded the Posse Comitatus movement in 1969. Gale was a virulent anti-Semite who, though lacking formal ordination, referred to himself as "reverend." Gale's message was consistently anti-Jewish, warning his listeners that Jews were children of Satan and that a Jewish conspiracy was acting to take over America. Gale is perhaps best known for a sound-bite from a sermon broadcast in Kansas in 1982: "If a Jew comes near you, run a sword through him."

Gale's racist views dated to the 1950s when he adopted the beliefs of Christian Identity, which teaches white superiority and Jewish inferiority. He preached and spoke continuously for the cause of white superiority until his death in 1988. At the time of his death, Gale was actively appealing his recent conviction for threatening an Internal Revenue Service agent. Ironically, Gales' parents had arrived in the United States in 1894, after fleeing Russian oppression. Gales' parents were both Jewish.

---

purpose of the legislation was to prevent military involvement in Southern elections following the Civil War; the application of the law has effectively prevented most uses of military personnel or equipment against U.S. citizens, reserving these actions for civilian law enforcement agencies.

Consistent with both of these definitions, Posse Comitatus organizations are unanimous in their belief in local self-rule; most groups claim independence from federal (and in many cases, state) authority, recognizing only the local level of governmental authority. Under this system of government, the local sheriff is the highest level of government authority and is charged with enforcing local laws. The sheriff also serves at the pleasure of the citizens and may be removed from office, if they so choose.

Given their disrespect of federal authority, it is hardly surprising that Posse Comitatus members frequently refuse to pay income taxes or purchase automobile license plates. In addition, they were generally unwilling to recognize even the local government's right to repossess property such as farmland. They also generally deny the worth of U.S. currency, claiming that because the country's paper money is not based on actual gold reserves, it is worthless. This belief has been offered as the justification for numerous incidents of Posse fraud and counterfeiting.

A second unifying characteristic of Posse members is anti-Semitism, or the contention that Jews are inherently inferior to whites. While white supremacists advance numerous theories about why Jews are inferior to whites, most of these justifications fall under two broad

---

PRIMARY SOURCE

Rooting for Armageddon

[A review of the book], ARMED AND DANGEROUS The Rise of the Survivalist Right. By James Coates. New York: Hill & Wang.

It was in early June 1983 that more than 40 armed Federal, state and local police surrounded a remote farmhouse in the Arkansas Ozarks and tried to arrest a bespectacled 63-year-old tax protester named Gordon Kahl.

In the shoot-out and conflagration that ensued, both Kahl and a sheriff who led a half-dozen officers into the concrete farmhouse-bunker died. The sheriff killed the elderly fugitive with a single shot to the head, but not before Kahl had squeezed off a barrage from an automatic rifle. The lawman reeled outside but bled to death. Fellow officers unleashed a fusillade of fire and tear gas, igniting thousands of rounds of ammunition and stores of explosives in the bunker that rocked the rainy hillsides like thunder for two hours.

It was the end of a violent odyssey for Gordon Kahl, a North Dakota farmer and anti-tax fanatic who had gone on the run four months earlier after another bloody confrontation.

In that incident, five armed officers, three of them Federal marshals, had come after Kahl at his rural North Dakota farm because he had violated his parole in a tax matter. Kahl, his 23-year-old son, and a third man opened fire, and when it was over all five lawmen lay on the ground, two dead and three wounded. Kahl himself had run straight at two of them with an automatic weapon, laying down a hail of fire. He managed to hide out for months until his fiery death in the bunker.

Kahl, it developed, was a disciple of Posse Comitatus, a neo-anarchist organization that is violent, anti-Semitic and antiblack as well as anti-government. The Jews, Posse leaders preached, were the fount of all evil, and the true Israelites were Aryans, destined to regain the Promised Land of America in a racial Armageddon that would establish the primacy of the white race.

Federal investigators began to uncover disturbing links between Posse adherents and other heavily armed racial extremists, including the Ku Klux Klan, the American Nazi Party and lesser-known neo-Nazi and anti-Semitic survivalist groups with names like Aryan Nations, the Christian Patriots Defense League and the Covenant, the Sword and the Arm of the Lord - the latter of which maintained a heavily armed compound some 60 miles from where Kahl died. But it was a year and a half before Federal investigators began to decipher the links and discover how dangerous the network they formed was.

That is also what James Coates's "Armed and Dangerous" is about—the rise of what he calls the survivalist right in America, a loosely linked network of armed racist revolutionaries

headings. First are biological rationales, which argue that Jews are somehow genetically inferior to people of European descent (whites). One such argument is the contention that the Jews of the Bible migrated to Europe, making today's Europeans the true Jews and today's Jews are imposters. This belief, called Ango-Israelism or British Israelism, is a central feature of a broader white supremacist movement known as Christian Identity. A more extreme biological argument made by some white supremacists is that Jews are not actually human beings; instead, though they appear human they are in fact a lower type of creature, so-called "mud people," or the soul-less descendents of Satan.

A second broad line of anti-Semitic reasoning rests on a seemingly endless stream of conspiracy theories that portray the Jews as plotting against white Americans. In some of these accounts, Jews, referred to as Zionists, are gradually taking over the U.S. banking and financial systems. In other versions of the story, the Zionists are working toward seizing control of the entire U.S. government. While these anti-Semitic assertions appear to have little basis in fact, they form one of the major

bent on the overthrow of what they call the ZOG, or Zionist Occupational Government, and the establishment of an Aryan nation, or White Bastion, in its place.

It is also about the odd, violently racist beliefs of these organizations and the curious people who adhere to such beliefs—from those who, like Gordon Kahl, died for them, to the spiritual leaders like 66-year-old Richard Girnt Butler, founder of the goose-stepping Aryan Nations in Idaho, and Robert Miles, a former Klansman who is pastor of the racialist Mountain Kirk in upstate Michigan. There are also gruesome side trips to such places as a cult hideaway in Rulo, Neb., where a deviant cultist was flayed alive in the course of his ritual murder—although the motives behind such acts may have been more psychopathic than ideological.

Eighteen months after the Kahl shoot-out in Arkansas, an almost identical drama played itself out 2,000 miles away on Whidbey Island in Puget Sound. There, 200 police officers surrounded a house where another fugitive, 31-year-old Robert Jay Matthews, died in a blaze set by a flare. He had held the men at bay for 36 hours with sproradic bursts from a machine gun.

Matthews was the charismatic leader of a group that calls itself the Bruder Schweigen, or Silent Brotherhood (it has come to be known as The Order), a fanatic band of racist revolutionaries later convicted of crimes ranging from armed robberies that netted more than $4 million to arson, counterfeiting and a host of other offenses. Two members of the group were convicted Nov. 17 in Federal District Court in Denver of civil rights violations in the 1984 machine-gun murder of the radio talk show host Alan Berg.

Investigators began to unravel a bizarre ideological affinity among the groups. Matthews plotted with his fellow racist warriors in the Bruder Schweigen, but there was no evidence that he knew Gordon Kahl. What possessed them both was the same anti-Semitic pseudotheology, called Christian Identity, or, more often, simply Identity. It holds that Jews are the offspring of Satan, have seized the land and the power of the true Aryan Israelites—white Christians—and must be exterminated, along with the "mud people," the blacks, browns and other minorities who are their purported henchmen. What also unites such people and the shifting groups they form is a kind of institutional paranoia that drives them into remote armed camps to prepare for the end.

Wayne King

Source: New York Times, 1987

elements of Posse Comitatus philosophy. In the Posse Comitatus and similar groups, white supremacist views extend to all non-whites, not just Jews.

Posse groups first began to attract attention in 1974, when Thomas Stockheimer, the leader of the Posse in Wisconsin, was tried and convicted for assaulting an Internal Revenue Service agent. Other Posse leaders in Wisconsin also attracted attention in the following years, including James Wickstrom, the self-appointed "national director of counterinsurgency" for the Posse. Wickstrom's base of operations was a farm in northeastern Wisconsin. There, he and others with similar views assembled a group of trailers, then declared the land the Constitutional Township of Tigerton Dells. In taking this step, Wickstrom and his comrades claimed that their property was no longer under the control of the U.S. government.

Wickstrom's message of defying the government and resisting foreclosing bankers resonated with farm families struggling to make ends meet during the farm crisis of the late 1970s and early 1980s. Wickstrom began offering paramilitary style instruction at Tigerton Dells around 1980, claiming

KEY EVENTS

1969: Henry Beach and William Potter Gale independently form the first two Posse groups.

1975: Thomas Stockheimer, leader of the Wisconsin Posse, is convicted of assaulting an Internal Revenue Service agent.

1980: James Wickstrom begins offering paramilitary training at the Tigerton Dells compound. That same year, Wickstrom runs for U.S. Senate.

1983: Gordon Kahl and U.S. Marshals exchange gunfire at a roadblock. Kahl escapes, but is later killed in a shoot-out in Arkansas.

1983: Wickstrom is sentenced to 13 ½ months for impersonating a city official.

1990: Wickstrom is convicted for his efforts to print $100,000 in counterfeit currency. He serves three years in prison.

2004: With the Posse Comitatus largely a memory, Wickstrom is named to the post of World Chaplain for the white supremacist group Aryan Nations.

that thousands of students were being trained by elite military veterans. Wickstrom also ran for the U.S. Senate in 1980, receiving 16,000 votes. Two years later, he ran for governor of Wisconsin.

Following its early years of relative quiet, the Posse Comitatus leaped into the headlines in 1983 when Gordon Kahl became a fixture on the nightly news. Kahl was a tax protestor and racist who had stopped filing his income tax returns in 1968; he frequently traveled the country, encouraging others to do the same. In February 1983, Kahl was traveling to his rural home following a meeting with supporters. Local police and federal marshals had obtained an arrest warrant for Kahl and attempted to serve the warrant, using a roadblock.

Kahl's vehicle stopped before reaching the roadblock, and some of Kahl's passengers, including his son, aimed rifles at the marshals, who were already aiming their weapons at

Kahl's vehicle. After a tense standoff, a firefight erupted; men on both sides of the standoff were hit, two officers died, and Kahl escaped. He was quickly added to the FBI's most wanted list, and a nationwide manhunt began. Kahl was eventually cornered in Arkansas, where both he and a sheriff died in a second gunfight.

Kahl's death provided a launching point for a massive publicity blitz in which Jim Wickstrom traveled the talk-show circuit, claiming that Gordon Kahl had been wrongfully killed and was therefore the movement's first martyr. Wickstrom's appearances on 20/20 and The Phil Donahue Show included little of his usual fiery rhetoric, instead serving to promote the Posse as a refuge for the working class and the oppressed.

Wickstrom's fame was short-lived. Soon after his Donahue appearance, he was charged with impersonating a public official, an accusation stemming from his actions in Tigerton Dells. Prosecutors argued that Wickstrom's claim of sovereignty was not only implausible, but that Wickstrom himself did not even believe it. The judge sentenced Wickstrom to thirteen and a half months in jail, the maximum sentence allowed. During his incarceration, Tigerton Dells was closed for zoning violations.

Wickstrom was released in 1985 and moved to Pennsylvania under a parole agreement that did not allow any involvement with the Posse Comitatus or other political groups for two years. Wickstrom, however, soon returned to Posse activities and was eventually arrested again. In 1990, he was convicted for his involvement in a plot to print $100,000 in counterfeit currency for use by white supremacists. With Wickstrom behind bars and no new leader emerging to take his place, the Posse foundered. By the time of Wickstrom's release in 1993, the Posse had largely disappeared.

Consistent with its core opposition to federal and state authority, the Posse Comitatus as an organization did not utilize any structure or authority above the local level. Given this inherent autonomy of each local chapter, the group never achieved the notoriety of other more organized hate groups. However the Posse Comitatus played a foundational role in the development of today's broader Christian Identity Movement, providing the early framework from which the current white supremacist movement evolved.

PHILOSOPHY AND TACTICS

The philosophy of the Posse Comitatus is consistent with most other white-supremacist, anti-government factions, and includes several key positions. Foremost among these is the illegitimacy of the U.S. government. Consistent with this position, Posse members were often involved in overt actions to challenge the federal government's authority. In some cases, they simply quit paying income taxes, then proceeded to boast about it and encourage others to follow suit, leading to numerous confrontations between group members and Internal Revenue Service representatives. In other cases, they threatened public officials. Most of these threats were directed at mayors, city council members, and other local authorities; judges and other court officials were also frequent targets of group threats.

The group attracted government attention in 1975 when a band of Posse members allegedly created a team for the purpose of assassinating Vice President Nelson Rockefeller. The discovery of this plot prompted the FBI to open a formal investigation of the group; investigators concluded that the group numbered around 15,000, with perhaps 150,000 others supporting them.

While the Posse Comitatus claimed to support American values and ideals, it repeatedly demonstrated a willingness to defraud other Americans in pursuit of its objectives. Like many other anti-government factions, Posse members frequently issued counterfeit checks to purchase equipment and weapons. Group leader James Wickstrom served three years in prison for his part in a scheme to produce $100,000 in counterfeit U.S. currency for use by white supremacists. Group leaders frequently justified these fraudulent tactics by claiming that the U.S. financial system is controlled by Jewish bankers and should therefore be disrupted.

Violence was also a preferred tactic of the Posse Comitatus, though the group as a whole appears to have invested more time in planning and training for combat than it did in actual fighting. Kenneth Stern, in his 1995 book *A Force Upon the Plain,* provided extensive descriptions of Posse efforts in Kansas. He revealed how William Potter Gale and James Wickstrom joined forces to sponsor "counter insurgency seminars" during the early 1980's. According to a report by the Kansas Attorney

General's office, training at these seminars included techniques for hand-to-hand combat, assassinations, night combat, the use of ambushes for murder, and bomb-making. William Gale also wrote a handbook on using guerilla warfare tactics which was widely distributed by Posse groups.

One of the more unusual tactics used by the Posse Comitatus was the establishment of so-called sovereign courts and government structures. Most notable was the group's Minnesota compound (Tigerton Dells), which leaders claimed was no longer part of the United States. In addition to his self-appointed role as head of counter-terrorism in the township, James Wickstrom also appointed himself its municipal clerk and judge. Wickstrom then exercised his self-appointed authority to grant a liquor license to township founder Donald Minniecheske, whose actual liquor license had been revoked two years earlier. For his actions in Tigerton Dells, Wickstrom was eventually convicted on two counts of impersonating a city official and sentenced to jail time.

Anti-government organizations like Posse Comitatus teach their members a variety of disruptive tactics for use in trying to avoid imprisonment or other legal sanctions. Many of the group's tactics appear rather juvenile, however, they can bring a routine judicial proceeding to a rapid halt. For example, Posse members will frequently deny that they are the person listed on a warrant or court docket, or in some cases, will simply refuse to identify themselves at all, leaving the court little recourse but to hold them in contempt.

In other cases, individuals refuse to sign court documents, again putting the proceeding on hold until a signature can be obtained. Some defendants have chosen to appear in court but have refused to speak or answer questions; conversely, defendants sometimes tie up the court by refusing to be silent, talking incessantly whenever given the floor. In one extreme case involving an anti-government activist, a defendant took the improbable step of convening his own court inside the actual courtroom. He then proceeded to ask the judge questions, issue rulings on motions, and conduct his own mock trial within a trial.

Anti-government factions also utilize intimidation as a weapon. In some cases, defendants pack courtrooms with their own supporters in an effort to sway the judge. In other cases, threats have been issued not just against judges and jurors but even court clerks. One of the most common anti-government intimidation tactics involves the use of fraudulent liens and lawsuits. Filing these legal motions against elected and judicial officials requires very little time or money for the anti-government activist. However, resolving the filing often requires a great deal of time and effort for the elected official, making these filings a potent harassment tactic. In many cases, defendants file a veritable mountain of paperwork, attacking the case judge, each juror, the prosecutor, and even such employees as the bailiff. They also frequently file to dismiss the case, since they claim not to be under the jurisdiction of U.S. courts.

OTHER PERSPECTIVES

While the Posse Comitatus has largely disappeared, its ideology remains strong, carried forward by a variety of contemporary white supremacist organizations. Although largely autonomous, these competing groups often support one another when it advances their purposes, and in many cases their roots run back through the same racist leaders. The staunch support of other racist groups, coupled with members' frequent postings to racist discussion sites, creates the impression that these crusaders are not alone or unrealistic in their objectives. However, outside the white supremacist community itself, only a handful of Constitutional advocacy groups such as the American Civil Liberties Union (ACLU) generally support the white supremacist cause in any way. In those circumstances the advocacy groups are careful to distance themselves from support of the

extremist ideology and restrict themselves to legal support of free speech rights.

SUMMARY

The Posse Comitatus, a loosely organized coalition of anti-government white supremacist groups, formed one of the earliest stages in the development of today's white supremacist movement. With a membership that peaked around 15,000 during the 1970s, the group lost momentum during its leader's incarceration and was eventually supplanted by better organized anti-government and racist organizations.

SOURCES

Books

Levitas, Daniel. *The Terrorist Next Door: The Militia Movement and the Radical Right*. New York: St. Martin's Press, 2002.

Stern, Kenneth S. *A Force upon the Plain: The American Militia Movement and the Politics of Hate*. New York: Simon and Schuster, 1995.

Web sites

Anti-Defamation League. "Paper Terrorism's Forgotten Victims: The Use of Bogus Liens against Private Individuals and Businesses." < http://www.adl.org/mwd/privlien.asp > (accessed October 21, 2005).

Anti-Government.com. "The Anti-Government Movement Guidebook: Posse Comitatus." < http://www.anti-government.com/ > (accessed October 21, 2005).

Southern Poverty Law Center. "Hate and Hypocrisy: What Is Behind the Rare-but-recurring Phenomenon of Jewish Anti-Semites?" < http://www.splcenter.org/intel/intelreport/article.jsp?aid = 73 > (accessed October 21, 2005).

Provisional Irish Republican Army

LEADER: Gerry Adams

USUAL AREA OF OPERATION: Northern Ireland; the Republic of Ireland; mainland Britain

OVERVIEW

The Provisional Irish Republican Army (universally known as the IRA, or "Provos") is Ireland's preeminent nationalist paramilitary organization. A modern successor of the "old" Irish Republican Army that had fought the Anglo-Irish War, it formed following a split with the Official IRA in 1969. Thereafter, its violent campaign of bombings, assassinations, kidnappings, and robberies—in the Republic and Northern Ireland, plus mainland Britain—followed almost uninterrupted for 25 years. During the 1990s, it entered two ceasefires, while its political wing, Sinn Fein, held peace talks with the British government, culminating in the Good Friday Agreement of 1998.

HISTORY

The origins of the IRA lie far back, within the Anglo-Irish War (1916–1921), which resulted in the creation of the Irish Free State. The use of force to push through ideals of Irish republicanism had tradition, extending back even further through the rebellions of 1798, 1803, and 1865 to the creation of the Irish Republican Brotherhood (IRB) and Irish Volunteers.

The impetus for the creation of the IRA came after the Easter Rising of 1916—at which

An 18-year old Catholic girl was killed in 1997 by Protestant extremists in the home of her Protestant boyfriend in Ulster, Northern Ireland. © *Abbas | Magnum Photos*

a Proclamation of the Irish Republic was read out and independence declared. The rising, organized by the IRB and the Irish volunteers, was militarily and politically unsuccessful and its ringleaders either executed or interned. Following its failure, in October 1917, Sinn Fein, a small republican political party under the leadership of Eamonn De Valera that had wrongly been accused of organizing the rising, set about reorganizing the defeated Irish Volunteers. It organized this new group, the Irish Republican Army (IRA), into hundreds of companies (estimates range between 162–390) throughout Ireland, and over the following four years it was at the forefront of the war to secure nationhood.

When this concluded with the Anglo-Irish Agreement of December 1921, Ireland was partitioned between the 26 predominantly Catholic counties of the south—the Irish Free State—and the six mostly Protestant counties of the north, which became Northern Ireland and remained part of the United Kingdom. The treaty split the IRA, and the Irish Free State descended into a

bloody civil war, between the pro-treaty IRA (which became the regular Irish National Army) and those who opposed the treaty as a betrayal of Irish nationalism.

This bloody civil war, which lasted a year, claimed more lives than the War of Independence, and ended in defeat for the anti-treaty IRA. Nevertheless, even after a ceasefire had been agreed with the Irish Free State in May 1923, a minority of the defeated IRA continued to insist that the Irish Free State was created by an "illegitimate" treaty and was an illegitimate state. As such, they refused to recognize it or its institutions, and claimed that the IRA Army Executive was the real government of the still-existing Irish Republic proclaimed in 1918. These would remain important principles for the IRA in decades to come.

An uneasy coexistence emerged between the Irish Free State and the IRA, and the organization flitted between periods of illegality and attempts by the Irish government to reach compromise. During World War II, it sought after

Smoke billows from a Londonderry, Northern Ireland, department store on January 4, 1972. The fire resulted from a bomb planted in the building by militant members of the Irish Republican Army. AP/Wide World Photos. Reproduced by permission.

A hooded man delivers the IRA's Easter Message at a rally in Crossmaglen, Northern Ireland, on April 7, 1996. The year marked the 80th anniversary of the 1916 Easter uprising.

AP/Wide World Photos

arms from Nazi Germany and passed on intelligence to them about bombing targets in Belfast. It also launched an armed campaign in Belfast in 1942.

Post-war, it initiated a campaign of border raids from the Irish Republic into Northern Ireland, which included attacks on security installations and attempts to disrupt the province's infrastructure. While this would be the basis for Provisional IRA attacks in later years, the border campaign was regarded as an annoyance rather than a threat and failed to attract significant support from populations on either side of the border. The campaign ended in 1962.

By the end of the 1960s, the IRA was in a state of disarray. It had become increasingly under the influence of left-wing thinkers, who espoused a Marxist analysis of partition, which its critics considered irrelevant, and deep divisions emerged over the issue of abstentionism (essentially, whether the Irish government be

recognized). A split came in 1969, and the two groups that emerged became known as the (Marxist-espousing) Official IRA and the Provisional IRA, which carried on the traditions set by the anti-treaty IRA four decades earlier. It continued the long-standing tradition of claiming that the IRA Army Council was the provisional government of a 32-county Irish Republic.

The Provisional IRA soon came to dominate the republican movement (the Official IRA, by contrast, was effectively dormant and declared a ceasefire in 1972), particularly in the north where the Catholic community had been under increased attack from loyalists.

As the intermittent fighting of the late 1960s became full-scale civil chaos, the IRA increased in size, prestige, and notoriety. Incidents such as "Bloody Sunday", in 1972, when British troops killed 13 unarmed civil rights protestors in Derry, and the introduction of internment without trial, boosted its ranks substantially and saw a flow of dollars coming in from a sympathetic Irish diaspora, particularly the United States. From being a poorly armed and demoralized organization in the late 1960s, the Provisional IRA had become, in a matter of years, a sophisticated and well-equipped paramilitary organization with a wide base of support.

The Provo's main strategy in the early 1970s was to disrupt the civil and economic life of Northern Ireland and to attack British military installations. It also set itself out as the defender of Catholics in the province. This manifested itself in a number of ways. British soldiers and Royal Ulster Constabulary (RUC) officers were routinely assassinated, both on and off duty. If loyalist paramilitaries targeted a Catholic, the IRA would seek reprisals either against the paramilitaries themselves or, more commonly, against Protestant civilians.

The group set out to disrupt civil and economic life in the province by starting a bombing campaign in town centers and on other key targets, such as rail and bus stations. Never were its efforts more notorious than on July 21, 1972, when it set off 22 bombs across Belfast. Nine deaths were caused by two of the bombs, including six people at Belfast's busiest bus station.

A year later, attempts to bring a political solution to Northern Ireland failed, and in 1974, the IRA began a bombing campaign in mainland Britain, with the express aim of

IRA riots in Londonderry, Northern Ireland, in 1985. © *Stuart Franklin, Magnum Photos*

sapping any political will to hold onto the province that existed within Westminster or the population at large. High-profile attacks included the bombing of a bus of soldiers and their families, killing 12; the bombing of pubs in Guilford and Birmingham, which killed a total of 23 people; and an attack on Harrods department store in Knightsbridge. Car bombs in Dublin and Monaghan also killed 33 people.

Rather than diminishing resolve in Britain, the IRA's sustained campaign of terror meant that no credible politician was willing to talk with them. Over subsequent years, the attacks would increase in notoriety and ambition: from the murder of Prince Philip's uncle, Earl Mountbatten, in 1979, to the attempt to kill British Prime Minister Margaret Thatcher in the bombing of a hotel in Brighton in 1984 during the Conservative Party Conference; the bombing of a Remembrance Day Parade in Enniskillen in 1987 that killed 11 civilians to the bombing of a fish and chip shop on Shankhill Road in 1993, which killed nine Protestant civilians.

Their political marginalization was such that British broadcasters were not even allowed to broadcast the voices of the leaders of its political wing, Sinn Fein. Given this shunning, the IRA was forced to launch audacious stunts to achieve political action. The most notorious of these were the Maze Prison hunger strikes in 1981, when convicted IRA members went on a hunger strike for "prisoner of war" status. Its most notorious advocate, Bobby Sands, died after 64 days without food. He became immortalized as a republican martyr.

Nevertheless, the election of Gerry Adams as Sinn Fein president in 1983 saw moves to bring the IRA back to within a modicum of electoral respectability and to bring a political solution to "The Troubles." In 1986, Adams brought an end to the long-standing principle of abstentionism, allowing Sinn Fein to sit in the Irish Dail (although not Westminster). This recognition that the IRA was not, in fact, the provisional government of Ireland paved the way for tentative negotiations with Dublin and Westminster.

Nevertheless, only in the mid 1990s would the stream of terrorist attacks in Northern Ireland and Britain begin to come to an end. Secret talks initiated by British Prime Minister

LEADERSHIP

GERRY ADAMS

Born to a staunchly nationalist Catholic family in West Belfast in 1948, Gerry Adams was embroiled in nationalist politics from his mid-teens, becoming a member of Sinn Fein at the age of 16. He rose swiftly through the ranks of the party and was an important part of the emergent civil rights movement in the early 1970s. He was interred without trial by the British authorities in 1971, and again between 1973 and 1977.

Ostensibly, this was for IRA membership, although Adams has always denied the accusation. Evidence, nevertheless, suggests otherwise. British and Irish governmental papers and the testimony of former IRA members point to Adams' membership, while Irish justice minister, Michael McDowell, claims Adams and his deputy, Martin McGuinness, were members of the IRA Council until July 2005. In *A Secret History of the IRA*, Ed Moloney describes in detail Adams' alleged IRA career: joined as an 18-year-old volunteer in D Company on the Falls Road in 1966; went with the Provisionals in 1970; commander in the West Belfast housing estate of Ballymurphy in 1971; member of the Belfast Brigade staff; second in command and then Belfast commander in 1972; interned in 1973; released in 1977 and joined the ruling Army Council; briefly, chief of staff in 1977; Northern commander in 1979; and so it goes on. Adams' supporters, nevertheless, decry such allegations as lies.

Either way, Adams proved an adept and skilled politician, taking a pragmatic long-term view of the seemingly indissoluble problems of Northern Ireland. He rose to vice president of Sinn Fein in 1978, and quickly extolled the controversial view that a military struggle alone would not bring the republicans its desired goals. Sinn Fein and the IRA began to work in synch, adopting a dual policy that became known as "the armalite and the ballot box"—in other words, the pursuit of republican goals through both violent and political means.

While he seemed a relentless hard-liner and a particularly unremorseful individual when faced with the horrors of the IRA's latest atrocity, Adams was slowly realigning Sinn Fein to a point where they could credibly enter the political process. He became president in 1983, and three years later dropped the principle of abstentionism. This meant Sinn Fein could speak to the Irish government, without claiming its authority. Secret trilateral talks with the British and Irish governments in the early 1990s paved the way for an IRA ceasefire in 1994, which held for 17 months. A further ceasefire in 1997 held, and led to the Good Friday Agreement, which provided Northern Ireland with a political settlement. Adams convinced the majority of republican community that this path would provide the mechanisms to eventually deliver a united Ireland by constitutional means.

Adams apparent resignation from the IRA Council in July 2005 and the IRA's disbandment shortly after effectively completed his journey from alleged terrorist to mainstream politician, and his realignment of Sinn Fein from the mouthpiece of the IRA to a genuine political force on both sides of the Irish border.

John Major led to a ceasefire in September 1994, which held for 17 months. A second ceasefire, called in July 1997, proved more long lasting and paved the way for talks on power-sharing in Northern Ireland, culminating in the Good Friday Agreement of 1998.

When devolved government started in the province later on that year, senior Sinn Fein figures took up roles within the government.

Although the Northern Ireland Assembly would be characterized by infighting and would be suspended in 2002 because of the IRA's reluctance to publicly decommission its arms, the IRA ceasefire held. Nevertheless, breakaway paramilitary groups, the Continuity IRA and the Real IRA, continued terrorist activity, sometimes to horrifying effect. The principles of the "old school" IRA still held strong in some quarters.

KEY EVENTS

1969: Formation of Provisional IRA after a split within the ranks of the former IRA.

1972: Bloody Sunday massacre leads to an upsurge in IRA attacks.

1972: Bloody Friday bombings in Belfast.

1974: Series of IRA outrages in Britain and the Irish Republic.

1983: Election of Gerry Adams as Sinn Fein president.

1984: IRA attempt to kill British Prime Minister Margaret Thatcher in Brighton bombing.

1986: Sinn Fein drops abstentionism, paving the way for negotiations with British and Irish governments.

1994: Ceasefire after secret talks with British and Irish governments.

1994: Second IRA ceasefire paves the way for political talks on Northern Ireland's future.

1998: Good Friday Agreement.

2005: IRA announces disbandment.

Northern Ireland continues to be divided along paramilitary lines, however. While overt sectarian killings carried out by paramilitaries have declined inexorably, the one-time terrorists maintain their hold over their communities in other ways. Gangsterism, drug dealing, and extortion are now a way of life for many former paramilitaries. The robbery of the Northern Bank in Belfast in December 2004 is widely believed to have been carried out by the IRA— a "retirement fund," as some have wryly observed. Moreover, the brutal murder (and cover up) of Robert McCartney a month later and the IRA's refusal to cooperate with the authorities in the pursuit of justice begged serious questions about its integrity and willingness to engage as a lawful organization.

On July 28, 2005, the Provisional IRA announced an end to its armed campaign and stated that it had instructed its members to dump all weapons, and to engage in no "other activities whatsoever" beyond "the development of purely political and democratic programmes through exclusively peaceful means." It also authorized its representatives to ensure the Independent International Commission on Decommissioning put its arms beyond use.

PHILOSOPHY AND TACTICS

The Provisional IRA is committed to the removal of British forces in Northern Ireland and the creation of a united Ireland. At various stages in its history, it has also adopted a socialist visage, although the Marxist rhetoric that precipitated its split with the Official IRA in 1969 has seldom been extolled in recent years.

For most of its history, the IRA's claims to be the provisional government of the Irish republic gave it a one-dimensional approach and meant it was unequivocally committed to regaining its perceived mantle by armed struggle only. The tactics of the Provisional IRA were initially threefold: the disruption of economic and civil life in Northern Ireland by targeted bombing; attacks on military and police installations to undermine the British presence; and the "protection" of Ulster's Catholic community.

A fourth strand emerged in 1974 with attacks on the British mainland, designed to test the political will of ordinary Britons and their government's readiness to hold on to the province.

The dropping of abstentionism and the claims to be Ireland's provisional government in 1986 meant it was able to see out a more dualistic policy, a so-called "armalite and ballot box" approach. This would culminate in a lasting ceasefire from 1997 and Sinn Fein's arrival as a mainstream political party shortly thereafter.

OTHER PERSPECTIVES

A leader in the conservative *Daily Telegraph* published in the wake of the IRA's call for disbandment in July 2005 viewed the move with suspicion. "The statement says that all IRA units have been ordered to 'dump arms,' without saying all their arms," it pointed out. "It gives no

PRIMARY SOURCE

Irish Republican Army (IRA) a.k.a.
Provisional Irish Republican Army
(PIRA), the Provos

DESCRIPTION

Formed in 1969 as the clandestine armed wing of the political movement Sinn Fein, the IRA is devoted both to removing British forces from Northern Ireland and to unifying Ireland. The IRA conducted attacks until its cease-fire in 1997 and agreed to disarm as a part of the 1998 Belfast Agreement, which established the basis for peace in Northern Ireland. Dissension within the IRA over support for the Northern Ireland peace process resulted in the formation of two more radical splinter groups: Continuity IRA (CIRA), and the Real IRA (RIRA) in mid to late 1990s. The IRA, sometimes referred to as the PIRA to distinguish it from RIRA and CIRA, is organized into small, tightly-knit cells under the leadership of the Army Council.

ACTIVITIES

Traditional IRA activities have included bombings, assassinations, kidnappings, punishment beatings, extortion, smuggling, and robberies. Before the cease-fire in 1997, the group had conducted bombing campaigns on various targets in Northern Ireland and Great Britain, including senior British Government officials, civilians, police, and British military targets. The group's refusal in late 2004 to allow photographic documentation of its decommissioning process was an obstacle to progress in implementing the Belfast Agreement and stalled talks. The group previously had disposed of light, medium, and heavy weapons, ammunition, and explosives in three rounds of decommissioning. However, the IRA is believed to retain the ability to conduct paramilitary operations. The group's extensive criminal activities reportedly provide the IRA and the political party Sinn Fein with millions of dollars each year; the IRA was implicated in two significant robberies in 2004, one involving almost $50 million.

STRENGTH

Several hundred members and several thousand sympathizers despite the defection of some members to RIRA and CIRA.

LOCATION/AREA OF OPERATION

Northern Ireland, Irish Republic, Great Britain, and Europe.

EXTERNAL AID

In the past, the IRA has received aid from a variety of groups and countries and considerable training and arms from Libya and the PLO. Is suspected of receiving funds, arms, and other terrorist-related material from sympathizers in the United States. Similarities in operations suggest links to ETA and the FARC. In August 2002, three suspected IRA members were arrested in Colombia on charges of helping the FARC improve its explosives capabilities.

Source: U.S. Department of State. *Country Reports on Terrorism.* Washington, D.C., 2004.

---

undertaking to co-operate with the forces of law and order, while renewing the IRA's commitment to ending British rule—majority rule—in Northern Ireland. The statement praises 'our patriot dead' and IRA men who have been sent to prison for murder... We hope passionately that a lasting peace will come to Northern Ireland. But, so far, the latest initiative looks like just the latest step in a macabre dance, in which the IRA offers only words, while the democratically elected Government immediately performs deeds in return. What sort of message does that send to terrorists all over the world?"

Colin Parry, a peace campaigner whose 12-year-old son, Tim, was killed in an IRA bomb attack in Warrington town center in 1993, gave the call for disbandment a cautious welcome. "I don't say anything other than I welcome these words, but I do think that, as ever, you look for the words that aren't there as much as the words that are. The absence of any absolute ending of violence was a shame. I rather hoped they would say, 'This is it for all time and under no circumstances will we ever return to the armed struggle'... Usually, words like 'sincerity' with the IRA are difficult for me, but I think it's been a clearly thought out tactical decision and one which is based upon the absolute, over-whelming proof that there's nothing to be gained from the continuation of the armed struggle.

"I don't think this war had any winners. There have been losers all round: more than 3,000 lives wasted, families torn apart and a political resolution to the problem halted by the continuation of the violence over 30 years. Those who say it's the violence which got the IRA and Sinn Fein to the table are, in my opinion, talking absolute rubbish. Britain's hands aren't clean as far as the history of Ireland is concerned. I wouldn't argue with that, because I think there's enough history to prove that point, but that didn't justify blowing up buildings and killing police officers, blowing up towns and city centres. Two wrongs don't make a right. The loss of my son never goes away. It's always at the fore..."

SUMMARY

Despite the call for the IRA's disbandment and despite Sinn Fein's relative electoral success, the IRA stands at a crossroads in its history. There seems to be three routes newly retired paramilitaries can take. Those hooked on violence and with an inherent belief that only an armed struggle can bring about ambitions as republicans and Irish nationalists may join the flagging ranks of IRA splinter groups, such as the Continuity IRA or the Real IRA, or even form their own paramilitary group. They could take the path trodden by former IRA activists like Gerry Adams and Martin McGuinness and pursue their goals via constitutional methods. There is also the prospect that they will continue operating—as they largely have since 1998—beyond the law and without political interest as gangsters, extorting, robbing, and continuing to make their reputations count financially. A final possibility is that the IRA will merely fade from consciousness, like other revolutionary organizations throughout history, their vision part of people's present, their role part of the past.

SOURCES

Books

McKittrick, David, and David McVeigh. *Making Sense of the Troubles*. London: Penguin, 2003.

Moloney, Ed. *Secret History of the IRA*. London: Penguin, 2003.

Taylor, Peter. *The Provos: The IRA and Sinn Fein*. London: Bloomsbury, 1998.

Toolis, Kevin. *Rebel Hearts, Journeys in the Republican Movement*. London: Picador, 1995.

Web sites

BBC News. "Provisional IRA: War, Ceasefire, Endgame?" < http://news.bbc.co.uk/hi/english/static/in_depth/northern_ireland/2001/provisional_ira/ > (accessed October 14, 2005).

PBS. "Behind the Mask: The IRA & Sinn Fein." < http://www.pbs.org/wgbh/pages/frontline/shows/ira/ > (accessed October 14, 2005).

SEE ALSO

Real Irish Republican Army

Continuity Irish Republican Army

Irish Republican Army

Real Irish Republican Army (RIRA)

YEAR ESTABLISHED OR BECAME ACTIVE: 1997

ESTIMATED SIZE: 150

USUAL AREA OF OPERATION: Northern Ireland; Republic of Ireland; mainland Britain

The Real IRA (RIRA) is a dissident Irish republican splinter group responsible for the Omagh bombing of August 1998—the single worst incident of Northern Ireland's thirty-year-long troubles—and several other attacks on mainland Britain. It was founded by several disgruntled members of the twelve-member executive group of the Provisional IRA in late 1997 as a response to the negotiations between its political wing, Sinn Fein, and the British and Irish governments. It regarded these talks, which would culminate in the Good Friday Agreement of April 1998, as a betrayal of republicanism and saw its mission as continuing the armed struggle.

HISTORY

The slow entry of Sinn Fein—and, in turn, the Provisional IRA—into Ireland's peacemaking process, begun when Gerry Adams was elected its president in 1983, had been regarded by sections of the republican movement with suspicion and contempt. In 1985, a former Sinn Fein president, Ruari O'Bradaigh, had led a breakaway group, Republican Sinn Fein, when the party's long-standing policy of abstention from the Irish Parliament, the Dail, ended. Republican Sinn Fein's military wing, the Continuity IRA

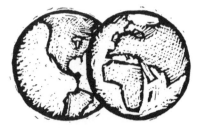

Real IRA graffiti on a wall in west Belfast, Northern Ireland. The Real IRA is thought to be responsible for the August 1998 Omagh bombing. AP/Wide World Photos. Reproduced by permission.

(CIRA), began terrorist activity following the Provisional IRA ceasefire in 1994.

Perhaps if O'Bradaigh had not been regarded as yesterday's man and his organization not seen as amateurish, his fledgling party may have made a deeper impact within republican politics at a time when closer cooperation with the British and Irish governments was raising concerns among parts of the republican community. Throughout late 1997 and on into 1998, the Continuity IRA made a number of bombings in an effort to disrupt peace talks, but these acts failed to make the desired impact.

It increasingly appeared that if any serious effort would be made to derail the peace process in accordance with historical principles of Irish nationalism, it would come from within the Provisional IRA itself. In late 1997, several of the IRA's twelve-member executive group left in opposition to Sinn Fein's backing of the Mitchell Principles on democracy and nonviolence. These were designed to act as a precursor

to full-scale political negotiations on power-sharing the following year. In the weeks running up to a special Provisional IRA convention, where it was expected that Sinn Fein would be given the go-ahead to enter into new political negotiations, the dissidents released a statement stating that the ceasefire was over and that there would be a return to military action. The dissidents called themselves the Real IRA and denounced the "old leadership" of the Provisional IRA, likening them to Michael Collins and Eamonn De Valera, men who many republicans believed betrayed their cause when forming the Irish Free State almost 80 years earlier.

In 1986, when Republican Sinn Fein had been formed, the nascent organization had been characterized by its relative weakness: a group with high ambitions of revolutionary insurrection, but without the power base or means to carry out such aims. Now, to the alarm of British intelligence, it was a group of

A large-scale car bomb destroyed much of Edward Street in Portadown, Northern Ireland, when it exploded on February 24, 1998. AP/Wide World Photos. *Reproduced by permission.*

KEY EVENTS

1997: IRA ceasefire prompts outrage in sections of the republican movement, leading to the formation of a splinter group, the Real IRA.

1998: Good Friday Agreement.

1998: Attack on Banbridge.

1998: Omagh mombing kills twenty-nine people in the worst act of violence in Northern Ireland's history.

2000: Real IRA attack on MI6 headquarters.

2002: Call by imprisoned Real IRA leaders for disbandment.

2005: Irish Justice Minister, Michael McDowell, claims that the Real IRA are down to just 150 members.

senior IRA men of similarly benign ambitions, but with the know-how, weaponry, and see-mingly, the manpower to perpetrate savage attacks.

In addition to the former members of the IRA executive, there was a former IRA Quartermaster—which indicated they probably had access to weapons—and the apparent back-ing of dissident members of the Provisional IRA's South Armagh Brigade, formerly its most important rural stronghold. It also had the backing of Bernadette Sands-McKevitt, sister of the late IRA terrorist and hunger striker, Bobby Sands, an iconic figure, deified in the eyes of the republican movement. His sister was a high-profile and vociferous addition to the ranks of this breakaway group.

Bombings on the towns of Moira and Portadown in early 1998 showed the Real IRA's deadly potential and the apparent use of splinter cells to carry out attacks, independent of a conventional command structure.

The Real IRA's early attacks had been rela-tively minor but, on August 1, 1998, a huge

bomb was set off at peak shopping time in the center of the town of Banbridge. A warning had been received shortly before the explosion, but it had not provided sufficient time to prevent injuries to more than thirty people or to prevent millions worth of damage.

In many ways, this attack was the Real IRA's first major attack, and loss of life was only narrowly averted. Two weeks later, how-ever, on August 15, 1998, the Real IRA would carry out a bombing that would secure their notoriety. In an almost identical attack, a 500-pound car bomb was set off at the height of shopping time in the small County Tyrone town of Omagh, killing twenty-nine people (including a woman pregnant with twins) and injuring another 200.

The bombing was the worst act of terrorism in the province's deeply troubled history and prompted outrage in Britain, Ireland, and across the world. For the Real IRA, it was the cause of intense political embarrassment and served to almost entirely marginalize them. This was heightened by a flood of arrests by British and Irish police in the huge operation that followed the bombing.

LEADERSHIP

MICHAEL MCKEVITT

Michael McKevitt was the Provisional IRA's dissident Quartermaster who left the organization in 1997 in protest at Sinn Fein's entry into peace talks. With several former members of the Provisional IRA Council, McKevitt formed the Real IRA. He was number one in a chain of command that placed his wife, Bernadette Sands-McKevitt, sister of the hunger striker, Bobby Sands, at number three.

McKevitt was already a hardened and deeply experienced terrorist when he helped form the Real IRA. His previous role with the Provisional IRA gave him the knowledge to acquire arms, and the involvement of a number of similarly experienced men made his organization uniquely dangerous.

Following the Omagh bombing, it was widely assumed that McKevitt had been behind the attack and he was forced to flee his home. Nevertheless, the police case against him was slow and it took until 2003 for McKevitt to be tried.

The case against him was based largely on the testimony of an undercover FBI and MI5 agent, David Rupert, who McKevitt had made head of the Real IRA's U.S. operations, after Rupert had infiltrated the organization. During the trial, it came out that McKevitt had hatched plans to assassinate British Prime Minister Tony Blair. Just days before the trial's conclusion, he issued a death threat to the Sinn Fein leader, Gerry Adams.

McKevitt was found guilty of "direction of terrorism" and "membership of an illegal organization" and sentenced to twenty years imprisonment.

Despite the Real IRA subsequently announcing a ceasefire, in September 2000 a missile attack on MI6's headquarters in Vauxhall, London, ended the apparent cessation in hostilities. Attacks on the BBC, Ealing Broadway tube station, and an attempt to blow up Hammersmith Bridge in West London followed

over the subsequent year, but these bombings were relatively low-tech, and disruptions and injuries minimal.

In fact, not until August 2002 would the Real IRA again claim a life, when a booby trap at a Territorial Army (British Army Reserves) base in County Londonderry killed a maintenance worker. The relatively minor nature of all these attacks hinted at the growing military weakness of the Real IRA after all the arrests and political marginalization following the Omagh outrage.

This sense grew further in autumn of 2002, when a message from Real IRA inmates at Portlaoise Prison in the Irish republic denounced the organization's leadership as corrupt, saying that it had "forfeited all moral authority" and called for its immediate disbandment.

More recently, the role of the Real IRA has been limited to punishment beatings and fire bombings, although its name is often linked to bank robberies and extortion, which suggest it may be raising funds for another offensive. Nevertheless in 2005, the Irish Justice Minister, Michael McDowell, told the Dail that the organization was down to a maximum of just 150 members.

PHILOSOPHY AND TACTICS

Like their precursors, the Continuity IRA, the Real IRA's mantra centers on the "old school" brand of Irish nationalism based on an unyielding belief in the creation of a thirty-two-county united Ireland on the back of an armed struggle. While its refusal to negotiate with either British or Irish governments—which they regard as illegitimate—give it a unique complexion, they also make the Real IRA a marginal force in a country no longer in the thrall of revolutionary foment. Maybe its ambitions were feasible in a different era, but with mainstream republicans engaged in Northern Ireland's intermittently successful power-sharing process, the violence propagated by the Real IRA in pursuit of its aims seems outmoded and deeply unsavory in the minds of most Irish people.

Like the Provisional IRA a generation earlier, the Real IRA's violent tactics center primarily on disrupting Northern Ireland's economic infrastructure by the detonation of bombs in

PRIMARY SOURCE
Real IRA (RIRA)

DESCRIPTION

RIRA was formed in the late 1990s as the clandestine armed wing of the 32-County Sovereignty Movement, a "political pressure group" dedicated to removing British forces from Northern Ireland and unifying Ireland. The RIRA also seeks to disrupt the Northern Ireland peace process. The 32-County Sovereignty Movement opposed Sinn Fein's adoption in September 1997 of the Mitchell principles of democracy and non-violence; it also opposed the amendment in December 1999 of Articles 2 and 3 of the Irish Constitution, which had claimed the territory of Northern Ireland. Despite internal rifts and calls by some jailed members—including the group's founder Michael "Mickey" McKevitt—for a ceasefire and disbandment, RIRA has pledged additional violence and continues to conduct attacks.

ACTIVITIES

Bombings, assassinations, and robberies. Many Real IRA members are former Provisional Irish Republican Army members who left that organization after the Provisional IRA renewed its cease-fire in 1997. These members brought a wealth of experience in terrorist tactics and bomb making to RIRA. Targets have included civilians (most notoriously in the Omagh bombing in August 1998), British security forces, police in Northern Ireland, and local Protestant communities. RIRA's most recent fatal attack was in August 2002 at a London army base that killed a construction worker. In 2004, RIRA conducted several postal bomb attacks and made threats against prison officers, people involved in the new policing arrangements, and senior politicians. RIRA also planted incendiary devices in Belfast shopping areas and conducted

a serious shooting attack against a Police Service of Northern Ireland station in September. The organization reportedly wants to improve its intelligence-gathering ability, engineering capacity, and access to weaponry; it also trains members in the use of guns and explosives. RIRA continues to attract new members, and its senior members are committed to launching attacks on security forces. Arrests in the spring led to the discovery of incendiary and explosive devices at a RIRA bomb making facility in Limerick. The group also engaged in smuggling and other non-terrorist crime in Ireland.

STRENGTH

The number of activists may have fallen to less than 100. The organization may receive limited support from IRA hardliners and Republican sympathizers dissatisfied with the IRA's continuing cease-fire and Sinn Fein's involvement in the peace process. Approximately forty RIRA members are in Irish jails.

LOCATION/AREA OF OPERATION

Northern Ireland, Great Britain, and Irish Republic.

EXTERNAL AID

Suspected of receiving funds from sympathizers in the United States and of attempting to buy weapons from US gun dealers. RIRA also is reported to have purchased sophisticated weapons from the Balkans, and to have taken materials from Provisional IRA arms dumps in the later 1990s.

Source: U.S. Department of State. *Country Reports on Terrorism.* Washington, D.C., 2004.

---

town centers. It has also targeted Northern Ireland's security forces and their bases. On mainland Britain, where they have also set out to disrupt economic targets, their attacks hold a dual purpose, namely to diminish the British will to hold onto Northern Ireland. Nevertheless, the Real IRA's weakness has seen it make more

symbolic attacks or choose easier targets, away from the comparatively well-guarded area of central London, such as Hammersmith Bridge and Ealing Broadway tube station, both in the west London suburbs, than carry out the sort of atrocities that would genuinely shake their victims.

As with the IRA, its funding has come largely from sympathetic Irish Americans and from bank robberies. Nevertheless, the U.S. Department of State's classification of the Real IRA as a terrorist organization has stymied the flow from the former in recent years.

OTHER PERSPECTIVES

"It's certain that the bombers did not intend to murder the twenty-nine people who were killed," wrote the BBC's Northern Ireland correspondent, Dennis Murray, in a deeply personal and at times angry essay on the Omagh bombing. "What they intended was that members of the security forces would die. The intention of the bombers was that people would die. To them, non-people. Human beings who were in the uniform of what they call 'Crown Forces'. Murder, plain and simple, murder. A plan that people, those in uniform, would die. And in the name of what? In the name of a crusade—a jihad—a holy war, to unite Ireland. To unite Ireland? Yes, to unite Ireland." Murray went on to say that the bombers achieved only one thing: "uniting all of the people of Ireland in disgust—at their out-of-the-past, unthinking stupidity."

"RIRA members follow an extreme, fundamentalist Republican ideology," wrote the intelligence expert Sean Boyne in *Jane's Intelligence Review* shortly after the Omagh atrocity in 1998. "They claim their historical mandate for violence goes back to the Declaration of Independence of the 1919 Dail. This alleged mandate from a long-dead electorate conveniently allows them to ignore the clear wishes for peace of the vast majority of living Irish people—north and south—as expressed through parliamentary elections and referendums.

"The RIRA is essentially a tiny fringe group, with no electoral mandate or popular support. It is not amenable to public opinion. Nevertheless, it would prefer to have public sympathy in the areas where it operates." Boyne believed even then that the Real IRA faced an uncertain future in light of the expected security clampdown. Nevertheless, he warned, "despite all this pressure, one can expect certain RIRA diehards to blithely ignore the clamour for peace and to cling to the policy of the bomb and the bullet."

SUMMARY

The Omagh bombing of August 1998 seemed to represent the sum of many people's fears about the Northern Irish peace process; yet rather than serving as the inspiration for further acts of terror, it attracted widespread revulsion and served as the prompt for extraordinary efforts by British and Irish security forces to infiltrate dissident republican groups. Moreover, the successful referendum on the Good Friday Agreement gave Northern Ireland's republican population a clear reminder of what they had overwhelmingly chosen: namely, a modern brand of republicanism that sought solutions by due political process.

By 2001, when its last attack was carried out in mainland Britain, the Real IRA was in disarray, beset by arrests and infiltration. When calls for its disbandment were made by senior members a year later, it surprised few people. Since then, the Real IRA has remained on the fringes, stymied but unbroken, a reminder of the extremes that still bubble under the surface of Irish politics.

SOURCES

Books

McKittrick, David, and David McVeigh. *Making Sense of the Troubles*. London: Penguin, 2003.

Mooney, John, and Michael O'Toole. *Black Operations: The Secret War against the Real IRA*. County Meath, Ireland: Maverick House, 2003.

Web sites

Jane's Intelligence Review. "The Real IRA: After Omagh, What Now?" < http://www.janes.com/regional_news/europe/news/jir/jir980824_1_n.shtml > (accessing October 14, 2005).

BBC News. "The Omagh Bomb." < http://news.-bbc.co.uk/1/hi/in_depth/northern_ireland/2000/the_omagh_bomb/default.stm > (accessed October 14, 2005).

SEE ALSO

Continuity Irish Republican Army

Provisional Irish Republican Army

Irish Republican Army

Red Army Faction

LEADERS: Gudrun Ensslin, and Andreas Baader
YEAR ESTABLISHED OR BECAME ACTIVE: 1978
ESTIMATED SIZE: 10–20
USUAL AREA OF OPERATION: West Germany (now Germany)

OVERVIEW

The Red Army Faction (RAF), or *Rote Armee Fraktion*, is a terrorist organization that is known to have targeted various government and business entities in Germany in the late 1970s and 1980s. Throughout this period, the group reportedly carried out numerous terrorist activities in Germany. As thought by analysts and monitor groups, the group has been inactive since the mid 1990s.

The Red Army Faction is also known as Baader-Meinhof Gang and Baader-Meinhof Group. As of 2005, the group has been excluded from the U.S. State Department Terrorist organizations list.

HISTORY

Although the Red Army Faction was claimed to have formed in 1978, its roots can be traced back to the late 1960s, according to published reports. During the 1960s, there were wide-ranging student protests in Germany, especially in the city of Berlin. The protests were reportedly in opposition to the Vietnam war as well as the aggressive tactics employed by the West German police.

Following the protests, a few German students, including Gudrun Ensslin and Andreas

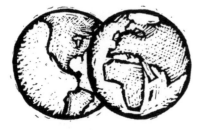

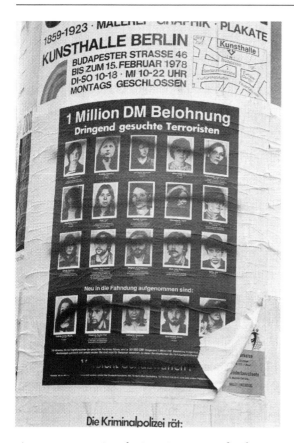

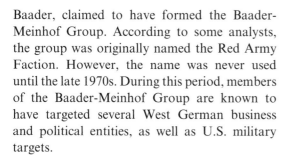

A poster protesting the imprisonment of militant Red Army Faction members. © Raymond Depardon / Magnum Photos.

KEY EVENTS

1968: Four students claim to form the Baader-Meinhof Group in West Germany.

1972: Several leaders of the group, including Baader, Ensslin, Meinhof, Holger Meins, and Jan-Carl Raspe, are caught by the West German police.

1975: The Stammheim Trial begins; Baader, Ensslin, and other RAF leaders are convicted and sentenced to life imprisonment. This trial is considered to be the longest and the most expensive in the history of Germany.

1976: Baader and Ensslin allegedly commit suicide in their prison cell on the same day.

1978: Remaining members of the reportedly dissolved Baader-Meinhof Group and form the Red Army Faction.

1992: RAF issues a public statement declaring ceasefire.

1998: The RAF officials announces the termination of the group.

Baader, claimed to have formed the Baader-Meinhof Group. According to some analysts, the group was originally named the Red Army Faction. However, the name was never used until the late 1970s. During this period, members of the Baader-Meinhof Group are known to have targeted several West German business and political entities, as well as U.S. military targets.

As thought by analysts, the Baader-Meinhof Group, following the arrest of several leaders, started losing steam by the mid 1970s. A few original members of the group committed suicide. The group was allegedly dissolved in 1977. Monitor groups state that the remaining members of the Baader-Meinhof Group formed the Red Army Faction in 1978, claiming to follow the same ideologies and philosophies as the Baader-Meinhof Group.

In the 1980s, the RAF was held responsible for numerous bombings, assassinations, kidnappings, and robberies. Some of these included the 1986 bombing of an IBM Corporation building in Heidelberg, West Germany. Government officials alleged that the attack was carried out by members of the RAF. The bombing caused significant structural damage to the building. During the same year, the West German government also accused members of RAF of shooting a manager of Siemens and his driver.

The late 1980s also witnessed a number of similar attacks, allegedly by the RAF. Among these were the bombing of Deutsche Bank chief, Alfred Herrhausen, in November 1989. On April 1, 1991, Detlev Karsten Rohwedder, leader of a West German Government organization was killed.

As thought by government officials and terrorism experts, the number of terrorist acts by

LEADERSHIP

GUDRUN ENSSLIN AND ANDREAS BAADER

The RAF and its parent group Baader-Meinhof is thought to have had numerous leaders over the years. Analysts, however state that the founding members, Gudrun Ensslin and Andreas Baader, were the key driving factors behind the formation and subsequent operations of the group.

Both Ensslin and Baader were thought to have strong communalist beliefs and had reportedly masterminded many of the operations of Baader-Meinhof in the 1970s. Baader and Ensslin were arrested by West German police in the mid 1970s. In 1975, Baader and Ensslin, along with other leaders of the RAF, were sentenced to life imprisonment after the Stammheim Trial—reportedly the longest and most expensive trial in German history.

Baader and Ensslin, in 1976, were found dead in their prison cells. West German officials ruled the deaths as suicide. However, supporters of the RAF allege that the two were killed by the police.

RAF decreased by the early 1990s. Experts attribute a number of reasons for this including the decline of communism around the world and the reunification of Germany in 1990.

According to published reports, RAF made a public announcement in 1992, declaring a ceasefire against the government. Reports also suggest that the group officially announced their dissolution in 1998.

PHILOSOPHY AND TACTICS

The Red Army Faction and its predecessor, Baader-Meinhof Group, are known to have a communist ideology. Terrorism experts state that the group was formed with an aim of creating separate socialist states in Germany and

throughout Europe. Members of the RAF have philosophies based on communism and Marxism, which can be defined as a state without social classes. Communists propagate a classless society that is not ruled by political governments or any other form of private ownership: everything is divided equally within a society.

According to anti-terrorism experts, the RAF aimed at reducing the "oppression" and the "hardcore tactics" of the West German authorities in the 1970s and 1980s. The group's tactics were also aimed at U.S. military operations and "imperialism" around the world.

According to published reports, over the years the RAF consisted of only ten to twenty members. However, their tactics were known to be quite deadly. During the 1970s and 1980s, RAF and Baader-Meinhof allegedly carried out several bombings, political killings, kidnappings of business leaders, and robberies. These were aimed mainly at West German and American government, business, and political establishments. Reportedly, the killings and bombings were carried out in protest against what the RAF calls a "monopoly capitalism and imperialism."

Since the 1970s, the group is thought to have formed alliances with other radical and extremist organizations. One such suspected ally was Action Directe, the terrorist organization from France. U.S. and West German government officials also allege that the RAF received financial support, logistic support, training, and shelter from the intelligence agency of East Germany (this was in the 1980s before the unification of Germany). Analysts and monitor groups claim that several members of the group received training from Palestinian and other Middle Eastern terrorist organizations.

By the early 1990s, the RAF is thought to have become ineffective. The reason for this, as suggested by experts, is the decline of communism worldwide, triggered by the fall of the Soviet Union. The group officially announced that it was disbanding in 1998.

OTHER PERSPECTIVES

The West German police officials often criticized the tactics of the Red Army Faction. Most experts state that the members of the RAF followed communist philosophies. However, a few argue that the RAF had edged towards anarchism later on—opposing any action and policy by the government.

There are many who supported the student protests of the 1960s. However, they were quick to criticize the strategies employed by the RAF. A German journalist, Guenter Zint who in the past lived with Ulrike Meinhof and other radical journalists, stated in an interview with BBC that "People know that the Sixties changed Germany for the good." However, referring to the Baader Meinhof gang, he mentioned, "The resort to terrorism killed the protest movement."

SUMMARY

The Red Army Faction is known to be inactive since the late 1990s. During the 1970s and 1980s, a period when the group was thought to be at its peak, the RAF allegedly carried out a number of terrorist acts against the West German government.

Since early 1990, the group reportedly saw a decline in its activities due to the fall of communism around the world. In 1998, the Red Army Faction officially announced that it was disbanding.

SOURCES

Web sites

BBC.com. "Full Circle for German Revolutionaries." < http://news.bbc.co.uk/1/hi/world/europe/ 1250944.stm > (accessed October 15, 2005).

BBC.com. "German Red Army Faction Disbands." < http://news.bbc.co.uk/1/hi/world/europe/80960.stm > (accessed October 15, 2005).

BBC.com. "Germany Recalls Its 'Autumn of Terror.'" < http://news.bbc.co.uk/1/hi/world/europe/ 2340095.stm > (accessed October 15, 2005).

MIPT Terrorism Knowledge Base. "Group Profile: Red Army Faction." < http://www.tkb.org/Group.jsp? groupID = 163 > (accessed October 15, 2005).

Red Brigades

LEADER: Renato Curcio; Giovanni Senzani
USUAL AREA OF OPERATION: Italy

OVERVIEW

The Red Brigades (*Brigate Rosse* [BR] in Italian) is a Marxist-Leninist group that formed in 1969 from student movements in Italy. The group split into two—the Communist Combatant Party (BR-PCC) and the Union of Combatant Communists (BR-UCC) in 1984.

HISTORY

The Red Brigades (BR) organization was one of Italy's most active extremist groups between the years of 1969 and 1984. Their agenda to destabilize the country and separate Italy from the Western Alliance included robberies, kidnappings, assassinations, and arson.

The founder, Renato Curcio, and his wife, Mara Cagol, launched an organization called the Metropolitan Political Collective (MPC) in September 1969. Their objective was to use the MPC as a means to radicalize workers and students towards Marxist-Leninist ideas. The Red Brigades was immediately created to concentrate on that objective. They announced their intentions for the BR in the MPC's journal, stating that they would use a grassroots revolution to overthrow capitalism.

The presence of the BR was first felt from the many attacks they carried out on the symbols

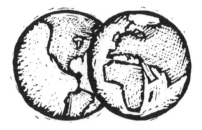

The body of Italian Premier Aldo Moro, riddled with bullets, lies in the back of a vehicle near his Christian Democrat Party headquarters on May 9, 1978. Fifty-five days earlier, Moro was kidnapped in a Red Brigade ambush in Rome. AP/Wide World Photos. Reproduced by permission.

of capitalism. They burned the personal vehicles of company directors and damaged company property. They were known to firebomb warehouses and factories. They abducted business executives and right-wing officials of the trade union, who were later released.

The group was influential. In December 1973, the BR kidnapped the personnel director of the Fiat automobile company. Fiat was forced to reinstate the employment of 600 laid-off workers in order to secure his release.

In April 1974, the BR kidnapped a right-wing judge, Mario Sossi, in Genoa. They held him for thirty-five days, until the government agreed to a prisoner exchange. However, after the release of the judge, the authorities did not follow through with their end of the bargain. A violent revenge was later carried out against the judge responsible for canceling the prisoner exchange.

The Red Brigades first began their deadly campaign in June 1974 while raiding the neo-fascist Italian Social Movement Party headquarters in Padua. The BR murdered two party officials who put up resistance. That same year, the group killed the inspector of Turin's anti-terrorism team.

The summer and autumn of 1974 saw the capture of many of the leaders of the BR, including Curcio. With Curcio in jail, his wife, Mara Cagol, took over leadership of the organization. In February 1975, the BR succeeded in freeing Curcio.

In May 1975, three members of the BR carried out the first of their trademark "kneecappings," by shooting Christian Democrat lawyer Massimo de Cairolis in the leg. Beginning that spring, violent attacks by the BR were commonplace. A month later, in June, Cagol was killed in a gun battle with the elite Italian police, the Carabinieri.

Curcio and several other BR leaders were taken back into police custody in January 1976.

LEADERSHIP

RENATO CURCIO

Renato Curcio, born in 1945, first set up a leftist group at the University of Trento in 1967. It was a thinking group devoted to the study of political thinkers Karl Marx, Mao Zedong, and Che Guevara. Curcio married Mara Cagol, also a radical. They moved to Milan, where they began to assemble other zealots who would eventually form the base of the Red Brigades. Curcio was put in prison for the second time in 1976. He was freed in 1993.

GIOVANNI SENZANI

Giovanni Senzani was considered the main leader of the Red Brigades during the peak of their violent campaign. He was a respected criminology professor at the University of Florence and had also worked at the University of California at Berkeley. For a period, Senzani was also a criminology consultant for the Italian government. After his arrest, many other Red Brigades began turning themselves in and became informers.

While their court cases were getting underway in Turin, members of the Red Brigades continued to carry out murders. They planned to sabotage the trials being held for the BR members.

First, the BR threatened all lawyers working on the proceedings. Then, the BR killed the president of the Lawyers' Association, Fulvio Croce, who selected the public defenders for the Red Brigades on trial. With the murder of two policemen, the trial was halted, due to the inability of the court to keep the right number of judges on the panel. A second trial was begun with 8,000 armed men surrounding the courthouse. Several big attacks, including the murder of Turin's marshal of public security, overshadowed the trial.

Attacks against individuals in the media whom the BR claimed were enemies, were carried out in 1977. The Red Brigades capped the knees of three conservative journalists. The BR accused them of spreading lies about the group. They also shot and killed Carlo Casalegno, the vice-director of *La Stampa*, one of Italy's largest newspapers.

The kidnapping and murder of former Prime Minister Aldo Moro in 1978 is considered one of the most notorious actions carried out by the Red Brigade. At the time, Moro was the leader of the ruling Christian Democratic Party and had facilitated a compromise leading to the formation of the first Italian government to be actively supported by the Communist Party. On the morning Moro was to institute this new government, all five of Moro's security forces were killed, and Moro was seized from his car. Then Prime Minister Giulio Andreotti refused to negotiate on Moro's behalf, claiming he would not negotiate with a terrorist organization. Moro's bullet-riddled body was eventually found in an automobile, in the center of Rome.

The authorities stepped up their operations against the Red Brigades in 1978. This caused further escalation in the knee-capping and murders of important Italian figures. The number of violent attacks in Italy reached a record 2,500 in 1979.

In 1981, the government adopted strict measures to try to catch terrorists, as they were labeled. This included automatic life sentences for the murder of a public official and the allowing of interrogation without the presence of a lawyer.

A 1981 decision gave reduced sentences to extremists who cooperated with police. These informants were called "pentiti," and are said to have brought about the final decline of the BR. The chief of the BR in Turin, Patrizio Peci, became the first pentiti.

The biggest break for police came with the capture of Giovanni Senzani, a respected professor of Criminology at the University of Florence. Many informers claimed he was the real leader of the Red Brigades. His arrest came at the same time the Red Brigades had kidnapped decorated Vietnam veteran, James Lee Dozier, who was the deputy chief of staff for logistics and administration at NATO. An informer revealed to police the address where Dozier was being held.

Following Dozier's rescue in 1981 and the capture of his kidnappers, many informers began coming forward. This led to even more raids and arrests of BR members. This caused the BR to lose the large following they previously had. However, they continued to murder and maim. By 1982, though, their attacks on politicians, professors, and military advisors became much more sporadic.

As the Red Brigades rapidly declined as a militant force, they began to link up with other European militant groups in promoting the Palestinian cause. In 1984, the BR killed US diplomat Leamon Hunt in Rome, in an attempt to weaken the Camp David Accords.

The Red Brigades continued to murder through the 1980s, but on a much-reduced scale. The final assassination was that of an advisor to the Christian Democrats, in 1988. Trials of Red Brigades members carried over into the 1990s.

There has been evidence that a new Red Brigades has formed. In 2003, nine suspected Red Brigades members were arrested in Rome, following an investigation of the murder of a labor consultant, Marco Biagi. Biagi was reportedly targeted for his help in drafting laws to make it easier to fire workers. The recent Red Brigades claimed responsibility for the Biagi killing and the murder of another labor advisor, which they say they did on behalf of the Combatant Communist Party.

Investigations into the new Red Brigades uncovered guns, 220 pounds of explosives, detonators, fake identity cards, and police uniforms at a house in an eastern suburb of Rome. Of the nine arrested members, many had normal jobs and were considered to be normal law-abiding citizens by their neighbors. The police were given a tip regarding this new wave of Red Brigades following a train shootout with two of the group's members. One of them was killed.

PHILOSOPHY AND TACTICS

The leaders of the Red Brigades considered themselves promoters of a pure form of Marxist-Leninism. The Bolsheviks, who were led by Lenin and Trotsky and who fought to establish communism in Russia, were one of the role models of the BR.

The BR was part of the Italian revolutionary left that developed at the time when a divide within the left-leaning political parties had formed. Differences came from disagreement between reformist policy designed by the Italian Communist Party (*Partito Communista Italiano*, PCI) and the Marxist-Leninist revolutionary ideology. It was these differences that shaped party activists, Italian intellect, and eventually the extremists.

At the time, the far left in Italy followed one of two trends. First, there were those Marxist-Leninists who placed emphasis on the doctrine of Lenin, which stated that the organization of political parties was most important. The second approach was called Worker's Autonomy (*Autonomia Operaia*, AO), which focused on the importance of political organization and awareness of the working class. To the AO mindset, political awareness was important for reaching the essential stage in the revolutionary process when the party could play an important role.

The BR thought of their organization as being related to the approach of the AO. The BR was not a party, but rather an armed avantgarde group working with the laborers to form a party.

One very important ideological leader for the Italian radical left, accepted by both leftwing student activists and the intellects, was Antonio Negri, a professor at the University of Padua. Negri's books and articles greatly influenced the leaders of BR and other extremist groups. Negri legitimized the use of shooting, arson, and other criminal behavior as tools for breaking down the structure of the capitalist economy. Negri was arrested and put on trial by Italian authorities, but his direct involvement in the criminal activity he legitimized was never proved.

In the first four or five years of its existence, BR focused their activities in Milan and Turin. They concentrated on what was happening in factories, where social disparities and labor disputes were obvious. They first targeted the far right and then began armed assistance for trade unionists.

The second stage of BR activity began to focus more on the state. They began working outside of factories and began to earn national recognition. As security forces were cracking down on the group, they had to focus less on the movement of the masses, and increase their secrecy.

PRIMARY SOURCE

New Red Brigades/Communist Combatant Party (BR/PCC) a.k.a. Brigate Rosse/Partito Comunista Combattente

DESCRIPTION

This Marxist-Leninist group is a successor to the Red Brigades, active in the 1970s and 1980s. In addition to ideology, both groups share the same symbol, a five-pointed star inside a circle. The group is opposed to Italy's foreign and labor policies and to NATO.

ACTIVITIES

In 2004, the BR/PCC continued to suffer setbacks, with their leadership in prison and other members under pressure from the Italian Government. The BR/PCC did not claim responsibility for a blast at an employment agency in Milan in late October, although the police suspect remnants of the group are responsible. In 2003, Italian authorities captured at least seven members of the BR/PCC, dealing the terrorist group a severe blow to its operational effectiveness. Some of those arrested are suspects in the assassination in 1999 of Labor Ministry adviser Massimo D'Antona, and authorities are hoping to link them to the assassination in 2002 of Labor Ministry advisor Marco Biagi. The arrests in October came on the heels of a clash in March 2003 involving Italian Railway Police and two BR/PCC members, which resulted in the deaths of one of the operatives and an Italian security officer. The BR/PCC has financed its activities through armed robberies.

STRENGTH

Fewer than 20.

LOCATION/AREA OF OPERATION

Italy.

EXTERNAL AID

Unknown.

Source: U.S. Department of State. *Country Reports on Terrorism.* Washington, D.C., 2004.

The group published a document describing its immediate strategic goals in 1975. Its stated plan was to weaken the central government of Italy and cause its political disintegration.

In 1977, the BR moved to their most violent period, when their almost daily attacks, or campaigns, took on different themes. The idea being to collapse the system. The BR was acting in the context of a larger movement of political protest—feminist movement, protests against transport price hikes, and others.

The Moro murder trials provided a detailed picture of the Red Brigades' organizational structure. It became clear how the group was managed, how it recruited, and how members were trained. The group had territorial columns, or brigades, based in Rome, Milan, Genoa, Turin, Naples, and other Italian cities. Each of the brigades had an independent chain of command. At the very top of the BR was the Strategic Direction, made up of representatives from each column. Under the Strategic Direction, the second level of leadership, the Executive Committee, implemented the decisions and plans developed by the Strategic Direction. There were different fronts for coordinating the different logistics required for the group's activities.

Within the different columns, there were two types of members. Those called regulars went underground, working only with their particular brigade. Irregulars were those who pursued normal careers but worked secretly for the Red Brigades.

BR recruited individuals from radical left-wing factions. The recruits had to complete a rigorous training before becoming full members. Despite the recruits, BR chose to maintain small numbers. They never had more than a few hundred active members at any one time. The thinking behind this approach was to keep the BR's status as an elite revolutionary group, in common with the Bolsheviks.

KEY EVENTS

1969: Red Brigades formed.

1974: BR launches its first deadly attack.

1974: BR founder, Renato Curcio, captured by police.

1975: Curcio's wife, Mara Cagol, killed in a gun battle.

1976: Curcio back in jail for a second time after being freed.

1976: BR members sabotage BR criminal trials by killing lawyers and policemen.

1978: BR kidnaps and kills former Prime Minister Aldo Moro.

1981: Informers help police capture Giovanni Senzani and other top Red Brigades leaders.

1982: BR is weakened, killings are fewer and more sporadic.

1984: BR turns their focus to the Palestinian cause.

1988: Last assassination by the original BR.

Being a small organization, the BR relied on sympathizers to give them support when needs came about. Many of these sympathizers were revolutionary groups that had taken hold in schools and factories across Italy. The actual number of these groups is unknown, but it appeared as though there were many throughout Italy. These groups looked to the Red Brigades as role models and for direction.

The Christian Democrats were the ruling political party in Italy during the time of the BR. Members of the party were often the primary target of the Red Brigades. However, in 1979, the BR killed a communist factory worker, Guido Rossa, who had actively supported Christian Democratic policy against the BR. The BR was also critical of the reformist Communist Party. Following Rossa's assassination, there were large protests by factory workers against what were labeled as "terrorist activities." This caused some damage to BR public relations.

The killing of Rossa, controversial among the radical left, began to create internal problems within the BR. Two leaders of BR who had taken part in the Rossa killing resigned. The BR Executive Committee was accused of looking beyond the interests of the working class, and the state of Italy was determined to defeat BR.

The tactical disagreements and personality clashes led to the creation of two additional splinter groups. The three organizations appeared to be in competition to outdo each other, as the number of violent attacks soared. At this same time, the Palestinians and BR began to be in contact. Acting on behalf of the Palestinian causes and the Marxist-Leninist causes, BR was pulled in even more directions. Eventually, with the capture of many members, the Red Brigades declined.

OTHER PERSPECTIVES

The Red Brigades are known for having one of the most consistent and well thought through ideologies of all extreme European leftist groups during the 1970s and 1980s. They thought of themselves as having a pure Marxist-Leninist approach. However, it is argued that the BR approach of fighting for the social inequities of the working class puts the group, today, in a category of the New Left and neo-Marxism. It has been argued further that the neo-Marxism tendencies, along with many of their activities, classify the group as an anarcho-communist organization.

There are disagreements as to the level at which the BR participated in activities with Palestinian organizations (POs). Much was published stating that POs and BR worked together in a close cooperation in various campaigns. Other evidence indicates that the BR's relationship with Palestine was not highly developed, although BR may have acted independently in the name of some causes of POs. This evidence says BR prisoners may have over-emphasized the relationship between the groups. This was at a time when there was growing fear in Italy of Middle Eastern-based terrorism.

It is said that the BR influenced politics in Italy, as well as the psyche of the Italian people, in its efforts to turn communist ideology into reality. However, the BR failed to reach this reality because of the resistance of the Italian people to heed the calls for a revolution. The Italian government and security forces were eventually able to defeat one of their greatest challenges and remove the threat of revolution.

SUMMARY

During the 1970s and 1980s, the BR was determined to destroy the Italian political scene with kidnappings, killings, and destruction of property. The time period has been labeled the "Years of Lead" for the enormous number of bullets that were used. The Red Brigades claimed to be fighting on behalf of the labor class and hoped to implement a Marxist-Leninist government in Italy.

The group, known as one of the most violent in Western Europe, was brought to a functional halt in 1988. However, after 1988, the group succeeded in assassinating a former Prime Minister, judges, businessmen, and diplomats.

A new Red Brigades group was uncovered in 2003. Its strength is unclear. This group appears to be targeting lesser-known people who shape public policy. This is in contrast to the BR, which specialized in high-profile targets.

SOURCES

Books

Crenshaw, Martha, and John Pimlott (editors). *Encyclopedia of World Terrorism, Volume 3.* Toronto: Sharpe Reference, 1996.

Periodicals

Stanley, Alessandra. "Rome Journal; Agony Lingers, 20 Years After the Moro Killing." *New York Times.* May 9, 1998.

Web sites

BBC History, Higher Bitesize Revision. "Why did the Bolsheviks win the Russian Civil War?" < http://www.bbc.co.uk/scotland/education/bitesize/higher/history/russia/russiancivil1_rev.shtml > (accessed October 20, 2005).

BBC News World Edition. "Italy's History of Terror." < http://news.bbc.co.uk/2/hi/europe/3372239.htm > (accessed October 20, 2005).

BBC News. "Police Seize 'Red Brigades' Cache.'" < http://news.bbc.co.uk/go/pr/fr/-/2/hi/europe/3337809.stm > (accessed October 20, 2005).

BBC News UK Edition. "Italy's Andreotti Cleared of Murder." < http://news.bbc.co.uk/1/hi/world/europe/3228917.stm > (accessed October 20, 2005).

International Policy Institute for Counter-Terrorism. "Red Brigades." < http://www.ict.org.il/inter_ter/orgdet.cfm?orgid = 36 > (accessed October 20, 2005).

International Policy Institute for Counter-Terrorism. "The Red Brigades: Cooperation with the Palestinian Terrorist Organizations." < http://www.ict.org.il/articles/red_brigades-palestinians.htm > (accessed October 20, 2005).

Republic of Texas

LEADER: Richard McLaren

YEAR ESTABLISHED OR BECAME ACTIVE: 1995

ESTIMATED SIZE: Less than 1,000

USUAL AREA OF OPERATION: Texas

OVERVIEW

The Republic of Texas is an extremist group formed in 1995, claiming that the state of Texas was never legally annexed by the United States and is therefore an independent country. Based on this claim, members of the group assert that both the federal and Texas state governments are illegitimate, making their laws and regulations non-binding. Like numerous other antigovernment groups, the Republic of Texas employs a variety of financial tactics, including bank fraud, issuing worthless checks, and filing fraudulent government claims to harass enemies.

In 1996, the year-old group split into three factions. One of these factions gained notoriety during a 1997 hostage-taking, which ended peacefully one week later, while members of a second faction were arrested for threats against the President. Several group members were subsequently tried and sent to prison for these two crimes, and other group members disavowed the violent tactics. Today, the reorganized group continues its efforts to assert Texas independence.

HISTORY

In 1995, former insurance salesman Richard McLaren made a startling claim: the state of

Republic of Texas members Robert "White Eagle" Otto, left, Gregg Paulson, center, and their leader Richard McLaren, right, flash victory signs from the back of a sheriff's car escorting them back to jail after their arraignment on July 10, 1997. The three were arrested for taking a hostage in May. AP/Wide World Photos

Texas, part of the Union since 1845, had been annexed illegally. Further, given that Texas used to be an independent nation, the current residents of Texas are not actually Americans but are legal citizens of the sovereign Republic of Texas. Finally, because Texans are not Americans, McLaren claimed they are not subject to U.S. laws, including the Internal Revenue Code.

While McLaren's claims were quickly dismissed by historians and legal experts, they created a modest stir, attracting a small band of disgruntled followers who began working for Texas independence. In 1996, the group split into three separate factions. The following year, McLaren led his group in kidnapping Republic of Texas opponents, Joe and Margaret Ann Rowe, who they held as "prisoners of war," while demanding the release of two imprisoned Republic of Texas members. The conflict was resolved peacefully one week later, with the

arrest of McLaren and the release of the hostages. McLaren and five others were tried and imprisoned for the kidnapping.

A second faction of the original organization was also involved in criminal activity. This group, led by Jesse Enloe, threatened to assassinate multiple government officials, including then-President Bill Clinton. An FBI informant, John L. Cain, infiltrated the group and discovered their plans, which involved the creation of a unique weapon. This weapon, a specially modified cigarette lighter, would have been used to shoot cactus thorns dipped in toxins such as the HIV virus and rabies. Three members of the group, including Enloe, were convicted and sent to prison for the plot.

Many of the Republic of Texas' members were outraged at the tactics used by McLaren and Enloe and openly criticized their actions. During the late 1990s, the remaining group shrank numerically and appeared to moderate

Richard McLaren walks in front of his home near Fort Davis, Texas, which he calls the "Embassy of the Republic of Texas, Office of Foreign Affairs." McLaren denies the legitimacy of the federal and state government, and considers himself an ambassador with duties similar to those of a secretary of state.
AP/Wide World Photos. Reproduced by permission.

its views somewhat. Following the September 2001 terrorist attacks on the United States, the President of the Republic of Texas called the American people "brothers" of the citizens of Texas and offered the group's assistance in the war on terror.

PHILOSOPHY AND TACTICS

The Republic of Texas bases its ideology on a contention that Texas is an independent country, rather than part of the United States, exempting Texas citizens from U.S. law. In addition to resisting federal taxes and regulation, some members have committed fraud and theft

in pursuit of their goals; prior to his standoff with police, McLaren had been court-ordered to stop filing spurious liens and was then found in contempt when he failed to comply with court orders.

The Republic of Texas, like numerous other antigovernment groups in the United States, is notorious for its use of liens, which members file against property owned by public officials. Property liens, which are simple and inexpensive to file, prevent the property holder from selling the property; while frivolous liens are relatively simple to remove, this action requires the property owner to appear in court, making these liens a powerful tool for harassment. In addition, the massive volume of liens filed often overloads the

LEADERSHIP

RICHARD MCLAREN

Richard McLaren is a native of Missouri and worked as an automobile repair manual author and sold insurance. McLaren is well known for his self-proclaimed opposition to taxation of any kind. In 1995, he publicized his belief that Texas' 1845 annexation into the United States was illegal, making Texans non-U.S. citizens. Further, he claims that as non-citizens they do not have to pay federal taxes or obey federal laws and that the federal government owes them war reparations.

McLaren and about fifty followers soon formed the Republic of Texas, with the goal of removing the state from U.S. control. Following his involvement in a 1997 kidnapping, McLaren and his associate, Robert Otto, were convicted; Otto was given a fifty-year sentence, while McLaren was sentenced to 99 years in prison. In 1998, McLaren, his wife, and several other members of the group were convicted of passing more than $3 billion in hot checks; McLaren received an additional twelve-year sentence for this conviction.

court system, further obstructing the working of the local government. In response to the use of frivolous liens, several states have since passed laws restricting the use of frivolous liens, although as of 2005, Texas is not among them. As of 2005, state governor Rick Perry has more than 200 liens filed against his property by various groups.

OTHER PERSPECTIVES

Given Texas' unique history as an independent nation prior to joining the United States, the claims of Texas continuing sovereignty raise interesting if not realistic legal issues. Ralph Brock, a practicing attorney and law school

KEY EVENTS

1845: The Republic of Texas becomes the twenty-eighth state of the Union by an act of Congress.

1995: Richard McLaren, an antigovernment activist, announces the formation of the Republic of Texas, claiming that Texas was never legally annexed by the United States.

1996: The group splits into three factions, two of which eventually commit terrorist acts.

1997: Police arrest two members, one for driving without license plates. McLaren and followers kidnap two individuals, demanding the members' release. The standoff is peacefully resolved.

1997: Republic of Texas faction leader, Jesse Enloe, and followers are arrested for threatening to kill government officials, including the President.

2003: The newly reunited group sets up its "capital" in the small town of Overton, RT (Republic of Texas).

teacher, notes several reasons that sovereignty claims by the Republic of Texas are legally defective. Foremost, international law states that no nation has the right to question agreements with other nations by claiming that the other nation violated its own laws.

Second, an 1868 case titled *Texas v. White* reached the U.S. Supreme Court, which held that once Texas became a state in 1845, its union with the remaining states was permanent and complete. A 1901 Supreme Court opinion also cited Texas' entry into the union as an example of an absolute annexation. Also, since Texas has failed to legally challenge its statehood in the many years since, its acquiescence removes any legal defects in the U.S. claim of sovereignty. Finally, because the people of Texas voted to join the Union, Texas cannot argue that the annexation was illegal.

PRIMARY SOURCE

Separatism: Texans promised (second) capitol

In a communiqué notable for its bravado if not its import, the leaders of the antigovernment Republic of Texas (ROT) told the world in October that they have secured forty-two acres on which they plan to build their "Provisional Capitol."

From this patch of land in Dewitt County, the group that says Texas never really joined the union will pursue its quest to convince Americans that their state is actually an independent nation.

To that end, they plan a home for the "General Council," an official state archive, and buildings to serve as meeting places "for various committees and branches of the Provisional Government and a symbol of the increasing growth and entrenchment of our independence movement."

Actually, ROT hasn't made too much real political progress, although a ROT faction did manage to get into a week-long standoff with several hundred Texas Rangers in 1997, ending with the death of one ROT member. But it has made a series of announcements that have at least the ring of authority.

In July, for example, the General Council announced that "the Republic of Texas Provisional Government is pleased to announce that Texas' newest Embassy and Consulate will open July 10, 2000, in Barcelona, Spain."

That news, like the September announcement that Daniel Miller had replaced Archie Lowe as president of ROT, was virtually ignored by the mainstream U.S. and foreign press.

Of course, some reporters may be thinking about the last ROT "embassy." It was there, in Ft. Davis, Texas, that ROT factional leader Richard McLaren held several hundred police and reporters at bay after followers kidnapped a neighbor couple. McLaren is now serving a sentence of 111 years in prison.

Source: Southern Poverty Law Center, 2000

Similar anti-annexation claims are also made by groups in the states of Alaska and Hawaii, claiming that the United States erred by failing to consult natives before annexing the two territories. In 1996, the Hawaiian secessionists managed to pass a nonbonding referendum calling for the state to secede from the Union, however the claim has made little progress.

SUMMARY

The Republic of Texas is one of several extremist groups throughout the United States that claims political sovereignty and the freedom to reject U.S. law. While the Texas group's claims are based on an interesting set of historical circumstances, most legal scholars and historical experts reject them outright. Since 2003, the reorganized group is headquartered in Overton, Texas, and is not considered a major threat by extremist watchdog groups.

SOURCES

Books

Griffin, D. *Radical Common Law Movement and Paper Terrorism: The State Response.* National Conference of State, 2000.

Web sites

Anti-Defamation League. "Paper Terrorism's Forgotten Victims: The Use of Bogus Liens against Private Individuals and Businesses." < http://www.adl.org/mwd/privlien.asp > (accessed October 16, 2005).

Houston Chronicle.com. "Still True Today: 'The Republic of Texas' Is No More." < http://www.chron.com/content/chronicle/editorial/97/05/01/brock.0-1.html > (accessed October 16, 2005).

MIPT Terrorism Knowledge Base . "Republic of Texas (ROT)." < http://www.tkb.org/Group.jsp?groupID=95 > (accessed October 16, 2005).

Slate.com. "The Republic of Texas." < http://www. slate.com/id/1057 > (accessed October 16, 2005).

Rescue America

LEADER: Donald Treshman

USUAL AREA OF OPERATION: United States

OVERVIEW

Rescue America, based in Baltimore, Maryland, was founded in the late 1980s by Don Treshman. The organization identifies itself as being anti-abortion and willing to use violent tactics such as bombings, harassment, explicit imagery, intimidation of people entering abortion clinics, and assassinations of abortion providers and women's clinic workers in the group's work to make abortion illegal in the United States.

Rescue America, like Randall Terry's Operation Rescue, uses aggressive tactics during protests, in threatening abortion providers and in gaining media attention for their cause. Rescue America, like Operation Rescue, has been the plaintiff as well as the defendant in a number of court cases, including *Madsen v. Women's Health Center*, in which the Supreme Court upheld strict rules about "buffer zones" that protestors must not enter near abortion clinic entrances, and *Planned Parenthood of the Columbia/Willamette Inc. v. American Coalition of Life Activists*, in which the Supreme Court found that the creation of abortion provider wanted posters and a web site called "The Nuremberg Files," with abortion providers' photos, home addresses, home phone numbers published on it, did not fall under protected free speech.

Openly advocating the murder of abortion providers, Rescue America is considered to be

Activists from both sides of the abortion issue clamor for space and attention in front of the New York City federal courthouse during a July 1992 protest. AP/Wide World Photos

one of the most extreme and militant groups in the pro-life movement.

HISTORY

Between 1982 and 1996, more than $13 million in damage was caused by more than 150 incidents of bombings, arson, and shootings perpetrated by anti-abortion groups and individuals in the United States. In recent years, the terms anti-abortion and pro-life have taken on specific political meanings: pro-life activists are against abortion and use protests, letter-writing, legislative activism, and grassroots efforts to end legal abortion; anti-abortion activists use all of these tactics, but also condone—and at times

promote—the use of violence and murder of abortion providers to accomplish the goal of making abortion illegal in the United States.

As violence at abortion and women's clinics began to rise in the United States in the late 1980s and early 1990s, a group of anti-abortion organizations issued what came to be known as the "defensive action statement." The statement was written just as the trial of Michael Griffin was beginning; Griffin was being tried for the 1993 murder of Dr. David Gunn, a doctor who performed abortions. The statement reads:

> We, the undersigned, declare the justice of taking all godly action necessary to defend innocent human life including the use of force. We proclaim that whatever force is legitimate to defend the life of a born child is legitimate to defend the life of an unborn child. We assert that if Michael Griffin did in fact kill David Gunn, his use of lethal force was justifiable provided it was carried out for the purpose of defending the lives of unborn children. Therefore, he ought to be acquitted of the charges against him.

The document was signed by at least thirty-one individuals, including members from Life Enterprises, Advocates for Life Ministries, the American Coalition of Life Advocates, the founder of Life Advocate Magazine, and members of Rescue America. Michael Griffin himself was a Rescue America member. Don Treshman, the founder and leader of Rescue America, allegedly was responsible for organizing the protest in front of the abortion clinic on the day that Dr. Gunn was killed, and publicly helped to set up a trust fund for the murderer's family. Rescue America members had allegedly harassed Gunn and made death threats against him in the week preceding his death. In addition, wanted posters with Gunn's photo and home telephone number were handed out at anti-abortion gatherings.

On the issue of David Gunn's murder, Treshman stated that, "While Gunn's death is unfortunate, it's also true that quite a number of babies' lives will be saved."

In March 1993, Treshman went to London to give press interviews on the issue of abortion in the United States. Within a few days, the British government deported him, stating that his presence on British soil was "not conducive to the common good," and that he was being ejected from the country for his "previous

Pro-choice demonstrators advocate keeping abortion legal and a matter of personal and private choice.
Leonard Lessin / Peter Arnold, Inc.

involvement in actions leading to violence." Treshman left the country and was banned from entering the U.K. for five years. In August 1993, an immigration appeal tribunal noted that Treshman "avoided condemning [violence] in unequivocal terms, and what he said could lead those who supported his aims to conclude that violence was justified."

A second "defensive action statement" was issued in 1994 after Paul Hill, who signed the first statement, killed Dr. John Britton and his escort, James Herman, at a Pensacola, Florida, women's clinic. The second defensive action statement reiterated the first statement, offering support for what Rescue America called Hill's "justifiable homicide" of Britton and Herman.

In 1994, the case *Madsen v. Women's Health Center* found its way to the Supreme Court. The case originated in 1991 in the Florida courts. The lower court ordered that anti-abortion protestors could not picket or protest within thirty-six feet of any abortion clinic, make loud noises within earshot of the clinic, display images or use posters that could be seen from the clinic, approach suspected patients within a 300-foot diameter around the clinic, and protest within 300 feet of any clinic employee's home. The Florida Supreme Court upheld the injunction in full, and the defendants, Don Treshman among them, appealed the case all the way to the United States Supreme Court.

In *Madsen v. Women's Health Center*, the Supreme Court upheld the thirty-six-foot "buffer zone" in front of the clinics' entrances, but permitted protestors to be within 300 feet of the clinic in non-entrance areas.

In the same year, a Texas court awarded $1.01 million in damages to a number of women's clinics named in the court case *Operation Rescue-National a/k/a Operation Rescue, Rescue America, Dallas Rescue, Rev. Phillip L. "Flip" Benham, Bob Jewitt, Don Treshman, and Rev. Keith Tucci, Petitioners v. Planned Parenthood of Houston and Southeast Texas, Inc., AAA Concerned Women's Center, Inc., Aaron's Family Planning Clinic of*

Anti-abortion activists hold caskets and lift posters bearing the number of abortions performed each year during a demonstration on January 22, 2003, in Washington, D.C. AP/*Wide World Photos*

Houston, Inc., A–Z Women's Health Services, P.A., Downtown Women's Center a/k/a Downtown Women's Clinic, Et Al., Respondents. The court decided against Rescue America, Don Treshman, and co-defendant Keith Tucci of Operation Rescue, and Operation Rescue itself on charges of conspiracy to blockade abortion clinics.

In 1998, the Texas Supreme Court upheld the award of $1.01 million, but ruled that some of the clinics must modify their buffer zones and that two abortion counselors must be permitted to approach patients—unless the patients ask to be left alone.

Overall, Rescue America is not as well known as Operation Rescue outside of the pro-life/anti-abortion movement. However, its use of the court system to attempt to bring systemic change and its willingness to use violence to end legal abortion sets it apart from some of the more mainstream pro-life groups.

Leader Donald Treshman has also been linked to Human Life International, an extreme-right Catholic organization that calls itself pro-life.

PHILOSOPHY AND TACTICS

Rescue America, like Operation Rescue, uses highly confrontational tactics to promote its anti-abortion agenda. Starting in the mid 1980s, pro-life protestors began employing 1960s-style protest techniques in the abortion debate. Chaining themselves to structures, protesting with graphic images and slogans on signs, calling people with telemarketing messages, developing grassroots religious campaigns in churches, and leafleting areas near their sites of protest, these radicalized groups used direct contact to prevent patients from entering abortion clinics and attempted to persuade abortion providers to stop offering their services as well.

Their explicit promotion of violent tactics, bombings, and homicide as a viable tool in fighting against legal abortion forced Rescue America, as well as other anti-abortion groups,

LEADERSHIP

KEY EVENTS

DON TRESHMAN

Don Treshman, the founder and leader of Rescue America, has also worked as a spokesman for Human Life International, a far-right Catholic pro-life organization, and has been linked to the American Coalition of Life Activists and Operation Rescue, both militant anti-abortion groups that advocate and use violence.

1993: Murder of Dr. David Gunn.

1993: Treshman deported from Britain.

1994: Paul Hill murders Dr. John Britton and his escort, James Herman, at a Pensacola, Florida, women's clinic.

2003: Paul Hill executed by the State of Florida for murders of Britton and Herman.

to splinter off from mainstream pro-life organizations such as the American Life League, Democrats for Life, the Pro-Life Action League, and others. By 1993, the division was clear: Rescue America set itself apart as an open promoter of violence against abortion clinics and abortion providers.

Shortly after Dr. David Gunn's murder in 1993, Daniel Ware, and a Rescue America member and friend of Paul Hill (later convicted and executed for the murders of Dr. John Britton and an escort, James Herman), was arrested in Pensacola, Florida, for possessing a large number of weapons, as well as more than 400 rounds of ammunition. He had vowed to "terminate" abortion providers gathered in Pensacola for a memorial service for Dr. David Gunn, who had been murdered by fellow Rescue America member, Michael Griffin. Ware stated publicly that he wanted "to take out as many child-killers in a Beirut-style massacre," and was tried but found innocent by the court.

Don Treshman used bold statements to gain press coverage for the anti-abortion issue. After David Gunn's death, Treshman issued a statement saying, "While we think Gunn's death is unfortunate, the fact is that a number of mothers would have been put at risk today and over a dozen babies would have died at his hands. Pro-lifers are asked to pray that he had a chance to ask for God's forgiveness for his part in the abortion holocaust before his demise."

Treshman also stated, in an article in *Boston Globe*, when asked about the murders of abortion providers: "[T]here are 30 million dead babies and only five people on the other side, so it's really nothing to get excited about."

Treshman has stated that a civil war may be necessary in the fight to end legal abortion. He defends the actions of Rescue America by claiming that the murder of one abortion provider prevents abortion of many fetuses, which in the group's view, is legalized murder. Their use of the concept of "justifiable homicide" and civil war analogies follows this train of thought.

With the 1994 and 1998 court cases involving Donald Treshman and Rescue America, the group's goal was to bring attention to their cause and to potentially build a series of lower court cases that would lead to the eventual overturning of *Roe v. Wade*, the landmark 1973 Supreme Court case that defined the constitutional right to privacy and used that right to prevent the individual states from making abortion illegal. All pro-life and anti-abortion groups seek to overturn *Roe v. Wade*. Various Supreme Court cases throughout the late 1980s and 1990s have, in the opinion of pro-choice activists, "chipped away" at abortion rights; most pro-life and anti-abortion groups consider these cases to be small victories.

The use of court cases as a tool for slowly eroding *Roe v. Wade* was part of a larger effort on the part of all pro-life organizations, and Rescue America's involvement in *Madsen v.*

PRIMARY SOURCE

"Justifiable Homicide": The Signers

Shortly before the trial of Michael Griffin for the 1993 murder of Dr. David Gunn, former Rev. Paul Hill and thirty-three others signed what has become known as the "defensive action statement."

The statement (text below) has become well known in the movement as one of the definitive lists of those who have seen murder of abortion doctors as "justifiable homicide."

Some of the signers, whose names were compiled by the Feminist Majority Foundation, have since withdrawn their names, and some have changed locations.

"We, the undersigned, declare the justice of taking all godly action necessary to defend innocent human life including the use of force. We proclaim that whatever force is legitimate to defend the life of a born child is legitimate to defend the life of an unborn child. We assert that if Michael Griffin did in fact kill David Gunn, his use of lethal force was justifiable provided it was carried out for the purpose of defending the lives of unborn children. Therefore, he ought to be acquitted of the charges against him."

* Paul J. Hill, prisoner, Pensacola, Fla. (* OTHER NAMES REDACTED.*)

Source: Southern Poverty Law Center, 1998

Women's Health Center was a crucial part of this strategy.

Another case that made its way to the Supreme Court, *Planned Parenthood of the Columbia/Willamette Inc. v. American Coalition of Life Activists*, named Donald Treshman and Rescue America directly as a defendant. The court case involved a group of physicians who sued various pro-life groups and individuals for creating wanted posters of doctors who performed abortions. The wanted posters included personal information about abortion providers, offered rewards to individuals who helped to persuade doctors to stop performing abortions, and for helping to close clinics. Members of the groups listed also created a web site called "The Nuremburg Files," which listed personal information about more than 200 abortion providers, including home addresses, telephone numbers, and personal details. The physicians who sued claimed that the web site and posters constituted "harassment, intimidation and threats of violence in order to cause violent acts and to drive plaintiffs out of business." On the "The Nuremburg Files" web site, murdered abortion providers were depicted with a line through their face, while those wounded were shaded gray.

Don Treshman, Rescue America, and the other groups and individuals claimed that the posters and the web site were protected speech under the First Amendment; according to the defendants, the posters did not directly advocate violence; none of the writings told people to harm any single person, nor did they make explicit threats to the doctors.

The Ninth Circuit Court of Appeals ruled that the posters and web site did not constitute protected speech; "The Nuremburg Files" was ordered to remain offline. Many of the defendants filed for personal bankruptcy, a common tactic among anti-abortion protestors who faced the payment of damages to plaintiffs.

Rescue America members used other dramatic measures to gain attention for their cause. On May 27, 1998, Treshman appeared wearing a trash bag, pretending to be a discarded fetus, in a protest at a luncheon featuring then-Surgeon General Jocelyn Elders. Security forces removed him from the event, which garnered some publicity for Treshman and Rescue America. Treshman has also been sighted following abortion providers, screaming at them and videotaping their reactions to his screaming and his questions. Members used dramatic images on posters, web site, and pamphlets as well.

OTHER PERSPECTIVES

While pro-choice organizations categorically condemn Rescue America's actions and even use them as an example of the extreme radicalism of the anti-abortion movement, mainstream pro-life organizations also strongly criticize Rescue America's tactics. In 1999, the American Life League, a Catholic organization that identifies itself as pro-life, created a document called the "Pro-life Proclamation Against Violence." In the document, which was signed by more than 120 pro-life organizations across the United States, the signers promise not to use violence as a means to ending abortion in the United States. High-profile organizations such as Operation Rescue, Rescue America, and the American Coalition of Life Activists refused to sign the document.

SUMMARY

The most recent information available on Rescue America indicates that it is still based in Baltimore, but it has not received much media coverage over the past five years. While not defunct, it is far less active than in the late 1980s and throughout the 1990s.

Paul Hill was executed on September 3, 2003, in a Florida prison by lethal injection. He was the first person executed in the United States for anti-abortion violence.

SOURCES

Books

Mason, Carol. *Killing for Life: The Apocalyptic Narrative of Pro-Life Politics.* Ithaca, NY: Cornell University Press, 2002.

Web sites

American Civil Liberties Union. "Planned Parenthood of the Columbia/Willamette Inc. v American Coalition of Life Activists (1999 decision)." < http://www.aclu.org/ReproductiveRights/ReproductiveRights/ > (accessed October 21, 2005).

FindLaw.com. "U.S. Supreme Court Madsen v. Women's Health Ctr., Inc., U.S. (1994)." < http http://caselaw.lp.-findlaw.com/cgi-bin/getcase/ > (accessed October 21, 2005).

FindLaw.com. "Operation Rescue-National a/k/a Operation Rescue, Rescue America, Dallas Rescue, Rev. Phillip L. 'Flip' Benham, Bob Jewitt, Don Treshman, and Rev. Keith Tucci, Petitioners v. Planned Parenthood of Houston and Southeast Texas, Inc., AAA Concerned Women's Center, Inc., Aaron's Family Planning Clinic of Houston, Inc., A–Z Women's Health Services, P.A., Downtown Women's Center a/k/a Downtown Women's Clinic, Et Al., Respondents." < http://caselaw.lp.findlaw.com/data2/texasstatecases/sc/970171d.htm > (accessed October 21, 2005).

Southern Poverty Law Center. "Anti-Abortion Violence: Two Decades of Arson, Bombs, and Murder." < http://www.splcenter.org/intel/intelreport/article.jsp?aid = 411 > (accessed October 21, 2005).

U.S. Court of Appeals for the Ninth Circuit. "Planned Parenthood of the Columbia/Willamette Inc. v American Coalition of Life Activists (2001 decision)." < http://www.ce9.uscourts.gov/web/newopinions.nsf/0/1b21cad7a2e437d988256a1d006a03a1?OpenDocument > (accessed October 21, 2005).

U.S. Court of Appeals for the Ninth Circuit. "Planned Parenthood of the Columbia/Willamette Inc. v American Coalition of Life Activists (2002 decision)." < http://www.ca9.uscourts.gov/ca9/newopinions.nsf/0F569EF00290007188256BC0005876E6/$file/9935320ebcorrected.pdf?openelement > (accessed October 21, 2005).

SEE ALSO

Operation Rescue

Resistance Records

LEADER: Erich Gliebe

YEAR ESTABLISHED OR BECAME ACTIVE: 1993

ESTIMATED SIZE: 1,500

USUAL AREA OF OPERATION: Europe; North America; South America; South Africa

OVERVIEW

Resistance Records is a white separatist music company that produces and distributes hate rock/country/folk music of neo-Nazi/skinhead musicians. It maintains an Internet web site, publishes *Resistance Magazine*, operates Internet radio station Resistance Radio, and sells video games, and other related merchandise. As a subsidiary of the neo-Nazi organization National Alliance, Resistance Records also manages several small music companies. Headquartered in Hillsboro, West Virginia, and headed by Erich Gliebe, the company is considered by music industry commentators and extremist group analysts as one of the largest commercial suppliers of racist music in the United States.

HISTORY

A small rock music distribution company called Resistance Records was founded in 1993 by George Burdi in Windsor, Ontario, Canada. He started with only a small number of album titles involving hate rock music (also called hate-core music and white power rock). Burdi incorporated the company in May 1994 with assets of about $48,000.

In order to evade Canadian anti-hate laws, Burdi moved his business office to the Detroit,

Right-wing extremist band leader Michael Regener, left, and his lawyer wait for sentencing on March 10, 2005, after the German Federal Supreme Court declared Regener's neo-Nazi music group a criminal organization. AP/Wide World Photos. Reproduced by permission.

Michigan, area. Burdi created a glossy, multi-colored music magazine to promote the company's music and his racist philosophy. Various news reports, along with research performed by the Southern Poverty Law Center, stated that the company had its first profit in 1996 from the sale of approximately $300,000 worth of products. In that year, Burdi distributed music for about twelve white power rock bands in Europe, North America, South America, and South Africa.

On April 9, 1997—while Burdi was serving a jail sentence for assault—the Michigan State Police raided Resistance Records' offices and the Ontario Provincial Police raided Burdi's residence. The two raids confiscated numerous boxes of materials, including about 200,000 compact discs, cassette tapes, and records, along with magazines, computers, T-shirts and other related merchandise, business records, and subscriber lists.

As a result, Burdi and other leaders were investigated in the United States for tax fraud (allegedly for not paying Michigan sales tax and

operating a business without a license). In September 1997, they were charged in Canada with conspiracy to promote hatred and willfully promoting hatred. By the end of 1997, the jailed Burdi was forced to terminate the business.

In 1998, Willis A. Carto (founder/leader of the anti-Semitic group, Liberty Lobby) and business partner Todd Blodgett (former-staffer, strategist, and advisor for presidential campaigns/administrations) acquired Resistance Records. During the first year, Carto had financial difficulties and passed control of the company to Blodgett.

Looking to expand his anti-Semitic, white separatist organization National Alliance into the music industry, William L. Pierce, in early 1999, sought a partnership with Blodgett. According to David Lethbridge of the Bethune Institute for Anti-Fascist Studies (Canada), Pierce and Blodgett were unable to agree on the final details. As a result, Pierce purchased the company in the fall of 1999 for $250,000.

LEADERSHIP

KEY EVENTS

GEORGE BURDI

Born in 1970, George Burdi became active with the white supremacist movement while a teenager. By the age of twenty-one, he was the leader of the Canadian unit of the white supremacist group, Church of the Creator. Under the alias Reverend George Eric Hawthorne, in 1989 he formed and was the lead vocalist of the skinhead band called RaHoWa (slang for Racial Holy War). Through most of the 1990s, the band was considered the most popular hate-rock band in North America. In 1993, Burdi became the founder and leader of Resistance Records, which distributed records and materials for his band and other white power bands. Four years later, he was convicted of assault and sentenced to one-year imprisonment for kicking an anti-racism female protestor while playing at a 1993 concert. Then, in 1998, Burdi was forced to sell Resistance Records to the neo-Nazi organization National Alliance. Cynical of the movement, Burdi renounced white supremacy and, as of 2005, is a musician in the Canadian multiracial rock band Novacosm.

With the acquisition of Resistance Records (to increase membership) and the purchase of Swedish record label Nordland Records (to increase inventory) at the end of 1999, Pierce now controlled a comprehensive media company that distributed newsletters, magazines, leaflets, books, Web sites, music, and a weekly radio show. Leaders of the Anti-Defamation League (ADL), a leading organization combating anti-Semitism, estimate that in 2000 Resistance Records had annual sales close to $1 million. With Pierce running the company, Resistance Records soon became one of the most profitable organizations in the United States that promoted hate-related music and accessories. One year later, according to research performed by ADL, annual gross revenues were approximately $1.3 million and membership was estimated to be about 1,500.

1993: Resistance Records is founded, primarily by George Burdi.

1994: Burdi incorporates the organization in Michigan.

1997: Burdi is convicted and sentenced to jail on a 1993 assault charge.

1997: The business offices of Resistance Records and residence of Burdi are raided by U.S. and Canadian law enforcement officials.

1997: Burdi and other leaders are charged by Canadian government with hate crimes.

1998: Carto and Blodgett acquire bankrupt Resistance Records but, due to financial difficulties, Carto passes control to Blodgett.

1999: Pierce takes over Resistance Records from Blodgett and the company becomes part of National Alliance.

2002: Pierce dies and Gliebe is appointed head of National Alliance.

On July 23, 2002, Pierce died, and Erich Gliebe was appointed as the new head of National Alliance. Since 2003, Resistance Records was forced to contend with more competition, especially Minnesota-based Panzeraust Records, which has degraded its profits.

PHILOSOPHY AND TACTICS

Resistance Records leaders advocate the establishment of a whites-only society in the United States. They also assert that the U.S. federal government should be abolished. Because of racial tensions, its leaders contend that a whites-only political society is a feasible political solution to those problems. Thus, they support and make associations with members of any organization that support racial separation.

PRIMARY SOURCE
Hatecore on the Web

When Canadian George Burdi founded one of the first North American racist music companies in 1993, he said a part of the goal of his Resistance Records would be to remedy a situation in which whites had "no clue where they could purchase a White Power CD or cassette."

Today, white youths have more than a clue; they have the Internet. Although Web-based commerce has grown more slowly than expected for many industries, it is critical for racist music, which is very difficult to find in music stores.

Here are two Web sites that make buying "hatecore" simple: Resistance Records (www.resistance.com). Styling itself "The Soundtrack for White Revolution," Resistance Records sells books, clothing, flags, and over 319 CD titles from bands around the world. A highlight is Resistance Radio, which streams white power music 24 hours a day.

The site also features the current issue of Resistance magazine, which is part of the music operation, and explains how to become a local distributor. Resistance, owned by neo-Nazi William Pierce and headquartered at his National Alliance compound in West Virginia, says that its mission goes beyond music.

"You are not merely consumers of a product," the site instructs its readers. "And we are not merely distributors of a product. Together we are fighting a war to awaken the survival instincts in a dying people. ... Ours is not just a culture worth preserving. It is the only one worth preserving."

Panzerfaust Records (www.panzerfaust.com). Featuring black-and-white photos of the Third Reich, this site boasts of the international bands among its 252 CD titles. Of one disc, it exhorts readers to "Get your copy now before it gets confiscated by the German government!"

Owner Anthony Pierpont, who has close ties to the extremely violent Hammerskin Nation, runs Panzerfaust Records from Minnesota.

The firm's name reflects how it sees its role. "During the fratricidal conflict of the Second World War," the Panzerfaust site says, "National Socialist Germany developed a portable, hand-held anti-tank weapon ... suitably dubbed 'Panzerfaust,' which in German means 'armored fist.' Effective only to 100 meters, it took tremendous courage to confront the enemy with [it.] Success was possible, but not guaranteed."

Its music, Panzerfaust adds, is "the audio ordnance [for] today's racial struggle."

Source: Southern Poverty Law Center, 2001

These leaders also view the music and related merchandise that they sell as a very important and formidable way to recruit new members, especially impressionable teenagers and young adults, into their ideology. The profits generated at Resistance Records are used to further the racist goals of the National Alliance.

Resistance Record leaders use hatecore music to attract younger customers who may be initially unaware of the company's racist and hate-based ideology. In many cases, troubled children and young adults are searching for alternatives to the mass-produced music selections available from established music labels. Once attracting such people to the music, leaders of Resistance Records make it easy to join their organization. Such a strategy, which involves racist and anti-government messages, is used as a way to attract troubled customers and converts.

OTHER PERSPECTIVES

Anti-Defamation League (ADL) leaders contend that Resistance Record's parent company National Alliance is one of the most dangerous hate groups in the United States. As its subsidiary, Resistance Records is in a position, through sales of its music and merchandise, to greatly strengthen the ability of the National Alliance to promote its racist ideals.

The music promoted by Resistance Records, according to ADL analysts, is not just rebellious music, like much heavy metal music, but is also dangerous. Its lyrics talk of hate and racism to susceptible minds. Such music, according to ADL analysts, encourages acts of violence.

Michael Barkun, an expert on right-wing extremist groups, stated in the 1998 article "Resisting Arrest" by the Southern Poverty Law Center that Resistance Records is able to attract customers because of its excellent leadership style. Barkun stated that most extremist organizations perform poorly due to inadequate leadership. However, Resistance Records leaders use very professional methods such as slick-looking magazines, compact discs, and web sites, which are especially attractive to youth who often feel like outcasts and desire to be part of a larger group. Once Resistance Records leaders have attracted their usually unsophisticated customers with their sophisticated media campaigns, the often-times unsuspecting customers are then easy recruitment targets to the company's political agenda.

Michelle Lefkowitz, an Oregon official with Communities Against Hate, stated in the same 1998 article "Resisting Arrest" that Resistance Records is one of the most successful organizing instruments used by white separatists to recruit new members.

SUMMARY

Since 1999, when Resistance Records was purchased by Pierce, the record company has seen strong growth in music and music-related sales of its merchandise. The company has been successful within the extreme right-wing, white separatist movement due to its appealing approach toward young people who are not attracted to the older, traditional leadership of well-established white separatist/supremacist organizations.

Its foreign sales are especially strong where hate movements and hate music are very popular. Its strong performing markets include Denmark, France, Germany, Greece, the Czech Republic, Poland, Serbia, Slovakia, and Sweden. Besides providing hate rock music, leaders of Resistance Records have recently branched out into hate country and hate folk music.

The strategy of Resistance Records leaders to attract members to their white separatist views with the use of hate music has been seen by extremist groups as an excellent way to recruit new members into their organizations. Resistance Records leaders, particularly Burdi and Pierce, have successfully molded the company into an effective way to sell hate music and promote their interests in the anti-government and national separatist movements.

SOURCES

Books

Merkl, Peter H. and Leonard Weinberg, editors. *Right-wing Extremism in the Twenty-first Century*. London and Portland, OR: Frank Cass, 2003.

Periodicals

Shepardson, David, Gary Heinlein, and Oralandar Brand-Williams. "White Supremacist Record Company in Oakland (Michigan) Raided in Tax-Fraud Probe." *The Detroit News*. April 11, 1997.

Web sites

Adam Cohen, *Time.com, Time, Inc.* "All You Need Is Hate: White-power Music Is Thriving Abroad—And Also in the U.S." < http://www.time.com/time/musicgoesglobal/na/mnoise.html > (accessed October 15, 2005).

Enzo Di Matteo, *NOW Magazine, NOW Communications.* "A Racist No Longer: Ex-White Rights Fan Just Wants to be a Rock Star." < http://www.nowtoronto.com/issues/2001-01-25/news.html > (accessed October 15, 2005).

Intelligence Report, Southern Poverty Law Center. "Resisting Arrest: Racist Resistance Records Isn't Slowing Down." < http://www.splcenter.org/intel/intel-report/article.jsp?aid = 452 > (accessed October 15, 2005).

Mark Potok, *Intelligence Report, Southern Poverty Law Center.* "The Year in Hate: A Period of Realignment and Rebuilding Follows a Tumultuous Year on the American Radical Right." < http://www.splcenter.org/intel/intelreport/article/ > (accessed October 15, 2005).

Revolutionary People's Liberation Party/Front (DHKP/C)

LEADER: Dursun Karatas

YEAR ESTABLISHED OR BECAME ACTIVE: 1978 as Dev-Sol; renamed DHKP/C in 1994

USUAL AREA OF OPERATION: Turkey, primarily in Istanbul, Ankara, Izmir, and Adana

OVERVIEW

The radical leftist organization Revolutionary People's Liberation Party/Front (RPLP/F; in Turkish, *Devrimci Halk Kurtulus Partisi/Cephesi*, abbreviated DHKP/C) was initially formed in Turkey in 1978 by Dursun Karatas. At that time, it was known as the Revolutionary Left (in Turkish as *Devrimci Sol*, abbreviated Dev-Sol). The Dev-Sol consisted of former members from factions of Turkish radical leftist groups. Before 1978, the group was a splinter group of the Revolutionary Voice (in Turkish *Devrimci Yol*, abbreviated Dev-Yol), which itself was a splinter group of the Turkish People's Liberation Party-Front (THKP-C). The THKP-C was part of the larger Turkish group called the Revolutionary Youth (in Turkish *Devrimci Genclik*, abbreviated Dev-Genc).

The Dev-Sol was renamed DHKP/C and formally established by Karatas in 1994 when disgruntled members split from the THKP-C after disputes with other members. The "Party" part of the group's name represents its political side, while the "Front" stands for its military operations. The anti-Western DHKP/C maintains a philosophy based on a Marxist-Leninist ideology. It strongly opposes such perceived imperialistic, oligarchic groups as the United States, the North Atlantic Treaty Organization (NATO), and the Turkish government and its established society. The DHKP/C uses violence

The founders of Turkey's Revolutionary People's Liberation Party-Front pose together in prison. From left to right: Bedri Yagan, Dursun Karatas, and Sinan Kukul. AFP/Getty Images.

against its enemies that it perceives to hinder independence and prevent favorable economic conditions for the Turkish people. Its primary goal is to establish a socialist state in Turkey and its secondary goal is to improve Turkish prison conditions.

HISTORY

Dev-Sol was formed in 1978. By the early 1990s, conflicts within the much-expanded group caused its founder, Dursun Karatas, to establish in 1994 the DHKP/C. At this time, Bedri Yagan, also a Dev-Sol founder, split from DHKP/C and formed THKP-C. (Although THKP-C represents the same name as the earlier group, it is a distinct organization.)

According to the MIPT article, "DHKP-C," and the associated articles that chronicled the group's activities, on April 14, 1995, DHKP/C firebombed a Turkish Airlines office in Vienna, Austria. Afterwards, the group claimed responsibility for the act, which left no one injured or dead, by leaving a red flag with a yellow star and the initials DHKC. The DHKP/C also firebombed five Turkish banks in Cologne, Germany. Similarly, no injuries or fatalities occurred. Later, the police arrested nine Turkish suspects believed associated with the incidents.

That same year, on July 14, DHKP/C members invaded Galata Tower in Istanbul, Turkey. They took thirty people hostage, including sixteen foreign tourists. To demonstrate its opposition to the imprisonment of fellow activists from the New Democracy Movement offices, DHKP/C members draped banners from a restaurant. No hostages were hurt or killed.

On October 6, 1995, DHKP/C attacked people working inside the Turkish Consulate in Hamburg, Germany. After taking over the building, members painted slogans on the walls. Again, no injuries or fatalities resulted.

In 1996, DHKP/C made what is generally considered its first significant terrorist attack

Revolutionary People's Liberation Party-Front members participating in a in May 1996 demonstration in Istanbul, Turkey. Mustafa Ozer/AFP/Getty Images.

when it fired a rocket at the U.S. Consulate in Istanbul. That same year, the group assassinated an important Turkish businessman and two associates. At various times in the first half of the year, DHKP/C attacked several Turkish communities. On July 30, the group firebombed a mosque in Leverkusen, Germany.

In 1997, police stopped DHKP/C from operating in the Adana and Osmaniye regions near the Mediterranean Sea. As a result, in 1998, DHKP/C leaders moved its operations to the Aegean region. In the process, the group gained many new members.

On August 14, 1998, DHKP/C exploded a bomb in front of the Istanbul University Literature Department. The incident injured four people, including one police officer. On September 19, DHKP/C members used an anti-tank weapon to attack the Instanbul Directorate of Police (Fatih locality). DHKP/C leaders claimed the attack was undertaken to publicize the disappearance of four members captured in

March 1998. On October 12, six members were captured in connection to the September incident.

On April 13, 1999, DHKP/C planted a time-delay bomb inside the True Path Party office in Kagithane (Istanbul province). Police officials defused the bomb before it exploded. On June 4, police killed two DHKP/C members when they attempted an attack on the U.S. Consulate in Istanbul. On September 10, DHKP/C attempted to detonate an explosive device in Istanbul Province at the Labor and Social Security Ministry. However, the bomb was thrown outside where it exploded harmlessly. A second blast later that day at another government building injured twenty people. In both cases, DHKP/C criticized U.S. imperialism as the primary reason for the attacks. On October 6, DHKP/C detonated a bomb on the seventh floor of the Public Works and Settlement Provincial Directorate in the Besiktas locality of Istanbul. Although damage resulted from the bomb, no injuries or deaths occurred.

Members of the Revolutionary People's Liberation Party-Front, a radical lefttist group, carry red flags as they march during May Day celebrations in Ankara, Turkey on Saturday May 1, 2004. AP/Wide World Photos. *Reproduced by permission.*

On March 29, 2000, DHKP/C members detonated a bomb in a bathroom of the Sehitkamil Telekom Directorate building (Gazinantep province). Minor damage resulted, but no one was injured or killed. On March 30, DHKP/C members attempted a bomb detonation at the State Statistic Institute's Istanbul Regional Directorate. Detonation experts defused the bomb without property damage or personnel injury. On May 11, a time-delay bomb was detonated in a bathroom of the TEDAS building (Gaziantep province). The resulting explosion at the building, which housed the state-run electricity company, did not injure or kill anyone.

On January 1, 2001, DHKP/C detonated a pipe bomb at a New Year Eve's celebration in Istanbul. The incident injured ten people. On January 3, DHKP/C conducted its first suicide bombing when it targeted people working on the fifth floor of the Sisli District Security Directorate in Istanbul. The bomb killed two men (one man and the bomber) and injured two police officers. DHKP/C leaders claimed responsibility in response to the imprisonment and subsequent murder of some of its members. On April 1, DHKP/C leaders claimed responsibility for an attack directed at a police vehicle that killed two police officers in the Bahcelievler district (Istanbul province).

On September 10, 2001, DHKP/C conducted its second suicide bombing when it attacked riot police officers at an Istanbul gathering place near the German Consulate. The explosion killed two police officers, a civilian, and the bomber.

DHKP/C did not conduct any known terrorist attacks during 2002.

On April 15, 2003, DHKP/C exploded a device at a McDonald's restaurant in the Sirkeci locality of Istanbul. One person was injured from falling debris. At the same time,

LEADERSHIP

DURSUN KARATAS

Dursun Karatas is the founder of the DHKP/C. He is considered to have been responsible for the death of thirty-seven people as the result of his involvement with terrorism. Karatas served nine years in prison for terrorism before escaping in October 1989, along with his second-in-command, Bedri Yagan. However, on March 6, 1993, Yagan was killed by Turkish police in a violent confrontation. Later, in April 1992, Karatas barely escaped a police raid in Kartal, Turkey, which killed twelve Dev-Sol members. Karatas is currently in exile somewhere in Western Europe.

another McDonald's restaurant in Istanbul province was bombed. A third attack that same day occurred at the Judge's Club in Tarabyes (Istanbul province). The attack caused the ceiling to collapse, but no casualties occurred. According to DHKP/C leaders, the three attacks were made to protest the Iraqi and Turkish massacres caused by American and allied forces.

On May 20, 2003, a DHKP/C member was killed when a bomb she was wearing exploded prematurely in a bathroom of the Crocodile Cafe (Ankara). One customer was injured. On June 3, five people—including the State Security Court Prosecutor and two police officers—were injured when their automobile was bombed in the Bakirkoy locality of Istanbul. The DHKP/C claimed responsibility, stating that the Turkish government was a "neocolony of America."

On August 10, 2003, DHKP/C exploded a bomb near an Istanbul office (Sisli locality) of the Justice and Development Party. No damage or injuries occurred. The bombing occurred to protest the marriage of the son of Turkey's prime minister.

On April 1, 2004, authorities arrested more than 40 DHKP/C members in raids held across Turkey and Europe. In October, ten of the forty were sentenced to life imprisonment while charges against another twenty were dropped due to the statute of limitations. Between 2002 and 2004, successful counter-attacks by police have significantly weakened the group's ability to carry out its activities.

On June 24, 2004, DHKP/C detonated a bomb (supposedly by mistake) aboard an Istanbul passenger bus. The attack killed four people, including the bomber, and injured at least fifteen others. The police suspected the bomb was intended for retaliation against killings that allegedly occurred in Turkish prisons.

On June 24, 2004, a DHKP/C operative prematurely detonated an explosive device aboard an Istanbul passenger bus. The bomb killed the bomber and three passengers. Police suspected the bombing was performed in connection with the nearby NATO summit.

On July 1, 2005, security guards prevented a suicide bombing at the office of Prime Minister Recep Tayyip Erdogan. After discovering the bomber, the police killed him as he was running away.

PHILOSOPHY AND TACTICS

The philosophy of the DHKP/C is similar to philosophies of other radical Turkish leftist groups. It contends that the Turkish government is a fascist-type government that is controlled by Western imperialistic organizations, especially the United States and NATO. The group is dedicated to attacking and eventually destroying these Western groups. The DHKP/C calls its actions "armed propaganda" and its fight against imperialism the "people's war." It targets its membership to the Turkish people such as peasant workers.

The DHKP/C has continued the ideology and goals of the original Dev-Sol group. The group regularly brings attention to its imprisoned members by staging hunger protests and other similar public displays. It actively publicizes the harsh conditions within one- to three-person prison cells that exist in Turkey. Such propaganda is an important strategy within the tactics of DHKP/C.

During its early years, DHKP/C focused largely on assassinations of political figures and

KEY EVENTS

1978: Dev-Sol is formed in Turkey by Dursun Karatas.

1994: Dev-Sol is renamed DHKP/C.

1995: DHKP/C firebombs Turkish Airlines office in Vienna; firebombs five Turkish banks in Cologne.

1996: DHKP/C makes first terrorist attack at U.S. Consulate in Istanbul. It assassinates Turkish businessman and two associates; attacks several Turkish communities, firebombs a Leverkusen mosque.

1997: DHKP/C moves from Adana and Osmaniye to Aegean.

1998: DHKP/C explodes bomb at Instanbul University Literature Department; uses anti-tank weapon on Directorate of Police (Istanbul). Later, six members are captured.

1999: DHKP/C plants bomb inside True Path Party office (it is defused); attacks U.S. Consulate in Istanbul (two members killed); tries to detonate device at Labor and Social Security Ministry (bomb exploded outside); explodes bomb at government building (twenty persons injured); and detonates bomb at Public Works and Settlement Provincial Directorate.

2000: DHKP/C detonates bomb at Sehitkamil Telekom Directorate building (minor damage); tries to detonate bomb at State Statistic Institute's Instanbul Regional Directorate (bomb defused); detonates bomb at TEDAS building (no injuries/deaths).

2001: DHKP/C detonates bomb in Istanbul (ten injured); conducts first suicide bombing at Sisli District Security Directorate (killing two, injuring one); and attacks police car (two killed); conducts second suicide bombing outside German Consulate in Istanbul (kills four).

2003: DHKP/C member is killed when bomb explodes in Ankara; five people injured when car bombed in Istanbul; explodes bomb near Istanbul office of Justice and Development Party.

2004: Authorities arrest over forty members.

2004: DHKP/C detonates bomb aboard Istanbul bus (killing four, injuring fifteen).

2005: Guards prevent bombing of prime minister's office.

---

attacks of Turkish military targets. However, a counter-terrorist strategy by the Turkish government in the early 1980s forced the group to end those activities. By the late 1980s, the group was able to resume its attacks against Turkish military and security targets.

The DHKP/C uses forests and mountainous regions as hiding places. These locations are highly prized by DHKP/C because enemy forces have difficulty locating its members and bases from such remote geographical locales.

Beginning in 1990, DHKP/C leaders began a new campaign of targeting foreign interests in Turkey. Included within these attacks were targets of U.S. military and diplomatic personnel, facilities, and materials. The DHKP/C has

publicly declared its opposition to U.S. military operations in Afghanistan and Iran. Its leaders have expressed their contentions that such actions show the imperialist goals of the United States.

Since the end of 2001, DHKP/C members have primarily used improvised explosive devices against Turkish and U.S. targets. Since this time, DHKP/C leaders finance their activities mainly through armed robberies and extortion. Leaders also raise funds through donations largely made from Western Europe, most likely because the majority of its leadership personnel come from countries in Western Europe.

DHKP/C has "several dozen" terrorist operatives inside Turkey and a sizeable support network throughout Europe. The DHKP/C is

PRIMARY SOURCE

Revolutionary People's Liberation Party/ Front (DHKP/C) a.k.a. Devrimci Sol, Dev Sol, Revolutionary Left

DESCRIPTION

This group originally formed in Turkey in 1978 as Devrimci Sol, or Dev Sol, a splinter faction of Dev Genc (Revolutionary Youth). Renamed in 1994 after factional infighting. "Party" refers to the group's political activities, while "Front" is a reference to the group's militant operations. The group espouses a Marxist-Leninist ideology and is vehemently anti-US, anti-NATO, and anti-Turkish establishment. Its goals are the establishment of a socialist state and the abolition of one- to three-man prison cells, called F-type prisons. DHKP/C finances its activities chiefly through donations and extortion.

ACTIVITIES

Since the late 1980s the group has targeted primarily current and retired Turkish security and military officials. It began a new campaign against foreign interests in 1990, which included attacks against US military and diplomatic personnel and facilities. To protest perceived US imperialism during the Gulf War, Dev Sol assassinated two US military contractors, wounded an Air Force officer, and bombed more than twenty US and NATO military, commercial, and cultural facilities. In its first significant terrorist act as DHKP/C in 1996, the group assassinated a prominent Turkish businessman and two others. DHKP/C added suicide bombings to its repertoire in 2001, with successful attacks against Turkish police in January and September. Since the end of 2001, DHKP/C has typically used improvised explosive devices against official Turkish

targets and soft US targets of opportunity; attacks against US targets beginning in 2003 probably came in response to Operation Iraqi Freedom. Operations and arrests against the group have weakened its capabilities. DHKP/C did not conduct any major terrorist attacks in 2003, but on June 24, 2004—just days before the NATO summit—an explosive device detonated, apparently prematurely, aboard a passenger bus in Istanbul while a DHKP/C operative was transporting it to another location, killing the operative and three other persons.

STRENGTH

Probably several dozen terrorist operatives inside Turkey, with a large support network throughout Europe. On April 1, 2004, authorities arrested more than forty suspected DHKP/C members in coordinated raids across Turkey and Europe. In October, ten alleged members of the group were sentenced to life imprisonment, while charges were dropped against twenty other defendants because of a statute of limitations.

LOCATION/AREA OF OPERATION

Turkey, primarily Istanbul, Ankara, Izmir, and Adana. Raises funds in Europe.

EXTERNAL AID

Widely believed to have training facilities or offices in Lebanon and Syria.

Source: U.S. Department of State. *Country Reports on Terrorism*. Washington, D.C., 2004.

---

believed to maintain training facilities and offices in Lebanon and Syria.

OTHER PERSPECTIVES

A December 18, 1999 article by the Canadian Security Intelligence Service reported that

Turkish law enforcement and security organizations continue to be concerned with the persistent threat of terrorism and its related violence. These organizations are aware that the DHKP/C, along with other terrorist groups, remains a negative influence on the state of the Turkish government and its citizens.

According to *The Turkish Times*, as of 2002, the DHKP/C and the radical Islamist group Hezbollah are considered two of the most active terrorist organizations in Turkey.

On September 5, 2003, Mr. M. Vecdi Gönül, the Minister of National Defense of the Republic of Turkey, gave a speech in which he stated that Turkey is located at the center of the problem areas within the Middle East, the Balkans, and the Caucasus. Since the 1960s, ideological, religious, separatist, state-sponsored, and other types of terrorism have frequently occurred in Turkey. Because of such disagreements within the various terrorist organizations, the DHKP/C was established. For "more than twenty years," Gönül stated that the DHKP/C has continued its "heinous acts of murder and violence." As the result of the DHKP/C and numerous other leftist extremist groups, the government of Turkey remains under a constant threat from terrorism.

SUMMARY

Since it was first established, the DHKP/C has carried out numerous violent attacks in Turkey, primarily targeting the established political and military sectors. Along with these violent activities, the DHKP/C is also very hostile toward the United States, England, and Israel, referring to what it calls "U.S. imperialism" and its close allies. As a result, the United States and the European Union have declared the DHKP/C a terror organization. Within a BBC article, the AFP news agency reported that since 1976, DHKP/C members (or members of predecessor groups) have killed dozens of people, including two retired generals, one former justice minister, and several important businesspersons.

Government officials in Ankara, Turkey, claim that about 100 police officers and soldiers and about eighty civilians have been killed. The BBC article reported that, according to a noted Turkish counter-terrorism expert, the DHKP/C has attempted to gain public notoriety since September 11, 2001 by imitating the terrorist style of Osama bin Laden. In 2005, many of the DHKP/C leaders and its prominent activists live in exile in the four Western European countries of Belgium, Germany, the Netherlands, and Italy.

SOURCES

Web sites

BBC News UK Edition, British Broadcasting Corporation. "Profile: Turkey's Marxist DHKP-C." < http://news.bbc.co.uk/1/hi/world/europe/3591119.stm > (accessed October 19, 2005).

Canadian Security Intelligence Service. "Perspectives: Trends in Terrorism." < http://www.csis-scrs.gc.ca/eng/miscdocs/200001_e.html > (accessed October 19, 2005).

International Policy Institute for Counter-Terrorism. "Revolutionary People's Liberation Party/Front Attacks: from 1988–the present." < http://www.ict.org.il/organizations/orgattack.cfm?orgid = 39 > (accessed October 19, 2005).

MIPT Terrorism Knowledge Base, National Memorial Institute for the Prevention of Terrorism. "DHKP-C." < http://www.tkb.org/Group.jsp?groupID = 38 > (accessed October 19, 2005).

Overseas Security Advisory Council. "Revolutionary People's Liberation Party/Front (DHKP/C)." < http://www.ds-osac.org/Groups/group.cfm?contentID = 1296 > (accessed October 19, 2005).

The Turkish Times. "PKK and DHKP-C in U.S. Terrorism Report." < http://www.theturkishtimes.com/archive/02/06_01/ > (accessed October 19, 2005).

The Turkish Times. "Shaping a Common Security Agenda for Southeast Europe: New Approaches and Shared Responsibilities." < http://www.anticorruption.bg/eng/news/artShow.php?id = 1112 > (accessed October 19, 2005).

Revolutionary Armed Forces of Colombia (FARC)

LEADERS: Fabio Vásquez Castaño; Felipe Torres; Manuel Marulanda Vélez

YEAR ESTABLISHED OR BECAME ACTIVE: 1964

ESTIMATED SIZE: 18,000 (30% of membership is female; 20–30% are children; the majority are under 19)

USUAL AREA OF OPERATION: Colombia

OVERVIEW

The *Fuerzas Armadas Revolucionarias de Colombia–Ejército del Pueblo* (Revolutionary Armed Forces of Colombia, or FARC) originally began as the military wing of the Colombian Communist Party. Founded between 1964 and 1966, the group now has a membership of 18,000 and is led by Manuel Marulanda Vélez, nicknamed "Tirojifo." The group has been actively fighting against the Colombian national government for nearly forty years in an armed struggle to forward its Marxist-Leninist goals. FARC claims to be Marxist-Leninist and also draws inspiration from Simon Bolivar, who "liberated" northern South America from Spanish colonial rule in the early 1800s.

FARC claims to represent the cause of the rural poor and fights against privatization of utilities, and foreign investment and influence in Colombia (especially from the United States), while battling against right-wing paramilitary groups such as *Autodefensas Unidas de Colombia* (United Self-Defense Forces of Colombia, or AUC). FARC's stated goal is to overthrow the national government and create a communist-agrarian state. FARC funds itself primarily with ransomed kidnappings, donations from supporters, and extortion in the narco-trafficking trade in Colombia.

International human rights organizations such as Amnesty International and Human

Rebels of the Revolutionary Armed Forces of Colombia march during a military practice in La Macarena, in the former rebel-controlled area in southern Colombia, in August 2001. AP/Wide World Photos. Reproduced by permission.

Rights Watch have noted FARC's violence against citizens, its use of children as soldiers in armed conflicts, and execution-style killings of farmers engaged in coca growing and the drug trade. It is estimated that FARC outright controls or has a military presence in as much as 30–40% of the land in Colombia.

HISTORY

FARC is the largest left-wing organization in South America. FARC's roots began in 1948, when the head of the Liberal Party in Colombia, Jorge Eliecer Gaitan, was assassinated; the country broke into chaos, with riots and insurrections in major cities. In the decade that followed, called *La Violencia* (The Violence), more than 200,000 people were killed and more than $1 billion in personal, government, and corporate property was damaged or destroyed. A peasant named Manuel Marulanda

Vélez joined with others to form a guerilla army to fight against conservatives and Colombian military during La Violencia.

As La Violencia continued, Marulanda formed a peasant cooperative in the Andean plains called Marquetalia. Many members of the communist and liberal parties had formed similar "independent republics" during La Violencia. With more than 1,000 members, Marquetalia became the largest of the cooperatives. This cooperative allegedly became the basis for the formation of FARC shortly after La Violencia ended.

In 1964, the Colombian government used napalm against Marquetalia in an attack. In response, Marulanda created a group called the Southern Bloc, which later turned into FARC. Marulanda became their military leader and remains leader to this day. By 1964, FARC had become active, under the banner of Marxist-Leninist ideology.

A soldier and passengers survey the remains of a truck set on fire by rebels of the Revolutionary Armed Forces of Colombia in Los Chorros, Colombia, on January 19, 2004. AP/Wide World Photos. Reproduced by permission.

Marulanda was joined in leading FARC by his friend Jacobo Arenas. Arenas' political vision joined with Marulanda's military strategies to form a movement devoted to creating an agrarian and communist state with local industries. Both Arenas and Marulanda believed that the Colombian national government was corrupt and exclusionary; FARC's mission was to overthrow the government.

FARC quickly grew in military force, eventually establishing twenty-seven battalions of armed fighters. In addition, throughout the 1970s and 1980s FARC charged a "war tax" to individuals and businesses in areas it controlled. The group used some of this money to provide needed social services in the poorer areas it controlled, opening hospitals and schools in remote areas in southern Colombia. Over time, FARC came to control or occupy 30–40% of Colombia.

By 1984, as FARC's popularity and strength coalesced, the national government, under President Belisario Betancur, offered a ceasefire, as well as other measures that would make FARC a part of the political process in

Colombia. In May 1984, FARC and Betancur signed the La Uribe peace accords, which granted FARC the right to form an accepted political party, called *Unión Patriótica* (Patriotic Union, or UP). The UP was comprised of communists, guerillas, and some liberals. Their platform consisted of the same goals FARC had aimed to achieve: land and income redistribution, the elimination of government corruption, and strong penalties against drug traffickers (at this point, FARC was not involved in the drug trade; Arenas would not permit it).

With FARC's increasing legitimacy came greater success in elections, and as the UP gained more seats in national government and won local elections, right-wing supporters became agitated. In the late 1970s and early 1980s, right-wing insurgent groups, local in nature, formed in direct response to FARC and another leftist group, the National Liberation Army (ELN). Organized in loose vigilante groups originally, this movement developed to allay the fears of national and foreign corporations and

A FARC rebel fighter sits in front of a billboard. AP/Wide World Photos

the elites. These vigilante groups, paramilitary in nature, formed to protect landowners and drug-traffickers; by the 1980s, the Colombian government viewed these groups as a viable response to FARC and ELN and began supplying the vigilante groups with arms.

When FARC's political party gained more power and attention, paramilitary groups began to crack down on leftists and suspected leftists. More than 3,000 UP members were killed by right-wing militias and death squads. FARC returned to using military violence, as its members came to believe that their participation in political parties and legitimate political systems would not be tolerated by the paramilitary groups.

By 1989, interactions between FARC and the paramilitary militias had become increasingly aggressive; the right-wing militias had organized into a loose coalition later referred to as United Self-Defense Forces of Colombia (AUC) and numbered more than 8,000 members. AUC faced accusations of attacking civilian villages without provocation and murdering

civilians they suspected were aligned with FARC or ELN. The Colombian government outlawed the groups, but they received unofficial financial support from the government, training from retired military members, and increased membership from former military soldiers and right-wing militants.

In 1990, Arenas died; FARC expanded dramatically into the coca trade and began to collect protection fees and "taxes" from narco-traffickers and coca farmers. FARC began to argue that Colombia should legalize narcotics as a political and economic strategy, so that Colombia could gain economically from the United States through the drug trade. Within a few years, the money from the drug trade represented 65% of FARC's funding. Because of FARC's growing prominence in narco-trafficking, the group gained more attention from the U.S. government as it fought its "War on Drugs."

The new source of funding provided FARC with the means to upgrade munitions, increase communications ability, and fortify and expand

LEADERSHIP

MANUEL MARULANDA VÉLEZ

Manuel Marulanda Vélez, nicked named Tirojifo, was born to peasant parents in the coffee-growing region of west-central Colombia. He is in his 70s or 80s at this point, though his exact birth date remains a question. Marulanda received an elementary school education and worked for a time as a candy maker and a wood-cutter. In 1948, when the head of the Liberal Party in Colombia, Jorge Eliecer Gaitan, was assassinated, Marulanda joined some cousins to form a band of guerilla fighters for the Liberal Party. During La Violencia, from 1948–1958, these peasant guerilla fighters fought the Colombian military and civil forces primarily in the countryside.

Marulanda established FARC in 1964 after the Colombian military used napalm against his village. Marulanda became FARC's military leader and remains the leader to this day.

its army. FARC launched a new campaign and reached out to universities to attract militant students; the "Bolivarian Movement for a New Colombia" drew on the image of Simon Bolivar, the colonial liberator, to tie FARC's actions in with the idea of liberation from what FARC perceived to be an oppressive, imperialist national government.

Between 1996 and 1998, FARC made major inroads in controlling more areas throughout the country. One major victory involved the capture of a military base at Las Delicias, a move that concerned the national government, international observers, and citizens alike. In response, Colombian citizens lobbied their government to open up peace talks with FARC. In 1999, the Colombian government gave FARC official control over a portion of Colombia with the understanding that FARC would enter into negotiations for peace. After three years, however, a period during which

KEY EVENTS

1984: FARC signs the La Uribe peace accords with the Colombian national government.

1987: FARC ambushes military convoys and small towns, fighting on more than five fronts.

1990: Jacobo Arenas dies; FARC expands into the coca trade.

2002: FARC kidnaps presidential candidate Ingrid Betancourt.

2002: FARC attacks during President Alvaro Uribe's inauguration.

2003: Grenade attacks in the Colombian capital of Bogota leave one dead, and 72 wounded. Military forces suspect FARC.

FARC was rumored to have been using the land to shore up its base, recruit new members, and increase its role in the coca trade, the Colombian government became discouraged. The kidnapping of presidential candidate Ingrid Betancourt in 2002 ended the peace talks; President Andrés Pastrana Arango ordered the Colombian military to reclaim the lands he had given to FARC. Ingrid Betancourt is still in FARC's custody as of this writing.

Like its leftist counterpart, the National Liberation Army, FARC uses kidnappings and ransoming of wealthy individuals, political figures, or executives from multinational companies as a form of revenue. In 1999, FARC kidnapped three U.S. citizens working in Colombia; the hostages were killed. The incident provoked international outcry, and FARC admitted that the killings had been a "mistake," and that those involved would be punished. To date, international human rights observers have not seen evidence of any punishment for the murders.

Between Ingrid Betancourt's kidnapping in 2002 and 2004, FARC was relatively quiet compared to past activity; it is believed the

PRIMARY SOURCE

Revolutionary Armed Forces of Colombia (FARC)

DESCRIPTION

Established in 1964 as the military wing of the Colombian Communist Party, the FARC is Latin America's oldest, largest, most capable, and best-equipped insurgency of Marxist origin. Although only nominally fighting in support of Marxist goals today, the FARC is governed by a general secretariat led by long-time leader Manuel Marulanda (a.k.a. "Tirofijo") and six others, including senior military commander Jorge Briceno (a.k.a. "Mono Jojoy"). Organized along military lines but includes some specialized urban fighting units. A Colombian military offensive targeting FARC fighters in their former safe haven in southern Colombia has experienced some success, with several FARC mid-level leaders killed or captured. On December 31, 2004, FARC leader Simon Trinidad, the highest-ranking FARC leader ever captured, was extradited to the United States on drug charges.

ACTIVITIES

Bombings, murder, mortar attacks, kidnapping, extortion, and hijacking, as well as guerrilla and conventional military action against Colombian political, military, and economic targets. In March 1999, the FARC executed three US indigenous rights activists on Venezuelan territory after it kidnapped them in Colombia. In February 2003, the FARC captured and continues to hold three US contractors and killed one other American when their plane crashed in Florencia. Foreign citizens often are targets of FARC kidnapping for ransom. The FARC has well-documented ties to the full range of narcotics trafficking activities, including taxation, cultivation, and distribution.

STRENGTH

Approximately 9,000 to 12,000 armed combatants and several thousand more supporters, mostly in rural areas.

LOCATION/AREA OF OPERATION

Primarily in Colombia with some activities—extortion, kidnapping, weapons sourcing, logistics, and R&R—suspected in neighboring Brazil, Venezuela, Panama, Peru, and Ecuador.

EXTERNAL AID

Cuba provides some medical care, safe haven, and political consultation. In December 2004, a Colombian Appeals Court declared three members of the Irish Republican Army—arrested in Colombia in 2001 upon exiting the former FARC-controlled demilitarized zone (despeje)—guilty of providing advanced explosives training to the FARC. The FARC often uses the Colombia/Venezuela border area for cross-border incursions and consider Venezuelan territory as a safe haven.

Source: U.S. Department of State. *Country Reports on Terrorism.* Washington, D.C., 2004.

organization was busy regrouping and training. In June and July of 2004, FARC was implicated in execution-style killings of peasants, and the UN High Commissioner for Human Rights condemned FARC's actions, calling it a violation of the Geneva Protocol. Since 1997, FARC has been listed by the U.S Department of State as a terrorist organization. On October 15, 2001, in the wake of the September 11 attacks, the United States listed FARC as a serious terrorist threat, claiming that the area of Colombia controlled by FARC was a training ground for terrorists.

PHILOSOPHY AND TACTICS

FARC is a hierarchical organization with the leader, Marulanda, at the top. Beneath him are seven "General Secretariats," each responsible for particular blocks or zones in Colombia.

PRIMARY SOURCE

Terror Trainers or Eco-tourists?

I slept next to the brothel.

The music and shrieks from that sad bordello drifted in the window until long past dawn, while I turned and sweated in the muggy swamp of my bed, the main attraction for squadrons of mosquitoes.

But I had some consolation. I was not the most uncomfortable Irishman in Colombia that night.

Far away in a high-security prison, three Irish Republican prisoners were enduring another night of captivity.

They are suspected to have trained the Colombian extreme left-wing FARC rebel group in terrorism techniques.

This week, a congressional report released in Washington alleged that links exist between the FARC and the Irish Republican Army—the IRA quickly denied that any of its operatives had been sent to Colombia to carry out training.

Safe Haven

I was, in fact, following a path those same Irishmen had blazed some months before.

For all I knew, they may even have stayed in the same hotel in San Vicente, the town in the Colombian jungle which until recently was the capital of the guerrilla safe haven.

Under a unique arrangement, the government had allowed the Marxist guerrillas of FARC to control a vast swath of territory, on condition that they were good chaps, and talked about a ceasefire.

They did talk, and talk.

Alas, they also kidnapped and killed, and continued to raise millions from taxing the cocaine which flourishes in the jungles of Colombia.

The FARC are the world's richest Marxists. The U.S. government believes they earn as much as US$300m a year from the drugs trade.

Guerrilla Needlework

The following morning, I set out for the big FARC base in the hills outside San Vicente.

The inquiry was launched after the arrest of three alleged terrorist trainers.

One of the group's leaders had agreed to an interview, news delivered to me by a bearded, motorbike-riding revolutionary with whom I dined the night before.

The guerrilla camp was a muddle. The commandant would be with us in a few minutes, a young guerrilla guard had announced—we should be patient.

The teenage fighter was polite, but she was preoccupied.

We had interrupted her morning needlework session. She had been busy stitching a holster for her pistol.

It was a scene of extraordinary incongruity. The Women's Institute meets Che Guevara.

Cautious Response

Commandant Raoul Rais turned out to be a very dreary man—plump, and dressed in immaculate fatigues, he sat with an armalite in his lap throughout the interview.

Marulanda and his commanders maintain tight control over FARC's activities in spite of the remote areas it controls and the problems with maintaining open communication lines.

FARC is best known for its use of kidnapping and ransoming as both a political and economic strategy. Colombia is the kidnapping capital of the world, and FARC is believed to be responsible for approximately one-third of all kidnappings in that country. FARC has been held responsible for the kidnapping of elected and appointed Colombian government officials, international and national aid workers, employees of multinational

But the commandant was very cautious when I brought up the question of the three detained Irishmen.

They came here for one reason only, to share political views.

They wanted to study the peace process in Colombia, and to share with us about the peace process in Ireland. And that was that.

The U.S. State Department, though, believes otherwise.

One of its officials told congress it was his information that the three had traces of explosives on their clothes.

They had also been traveling on false passports. And the FARC had of late been using bombing tactics familiar to anybody who had studied the IRA in Northern Ireland.

The White House seems disinclined to accept that the men were on a mission of peace.

Rather, it believes they were training a group which has threatened American lives, and which is now a target of the war on terror.

Eco-tourists?

Why would three Irish Republicans go to one of the most dangerous countries on earth, traveling on false passports, into the stronghold of a guerrilla group notorious for kidnapping, drug trafficking and murder?

It is a question the three defendants will attempt to answer at their trial in Colombia, but one which has caused untold embarrassment for Sinn Fein, and considerable anger for the White House.

There may indeed be a simple explanation.

They might have been there as eco-tourists, the first explanation offered, or to study the Colombian peace process—the subsequent explanation.

The notion of convicted terrorists James Monaghan and Martin McCauley chasing butterflies in the jungle or listening to the warbling of parrots is charming. But am I alone in wondering if it is true?

For all that, I doubt that Mr. Bush will want action against Sinn Fein that might in turn precipitate a crisis in the Irish peace process.

There is, it needs to be said, no proof that the party, or indeed, the IRA, sent the men to Colombia.

Big American Stick

And with the Middle East in flames, the last thing the White House needs is trouble in a place where the U.S. has gained so much credit for its peacemaking role.

There already have been some very tough words in private, but my guess is it will not go much further than that.

As far as the commandant and his comrades are concerned, stand by not for words, but for a very big American stick.

In George W. Bush's world of friends and enemies, the commandant knows exactly where he stands.

Source: BBC News, 2002

---

corporations, and wealthy Colombians and nonnative individuals.

In addition, FARC's use of traditional military tactics, and the formation of fully armed army battalions, has given rise to its status as the largest leftist, independent army in South America. FARC trains volunteers in its political

ideology and in military maneuvers and methods for combat in the areas it currently holds and protects or in areas it seeks to capture. FARC then goes into an area and attacks local police and army targets to gain control.

The group uses murder as a political tool as well. Although the vast majority of its kidnapping victims are returned alive, nonpayment of a ransom results in death. In addition, FARC has been accused of execution-style killings of various kidnapping victims, such as the killing of three activists from the United States in 1999.

According to human rights groups, FARC frequently violates international law by conscripting children as fighters into its armies, creating booby traps by hiding bombs in the bodies of fallen opponents, and burning civilians alive in their homes. FARC's response has vacillated between agreeing to follow international humanitarian law and claiming that they are not bound by such conventions as FARC is not the official government of Colombia.

Along with kidnappings and military actions, FARC uses bombings to damage the energy sector, with a particular focus on oil pipelines. The organization focuses also on water reservoirs, electricity plants, and transportation centers.

FARC has been accused of murdering high-ranking politicians and their family members as well. In 2001, FARC stepped up violent acts against kidnapping victims, murdering hostage Consuelo Araújonoguera, a former Colombian minister of culture and the wife of the attorney general. In 2002, in addition to kidnapping presidential candidate Ingrid Betancourt, FARC hijacked a Colombian jet and took passenger Sen. Jorge Gechem Turbay as hostage, the fifth congressmen kidnapped by FARC since June 2001.

On August 7, 2002, FARC attacked the presidential palace, where President Alvaro Uribe was being inaugurated. Dignitaries from around the world were present but not injured, although twenty-one civilians died in the attack from stray bullets.

In recent years, FARC has begun to use kidnapping victims as leverage for prisoner exchange demands. President Uribe prefers to use rescue operations to save the seventy or so hostages being offered in the exchange, but family members have balked at the idea, pointing to the failure to save Governor Guillermo Gaviria Correa, his peace advisor, and numerous soldiers, who were kidnapped by FARC in 2003. FARC reportedly killed all the hostages when the Colombian army initiated a rescue into the area of the jungle where they were being held.

FARC continues to hold the hostages, including three Americans, presidential candidate Ingrid Betancourt, her running mate Clara Rojas, and a German citizen, Lothar Hintze. Negotiations with the Colombia government have failed to come to any resolutions that would lead to their release.

OTHER PERSPECTIVES

Human Rights Watch, a nonpartisan, nongovernmental organization, has long criticized FARC for their poor human rights record. Human Rights Watch states that:

> ... Human Rights Watch has found little evidence that the FARC makes an attempt to conform its methods to international standards, which its members flagrantly violate in the field. Despite repeated requests, the FARC has not provided Human Rights Watch with a copy of its regulations, current combat manuals, trial procedures, or rules of engagement, nor has it responded to our submission of a list of detailed cases ... of alleged violations committed by the FARC.

> When the FARC perceives a political advantage, it emphasizes its respect for international humanitarian law, as in the case of sixty soldiers captured after an armed forces–FARC clash at the Las Delicias base in the department of Putumayo in 1996 and released ten months later. The laws of war applicable in Colombia give captured combatants no special status but provide for their humane treatment and safe release, which the FARC respected.

> However, in dozens of other, less publicized cases, when no political advantage is apparent, the FARC makes little if any attempt to abide by international humanitarian law.

At the same time, international observers also note that Colombia's role in the United States' War on Drugs complicates internal politics in Colombia. FARC seeks to eliminate U.S. involvement in Colombia, and yet FARC derives significant income from drug interests. Experts point to this paradox: until drug activities decrease, U.S. pressure will continue or possibly increase. FARC will not voluntarily reduce the drug trade, as such action would lower its funding.

Garry Leach, of *Colombia Journal Online*, notes that although demands are made for FARC to cease all political violence in Colombia: "...there was never an agreement that the Colombian military cease its military activities throughout the rest of the country. And yet, politicians and the media in the United States and Colombia repeatedly lambasted the FARC for continuing to fight a war against an enemy that was actively seeking to defeat it on the battlefield. The rebels also had to contend throughout the peace process with the growing military threat of right-wing paramilitaries closely allied to the Colombian army."

SUMMARY

FARC continues to face conflict with right-wing paramilitaries from the AUC. In addition, FARC has been holding Ingrid Betancourt hostage since 2002. Betancourt had condemned government corruption and had written extensively about the need for a peace process prior to her kidnapping; negotiations for her release are ongoing as of this writing.

In 1997, one of the strongest right-wing paramilitary groups, under the leadership of Carlos Castano, formed to create the AUC officially—until this time the groups had operated as a very decentralized whole. AUC has been accused of destroying entire villages solely because they were suspected supporters of FARC. Approximately 3,500 civilians die in Colombia each year as a result of FARC, ELN, AUC, and Colombian military actions. Experts believe AUC is responsible for 75% of those deaths.

On December 13, 2004, a FARC leader named Ricardo Gonzalez (also known as Rodrigo Granda) was arrested. The incident caused conflict between Venezuela and Colombia; some FARC members claim that Colombian authorities arrested Granda in Venezuela illegally. Colombian officials have previously accused Venezuela of harboring terrorists; this incident aggravated tensions between the two countries and brought FARC to the forefront once more.

The discrepancy between the way the Colombian national government treats FARC and AUC has been the center of controversy. In 2005, Colombian President Alvaro Uribe granted limited immunity to right-wing AUC insurgents—but the order does not give the same rights to members of FARC, although AUC is responsible for significantly more civilian deaths in recent years. Critics charge that President Uribe is using the agreement to increase foreign aid and investment and that by disengaging the AUC, he opens the door for an increase in leftist political violence.

SOURCES

Books

Murillo, Mario Alfonso, and Jesus Rey Avirama. *Colombia and the United States: War, Terrorism, and Destabilization.* New York: Seven Stories Press, 2003.

Pearce, Jenny. *Inside Colombia: Drugs, Democracy, and War.* New Brunswick, NJ: Rutgers University Press, 2004.

Safford, Frank, and Marco Palacios. *Colombia: Fragmented Land, Divided Society.* Oxford: Oxford University Press, 2001.

Web sites

Amnesty International. "Colombia, A Laboratory of War: Repression and Violence in Arauca." < http:// web.amnesty.org/library/index/engamr230042004 > (accessed September 30, 2005).

Amnesty International. "Colombia: Report 2005." < http:// web.amnesty.org/report2005/col-summary-eng > (accessed September 30, 2005).

Foreign Policy Research Institute. "E-Notes: Terrorism in Colombia." < http://www.fpri.org/enotes/latin.20020121. posada.terrorismincolombia.html > (accessed September 30, 2005).

Colombia Journal Online. "The Hypocrisy of the Peace Process." < http://www.colombiajournal.org/ colombia103.htm > (accessed September 30, 2005).

Audio and Visual Media

National Public Radio's Weekend Edition (audio clip). "FARC." < http://www.npr.org/templates/story/story. php?storyId = 1127278 > (accessed September 30, 2005).

SEE ALSO

National Liberation Army (ELN)

Revolutionary Front for an Independent East Timor

ALTERNATE NAME: Fretilin

LEADERS: Xanana Gusmao; José Ramos-Horta

USUAL AREA OF OPERATION: East Timor

OVERVIEW

The Revolutionary Front for an Independent East Timor (in Portuguese, *Frente Revolucionária de Timor Leste Independente*, or Fretilin) was formed as a radical left-wing party supporting the independence of East Timor in 1974. The group's original name was Timorese Social Democratic Association (*Associação Social Democrática Timor*, ASDT), and its military wing was the Armed Forces for the National Liberation of East Timor (*Forças Armadas de Libertação Nacional de Timor-Leste*, Falintil).

HISTORY

The Revolutionary Front for an Independent East Timor (Fretilin) led the fight for East Timor's independence from Indonesia. The group was originally organized in 1974 as a radical left-wing party to promote the independence of East Timor at the end of Portuguese rule in the Indonesian colony.

Portugal considered East Timor an overseas province for more than 400 years, when it first established colonial authority. In 1960, the United Nations (UN) General Assembly declared that territories under Portuguese control did not fit the definition of non-self-governing territories, according to Chapter XI of the UN Charter.

East Timorese listen to a speech on May 15, 2000, the first day of the Revolutionary Front for an Independent East Timor (FRETILIN) national congress in Dili. AP/Wide World Photos. Reproduced by permission.

Militant members of the anti-independence East Timorese group known as Besi Mera Putih (Iron Red and White), patrol with makeshift weapons in April 1999 before attacking pro-independence supporters in Liquica, a town east of Jakarta. AP/Wide World Photos

It was not until a 1974 government change in Lisbon, the capitol of Portugal, that Chapter IX was recognized in Portuguese law. This change began a period called the "Carnation Revolution," when Portugal modified its Constitutional definition of an overseas province. The new definition meant Portugal recognized that its colonies, including East Timor, should be allowed to determine their sovereignty status. Portugal was presenting the opportunity for its colonies to gain independence.

A law was passed in 1975, which called for the formation of a transitional government in East Timor. The transitional government would assist East Timor in holding an election of a popular assembly in 1976. Finally, termination of Portuguese administration was planned for October 1978.

The people of East Timor began to prepare for their self-determination by organizing politically. The Fretilin party came into existence as an advocate for immediate independence from

Portugal. Additional parties were also formed. The Timorese Democratic Union (*União Democrática Timorense*, UDT) favored continued association with Portugal throughout the independence process. The Timorese Popular Democratic Association (*Associação Popular Democrática Timorense*, Apodeti) pushed for East Timor to become an autonomous province within Indonesia.

Fretilin and UDT tried to forge a coalition on the common objective of independence. This was short-lived, though, as Fretilin appeared to be increasingly left wing, and UDT moved into closer contact with Indonesia.

In June 1975, Fretilin boycotted a conference convened by Portugal in Macau to discuss a gradual plan for decolonization. UDT and Apodeti both attended the meetings. Fretilin was unhappy with the inclusion of Apodeti. Fretilin claimed factions within Indonesia supported the party.

LEADERSHIP

XANANA GUSMAO

Xanana Gusmao, born in 1946, was a prominent member of the Fretilin party. As the leader of Falintil, Gusmao fought against the Indonesian military forces from the bush. He spent more than six years in prison or under house arrest. Just before East Timor received its independence in 2002, Gusmao was elected president. However, he ran as an independent, not as a member of the Fretilin party. Prior to being elected, he said he did not want the job of president, saying he would rather farm pumpkins or be a photographer. However, there was no other serious contender when the time came for an election. As President, he has appealed for reconciliation with those who carried out violent acts during the fight for independence. He was born in the town of Manatuto, the second of nine children. He studied for four years at a Jesuit seminary in Dare and did three years of required service with the Portuguese. Later, he worked with a department in the local government during the colonial administration.

JOSÉ RAMOS-HORTA

José Ramos-Horta, born on December 26, 1949, in Dili, was one of the most influential leaders of the Fretilin organization in bringing attention to the issues of self-determination of East Timor. Just before the invasion of Indonesia in East Timor, Ramos-Horta was named the Minister of External Relations and Information for the Fretilin Party. Ramos-Horta left East Timor in 1975, but served as an active spokesperson for East Timor issues at the UN and in front of other international bodies. He was named the Permanent Representative to the UN for the East Timorese independence movement for over ten years, beginning in 1975. He has studied International Relations, International Law, and Peace Studies. He is the author of *Funu: The Unfinished Saga of East Timor*, and other books. In 1996, Ramos-Horta won the Nobel Peace Prize.

Relations between these three parties worsened rapidly in the second half of 1975. Open hostilities began, and East Timor fell into a civil war. In August, the Portuguese governor and administration withdrew from the mainland of East Timor to the island of Atauro. At the same time, covert Indonesian forces began operating in nearby West Timor.

In November 1975, Fretilin, which was reported to control most of the territory, declared the independence of East Timor. Fretilin was relying on the support of the Portuguese local military forces and on weapons left by the Portuguese. Two days later, though, a coalition of pro-Indonesian parties (primarily UDT and Apodeti) proclaimed East Timor independent and integrated with Indonesia. On December 7, Indonesia launched a naval, air, and land invasion of East Timor. Indonesia fought against Fretilin resistance and was able to increase its territorial control. Indonesia claimed to be fighting against a threat of communism in East Timor.

Indonesia claimed to establish a Regional Popular Assembly. At the Assembly's only meeting in May 1976, those gathered decided to ask Indonesia to formally integrate East Timor into the country. Indonesian President Suharto declared Law 7/76, which named East Timor the twenty-seventh province. Indonesia claimed that the people of East Timor, through the Assembly, had exercised their self-determination rights.

The UN did not recognize the authority of the Popular Assembly and therefore did not endorse its decision to integrate East Timor into Indonesia. Likewise, Portugal did not give up its power of administration over East Timor. It made a constitutional amendment, saying Portugal was bound to promote and safeguard the right to self-determination and independence of East Timor. The Portuguese president was given authority to achieve these goals.

KEY EVENTS

1974: Portugal promises to allow colonies self-determination; Fretilin and other parties form.

1975: Civil war breaks out between pro-independence and pro-Indonesian parties; independence declared separately by Fretilin and pro-Indonesian parties; Indonesia invades and annexes East Timor; period of armed struggle begins, killing 200,000 people.

1991: Over 100 independence activists killed at a funeral.

1992: Gusmão is captured.

1999: Indonesia reconsiders granting East Timor independence; Gusmão moved to house arrest; anti-independence violence erupts in East Timor; East Timorese vote for independence; 1,000 people killed by anti-independence militia backed by Indonesian military; Australian peace-keeping forces arrive; UN Transitional Administration in East Timor established.

2001: Fretilin wins fifty-five of eighty-eight Constituent Assembly seats.

2002: Xanana Gusmão wins presidential election; East Timor officially becomes independent.

Fretilin named José Ramos-Horta a minister for communications and external affairs in 1975. He became the primary contact between journalists and Fretilin. He was also an important link to the UN. Ramos left East Timor just before the attack by Indonesia in 1976. He helped convince the UN Security Council to pass resolutions calling on Indonesia to withdrawal its forces from East Timor.

Fretilin continued to resist East Timor's integration into Indonesia by means of its armed wing, the Armed Forces for the National Liberation of East Timor (Falintil). In 1981, Xanana Gusmão became the leader of Falintil. Falintil used guerilla warfare to carry

out its campaign. There are estimates that up to 200,000 people were killed as a result of the fighting. Many displaced citizens died of famine and disease.

The pro-independence activists suffered many human rights violations by the Indonesian forces, but there was little international attention given to the situation. This changed in November 1991, when Indonesian forces opened fire on a pro-independence demonstration near a cemetery in the capital, Dili. As many as 200 people were reported killed in the attack. Images and reports from journalists on the scene impacted international opinion of the situation. Many foreign governments, particularly in the West, began making policies supporting the self-determination of East Timor.

Gusmão was captured in 1992 and convicted in 1993 of trying to overthrow the Indonesian Government. He was given a life sentence, which was later reduced.

The resignation of Suharto as president of Indonesia was a turning point towards self-determination for East Timor. In January 1999, after President Habibie came into power, Indonesia indicated it would revisit the idea of East Timor independence.

Gusmão was released in February 1999 and placed under house arrest. Because of violence from anti-independence activists, Gusmão ordered guerrillas to continue fighting.

Indonesia and Portugal signed an agreement in May 1999 to allow the people of East Timor to vote on their future. The UN organized a referendum which took place the following August. The results showed 78% of voters favored independence. However, anti-independence militia, aided by the Indonesian military, carried out attacks that killed over 1,000 people. An Australian peacekeeping force arrived to restore order. Later in 1999, the Indonesian parliament recognized the outcome of the referendum, and the UN Transitional Administration in East Timor was established. Gusmão was released in October 1999.

In 2001, the Fretilin party candidates won fifty-five of eighty-eight seats in East Timor's Constituent Assembly. Gusmão was elected president in 2002. East Timor's official independence was declared on the May 20, 2002.

PHILOSOPHY AND TACTICS

The leftist coup that took over Portugal in 1974 was responsible for the change in policy for dealing with its colonies. Fretilin was also a Marxist organization, given arms by Portugal when hostilities began in 1975. This gave Fretilin the much-needed support in the beginning of its conflicts with the pro-integration militias. Marxist leadership and civil war was also taking place in the former Portuguese colonies of Mozambique and Angola.

Falintil acted on behalf of Fretilin throughout the party's ongoing struggle for East Timor independence. They followed the lead of Gusmão, who referred to the struggle as the "sacred ideal" of independence. There were many Falintil camps in the East Timorese bush, planning and organizing their next moves. Many of the fighters left their families and were always on the run in the harsh terrain of East Timor. Compared to the militia forces, the Falintil were often outnumbered, and were not as well armed. Falintil fighters were subject to sickness and starvation and were tortured when caught. The Falintil fighters numbered over 27,000 during the entire conflict. These numbers were reduced during the militia violence that followed the vote for independence.

Falintil actively targeted the pro-integration militias, which grew in number as pro-independence campaigning increased in strength and effectiveness. Falintil killed Indonesian soldiers and seized army weapons in East Timor. These techniques were met with reprisal attacks, which included attacks on civilian supporters of independence.

Gusmão had close control of Falintil. As tensions between the pro-independence and pro-integration sides escalated toward the time to vote on independence, it became clear that steps needed to be taken to disarm the militias. At the time, Falintil was already operating under a ceasefire that Gusmão had ordered, which was being maintained. However, when the Indonesian military openly endorsed the militia and admitted to providing supplies and training, Gusmão authorized Falintil to fight the militias. Fretinil claimed it was protecting the people of East Timor.

In 1998, a UN team determined in an annual All-Inclusive Intra-East Timorese Dialogue that many former advocates for the integration of East Timor had become dissatisfied with Indonesian rule, and were pushing for independence. The UN discovered that the generation that had been educated during Indonesian rule were even more adamant about independence than their parents. Outward activism for independence was growing in the mid 1990s. This provided pro-independence forces in East Timor with further international support.

Fretilin and other independence movements worked together under Gusmão to form the National Council of Timorese Resistance (CNRT). The CNRT solidified the coalition of movements for independence in East Timor.

Gusmão, while under house arrest, provided input to the negotiations for self-determination between Portugal, Indonesia, and the UN in 1999. Gusmão was uncompromising in his determination to ensure that a referendum would be carried out to determine East Timor's fate. He also agreed to the ongoing participation of Indonesia in the process.

When concerns over security grew stronger leading up to the referendum, a UN representative in East Timor called for the creation of a peace commission involving both pro-independence and pro-integration factions. This was something Gusmão advocated. He saw it as a way to calm the situation and a good opportunity for the UN to begin establishing a presence in East Timor. However, the Indonesian government did not want the commission to proceed, claiming it was too early to involve all concerned parties in discussions about East Timor's future.

During the formation of the East Timor political system after the independence vote, Fretilin provided much guidance. The prominence of the organization was further demonstrated by the large number of seats won by the Fretilin party in East Timor's Constituent Assembly.

OTHER PERSPECTIVES

During the 1970s, Indonesia denied any claims to East Timor territory. Indonesia was a former Dutch colony, and East Timor had always been aligned with Portugal. The Indonesian government claimed the threat of communism in the region as reason for resisting the struggle of Fretilin and other organizations to make East Timor independent.

Australia sided with Indonesia on the issue of integration in 1978. They were eager to settle disputes concerning the borders of the seabed in the Timor Sea and felt this was easier to accomplish if East Timor was part of Indonesia. It was known for some years that oil and other minerals were abundant in the Timor Sea. Even during the late 1990s, Australia claimed the interests of all—East Timor, Indonesia, and Australia—were best served if East Timor remained part of Indonesia. However, Australia began pushing for the importance of self-determination. The issue of natural resources may have been a driving factor as to why Indonesia wanted to annex East Timor.

The United States supported Indonesia in the 1970s. *The Nation* reports that the United States continued to give aid, including military aid, to Indonesia as they took on the pro-independence group in East Timor. However, the United States began contributing to, and supporting the efforts of, the UN to guide the process of self-determination in East Timor.

There are arguments that a long struggle for East Timor was unavoidable considering its state of development following colonization. East Timor is said to have been unprepared for self-governance in 1975. Very few East Timorese were educated. There was one secondary school for a population of over 700,000. The literacy rate was 10%.

SUMMARY

Fretilin began the fight for East Timor's independence in 1975. The continued struggle of Falintil guerrillas over two and a half decades, eventually gave the people of East Timor a chance for self-determination.

The chaos in East Timor during the 1990s forced all sides to work on a solution. The impact on civilian life grabbed the attention of the international community and persuaded them to get involved. The assistance of the UN was vital in making headway towards peace and eventually proved instrumental in assisting East Timor in becoming a self-governing state.

Fretilin continues to remain a strong force in East Timor. They hold a large number of seats in the country's Constituent Assembly, and the party's former leader, Gusmão, is still in power. In April 2005, East Timor and Indonesia settled border agreements. East Timor and Australia agreed on a strategy for sharing the billions of dollars in revenue that is expected from Timor Sea resources—primarily oil and natural gas deposits.

SOURCES

Books

Martin, Ian. *Self Determination in East Timor*, International Peace Academy Occasional Paper Series. Boulder, CO: Lynne Rienner Publishers, 2001.

Periodicals

"Fighters on the ropes." *Time International*. May 26, 2003: vol. 161, i. 21, p. 46.

"East Timor, Indonesia, and U.S. Policy." *U.S. Department of State Dispatch*. March 16, 1992: vol. 3, no. 11, p. 213(4).

Kohen, Arnold S. "Making an Issue of East." *The Nation*. Feb. 10, 1992: vol. 254, no. 5, p. 162(2).

Web sites

BBC News World Edition "Victory for Timor Freedom Party." < http://news.bbc.co.uk/2/hi/asia-pacific/1526725.stm > (accessed October 1, 2005).

BBC News World Edition. "Timeline: East Timor." < http://news.bbc.co.uk/2/hi/asia-pacific/country_profiles/1504243.stm > (accessed October 1, 2005).

BBC News World Edition. "Profile: Xanana Gusmao." < http://news.bbc.co.uk/1/hi/world/asia-pacific/342145.stm > (accessed October 1, 2005).

Nobel Prize. "José Ramos-Horta—Curriculum Vitae." < http://nobelprize.org/peace/laureates/1996/ramos-horta-cv.html > (accessed October 1, 2005).

Revolutionary Nuclei

OVERVIEW

The Revolutionary Nuclei is a relatively new group. Its first terrorist activity was reported in 1996. The group is thought to be an offshoot of the terrorist group *Espanastatikos Laikos Agonas* (ELA). The ELA reportedly targeted various government entities in Greece. It also claimed responsibility for numerous attacks against U.S. establishments in Greece. Like its predecessor, the Revolutionary Nuclei (RN) is also thought to have similar ideologies and objectives.

On account of its reported attacks against the United States and Greek establishments, the U.S. Department of State has categorized RN as a terrorist organization in 1997. It was again added to the list of foreign terrorist organizations in 2000 and 2001. The group is also known by many other names. Some of these are Revolutionary Cells, Revolutionary Popular Struggle, and ELA.

YEAR ESTABLISHED OR BECAME ACTIVE: 1995

ESTIMATED SIZE: less than 100

USUAL AREA OF OPERATION: Greece, primarily the Athens metropolitan area

HISTORY

The Revolutionary Nuclei is thought to be the successor of the more prominent *Espanastatikos Laikos Agonas* (ELA), which was formed in Greece in 1975. ELA was allegedly formed with the aim of resisting the military government in

LEADERSHIP

NOT KNOWN

The terrorist outfit Revolutionary Nuclei is thought to be a small group of less than 100 members. Not much has been reported or written about any of its leaders. Unlike other terrorist organizations, no member of the group has reportedly made claims of leading the Revolutionary Nuclei.

Interestingly, news reports, anti-terrorism experts, and government officials have not mentioned any names of masterminds of various terrorist attacks carried out by the Revolutionary Nuclei. The group is thought to be secretive about its members and other issues such as total strength and funding.

Greece that existed at the time. The group claimed that it was against "capitalism," and "imperialism."

Experts state that the ELA also turned its attention to anti-American activities. Reports indicate that the cause of such a shift was due to U.S. support for the military regime in Greece. ELA, during the late 1970s, 1980s, and early 1990s claimed responsibility for hundreds of bombings throughout Greece. These included Greek government targets as well as those owned by Americans in Greece.

According to U.S. government officials and monitor groups, the last known attack by the ELA occurred in 1995. Shortly after this, the group is thought to have been disbanded. Experts allege that most members of the ELA formed a new group in 1995, known as the Revolutionary Nuclei.

The Revolutionary Nuclei reportedly has similar views as the ELA. Since 1996, the group has allegedly carried out dozens of bombings and arson attacks, again on Greek government establishments as well as businesses and offices owned by American institutions based in Greece, mainly around the

Athens area. Analysts state that the years 1997–1999 saw maximum operations carried out by the group. The most prominent attack by RN came in 1999, when members of the group set off a bomb at the Athenaeum Intercontinental Hotel in Athens. At the time, the hotel was to hold an international economic conference by Leon Brittan, Vice President of the European commission. The bomb killed a Greek woman and injured an employee of the hotel. Considerable damage was reportedly done to the building.

Apart from the above, there have been many other similar attacks during this period. In 1996, the group claimed responsibility for bombing of a branch office of Citibank in Athens. According to news reports, the bombing did not kill or injure anyone and caused minor structural damage to the office. In the same year, members of RN are thought to be behind the attack on a travel agency in Paris, which arranged group tours to Denmark. The attack was allegedly carried out as a protest against the imprisonment of a fellow extremist in Denmark. Some experts dispute that the attack was carried out by other terrorist groups affiliated to the RN.

The year 1998 saw numerous terrorist attacks in Greece. Most of these were attributed by government officials to Revolutionary Nuclei and 17 November, another terrorist outfit operating in Greece. In June, the group was suspected behind the bombing of the office of the Supreme Council of Personnel Selection—a Greek government organization. A month later, members of Revolutionary Nuclei claimed responsibility of bombing another government entity, the ASEP, or Civil Service Employment Agency (the state agency responsible for public employment in Greece). Both these attacks caused structural damage to the buildings. No one was killed or injured.

Later in 1998, the RN shifted its focus to American establishments. Two bombs exploded within a short timeframe at two different offices of American Express in Piraeus, Greece. The subsequent year also saw a few attacks carried out by the group. The group also claimed responsibility for bombing a Texaco gas station in Athens. Like all their other attacks, there were no casualties reported.

In early 2000, the RN claimed responsibility for bombing a Greek mining and metal

KEY EVENTS

1995: The last reported attack by ELA carried out; the Revolutionary Nuclei, an offshoot of the ELA is thought to have been formed at this time.

1996: Members of the RN reportedly carry out their first attack by bombing Citibank in Athens.

1997: The group is designated as a terrorist organization by the U.S. Department of State.

1998: Many more bombings claimed by the group, including attacks on Greek government buildings.

1999: Bomb explodes in the Athenaeum Intercontinental Hotel in Athens during an international economic conference. The attack claimed by the RN kills one person and injures another, the only instance of human casualties among all attacks attributed to the group.

2000: The last reported attack by the group occurs on November 12. The group is thought to have dismantled after this attack.

---

company, METKA. Later in the year, police authorities were reportedly able to prevent a bomb attack on the office of Stavros Soumakis, a minister with the Greek government. The last reported attacks by the group occurred in November 2000. On November 12, 2000, three bombs exploded within a short time of each other. The first bomb exploded in the studio of a Greek-American sculptor in Athens. The other two exploded shortly after the first bomb, one at an office of Citibank, and the other in the office of Barclay's (a British bank).

In subsequent years, there were no attacks reported or claimed by Revolutionary Nuclei. However, during this time, activities by other terrorist organizations such as 17 November that are thought to be affiliated with the RN increased. After 2000, Greek police officials arrested people suspected to be members of Revolutionary Nuclei and other terrorist outfits.

Most experts allege that members of Revolutionary Nuclei have joined other prominent terrorist organizations since 2000. The group was thought to have disbanded in the early 2000s. However, in 2003, a bomb at the Insurance Company Alico reportedly caused the police to look at Revolutionary Nuclei again. According to published reports, the bomb strongly resembled bombs used by members of the RN in the past. The group did not claim responsibility. In contrast, during this period there were other bombings and arson attacks that were claimed by the Revolutionary Nuclei. The Greek police have reportedly disputed these claims.

Greek government and police officials also reportedly received threats from the RN and other such groups before the 2004 Summer Olympics in Athens. Experts claim that such threats would suggest that the group is alive and is planning more attacks in the future.

PHILOSOPHY AND TACTICS

The Revolutionary Nuclei is thought to be an offshoot of the *Espanastatikos Laikos Agonas*. As analysts suggest, the Revolutionary Nuclei shares the same beliefs as the ELA. These include views of anti-capitalism and anti-imperialism. Although, the ELA was reportedly formed to resist the military government in Greece in the 1970s and 1980s, even after the fall of the military junta, the ELA and later the RN continued their activities against the Greek government.

The Revolutionary Nuclei is also known to be anti-American. Experts maintain that the group's anti-American sentiment is mainly due to U.S. policies of imperialism, especially those in Iraq and Yugoslavia. The group reportedly has a few members and not much is known about any of the leaders or masterminds behind the attacks carried out.

According to news reports, the group engages in bombings and arson attacks. Almost all of their known attacks use advanced weapons such as time bombs. Since its inception in 1995, the group has targeted buildings owned by the Greek government and U.S.-owned offices, businesses, and banks. Experts state that the main objective of the group is to cause structural damage to buildings and property and not kill people. Apart from the attack on the Intercontinental Hotel in 1999, where one woman was killed, no other reported attacks by the Revolutionary Nuclei have caused death or major injuries.

One of the strategies group members have reportedly employed for every attack is to call the news media and warn them about an impending attack. Every attack has been preceded by a call by someone claiming to be a representative of the Revolutionary Nuclei, informing the media about the place of attack. In some cases, according to news reports, the Greek police have been able to successfully evacuate the building or office before the bomb explodes. Similarly, the group is also thought to have sent letters to the press after every attack. The letter usually states the purpose of the attack. Anti-terrorism experts and monitor groups assert that these make the point that the main purpose of the Revolutionary Nuclei's terrorist activities is to cause structural damage to government- and U.S.-owned buildings rather than kill people. As has been reported, all bombings by the group have occurred either late at night or early in the morning. There have no reported incidents of bombings during the day.

The group's tactics involves calling or sending letters to the press after an attack, stating the purpose of the attack. For instance, shortly after the attack on the Athenaeum Intercontinental Hotel in Athens, members of the press received a letter allegedly from the Revolutionary Nuclei. The hotel was host to the Third Economist Roundtable with the government of Greece Conference. This was an annual conference and, the day of the attack, Leon Brittan, the Vice President of the European Commission, was scheduled to hold a conference. The letter stated that the objective of the bombing was to protest against the NATO air strikes against Yugoslavia. Reportedly, the air strikes faced considerable criticism in Greece. A number of anti-war rallies were also held at the time.

Similarly, a person claiming to be a member of the group called up the press after the attack on an American Express office in 1998. Apparently, the attack was in response to "the criminal NATO coalition that bombed Iraq." A call made to a radio station after the bombing of a building that accommodated the Supreme Council of Personnel Selection (a Greek government organization that is responsible for education and employment related policies) claimed that the bombing was due to the "unfair" practices employed by the government while hiring teachers. All other attacks were reportedly carried out in the same manner, with each bombing preceded and followed by phone calls/letters to the media.

The last reported attack by the Revolutionary Nuclei was in late 2000. Greek officials claimed afterwards that they had been successful in eliminating the group. However, since 2003, there have been contradictory reports in the media about the existence of the group. Anti-terrorism experts and monitor groups claim that the group, although it has not claimed responsibility for any attack after 2000, is still active. According to news reports, the 2004 Summer Olympics held in Athens had unprecedented security due to alleged threats received from various terrorist organizations operating in Greece, including the Revolutionary Nuclei. Additionally, in 2003, a bomb explosion in an insurance company was also thought by police authorities to be the work of RN members. These attacks and threats are thought to be acts of resistance against the U.S-led wars in Afghanistan and Iraq.

The Revolutionary Nuclei, throughout its period of existence, has been associated with other terrorist organizations operating in Greece. Some of these include 17 November, May 1, and Popular Revolutionary Action. However, none of the alliances have been confirmed by the group itself or by government and police authorities. The news media have suggested that various terrorist activities are being jointly organized by members of the RN and other groups. Some reports also claim that the organization has links with known international terrorist, Carlos the Jackal. These are unconfirmed.

Monitor groups, anti-terrorism experts, and Greek and U.S. government officials are also not clear about the funding sources of the Revolutionary Nuclei. According to news reports, police investigations have not revealed funding from any sources, as is the case for many terrorist organizations around the world. The group is thought to be self-sustaining, with some donations from locals.

OTHER PERSPECTIVES

U.S. government officials as well as Greek government officials have repeatedly condemned various acts of terror organized by the Revolutionary Nuclei. Reacting to the bombing in the Intercontinental Hotel in Athens in 1999, Greek officials called it a "murderous act of terrorism."

The Prime Minister of Greece at the time, Costas Simitis, strongly condemned the actions of the Revolutionary Nuclei and the attack on the hotel. He stated "that the government would do its duty," and called on the Greek people "to resist and condemn such phenomena which were counter to the country's interests." He added, "those who use such methods maintain that they supposedly condemn violence, but they use blind violence or kill innocent citizens, and the bottom line is that they use violence as a means of destabilising the country's political life and democratic form of government."

The bombing was allegedly carried out as a protest against the NATO bombings in Yugoslavia. Reacting to this, the Prime Minister said "such actions harm the Greek people, the country's interests, the economy and tourism, aspiring to more tension and a climate of blind hate. Such practices, however, do not stop the bombings against Yugoslavia."

Greece's opposition leaders, as well as other world leaders, have also condemned terrorist acts by the group. Leaders of the main opposition party in Greece, in a public statement after the attack on the hotel in Athens, said "We express our abhorrence over yesterday's blind terrorist hit, which had human victims. We reiterate our complete support for every action of the police authorities in effectively tackling terrorism. It is necessary, with the common effort of all of us, to permanently neutralise the criminal action of terrorists, which harm the country's interests."

According to other officials, members of the RN intended to "impose their views through barbaric methods."

The U.S. government has also reportedly denounced activities of the Revolutionary Nuclei and has designated it as a terrorist organization. They have, however, also been critical of the way the Greek government has handled such activities. In 2001, the U.S. government stated that the government of Greece "has not yet arrested or convicted those terrorists responsible for attacks conducted by revolutionary Organization 17 November (17N) or Revolutionary Nuclei over the past two decades."

In 2001, the United Kingdom also added the Revolutionary Nuclei to its list of terrorist organizations with a purpose of freezing its funds and assets. Soon after designating the RN (and others) as terrorist organizations, United Kingdom Chancellor Gordon Brown commented, "Those named have committed or pose a real risk of committing or funding acts of terrorism." He added, "Those who finance terrorism are as guilty as those who commit it . . . we will do whatever is necessary to deprive terrorists of the funds they rely on. Just as there is no safe haven for terrorists there is no safe hiding place for their funds."

SUMMARY

The Revolutionary Nuclei has reportedly had a short period of existence. It is thought to have formed in 1995, as an offshoot of the ELA, another Greek terrorist organization with the same philosophies and ideologies. Throughout the late 1990s, the group claimed responsibility for several low-intensity bombings as well as arson attacks, mainly on Greek government-owned structures as well as offices of American businesses.

Most attacks caused structural damage to buildings, but there were no human casualties. Greek government officials and anti-terrorism analysts are of the opinion that the group has been effectively taken apart after 2000. However, as news agencies have reported in 2003 and 2004, the group may still be alive and poses a threat to the security in Greece.

SOURCES

Web sites

BBC News. "World: Europe: Bomb Rips through Greek Hotel." < http://news.bbc.co.uk/1/hi/world/europe/330024.stm > (accessed October 4, 2005).

The Athens News Agency. "Athens News Agency: News in English (PM), 99-04-28." < http://www.hri.org/news/greek/apeen/1999/99-04-28_1.apeen.html > (accessed October 4, 2005).

CDI Terrorism Project. "In the Spotlight: The Revolutionary Nuclei (RN)." < http://www.cdi.org/terrorism/rn-pr.cfm > (accessed October 4, 2005).

BBC News. "UK Expands Terror Funds List." < http://news.bbc.co.uk/1/hi/business/1635382.stm > (accessed October 4, 2005).

MIPT Terrorism Knowledge Base. "Group Profile: Revolutionary Nuclei." < http://www.tkb.org/Group.jsp?groupID = 100 > (accessed October 4, 2005).

SEE ALSO

17 November Organization

Revolutionary United Front (RUF)

OVERVIEW

The Revolutionary United Front (RUF) was organized in 1991 by Foday Sankoh and two partners, Abu Kanu and Rashid Mansaray, along with financial assistance from future Liberian leader Charles Taylor. Its goal was to overthrow the dictatorial government of Sierra Leone, headed by President Joseph Saidu Momoh.

Although initially promising to solve the country's problems and bring a just leadership to Sierra Leone, Sankoh, instead, was extremely cruel to his enemies and to the innocent citizens of the country. Sankoh also took control of the lucrative diamond-producing regions of Sierra Leone for his own personal use and to fund RUF activities. After a ten-year fight that killed thousands of people, Sankoh's band of rebel fighters was defeated in 2001. The RUF was disbanded but not totally dissolved, and Sankoh imprisoned. In 2005, with Sankoh deceased, the RUF remains in existence but in a diminished state.

HISTORY

The origins of the RUF began in Libya between the years 1987 and 1988 when a group of Sierra Leoneans received guerilla training under the

LEADER: Foday Sankoh

YEAR ESTABLISHED OR BECAME ACTIVE: March 1991

ESTIMATED SIZE: Probably less than a few hundred

USUAL AREA OF OPERATION: Sierra Leone, Liberia, and Guinea

Foday Sankoh, a rebel leader for the Revolutionary United Front, visits soldiers at a camp in Port Loko, Sierra Leone in December 1999. Photograph by Tuen Voeten. Reproduced by permission.

regime of Muammar el-Qaddafi, the Libyan revolutionary leader. At one of Gadhafi's rebel training camps, Sankoh met Charles Taylor, then leader of the National Patriotic Front for Liberia, and future president of Liberia and future ally of Sankoh. Returning to Sierra Leone in March 1991, Sankoh, with the help of two allies, Abu Kanu and Rashid Mansaray, established the RUF.

When first organized, RUF was popular with Sierra Leone citizens because Sankoh promised many improvements such as free health care and public education and a share of the diamond revenues if he overthrew the government. The Momoh-led government was widely perceived by its citizens as being corrupt and having caused widespread unemployment, crime and violence, drug profiteering and abuse, and other societal ills.

The first attacks by RUF guerrillas were inflicted in 1991 upon the villages that bordered the countries of Sierra Leone, Liberia, and Guinea. At this time, according to a report from the United Nations (UN) that was noted in the article, "Revolutionary United Front (RUF)," in the Federation of American Scientists (FAS), the RUF was provided support and guidance from Liberian President Charles Taylor, along with weapons and other needed military materials from Burkina Faso, Gambia, and Libya. Specific examples of such assistance were contained in documents in numerous British Broadcasting Corporation (BBC) investigations that reported, for instance, large supplies of small arms and ammunition being delivered to the RUF from Liberia in June 2000.

In 1992, Sankoh gained control of many of Sierre Leone's diamond fields. However, counter to what he promised, Sankoh used the funds, not for the citizens, but to buy military supplies for Taylor and himself. Sankoh eventually used all of the country's financial resources to maintain control over the diamond fields and other RUF activities. These actions over the next four years destroyed the country's economy and lead to starvation for many of its people.

In March 1996, Sierra Leone held its first multi-party election in over twenty years. Alhaji Ahmad Tejan Kabbah, the leader of the Sierra Leone Peoples Party, was elected president. His first political goal was to end the devastating rebel war with RUF. A private South African security company, Executive Outcomes (EO), was hired by Kabbah to counter the rebels. The experienced EO troops succeeded in removing the RUF out of the capital of Freetown. The retreat forced Sankoh with a weakened RUF to sign a peace treaty with President Kabbah later that year. However, the peace negotiations unexpectedly gave Sankoh more legitimacy with his cause. Thus, seeing his military strength increase, Sankoh resumed his attacks and broke off the peace talks.

In 1997, according to the May 2000 BBC article, "Brutal Child Army Grows Up," the RUF and the Armed Forces Revolutionary Council (AFRC), a group of junior army soldiers, joined forces in a bolder attempt to overthrow the government of President Kabbah. By May 1997, the excessive amount of fighting by this coalition forced Kabbah into exile in Guinea. During this time, the war in Sierra Leone—as explained in the biography of President Kabbah contained within the Sierra

The body of a Revolutionary United Front (RUF) soldier lies in the back of a truck on June 11, 1997. The soldier was killed in a clash with Nigerian peacekeeping soldiers north of Freetown, Sierra Leone. AP/Wide World Photos.

Leone Web site—was commonly considered as one the world's most devastating civil conflicts.

By this time, Sankoh and his rebel troops were well known for their brutality and cruelty—using children as soldiers and prostitutes; raping women; amputating limbs to assure farmers could not grow crops for government troops; killing thousands of innocent civilians, including children; (supposedly) practicing cannibalism; and other such atrocities.

In February 1998, just nine months after Kabbah was forced out, the RUF again attacked Freetown, but this time was overtaken by troops of the ECOMOG (Monitoring Group for Economic Community of West African States). The ECOMOG leaders reinstated the presidency of Kabbah, who signed another peace agreement with Sankoh in July 1999.

However, Sankoh broke the Lome Peace Agreement, as it was called, as RUF forces pushed their Operation No Living Thing

campaign into all of Sierra Leone where they killed thousands. As a result of the brutal campaign, the government controlled only the capital city and small areas scattered about the country. Various RUF factions held most of the rural areas, along with the country's diamond mines. The siege forced the United Nations to bring in a peacekeeping force, which according to the May 2000 BBC article, "Can the UN Force Restore Peace?," was eventually composed of 11,000 soldiers from the Middle East, South Asia, and the sub-Saharan Africa. Sankoh repeatedly broke the agreement and continued his violence during the next two years. For example, later in 2000, the RUF captured hundreds of members of the UN peacekeeping force stationed in Sierra Leone. President Kabbah eventually negotiated the release of the captives with the help of RUF-allied, Liberian president Charles Taylor.

Sankoh was arrested in 2000 by British and Guinean forces outside his Freetown home. He

LEADERSHIP

FODAY SANKOH

Foday Sankoh was the leader of the rebel forces that attempted to overthrow the Sierra Leone government in the decade-long civil war that began in 1991. Formerly a corporal in the Sierra Leonean army, wedding photographer, and television cameraman, Sankoh began his rebellious ways in the 1970s while a student activist demonstrating against the government's suppression of its citizens. After a prison term for participating in student demonstrations, Sankoh joined a Libyan guerilla camp sponsored by Muammar el-Qaddafi. Returning to Sierra Leone, Sankoh formed the RUF and began his rebellion that ultimately failed. However, for ten years, Sankoh and his troops brutally killed and tortured his enemies, both civilian and military. He died in 2003 of complications from a stroke while waiting for a UN-based war crimes trial for his alleged human rights abuses.

was turned over to British forces, which arranged a UN war crime tribunal to try him on numerous war crimes, including crimes against humanity, extermination, rape, and sexual slavery. After its leader was jailed, the RUF was weakened. Its last known attack, according to the National Memorial Institute for the Prevention of Terrorism (MIPT), was on September 5, 2000. The RUF was further weakened when a program of disarmament, demobilization, and reintegration was begun in mid 2001 by the Sierra Leone government.

On January 18, 2002, the rebel forces were officially disarmed and demobilized under the authority of the United Nations Mission in Sierra Leone (UNAMSIL), which resulted in the official end of the civil war. At this time, the war was estimated to have killed between roughly 50,000 and 200,000 people.

In May 2002, the RUF—under the name Revolutionary United Front Party (RUFP)—entered the May 2002 presidential elections, but performed poorly in the results. At that same time, the Sierra Leone Special Court, which was sponsored by the UN, continued its investigation of the RUF and Sankoh for war crimes. Both of these events further weakened the position of the group. In July 2003, Sankoh died from complications of a stroke while waiting for his war crimes trial to begin.

The group's membership ranks were reduced to several hundred members by the end of 2003. In 2005, with the RUF essentially disbanded, it is unknown exactly how many former members still exist.

PHILOSOPHY AND TACTICS

The RUF was formed by Sankoh primarily out of anger and frustration with the dictatorial government of Sierra Leone, which had caused years of widespread problems among its citizens due to corrupt leadership. The RUF philosophy, according to the manifesto written by Sankoh as noted in the MIPT article, "Revolutionary United Front (RUF)," was "committed to peace," but not committed to becoming "victims of peace."

According to the ideals spoken by Sankoh (initially in 1995) within "Footpaths of Democracy," as found on Peter C. Andersen's Web site, the RUF's goal was to solve problems such as poverty that had troubled the Sierra Leone citizens due to the degraded condition of the government. Because Sankoh personally felt that poverty does not honor the Supreme Being, he was strongly convinced that the people of Sierra Leone had the right to organize themselves against a tyrannical government in order to regain their dignity and human rights.

On the other hand, many media articles reported that the RUF possessed no idealized principles—only a goal to overthrow the current government of Sierra Leone in order to control the profitable diamond-producing regions of the country.

The RUF appeared to be a loosely organized group of soldiers but, in reality, possessed strict discipline and a tight loyalty to its leaders. The RUF maintained that loyalty, according to the BBC, with drugs such as cocaine, which were

KEY EVENTS

1988: Sankoh meets Charles Taylor who eventually becomes Sankoh's major ally.

1991: Sankoh returns to Sierra Leone and, with the help of Abu Kanu and Rashid Mansaray, forms the RUF.

1991: First attacks by RUF guerrillas are made on villages bordering Liberi, Sierra Leone, and Guinea.

1992: Sankoh achieves a major victory by gaining control of parts of the diamond-producing areas.

1996: Alhaji Ahmad Tejan Kabbah is elected president of Sierra Leone.

1996: Executive Outcomes is hired to counter the rebels. Its troops expel RUF from the capital, which forces Sankoh, later that year, to sign a peace treaty.

1997: RUF and the Armed Forces Revolutionary Council join together in an attempt to control all the country.

1997: President Kabbah is forced into exile.

1998: RUF attacks Freetown, but is overtaken by a coalition of western African troops.

1999: The coalition reinstates President Kabbah, who signs another peace agreement with Sankoh.

1999: Sankoh breaks the peace treaty and RUF forces bombard the country with its Operation No Living Thing campaign. The action forces UN peacekeepers to enter the country.

2000: Sankoh is arrested outside his Freetown home.

2000: The last known RUF attack is recorded.

2001: A disarmament, demobilization, and reintegration program further weakens the RUF.

2002: Rebel forces are officially disarmed and demobilized, resulting in the end of the civil war.

2003: Sankoh dies from a stroke while waiting for his war crimes trial.

---

rampant inside the rebel force as ways to attract new recruits and to control existing members.

The tactics of the RUF were largely very effective against enemy forces due to the flexibility of its structure, along with the brutality it constantly used with civilian and military opponents as a way to maintain control of its strongholds. The RUF used criminal, guerrilla, and terrorist tactics such as intimidation, murder, mutilation, rape, and torture to fight the Sierra Leonean army, control the country's civilians, and keep UN peacekeeping units from gaining control.

The organization funded its operations through three major means, including the mining and sale of diamonds obtained within the areas it controlled in Sierra Leone, the financial assistance of President Charles Taylor of Liberia, and the military weapons and materials received from the countries of Libya, Gambia, and Burkina Faso. At the height of its power, the government of Sierra Leone estimated the RUF to possibly possess three to four thousand soldiers (but only five or six hundred hardened rebel fighters), along with a similar number of supporters and sympathizers.

OTHER PERSPECTIVES

On May 3, 2000, Peter Takirambudde, the executive director of the African division of Human Rights Watch wrote a letter to Sankoh. Although he applauded Sankoh in his cooperation with UNICEF (United Nation's Children Fund) and ECOMOG in order to stop using children as soldiers in his civil war with Sierra Leone, Takirambudde was still very concerned that thousands of children remained under his control. Takirambudde suggested in his letter that Sankoh release the abducted children and stop using children in the future.

Members of the U.S. Senate, on May 25, 2000, under the leadership of Senators Jesse Helms, Joe Bidden, Bill Frist, and Russ Feingold, submitted a resolution concerning the crimes and abuses of the RUF upon the citizens of Sierra Leone. Along with a multitude of stated grievances, the resolution declared that the government of the United States would make every effort to assure that the RUF and its leaders be held legally responsible for the human rights abuses committed against the people of Sierra Leone.

According to the United Nations General Assembly, on December 1, 2000, the international group adopted—unanimously—a resolution to levy sanctions against the RUF due to its continued use of "conflict" diamonds in funding its revolution in Sierra Leone. The UN found that the use of conflict diamonds (that is, diamonds originally controlled by a recognized government but subsequently taken over by a military force in opposition to that government) helps to prolong wars and reduce the likelihood of peace in parts of Africa.

According to the May 17, 2000 article in *The Guardian Unlimited* called "Who is Foday Sankoh?" Sankoh regularly responded to criticisms against himself or the RUF by either denying the accusation or, when possible, by putting to death the critics. For example, even though Kanu and Mansaray helped Sankoh form the RUF, when they tried to minimize the atrocities happening within the RUF, Sankoh executed both men.

SUMMARY

The initial reason for the founding of RUF was to overthrow a cruel dictatorial government. Along the way, Sankoh used tactics of murder and other brutal violence against innocent people in his unsuccessful coup for the government of Sierra Leone.

The RUF, now called the Revolutionary United Front Party (RUFP) is, as of 2005, a small political party that participates in electing members of its organization and influencing the Sierra Leone government. In the May 14, 2002, election in Sierra Leone, the RUFP won only 2.2% of the popular vote count, garnered no seats within the government body, and won only 1.7% of the popular vote by its presidential candidate.

Although the RUF is considered a weak organization by leaders of the Sierra Leone government, many of its former fighters are either in exile within other countries or have yet to be merged into Sierra Leone society. As a result, these still-capable fighters are seen as a viable threat to the government of Sierra Leone.

President Kabbah, reelected in 2002 for a five-year term as president of Sierra Leone, is attempting to turn around the country's future after its ten-year conflict with the RUF. He has been successful at bringing in foreign financial and technical assistance to the country. However, past problems with poverty, rebellions such as the one with the RUF, rivalry among tribes, and corrupt government leaders make this time of reconstruction slow and tedious.

SOURCES

Books

Ibrahim Abdullah, editor. *Between Democracy and Terror: The Sierra Leone Civil War*. Dakar, Senegal: Council for the Development of Social Science Research in Africa, 2004.

Web sites

BBC News, British Broadcasting Corporation. "Can UN Force Restore Peace?" < http://news.bbc.co.uk/1/hi/world/africa/742196.stm > (accessed October 3, 2005).

Federation of American Scientists. "Revolutionary United Front (RUF)." < http://www.fas.org/main/home.jsp > (assessed October 3, 2005).

GlobalSecurity.org. "Revolutionary United Front (RUF)." < http://www.globalsecurity.org/military/world/para/ruf.htm > (accessed October 3, 2005).

Government of Sierra Leone. "Bio Data of The President of Sierra Leone." < http://www.statehouse-sl.org/biodata.html > (accessed October 3, 2005).

Guardian Unlimited. "Who is Foday Sankoh?" < http://www.guardian.co.uk/sierra/article/0,2763,221853,00.html > (accessed October 3, 2005).

Jonathan Marcus, *BBC News, British Broadcasting Corporation.* "Brutal Child Army Grows Up." < http://

news.bbc.co.uk/1/hi/world/africa/743684.stm >
(accessed October 3, 2005).

MIPT Terrorism Knowledge Base, National Memo-rial Institute for the Prevention of Terrorism. "Revolutionary United Front (RUF)." < http://www.tkb.org/Group.jsp?groupID = 4247 > (accessed October 3, 2005).

Peter C. Andersen's Sierra-Leone.org. "Footpaths to Democracy: Toward a New Sierra Leone." < http://www.sierra-leone.org/footpaths.html > (accessed October 3, 2005).

United Nations. "Conflict Diamonds: Sanctions and War." < http://www.un.org/peace/africa/Diamond. html > (accessed October 3, 2005).

Salafist Group for Call and Combat

LEADERS: Abu Mossaab Abdelouadoud; Mokhtar Belmokhtar

USUAL AREA OF OPERATION: Algeria

OVERVIEW

In 1996, militants from the Algerian Armed Islamic Group (GIA) created a splinter faction called *Groupe Salafiste pour la Predication et le Combat* (GSPC), or the Salafist Group for Call and Combat (also called the Salafist Group for Preaching and Combat). The GSPC promised Algerians that it would deviate from the GIA practice of targeting civilians. Based on this promise, the group developed support throughout Algeria and has become the largest and most significant anti-government movement in that country.

The group is a salafist organization that operates throughout northern Africa, specifically Algeria. Salafist comes from the term *salafi*, which refers to fundamentalists. Salafists adhere to a strict and "pure" interpretation of the Koran. The GSPC objective is the removal of the present government in Algeria to be replaced with an Islamic state that adheres to a strict interpretation of Islam. Although committed to its principal goal of an Algerian Islamic state, the GSPC has publicly pledged its support for groups such as al-Qaeda, and its members have been participants in plots on European targets.

Amari Saichi, the Salafist Group for Call and Combat's second-in-command, who was reported to have kidnapped 32 European tourists in the Sahara desert in February and March 2003.

AP/Wide World Photos. Reproduced by permission.

HISTORY

After centuries under French rule, Algeria sought independence from the colonial power, resulting in an eight-year conflict. The independence movement in Algeria was led by *maquisards* (guerillas) from the Front de Liberation Nationale (FLN) or National Liberation Front. On July 3, 1963, France declared Algeria independent. By September 1963, a constitution had been passed and the presidential election placed Ahmed Ben Bella into power. By 1965, a bloodless coup was led by the minister of defense, Colonel Houari Boumediene, who was elected president in 1976. The FLN then nominated and backed the election of Colonel Chadli Bendjedid in 1979. Bendjedid remained in power through the 1984 and 1988 elections due to the support of the FLN. In 1989, a new constitution allowed for the formation of political parties other than the FLN. As a result, the

Front Islamique du Salut (FIS), or Islamic Salvation Front, was established. In 1991, the FIS won the first round of elections, prompting the army to nullify the election and cancel the next round scheduled for 1992.

With economic uncertainty prevailing in the country and the political unrest caused by the election, violence broke out throughout the country, led by Islamists. President Bendjedid declared a state of emergency and created the High Council of State (HCS) to lead the country in the interim. The HCS moved quickly to dissolve and make the FIS an illegal organization. In the midst of violence sweeping the country, the leader of the HCS, Lamine Zeroual, called for elections to occur in 1995. The FLN-backed candidate, Zeroual, won 75% of the vote due in large part to FIS not being able to participate. During this time, the Armed Islamic Group (GIA) began its campaign of assassinations, bombings, and massacres, which included targeting civilians thought to be supporters of the government. In 1999, on the eve of the election, six out of the seven candidates withdrew from the race under suspicion of fraud. As a result, Abdelaziz Bouteflika won the election with the support of the military. Bouteflika moved quickly to curb the violence and proposed a referendum to grant amnesty to those who took up arms against the government, except in the case of rape and murder. The referendum, called a Civil Accord, was approved in 2000 and many of the militant groups in Algeria accepted the amnesty and relinquished their weapons.

One of the few groups that did not accept amnesty was the GSPC. Between 1996 and 1997, Algerian Salafist groups, such as the GIA, had perpetrated an estimated 150,000 deaths, including civilian women and children thought to support the government and oppose their *jihad* (holy war). This resulted in significant fragmentation among the groups. In 1998, one of the GIA members, Hassan Hattab (or Abu Hamza), left the group to form the GSPC, taking many defectors with him. Hattab vowed to put an end to the policy of attacking civilians. In 2000, as an estimated 5,000 militants surrendered their weapons under the Civil Accord, the GSPC refused to do so and gained support among the Salafists. As a result, the GSPC surpassed its parent organization in membership.

The GSPC operates a campaign of bombings, attacks on military, police, and government

LEADERSHIP

ABU MOSSAAB ABDELOUADOUD

Abu Mossaab Abdelouadoud was appointed the leader of the GSPC in 2004. Abdelouadoud assumed command of the group several months after the previous leader Nabil Sahraoui was killed by the Algerian army. Abdelouadoud's real name is Abdelmalek Dourkdal.

MOKHTAR BELMOKHTAR

Mokhtar Belmokhtar was born in Gardhaïa, which is on the edges of the Sahara desert. He joined the military and fought against the Soviet Union in Afghanistan. After Belmokhtar left the army, he developed a smuggling operation in the southern region of Algeria. He is believed to be leading the faction of the GSPC that kidnapped thirty-two European tourists in 2003.

---

convoys, and false roadblocks. In March 2000, the GSPC took responsibility for a bombing at an oil pipeline in Der Chouyoukh. The bomb and subsequent fire damaged the pipeline and many trucks. The GSPC attacked a military convoy in July 2002, killing six soldiers. Also in 2002, members of the GSPC looted and burned a professional training center in rural Algeria. The group also engaged in bombing attacks on police patrols in August and October 2002, resulting in the death of one police officer. The GSPC also targeted civilians in October 2002, by raiding rural neighborhoods and extorting money from the residents. In May 2003, a total of 32 European tourists were taken hostage in six separate incidents. The tourists were held in two groups of 17, with the intention of obtaining ransom for their release. One of the groups was discovered and after a firefight with the Algerian Army, the tourists were released. The other group, however, remained in captivity until August, when the German government reportedly paid a $6 million ransom. In March 2004, the GSPC successfully assassinated Abdennacer

Abou Hafs—an imam from el-Harrah considered to be in collusion with the Algerian government. In June 2004, a truck bomb was used to target a utilities facility in the city of Algiers, resulting in injuries to eleven people. In June 2005, the GSPC assassinated the head of Djelfa Judicial Police Mobile Brigade by using a homemade bomb. Also in June 2005, a road block was set up between Tizi Ouzou and Boghi. For two hours, twenty armed militants harassed and looted vehicles. Three soldiers were killed and one civilian was shot in the incident.

The GSPC also engages in alliances with other Islamic fundamentalist groups, such as al-Qaeda. The group's ties to al-Qaeda are decades-old and rooted in its parent organization, GIA. Many of the GIA members and participants fought in the Afghan-Soviet war and had ties to Osama bin Laden. However, as GIA employed mass killings—which included moderate Muslims—al-Qaeda remained a distant source for support. As the GSPC rejected these tactics, the group gained the financial and logistical support of al-Qaeda. As a result, the GSPC operates as a recruiting center for the organization.

In 2004, the leader of GSPC, Nabil Sahraoui, was killed by the Algerian army. The group entered a period of disarray due to a lack of leadership until Abu Mossaab Abdelouadoud assumed the leadership. However, the group appears to have divided into two factions. Abdelouadoud operates the GSPC out of the northern region of Algeria, while a former GSPC member, Mokhtar Belmokhtar, is leader of the splinter group called the Free Salafist Group out of the southern region of the country.

PHILOSOPHY AND TACTICS

The GSPC identifies itself as a salafist organization, referring to the salafist sect of Islam. As salafists, the group seeks to overthrow the current government in Algeria and replace it with an Islamic state that adheres to a strict interpretation of Islam. In order to accomplish this, the group employs tactics ranging from assassinations to alliances with other Islamic fundamentalists. The GSPC targets the Algerian government and security forces, particularly in rural regions. Although the group promised to end targeting civilian, approximately 900 people

KEY EVENTS

1989: Change in the Algerian constitution allows for the formation of political parties other than the FLN.

1991: Islamic Salvation Front (FIS) wins first round of elections, which prompts the military to nullify the election results and cancel subsequent elections.

1992: Bendjedid declares a state of emergency as violent protests erupt throughout the country. The High Council of State (HCS) is created to lead the government.

1994: The Armed Islamic Group (GIA) becomes the most active group participating in assassinations, bombings, and massacres of civilians thought to support the FLN government.

1995: Leader of the HCS, Lamine Zeroual, calls for elections and wins 75% of the vote. The FIS is not permitted to participate in the election.

1998: GSPC, under the leadership of Hassan Hattab, splits from the GIA and promises to end the practice of targeting civilians.

1999: Bouteflika, the FLN and military backed candidate, is elected president and proposes a Civil Accord to offer amnesty to Islamic militants willing to disarm.

2000: Referendum called Civil Accord is passed, and many militants turn in their weapons and disarm. The GSPC rejects amnesty.

2000: The GSPC bombs a pipeline in Der Chouyoukh, causing damage to the trucks and pipeline.

2001: GSPC leader, Hattab, issues a statement in support of Osama bin Laden and al-Qaeda after the September 11 attacks on the United States.

2002: GSPC kills six soldiers during an attack on a military convoy.

2002: GSPC militants target civilians in rural neighborhoods and set fire to a professional training center.

2003: Thirty-two European hostages are taken by the GSPC. After some are released, the remaining hostages are held until the German government pays a $6 million ransom.

2004: Abdennacer Abou Hafs, an imam, is assassinated by GSPC members.

2004: GSPC leader, Nabil Sahraoui, is killed by the Algerian army. Abu Mossaab Abdelouadoud is appointed the new leader.

2005: The GSPC assassinated the head of the Djelfa Judicial Police Mobile Brigade.

---

have been killed in raids conducted by the GSPC. The group generates funds by operating false roadblocks and participating in petty crimes, credit card fraud, document fabrication, and the smuggling of cigarettes, drugs, vehicles, and arms. The U.S. State Department asserts that the group is also funded by Algerians living abroad, and by Iran and Sudan. In addition, the GSPC has emerged as a recruiting site for al-Qaeda. After the group offered its support to Osama bin Laden after the September 11 attacks, the GSPC pledged to attack U.S. and European targets. As a result, the group has been linked to several foiled plots against Western targets.

OTHER PERSPECTIVES

The GSPC went largely unnoticed by outside sources until after the September 11 attacks on the United States. After the group pledged its support to Osama bin Laden and al-Qaeda, the group slowly came under scrutiny. In September 2001, U.S. President George W. Bush issued Executive Order 13224, which froze the assets of organizations believed to operate terrorist activities, against the GSPC assets. The next year, the U.S. State Department designated the GSPC as a terrorist organization and determined that "civilians have been attacked" in activities undertaken by the GSPC. In that

PRIMARY SOURCE

Salafist Group for Call and Combat (GSPC) a.k.a. Salafist Group for Preaching and Combat

DESCRIPTION

The Salafist Group for Call and Combat (GSPC), a splinter group of the Armed Islamic Group (GIA), seeks to overthrow the Algerian Government with the goal of installing an Islamic regime. GSPC eclipsed the GIA in approximately 1998, and is currently the most effective and largest armed group inside Algeria. In contrast to the GIA, the GSPC pledged to avoid civilian attacks inside Algeria.

ACTIVITIES

The GSPC continues to conduct operations aimed at Algerian Government and military targets, primarily in rural areas, although civilians are sometimes killed. The Government of Algeria scored major counterterrorism successes against GSPC in 2004, significantly weakening the organization, which also has been plagued with internal divisions. Algerian military forces killed GSPC leader Nabil Sahraoui and one of his top lieutenants, Abbi Abdelaziz, in June 2004 in the mountainous area east of Algiers. In October, the Algerian Government took custody of Abderazak al-Para, who led a GSPC faction that held 32 European tourists hostage in 2003. According to press reporting, some GSPC members in Europe and the Middle East maintain contact with other North African extremists sympathetic to al-Qa'ida. In late 2003, the GSPC leader issued a communiqué announcing the group's support of a number of jihadist causes and movements, including al-Qa'ida.

STRENGTH

Several hundred fighters with an unknown number of facilitators outside Algeria.

LOCATION/AREA OF OPERATION

Algeria, the Sahel (i.e. northern Mali, northern Mauritania, and northern Niger), Canada, and Western Europe.

EXTERNAL AID

Algerian expatriates and GSPC members abroad, many residing in Western Europe, provide financial and logistical support. GSPC members also engage in criminal activity.

Source: U.S. Department of State. *Country Reports on Terrorism.* Washington, D.C., 2004.

---

report, the State Department identified the group as one of the "most effective remaining armed groups" and "the largest, most active terrorist organization in Algeria." In addition, the State Department stressed that one of the concerns surrounding the GSPC is its alliance with al-Qaeda. The report states that the group has fostered and developed continued alliances first established by the GIA.

SUMMARY

In the Algerian war for independence, the guerilla organization, the FLN, led the struggle against France. Once independence was granted, the FLN then became the leading, and only, political organization in the country. The GSPC seeks to follow the same path on its quest to create an Islamic state in Algeria. The group was formed by Hassan Hattab in 1998 after many members of the GIA became disillusioned by the civilian massacres taking place during the struggle. Although the GSPC promised to end the policy of targeting civilians, this has not happened—although the civilian deaths attributed to the GSPC are much smaller than those attributed to the GIA. The group rose to prominence after declining the government-offered amnesty in 2000 and surpassed its parent organization, GIA, in membership and support. Many of the defectors from the GIA fought in Afghanistan against the Soviet Union and, as a result, the group developed close ties to Osama bin Laden and al-Qaeda. The membership of the GSPC is estimated around 800, although that number does not take into account the rumor that the group has split. Members of the GSPC residing in the southern region have developed a group called the Free Salafist Group and are believed to be led by Mokhtar Belmokhtar.

SOURCES

Periodicals

Daly, Sara. "The Algerian Salafist Group for Call and Combat: A Dossier." *The Jamestown Foundation.* March 11, 2005: vol. 3, i. 5

Schanzer, Jonathan. "Algeria's GSPC and America's War on Terror." *Washington Institute.* October 15, 2002.

Web sites

Australian Broadcasting Corporation. "The Salafist Group for Call and Combat." < http://abcasiapacific. com/cause/network/salafist.htm > (accessed October 16, 2005).

BBC News Online. "Profile: Algeria's Salafist Group." < http://news.bbc.co.uk/1/hi/world/africa/ 3027621.stm > (accessed October 16, 2005).

Center for Defence Information. "In the Spotlight: The Salafist Group for Call and Combat." < http:// www.cdi.org/terrorism/gspc-pr.cfm > (accessed October 16, 2005).

Global Security. "Algerian Insurgency." < http:// www.globalsecurity.org/military/world/war/algeria-90s.htm > (accessed October 16, 2005).

MIPT Terrorism Knowledge Base. "Salafist Group for Call and Combat." < http://www.tkb.org/ Group.jsp?groupID = 3777 > (accessed October 16, 2005).

SEE ALSO

Al-Qaeda

Scriptures for America

ALTERNATE NAME: Scriptures for America
   Worldwide

LEADER: Peter (Pete) J. Peters

YEAR ESTABLISHED OR BECAME ACTIVE: 1977

ESTIMATED SIZE: 100

USUAL AREA OF OPERATION: LaPorte, Colorado

Scriptures for America Worldwide is an organization based in the United States that allegedly claims to be devoted to preaching the gospel of Jesus Christ. The organization was earlier known to be a part of the Christian Identity Movement (an affiliation of extremist groups) that claimed that Christians, and not Jews, are the "true Israelites" and are favored by God. However, reportedly, the Scriptures of America (SFA) later denounced the association.

Peter J. (Pete) Peters, the pastor of the LaPorte Church of Christ in LaPorte, Colorado, heads the Scriptures for America ministries around the world. The organization is also referred to as SFAW.

HISTORY

Peter J. Peters, the pastor of the LaPorte Church of Christ in LaPorte, Colorado, is the self-proclaimed head of Scriptures for America Ministries Worldwide. Peters became the pastor of LaPorte Church, allegedly a Christian Identity church with nearly 100 worshippers in the state of Colorado, in October 1977. Peters' position as the pastor is thought to have provided him a platform to illustrate and expand his extremist views. LaPorte Church claims that it is

LEADERSHIP

PETER J. PETERS

Pastor Pete J. Peters, the self-proclaimed leader of the Scriptures for America, claims to own a ranch in western Nebraska. He graduated from the School of Agriculture, University of Nebraska, and holds a Bachelor's degree in Agricultural Business and Economics from Colorado State University.

It is reported that Peters had served the U.S. Department of Agriculture before he formed Scriptures for America. Additionally, Peters has a baccalaureate degree in Sacred Literature in Bible and Bible-related Studies from the Christ Bible Training School in Gering, Nebraska. His wife, Cheri, is also known to support her husband and adopt his philosophies.

an autonomous, nondenominational Christian church that was inspired by the New Covenant Scriptures (thought by many to be another extremist entity).

According to published reports, the activities of SFA first came into the picture in 1985 after the local media in Colorado reported that the members of The Order, a terrorist group of the 1980s, had attended the LaPorte Church. The media also provided information that claimed that this visit by The Order came during a period when the group was thought to be very active. It was during this time (the mid 1980s) that The Order was allegedly accused by U.S. government authorities for involvement in various terrorist activities including bombings, robberies, and forgeries. This incident was followed by reports in 1987, when two prominent members of The Order were found guilty under charges of murdering Alan Berg, a Jewish talk-show host in Denver, Colorado. Media reports further mentioned that in 1984, Berg had interviewed Peters, the alleged head of SFA, and had challenged him on his views of white supremacy. Allegedly, this did not sit well with Peters, who according to

the media played a prominent role in the murder of Alan Berg.

In 1988, the state of Colorado held a vote to determine whether gays and lesbians should be provided civil rights. The SFA, under LaPorte Church, reportedly acquired the advertising and broadcast rights for this event. However, allegedly, members of SFA propagated anti-gay ideologies in a bid to prevent homosexuals from being provided civil rights. The state government ruled that the church was not following the regulations prescribed by the campaign reform law, which imposes rules on what can and what cannot be broadcasted, and fined the institution. After repeated reminders, the church reportedly failed to pay the required fine amount and eventually in 1992, the savings account of the church was acquired by the state government. Political experts state that the government also auctioned off the assets of the church in order to settle the account. Peters was allegedly displeased with the proceedings and blamed the government for the entire debacle.

PHILOSOPHY AND TACTICS

Experts on religious extremism allege that Pete J. Peters has often misused his authority as the pastor of LaPorte Church and proclaims the belief that Jews and people of color, including African Americans, are inferior to Caucasians. Allegedly, SFAW states that people of all races, excluding Caucasians, pose a threat to human civilization. Furthermore, SFA appears to condemn homosexuality and encourage its followers to renounce homosexuals.

The organization reportedly pronounces itself to be dedicated to advocating the gospel of Jesus Christ as well as proclaiming the "true biblical identity" of the Anglo-Saxon, Germanic, and other races that have settled globally. According to proclamations made by Scriptures for America, there are twelve tribes of Israel consisting of the Anglo-Saxon, Germanic, Celtic, Scandinavian, as well as similar sects. Members of these, especially the white-skinned people who have settled in North America, form the basic and "true" population of the United States. SFA allegedly claims that they are "genuine Christians," even asserting that Jews have openly opposed the truth and

KEY EVENTS

1985: Media reports suggested that a violent extremist group, The Order, visited the SFAW Church and created a national controversy.

1987: Two members of The Order allegedly linked with Peters of SFAW were convicted of murdering a Jewish talk show host.

1992: The La Porte Church that harbored the SFAW reportedly lost its savings account and most of its assets in a government auction.

2004: SFA allegedly continued its efforts in propagating its pro-Christianity ideology through seminars, taped recordings, and radio sermons.

---

have made the Christians around the world appear evil.

To promote its propaganda, the SFA uses a number of mediums and strategies. The most prominent medium is thought to be radio and television shows. Monitor groups state that the SFA also uses audiocassettes for this purpose. According to reports, another mode of propagation is through seminars. The organization allegedly hosts frequent seminars and encourages the mingling of individuals with similar extremist ideologies. SFA also reportedly publishes newsletters and has an active web site. Other means of propagation include newsletters, brochures, taped recordings, and books.

In 1993, a few prominent members of SFA launched a controversial semiweekly radio show called "Truth for the Times." Analysts argue that, due to its controversial content matter, the show was pulled off the air in 1995. However, it was aired again later through several local radio stations.

There are reports that during a conference of white supremacists in 1992, the SFA and other similar organizations formed a coalition against

the state government. Experts are of the opinion that this coalition was involved in several acts of terror against the government and its allies.

Peters is also reported to have participated in several acts of defamation of other religions, especially Judaism.

OTHER PERSPECTIVES

In 2004, an FBI strategic assessment report about the potential for domestic terrorism in the United States focused on movements associated with Christian fundamentalism, including Scriptures for America. The report mentioned that, "One of the greatest threats posed by the right-wing in terms of millennial violence is the formation of a conglomeration of individuals that will work together to commit criminal acts." The report was targeted at many Christian extremist groups—the Scriptures for America being one of them.

The report also mentioned that, "Law enforcement officials should be particularly aware that the new millennium may increase the odds that extremists may engage in proactive violence specifically targeting law enforcement officers. Religiously motivated extremists may initiate violent conflicts with law enforcement officials in an attempt to facilitate the onset of Armageddon, or to help fulfill a prophesy. For many on the extreme right-wing, the battle of Armageddon is interpreted as a race war to be fought between Aryans and the satanic Jews and their allies."

These comments were directed at Pete Peters and his SFA, among other such organizations.

SUMMARY

The Scriptures for America Worldwide promoted its ideology mainly through radio programs and conferences during the 1980s and 1990s. Scriptures for America reportedly continues to broadcast its philosophies through digital satellite twenty-four hours a day. In addition, it is also thought to spread its message through its web site, LaPorte Church sessions, and workshops to motivate new members to join.

As of 2005, analysts claim that the SFA has been growing. It is also thought to organize activities jointly with other extremist groups.

SOURCES

Web sites

Anti-Defamation League. "Peter J. 'Pete' Peters." < http://www.adl.org/learn/ext_us/Peters/ > (accessed September 30, 2005).

Center for Studies on New Religions. "Project Megiddo." < http://www.cesnur.org/testi/FBI_004.htm > (accessed September 30, 2005).

SEE ALSO

Christian Identity Movement

Order, The

Sea Shepherd Conservation Society

LEADER: Paul Watson
YEAR ESTABLISHED OR BECAME ACTIVE: 1977
USUAL AREA OF OPERATION: Worldwide

OVERVIEW

Founded in 1977 as a more extreme alternative to Greenpeace, the Sea Shepherd Conservation Society has amassed a lengthy record of attacks on whaling and fishing vessels. The group's leader is wanted in several countries for his work, and he has frequently bragged about his organization's numerous attacks on whaling ships. The group considers itself a self-appointed enforcer of international maritime law.

HISTORY

By the mid 1970s, the environmentalist group known as Greenpeace had gained substantial attention for its efforts to stop commercial whaling, nuclear testing, and other anti-environmental practices. Typical of the group's efforts was a 1975 mission in which a Greenpeace vessel confronted Soviet whaling vessels off the coast of California, with Greenpeace members steering their inflatable speedboats between the whalers and their targets. While Greenpeace's actions often shocked the general public, some within the group believed that its tactics were actually far too tame.

Paul Watson, a charter member of the organization, was among these disgruntled members. In 1977, Watson left Greenpeace to begin his

A crew member stands next to the Ocean Warrior, which belongs to the marine conservation group, Sea Shepherd. The Ocean Warrior, seen here on July 11, 2001, will attempt to stop whale hunting and turtle poaching when it docks in the Caribbean. AP/Wide World Photos

own organization. While controversy remains over whether this departure was voluntary or not, Watson's new organization was founded with the simple purpose of prosecuting the Greenpeace battle, using more violent tactics. Watson's efforts led to the founding that same year of the Sea Shepherd Conservation Society, which describes itself as a self-appointed policing organization of the high seas.

In 1979, Watson's vessel (also named Sea Shepherd) was patrolling off the coast of Portugal when it encountered the Sierra, a commercial whaling ship that was allegedly operating in violation of international whaling guidelines. Watson's ship had been uniquely prepared for this encounter: her bow compartments were entirely filled with concrete, making the front of the Sea Shepherd a lethal weapon. Watson took aim at the Sierra and rammed it, seriously damaging the vessel.

Portuguese officials soon confiscated the Sea Shepherd and announced plans to give it to the Sierra's owners as compensation for the

ramming. In response, Watson covertly boarded the Sea Shepherd and scuttled her, though two later vessels in the Sea Shepherd "navy" would be christened with the same name. The Sierra, while surviving this initial attack, would not survive long. While docked in Lisbon harbor in 1980, the vessel was attacked. Divers attached magnetic mines to the ship's hull, and the resulting explosions sank the vessel. Sea Shepherd statements claimed credit for the attack.

Throughout the 1980s, Sea Shepherd Conservation Society was linked to numerous acts of violence. In several cases, Watson openly bragged about the attacks, claiming credit for sinking whaling and fishing vessels flying the flags of Spain, Iceland, and other nations. While not all of Watson's claimed attacks have been verified by independent sources, the government of Norway found sufficient evidence of his involvement to confront him at sea. In 1994, as a Sea Shepherd vessel followed whaling ships off the coast, the Norwegian coast guard ship

Captain Paul Watson, (right), founder of the Sea Shepherd Conservation Society, speaks with Makah Indian Elder Jeff Ides in front of the group's flagship, the Sea Shepherd, on October 20, 1997. Ides opposes a U.S. proposal at the meeting that would allow his tribe to hunt a few gray whales a year. AP/Wide World Photos

Andenes approached, intending to stop the vessel and arrest Watson.

The incident that followed remains in dispute. Watson claims his ship was in international waters and that the Andenes rammed him. Norwegian authorities, citing videotape and eyewitness accounts, claim Watson was in Norwegian coastal waters at the time and that he in fact rammed the coast guard vessel. Following the collision, Watson's vessel limped away with the Andenes in pursuit. The Andenes eventually broke off the chase, and Watson escaped.

Later that same year, Sea Shepherd claimed responsibility for the attempted sinking of another fishing and whaling vessel off the coast of Norway; though it sustained massive damage, the vessel Senet was prevented from sinking. In his press release after the sinking, Paul Watson claimed that former U.S. Navy Seals had participated in the attack. Following this incident, the

Norwegian foreign secretary summoned U.S. officials to his office to discuss the United States' responsibility in dealing with Sea Shepherd. In later public statements, a Norwegian official pointed out that not only is the group headquartered in the United States, but that it also receives "financial support" in the form of tax breaks associated with its status as a non-profit entity. He also suggested that U.S. authorities enjoy a tacit agreement to ignore the group's actions as long as U.S. interests are not targeted.

As of 2005, Sea Shepherd remains at the extremist edge of the environmental conservation movement. Paul Watson continues to lead the organization, and several celebrities are among the group's supporters. The group's current priorities include protecting sea turtles in the Galapagos Islands, intercepting so-called long-line fishing nets, and raising funds to intercept the Japanese whaling fleet near Antarctica.

LEADERSHIP

PAUL WATSON

Born in 1950 in Toronto, Paul Watson is the founder and current leader of the Sea Shepherd Conservation Society. Watson grew up in a coastal region and soon took to the sea, working in the Canadian Coast Guard and on merchant vessels. His first known environmentalist effort came in 1969, when he participated in a Sierra Club antinuclear protest. He soon joined the fledgling group Greenpeace, where he served as an officer and sailor on several missions during the 1970s.

Watson left Greenpeace in 1977, reportedly because he found Greenpeace's tactics insufficiently violent. Watson was later quoted as saying that Greenpeace lost sight of its original mission and degenerated into "a bunch of wimps." In response, Watson founded the Sea Shepherd Conservation Society, which works to end whaling, seal hunting, and other abuses of the seas. Watson is often described as flamboyant, flying a skull and crossbones above his ship and painting the names of rammed vessels on its hull. According to one account, Watson's ship often plays Wagner's "Ride of the Valkyries" to intimidate his intended victims.

In 1983, Watson was sentenced to fifteen months in prison for interfering with a seal hunt in Canada. In later years, he was repeatedly charged by nations around the world, though he has largely managed to avoid jail time, despite admissions of his involvement in numerous acts of eco-terrorism. As of 2005, Watson remains at sea.

Sea Shepherd's tactics appear more extreme and far more violent. Watson and his associates claim responsibility for numerous sinkings and attempted sinkings on their website. Watson is also well-acquainted with the more traditional tools of publicity, admitting during a Canadian Broadcasting Company interview that his group uses photos of seals simply because the animals appear so cuddly.

Sea Shepherd currently maintains two ocean-going vessels at its home port in Friday Harbor, Washington. Crewmembers on Sea Shepherd missions pay the organization $1,000 for the right to participate. Because of its past actions, Sea Shepherd was banned from attending the 2005 International Whaling Commission Meeting in Ulsan, Korea. The group announced that it would instead send undercover delegates to the meeting.

OTHER PERSPECTIVES

Though it relies on extremist tactics to achieve its goals, some members of the more-radical environmental and animal rights movement praise Sea Shepherd's mission to stop whaling. Many supporters assert that Sea Shepherd acts primarily to stop whaling that is in violation of international law or treaties. However, critics counter-argue that such actions, even if directed against illegal whaling operations, constitute vigilantism.

Sea Shepherd took their mission to stop legal seal hunting into Canadian courts on September 15, 2005. A lawsuit filed on behalf of eleven Sea Shepherd members challenged the constitutionality of laws protecting hunters from being observed and documented by environmental and animal rights organizations without government permission. The suit was filed in response to charges that the organization violated such laws in the past.

PHILOSOPHY AND TACTICS

Like many other environmental activist groups, the Sea Shepherd Conservation Society believes that commercial uses of animal resources should be severely curtailed or eliminated. In comparison to most other environmental action groups,

SUMMARY

Like its gregarious founder, the Sea Shepherd Conservation Society at times appears to crave the spotlight. While many activist groups appear reluctant to discuss their use of violence, Paul Watson openly brags about his group's exploits

KEY EVENTS

1977: Paul Watson leaves Greenpeace and launches the Sea Shepherd Conservation Society.

1979: Sea Shepherd rams whaling vessel Sierra, crippling it. When Portuguese officials seizes the Sea Shepherd, Paul Watson sneaks aboard and sinks it.

1994: Norwegian coast guard vessel and Sea Shepherd ship collide. Both sides claim the other was at fault.

1994: Norwegian authorities demand that the U.S. government take action against Sea Shepherd, which is currently headquartered in Washington state.

2005: Sea Shepherd makes plans for a winter mission to intercept Japanese whaling vessels near Antarctica.

and the destruction they cause. Sea Shepherd has been able to escape legal problems largely because its actions take place on the open seas, a region that lies largely outside the jurisdiction of any single national government. The group has become increasingly bold in pre-announcing its campaigns, raising the likelihood that its intended victims may take steps to fight back in the future.

SOURCES

Books

Morris, David B. *Earth Warrior: Overboard With Paul Watson and the Sea Shepherd Conservation Society.* Golden, Colorado: Fulcrum Publishing, 1995.

Wright, Richard T. *Environmental Science: Toward a Sustainable Future (9th edition).* NY: Prentice Hall, 2004.

Web sites

Activist Cash.com. "Norway to the USA: Stop Sea Shepherd." < http://www.activistcash.com/organization_overview.cfm/oid/347 > (accessed September 30, 2005).

The High North News. "Sea Shepherd Conservation Society." < http://www.highnorth.no/Library/Movements/Sea_Shepherd/st-se-sh.htm > (accessed September 30, 2005).

The Institute of Cetacean Research. "Sea Shepherd's Violent History." < http://www.icrwhale.org/eng/history.pdf > (accessed September 30, 2005).

SEE ALSO

Greenpeace

Sendero Luminoso (Shining Path)

OVERVIEW

Sendero Luminoso (Shining Path in Spanish; SL), an extension of the Peruvian Communist Party (PCP), was a band of insurgents that formed in the 1970s, led by philosophy professor Abimael Guzmán. SL formed in reaction to socioeconomic underdevelopment in the Peruvian highlands and promoted the idea of a "people's war" to end economic and social repression. SL's message spoke to the Amerindian of Peruvian society, as the revolutionaries spread ideas of Indian agrarian/communal rule in the hopes of returning to pre-Incan societal structures.

Advocating armed insurgency against the established Peruvian national government, Guzmán led Sendero Luminoso on a twelve-year campaign of political violence, with the express goal of gaining control and converting society to a pre-Incan cooperative agricultural structure. Through bombings, electrical and water supply disruptions, and armed conflict, Sendero presented a major obstacle for the president in sending an international message about Peru's stability and reliability as a place for foreign investment.

Between 1980 and 1993, the group's insurrection was responsible for 23,000 civilian, member, and military deaths, and more than $20 billion in state and personal property damage.

Esteban Barboza, second from the left, a 58-year-old "rondero," or member of the community patrol, joins other ronderos in displaying their rifles during a ceremony in the city of Ayacucho, 250 miles southeast of Lima, Peru, on July 25, 2003. Ronderos have been reorganizing because of Shining Path's recent activity.
AP/Wide World Photos. Reproduced by permission.

HISTORY

Peru suffered from a host of socioeconomic problems in the 1970s and 1980s. Dramatic income disparity, high infant mortality rates, runaway inflation, and chronic economic problems plagued the nation. The highland and mountain areas, where Quechua Indians reside, experienced the most crushing poverty and development problems.

Sendero Luminoso's ideology has been described by Daniel Masterson as "an amalgam of the socialist communal teachings of Jose Carlos Mariategui" (the Peruvian philosopher who founded the Peruvian Communist Party, PCP, in 1928), Marxism, and Abimael Guzmán's interpretation of these ideas. The unique ideology separated SL from blending with other international leftist organizations, and in fact SL scorned other communist movements and governments, including Cuba, China, and the USSR.

In 1964, a pro-Chinese faction within the PCP split from the party. Guzmán disagreed with Chinese communism, and by 1970 Guzmán split with the PCP and the pro-Chinese group, instead forming his own organization Sendero Luminoso, whose name comes from the "shining path" that leads to a return to pre-Incan, cooperative agriculture in Mariategui's writings.

Guzmán determined that the current government was imperialist and that the indigenous population in Peru should rise up in armed struggle against the state and place power in the hands of the peasants. Ayacucho, an area in the highlands populated mostly by Quechua Indians, became SL's center of operations. The peasants felt neglected by the national government; the government's failure to provide proper funding for basic human services, sanitation, refusal to institute land reform requests, and failure to stop the beginnings of SL violence in the countryside created support for the ideology

The bodies of two policemen killed in a Shining Path ambush lie on the side of a road in Tingo Maria, Peru on February 20, 2005. It was the first attack by the rebels against local police in several years. AP/Wide World Photos. Reproduced by permission.

behind SL. In 1991, eleven years after SL's armed struggle began and violence swept the countryside, 7% of all Peruvians and 11% of the poorest citizens still viewed the insurgency favorably.

For the first decade of SL's existence (1970–1980), Peru was ruled by a strong military government. Nationalization, land reform, and extreme changes in international relations were the cornerstones of the military's "Peruvian Experiment." However, the promised land reform did not unfold as SL had expected. The failure of this land restructuring provided an example for SL of how not to initiate and implement strategies for change. In fact, Sendero's first political action, the burning of ballot boxes and the boycotting of elections in 1980, was a careful move to make clear to society that change must be swift and intense.

From the standpoint of the national government, controlling Sendero Luminoso was

difficult at first. As of 1980, the only laws applicable to terrorist trials and political violence were "disturbing internal peace," "disruption of public order," or "conspiracy to introduce terrorism" charges. The national government worked to pass a series of laws to give them legislative and judicial clout when arresting, trying, and sentencing SL members.

In addition, the Peruvian government used local and national police, as well as military forces, to fight against the SL in the countryside and in urban areas as needed. In both 1982 and 1983, military forces were ordered into Ayacucho, Apurimac, and Huancavelica to establish control and defeat the insurgents. At the same time, police organized voluntary, locally based peasant groups. These groups, patterned after the voluntary and successful peasant patrol groups used in the northern highlands, helped to alert the police of SL activities and strongholds. Also, as migration

LEADERSHIP

ABIMAEL GUZMÁN

Abimael Guzmán, the leader of SL, began his teaching career in philosophy and the University of San Cristobal de Huamanga in Ayacocho, Peru, a center of communist activity in the rural highlands. Three key factors influenced Guzmán's politics: deteriorating social conditions in Ayacucho, reading the work of Jose Carlos Mariategui, and his wife's encouragement to become more politically active in leftist causes. Guzmán became convinced that an armed struggle was required for the overthrow of the current Peruvian government and appealed to peasants to join him in the fight.

After more than twelve years of violent activity from SL and its cells, Abimael Guzmán was captured on September 12, 1992, and sentenced to life in prison. The cult of "Chairman Gonzalo," as he was nicknamed, continues to this day, as groups in Peru and the United States work for his freedom from imprisonment.

increased from Ayacuhco to urban centers, sparked by the violence and by the search for jobs, these peasants served as unofficial "troops" in the battle against SL.

However, when the military stepped in, the tone of these groups changed dramatically. The Peruvian military began obligating peasants to join the civil defense patrols, and those who were resisted were often labeled subversive. In addition to creating these forced peasant patrols, the military formed detention centers in peasant areas, such as Ayacucho, Apurimac, Huanta, and LaMar. These actions on the part of the military alienated peasants. The same peasants who fled SL's violence were now confronted with a difficult choice: support Sendero or face forced, unofficial military conscription.

SL was most active from 1984 through 1990, a period when Sendero increased attacks on Peru's capital, Lima. By 1990, when President

Alberto Fujimori took power, SL was considered the greatest challenge facing the new president. President Fujimori publicly stated that SL would be eradicated by 1995. With the capture of Abimael Guzmán on September 12, 1992, Fujimori claimed victory over the insurgent group.

PHILOSOPHY AND TACTICS

From 1970 through 1980, Guzmán used SL to gather support among rural Indians in Ayacucho. The failure of Peru's military regime to fulfill promises of land reform reinforced SL's conviction that violence was necessary for revolution. SL began to provide services in Ayacucho that the national government would not provide, such as medical services, education, and communal farming assistance. This decade was SL's gestation period, a time for garnering ideological support and gaining activists. By 1980, SL was ready for action.

On May 17, 1980, SL claimed responsibility for instigating the burning of ballot boxes and boycotting of elections in the town of Chuschi in Ayacucho. Although this action was accompanied by little violence, by the end of 1981, SL had claimed responsibility for more than 400 separate actions of political violence in Peru.

SL used three main forms of activity: sabotage, security force attacks, and town and village occupation. The main targets for sabotage were the Peruvian infrastructure and power structure, with roads, rail links, telephone lines, water sources, and electrical sources attacked. In addition, SL targeted security force bases and government workers' homes.

Sendero Luminoso also used displays of power in terms of political and economic manipulation, planning and causing blackouts and brownouts in Lima on key "holidays" within the SL movement, such as Guzmán's birthday, or the anniversary of political violence events.

According to James Anderson, in his book *Sendero Luminoso: A Revolutionary Model?*, SL's campaign to overthrow what it called the "imperialist, Eurocentric" Peruvian government involved five key stages of armed struggle, including mobilization and propaganda dissemination, to gain solid support in the countryside; sabotage and rural guerilla activity; political

KEY EVENTS

1970: Sendero Luminoso began.

1980: The group's first political act occurred.

1980–1992: Active in terms of political violence.

1992: Guzmán was captured and imprisoned for life.

---

violence and confrontation of security forces; expansion of bases into "enemy" zones; and blockading towns with peasant armies, and deployment of members to provoke a civil war.

In 1992, when Guzmán was captured, SL leaders were publicly stating that they believed themselves to be in the fifth and last stage, ready to provoke a civil war.

SL's activities in the countryside, however, alienated many of the peasants that provided the foundation of support for SL. In the early years of their activity, SL aided peasants in obtaining land. However, within a few years, the SL operatives became increasingly restrictive, controlling commerce and external trade, even controlling peasant access to the ocean for trade purposes. SL also prevented voting in various towns and used political violence against local leaders, claiming to have murdered politicians and forced hundreds out of office through threats.

SL was unique in terms of extremist groups in that it was not dependent on any outside organization for financial or arms support. Most of its money was received from extortion of coca farmers and plantation owners. SL received money and goods in exchange for protecting peasants that farmed small lots from drug traffickers. In addition, SL controlled critical airline runways for drug exports. Farming coca produced as much as forty times the average income per year for a peasant in Ayacucho; SL's protection of these activities helped them to gain support among this population.

SL was organized in a cell formation, with individual cells containing between five and eight members. Each unit contained an explosives expert, a munitions expert, four or five members, and a commander. The commander was the only contact person for the next level of the organization. By structuring itself in this manner, SL avoided large-scale captures by the military until 1992. SL viewed sympathizers and members as falling into five distinct categories: sympathizers—peasants or individuals who provided funds, food, medicine, etc. and who acted as messengers; activists—those who hung posters, painted slogans, and spread propaganda; militants—people who participated directly in violent actions (SL frequently referred to these people as their "militia"); *cuadros* (commanders)—individuals who managed regions and zones, or cells; and *cupola* (top leaders)—Guzmán and the Central Committee for SL.

SL membership ranged between an estimated 5,000 and 15,000. Membership was drawn largely from the working class, with disenchanted students, peasant farmers, miners, street vendors, domestic servants, and unskilled and semi-skilled laborers filling the ranks. At the higher levels, academics like Guzmán assumed most leadership positions. Women filled about 30% of the leadership positions in SL, part of an expressed tactic on the part of Guzmán. In Ayacucho and the peasant areas, the societies are highly paternalistic, and women are rarely considered subversive or threatening; SL used female members to maintain an element of surprise.

Sendero Luminoso was aided by the military's approach to rural peasants. In addition to the use of forced patrols, military groups would enter the sections of the countryside labeled "red zone" areas, where SL had control or was fighting to gain control. The security forces gathered peasants and cleared the area of civilians, hoping to eliminate SL's support base. These uprooted peasants were often forced to relocate to other villages, breeding intra-Quecha village rivalry and angering peasants.

In 1984, the Peruvian government put the "Internal Defense of the Territory Plan" in place. Phase one of this plan was implemented immediately: 7,000 troops were deployed to begin a "containment strategy" in areas of high Sendero activity. In addition, Amnesty International and other human rights organizations began to document disappearances and human rights abuses against suspected leftists in Peru.

Between 1982 and 1990, Ayacucho was under a declared state of emergency. The crackdown on SL operatives in the countryside led to more attacks on Lima.

In 1985, when Alan Garcia assumed the presidency, he implemented a wide range of reforms, including redevelopment, funding programs to aid the unemployed and underemployed, and a peace commission to address the issue of the "disappeared" leftists. SL activity dropped in 1985, but by 1986 SL scaled up its activities and targeted Lima once again. Garcia placed Lima under a state of emergency and enforced a curfew for the entire city.

Sendero Luminoso's tactics resulted in a wide range of acts of political violence, including attacking Civil Guard officers in a pro-active offensive movement, starting around 1983. The Civil Guard claims that SL members attacked and killed guard members to take their weapons and uniforms, using both to impersonate officers. Confusion spread quickly as SL members were able to infiltrate military bases of operation and attack Civil Guard groups while in uniform.

In 1983, SL caused a blackout in Lima and set fire to the Bayer industrial plant, gutting it. In June 1985, SL detonated several bombs near a power transmission center and produced a blackout in Lima once more. They detonated several car bombs and set off bombs in popular shopping malls. In 1986, a prison rebellion instigated by SL members resulted in the deaths of more than 300 members. In 1993, a street bomb detonated in Lima killed 40 people and destroyed numerous buildings. Many of the attacks took place when foreign dignitaries visited Peru's president, a message from SL about its views on foreign investment and influence.

By 1991, Sendero controlled various parts of the countryside in the south and central sections of Peru. However, SL's use of violence had alienated many of the peasants who formed their support base. When SL's leader was captured in 1992, Sendero had been responsible for a twelve-year stretch of political violence that threatened Peru's political system, economic development, infrastructure, and rural society. Through guerilla tactics, cell formation, propaganda, mafia-like methods, and violence, the group kept three different Peruvian presidents very busy with initiatives and orders to eradicate the group.

After Guzmán's arrest, a group calling itself *Proseguir* (Onward) claimed to be the continuation of SL. The Peruvian government claims that the group numbers no more than 100, and that they are working with narco-traffickers as a funding source.

Isolated bombings, including a car bomb attack in Lima in 2002 that killed nine people shortly before a visit from U.S. President George W. Bush, have been attributed to SL. While isolated cells may be operational, Sendero Luminoso ceases to be a major actor in Peruvian politics today.

OTHER PERSPECTIVES

The Committee to Support the Revolution in Peru, a Berkeley, California-based organization, is an American group that identifies itself as being a continuation of the Peruvian Communist Party and Sendero Luminoso. According to the group's web site, "The Committee to Support the Revolution in Peru (CSRP) works in our communities to build political support for the People's War and active resistance to the Peruvian regime. The People's War is led by the Communist Party of Peru (PCP)—often referred to as Sendero Luminoso, or Shining Path, by the media. We distribute the writings of the PCP (Partido Comunista del Peru) and other materials that help people understand what this revolution is about."

The organization claims that the capture and imprisonment of Abimael Guzmán (nicknamed Chairman Gonzalo) is unjust. The group's web site also states that, "After his capture and a secret, summary military trial before faceless judges in 1992, Chairman Gonzalo, leader of the Communist Party of Peru (PCP) and the People's War in that country, was thrown into an isolation cell in an underground military prison. He and other PCP leaders are still being held there today. He was last seen in public on 24 September 1992."

In 2003, Peru's Constitutional Court ruled that the terrorist laws under which Abimael Guzmán and others had been tried and convicted were unconstitutional. More than 1,900 alleged terrorists were given an opportunity for new trials in Peru. Chairman Gonzalo was one of those permitted a new trial. The proceedings, scheduled for November 5, 2004, were postponed. The Committee to Support the

PRIMARY SOURCE
Shining Path (SL) a.k.a. Sendero Luminoso People's Liberation Army

DESCRIPTION

Former university professor Abimael Guzman formed SL in Peru in the late 1960s, and his teachings created the foundation of SL's militant Maoist doctrine. In the 1980s, SL became one of the most ruthless terrorist groups in the Western Hemisphere. Approximately 30,000 persons have died since Shining Path took up arms in 1980. The Peruvian Government made dramatic gains against SL during the 1990s, but reports of recent SL involvement in narco-trafficking and kidnapping for ransom indicate it may be developing new sources of support. Its stated goal is to destroy existing Peruvian institutions and replace them with a communist peasant revolutionary regime. It also opposes any influence by foreign governments. Peruvian Courts in 2003 granted approximately 1,900 members the right to request retrials in a civilian court, including the imprisoned top leadership. The trial of Guzman, who was arrested in 1992, was scheduled for November 5, 2004, but was postponed after the first day, when chaos erupted in the courtroom.

ACTIVITIES

Conducted indiscriminate bombing campaigns and selective assassinations.

STRENGTH

Unknown but estimated to be some 300 armed militants.

LOCATION/AREA OF OPERATION

Peru, with most activity in rural areas.

EXTERNAL AID

None.

Source: U.S. Department of State. *Country Reports on Terrorism.* Washington, D.C., 2004.

Revolution in Peru condemned the postponement, declaring Guzmán innocent of all charges.

defunct, although the activities of Proseguir remain to be seen. Guzmán remains in prison, waiting for a new trial to be scheduled.

SUMMARY

The impact of Sendero Luminoso on Peru in the 1980s and early 1990s was extreme. Presidential preoccupation with the rebels was intense, and financial, political, and military resources were diverted from development into fighting SL. Sendero also garnered international attention for its activities as a rebel group and for its association with narco-traffickers.

Although there were pockets of SL activity following Guzmán's arrest, trial, and conviction, the group is now considered to be largely

SOURCES

Books

Goritti, Gustavo. *The Shining Path: A History of the Millenarian War in Peru.* Durham, North Carolina: University of North Carolina Press, 1999.

Web sites

Truth and Reconciliation Commission (in Spanish). "Final Report." < http://www.cverdad.org.pe/ifinal/index.php > (accessed October 4, 2005).

Human Rights Watch. "Peru." < http://hrw.org/english/docs/2004/01/21/peru6988.htm > (accessed October 4, 2005).

Shiv Sena

LEADER: Bal Thackeray
YEAR ESTABLISHED OR BECAME ACTIVE: 1966
ESTIMATED SIZE: Several hundred
USUAL AREA OF OPERATION: Maharashtra, India

OVERVIEW

Shiv Sena (Army of Shivaji, an ancient fighter belonging to the region of Maharashtra, India) was allegedly formed in 1966 by Bal Thackeray, in Mumbai (formerly known as Bombay), India. Ever since, Shiv Sena has been actively promoting its ideology in Maharashtra and other states in India. The members and followers are allegedly considered to be staunch Hindu extremists.

Experts consider Shiv Sena to be extremely conservative and anti-Muslim. Bal Thackeray is often referred as a controversial and militant leader. The party is active on the political front and reportedly has a huge presence and following in Mumbai. The employment faction of Shiv Sena is known as *Shiv Udyog Sena. Bharatiya Kamgar Sena* (Indian Worker's Army), a labor union supporting mostly lower-income worker class communities, is allegedly affiliated to the Shiv Sena. The youth wing of Shiv Sena is known as the *Bharatiya Vidyarthi Sena* (All India Students' Army).

HISTORY

Shiv Sena was formed in June 1966 by Bal Thackeray, allegedly to protect the interest of the native youths in Maharashtra. According to reports, Mumbai, the capital city of

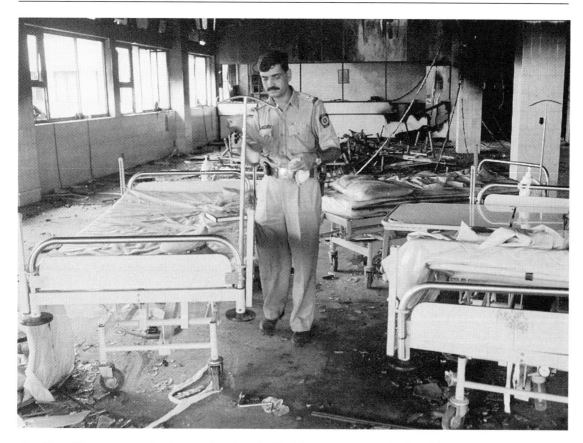

A police officer surveys the damage in a hospital in Thane, a city north of Bombay, on August 27, 2001. Several patients were discovered missing after members of Hindu nationalist Shiv Sena party reportedly torched the hospital and ambulances in response to the death of a local party leader. AP/Wide World Photos. Reproduced by permission.

Maharashtra, was getting crowded, especially because of ethnic immigrants moving into the city. The primary focus of the Shiv Sena was allegedly to motivate the Marathi (native of Maharashtra) youths to drive out non-Marathis from their city and state. This campaign was especially targeted towards the South Indians, Gujaratis (natives to the western Indian state of Gujarat), and Muslims from Mumbai.

Soon after it was formed, the organization ventured into politics and began their drive to reform the city. Several of Shiv Sena members held prominent positions in the Mumbai Municipal Corporation. During the late 1980s and early 1990s, Shiv Sena allied with the Bhartiya Janta Party, a national party that, as of 2005, has been part of the central government of India a few times and featured prominently in the State Assembly polls, which are held to elect the state government.

Shiv Sena was in favor of establishing the Hindu Temple at the controversial Babri Mosque site in the northern Indian state of Uttar Pradesh. Members of Shiv Sena and other Hindu fundamentalist groups claim that the mosque was made at the birth site of Lord Ram, a revered Hindu god. In 1989, the foundation stone for the temple was laid, which caused anti-Hindu riots even in neighboring Bangladesh and Pakistan. The party followed the proceedings of the controversy carefully and propagated *Hindutva* (Hindu fundamentalism) throughout the state of Maharashtra, allegedly with the support of Bharatiya Janata Party (BJP), the *Vishwa Hindu Parishad* (World Hindu Council), and *Rashtriya Swayamsevak Sangh* (National Volunteers Association).

LEADERSHIP

BAL THACKERAY

Shiv Sena was founded and presided over for a long time by Bal Thackeray, also known as Balasaheb Thackeray. As of 2005, his son, Uddhav Thackeray, is the working president of the party. However, Bal Thackeray is considered by most to be the supreme leader of the organization.

Bal Thackeray, born on January 23, 1927, started his career as a cartoonist for a newspaper during the 1950s. He later started his own weekly where his sarcastic cartoons were allegedly aimed to awaken the Marathi youths of Maharashtra. He subsequently formed Shiv Sena, an organization that claims to have a mission of protecting the rights of the natives of Maharashtra. The party, under Thackeray, opposed the infiltration of the state of Maharashtra by South Indians and Gujaratis. Thackeray himself never ran in any election, but allegedly influenced the political situation in Maharashtra greatly by supporting the pro-Hindu political party BJP.

Bal Thackeray claims to be a conservative nationalist believing in Hindu fundamentalism. He and his party have allegedly attacked civil liberties of individuals, especially minorities. Some of the activities opposed by his party are Valentine Day celebrations, movies with radical subjects, cricket matches involving Pakistani players, and more.

Over the years, the party has allegedly developed into a Hindu fundamentalist party with staunch anti-Muslim beliefs. On December 6, 1992, the Babri Mosque was demolished allegedly by Hindutva-driven volunteers. This led to a series of riots across the country, especially in Mumbai where the riots lasted for two months. More than 800 people reportedly died in Mumbai alone. Several human rights groups claim that the anti-Muslim riots in Mumbai were incited by Bal Thackeray and his Shiv Sena party. In February 1998, Justice B.N. Srikrishna (a former judge of the Supreme Court of India) submitted a report that investigated the communal riots in Mumbai to the state government of Maharashtra. The report implicated the hand of Bal Thackeray and *Shiv Sainiks* (the members of Shiv Sena) in intensifying the riots. In retaliation, Shiv Sena claimed that the report was biased and that they had no agenda in the Mumbai riots.

According to media reports, there were several campaigns carried out by the opposition parties and human rights groups supporting the prosecution of the offenders. The ruling BJP–Shiv Sena party allegedly refused to accept the recommendation of the report and labeled the report "anti-Hindu."

That said, in the 1990s, political experts also attribute a number of economic growth-oriented developments to the Shiv Sena. During the reign of the BJP-Shiv Sena state government (in Maharashtra), there were several reforms made by the party. This included completion of the Mumbai–Pune expressway that bridged the gap between the two most prominent cities of Maharashtra, construction of several flyovers in Mumbai to ease the traffic congestion problems in the city, improved water and irrigation supply in several urban and rural areas of Maharashtra, as well as providing a safe haven for the elderly.

The coalition, however, did not win the 2004 state elections and, as of 2005, is the opposition party in the state.

PHILOSOPHY AND TACTICS

Shiv Sena is a right-wing political party with staunch Hindu fundamentalist beliefs. Soon after the formation of the party, its members allegedly fought for the rights of Marathi youths of Maharashtra by campaigning extensively against immigrants from other areas of India. The party reportedly gave an ultimatum to South Indians working in Mumbai to move out of the city or face the consequences. The same stance was then applied against Gujaratis and Muslims. In their bid to drive away immigrants, the party allegedly ran several violent campaigns to terrorize non-Marathi individuals. There were also reports of attacks by Shiv Sena members on

KEY EVENTS

1966: Shiv Sena displayed regional chauvinism and an anti-communism stance in Mumbai and other areas of Maharashtra.

1970s: Shiv Sena members accused to have played a prominent role in communal riots in Bhiwandi-Jalgaon areas of Maharashtra.

1984: Mumbai–Bhiwandi riots, both between Hindus and Muslims.

1992: After the fall of Babri Mosque, there were widespread riots at several places in India, especially in Mumbai.

1995: The BJP–Shiv Sena alliance first formed the Maharashtra state government.

1998: The Sri Krishna commission report submitted to the Maharashtra state government implicated the role of Shiv Sena members and especially its chief, Bal Thackeray, in the 1992–1993 riots.

2003: Shiv Sena underwent organizational changes when Bal Thackeray's son, Uddhav, was appointed as the executive president of the party.

---

trade unions that supported the rights of non-Marathis.

However, during the 1970s, the party shifted its focus to Hindu fundamentalism. According to the Census Bureau of India, about 80% of the population of India follows Hinduism (since the early 1970s). Political experts claim that several political parties and religious organizations, including Shiv Sena, support Hindutva (Hindu nationalism). In May 1970, Hindu-Muslim riots erupted in the Bhiwandi-Jalgaon area of Maharashtra that reportedly claimed the lives of more than 250 people. Several monitor groups indicate that Shiv Sena played a major role in intensifying the riots as part of their strategy to promote Hindu fundamentalism.

Later in 1984, Shiv Sena reportedly organized a Hindu congregation rally in Mumbai in which Bal Thackeray made derogatory remarks about Islam, subsequently provoking the Muslims. Media reports have claimed time and again that Shiv Sena receives unabashed support from specific members of the local law authorities that let the party carry out its operations. In 1989, Shiv Sena started publishing a Marathi daily, *Saamna* (Confrontation), that acted as a mouthpiece of the party and featured provocative pro-Hindu editorials by Bal Thackeray. Experts claim that the party also started a student cell and a worker's union cell to expand its influence.

The December 1992 Babri Mosque demolition in Ayodhya was applauded by Shiv Sena leader Bal Thackeray. His heated speeches reportedly played a major role in provoking the communal riots in Mumbai that claimed the lives of more than 800 people. An inquiry into the 1992–1993 riots in Mumbai pinpointed the involvement of Shiv Sena leader, Bal Thackeray, and the then-Chief Minister of Maharashtra, Manohar Joshi, thought by many to be an avid Shiv Sena supporter. The report stated that Shiv Sena deliberately and systematically planned the riots and the subsequent chaos in the city. The then-ruling BJP–Shiv Sena coalition government in the state of Maharashtra disregarded the inquiry report by calling it biased.

Apart from various Hindu fundamentalist activities, the Shiv Sena also continued its campaign against immigrants. In 1995, the Maharashtra state government that was led by the BJP–Shiv Sena coalition proposed renaming the city of Bombay as Mumbai, as they claimed that the name Bombay was a "corruption" of the original name. In its drive against non-Marathis and Muslims, changing the official name of the city of Bombay allegedly was the next step in asserting that the Shiv Sena was firm in its resolve.

In 2003, the party launched *Mee Mumbaikar* (I belong to Mumbai) campaign, another tactic to discourage immigrants from other states to come to Mumbai. According to Shiv Sena, the campaign was targeted to instill pride among the Mumbai natives for being a part of the city of Mumbai, but skeptics think otherwise. Shiv Sena party members argue that the real *Mumbaikar*, or someone belonging to Mumbai, is a person who contributes towards the fortification of the city and does not take advantage of it.

Shiv Sena is accused by the authorities and media of exhibiting fanatical Hindu ideology by lashing out at minorities and carrying out violent acts against them. In spite of these allegations, the party claims that it is a nationalistic party and is not against any specific religion, caste, or creed, but only against the "traitors" of India and would go to any length to punish them. The party has allegedly resorted to demonstrations and rallies, protest marches, calling for strikes, forcing the local business to stay closed, and arrogant self-righteous attitude. Party followers and members have also reportedly lashed out against movies that display controversial themes and reacted strongly to any anti-Hindu or pro-Muslim statements made by political leaders.

Prominent members of the party are known for their inflammatory public remarks as well as articles in publications sponsored by Shiv Sena. Its members have also reportedly used economic and social issues to win the confidence of common people. Issues such as prices and tax hike, cleanliness, elder homes, traffic problems, water supply troubles, ethics and morality, Hindu causes, and several others are seemingly prominent features in Shiv Sena periodicals, billboards, speeches, and protests.

OTHER PERSPECTIVES

In the 1990s, the Shiv Sena government in Maharashtra was severely criticized by the media as well as human rights organizations for their alleged failure to control the 1992–1993 Mumbai riots. Prominent members of Shiv Sena were also under scrutiny for their alleged involvement in the riots. The Sri Krishna Commission report stated that, "As far as the December 1992 phase of the rioting by the Muslims is concerned, there is no material to show that it was anything other than a spontaneous reaction of leaderless and incensed Muslim mobs, which commenced as peaceful protest, but soon degenerated into riots. The Hindus must share a part of the blame in provoking the Muslims by their celebration rallies, inciting slogans and *rasta roko* (stop-the-traffic protests) which were all organized mostly by *Shiv Sainiks* (Shiv Sena members), and to a marginal extent by BJP activists."

Additionally, the report went on to say that "large-scale rioting and violence was commenced from 6th January 1993 by the Hindus brought to fever pitch by communally inciting propaganda unleashed by Hindu communal organizations and writings in newspapers like *Saamna* and *Navakal*. It was taken over by Shiv Sena and its leaders who continued to whip up communal frenzy by their statements and acts and writings and directives issued by the Shiv Sena *Pramukh* (leader) Bal Thackeray."

According to the International Religious Freedom Report 2004 released by the U.S. Bureau of Democracy, Human Rights, and Labor, in 2002, Shiv Sena leader Bal Thackeray called upon his followers to form Hindu suicide squads to combat Muslim extremists. The Maharashta government filed charges against Thackeray under the Penal Code for "causing a rift amongst two communities."

SUMMARY

As of 2005, media reports claim that the stronghold of Shiv Sena on the Maharashtra political scene is losing its grip. The Shiv Sena–BJP coalition could not win the 2004 election, in spite of the claims and promises made by both the political parties to the people of Maharashtra. Also, political analysts speculate whether it was Bal Thackeray's charm or threatening personality that lured hundreds into being ardent followers of Shiv Sena. It is quite evident that Shiv Sena could exercise its influence, mainly over Mumbai and nearby areas and not the greater region of Maharashtra. Also, there is very little presence of Shiv Sena in the Indian parliament. Critics of Shiv Sena argue that the current face of Shiv Sena is nothing compared to what it was during the 1990s. There have been reports about conflict among prominent members of the party. The successors of Bal Thackeray's legacy allegedly lack the charisma and wisdom that made Shiv Sena hugely popular.

SOURCES

Web sites

BBC News, South East Asia. "Profile: Bombay's Militant Voice." < http://news.bbc.co.uk/1/hi/world/south_asia/841488.stm > (accessed October 4, 2005).

BBC News, South East Asia. "Shiv Sena: Profile." <http://news.bbc.co.uk/1/hi/world/south_asia/ 3551067.stm> (accessed October 4, 2005).

Countercurrents.org. "Shiv Sena On The Threshold Of Disintegration." <http://www.countercurrents.org/ comm-ketkar011104.htm> (accessed October 4, 2005).

Frontline. "A Parochial Project." <http://www.flonnet. com/fl2010/stories/20030523004803200.htm> (accessed October 4, 2005).

Human Rights Watch. "Human Rights Developments, India." <http://www.hrw.org/worldreport99/asia/ india.html> (accessed October 4, 2005).

Sikh Militants

ALTERNATE NAMES: Babbar Khalsa International, International Sikh Youth Federation, Khalistand Zindabad Force, Khalistan Liberation Front, Dal Khalsa

LEADERS: Lakhbir Singh Rode (ISYF); Ranjit Singh Neeta (KZF)

YEAR ESTABLISHED OR BECAME ACTIVE: 1980s

USUAL AREAS OF OPERATION: Northern India, especially Punjab

OVERVIEW

Sikh (a sect) terrorism is allegedly sponsored by Sikh militant groups who demand the creation of a Sikh state called *Khalistan* (Land of the Pure), independent of India. Some of the prominent Sikh militant groups include organizations like Babbar Khalsa International, International Sikh Youth Federation (ISYF), Khalistan Zindabad Force (KZF), Dal Khalsa, Khalistan National Army (KNA), and several others. Terrorism experts are of the opinion that their major areas of operation include Northern India, Western Europe, Southeast Asia, and North America.

After the September 11, 2001, attacks in the United States, the U.S. Department of State assigned Babbar Khalsa International and International Sikh Youth Federation as terrorist organizations.

HISTORY

After India's independence from British rule in 1947, the province of Punjab was split into two, with parts of it being allotted to Pakistan and India. Published reports mention that after the Indian independence, a group of Sikhs demanded a separate Punjabi-speaking state (the native language of Sikhs) and a special

Mother Teresa prays as she is led through Trilokpuri, a Sikh section of Delhi where many Sikhs were burned alive by mobs after Indira Gandhi's assassination. AP/Wide World Photos. Reproduced by permission.

place in the constitution of India. They reportedly felt that the Indian government was not treating them fairly by denying them a separate state. This was followed by the formation of an organization known as Patiala and East Punjab States Union (PEPSU) that had a Sikh majority. PEPSU, allegedly, encouraged the Sikhs to demand for an independent Sikh state within India.

However, the Indian government formed a larger state with a population consisting of both Hindus and Sikhs—a move that is thought to further dissatisfy the Sikhs. Eventually, in 1966, a separate state of Punjab was formed with Punjabi as the official language of the state. However, it has been reported that various fundamentalist Sikh groups were disgruntled as many regions that they claimed were rightfully theirs were allotted to the neighboring states of Haryana and Himachal Pradesh.

News and media agencies report that during the early 1980s, with an intention of winning over the Hindu voters of northern states, the reigning Congress Party led by Indira Gandhi, the then Prime Minister of India, allegedly used the differences between the Hindus and Sikhs of Punjab to their political advantage. Sant Harchand Singh Longowal, the leader of Akali Dal (ruling Sikh political party of Punjab at that time) allegedly started the *Dharma Yudh* (Religious War) in August 1982, and all the Akali Dal members resigned from the Legislative Assembly and the Parliament.

The tension reached its peak during 1983–1984 when the government of India, as alleged by various Sikh organizations, did not pay attention to the grievances of the Sikhs and their supporting political parties. Sant Jarnail Singh Bhindranwale, a radical Sikh leader, gained huge popularity during this period. He and his armed followers, allegedly, carried out various terrorist activities in the state to drive out the Hindu population from India. It is thought that most of the militant groups can trace their origins to Jarnail Singh Bhindranwale. During 1984, Bhindranwale and his supporters occupied the Golden Temple, a

Broken glass is scattered on the pavement outside a restaurant damaged by a blast inside two New Delhi movie theaters on May 22, 2005. At least 50 people were injured by the blasts at the two theaters, which were showing a "Bollywood" film that has been criticized by Sikh religious leaders for debasing their faith. AP/Wide World Photos. Reproduced by permission.

holy place of the Sikhs at Amritsar (in Punjab), and established their headquarters in the temple premises. Indira Gandhi, the then Prime Minister of India, launched the "Operation Blue Star" to flush out the terrorists from the besieged temple. This attack on the Sikh religious shrine that reportedly killed hundreds is thought by most experts to have infuriated the ardent Sikhism followers, subsequently leading to increased extremist activities. Eventually, in October 1984, the central government laid down the President's Rule in the state of Punjab. (In other words, the state of Punjab would be ruled by the President of India, rather than the democratically elected state government.)

The Indian government claims that the intention behind Operation Blue Star was not to attack the religious identity of the Sikhs, but to get hold of the armed Sikh Militants. However, the assassination of Indira Gandhi on October 31, 1984, by her Sikh bodyguards reportedly ignited anti-Sikh riots and claimed the lives of thousands of Sikhs. After the 1984 carnage, the number of militant groups operating in Punjab, allegedly, multiplied.

Babbar Khalsa International (BKI) is considered by the Indian authorities as one of the oldest (with its roots in the 1920's Babbar Akali Movement) and most prominent organizations that, as of 2005, continue to spread the ideology of Khalistan.

Babbar Khalsa International was reportedly founded in Canada by Sukhdev Singh Babbar and Talwinder Singh Parmar in early 1980s. The BKI claims that their objective is to have an independent Sikh state Khalistan. In 1992, the group seemingly split because of ideological differences among the leaders, and Talwinder Singh Parmar became the leader of the Babbar Khalsa Parmar faction (The original BKI was still reportedly led by Babbar). As of 2005, intelligence reports state that BKI is a part of Germany-based terrorist organization and also has established close links with Inter Services Intelligence (ISI)—Pakistan's external intelligence agency, accused by the Indian government of encouraging terrorism activities in the Indian-administered Punjab. Authorities blamed the BKI for the 1985 Air India plane bombing that took place near the Ireland coast and reportedly claimed more than 300 lives.

Babbar Khalsa members are also accused by the Indian government of masterminding and executing the assassination of the Punjab Chief Minister Beant Singh, in 1995. As thought by most analysts, as of 2005, even though the terrorist activities of Babbar Khalsa are not as prominent as they were in the 1980s, the movement still allegedly garners support of Sikh communities all over the world, including the United Kingdom, the United States, and Canada. Babbar Khalsa is, as of 2005, listed as a terrorist organization by India, the United States, and Canada.

After Operation Blue Star was carried out by the Indian army, in 1984, against the Sikh militants occupying the Sikh shrine Golden Temple, the Indira Gandhi government bore

LEADERSHIP

LAKHBIR SINGH RODE

A prominent Sikh militant, Lakhbir Singh Rode is the leader of International Sikh Youth Federation, as of 2005. Rode is regarded as a "hardcore terrorist" by the authorities in Punjab, India, where most of his terrorist activities were reported. Most analysts argue that he stays in Pakistan and is considered as a "most wanted" terrorist by the government of India.

RANJIT SINGH NEETA

Ranjit Singh Neeta of the KZF reportedly started as a petty felon and later formed associations with smugglers and other more influential criminals. Authorities claim that Neeta was involved in a series of bomb blasts on buses and trains in the north east region of India, between 1988 and 1999.

OTHER LEADERS

Talwinder Singh Parmar is founder and one of the leaders of the Babbar Khalsa International. Parmar was killed in an encounter with the Punjab police, in 1992. Sukhdev Singh Babbar, another founder member of BKI, was also killed earlier that year. Reports suggest that Wadhwa Singh, who is allegedly at an undisclosed location in Pakistan, as of 2005, heads the Babbar Khalsa organization and Mehal Singh, is employed as his deputy chief.

Apart from Lakhbir Singh Rode, the Indian government has declared Wadhwa Singh and Mehal Singh of Babbar Khalsa International, and Ranjit Singh Neeta of KZF as "most wanted" terrorists and has demanded that the Pakistan government take actions to extradite them to India.

severe criticism from staunch Sikhs all over the world. The International Sikh Youth Federation (ISYF) was allegedly founded by Amrik Singh and Jasbir Singh Rode (nephew of Bhindranwale, a key Sikh fundamentalist who got killed in Operation Blue Star) in the United Kingdom after the Golden Temple crisis.

Soon after it was founded, the group is thought to have undergone a series of splits. Several splinter groups emerged with offices reportedly in the United Kingdom, the United States, Canada, and Germany. The organization was allegedly involved in several terrorist activities in Punjab, including the assassination attempt on the Chief Minister of Punjab in 1997. The British government declared the ISYF as a proscribed organization, which was followed by the ban on the organization by the Indian government. The group was declared disbanded by one of the representatives of the ISYF in 2002. Amrik Singh proclaimed, in 2002, that the group had been disbanded as it was categorized as a terrorist organization. On April 30, 2004, the United States included ISYF in its Terrorist Exclusion List.

Khalistan Zindabad Force (KZF) was allegedly founded with the help of Sikhs based in Jammu, India. There is limited information about the strength and organization of this group. Reports suggest that Ranjit Singh Neeta, allegedly based in Pakistan, is the self-proclaimed leader of this terrorist outfit.

The group is thought to operate mainly in Punjab, Delhi, and Jammu (in northern India), but there are reports citing the operations of the group in Nepal as well. Law enforcement officials in Punjab have claimed, on several occasions, that KZF has links with Pakistan's ISI, along with several terrorist groups active in Jammu and Kashmir, including the Hizb-ul-Mujahideen.

PHILOSOPHY AND TACTICS

Experts on Sikh militancy indicate that, in the 1970s, the radical ideologies of Sant Jarnail Singh Bhindranwal caused friction among the followers of the Sikh religion. It is thought that the ideologies of Sikh religion, such as the doctrine of one God and tolerance towards other religious followers, were not acceptable to certain fundamentalists who were in favor of creation of a separate state of Punjab and name it Khalistan. Bhindranwale reportedly advocated fundamentalism and encouraged armed struggle for the liberation of Khalistan. Most of the

KEY EVENTS

1984: Sikh militants occupied the Golden Temple; Operation Blue Star was launched by Prime Minister Indira Gandhi to drag out the militants from the Golden Temple; thousands lost their lives.

1984: Prime Minister Indira Gandhi was assassinated by her two Sikh bodyguards; this ignited the anti-Sikh riots and claimed a minimum of 2,000 lives in New Delhi and other northern Indian states.

1985: Sikh extremists belonging to the Babbar Khalsa organizations were accused by the Indian government of planning the Air India bombing over the Irish coast in June 1985, killing 329 passengers and crew onboard; on the same day, a bomb allegedly planted by Sikh militants on an Air India flight from Vancouver exploded in Tokyo's Narita Airport, claiming the lives of two Japanese baggage handlers.

---

militant groups can trace their origins to Jarnail Singh Bhindranwale and adopt his philosophies.

The main focus of all the Sikh militant groups is thought to be the creation of Khalistan. Media reports have quoted most Sikh militant group leaders proclaiming that *Khalsa Raj* (Rule of the Sikh Brotherhood) is free from evil as well as evildoers and eradicates all pains and sufferings. Additionally, these leaders reportedly propagate their belief by proclaiming that Khalistan would be an idyllic land free from cultural and economic exploitation.

Another Sikh militant organization *Khalistan Zindabad* Force (Victory to the Land of the Pure) reportedly aims at the creation of an independent Punjab and, as of 2005, is also focusing on the Jammu and Kashmir cause. KZF allegedly has support from the ISI of Pakistan and other Islamic fundamentalist terrorist organizations based in Pakistan and Kashmir.

The Sikh militants belonging to organizations such as Babbar Khalsa International, Khalistan Commando Force, and the International Sikh Youth Federation have, in the past, been accused by the Indian government of using violence to take charge of fund committees of temples and other charitable institutions (these funds are then allegedly used for their operations). They have also been accused of using threats and aggressive behavior to coerce Sikhs into accepting their orthodox ideals.

The tension between the Sikhs and Indian government reached its highest point in the 1980s. It is reported that between 1981 and 1992, seven major (and about a dozen smaller) Sikh militant organizations attacked and killed unarmed civilians, and also engaged themselves in random (as well as planned) acts of violence against individuals and groups with conflicting ideologies. They were also accused of assassinations and killings of political leaders and Hindu religious leaders. In 1982, as claimed by the Indian government, some 10,000 Sikhs took an oath on the premises of the Golden Temple, Amritsar, India, under the auspices of Bhindranwale, that they would rather attain martyrdom in their battle for Khalistan than give in to government pressure. The central government took charge eventually in 1984, and conducted a siege on the Golden Temple. This siege (Operation Blue Star) is thought to have incited Sikh militancy further. It also reportedly aggravated the Sikh–Hindu communalism and gave a push to extremism and political assassinations.

According to published reports, incidents as a result of Sikh terrorism include attacks on Indian officials and civilians (mainly Hindus, but also Sikhs who opposed extremism). Other tactics followed by militant groups range from kidnappings to bombings and assassinations.

According to terrorism experts and monitor groups, these militant movements are characterized according to their ideologies. During the 1980s when Sikh militancy was causing a great deal of concern for the Indian government, the leading political party, Indian National Congress, categorized these movements as "separatists" (separation from India), "disintegrationist" (breaking the integrity of the Indian nation), "fundamentalist," and "terrorist movements." Other political parties, including the opposition parties, reportedly labeled the Sikh militant organizations as "anti-Hindu," "anti-national," "undemocratic," and "extremist" movements, based on their philosophies.

As thought by these experts, one of the most organized tactics by Sikh militants was carried out on June 23, 1985. New Delhi-bound Air India flight *Kanishka* that took off from Toronto was bombed near the Irish coast, while it was preparing to land at the Heathrow Airport. This mid-air explosion claimed 329 lives, including passengers and crew. Indian investigations revealed that the explosions were carried out by two Sikh terrorists allegedly belonging to the Babbar Khalsa Organization. The Canadian authorities suspected that the bombing was conducted to avenge the 1984 Operation Blue Star. Ripudaman Singh Malik, 57, and Ajaib Singh Bagri, 55, both allegedly belonging to Babbar Khalsa Organization were charged with planting bombs on the plane. On March 17, 2005, the accused were however acquitted due to "lack of evidence." The British Columbia Supreme Court Justice, Ian Josephson, said that the key prosecution witnesses were "too late to be credible."

Experts and government authorities have also accused Sikh militants of engaging in random as well as targeted acts of violence against civilians and government, such as bombing and shoot-outs at marketplaces, movie theaters, restaurants, as well as at public and private properties. Some of these attacks have reportedly occurred outside Punjab in neighboring states of Himachal Pradesh and New Delhi.

Sikh militants have also been often accused by the Indian government for conspiring to disrupt, on a routine basis, the Indian Republic Day celebrations (the Republic Day is celebrated on January 26 every year to mark the day in 1950 when the Indian constitution took effect). It is alleged that the Sikh militant groups are funded by their internationally active cells and other overseas Sikh communities. In addition, authorities claim that International Sikh Youth Federation and World Sikh Council are their other major funding sources.

Media reports also claim that the Pakistan Gurudwara Prabandhak Committee (PGPC), the body that administers Sikh shrines in Pakistan, has been administered by the ISI. The PGPC was formed in 1999 and, according to intelligence reports, Sikh terrorists camping in Pakistan are working under the direct supervision of ISI. There are also claims by the Indian media that ISI has assigned the Islamic extremist militia Lashkar-e-Tayyiba (LeT) the charge of reviving terrorism in the state of Punjab. LeT is also blamed for providing arms and ammunitions as well as training to the groups of BKI, the KZF, and the ISYF.

OTHER PERSPECTIVES

In published research papers, Wassan Singh Zaffarwal, a leader of Khalistan Commando Force (KCF), has been quoted declaring: "We will not create a society where one human being is poor and sleeps in the street while his neighbor sleeps in the palace or a luxurious building. We shall remove all remaining feudal and monopolist forces." Another leader of KCF has declared that "You cannot take money from any poor person, ever. We're clear on that. However, we shall impose a tax of Khalistan government on the wealthy. We don't force money out of them. We shall tax them."

According to some reports, the Sikh Students Federation has laid out the "real" reason for the Khalistan movement, which is also allegedly supported by several Sikh militant organizations. The Sikh Students Federation declares that "The Sikh struggle is only against those blood-sucking leeches, wicked, tyrants, sinners, and destructive raiders who have made fatal assaults on their *Guru Granth*, dress, *Gurudwaras*, cultural, and truthful earnings."

A January 2004 foreign relations statement released by the Indian Ministry of External Affairs talks about the Indo-Canadian bilateral relations. The statement explicitly declares that "the problem of Sikh terrorism originating in Canada has been an important issue in India-Canada relations. Talwinder Singh Parmar of the Babbar Khalsa arrived in Canada in 1979 and began to conduct extremist activities. Lakhbir Singh Brar, a relative of Jarnail Singh Bhindranwale, who joined Parmar in Canada in 1985, formed the International Sikh Youth Federation that came to control nearly 75% of the Gurdwaras in Canada by 1988. Canadian-based Sikh extremists bombed the Air India aircraft Kanishka in June 1985 and a bomb planted on another Air India aircraft exploded at Narita Airport, Tokyo."

In the 1991 report on Patterns of Global Terrorism submitted by the U.S. State Department Office of the Coordinator for Counterterrorism, it is mentioned that "the level of indigenous terrorism was high throughout 1991, as Punjabi, Kashmiri, and Assamese separatists conducted attacks in a bid to win independence for their states. Violence related to separatist movements claimed at least 5,500 lives in Punjab and over 1,500 lives in Kashmir." The report went on to mention that "in January, Sikh extremists declared war on the press in Punjab and forced reporters to stop calling them terrorists. Newsmen critical of Sikh terrorist tactics received death threats."

SUMMARY

The Sikh militant groups have denied the accusations by the Indian government authorities and opposed the inclusion of their organizations in the list of terrorist organizations by governments around the world. It has been reported that most of these organizations consider themselves to be "fighting for a just cause" and claim that they have a "distinct goal" and a "professed logic for violence" in their movements. Terrorism experts state that many Sikh militants believe that the *Khalsa* (Sikh) has been created only to destroy the tyrant and the tyranny and for the protection of the poor.

However, after 1992, the instances of terrorism by Sikh militants have decreased significantly. This has been attributed to the success of the Indian government as well as the Punjab police. Indian authorities assert that peace has finally returned to Punjab.

SOURCES

Web sites

Federation of American Scientists. "Sikh Terrorists." < http://www.fas.org/irp/world/para/sikh.htm > (accessed October 11, 2005).

GlobalSecurity.org. "Sikh Terrorists." < http://www.globalsecurity.org/military/world/para/sikh.htm > (accessed October 11, 2005).

GlobalSecurity.org. "Sikhs in Punjab." < http://www.globalsecurity.org/military/world/war/punjab.htm > (accessed October 11, 2005).

Office of the Secretary of State, Office of the Coordinator for Counterterrorism. "Patterns of Global Terrorism: 1991." < http://www.fas.org/irp/threat/terror_91/asia.html > (accessed October 11, 2005).

South Asia Terrorism Portal. "Terrorist Groups in Punjab." < http://www.satp.org/satporgtp/countries/india/states/punjab/terrorist_outfits/index.html > (accessed October 11, 2005).

The Mackenzie Institute. "Babbar Khalsa Banned at Last." < http://www.mackenzieinstitute.com/2003/terror060403.htm > (accessed October 11, 2005).

Sipah-e-Sahaba Pakistan (SSP)

OVERVIEW

Sipah-e-Sahaba Pakistan (SSP) is an extremist outfit claiming to fight for the rights of the Sunni sect in northern Pakistan, especially in the state of Punjab. The political and social scenario in Punjab has been dominated by a Shia community (a rival community of the Sunnis, a Muslim sect), comprising of high-profile landlords and businesspersons since the early 1980s.

The SSP has resorted to violent means to promote its ideologies and objectives. As of 2005, it has been banned by Pakistan as a terrorist organization.

LEADERS: Maulana Nawaz Jhangvi; Maulana Zia-ur-Rehman Farooqi; Maulana Eesar-ul-Haq Qasmi; Maulana Azam Tariq

YEAR ESTABLISHED OR BECAME ACTIVE: 1985

ESTIMATED SIZE: Thousands

USUAL AREA OF OPERATION: Pakistan, primarily the state of Punjab

HISTORY

SSP was originally known as Anjuman Sipah-e-Sahaba (ASSP) when it was formed in 1985 by *Maulana* Haq Nawaz Jhangvi, a Sunni cleric (Maulana is a term used to address scholarly Muslims). The ASSP came into existence in region of Jhang (in Pakistan) by the efforts of Maulana Zia-ur-Rehman Farooqi, Maulana Azam Tariq, and Eesar-ul-Haq Qasmi. The state of Punjab was then publicly known to have been dominated by feudal setup, which relates to a system wherein nobles (or influential people) allow people to work on their land in exchange for their labor and military service.

Police officers take away the bodies of shooting victims, one of whom is Maulana Azam Tariq, the one-time leader of the outlawed Sunni extremist group Sipah-e-Sahaba. AP/Wide World Photos

The Anjuman Sipah-e-Sahaba was soon renamed to Sipah-e-Sahaba Pakistan (SSP). The base of SSP, Jhang, is a province located between the central and southern Punjab. This region has very high numbers of landholdings by the Shi'ite landlords, and the people working for them are primarily Sunnis. The SSP, reportedly known as the voice of the Jhang-Sunni sect, is allegedly initiating violent means to achieve its goals, making the issue confrontational against the Shi'ite sect.

Since the late 1980s, the SSP has been reportedly involved in various terrorist activities such as bombings that have killed hundreds of policemen and civilians (mainly Shi'ites). SSP has been operating in all the regions of Pakistan and has been reported as one of the most influential extremist outfits in Pakistan politics. According to analysts, it managed to create a large vote bank in the state of Punjab and North-West Frontier Province (NWFP) of Pakistan.

However, by the mid 1990s there were reports of a reduction in the aggressive tactics of the group. As thought by anti-terrorism experts, owing to such moderation, many radical members left the group in 1996 to form another organization known as the Lashkar-e-Jhangvi (LeJ). Some reports also suggest that LeJ is an extension of the SSP.

As of 2005, SSP is thought to have set up more than 500 offices throughout the districts of Pakistan—a statistic that analysts claim makes it one of the most spread-out and well-networked terrorist organizations in Pakistan. According to Pakistani government officials, the founders of SSP, Maulana Tariq, Allama Ghazni, and Maulana Jhangvi, have been instrumental in the various terrorist acts organized by the group.

Pakistani President Pervez Musharraf declared the SSP a terrorist organization in 2002. According to media reports, the group renamed itself Millat-e-Islamia Pakistan in order to avoid the ramifications of the proscription. However, the group was re-designated a terrorist organization in 2003.

LEADERSHIP

MAULANA NAWAZ JHANGVI

The original founder of ASSP (later renamed to Sipah-e-Sahaba Pakistan, SSP), Maulana Nawaz Jhangvi is thought to be the most prominent SSP leader. Jhangvi, according to many, has masterminded most operations of the SSP. He reportedly contributed to what was known as the Deobandi movement against the feudal system of Shi'ites in Pakistan to resurrect the Sunni caste and its identity.

Jhangvi was killed in 1990, allegedly by Shi'ites. Although he served as leader of the SSP for a short time, most analysts state that he was responsible for the extensive propagation of the philosophies of SSP. According to Pakistan government officials, Jhangvi made numerous inflammatory remarks during his public speeches. These were thought to have instigated Sunnis to adopt terror tactics against Shi'ites and the Pakistan government.

In 1990, Maulana Jhangvi reportedly contested the election for the National Assembly seat that he eventually lost. Media reports claim that Jhangvi instructed his followers and activists to create an atmosphere of terror and violence in Pakistan and to constitute this act as a war toward establishing the Sunni state of Punjab.

PHILOSOPHY AND TACTICS

As claimed by the group, the Sipah-e-Sahaba's main objective is to create a separate Sunni state of Punjab. Reportedly, feudalism is highly prevalent in Punjab—Sunnis being at the suffering end. Members of the SSP are thought to vehemently oppose the Shi'ite sect as well as the Pakistan government.

In order to attain its objectives and promote its philosophy, the SSP has allegedly resorted to violent tactics, including bombings. Since its

KEY EVENTS

1990: Leader of SSP, Maulana Nawaz Jhangvi was allegedly killed by Shi'ites.

1994: SSP was suspected behind a terrorist attack that killed more than 70 people and injured another 300; this attack in the state of Punjab is thought to be one of the worst terrorist attacks in Pakistan.

1996: Many radical members of the SSP reportedly left the group to form another extremist outfit, the Lashkar-e-Jhangvi.

2002: Pakistan President Pervez Musharraf declared SSP a terrorist organization.

inception, SSP has been held responsible for targeted killings of high-profile members of opponent groups, prominent Shi'ite nationals, and Pakistan government officials. The group has reportedly also bombed religious places such as those belonging to Shi'ites and other opposing sects.

SSP self-proclamations often contain derogatory comments against Shi'ites and others who oppose their strategies and beliefs. Members of the SSP claim that Iran is a major sponsor of Shi'ite activitists. Reportedly, Iranian nationals residing in Pakistan and other countries are also targeted by the group.

In 1999, during the military coup in Pakistan (led by General Pervez Musharraf—now the self-appointed President of Pakistan), SSP, like other extremist organizations, also reportedly chose to keep a low profile. Anti-terrorism experts state that the SSP and many other similar outfits act only when they sense a neutral environment—an environment where they are more likely to make a bigger impact. According to news reports, the internal disorder within Pakistan, as a result of the various extremist organizations, saw a drastic reduction during this period.

PRIMARY SOURCE

Sipah-i-Sahaba/Pakistan (SSP)

DESCRIPTION

The Sipah-I-Sahaba/Pakistan (SSP) is a Sunni sectarian group that follows the Deobandi school. Violently anti-Shia, the SSP emerged in central Punjab in the mid–1980s as a response to the Iranian Revolution. Pakistani President Musharraf banned the SSP in January 2002. In August 2002, the SSP renamed itself Millat-i-Islami Pakistan, and Musharraf re-banned the group under its new name in November 2003. The SSP also has operated as a political party, winning seats in Pakistan's National Assembly.

ACTIVITIES

The group's activities range from organizing political rallies calling for Shia to be declared non-Muslims to assassinating prominent Shia leaders. The group was responsible for attacks on Shia worshippers in May 2004, when at least fifty people were killed.

STRENGTH

The SSP may have approximately 3,000 to 6,000 trained activists who carry out various kinds of sectarian activities.

LOCATION/AREA OF OPERATION

The SSP has influence in all four provinces of Pakistan. It is considered to be one of the most powerful sectarian groups in the country.

EXTERNAL AID

The SSP reportedly receives significant funding from Saudi Arabia through wealthy private donors in Pakistan. Funds also are acquired from other sources, including other Sunni extremist groups, madrassas, and contributions by political groups.

Source: U.S. Department of State. *Country Reports on Terrorism.* Washington, D.C., 2004.

However, in a tactical move in 2001, SSP joined hands with members of the Afghan Jehad Council after learning about the United States–Pakistan alliance on the "War on Terror" against the Taliban regime of Afghanistan. Anti-terrorism experts and monitor groups claim that the SSP is known to have close links with the Taliban regime. This move allegedly garnered considerable support from other groups that were also against the alliance. According to Pakistan government officials, such strategies have helped the group in intensifying their terrorist operations in Punjab and elsewhere.

The Sipah-e-Sahaba, in the past, is thought to have strong associations with a number of other terrorist outfits, both in Pakistan as well as other countries. According to news reports, the group has received financial funding as well as training support from many of these other organizations. Some of the alleged connections of the SSP are with Pakistan-based terrorist outfits—Harkat-ul-Mujahideen (HuM) and Jaish-e-Mohammed (JeM). According to published

reports, SSP also has links with al-Qaeda and the Taliban regime. Apart from these, monitor groups assert that Sipah-e-Sahaba has strong relations with numerous pro-Sunni political parties in Pakistan, including the Jamat-e-Islam (JeL) and Jamat-Ulema-e-Islam.

OTHER PERSPECTIVES

Pakistani government officials have condemned the terrorist acts performed by the SSP, especially since the early 2000s. As reported by the *Guardian* in 2001, after several attacks allegedly organized by the SSP, Pakistan's Interior Minister General Moinuddin Haider stated, "Over the years many people have been killed in the name of sects and we cannot allow this to continue."

Pakistan President Pervez Musharraf as well as other officials have also publicly criticized SSP and other similar militant groups, claiming that "terrorist acts of such organizations would not be tolerated."

and its establishment as an independent state still remains in the forefront.

SUMMARY

The Sipah-e-Sahaba is thought to have been most active during the 1990s. It has been suspected of numerous terror operations that were responsible for killing hundreds of people—mainly Shi'ites. Although the group was banned by President Pervez Musharraf in 2002 (and later re-designated in 2003), it is thought to be active.

As of 2005, reports claim that SSP has been involved in joint terrorist operations in Punjab and other parts of Pakistan. Their goal of Sunni liberation from Shi'ite community in Punjab,

SOURCES

Web sites

Guardian Unlimited. "Arrests Rack Up Tension Ahead of Execution." < http://www.guardian.co.uk/elsewhere/ journalist/story/0,7792,443781,00.html > (accessed October 1, 2005).

MIPT Terrorism Knowledge Base. "Group Profile: Sipah-e-Sahaba/Pakistan (SSP)." < http://www.tkb.org/ Group.jsp?groupID = 3870 > (accessed Octo 1, 2005).

South Asian Terrorism Portal. "Sipah-e-Sahaba Pakistan, Terrorist Group of Pakistan." < http://www.satp.org/ satporgtp/countries/pakistan/terroristoutfits/ssp.htm > (accessed October 1, 2005).

Skinheads

LEADER: Jimmy Miller, leader of one of the
Skinhead groups: Hammerskin Nation

YEAR ESTABLISHED OR BECAME ACTIVE: late 1960s
(in Great Britain)

ESTIMATED SIZE: Several thousand

USUAL AREA OF OPERATION: Europe, United
States, Russia, South America, Australia,
New Zealand

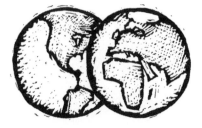

OVERVIEW

The Skinheads is a commonly used term for
members of various groups that reportedly originated in Great Britain in the 1960s. All members of this movement have shaved heads, thus
the name. Unlike other extremist organizations,
the Skinheads are divided into numerous factions and units. As anti-racism experts suggest,
the various groups are decentralized. In other
words, there is no single group controlling or
monitoring all the other groups that are part of
the Skinhead movement.

There are a few factions that are thought to
be more powerful and influential than others.

HISTORY

The Skinhead phenomenon started in Great
Britain, reportedly in the late 1960s. Members
of this group have shaved heads, an attribute
that was responsible for the name of the group.
Published reports and analysts state that all
members of this group were whites who came
from lower-middle-class families in the United
Kingdom. The group was thought to be formed
in protest of the rising numbers of Asian immigrants and homosexuals in the country.

The late 1960s and early 1970s saw a number
of racist attacks against the non-white

Skinheads walk through the gates of the former Nazi concentration camp, Auschwitz, on April 6, 1996. They are part of a demonstration organized by the Polish National Community-Polish National Party to protest a ban on the construction of a shopping center nearby. AP/Wide World Photos

community, especially Asians. Subsequently, a number of smaller groups were formed. Other white youths also formed their own Skinhead units, in different parts of the country. Members of all these groups bore similar styles and physical appearances. However, according to a few experts, many youths during this time merely adopted the appearance of Skinheads, and were known for minor incidents of rioting and hooliganism, for no specific reason.

The hard rock culture, prevalent during the 1960s and 1970s, is also thought to have played a part in the growth of the various Skinhead groups. Members, allegedly, spread their message through rock bands that played "Oi," white power music. These are pro-white songs

that have lyrics supporting racism and violence. Analysts and monitor groups assert that members of such bands also sport head styles and clothing similar to those used by the Skinheads.

In the 1980s, the Skinhead phenomenon started spreading to other countries and continents. Among these were Germany, Italy, Russia, and the United States. The United States reportedly saw a steep rise in the number of Skinheads in the mid 1980s. This was matched by a growing number of racist and violent incidents in the country. Such trends were also reported from the other countries.

At this time, according to published reports, many new groups associating themselves with the Skinheads were also being formed. However, analysts and experts state that although the groups had similar objectives, their tactics and ideology differed significantly. The media reported a number of killings and other crimes allegedly carried out by various Skinhead factions. Consequently, most people termed all Skinhead groups as racist and violent. As thought by hate crime experts, certain Skinheads who did not agree with the violent tactics of other members formed their own organizations.

Most Skinhead groups could now be divided into two major categories: the neo-Nazis, or racist Skinheads, and the non-racist groups such as Skinheads Against Racial Prejudice (SHARPs), formed in New York in 1987; Anti-Racist Action (ARA), formed in 1988; and Red and Anarchist Skinheads (RASH), formed in 1993. These groups believed in anti-racism and were against the use of violence. Groups that were against homosexuality were also thought to be formed during this period.

According to reports, the neo-Nazi groups gained considerable prominence in the 1980s and 1990s. Many such factions claimed responsibilities for a number of hate crimes against African Americans, Asians, gays, and even anti-racist Skinheads. Among these groups, the most prominent sub-groups were the Hammerskins, the Redskins, the Anarchists, and the White Racialists.

Most hate crime analysts and experts assert that Hammerskin Nation, a Hammerskin group formed in Dallas, Texas, in the late 1980s, is the most ruthless, feared, and violent neo-Nazi Skinhead unit in the United States. Its members have reportedly organized and

About 500 neo-Nazis chanting anti-foreigner maxims marched through central Berlin on March 12, 2000, to show support for far-right Austrian leader Joerg Haider on the anniversary of the 1938 Nazi annexation of Austria. AP/Wide World Photos. Reproduced by permission.

carried out various racist operations targeting non-whites in the country. The group is reportedly supported by some racist rock bands as well. The Hammerskin Nation claims to be a parent organization of a number of smaller Hammerskin groups located in the United States, as well as in other countries that have a predominantly white population (Germany, Canada, France, Australia, New Zealand, the Czech Republic, Great Britain, the Netherlands, Poland, Serbia, Slovenia and Russia.) Some of these smaller units are the Confederate Hammerskins, Eastern Hammerskins, the Northern Hammerskins, and the Arizona Hammerskins—all of these were reportedly formed in the late 1980s and

early 1990s. As of 2005, most of these groups are thought to be active and dangerous.

The Hammerskins and other neo-Nazi Skinhead organizations have allegedly organized and carried out operations and rallies in association with other prominent racist groups in the United States. These include the Ku Klux Klan, the Aryan Nations, the White Aryan Resistance (WAR), and the World Church of the Creator. According to published reports, the neo-Nazi Skinheads between 1987 and 2000 killed at least forty-three people in the United States itself. Apart from this, there have been hundreds of other hate crime incidents reported in the United States.

A Moscow police officer escorts demonstrators from the Russian National Union, a skinhead political group, as they march and carry neo-Nazi flags in Moscow, on May 12, 1998.

AP/Wide World Photos

According to reports, since 2001, the number of groups in the United States affiliated with racist Skinheads has been on the rise. Between 2002 and 2003 alone, the number increased from eleven groups to twenty-two groups. Worldwide, there are many more. As of 2005, most reports estimate the total number of Skinhead members within the United States to several thousands. It is thought by analysts that more racist Skinhead groups have also been formed in the recent past. The most prominent of these is the White Power Liberation Front (WPLF).

The various anti-racist Skinhead organizations such as SHARP and RASH have also spread to other countries since early 1990. As of 2005, these organizations reportedly have several members in the United Kingdom, Germany, France, Canada, Australia, and Brazil.

It should be noted that to counter the hate crimes of Skinhead groups in the United States, the U.S. Department of Justice (DoJ) formed, in 1989, the Skinhead Task Force as part of its Civil Rights Division. Ever since, this task force has prosecuted numerous youths (alleged members of Skinhead groups) on charges of murder, beatings, vandalism, and other crimes.

PHILOSOPHY AND TACTICS

The Skinheads are thought to be young white males ranging from 11–25 years. The main ideology of most Skinhead groups is white supremacy. A majority of Skinhead groups are racist and target their operations and activities at minorities, including blacks, Hispanics, Asians, and Jews. Some Skinheads also target homosexuals. Skinheads reportedly follow Nazi ideologies, thus being commonly categorized as neo-Nazi groups.

Analysts speculate that the youths who joined various Skinhead groups in the 1970s and 1980s came from lower income families. The groups at the time also comprised of a number of school dropouts and other youths with seemingly violent behavior.

Since the mid 1990s and early 2000s, although such characteristics hold true for most members of racist Skinhead units, experts suggest that considerable groups have started seeing an influx of older white males (above thirty years of age), and even those who are educated with college degrees. The racist Skinheads claim to be superior and pride themselves in being white. Some analysts even assert that one of the reasons for the formation of such groups is that most Skinheads felt that minorities were given privileged treatment in certain areas.

The physical appearance and attire is similar among most, if not all, Skinhead factions. Skinheads usually have shaved heads, wear suspenders, jackets, and boots, in addition to having heavily tattooed bodies. Much of their clothing consists of numerous emblems, including the swastika and Celtic cross.

The Skinhead groups employ a number of tactics to spread their message. As thought by

LEADERSHIP

JIMMY MILLER

The Skinheads is not a single group. Skinheads consist of numerous factions located around the world. Accordingly, they are not lead by a particular leader or a group of leaders. Many groups, seemingly, do not even have a leader. However, there are some members from racist Skinhead groups (such as the Hammerskin Nation), who are thought by media and analysts, to be more influential and feared than others. Jimmy Miller is one such member.

Miller is reportedly the leader of the Hammerskin Nation since 1996. According to anti-hate crime organizations, Jimmy Miller joined the neo-Nazi group White Aryan Resistance (WAR) at the age of 15. He subsequently joined the Arizona Hammerskins, a unit part of the Hammerskin Nation. Experts state that, as a member of the Arizona Hammerskins, his skills for organizing racist rallies and parades became well known. Subsequently, he became the leader of the Arizona Hammerskins. In the early 1990s, Miller was arrested and convicted of a number of hate crimes. He reportedly spent a few years in prison.

Within a short time of his release from jail (in the mid 1990s), he is thought to have become the leader of Hammerskin Nation. According to published reports, the Hammerskin Nation under Jimmy Miller has hired white youths extensively.

Other known prominent leaders of racist Skinhead groups include Louis Oddo and Sean Tarrant.

hate crime monitor groups and organizations, the most prominent medium Skinheads use is white power music. A large number of racist rock bands are associated with certain Skinhead units. For instance, the Hammerskin Nation allegedly sponsors numerous rock concerts that play white power music. The lyrics of all songs that form a part of such music are known to be violent and racially prejudiced. Monitor groups claim that these kinds of rock concerts are an easy way for Skinheads to attract and employ disgruntled white youths.

Most Skinhead factions are thought to use the Internet extensively for propagating their ideology. The more prominent organizations reportedly have web sites. They are also known to use online message boards and mailing lists (through email) as part of their overall campaign. In fact, according to hate crime experts, Skinheads have been using the Internet even before the World Wide Web was formed. They would use several Usenet Newsgroups (a worldwide network on newsgroups) to proclaim their philosophies. As reports would suggest, as of 2005, bigger organizations such as the Hammerskin Nation have their own publications.

The different mediums are supposedly also used to recruit new members. In addition, monitor groups allege that members are directly recruited from juvenile detention facilities. Hammerskin Nation is one group that allegedly recruits in this manner extensively. However, most Skinhead units are thought to be rather selective in their approach to recruiting. Leaders of some units have stated in public that they prefer "quality over quantity." New recruits reportedly undergo significant trial periods and are employed only if they can "prove" themselves.

Hate crime monitor groups argue that, often in the past, there has been internal fighting within Skinhead units. Members of various racist Skinhead factions are thought to have opposed certain tactics of their leaders. Subsequently, they have either left (forming their own units) or have been kicked out. The monitor groups suggest that such members are termed as "cowards" who have "not lived up to their oath." Such tactics, experts claim, again point to the fact that most Skinhead groups prefer "quality over quantity."

The racist, or neo-Nazi, Skinheads use violent tactics to assert their propaganda. This includes murders, beatings, harassment, and vandalism. Since 1970, racist Skinheads have been charged and/or convicted of several hundred murders and hate crimes around the world. Many of these are violent in nature. Hate crime monitor groups assert that a large number of

KEY EVENTS

Mid 1980s: The first Skinhead groups formed in the United States; a rise in the number of hate crimes reported.

1990s: Hammerskin Nation, a racist Skinhead group consisting of several Hammerskin groups formed in the United States.

---

killings by Skinheads are only because the other person is not white. For instance, in 1991, a few members of the Confederate Hammerskins claimed that after getting drunk they simply felt like "doing a drive by" and "shooting a black person." Many groups, especially the larger ones, have also organized anti-minority rallies and processions. Analysts claim that, in the past, a number of such rallies were held in cooperation with other white supremist organizations such as the Ku Klux Klan and White Aryan Resistance. Skinhead groups are also thought to receive funding from these organizations.

However, not all Skinhead groups are racist. A large number of Skinheads have in the past formed their own organizations that reportedly oppose racist Skinheads. These organizations (such as SHARP, ARA, and RASH) are thought to be anti-racists. According to monitor groups, such anti-racist Skinheads also organize their own rally with the mission of propagating ideologies of anti-racism. Reports suggest that there have been clashes between the anti-racist and neo-Nazi Skinheads. However, none of these are considered significant.

In the past, Skinheads have also reportedly targeted homosexuals. Analysts claim that certain Skinhead factions consider homosexuals to be "equal" with non-whites, even though the homosexual may be white. Alternatively, reports suggest that there are also Gay Skinheads—groups that consist of homosexuals seemingly formed to oppose anti-gay Skinheads.

OTHER PERSPECTIVES

The acts of violence carried out by various racist Skinhead groups have been condemned the world over. Governments, civil rights organizations, hate crime experts, and analysts have been vocal about the tactics and ideology of these groups.

The Anti Defamation League (ADL), one of the prominent organizations fighting hate crimes and hate groups, carried out a survey titled "The Skinhead International: A Worldwide Survey of Neo-Nazi Skinheads," in 1995. The purpose of the survey, according to the ADL, was to assess the threat posed by racist Skinhead groups around the world. After the release of this survey, the then-director of ADL, Abraham H. Foxman, stated "It is unbelievable that three generations after the Holocaust, we still hear the deadly march of Nazi thugs around the world. Cruel history has taught us that we dare not ignore the first sounds of jackboots. The violent and racist Skinhead movement must be countered by government, law enforcement and all decent people."

Foxman continued: "Of great concern is the extent to which disparate neo-Nazi Skinhead groups are globally linked. Through technology and travel, neo-Nazi Skinheads are able to share and promote their ideology beyond borders. They are linked by the travels of popular Skinhead rock bands, the worldwide marketing of Skinhead paraphernalia and music, the sale and trading of publications known as skinzines, and the use of computer bulletin boards and the Internet."

The U.S. Department of Justice that formed a special task force to deal with the crimes carried out by the Skinheads has also made strong statements against the group. In 2002, after eight members of Montana Skinheads were sentenced for civil right crimes, Ralph F. Boyd, Jr., Assistant Attorney General for Civil Rights, stated: "These convictions and sentences send a strong message that acts of violence based on race and national origin have no place in our society. The Justice Department will continue to vigorously pursue and prosecute those who commit crimes because of the color of a person's skin."

During the National Conference of Editorial Writers, held in Washington D.C., in April 2005, U.S. Secretary of State Condoleezza

Rice was asked to comment on an incident that involved members of a certain Skinhead group beating up an African-American diplomat in Ukraine. In response, Rice stated: "It's a very ugly incident. It is not an unknown fact about Eastern Europe, the former Soviet Union, that this kind of behavior by skinheads, particularly against people of color, has been a problem in the past. This is an area of the world I know really well both as a specialist and as a person of color, and so I'm very aware of these problems."

On the other hand, members of most racist Skinhead groups are thought to be highly committed to their cause. Jimmy Matchette, one of the leaders of Hammerskin Nation, in a statement to other members of the group said, "Being a Hammerskin is the distinct feeling of being set apart from the entire planet. And of knowing we will conquer & overcome all obstacles to achieve our goals and accomplish our great work, knowing that if we fail, all is lost forever and the west will perish." He adds: "Even though I am locked down in a maximum security federal penitentiary, I wouldn't [have] traded the opportunity for all the gold in the world. You my true comrades hold all the glory of victory at your fingertips. We really are the most notorious White power Skinhead group in the entire World!"

SUMMARY

The Skinhead movement that reportedly started in the 1960s, in the United Kingdom has, as of 2005, spread to many countries across most continents. Various Skinhead factions have been held responsible for several hate crimes, including murders against minorities, including blacks, Hispanics, and Asians. Members of the racist Skinhead groups are thought to be young white males, mostly from lower income families. Most of these groups are known to borrow their ideology from the Nazis.

Governments around the world have formed task forces to combat the operations of these groups. Alternatively, a number of anti-racist Skinhead groups have also been formed since the late 1980s. These groups aim at opposing their racist counterparts.

SOURCES

Web sites

Anti-Defamation League. "ADL Survey Documents and Analyzes Growing Menace of Neo-Nazi Skinheads and Their International Connections." < http://www.adl.org/ PresRele/NeoSk_82/2477_82.asp > (accessed October 4, 2005).

U.S. Department of Justice. "Eight Montana Skinheads Sentenced for Civil Rights Crimes." < http://www. usdoj.gov/opa/pr/2002/March/02_crt_114.htm > (accessed October 4, 2005).

Anti-Defamation League. "The Hammerskin Nation." < http://www.adl.org/learn/ext_us/Hammerskin.asp/ > (accessed October 4, 2005).

U.S. Department of State. "Remarks Secretary of State Condoleezza Rice To the National Conference of Editorial Writers." < http://www.ncew.org/member_services/State %20Department%20Briefing/C%20Rices%20Comments. pdf > (accessed October 4, 2005).

SEE ALSO

Ku Klux Klan

Aryan Nations

World Church of the Creator

White Aryan Resistance (WAR)

Sons of Liberty

LEADER: Samuel Adams

YEAR ESTABLISHED OR BECAME ACTIVE: 1765

USUAL AREA OF OPERATION: Great Britain's American colonies, especially the cities of Boston, New York, and Providence

OVERVIEW

The Sons of Liberty refers to a terrorist organization as well as to scattered groups and individuals who employed terror during the American Revolution. Some of the groups were known as the Sons of Liberty, while others used such names as Liberty Boys, but all of these loosely organized groups had the same philosophy and used the same tactics to achieve the same end. A Son of Liberty was also a generic term for anyone violently opposed to British rule.

The best-known Sons of Liberty organization began in Boston in 1765 as the Loyal Nine. They used intimidation and violence to protest the Stamp Act that had been imposed on American colonists by the British government. Enormously effective at stopping tax collection by the British, the Sons of Liberty were instrumental in starting the Revolutionary War. When the war officially began in 1776, the various Sons of Liberty disbanded.

HISTORY

The Sons of Liberty were secret colonial societies that emerged in 1765 in response to the widely hated Stamp Act. Great Britain's national debt had doubled in the decade after 1754, partly because of the expenses of supporting troops in

LEADERSHIP

SAMUEL ADAMS

Samuel Adams, one of the most important radicals of the American Revolutionary era, helped start the Sons of Liberty in 1765. Born in Boston on September 27, 1722, he attended Harvard. After the family brewery business failed, Adams became the tax collector of Boston from 1756–1764. When he founded the Sons of Liberty, he became a leading patriot. In the decentralized politics of colonial America, Adams typically collaborated closely with others and deliberately sought to obscure his own political role. It is known that after the Townshend Acts were passed in 1767 in an attempt to generate the revenue never raised by the failed Stamp Act, Adams formed the Non-Importation Association to boycott British goods. He also drafted the Circular Letter that Massachusetts sent to the legislatures of other colonies to drum up opposition to the new taxes.

When the Townshend Acts were repealed in 1770, Adams continued to agitate against the British and in favor of the rights of colonists. After the British East India Company was granted a monopoly on the sale of tea in the colonies, Adams supported the patriots who dumped the tea in Boston Harbor in 1773. When the British responded to this action by closing Boston Harbor, Adams organized a confederation of the colonies. He joined the Continental Congress in 1774, persuaded it to support the Bostonians, and served in that body until 1782. He signed the Declaration of Independence and participated in the convention called to ratify the new Constitution of the United States. Although he approved the Constitution, he believed that it needed a bill of rights to protect the citizens against tyranny. Adams concluded his public life as governor of Massachusetts. He died on October 2, 1803.

---

the colonies in the wake of the French and Indian War (also known as the Seven Years' War). Believing that the colonists should pay more for their protection instead of further burdening the British taxpayer, Britain's Parliament placed a tax on legal documents, customs papers, newspapers, almanacs, college diplomas, and playing cards. The American colonists viewed the Stamp Act as a serious danger to liberty. To them, property was the source of strength for every individual because it provided the freedom to think and act independently. The Stamp Act threatened to destroy liberty because it deprived a person of property. It also insulted the colonists by implying that they were second-class citizens who were not entitled to consent to their own taxation.

The Sons of Liberty, centered in the colonial seaports, protested against the Stamp Act legislation and sought to nullify the tax through terrorism. They took their name from Isaac Barré's speech opposing the act in the British House of Commons. Barré had closed with a reference to the American colonists as "these sons of liberty." The resisters consisted mostly of traders, lawyers, and prosperous artisans. These men violated the Stamp Act by refusing to purchase stamps. They organized the lower classes such as sailors, dockworkers, poor artisans, apprentices, and servants. In every colonial city, mobs instigated by the Sons of Liberty burned stamp collectors in effigy, insulted them on the streets, demolished their offices, and attacked their homes. All stamp agents in the American colonies, with the exception of ones in sparsely settled Georgia, had resigned before the Stamp Act officially became law on November 1, 1765. It was repealed in 1766.

The Sons of Liberty died down after the Stamp Act's repeal, although some leaders such as Silas Downer of Rhode Island tried to keep the organization alive. Downer wanted the Sons of Liberty to stay mobilized for immediate action against any future threats to colonial liberties by the British government. He began a Committee of Correspondence to alert other Sons of Liberty chapters about British misgovernment.

Most of the Sons of Liberty opposed the various revenue acts that the British Parliament passed in the wake of the failure of the Stamp Act, though subsequent resistance was not as violent. Besides opposing the Townshend Acts and the tea tax, the group may have played a role in the Boston Massacre. The Sons of Liberty were strongest in Boston, and British soldiers in the city were constantly cursed by citizens and frequently pelted with stones, dirt, and

KEY EVENTS

1765: The Sons of Liberty formed to protest against the Stamp Act.

1765: On August 14, the Boston chapter of the Sons of Liberty attacked property belonging to stamp collector Andrew Oliver and prompted his resignation.

1765: On August 26, a Boston mob that included Sons of Liberty members destroyed the homes of Stamp Act supporters and Massachusetts Lieutenant Governor Thomas Hutchinson.

1765–1766: The New York chapter of the Sons of Liberty joined in periodic rioting in New York City and sacked a newly opened theater.

1766: Great Britain repealed the Stamp Act.

1776: Sons of Liberty disbanded.

---

excrement. On March 5, 1770, a crowd surrounded ten British soldiers, who then panicked and fired into the mob, killing five men. Samuel Adams, the Boston Sons of Liberty leader, termed the incident a "massacre," and publicized the incident throughout the colonies. Whether or not the Sons of Liberty triggered the incident, Adams certainly took advantage of it.

The term Sons of Liberty also applied to popular leaders. The first street radical identified as a Son of Liberty was Scottish immigrant Alexander McDougall. He did not take a stand on the Stamp Act and did not join the original organized Sons of Liberty. In 1769, McDougall published a broadside, *To the Betrayed Inhabitants of the City and Colony of New York*, under the pseudonym, "A Son of Liberty." He charged the provincial assembly with sacrificing New Yorkers' rights for partisan advantage. When he was revealed as the author, the assembly imprisoned McDougall for a total of 162 days, although he was never convicted of an actual crime. Thereafter, McDougall was very

active in the politics of resistance and revolution. He helped form a New York City Sons of Liberty branch for direct resistance to the Tea Act at the end of 1773. The city's initial tea ship turned around at Sandy Hook after a committee, including McDougall, warned its captain of the consequences should he enter the harbor. When a second vessel did try to bring in taxed tea in April 1774, the Sons of Liberty dumped the cargo into the sea.

When the American Revolution officially began in 1776, the Sons of Liberty still in existence disbanded. They had achieved their aim of promoting resistance to British rule.

PHILOSOPHY AND TACTICS

The Sons of Liberty were responsible for many acts of mob violence. They typically tarred and feathered tax collectors. Contrary to popular conceptions and British propaganda, being tarred and feathered did not kill anyone. A tax collector would be roused out of his home, painted with warm tar, and then covered with chicken feathers. The stamp agent was not stripped of his clothing and the tar was never hot enough to burn his skin. However, he was covered with chicken feathers, which, unlike duck or goose down, are scratchy and uncomfortable. The tax collector was then placed on a wooden rail and carried out of town. As he was carried, the Sons of Liberty and other townspeople would shout abuse at him. The process was frightening and humiliating. The taxman would be left with bruises, scratches, ruined clothes, as well as emotional trauma.

The Sons of Liberty never deliberately killed anyone. They sought to scare tax collectors into quitting their job. In this, they succeeded. One of the best known tax collectors in the colonies was Andrew Oliver of Boston. On August 14, 1765, the Loyal Nine, the Boston Sons of Liberty, staged a public drama beneath the Liberty Tree on Boston Neck, a strip of land that connected the city to the mainland. The play illustrated the impact of the Stamp Act on the daily lives of Bostonians. The show ended, and the men gathered under the leadership of Ebenezer Macintosh, a shoemaker who was not a member of the Loyal Nine. The crowd then attacked property belonging to Oliver, who resigned his post as a direct result.

The various Sons of Liberty organizations disagreed about the use of violence, as seen in events of 1765. Lieutenant Governor Thomas Hutchinson of Massachusetts, brother-in-law of Oliver, privately opposed the Stamp Act, but publicly supported it because he felt an obligation to do so as a British Crown official. A mob that likely included Sons of Liberty members attacked Hutchinson's home on August 26, 1765. Hutchinson and his family barely escaped the mob's wrath, but saw their home and possessions completely destroyed. The Boston Sons of Liberty subsequently disavowed the destruction of Hutchinson's home. The lack of respect for private property evident in the attack shocked the many men of property and standing who belonged to the Sons of Liberty. Afterwards, they took care to keep crowds under tighter control. However, the New York Sons of Liberty approved of such rioting and participated in the riots that swept New York City from October 1765 to May 1766.

OTHER PERSPECTIVES

Relatively few colonists chastised the Sons of Liberty for fighting against the Stamp Act in 1765. An anonymous New York writer summed up the view of many colonists when he or she placed a short advertisement of thanks in *Rivington's New-York Gazetteer* of November 11, 1774. This notice complimented the New Yorkers for persevering in the cause of liberty and acting quickly to oppose the "dark, and futile, scheme" of Great Britain.

However, those who were loyal to the British Crown did speak up in defense of the governors of the colonies who were appointed by the English. When Massachusetts Lieutenant Governor Hutchinson came under attack from an anonymous Son of Liberty with a poisonous pen, a friend defended him in Boston's *The Censor* on November 23, 1771. The friend declared that the Sons acted to increase their own importance and took pleasure in "producing disorder in the machine of government."

They suffered from "unbridled ambition" and colonists had "something to lose, but nothing to gain, by uniting in the cry of the seditious ... How despicable is the swagger of a presumptuous demagogue!"

SUMMARY

The historical Sons of Liberty group was an extremist group that was essential to the success of the American Revolution. They turned a debate about Great Britain's right to tax the American colonists into outright resistance to British control over its colonies. They brought a range of people into street politics, giving them both direction and discipline. When the various Sons of Liberty disbanded with the start of the American Revolution, it is possible that some of the members continued to harass British loyalists. The better known Sons of Liberty, such as Samuel Adams, joined the new government of the United States. The Sons of Liberty provide an example of how some extremist groups are often hailed as revolutionary heroes as members help transform the social-political order through what are considered extremist measures.

SOURCES

Books

Alexander, John K. *Samuel Adams: America's Revolutionary Politician.* Lanham, MD: Rowman & Littlefield, 2002.

Copeland, David A. *Debating the Issues in Colonial Newspapers: Primary Documents on Events of the Period.* Westport, CT: Greenwood Press, 2000.

Dawson, Henry B. *The Sons of Liberty in New York.* New York: Arno Press and the New York Times, 1969.

Hoerder, Dirk. *Crowd Action in Revolutionary Massachusetts, 1765–1780.* New York: Academic Press, 1977.

Maier, Pauline. *From Resistance to Revolution: Colonial Radicals and the Development of American Opposition to Britain, 1765–1776.* New York: Knopf, 1972.

Stop Huntingdon Animal Cruelty (SHAC)

OVERVIEW

Stop Huntingdon Animal Cruelty (SHAC) is an animal rights campaign group formed in November 1999 with the aim of closing down Europe's largest animal-testing laboratory, Huntingdon Life Sciences (HLS), near Cambridge, England. SHAC's controversial campaign has seen a variety of tactics used and it has been widely imitated by other animal liberation campaigns throughout the world. Despite claims that it uses and supports only nonviolent methods, SHAC has been tainted by frequent accusations of extremism.

LEADER: Greg Avery

YEAR ESTABLISHED OR BECAME ACTIVE: 1999

USUAL AREA OF OPERATION: Britain, the United States, Portugal, the Czech Republic, Australia, New Zealand, Switzerland, Italy, Germany, the Netherlands, Ireland

HISTORY

Huntingdon Life Sciences (HLS) is Europe's largest animal-testing laboratory. It is situated near Cambridge, in the heart of Britain's chemical and pharmaceuticals research industry. HLS tests products such as pharmaceuticals, pesticides, domestic cleaners, and food additives on around 70,000 animals every year, including primates, rats, rabbits, cats, and dogs. HLS also has an operation in the United States, in New Jersey. The importance of laboratories like HLS to the British pharmaceutical industry alone is enormous: in 2003, pharmaceuticals were worth a net total of £3.6 billion to the British economy.

An animal rights advocate protests against vivisection outside a Huntingdon Life Sciences laboratory in Eye, Suffolk, United Kingdom.

Philippe Hays / Peter Arnold, Inc.

KEY EVENTS

1997: Screening of "A Dog's Life" on television 4, showing abuses of animals at HLS.

1999: Greg Avery and Heather James form SHAC with the intention of closing down HLS within three years.

2000: SHAC obtains and publishes a list of HLS shareholders. Many withdraw their stake in the company, including the Labour Party.

2001: Royal Bank of Scotland revokes HLS's banking facilities after a campaign of protests at its branches. The Bank of England steps into its place.

2001: Brian Cass, HLS Managing Director, is beaten by three men.

2001: Avery jailed for six months for "conspiracy to cause a public nuisance."

2005: The British government proposes to establish crimes of "acts preparatory to terrorism" and "indirect incitement to terrorism." The laws could be available to pursue SHAC.

Britain, nevertheless, boasts a long-standing tradition as a nation of animal lovers. As far back as 1863, British women in Florence are commonly credited to leading the first organized protest against vivisection, and the Cruelty to Animals Act was passed as early as 1876. Animal testing in the U.K. peaked in the 1980s, but as a result of the development of alternatives and public pressure, has been on the decline since. A European Directive on Scientific Procedures on Animals in 1986 brought in more stringent regulation on testing laboratories.

Nevertheless, work by organizations such as People for the Ethical Treatment of Animals (PETA) and the more radical Animal Liberation Front (ALF) that uncovered abuses in testing laboratories continued to prompt periodic outrage even as the number of animals being tested declined. One such investigation, "A Dog's Life," screened by Channel 4 TV in 1997 showed in graphic detail abuses carried out at Huntingdon Life Sciences. One particularly unseemly piece of footage showed a laboratory worker punching a beagle in its face.

Unsurprisingly, the film evoked outrage among Britain's animal lovers and helped increase the ranks of protestors. Following the film, three of the laboratory technicians filmed were suspended from HLS and the two men shown hitting and shaking the dogs were later arrested and prosecuted under the Animals Act of 1911. HLS also saw its work drop by a third in the flurry of bad publicity that followed.

It nevertheless took more than two years for animal rights protestors to turn their ire on HLS in earnest, when, in November 1999, a campaign entitled Stop Huntingdon Animal Cruelty was born. Founded by Greg Avery and his first wife

An animal rights protestor is pinned down by police on October 29, 2001, in front of Stephens Group Inc., in Little Rock, Arkansas. The company later announced in 2002 that it was selling its interest in Huntingdon Life Sciences, a controversial medical testing group. AP/Wide World Photos.

Heather James, they both were hardened animal rights campaigners, who had served prison terms for their work. SHAC's foundation coincided with the successful conclusion of a long-running operation against an Oxfordshire cat farm that bred cats for laboratory testing. This huge campaign, which often teetered over into overt violence and intimidation, involved not just protests outside the farm's gates, but the targeting of its employees and their homes, as well as suppliers and businesses even only tentatively associated with the farm. During the two years of these targeted protests, police arrested 350 people involved with the campaign and twenty-one were jailed.

When the full attention of Britain's animal rights movement was turned to HLS, SHAC soon came to include many of these facets in its campaign against the laboratory—despite its repeated insistence that it only used nonviolent means.

Setting itself the goal to close down HLS within three years, SHAC waged an extraordinary war of protest, propaganda, and intimidation.

Employees were followed home, shouted at, spat on, and threatened. On one occasion, ten employees had their cars firebombed during the middle of the night. Posters were plastered around the neighborhoods featuring employees and personal details divulged. HLS's Managing Director, Brian Cass, was set upon outside his home by three masked men wielding pickaxe handles and seriously injured; HLS's Marketing Director, Andrew Gay, was attacked on his doorstep in front of his three-year-old daughter with a chemical spray that temporarily blinded him.

LEADERSHIP

GREG AVERY

Greg Avery founded SHAC in November 1999 with his first wife Heather James, when he was thirty-one. Along with his second wife, Natasha Avery, he acts as spokesperson for SHAC. For legal reasons, SHAC is not a registered organization nor does it have a formal leadership, but Avery is its most famous and infamous protagonist.

A committed animal liberation activist, for twenty years Avery has been at the forefront of direct action campaigns against hunting, the fur industry, and latterly, vivisection. He likens himself to Nelson Mandela on account of his strong beliefs, commitment to resistance, and the fact that he has been imprisoned for his beliefs, and claims that he has devoted his life to saving 2.7 million animals that die every year in scientific research laboratories. On several occasions, Avery has been jailed because of his actions: He spent eighteen months on remand after police found 100 incendiary devices in the Birmingham house he was staying at with another activist, but was later acquitted; in 1998, he served six months for affray; and was jailed for "conspiracy to cause a public nuisance" in 2000 and in 2001.

Nevertheless, he claims to not condone or agree with violence, though conversely asserts that a "realistic" attitude has to be taken and that companies have "made things worse for themselves" by taking legal measures to try and stop protests. Speaking to the *Guardian* in 2004, he said, "That's why people are turning up at 2am or 3am and throwing bricks through windows, throwing paint over cars."

SHAC also turned its attention to other companies and investors that had a connection with HLS. Many, including the embarrassed Labour Party (which held shares in HLS through its pension fund), moved their money out to avoid further harassment. Institutional investors, including Shroeders, also withdrew.

Not surprisingly, the value of the company plummeted: being valued at £360 million in 1990, its market valuation fell to £5 million in 2001. HLS was also dropped from the New York Stock Exchange. When protests directed at its bankers, the Royal Bank of Scotland, led to its account being closed, the Bank of England—at the request of the British government—was obliged to step in and provide banking facilities. This was an unprecedented step.

SHAC remained unrepentant, despite its continued avowal of nonviolent means. Greg Avery said, "They've made their beds and now it's time to lie in them, and they're all whining." Nevertheless, SHAC inferred that the attacks were carried out by Animal Liberation Front (ALF) activists, with which it said it had no connection. This was a curious claim given that ALF news was carried on the SHAC web site and several of its senior members gave unequivocal support to the ALF. Indeed, Avery, together with his first wife and SHAC co-founder, Heather James, and his second wife and SHAC spokesperson, Natasha Avery, were jailed in December 2001 for criminal incitement.

As SHAC's three-year target for the closure of HLS neared, criticism about its methods mounted. One monitor of extremist groups likened its "frankly terroristic tactics" to those of "anti abortion extremists," while others seized upon its policy of publishing names and addresses of employees.

SHAC, for its part, maintained that it did not condone illegal activities and only published names and addresses so that people could protest peacefully and legally. However, testifying before a House of Commons Committee in March 2003, Dr. Ian Gibson, MP, quoted from a SHAC internal document on tactics: "A simple tactic has been adopted recently. Pick your target. Throw a couple of rape alarms in their roof guttering or thick hedgerow, and leg it ... Being kept awake at night hardly puts you in a good mood at work or with your family ... Another idea is to set off extra loud fireworks from a safe distance that will wake up the HLS scum and everybody else for miles around ... From the comfort of your own home, you can swamp all these bastards with send no money offers. They cause huge inconvenience and can give them a bad credit rating. Order them taxis, pizzas, curries, etc, the possibilities are endless. Above all, stay free and safe, and don't get caught. The more preparation you do the better... Think, think, think. Don't lick stamps, use gloves when pasting stuff... No idle talk in pubs. Burn your shoes and clothes after your night of action."

"Such activities may sound like a bit of fun or undergraduate play," said Dr Gibson. "But they are serious. They intimidate people, and they can lead to people with baseball bats getting stuck into managing directors, and so on."

Yet, SHAC had seen its campaign make huge inroads. By the middle of 2002, it claimed it had effectively wrecked the viability of HLS and that only the intervention of the British government and HLS's directors was keeping the company afloat. "Out of all the tens of thousands of banks and financial institutions world wide," it boasted on its web site, "Huntingdon cannot find just one to lend them money."

Moreover, it had seen its campaign internationalized with SHAC groups forming in eleven different countries outside the U.K. The highly effective tactics adopted by its protestors had also been copied in other campaigns, most notoriously in the U.K. against Darley Oaks farm in Staffordshire. The farm, which bred guinea pigs, suffered an appalling catalogue of intimidation and violence before closing in July 2005. This included the desecration of a grave of a distant relation of one of the farm's owners.

To help counteract SHAC and its various imitators, the British government introduced a raft of legislation designed to limit the rights of protestors and to increase police powers when dealing with threatening behavior. Judges and magistrates have also begun to treat each incident as part of a wider campaign of harassment, rather than as isolated breaches of public order. Nevertheless, SHAC apparently remains undeterred and has hinted darkly that its campaign may yet reach another level. Quoting John F. Kennedy, Kevin Jonas, leader of SHAC-USA has said: "If you make peaceful revolution impossible, you make violent revolution inevitable."

PHILOSOPHY AND TACTICS

Although animal welfare has a long tradition in Britain and elsewhere, SHAC gives no philosophical basis for its campaign. While its stated aim is to close Huntingdon Life Sciences down,

they provide no explanation on their web site as to why animal cruelty is wrong, nor what rights they should expect. This is entirely assumed.

Instead, its campaign "... is all about action. Words and tears mean nothing to the animals trapped in their cages inside HLS waiting to die," says its web site. "They deserve nothing less than our utmost commitment to take action every day to close down the lab that holds them captive and slowly kills them."

This action takes on many forms. Most visibly, it comes in the way of demonstrations, organized at short notice and by cell phone technology to avoid police detection. In reality, SHAC's direct action manifests itself in other, more insidious, ways. Despite its repeated claim that it does not condone violence, its publication of the names and addresses of HLS employees or investors so that its supporters might "protest" often sees its campaign teeter over this boundary. Protest tactics have included physical assaults on targets; intimidation (e.g., the photographing of a target's family such as dropping the children at school; phone calls in the middle of the night; fake bombs delivered; and so on); vandalism (e.g., the firebombing of cars; paint stripper poured on cars; red paint thrown on a target's home); and other disruptive tactics (e.g., ordering unwanted pizzas or taxis to a target's address; diverting mail.).

The SHAC web site reveals that it is explicitly clear about where it stands on the issue of violence against targets. Each page carries the disclaimer: "Please note that SHAC does not encourage illegal activities." Yet, much of its content is incendiary. As well as the publication of targets and their names and addresses, it contains much invective that may incite. A typical passage reads: "We know that violence is happening inside HLS on a daily basis as hundreds of beautiful animals are terrified and abused at the hands of their tormentors. It is violent to force a tube down animals' throats or jab needles into their veins and pour toxic poisons into their systems, it is depraved to poison animals and dispassionately make notes as they suffer and die, it is violent to kill and dismember puppies while other dogs sit waiting their turn, trembling in fear, it is abusive to punch dogs in the face while other people sit around laughing—these people are monsters and they are the violent ones, not us. SHAC does not support violence of any kind."

PRIMARY SOURCE

Threats.com: Radical Animal Rights Activists Set the Stage for a First Amendment Showdown

In 2002, Kevin Jonas, president of the extremist animal rights group Stop Huntingdon Animal Cruelty USA (SHAC USA), told the Intelligence Report, "[W]hen push comes to shove, we're ready to push, kick, shove, bite, do whatever to win."

But after a series of SHAC USA-sponsored harassment campaigns resulted in substantial property destruction and threats of personal injury, the federal government is now doing the shoving.

On May 27, 2004, SHAC USA, Jonas and six other members of the radical group were indicted for engaging in a conspiracy to violate the Animal Enterprise Protection Act [18 U.S.C. § 43] and other federal laws. The "SHAC Seven" are accused of using the Internet to terrorize the employees and business associates of Huntingdon Life Sciences (HLS), a pharmaceutical research company that uses animals to test drugs and chemicals.

As the SHAC Seven head to court, so too does the First Amendment. The ultimate question: Does the First Amendment shield individuals from criminal liability for Web site postings that encourage third parties to engage in campaigns of harassment?

SHAC ATTACK

Over the past four years, SHAC USA activists have harnessed the power of the Internet to harass Huntingdon's employees and its business associates across the country. But the online campaigns have made life difficult for SHAC USA as well. The group faces civil actions in at least two states and the federal criminal indictment naming the SHAC Seven.

A New Jersey state court has enjoined SHAC USA, its officers and "all persons acting in concert with it" from engaging in harassing tactics against HLS business associate TEVA Pharmaceuticals and one of its employees. Meanwhile, thousands of miles away, the California Court of Appeals has permitted a suit against SHAC USA for trespass and harassment to proceed to trial. [See Huntingdon Life Sciences, Inc, v. Stop Huntingdon Animal Cruelty USA (Cal. Ct. App. June 1, 2006).] SHAC USA's criminal prosecution in federal court only adds to the radical group's mounting legal woes.

According to the federal government's lengthy criminal indictment, the SHAC USA Web site encouraged members and sympathizers to engage in "direct action"—activities that "operate outside the confines of the legal system." SHAC USA suggested "top 20 terror tactics," including threatening to injure or kill a person's family members, assaulting a person by spraying cleaning fluid in their eyes, vandalizing or flooding a person's home, firebombing a person's car, breaking the windows of a person's home while family members are inside, and sending e-mail "bombs" to crash computers.

Despite its continued disavowal of violent means, SHAC is not a registered organization, instead a loose affiliation of individuals—essentially so it cannot be prosecuted or sued. This has also made it difficult for HLS to obtain injunctions to prevent protests outside its gates. Nevertheless, SHAC retains many of the characteristics of a corporate or charitable body and maintains a web site, mailing address, telephone information line, mailing list, and bank account. It is also split regionally across the U.K., with campaigns against suppliers and associated businesses conducted on a local level.

SHAC has international offshoots in eleven other countries too, most notably the United States, but also in more unexpected places such as Portugal and the Czech Republic. There, they carry out demonstrations against supplier companies and other affiliates. Recent targets have included UPS in Italy, Glaxo Smithkline in the United States, and Hotelplan in Switzerland.

And for SHAC USA activists' convenience, the Web site provided nifty features called "Target of the Week" and "Ongoing Targets." With a click of a mouse, Web site visitors could find addresses for HLS employees and executives, telephone and fax numbers and, in some instances, the names and ages of the targets' children and where they attended school.

TRUE THREATS AND THE INTERNET

The SHAC Seven certainly have a First Amendment right to be free from government censorship of their political viewpoints. But this right is not absolute. [See Virginia v. Black, 538 u.s. 343, 358 (2003); R.A.V. v. City of St. Paul, 505 u.s. 377, 382 (1992).] If the words on the SHAC USA Web site constitute "true threats," as the government argues, the SHAC Seven will find no First Amendment refuge from criminal prosecution. [See Watts v. United States, 394 u.s. 705, 705 (1964).]

The best-known case to address threats over the Internet is *Planned Parenthood of Columbia/ Willamette, Inc. v. Am. Coalition of Life Activists*, 290 f.3d 1058 (9th Cir. 2002) (en banc). In 1994, the American Coalition of Life Activists (ACLA), an anti-abortion extremist group, released a "Deadly Dozen" poster, designed in a wanted-style format with "guilty" captioned at the top and a list of names and addresses of thirteen abortion providers.

In 1997, a pro-life activist affiliated with ACLA gave a much longer list of more than 200 "abortionists" to anti-abortion hardliner Neal Horsley, who then posted them on a section of his Christian Gallery Web site labeled "Nuremberg Files." Horsley highlighted the names of those doctors and others murdered by anti-abortion terrorists by striking through their names on the list; those who were merely wounded had their names grayed out [Planned Parenthood, 290 f.3d at 1065.]

Several abortion providers listed on the posters and the Nuremburg Files site sued ACLA and twelve anti-abortion activists. A jury later found that the defendants violated the Freedom of Access to Clinic Entrances Act, awarding the plaintiffs $107 million in actual and punitive damages. The judge enjoined the posters and restricted the content on the Web site. [See Planned Parenthood, 290 f.3d at 1058.]

On appeal, the defendants argued that the content of the posters and Web site were protected speech under the First Amendment. But the full Ninth Circuit Court of Appeals upheld ACLA's liability, finding that the content on the posters and Web site constituted an unprotected true threat.

The court defined a true threat as a statement made when a "reasonable person would foresee that the statement would be interpreted by those to whom the maker communicates the

(continued on next page)

The stated aim is to stop these companies from having any involvement with HLS, but sometimes the connections are looser. Hotelplan, for instance, sells package vacations to the island of Mauritius. Mauritius is the largest supplier of primates to HLS. Therefore, the entire country and anyone who does business with it is a target. "Our policy," a SHAC spokesperson told Associated Press in February 2001, "is that anybody with any connection at all with Huntingdon Life Sciences is a target."

OTHER PERSPECTIVES

"The cowardice is breathtaking. At the first whiff of gunpowder the captains of industry, the big banks, stock brokers, financiers, pharmaceutical companies and even cancer research charities turned tail and fled," wrote the social commentator, Polly Toynbee, in the *Guardian*, in January 2001 following the Royal Bank of Scotland's withdrawal of HLS's banking facilities. "There are precious few famous scientists and doctors

PRIMARY SOURCE

Threats.com: Radical Animal Rights Activists Set the Stage for a First Amendment Showdown (continued)

statement as a serious expression of intent to harm." [See Planned Parenthood, 290 f.3d at 1074, 1088.] The test is an objective one; the defendant does not have to actually intend to, or be able to, carry out the threat. [Id. at 1076.] In the Planned Parenthood case, the Ninth Circuit found that it was reasonable for ACLA members to foresee that the named abortion providers would interpret the posters and Web site postings as a serious expression of ACLA members' intent to harm them.

In a more recent case, a panel of the Ninth Circuit took a more restrictive view of the true threats doctrine when dealing with criminal prosecutions. [See United States v. Cassel, 2005 Wl 1217387 (9th Cir. May 24, 2005).] In Cassel, the defendant was convicted of interfering with a federal land sale after he threatened to burn down any home built on federal property adjacent to his home. The court held that in order to prove that a true threat is unprotected by the First Amendment, the prosecution must show that the defendant subjectively intended the speech as a threat, something not required by the Planned Parenthood case.

Whether the SHAC Seven face the objective true threats test from Planned Parenthood or the more restrictive subjective test from Cassel, it is likely that the Web postings will be deemed true threats. In the California civil case against the SHAC Seven for harassment of an HLS employee, the state Court of Appeals found that the Web postings, as described in the complaint, "would [likely] intimidate [the plaintiff] and cause her to fear [Jonas, the SHAC USA president] and other persons affiliated with SHAC USA ... and indeed [Jonas] knew as much and that was the desired result." [See Huntingdon Life Sciences, Inc, v. Stop Huntingdon Animal Cruelty USA, at 27-28.]

In the federal criminal case, SHAC USA's "targets" suffered real-life, off-line consequences as a result of the online threats. Shortly after the Web site postings, the identified targets' homes, cars and personal property were vandalized—rocks thrown through windows, the exterior of homes spray-painted with slogans, cars and boats vandalized, and, in one instance, a target's car overturned in his driveway. HLS and its business associates' facilities also experienced vandalism and smoke bombs, while online attacks shut down computer systems. To make matters worse, the SHAC USA Web site reported many of these harassing acts after they occurred, fueling the fire.

By the time the criminal trial begins, the jury is likely to find it hard to believe that the SHAC Seven didn't intend to intimidate their targets.

Catherine E. Smith is an assistant professor at the University of Denver's Sturm College of Law and teaches a course on extremism and the law.

Catherine E. Smith

Source: Southern Poverty Law Center, 2005

---

putting their heads above the parapet either. The vigilante terror campaign of the animal rights lunatics has all but silenced the voice of reason. Huntingdon Life Sciences is being hung out to dry, taking the strain for the whole world of scientific research—or indeed sanity in general: a fish and chip shop got a nail bomb this week from animal madmen—a 'legitimate target' because fishing is cruel… If everyone runs away, the animal terrorists will win. What matters now is gaining wide public support for essential animal research. This craziness can only be seen off by a public hardening of attitudes which requires vigorous advocacy from cancer charities, scientists, politicians, doctors, nurses, teachers and all who are alive because of research."

"Anti-vivisection rallies in the early 1990s attracted thousands, but many have since been put off by the violence and fanaticism of the hard core," reported the *Economist* in April 2004. "The remaining militants have now figured out that outright violence loses sympathy and gets them arrested. So no real bombs have been sent to researchers for a while, though pretend ones abound. Physical assaults are now rare, while threats of thuggery are more common. The key to survival is to be extreme enough to attract money from the small number of supporters who want violence, while staying anonymous enough to evade the police." Despite the switch in tactics from overt violence to a more intimidating brand, it is still "bad news for drugs research in Britain, a business that turns over £9m ($16m) a day."

achieved so far—we have decimated their shareholder base, forced their bank to forclose (sic.) on their 22 million pound loan, persuaded any other commercial bank worldwide from giving them a bank account, and virtually every financial institution worldwide from dealing with them, forced them off the London and New York stock exchanges, crashed their share price and made the words Huntingdon Life Sciences synonymous with animal cruelty worldwide."

SUMMARY

Despite SHAC's founding aim in November 1999 that it would enforce the closure of HLS within three years, it has failed to achieve this objective, although the company remains financially wounded by what has become an international campaign of direct action, harassment, and intimidation. Moreover, SHAC's relative successes in highlighting what it terms "abuses" and targeting of loosely associated individuals and businesses have served as an inspiration for other animal liberation protestors. Although it has not effected the closure of HLS, SHAC remain convinced that it will achieve its objective and is aware of the catalog of victories its campaign has already achieved: "HLS will close," states its web site. "It is just a question of when, and only a matter of time. Look at what we have

SOURCES

Books

Best, Steven (ed.). *Terrorists or Freedom Fighters?: Reflections on the Liberation of Animals.* New York: Lantern Books, 2002.

Leahy, Michael. *Against Liberation: Putting Animals in Perspective.* Oxford: Routledge, 1993.

Web sites

SHAC. "News Index." < http://www.shac.net/ > (accessed October 22, 2005).

SEE ALSO

People for the Ethical Treatment of Animals (PETA)

Animal Liberation Front (ALF)

Stormfront.org

LEADER: Don Black

USUAL AREA OF OPERATION: United States; worldwide

OVERVIEW

Stormfront.org is a white nationalist web site that has been online since 1995. It was created, and is managed, by former Ku Klux Klan leader, Don Black. The site is intended both as a way of informing and supporting current white nationalists and as a way of attracting and recruiting new white nationalists.

The site describes itself as a resource for the courageous men and women fighting to preserve the white Western culture and as a forum for planning strategies and forming groups to ensure victory.

HISTORY

The Stormfront web site was created by white nationalist and former leader of the Ku Klux Klan, Don Black. It has been online since 1995.

The site was created mainly as a discussion board for white nationalists. The forums remain the most significant portion of the web site and are a way for white nationalists to interact, communicate, gain information, and learn about becoming activists. Since starting in 1995, the forums have grown in membership. As of 2005, the forums had over 50,000 members from around the world.

Don Black, Ku Klux Klan grand wizard of Birmingham, Alabama, is taken to a police van in New Orleans on May 14, 1981. He is arraigned on charges of conspiring with nine others to overthrow the government of Dominica in the Caribbean. AP/Wide World Photos

KEY EVENTS

1975: Don Black joined the Ku Klux Klan.

1978: Black became the leader, or Grand Wizard, of the Ku Klux Klan.

1981: Black was arrested for his part in a plan involving the invasion of Dominica. Black was sentenced to three years in prison and released in 1984.

1987: Black resigned from the KKK.

1995: Don Black created the Stormfront.org web site.

Another way the white nationalist message is disseminated is via articles on the site. The site initially started with several articles from well-known white nationalists, including William Pierce and David Duke. These essays communicated white nationalist propaganda designed to influence people to accept a white nationalist view and reject the mainstream view. As the site continued, the text library has expanded, steadily adding more essays. These essays promote anti-Semitism, white supremacy, and racism, while renouncing homosexuality and illegal immigration.

The site also contains a women's section with information intended to interest women and attract them to the white nationalist cause. Another section of the web site that has been added is the "white singles" section. This section allows members seeking a partner to post personal ads and find a partner with the same white nationalist views.

As the Stormfront web site expanded, it also added a section for kids. This section contains puzzles, music, and articles designed to attract children to the white nationalist cause.

The web site has also developed by adding links to various other web sites promoting the same cause, with some of these also owned by Don Black. Two of the web sites owned by Don Black are the White Nationalist News Agency (NNA), which posts articles from the mainstream news accompanied by white nationalist commentary on them, and The Truth at Last, which is the web site for the newspaper of the same name that claims to report the news suppressed by the daily press. Stormfront also links to various other sites, including White Pride World Wide and Blitzcast.

PHILOSOPHY AND TACTICS

In an article by the BBC titled *Battling Online Hate*, Black is described as stating that the Stormfront web site has been invaluable in recruiting new people to the white nationalist cause.

A large portion of the forums is made up of general topics, including theology, poetry, business and finance, health and fitness, homemaking, music and entertainment, and youth. These various sections allow people to communicate about issues that interest them and interact with other members who share the same issues or

PRIMARY SOURCE

Electronic Storm: Stormfront Grows a Thriving Neo-Nazi Community

On most days, the man once labeled a "near genius" in a *Time* magazine article spends the bulk of his time in an office of the Mandeville, La., home of infamous white supremacist David Duke.

There, Jamie Kelso whips across Duke's hardwood floors on a wheeled office chair as he attends to his work: monitoring the burgeoning community of the racist Stormfront Web site on one of six different computers.

To the thousands of white supremacists who regularly visit Stormfront and its forum, Kelso is best known by his e-moniker, "Charles A Lindbergh." He signs off all his posts with a quote from Lindbergh, a well-known racist and anti-Semite: "We can have peace and security only as long as we band together to preserve that most priceless possession, our inheritance of European blood." "I admire the aviator so much, " Kelso says.

The aviator, were he still alive, might well admire Kelso. As Stormfront celebrates its 10th birthday—the first major hate site on the Internet, it was created by former Alabama Klan leader Don Black in 1995—Kelso has much to be proud of. In the three years he's been a senior moderator of the site, it has grown from fewer than 10,000 registered users to, as of mid-June, an astounding 52,566. And while many thousands of that ever-growing total probably haven't visited in years, independent Web monitors recently ranked Stormfront the 338th largest electronic forum on the Internet, putting it easily into the top 1% of all sites on the World Wide Web.

Black and Kelso have created something more than just another hate site that draws people for a few months, then fades for lack of interest. Using everything from good manners to "white scholarships" to such catchy gimmicks as highlighting its members' birthdays, these two men have built something that very few people on the entire Internet have—a genuine and very large cyber-community. That they did it at a time when major neo-Nazi groups are on the decline is merely icing.

"Without a doubt," Bob DeMarais, a former staff member of the neo-Nazi National Alliance, wrote recently, "Stormfront is the most powerful active influence in the White Nationalist movement."

Want to find the latest headlines on black-on-white crime? Go to Stormfront. New developments in the National Alliance's leadership woes? Go to Stormfront. Details of yet another nefarious Jewish conspiracy? Go to Stormfront.

Stormfront's recent growth spurt is only the beginning, Kelso says. He and Black share a larger goal, one that their friend Duke also tried with a fair measure of success—establishing real legitimacy in the realm of public opinion.

FADE TO BLACK

It began with Don Black.

Going back to high school, Black had always been one of the more enthusiastic concerns. When it is noted that Don Black describes Stormfront as appealing to whites who feel discriminated against and who feel like they have been isolated by society, the general topics allowing people to connect with others over shared interests is important because it helps to create a feeling of shared community and belongingness. In an article by the Anti-Defamation League, Don Black is described referring to the Stormfront forums as a place for people who are attracted to his ideas to talk and form an online community. These forum topics also tend to have a white nationalist slant, but even without any particular white nationalist information being included, taking part in any discussion is likely to further the white nationalist cause simply because it makes people feel like part of the community and keeps them feeling positive about the cause.

proponents of white power. One of his first forays into the organized movement was in the 1970s, when he volunteered for the late white supremacist J.B. Stoner's unsuccessful run for governor of Georgia.

That was until Stoner's campaign manager, Jerry Ray, the brother of Martin Luther King Jr. assassin James Earl Ray, shot him in the chest. The shooting apparently stemmed from accusations that Black had broken into Stoner's office to steal a mailing list for the National Socialist White People's Party.

After recovering, Black went on to join the Knights of the Ku Klux Klan, the group headed by Duke in the 1970s. Working on Duke's unsuccessful campaign for Louisiana state senate, Black won Duke's trust, moving up to become his mentor's right-hand man. When Duke left the group amid allegations that he'd tried to sell its membership list to another Klan group for $35,000, Black took over.

But Black quickly got into trouble himself. In 1981, he and nine other white supremacists were arrested as they prepared to board a yacht with which they intended to invade the tiny Caribbean island of Dominica, oust its black-run government, and transform it into a "white state."

Black's resulting three-year prison sentence was time well spent. He took classes in computer programming that would provide the basis for his future.

Not long after his release, Black launched an abysmally unsuccessful campaign for a U.S. Senate seat from Alabama. He wound up marrying Duke's ex-wife, Chloe, and moving to West Palm Beach, Fla. Once there, he began dabbling with his computer, eventually setting up a dial-up bulletin board service for the radical right. By March 1995, that service evolved into Stormfront, the Net's best-known hate site.

Black saw clearly that with this new technology, white supremacists might finally bypass the mainstream media and political apparatus, getting their message out to people who otherwise would never hear it—people who now could listen in the privacy of their own homes without fear of embarrassment or reproach. "The potential of the Net for organizations and movements such as ours is enormous," Black told the *Philadelphia Inquirer* in 1996. "We're reaching tens of thousands of people who never before had access to our point of view."

Being the first of its kind helped Stormfront win enormous publicity. Black and his site were written up in newspapers around the country and the world, and he frequently appeared on major network news shows like ABC's "Nightline," where, clad in suit and tie, he talked politely about allowing people access to information not filtered by the "media monopoly." Though he undoubtedly turned off many viewers, each major TV appearance led to a spike in visitors to Stormfront.

T. K. Kim

Source: Southern Poverty Law Center, 2005

The web site forums also show a focus on promoting the white nationalist cause worldwide. This includes having separate threads for the following countries or regions: Europe; Great Britain; Canada; Australia and New Zealand, Latin America; the Netherlands; Sweden, Norway, Denmark, and Finland; Serbia; Russia; and South Africa. This feature allows individuals worldwide to discuss issues and communicate with other members in their local areas. This assists in creating a sense of unity and community, while making the Stormfront site seem relevant to all users regardless of their nation.

In a report presented at a meeting of the UN in 2000, international expert David Rosenthal referred to web sites such as Stormfront as being able to exist and flourish in the United States because the First Amendment protects people's right to free speech. Rosenthal described the

LEADERSHIP

DON BLACK

Don Black is the owner of the Stormfront.org web site and the leader of the Stormfront organization. Black first became involved in the white nationalist movement when he joined the White Youth Alliance at age 15.

In 1975, Black joined the Ku Klux Klan (KKK) and became the KKK's organizer for Alabama. In 1978, the leader of the KKK, David Duke, resigned and Black became the national director of the KKK. This position is referred to within the KKK as the Grand Wizard.

In 1981, Black was arrested while preparing to board a boat stocked with weapons. The weapons were intended to be used to invade Dominica. Black was sentenced to three years in prison and released in 1984.

In 1987, Black resigned from the KKK, stating that the group had a reputation for random violence and could never be a viable political movement. Black's plan was to promote the white nationalist cause via mainstream methods, with the intention of increasing the legitimacy of the cause and attracting new members.

In 1995, Black created the Stormfront web site. Black remains an active member on the Stormfront forums, providing information to members and engaging in discussions with members. Black has described the success of the Stormfront web site as a victory for the white nationalist movement.

United States as a safe haven for racists wanting to spread their message worldwide. Creator Don Black has described Stormfront as an effective method of reaching white people in America and throughout the world who feel they are being discriminated against. This suggests that Black has recognized that the Internet offers the possibility of reaching a global audience of current white nationalists, as well as individuals who can be drawn into the cause.

The Stormfront forums also have a section titled "Activism." This section has seven categories, all aimed at helping members carry out actions to assist the cause. There is an events section, where members can list news of white nationalist demonstrations, rallies, conferences, and media interviews. A strategy and tactics section is also included, allowing members to share information. In the local and regional section, individuals can leave their contact information so that others in the area can contact them and form an action group. There is also a section specifically for webmasters, with webmasters exchanging ideas and information on how to promote white nationalism via the Internet. In the legal issues section, individuals are informed about legal matters that might impact activists. The final section is called Pioneer Little Europe (PLE). A PLE is a term used to refer to a white community where whites live in close proximity to businesses supporting the white nationalist cause. This section of the forums invites individuals to state their interest in being part of a PLE and to describe the role they would play in the PLE. In total, this section of the forums invites individuals to become activists, gives current activists the opportunity to gain information, and allows for activists to unite and act together.

The web site also shows evidence of efforts to attract certain groups of individuals to the cause. This includes women, with a section of the web site dedicated to topics aimed at women. This also includes children, with a section of the web site aimed at promoting the white nationalist message to an audience of children. This is done with activities likely to interest young people, including puzzles and games. This section of the web site is also claimed to be created by Black's young son, Derek. It is unknown whether Derek actually provides the content, but the section is written as if coming from him. The kid's sections also presents the white nationalist message via references that children can relate to, such as Pokemon. In addition, the kid's section provides a history of the white race from a white nationalist view. This material is designed to educate children on this view before they learn the mainstream view of white history.

Overall, the web site is largely interactive, inviting members to be part of the community, rather than to just read information. This matches with the web site's purpose of supporting and encouraging white individuals who feel discriminated against and isolated in society. If white individuals feel that they do not have a voice and have been ignored by society, the web site gives them an opportunity to be part of something greater. This strategy is considered an effective method for attracting new members, regardless of whether they specifically accept a white nationalist view of society.

OTHER PERSPECTIVES

The Anti-Defamation League (ADL) describes the Stormfront web site as a supermarket of online hatred, stocking its shelves with anti-Semitism and racism. While noting that Don Black does not consider himself a hatemonger, the ADL describes Black's version of white pride as involving demeaning and demonizing Jews and non-whites.

In a book on cybercrime, authors Brian Loader and Douglas Thomas describe the threat of web sites such as Stormfront as being substantial. The authors describe how web sites are used to promote neo-Nazi ideas, including that messages can reach an unlimited number of possible supporters, that messages can be presented without any form of approval, and that members can easily share information, including across national borders. The authors also note that groups have used the medium of the Internet specifically to attract new members to the group. The Internet is an effective medium for achieving this goal because anyone who accesses the Internet is able to find the web site, including individuals finding it by accident and without an initial awareness of the cause of the web site. This allows individuals like Don Black to promote their message to a larger audience than ever before. It is also noted that web sites such as Stormfront are specifically designed to appeal to the needs of individuals likely to become members. This means that potential members do not necessarily need to have white nationalist ideals to be attracted to the organization and its cause. Instead, they may be unemployed white people frustrated with the lack of employment. If the Stormfront web site then presents information describing how undocumented immigrants have stolen jobs and suggests that it is the white person who is being discriminated against, the person who was already disgruntled may accept this solution and become a supporter of white nationalism.

One significant supporter of the Stormfront web site is David Duke. David Duke is a white supremacist, was Don Black's mentor, and is the leader of the European-American Unity and Rights Organization (EURO). Duke's strategy has been to mainstream the cause of white nationalists, including disguising the ideas of white nationalists. The Stormfront web site fits into Duke's strategy, with Duke supporting the web site and considering it to be an effective tool for educating people.

SUMMARY

Don Black has remained committed to the Stormfront web site since 1995 and has continually expanded it. There is no suggestion that this trend will not continue, with Stormfront expected to expand both in the offerings of its site and in the number of members.

SOURCES

Books

Loader, B., and D. Thomas. *Cybercrime: Law, Security And Privacy in the Information Age.* New York: Routledge, 2000.

Rosenthal, David. *Racism on the Internet.* Geneva: World Conference Against Racism, Racial Discrimination, Xenophobia, and Related Intolerance, 2000.

Web sites

Anti-Defamation League. "Don Black: White Pride World Wide." < http://www.adl.org/poisoning_web/black.asp > (accessed October 2, 2005).

BBC News. "Battling Online Hate." < http://news.bbc.co.uk/1/hi/world/americas/1516271.stm > (accessed October 2, 2005).

BBC News. "Cyber-racists 'Safe in US.'" < http://news.bbc.co.uk/1/hi/world/americas/645262.stm > (accessed October 2, 2005).

SEE ALSO

Ku Klux Klan

Students Islamic Movement of India (SIMI)

LEADER: Dr. Shahid Badar Falah
YEAR ESTABLISHED OR BECAME ACTIVE: 1977
USUAL AREA OF OPERATION: India

OVERVIEW

The Student Islamic Movement of India (SIMI) is an Islamist extremist group based in India. It was reportedly formed in the late 1970s, and a few years from its inception, the group evolved into an extremist group promoting its objectives through violent measures.

The SIMI is banned by the government of India due to its alleged part in several terrorist operations carried out in the country. Throughout its history, Indian government and security officials have associated the group with much larger terrorist groups operating out of Pakistan and Bangladesh.

HISTORY

The Student Islamic Movement of India (SIMI) was reportedly formed by a group of students in Aligarh, Uttar Pradesh (an eastern state in India) on April 25, 1977. At the time of its formation, the group was headed by Dr. Mohammad Ahmadullah Siddiqi, who had previously served as a professor of Journalism and Public Relations at the Western Illinois University in Macomb, Illinois. At the time, Dr. Siddiqi claimed that SIMI was formed with a purpose of propagating Islam in India and other countries through educational means.

LEADERSHIP

DR. SHAHID BADAR FALAH

Dr. Shahid Badar Falah reportedly served as the President of SIMI from the late 1980s until 2001. Falah was arrested by the Indian police in 2001 on a number of charges. According to analysts, Falah was instrumental in disseminating extremist ideologies among the members of SIMI. He is thought to have close links with several militant groups in Pakistan.

During the 1990s and early 2000s, the Indian government accused Dr. Falah of being the mastermind of numerous bombings that were carried out by group members during this period. Falah is thought to be a staunch Muslim with anti-Hindu and anti-Western philosophies.

In the 1980s, the group is known to have organized peaceful rallies and other educational programs to serve its objectives. Anti-terrorism experts state that by the late 1980s and early 1990s, the group started transforming into a more radical and aggressive organization. This, as thought by analysts, was due to the increasing influence of various militant groups based in Pakistan. By the 1990s, the Indian government started accusing SIMI members of anti-Hindu tactics. During this time, the group was suspected to have a part in many terrorist activities in the states of Punjab and Jammu & Kashmir.

In the 1990s, the group reportedly formed a schoolchildren's wing known as the *Shaheen* Force. This wing is thought to be targeting Muslim schoolchildren across India with the aim of promoting SIMI's aggressive ideologies. According to published reports, the terrorist operations attributed to SIMI increased towards the late 1990s. In 2000, the Indian government held members of SIMI responsible for a number of bombings in the state of Uttar Pradesh. These bombings reportedly killed more than fifty civilians. Additional bombings took place in 2001.

In the same year, government and police officials alleged that SIMI members had played a major role in inciting communal riots between Hindus and Muslims in the western state of Maharashtra. Subsequently, in September 2001, the Indian government banned the Students Islamic Movement of India under a Prevention of Terrorism Act (POTA).

Anti-terrorism experts and government officials claim that members of SIMI carried out terrorist activities even after the ban. Police authorities alleged SIMI to be involved in the bombings in Mumbai, in 2003. Uttar Pradesh police arrested some members of SIMI in 2005 on the charge of carrying out the foiled attack on the Ramjanmbhoomi-Babri Mosque complex in Ayodhya (Uttar Pradesh).

Since the ban, many members of SIMI have been reportedly arrested. As thought by analysts, the group as of 2005 comprises a few members. However, it is still considered by most to be a major security threat to various Indian states.

PHILOSOPHY AND TACTICS

The Students Islamic Movement of India, as claimed by its leader Dr. Siddiqi, was formed with the purpose of promoting Islam in India and other countries through educational means. The group was reportedly known to have organized various special programs in universities for this purpose.

However, according to published reports, the group's ideologies and tactics changed drastically throughout the 1980s. By the early 1990s, the group advocated *jihad* (a term for holy war against those who do not believe in Islamist fundamentalism). Its philosophies were allegedly anti-Hindu as well as anti-West. Self-proclamations by leaders of SIMI stated that their purpose was to establish Islamic rule in India and other non-Muslim countries. Anti-terrorism experts suggest that SIMI ideologies opposed secularism and democracy and propagated the idea of a single Islam nation. The group also disagreed with Western tactics claiming them to be "suppressors" of Muslims.

KEY EVENTS

1977: The Students Islamic Movement of India is formed on April 25, under the leadership of Dr. Mohammad Ahmadullah Siddiqi.

1980s: SIMI organizes numerous rallies and educational programs to promote Islam in India.

2001: SIMI is suspected to be involved in a number of bombings that kills many civilians in Uttar Pradesh.

2001: On September 27, the government of India bans SIMI as a terrorist organization under its Prevention of Terrorism Act.

2001: On September 28, the day following the terrorist ban, New Delhi police arrest Dr. Shahid Badar Falah, the National President of SIMI.

SIMI allegedly had several associations with militant groups based in Pakistan. Indian government and intelligence officials claim that the group received funding as well as arms training from banned outfits such as the Hizb-ul-Mujahideen and the Lashkar-e-Tayyiba. Intelligence officials also claim that Pakistan's intelligence agency, the ISI, has often provided such support to group members.

During the 1990s and early 2000s, the group reportedly carried out various terrorist operations to promote its philosophies. This included a number of bombings and killings in Uttar Pradesh, Punjab, Jammu & Kashmir, and other states of India. Hundreds of civilians were killed as a result of such bombings. The Indian government also accused SIMI members of inciting communal tension between Hindus and Muslims in many parts of India.

SIMI was also thought to promote its philosophies through many in-house publications and posters. These publications reportedly endorsed anti-Hindu policies and were thought to be one of the group's key strategies in promoting Hindu-Muslim riots in India.

After the September 11, 2001, attacks in the United States, SIMI leaders publicly made anti-American statements claiming that the entire attack was a conspiracy of Israel. Proclamations also stated that Osama bin Laden was a "true Muslim" fighting for the cause of followers of Islam around the world.

OTHER PERSPECTIVES

The Indian government has often criticized the tactics of SIMI and accused group members of committing innumerable terrorist acts. In 2001, after imposing a ban on SIMI, the government issued a statement saying that they had "enough evidence" indicating an association between the group and the al-Qaeda.

The Union Home Secretary of India at the time, Kamal Pande, while justifying the ban, stated: "The banning of SIMI was not a knee-jerk reaction. We had been watching the activities of the organization closely for the past several months." He continued by saying that considerable evidence showed that the objective of the group was "governing of human life on the basis of Quran, propagation of Islam, 'jehad.' (religious war) for the cause of Islam and destruction of nationalism and establishment of Islamic rule or caliphate."

SUMMARY

As of 2005, SIMI is thought to have a few members. Many of its leaders and others were arrested by the Indian police between 2001 (after the ban on the group) and 2003. However, analysts state that the group is still associated with militant organizations based in Pakistan and elsewhere. The Indian government also suspects SIMI has been involved in some terrorist acts since the ban.

SOURCES

Web sites

MIPT Terrorism Knowledge Base. "Students Islamic Movement of India (SIMI)." < http://www.tkb.org/

Group.jsp?groupID=4255> (accessed October 21, 2005).

South Asian Terrorism Portal. "Students Islamic Movement of India (SIMI)." <http://www.satp.org/satporgtp/countries/india/terroristoutfits/simi.htm> (accessed October 21, 2005).

South Asia Analysis Group. "Students Islamic Movement of India (SIMI)." <http://www.saag.org/papers9/paper825.html> (accessed October 21, 2005).

The Tribune. "Organisation Had Links with Laden." <http://www.tribuneindia.com/2001/20010929/main2.htm> (accessed October 21, 2005).

SEE ALSO

Lashkar-e-Tayyiba (Army of the Righteous)

Taliban

LEADER: Mullah Mohammed Omar
YEAR ESTABLISHED OR BECAME ACTIVE: 1994
USUAL AREA OF OPERATION: Afghanistan

OVERVIEW

The Taliban, an Islamic and Pashtun movement within Afghanistan, consolidated as a political and military force in 1994 and ruled Afghanistan from 1996 until early 2002. Noted for its record of extreme control over women and a strict interpretation of *shari'a* (Islamic law), the Taliban also openly invited acknowledged terrorists such as Osama bin Laden to reside within Afghanistan. The group lost control of Afghanistan in early 2002 after U.S. military forces invaded Afghanistan in search of bin Laden, the leader of al-Qaeda, the group that claimed responsibility for the September 11, 2001, attacks in New York, Washington D.C., and Pennsylvania.

HISTORY

In 1979, the USSR invaded Afghanistan as part of a policy of shoring up socialist/communist states. Afghanistan's turmoil after a 1978 military coup was of great concern, both politically and strategically, to the USSR. In 1980, U.S. President Jimmy Carter offered military and economic aid to Afghanistan's neighbor, Pakistan, in exchange for access to Afghanistan. The United States provided support to the *mujahedin* (fighters), Islamic Afghans who opposed the Soviet

Afghan warlord Gulbuddin Hekmatyar speaks with Ustad Abdul Rab Rasul Sayaf, leader of Itehade Islami Afghanistan, in Peshawar, Pakistan. The January 17, 1987, meeting they are attending led to the rejection of Kabul's offers of coalition government and ceasefire. Dimitri Kochko/AFP/Getty Images

invasion. Osama bin Laden, a Saudi with extensive financial resources, helped to funnel U.S. aid to the mujahedin via his organization, *Maktab al-Khadamat* (Office of Services). Pakistan, Saudi Arabia, and China all provided support to the mujahedin as well.

Most of the leaders of the mujahedin were local warlords. When the Soviets withdrew from Afghanistan in 1989, the country erupted into chaos as these warlords made power grabs for national control. Two groups emerged from the mujahedin: the Afghan Northern Alliance and the Taliban. By the early 1990s, the Taliban was emerging as the strongest group, helping economically by ending warlord extortion, and politically by providing stability within Afghanistan. In 1994, the group was asked by Pakistan to protect trade convoys, and by 1996, the Taliban controlled most of Afghanistan.

The Taliban established an Islamic state, ruled by shari'a. Women lost many rights within civil society, such as the right to work, vote, or be in public without a male relative; access to education was curtailed for women as well. While international outcry against these policies was widespread, it was the Taliban's approach to terrorists that drew the most international attention.

In 1996, the Taliban invited Osama bin Laden, now the leader of the terrorist group, al-Qaeda, to reside in Afghanistan. On August 7, 1998, U.S. embassies in Tanzania and Kenya were bombed by al-Qaeda, and the United States demanded that Afghanistan hand over Osama bin Laden for trial. When the Taliban held their own trial and declared Osama bin Laden to be "without sin," the United States bombed alleged al-Qaeda sites in Afghanistan.

After al-Qaeda claimed responsibility for the September 11, 2001, attacks in New York City, Washington, D.C., and southwestern Pennsylvania, the United States once again demanded that the Taliban turn over bin Laden. In October 2001, the United States

PRIMARY SOURCE

U.S. Official Praises Afghan Elections

The U.S. national security adviser on Sunday praised Afghanistan's legislative elections and said they sent neighboring countries a message that "democracy and freedom are possible today."

As officials began releasing partial preliminary results from the vote a week ago, Stephen Hadley urged winning and losing candidates to accept the outcome peacefully in a country still struggling to emerge from decades of bloodshed.

Standing beside the chairman of the U.N.-Afghan body that ran the country's first parliamentary elections since 1969, Hadley praised organizers for handling logistical and security challenges.

He called the poll "a tribute to the courage of the Afghan people" and a "remarkable success story."

When the outcome is final, "there will be a burden on the candidates—both those who won and those who lost—to accept the results peacefully and to show responsible behavior," Hadley said.

U.S. and other Western officials hope the elections will help Afghanistan move toward stability after decades of war. But there is concern that its legacy of violence could persist, deepening divisions that have worsened past conflicts.

More than 5,600 candidates contested 249 seats in the Wolesi Jirga, or lower house of Parliament, and 420 seats in provincial councils.

There has been some concern over a rule that says a winning candidate who dies is replaced by the next-highest vote-getter.

The voting was the last formal step on a path to democracy laid out after U.S.-led forces ousted the Taliban in 2001, when the hardline Islamic group's leaders refused to hand over al-Qaeda leader Osama bin laden after the Sept. 11 terror attacks.

Hadley was upbeat about the estimated turnout of 6.8 million, or about 55%—though it was a significant drop from the 70% for U.S.-backed Hamid Karzai's election as president last October.

Afghans "turned out in impressive numbers to vote," said Hadley, who later met with Karzai.

He said the election was "terribly important, not just for the future of Afghanistan, but also for the region as a whole. Because it says to every country in this region that democracy and freedom are possible today."

Afghanistan borders Pakistan, U.S. foe Iran and Central Asian countries with authoritarian governments—including Uzbekistan, whose leadership has been at odds with Washington after a bloody government crackdown on protesters in May.

The U.N.-Afghan electoral board began releasing partial provisional results Sunday, and chief electoral officer Peter Erben said the count was nearly finished in some of Afghanistan's 34 provinces, but only about 10% complete in others. The board hopes to issue complete provisional results by Oct. 4 and certified results by Oct. 22, after a complaint period.

Source: New York Times 2005

A portrait on an Indonesian truck in 2004 lauds Osama bin Laden and the Taliban as heroes. © *Abbas | Magnum Photos*

invaded Afghanistan and overthrew the Taliban within three months. Taliban insurgents remain in Afghanistan to this day, though Afghan voters elected Hamid Karzai to the presidency and he was sworn in on December 7, 2004.

PHILOSOPHY AND TACTICS

Driven largely by religion, the Taliban used Islamic law as a foundation for government. The Taliban gained popularity for its ability to establish control over chaotic regions of Afghanistan, for its Pashtun roots, and for weeding out corruption throughout Afghanistan.

Restrictions on the role of women, access to media, and Western ideas were part of the Taliban's philosophy. In ruling as an Islamic state, the reach of the government stretched into nearly every facet of civil society. Most Taliban members were educated in *madrassas* (religious schools) in Pakistan, and the combination of

these members and the mujahedin from the conflict with the USSR comprised the government.

Standard tactics used to gain power included alliances with Pakistan to act as a security force for trade convoys, and paying off warlords in return for control of areas. By 2001, the Taliban controlled 90–95% of Afghanistan, although it was recognized as the legitimate government only by three nations: United Arab Emirates, Saudi Arabia, and Pakistan.

The Taliban increased its visibility and stature among Islamic extremists and terrorist groups by defying Western opinion and offering safe haven to Osama bin Laden. Since being ousted from power in early 2002, the Taliban has claimed responsibility for the deaths of non-governmental organization workers, security force officers, foreign military officers, Afghan civilians, and government officials. In addition, the group's targets include transportation facilities, religious buildings, private citizens and property, and police officers. In 2004, President Hamid Karzai experienced an

Taliban supporters protest at a parade in New York City celebrating Pakistani Independence Day.
© *Thomas Dworzak | Magnum Photos*

assassination attempt at the hands of a Taliban member; police officers shot and killed the would-be assassin.

OTHER PERSPECTIVES

In a November 22, 2001, interview with BBC News correspondent Marc George, Taliban fighters give their viewpoint. One states that, "If the conflict is a civil conflict in Afghanistan, I will stop fighting and go home. But if the Americans continue bombing in Afghanistan the jihad (holy war) will continue and I will have carry on." Many fighters were ordered to join the jihad by local mullahs, or religious leaders. Rather than seeing the conflict in terms of terrorism, their viewpoint is one of religion; the invasion by the United States was viewed as a clash between the "infidel" United States and the holiness of Islam.

SUMMARY

The Taliban is still in operation in small pockets throughout Afghanistan as a loose rebel organization; new recruits feed the group. Their leader, Mullah Mohammed Omar, remains in control of much of the group, and 2005 was considered the bloodiest year since 2001 in terms of the insurgency. While Afghanistan is under an elected government's control along with U.S. support, the Taliban remains a solid force among extremist Muslims who disagree with U.S. intervention.

SOURCES

Books

Marsden, Peter. *The Taliban: War and Religion in Afghanistan.* London: Zed Books, 2002.

Rashid, Ahmed. *Taliban: Militant Islam, Oil and Fundamentalism in Central Asia.* New Haven: Yale University Press, 2001.

KEY EVENTS

1979: Soviet Union invades Afghanistan.

1980: The United States, among other countries, offers support to the freedom fighters (mujahedin) to fight against the Soviets.

1989: The Soviet Union troops withdraw.

1994: The Taliban appointed by the Pakistan government to protect trade envoys.

1996: The Taliban gains control of Kabul. They remove the Soviet-controlled government and create an Islamic state. They offer Osama bin Laden refuge in Afghanistan as the Taliban acquires control over large sections of the country.

1999: The UN imposes an embargo on the Taliban for the Taliban's refusal to hand over Osama bin Laden. The United States wants bin Laden for his role in the 1994 World Trade Center attack and the 1998 bombings of embassies in Africa.

2001: Following the September 11 attacks in the United States, Afghans flee Kabul, fearing U.S. retaliation. The United States demands that the Taliban hand over bin Laden.

2001: The United States begins bombings and ground operations in Afghanistan in an armed conflict.

2001: The Taliban loses control of various cities. Hamid Karzai is chosen as the interim leader.

2002: The Taliban officially loses power. Top Taliban officials surrender at Kandahar, and other Taliban fighters considered prisoners of war are taken to Guantanamo Bay in Cuba, under U.S. control.

2002: A Taliban activist attempts to assassinate Hamid Karzai.

2004: Taliban insurgents are suspected in a string of attacks on international aid workers.

LEADERSHIP

MULLAH MOHAMMED OMAR

Known as "Commander of the Faithful," Mullah Mohammed Omar founded the Taliban and presided over its control of Afghanistan from 1996 through early 2002. The son of a poor farmer, Omar is reportedly married to one of Osama bin Laden's daughters. Although Omar is not a cleric, he is a *mullah* (a spiritual leader), and allegedly created the Taliban as a religious and political response to Afghanistan's chaos during Soviet rule. Omar is elusive, and few photographs of him exist; according to rumor, he lost an eye while fighting against the Soviets, and his eyelid is sown shut. He fled Afghanistan sometime in late December 2001 and remains in hiding.

Web sites

BBCNews.com. "Profile: Mullah Mohammed Omar." < http://news.bbc.co.uk/2/hi/south_asia/1550419.stm > (accessed October 16, 2005).

BBCNews.com. "Meeting Taleban's Foreign Fighters." < http://news.bbc.co.uk/1/hi/world/south_asia/1669996.stm > (accessed October 16, 2005).

Time.com. "Time.com Primer: The Taliban and Afghanistan." < http://www.time.com/time/nation/article/0,8599,175372,00.html > (accessed October 16, 2005).

Audio and Visual Media

National Public Radio . "Afghanistan Takes Steps to Reconcile with Taliban Fighters." < http://www.npr.org/templates/story/story.php?storyId = 4469449 > (accessed October 16, 2005).

SEE ALSO

Al-Qaeda

Tamil Tigers

ALTERNATE NAME: Liberation Tigers of Tiger Eelam

LEADER: Veluppillai Prabhakaran Osman

YEAR ESTABLISHED OR BECAME ACTIVE: 1976

ESTIMATED SIZE: 8,000

USUAL AREA OF OPERATION: Sri Lanka, particularly the state of Tamil Eelam in the northeast of the country

A U.S. TERRORIST EXCLUSION LIST DESIGNEE: The U.S. Department of State declared the Tamil Tigers to be a terrorist organization in 1997

OVERVIEW

The name Tamil Tigers is used by over twenty-five different Tamil guerrilla organizations fighting the Sinhalese-dominated government of Sri Lanka. The Tigers use terrorism to push for the creation of an independent Tamil state.

The best-known and most influential of these terrorist groups is the Liberation Tigers of Tiger Eelam (LTTE). An outgrowth of the Tamil United Liberation Front and originally known as the Tamil New Tigers, LTTE formed on May 5, 1976. By April 1989, the LTTE and the remnants of three other Tiger organizations had formed an umbrella group, the Eelam National Liberation Front.

HISTORY

The Tamil Tigers are the product of ethnic conflict in Sri Lanka, the country known as Ceylon under British rule. The Sinhalese were the first Indians to arrive in Sri Lanka, landing in the sixth century. The Tamils seized power on the tropical island when they arrived from southern India in the early sixteenth century. The Portuguese then subdued the Tamils before losing control of Sri Lanka to the Dutch. The British held the territory from 1802–1948.

Masked women suicide squad members of the Liberation of Tamil Tigers " Black Tigers," left, arrive to celebrate "Heroes Day" in Sri Lanka, Nov. 27, 2002. AP/Wide World Photos. Reproduced by permission.

During British rule, the Tamils held great standing in Ceylon society.

When Sri Lanka gained independence on February 4, 1948, the majority (74% in 2002) Sinhalese and the minority (18% in 2002) Tamils began to drift apart. The Sinhalese were Buddhist while the Tamils were Hindu. The rift started initially because of economic competition. The break increased because of the rise of Sinhalese–Buddhist nationalism, in which the Sinhalese argued that the future of Sri Lanka depended on the unity of the government with Buddhism and the Sinhala language. They saw the Tamils as only invaders from South India. Successive Sri Lankan governments gave in to the sentiments of the nationalists and approved legislation that the Tamils viewed as discriminatory. In 1956, Sri Lanka passed legislation to disenfranchise the Tamils of Indian origin and to make Sinhala the sole official language. As a result, the Tamils were excluded from receiving the best education and denied the opportunity to hold government jobs.

By the mid 1970s, the Tamils began to push for a separate state in the areas of Sri Lanka in which they are a majority. When the Sri Lankan government standardized education, thereby making Sinhala compulsory in all schools, the demand to separate became stronger. In 1972, the Tamil United Liberation Front (TULF) was begun as an advocacy group for the Tamil people in Sri Lanka. A group of young, radical TULF members under the leadership of Velluppilai Prabhakaran created the Tamil New Tigers (TNT) in the belief that only armed struggle could free the Tamils from oppressive Sinhalese rule. In 1975, Prabhakaran committed the group's first act of violence by killing the mayor of Jaffna. Prabhakaran turned TNT into LTTE in 1976.

The Tamil Tigers began fighting in earnest in 1983 for a separate homeland for the island's Tamil minority. In the first LTTE attack, an ambush of a Sri Lankan army patrol in Jaffna killed 13 soldiers and sparked anti-Tamil riots in Colombo by Sinhalese mobs that butchered

Tamil Tigers march on the road to Thopigila Camp, the main military camp of the splinter group of the Liberation Tigers of Tamil Eelam (LTTE). AP/Wide World Photos. Reproduced by permission.

about 2,000 people. On May 14, 1985, the Tamil Tigers gunned down 146 Sinhalese civilians at Anurahhapura. Violence between the Tamil Tigers and the Sri Lankan forces killed nearly 65,000 people in a country of nineteen million before both sides agreed to a 2002 ceasefire negotiated by Norway. However, talks on a permanent settlement broke down in 2003. At that time, Tamil Tigers controlled key portions of northern Sri Lanka, including Trincomalee Harbor, a port on the Bay of Bengal that is seen as a key military staging point in Southeast Asia.

The devastation of Sri Lanka by the tsunami of 2004 offered the hope that the calamity might force cooperation between the government and the LTTE that would also revive the peace process. Instead, the Tigers initially fought the government and themselves over the distribution system for sharing international relief supplies. They then took advantage of the situation to establish themselves as the administrators of Tamil. They also enhanced their military capacity by expanding their navy and adding a

fledgling air force. Sri Lankan officials hesitated to collaborate with the Tigers to distribute aid because doing so would give the Tigers some international recognition. The government argued that allowing the Tigers to control aid supplies would also recognize them as the Tamils' sole representatives and give them a say in the areas that they did not control, such as Muslim settlements in Tamil. On June 24, 2005, the Sri Lankan government signed a deal, the Post-Tsunami Operational Management Structure (P-TOMS), sharing relief aid with the Tamil Tigers. Furious Muslims, Buddhists, and officials of parties that had exited the government upon the signing of the accord then went to the courts and blocked implementation of P-TOMS.

Perhaps because of their strengthened position as a result of the political aftereffects of the tsunami, the Tamil Tigers elected to end the ceasefire. By killing Sri Lankan Foreign Minister and Tamil Lakshman Kadirgamar, with sniper fire as he came out of the swimming pool at his private residence on August 12, 2005,

LEADERSHIP

VELUPPILLAI PRABHAKARAN

Veluppillai Prabhakaran is the head of the LTTE. He was born in 1954 in Valvettiturai as the youngest of four children of a government clerk and his wife. The family belonged to the Karaiyar fishing and pearl-diving caste. The Karaiyars, with a reputation for toughness and a spirit of enterprise, often served as soldiers of the Tamil kings. It is this Karaiyar background that raises doubts about Prabhakaran's leadership abilities among high-caste supporters of the Tamil Tigers, although they recognize his military prowess.

Typical of most LTTE leaders, Prabhakaran lacks a university education. He attended school for seven years before leaving to join Tamil Ilainar Peravai (TIP), the youth league of the Tamil United Liberation Front, in 1972. When the TIP leader was arrested by Sri Lanka government forces and gave away the names of top TIP officials under torture, Prabhakaran was elected leader because he was unknown to the security forces. He briefly fled to India before returning to found the Tamil New Tigers in 1972. This group became the LTTE in 1976. A traditional Tamil as well as one of the world's most prolific terrorists, Prabhakaran prohibits alcohol, tobacco, stimulants, and extramarital or premarital affairs among the Tamil Tigers.

Married in 1984 and with two children, he is known as a charismatic man. He has been in hiding for years, in part because he is widely suspected of arranging the murder of Indian Prime Minister Rajiv Gandhi in revenge after Gandhi sent Indian troops to the Tamil-dominated sections of Sri Lanka in accordance with India's 1987 agreement with the island nation. In 2002, Prabhararan made a rare public appearance at a tightly guarded press conference to announce his support for peace and a negotiated settlement. At the same time, he began making efforts to mend fences with the Muslims of Tamil.

---

the Tamil Tigers seriously jeopardized the peace agreement. The murder of the minister, a key participant in the peace process, enraged much of non-Tamil Sri Lanka. Most of the fifteen political parties represented in the Sri Lankan government as well as Buddhist priests and ordinary Sri Lankans condemned the Tamil Tigers for the assassination.

PHILOSOPHY AND TACTICS

The Tamil Tigers aim to create a separate state for Sri Lanka's Tamil people out of the nation's northern and eastern provinces. In these provinces, the Tamil people are the majority. In 1976, LTTE began a guerrilla terrorist movement to target the "enemies" of a Tamil state. These enemies include members of rival Tamil radical groups, ex-Tamil Tigers, Sri Lankan government officials, Muslims, Buddhists, and Indians. The tactics of the Tamil Tigers include assassinations and bombings as well as armed assaults on enemy forces. In their most successful military attack, the Tamil Tigers overran a Sri Lankan army camp in the northeastern town of Mullativu on July 18, 1996, and killed 1,200 troops.

The Tamil Tigers have denied using child soldiers, but human rights organizations, including Human Rights Watch and UNICEF, claim that LTTE has filled out its ranks by kidnapping an estimated 1,200 children and forcing them to fight. Families that refuse to hand over children are reportedly subjected to coercive methods, including threats against the child's parents, the burning of houses, and abduction. Children who refuse to fight are beaten and threatened. LTTE's reliance on child soldiers has badly stained its international reputation and prompted the European Union to block Tamil Tigers delegations from visiting member countries in 2005.

Rumors also abound that LTTE has imposed a monthly war tax on Tamils around the world that raised $2 million a year, but no

KEY EVENTS

1972: Velupillai Prabhakaran forms the Tamil New Tigers.

1976: The Tamil New Tigers become the Liberation Tigers of Tamil Eelam (LTTE).

1983: LTTE commits its first act of violence by ambushing a Sri Lankan army patrol in Jaffna that kills thirteen soldiers and sparks anti-Tamil riots.

1987: India and Sri Lanka sign a pact to end Tamil separatism, and India sends peace-keeping troops to Tamil; 1,500 Indians die in subsequent fighting.

1991: Indian Prime Minister Rajiv Gandhi is blown up by a Tamil Tiger suicide bomber.

1998: Sri Lanka outlaws the LTTE.

2002: Sri Lanka and LTTE signed a long-term ceasefire agreement.

police force has filed charges. The organization is also known as the "cyanide cult" because each Tamil Tiger carries a cyanide capsule around his or her neck to commit suicide in the event of capture by the Sri Lankan government. (The Sri Lankan government has been accused by human rights organizations and Tamils of using torture against political opponents, making cyanide a reasonable rebel defensive tactic.)

LTTE was one of the first modern groups to use suicide bombers. Mostly the Tamil Tigers specialize in suicide attacks, with about 230 such attacks recorded, including the murder of India's Rajiv Gandhi and the May 1, 1993, assassination of Sri Lanka President Ranasinghe Premadasa. On October 13, 1994, LTTE killed presidential candidate Gamini Dissanayake and fifty-one others in a suicide attack. In 1999, the Tamil Tigers nearly killed Sri Lankan President Chandrika Kumaratunga in a suicide attack that cost her an eye and left twenty-two people dead.

One of the first terrorist organizations to realize the importance of good public relations,

the Tamil Tigers targets the Tamils in Sri Lanka. They have a news office that provides information from LTTE-affiliated social service agencies and use radio to promote their message. They also sponsor contests and anniversary celebrations in schools that encourage students to join the LTTE ranks.

The Tamil Tigers were one of the organizations affected by the worldwide attack on terrorism that followed the September 11, 2001, terrorist attacks on the United States. LTTE had received funds estimated to be in the millions from Tamils that settled abroad, especially in Canada, and from revenues generated by businesses around the world that were operated by the Tigers under fictitious names. The anti-terrorist crackdown dried up many of these funds. The LTTE leaders subsequently became more interested in a peace agreement. They agreed to a ceasefire in 2001, but repeatedly broke the truce. Norwegian monitors estimated that there were 3,000 violations of the truce by the LTTE as well as 150 violations by the Sri Lankan government. Most of the LTTE violations involved recruitment of child soldiers.

OTHER PERSPECTIVES

The largest settlement of Tamils outside of Sri Lanka is in Canada. These people responded on August 15, 2005, to the murder of the Sri Lankan foreign minister by the Tamil Tigers. The Sri Lanka United National Association of Canada told the *National Post* of Canada that "We call on the Sri Lankan authorities to leave no stone unturned in arresting not only the gunmen who fired the shots, but also those leaders of the terrorist movement directing the gunmen."

In response to the European Union's banning of LTTE delegations from its member countries, the Tamil Tigers posted an interview on the Tamilnet web site on September 30, 2005. LTTE political wing leader S.P. Tamilselvan declared that the Tamil people rallied under one leadership, that of the Tamil Tigers, to fight for their basic human rights. He further stated that the Sinhalese people who refused to acknowledge injustices to Tamils in the past were unlikely to provide justice to Tamils in the future. Rather than seeing LTTE as a terrorist

PRIMARY SOURCE

Liberation Tigers of Tamil Eelam (LTTE) a.k.a. The Tamil Tigers, The Ellalan Force

DESCRIPTION

Founded in 1976, the LTTE is the most powerful Tamil group in Sri Lanka. It began its insurgency against the Sri Lankan Government in 1983 and has relied on a guerrilla strategy that includes the use of terrorist tactics. The LTTE currently is observing a cease-fire agreement with the Sri Lankan Government.

ACTIVITIES

The LTTE has integrated a battlefield insurgent strategy with a terrorist program that targets key personnel in the countryside and senior Sri Lankan political and military leaders in Colombo and other urban centers. The LTTE is most notorious for its cadre of suicide bombers, the Black Tigers. Political assassinations and bombings were commonplace tactics prior to the cease-fire.

STRENGTH

Exact strength is unknown, but the LTTE is estimated to have 8,000 to 10,000 armed combatants in Sri Lanka, with a core of 3,000 to 6,000 trained fighters. The LTTE also has a significant overseas support structure for fundraising, weapons procurement, and propaganda activities.

LOCATION/AREA OF OPERATIONS

The LTTE controls most of the northern and eastern coastal areas of Sri Lanka but has conducted operations throughout the island. Headquartered in northern Sri Lanka, LTTE leader Velupillai Prabhakaran has established an extensive network of checkpoints and informants to keep track of any outsiders who enter the group's area of control.

EXTERNAL AID

The LTTE's overt organizations support Tamil separatism by lobbying foreign governments and the United Nations. The LTTE also uses its international contacts and the large Tamil diaspora in North America, Europe, and Asia to procure weapons, communications, funding, and other needed supplies.

Source: U.S. Department of State. *Country Reports on Terrorism.* Washington, D.C., 2004.

---

organization, Tamilselvan viewed it as a protector of human rights.

SUMMARY

The Tamil Tigers appear no closer to achieving a separate state than they were at the time they formed in the 1970s. However, there is a growing acceptance of federalism in Sri Lanka that would permit the establishment of such a state. While the tenuous ceasefire agreement between the Tigers and the government continues to hold, most observers expect that hostilities will resume in the absence of peace talks and continuing violations of the truce.

SOURCES

Books

Balasingham, Anton. *The Politics of Duplicity: Revisiting the Jaffna Talks.* Mitcham, England: Fairmax Publishing, 2000.

Hellmann-Rajanayagam, Dagmar. *The Tamil Tigers: Armed Struggle for Identity.* Stuttgart: Franz Steiner Verlag, 1994.

Mukarji, Apratim. *Sri Lanka: A Dangerous Interlude.* Chicago: New Dawn Press, 2005.

Web sites

Tamil Tigers. "Southern Journalists on Goodwill Mission to Trincomalee." < http://www.tamilnet.com > (accessed October 10, 2005).

Tunisian Combatant Group

LEADERS: Seifallah Ben Hassine; Tarek Ben
Habib Maaroufi

USUAL AREA OF OPERATION: Tunisia

OVERVIEW

The Tunisian Combatant Group (TCG) was
formed in 2000 by Seifallah Ben Hassine and
Tarek Ben Habib Maaroufi. Known in Tunisia
as Jama'a Combattante Tunisienne, the group
has also been called the Groupe Combattant
Tunisien, Tunisian Combat Group, and the
Tunisian Islamic Group. The TCG is comprised
mainly of Islamic Tunisians living outside their
country who operate in small-sized cells
throughout Afghanistan and Western Europe.
Although the goal of the group is the creation
of a fundamentalist Islamic state in Tunisia, the
TCG has been involved with attacks on Western
targets and supports the activities of other international *jihadist* (holy warriors) organizations,
such as the Algerian organization the Salafist
Group for Call and Combat, and al-Qaeda.
Members of the TCG have been implicated for
providing false documents and are believed to
serve as recruiters for the larger salafist
organizations.

HISTORY

Tunisia is located in northern Africa bordering
Algeria, Libya, and the Mediterranean Sea. The
country was ruled by France until 1956, when it
was granted independence. In the first election,

Tarek ben Habib Maaroufi, co-founder of the Tunisian Combatant Group, is serving time in Brussels, Belgium, for selling false documents to terrorists in 2001. Thierry Roge/Reuters/Landov

Habib Bourguiba won the presidency and, in 1975, proclaimed himself to be "president for life." During his regime, Bourguiba dominated the country by creating a one-party state, repressing Islamic fundamentalism, and establishing rights for women unparalleled in the Arab world. In 1987, Bourguiba was placed under house arrest by the prime minister, Zine el Abidine Ben Ali, who then took over the presidency. Ali proceeded to implement political reforms that allowed for the creation of opposition political parties and passed a constitutional amendment that reduced the presidential office term to three five-year terms. In 1989, the state held its first multiparty election since Tunisia gained its independence from France. During this election, the Islamic fundamentalist group represented in the party an-Nahda, or renaissance, had a strong showing in the results. Although an-Nahda had a strong showing, Ali won the presidency with no opposition. As a result, he moved to outlaw Islamic fundamentalist political parties and continued a policy of censorship and imprisoning those supporting fundamental activities. In 1990, approximately 100 people were arrested on charges of trying to create an Islamic state in Tunisia. In 1991, prior to the Gulf War, thousands of protestors demonstrated in support of Iraq, leading to violence between the government and the protestors.

During this time, Tarek Ben Habib Maaroufi was living in Belgium and had become a naturalized citizen. Maaroufi was working at a radio station, el-Watan, which catered to immigrants from northern Africa, particularly Morocco. During this time, Maaroufi had become a contact for major Islamic fundamentalist organizations from northern Africa. In 1992 and 1996, the Tunisian government requested that Maaroufi be extradited on charges of his involvement with an-Nahda's armed movement to create an Islamic state in Tunisia. The Belgium government declined these requests on the grounds that he was now a Belgian citizen. However, in 1995, Maaroufi was arrested along with twelve members of the Algerian organization, the Armed Islamic Group, an organization with the stated goal of creating an Islamic state in Algeria. The group has been linked to violence against government officials and civilians in Algeria. He was released in December of 1996 and given three-years probation.

By 2000, Maaroufi and Hassine had formed the Tunisian Combatant Group (TCG) by drawing from Tunisians in Europe and elsewhere in the world. In December 2000, the United Nations had designated the group for sanctions under United Nations Security Council Resolution 1333. This resolution identifies the Taliban and al-Qaeda, and those groups operating with Osama bin Laden, as terrorist organizations that should be sanctioned and have their assets frozen. By January 2001, the group was suspected for participation in planning the foiled attacks on U.S., Algerian, and Tunisian diplomatic missions in Rome. In December 2001, Maaroufi was arrested in Belgium for his participation in the September 9 assassination of Ahmed Shah Massoud, the leader of the Afghan Northern Alliance. Maaroufi was charged with providing forged Belgian passports to the two men who carried out the assassinations. He was convicted in 2003 and sentenced to six years in prison. In April 2002, members of the TCG embarked on a suicide mission outside the el-Ghriba synagogue in Djerba, Tunisia. The suicide truck bomb was detonated outside the synagogue and killed approximately twenty people. By October 2002,

LEADERSHIP

SEIFALLAH BEN HASSINE

Seifallah Ben Hassine is the co-founder of the Tunisian Combatant Group. The Tunisian is believed to have established ties to Osama bin Laden and al-Qaeda while living in Afghanistan prior to 2001. After the fall of the Taliban, Hassine traveled throughout the Middle East until he was detained by Turkish authorities in 2003. The U.S. State Department believes Hassine spent time in London creating operating cells for al-Qaeda; however, his whereabouts are currently unknown.

TAREK BEN HABIB MAAROUFI

Tarek Ben Habib Maaroufi is the other co-founder of the Tunisian Combatant Group. Maaroufi, born in Tunisian in 1965, immigrated to Belgium where he obtained naturalized citizenship. He worked at an Arabic radio station, el-Watan, until 1991. During this time, Maaroufi became a point of contact for northern African Islamic jihadists. In 1992 and in 1996, the Tunisian government requested that Maaroufi be extradited by Belgium for participation in the Islamic fundamentalist group, an-Nahda. The Belgian government declined these requests. However, in 1995, Maaroufi was arrested along with twelve members of the Armed Islamic Group, a group dedicated to the creation of an Islamic state in Tunisia's neighbor, Algeria. Maaroufi was released in 1996 and sentenced to three years of probation. In the late 1990s, Maaroufi became a recruiter for al-Qaeda. In 2001, he was arrested in Belgium after the assassination of the leader of the Afghan Northern Alliance, Ahmed Shah Massoud. Maaroufi was convicted of providing the assassins fabricated Belgian passports and sentenced to six years in prison.

the United States designated the TCG as a terrorist organization under presidential Executive Order 13224, and expressed that the organization has ties with other northern African Islamic jihadist groups, al-Qaeda, and Osama bin Laden. As a direct result of those alliances, the executive order freezes the assets of the group and blocks further transactions from occurring within the United States. Also in 2002, the Italian court sentenced several TCG members on convictions relating to operations carried out by al-Qaeda.

PHILOSOPHY AND TACTICS

The members of the TCG are committed to the creation of an Islamic state in Tunisia. The group is closely allied with salafist organizations, like the Algerian Salafist Group for Call and Combat. Salafists believe in a strict interpretation of the Koran. The Islamic state created by salafists would adhere to this strict interpretation. In order to reach this goal, the group has developed ties with other international Islamic fundamentalists. The Algerian organization, the Salafist Group for Call and Combat, is seeking the creation of an Islamic state in Algeria, the neighbor of Tunisia. The group has targeted moderate Muslims within Algeria and attacked the government and civilians believed to support the government. Both the TCG and the Salafist Group for Call and Combat have become recruiting grounds in northern Africa for larger Islamic jihadist organizations, such as al-Qaeda. Al-Qaeda believes in a "defensive jihad," one that promotes the philosophy that each Muslim must fight attacks on Islam throughout the world. In doing so, al-Qaeda seeks the overthrow of secular regimes that are considered repressive to Muslims. These regimes, al-Qaeda believes, should be replaced by an Islamic government. As a result, al-Qaeda and the TCG have become allies in reaching their goals. To aid al-Qaeda in its mission, the TCG participates in recruiting, logistics, and providing forged documents to jihadists throughout Europe.

OTHER PERSPECTIVES

The TCG is comprised mainly of Tunisians living in Western Europe. Within Tunisia, 98% of the population is Muslim, and Islam is considered the state religion. However, the Tunisian government has banned Islamic political parties in an effort to hamper the activities of self-declared radical Islamists who seek to create a

KEY EVENTS

1956: Tunisia is granted independence from France. Habib Bourguiba is elected president and creates a one-party state. Bourguiba begins policy of banning Islamic fundamentalists from creating political parties.

1975: Bourguiba declares himself president for life.

1987: Bourguiba is placed under house arrest by the prime minister, Zine el Abidine Ben Ali, who begins to institute changes to political structure.

1989: The first multiparty elections since 1956 are held in Tunisia. The Islamic fundamentalist group, an-Nahda, wins more support than expected. Ali wins the presidency with no opposition and proceeds to ban an-Nahda and other Islamic groups.

1990: Approximately 100 people are arrested on charges of trying to overthrow the government and create an Islamic state.

1991: Violent clashes erupt during the Gulf War between government forces and Islamic supporters of the Iraqi regime led by Saddam Hussein.

1992: The Tunisian government requests from Belgium the extradition of the future co-founder of the TCG, Tarek Ben Habib Maaroufi, for his involvement in activities related to an-Nahda. Belgium declines.

1995: Maaroufi is arrested in Belgium with twelve members of the Armed Islamic Group.

Maaroufi is released with a sentence of three-years probation.

1996: The Tunisian government again requests the extradition of Maaroufi from Belgium. Belgium refuses.

2000: The TCG is formed by Tarek Ben Habib Maaroufi and Seifallah Ben Hassine with the stated goal to create an Islamic state in Tunisia.

2000: TCG is designated for sanctions under the UNSCR 1333 due to its ties with the Taliban and al-Qaeda.

2001: TCG is suspected in planning and attempting to carry out the foiled attacks on U.S., Algerian, and Tunisian diplomatic missions in Rome.

2001: Maaroufi is arrested in Belgium for providing false documents to the assassins of the Afghan Northern Alliance leader, Ahmed Shah Massoud.

2002: TCG suicide bombers on Tunisian island of Djerba detonate bomb outside a synagogue, killing twenty people.

2002: United States designates TCG as a terrorist organization under Executive Order 13224 and freezes the assets of the organization within the United States.

2002: Italian court convicts TCG members on activities with al-Qaeda.

2003: Maaroufi is sentenced to six years for his involvement in the 2001 assassination.

---

fundamentalist Islamic state in Tunisia. These campaigns seeking to repress Islamic fundamentalism in the county have resulted in thousands imprisoned, although many were released when President Ali began to open the political system in 1989. However, the TCG is viewed as a threat to the national security of Tunisia due to the stated goal of wanting to overthrow the government and replace it with a salafist regime. In addition, the TCG is close allies with al-Qaeda and virulently anti-American, anti-Western, and

anti-Israel. As such, the U.S. State Department has listed the group as a terrorist organization. Under Executive Order 12334, the assets of the organization within the United States are frozen.

SUMMARY

In 2000, the Tunisian Combatant Group was formed by Tarek Ben Habib Maaroufi and Seifallah Ben Hassine with the expressed goal

PRIMARY SOURCE
Tunisian Combatant Group (TCG)

DESCRIPTION

The Tunisian Combatant Group (TCG), also known as the Jama'a Combattante Tunisienne, seeks to establish an Islamic regime in Tunisia and has targeted US and Western interests. The group is an offshoot of the banned Tunisian Islamist movement, an-Nahda. Founded around 2000 by Tarek Maaroufi and Saifallah Ben Hassine, the TCG has drawn members from the Tunisian diaspora in Europe and elsewhere. It has lost some of its leadership, but may still exist, particularly in Western Europe. Belgian authorities arrested Maaroufi in late 2001 and sentenced him to six years in prison in 2003 for his role in the assassination of anti-Taliban commander Ahmad Shah Massoud two days before 9/11. The TCG was designated under EO 13224 in October 2002. Historically, the group has been associated with al-Qaeda as well. Members also have ties to other North African extremist groups. The TCG was designated for sanctions under UNSCR 1333 in December 2000.

ACTIVITIES

Tunisians associated with the TCG are part of the support network of the broader international jihadist movement. According to European press reports, TCG members or affiliates in the past have engaged in trafficking falsified documents and recruiting for terror training camps in Afghanistan. Some TCG associates were suspected of planning an attack against the US, Algerian, and Tunisian diplomatic missions in Rome in April 2001. Some members reportedly maintain ties to the Algerian Salafist Group for Call and Combat.

STRENGTH
Unknown.

LOCATION/AREA OF OPERATION
Western Europe and Afghanistan.

EXTERNAL AID
Unknown.

Source: U.S. Department of State. *Country Reports on Terrorism.* Washington, D.C., 2004.

---

being the creation of an Islamic state in Tunisia. The group was created in response to nearly 50 years of repression of Islamic fundamentalists within Tunisia. However, most of the groups members are Tunisians living in Europe and most of the group's activities have occurred outside the country. The U.S. State Department describes the TCG as a loosely based organization that operates in small cells throughout Europe and the Middle East. One of these cells was suspected in the 2001 attempted attacks on the U.S., Algerian, and Tunisian diplomatic missions in Rome. Much of the organization's other activities surround its alliances with other international Islamic jihad organizations, such as the Algerian Salafist Group for Call and Combat and al-Qaeda. The TCG provides recruiting, logistics,

planning, and false documents for operatives of these other organizations. The TCG has been sanctioned under both the United Nations Security Council Resolution 1333 and the U.S. presidential Executive Order 13224 for its connections with the Taliban and al-Qaeda. The organization has successfully launched operations within Tunisia. In 2002, operatives from the TCG participated in a suicide bombing of a synagogue in Djerba, an island off of Tunisia. The bombing killed twenty people.

The TCG is still considered to be active. Of the co-founders, Maaroufi is serving a six-year sentence for his participation in an assassination in 2001. Hassine, the other co-founder, is believed to still be leading the organization, although his whereabouts are currently unknown.

SOURCES

Web sites

CIA Government Factbook. "Tunisia." < http://www.cia.gov/cia/publications/factbook/geos/ts.html > (accessed October 16, 2005).

Flemish Republic. "Brussels: Europe's Hub of Terror." < http://www.flemishrepublic.org/extra.php/ > (accessed October 16, 2005).

MIPT Terrorism Knowledge Base. "Tunisian Combatant Group." < http://www.tkb.org/Group.jsp?groupID = 4346 > (accessed October 16, 2005).

Overseas Security Advisory Council. "Tunisian Combatant Group." < http://www.ds-osac.org/Groups/group.cfm?contentID = 1335 > (accessed October 16, 2005).

U.S. State Department. "Patterns of Global Terrorism." < http://www.state.gov/s/ct/rls/pgtrpt/2003/31638.htm > (accessed October 16, 2005).

SEE ALSO

Al-Qaeda

Tupac Amaru Revolutionary Movement (MRTA)

LEADERS: Victor Polay; Néstor Cerpa Cartolini
YEAR ESTABLISHED OR BECAME ACTIVE: 1984
ESTIMATED SIZE: 300–600
USUAL AREA OF OPERATION: Peru

OVERVIEW

The Tupac Amaru Revolutionary Movement (Tupac Amaru, or MRTA, which is the acronym for the Spanish name) was a Peruvian Marxist-Leninist revolutionary movement that was founded in 1984. MRTA's objective was to rid Peru of the national "imperialist" government and establish a Marxist regime. Tupac Amaru's political actions include bombings, ambushes, kidnappings for ransom, armed conflict, and assassinations. MRTA's political violence was focused on forwarding its anti-U.S. and anti-foreign investment message in Peruvian society. Throughout the late 1980s and early 1990s, many of its militants were arrested and imprisoned.

Tupac Amaru's membership included some 300 and 600 members as its peak. The group's base of operations was primarily in the upper Huallaga Valley, a jungle area in eastern Peru that is under the control of political rebels and narco-traffickers.

In December 1996, Tupac Amaru attacked the Japanese ambassador's residence in the Peruvian capitol of Lima, taking hundreds of diplomats and top government officials (including the Peruvian president's brother) hostage. The standoff ended on April 22, 1997, when the Peruvian special forces raided the Japanese ambassador's residence (which was part of the

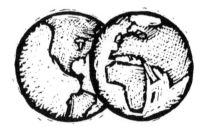

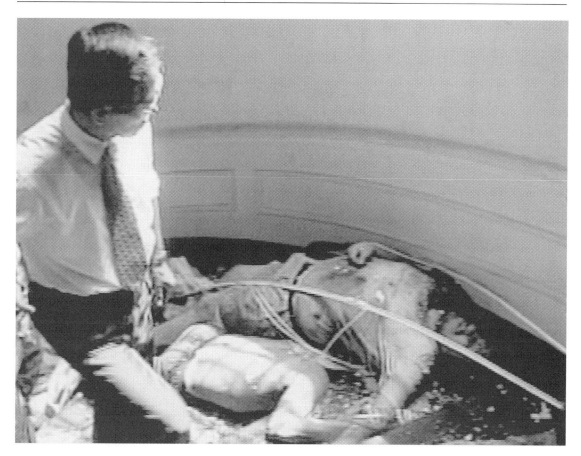

Alberto Fujimori, former Peruvian president, passes the bodies of two Tupac Amaru rebels who were killed in the storming of the Japanese ambassador's residence in Lima on April 23, 1997. The fourteen rebels held 72 hostages when they seized the residence on December 17. AP/Wide World Photos. Reproduced by permission.

Japanese embassy), and freed the remaining seventy-two hostages, killing all fourteen rebels.

HISTORY

The Tupac Amaru Revolutionary Movement was named after an indigenous leader who fought the Spanish colonial rulers in the 1700s. The group assumed the name Tupac Amaru because Tupac Amaru II symbolized success over imperialist leaders; his rebellions nearly toppled the Spanish stronghold in the largest Incan uprising against the Spaniards in nearly two centuries. Tupac Amaru was tortured and then drawn and quartered in Cuzco in 1782. He is revered by indigenous peoples in the highlands of Peru.

The Tupac Amaru movement formed in the shadow of *Sendero Luminoso* (Shining Path), a fellow revolutionary organization that used armed conflict as a means to accomplishing a complete overthrow of the national government and a return to pre-Incan communal agriculture. In the four years before Tupac Amaru was founded, Sendero developed a series of political violence events, including power supply disruptions, bombings, and violence in the rural highlands of Peru. As Peru's President Terry Fernando Belaúnde fought to maintain control, leftists widely claimed that a military *coup d'etat* would soon be enacted by the armed forces. This coup would force leftist organizations like Sendero and Tupac Amaru underground.

Sendero, however, pressed on with the violence; with strong support in the countryside, it

Two Tupac Amaru rebels flash victory Vs from atop the roof of the Japanese ambassador's residence after hanging banners during their seige of the property. AP/Wide World Photos. Reproduced by permission.

was establishing bases of operation and control over growing sections of the country. Both Tupac Amaru and Sendero Luminoso fought a guerilla war with the established government, using tactics such as kidnappings, bombings, and power supply disruptions to gain attention for their cause as they attempted to force governmental change or to oust the current government. Tapping into the alienation of the poor, indigenous population, movements like Sendero Luminoso and Tupac Amaru fought for a dramatic leftist change, one that embraced income redistribution, a return to indigenous rule, and a society and government that followed communal ideals.

Tupac Amaru, however, claimed that Sendero's violence was not productive in creating change. Sendero, in turn, criticized Tupac Amaru's willingness to negotiate with the Peruvian government, and to accept money from international organizations and supporters. For a

brief time, the two organizations engaged in armed conflict with each other, fighting a two-front war.

Tupac Amaru, or MRTA, financed its actions through bank robberies, extortion, and ransomed kidnappings, as well as through assistance from Cuba and other communist organizations outside of Peru. Tupac Amaru's international contacts were matters of concern to both the Peruvian military and U.S. officials. With connections to leftists in Cuba, Colombia, and El Salvador, the group had enough support from abroad to continue to operate. MRTA may also have received munitions from international allies.

Unlike Sendero Luminoso, though, Tupac Amaru did not use the rural highlands as a base of operations for penetrating an area with the eventual goal of taking charge. Their activities were more traditionally Marxist or communist, in working to disrupt the existing power structure to take control and implement political change.

LEADERSHIP

VICTOR POLAY CAMPOS

Victor Polay Campos was one of Tupac Amaru's founders in 1983. In 1989, Polay was arrested and imprisoned, but managed to tunnel his way out of prison in 1990. Two years later, he was recaptured and remains in prison, convicted of kidnapping and sabotage charges. He has been sentenced to life in prison.

In 2004, he was permitted a new trial, part of a wave of retrials given to more than 1,900 people convicted under questionable constitutional circumstances during the 1990s. As of this writing, the trial was still underway.

NÉSTOR CERPA CARTOLINI

Néstor Cerpa Cartolini, one of Tupac Amaru's founding members, was the leader of MRTA from 1992 until his death on April 22, 1997, when he was killed by Peruvian forces during the siege on the Japanese ambassador's residence.

Most members of MRTA were from the middle class, but Cerpa was from a working-class family. Active in the labor movement of the 1970s, he worked as a union organizer and served time in prison for taking over a bankrupt textile factory illegally. Four people died in the conflict, and Cerpa spent a year in prison. After serving his time, Cerpa joined the leftist movement in Peru, eventually helping to form MRTA in the early 1980s.

Cerpa was the military leader of the group of 14 MRTA members who stormed the Japanese ambassador's residence in Lima on December 17, 1996, and took more than 490 people hostage. He died during the Peruvian military's counterattack on April 22, 1997.

In 1995, a twenty-five-year-old American woman, Lori Berenson, was arrested for her connection to MRTA and for conspiracy charges. Berenson posed as a freelance journalist for magazines in the United States and brought a woman with her who posed as a photographer.

The woman, Nancy Gilvonio, was the wife of one of MRTA's leaders, Néstor Cerpa. In 1995, Berenson had attended public meetings of the Peruvian legislature several times, allegedly as a spy for MRTA. She was accused of "casing" the floor of the Peruvian legislature, and providing the MRTA with the floor plans of the Peruvian Congress. Other charges against her included providing information to Tupac Amaru about the congresses' security and members, as well as paying for rent on an apartment and harboring MRTA members.

Police specifically claimed that, during a raid on a Tupac Amaru safe house that same day, they found evidence of Berenson's conspiracy, including diagrams and notes related to the Peruvian Congress; a coded floor plan of Congress, drawn in Berenson's hand; a forged election ID for Berenson; police and military uniforms; and guns and munitions.

Berenson was also charged with participating in MRTA indoctrination courses, helping to provide members with food and money, and buying beepers and electronic equipment for her and Tupac Amaru members. Berenson was tried by a hooded tribunal and sentenced to life in a Peruvian prison.

A little over a year later, Tupac Amaru surprised Peru and the world by invading the Japanese ambassador's residence during a birthday party for the Japanese envoy on December 17, 1996. Fourteen Tupac Amaru members, including leader Néstor Cerpa, took control of over 490 hostages. The Japanese Embassy was technically under Japanese control, and yet the crisis took place on Peruvian soil. Promising to take no action that might harm the hostages, President Alberto Fujimori, whose brother was among the hostages, first negotiated for the release of some or all of the 490 captives. Tupac Amaru released all but seventy-one hostages over the next two months. Tupac Amaru kept Fujimori's brother, the Japanese ambassador, Peruvian Supreme Court justices, members of the Peruvian Congress, and other high-ranking officials. MRTA demanded the release of all their imprisoned members, including the wife of current leader Néstor Cerpa Cartolini; Nancy Gilvonio had been imprisoned for more than a year since her capture with Lori Berenson. Fujimori refused to agree to release the imprisoned Tupac Amaru members. He negotiated with MRTA members during the

KEY EVENTS

1987: The MRTA took control over a provincial capital, Juanji, a city of 25,000 inhabitants.

1987: The MRTA occupied seven radio stations in Lima; broadcasted statement against increasing militarization of Peruvian society.

1989: Police arrested and imprisoned Victor Polay.

1990: MRTA soldier shot former Defense Minister E. Lopez Albujar.

1990: Victor Polay and forty-six other inmates escaped from prison after digging a tunnel.

1992: Victor Polay was recaptured.

1995: Thirty Tupac Amaru members, including alleged member Lori Berenson, were arrested on conspiracy charges involving a plot against the Peruvian Congress.

---

four-month-long standoff, all while planning a possible military assault on the palace.

On April 22, 1997, Peruvian military commandoes stormed the palace in a carefully planned counter-terrorism siege. All fourteen Tupac Amaru hostage-takers were killed by the military forces, and one Supreme Court justice and two soldiers died in the attack as well.

PHILOSOPHY AND TACTICS

The stated goal of Tupac Amaru was to replace representative democracy with a more direct role for people in society and politics. According to MRTA's leader from 1983–1992, Victor Polay, Peru had become a dependent capitalist country with an imperialist national government. With a nod to the French Revolution, Polay believed that there is a bourgeoisie and upper class that promoted imperialist ideals, with a large working class; the MRTA incorporated anti-capitalist elements into its campaigns. These ideas appealed as well to the rural peasantry, with

the imagery of Tupac Amaru and the leftist goals of income and land redistribution.

MRTA was organized around three levels of membership: soldiers; part-time, ad hoc militia members; and self-defense committees in villages, organized to work on social, political, and legal issues.

According to MRTA's philosophy and tactics, in every institution—business, education, government—the people must control the operations directly. The people must collectively own and control all property; state control would lead to bureaucratization and corruption. Even private corporations function under the hand of the national government; MRTA found their existence unacceptable.

Tupac Amaru began its armed struggle in San Martin province, where farmers were reasonably well organized; the CCP (*Confederación Campesina del Peru*, or Farmer's Confederation of Peru) provided a sympathetic base from which to start. Starting in 1985, Tupac Amaru began building and organizing forces, and in 1987 initiated the first of many actions.

The MRTA had originally confined its activities to urban areas and a few coastal areas such as Lima, Ica, and Trujillo. The group frequently pressured the national government to increase investment in areas where it was popular among the local residents. In 1985, the MRTA offered a ceasefire to new President Alan Garcia if the new government would make fair settlements with unions and increase the minimum wage. They also requested that other nations suspend debt payment requirements and that Garcia nationalize the property of foreign companies. Tupac Amaru kidnapped and ransomed the president of the San Martin development corporation in 1988 to pressure the government to accomplish some of these investment goals.

Tupac Amaru took a more reformist approach in its dealings with the national government, hoping to work somewhat within the system to achieve its goals. Unlike Sendero Luminoso, the MRTA was willing to accept money from groups outside of Peru, and to attempt to negotiate with Peru's president. Sendero openly criticized both approaches, and open confrontations and armed fighting occurred between the two groups, especially in the Upper Huallaga, JunUn, and the lower jungle foothills. In 1989, Tupac Amaru and

PRIMARY SOURCE
Tupac Amaru Revolutionary Movement (MRTA)

DESCRIPTION

MRTA is a traditional Marxist-Leninist revolutionary movement formed in 1983 from remnants of the Movement of the Revolutionary Left, a Peruvian insurgent group active in the 1960s. It aims to establish a Marxist regime and to rid Peru of all imperialist elements (primarily US and Japanese influence). Peru's counterterrorist program has diminished the group's ability to conduct terrorist attacks, and the MRTA has suffered from infighting, the imprisonment or deaths of senior leaders, and the loss of leftist support.

ACTIVITIES

Previously conducted bombings, kidnappings, ambushes, and assassinations, but recent activity has fallen drastically. In December 1996, fourteen MRTA members occupied the Japanese Ambassador's residence in Lima and held seventy-two hostages for more than four months. Peruvian forces stormed the residence in April 1997, rescuing all but one of the remaining hostages and killing all fourteen group members, including the remaining leaders. The group has not conducted a significant terrorist operation since and appears more focused on obtaining the release of imprisoned MRTA members, although there are reports of low-level rebuilding efforts.

STRENGTH

Believed to be no more than 100 members, consisting largely of young fighters who lack leadership skills and experience.

LOCATION/AREA OF OPERATION

Peru, with supporters throughout Latin America and Western Europe. Controls no territory.

EXTERNAL AID

None.

Source: U.S. Department of State. *Country Reports on Terrorism.* Washington, D.C., 2004.

Sendero fought in open, armed conflict on the campus of San Marcos University.

At that point, however, the MRTA had suffered losses between fighting with Sendero Luminoso and with Peruvian forces. Police captured then-leader Victor Polay. However, within a year, Polay, along with forty-six other inmates, had dug a tunnel out of the prison, and escaped in 1990. He was recaptured in 1992, and Néstor Cerpa took control of the MRTA.

By 1996, the year after Lori Berenson and thirty other MRTA members were arrested and imprisoned, Tupac Amaru executed a raid on the Japanese ambassador's residence on December 17, 1996. The size of the operation diverged sharply from past actions; more than 490 people were initially held hostage. Tupac Amaru's siege on the Japanese ambassador's house was calculated to send a national and international message. Japan had invested more then $280 million in Peru's economy in 1995; the MRTA was violently opposed to foreign investment and foreign influence in Peru. The hostage crisis was viewed as an attack on President Fujimori's strength as president and on his Japanese heritage as well.

Four months later, the Peruvian military invaded the compound and ended the siege, killing all fourteen MRTA members involved, including their leader, Néstor Cerpa. This effectively ended the group's activity, and Tupac Amaru is now considered to be largely defunct.

OTHER PERSPECTIVES

In 2000, President Alberto Fujimori fled the country and moved to Japan, faxing his resignation to Peru. The Peruvian Congress rejected the resignation and declared him "morally unfit to serve." On September 5, 2001, Peru's Attorney General filed homicide charges against ex-President Fujimori for killings that took place from 1990–1995 in the name of fighting terrorism in Peru. In 2002, new forensic evidence revealed that thirteen of the fourteen Tupac Amaru rebels killed in the military raid on the Japanese ambassador's home were shot in the back, evidence that they had surrendered but were killed afterward.

While public sentiment was still against the MRTA rebels and against other extremist groups such as Sendero Luminoso, the new evidence changed the opinions of some Peruvians concerning the national government's acts in fighting terrorism. Support grew for the retrials that had been ordered for more than 1,900 prisoners.

SUMMARY

Following the Peruvian armed forces' storming of the Japanese ambassador's residence, and the death of MRTA's leader, the group became essentially defunct. The Peruvian Truth and Reconciliation Report issued in 2003 holds Tupac Amaru responsible for approximately 1.5% of all deaths it investigated; by comparison, the report states that Sendero Luminoso is responsible for more than 20% of deaths.

Lori Berenson, however, remains in prison for her alleged role in spying for Tupac Amaru and for helping to put in place a plot to kidnap members of the Peruvian Congress. In 2001, Berenson was given a second trial, in which her sentence was lessened from life in prison to twenty years; her release date would be in 2015, at which time she would be deported from Peru.

Victor Polay remains in jail. He is, as of this writing, going through a new trial.

SOURCES

Books

Conaghan, Catherine M. *Fujimori's Peru: Deception In The Public Sphere*. Pittsburgh: University of Pittsburgh Press, 2005.

Web sites

Amnesty International. "PERU: Summary of Amnesty Internationals concerns 1980–1995." < http://web.amnesty.org/library/Index/ > (accessed October 5, 2005).

PBS.org. "Hostage Crisis." < http://www.pbs.org/newshour/bb/latin_america/december96/peru_12-19.html > (accessed October 5, 2005).

SEE ALSO

Sendero Luminoso (Shining Path)

Turkish Hezbollah

OVERVIEW

The Turkish Hezbollah is a radical Islamic group with no known links to the Hezbollah group based in Lebanon. Variations of the spelling of *Hezbollah* (which translates to Party of God) include Hizbollah and Hizballah, and the group has been called Ilim and Kurdish Revolutionary Hizballah.

HISTORY

The Turkish Hezbollah is a violent radical Kurdish Islamic group established in the 1980s, with the objective of establishing a separate Islamic state in Turkey. The group began by fighting against the communist Kurdish Workers' Party (PKK) and the Kurdish separatist movement. Hezbollah is primarily made up of Kurdish Sunni Muslims, and is predominantly active in the heavily Kurdish regions of southeastern Turkey. The Turkish Hezbollah has no apparent direct links to the radical Islamic groups in Lebanon or Iran, which are also called Hezbollah.

The group received its initial military training in the camps of the communist Kurdish Worker's Party (PKK). The cooperation between PKK and Hezbollah did not last long. Hezbollah accused the PKK of killing Muslims,

LEADER: Huseyin Velioglu

USUAL AREA OF OPERATION: Mainly in southeastern Turkey

Officials carry the dead body of a businessman in Istanbul, Turkey, on Jan. 19, 2000. Turkish police found the bodies of 10 businessmen believed to have been kidnapped by the militant Islamic group, Turkish Hezbollah. AP/Wide World Photos. Reproduced by permission.

working with the Armenians, and having communist tendencies. Hezbollah also accused PKK of trying to divide the Muslim community.

Hezbollah began its attacks in 1984 by targeting members of pro-PKK political parties, newspaper workers, and leading Kurdish figures. The group killed over 500 people in the PKK and other Kurdish groups. Hezbollah became well known for its distinct method of assassinations carried out in broad daylight. Operatives killed more than 1,000 people in street shootings between 1992 and 1995.

In the middle of the 1990s, Hezbollah began targeting brothels, liquor stores, and other places considered by the group to be promoting anti-Islamic livelihoods. The group also began targeting moderate Muslims and others who refused to give money to Hezbollah.

Hezbollah is known to use kidnapping, torture, and killing against its targets. Victims' bodies are often mutilated. Victims have been buried alive by the group. The group has made video recordings of its activities. Operatives have dressed as women to avoid suspicion while carrying out their activities.

As the group gained strength in the 1990s, Hezbollah began to move into other parts of Turkey, including Istanbul. Mosques and safe houses were used as places to spread the group's message, recruit members, and house militants and equipment. Bookstores were also set up as places to distribute religious information and Islamic publications.

An attack in 1997 on the Ecumenical Patriarchate of Constantinople was one of the first incidents that gave Hezbollah widespread

LEADERSHIP

HUSEYIN VELIOGLU

Huseyin Velioglu was the original leader of the Turkish Hezbollah. He attended the same University as the leader of the PKK, Abdullah Ocalan. Velioglu was a Sunni Kurdish Islamist who was against the revolutionary teachings of the Iranian Ayatollah Khomeini. Velioglu was also anti-Shi'ite. Despite his weak religious background and training, Velioglu served as a spiritual and political leader for the Turkish Hezbollah. He was killed in January 2000 during a police operation that captured two other Hezbollah operatives in Istanbul.

---

attention, as the Patriarchate was a spiritual leader for millions of Orthodox Christians throughout the world. A 2000 attack that killed five police officers in southeastern Turkey gave the group further attention.

Hezbollah has stated that its financial and logistical support comes from contributions from small businesses and other donations. However, the organization gets much of its financial and logistical support through extortion. More than 200 Kurdish businessmen who were connected to other Islamic groups were kidnapped during the second half of 1999.

Two main factions within the Hezbollah organization were the cause of internal conflicts that resulted in the death of over 400 people. The factions disagreed on how to go about implementing the goal of an Islamic state in Turkey. The *Ilimciler* (translated to the Scientists) was the larger of the factions, and it advocated an armed struggle with the use of violence to implement an Islamic state in Turkey. The *Menzilciler* (translated to the Rangers) argued that it was too early for an armed struggle, and that a more intellectual approach should be tried first. The Ilimciler came out stronger, particularly after the death of the Menzilciler leader.

Hezbollah had a relatively low profile in Turkish politics until January 2000, when the Ilimciler leader, Huseyin Velioglu, was killed and two other operatives were captured during a police operation in Istanbul. The captured men were used as informants by the Turkish police. This led to a year of police raids throughout Turkey. Many of the group's victims were found, and information about the group was uncovered. The magnitude of the group's brutality was recognized through the numerous video recordings that were confiscated. Hundreds of Hezbollah members were arrested. Hundreds of other Hezbollah members escaped to Iran and northern Iraq.

The media revealed links between the Turkish Hezbollah and the Iranian government in the spring of 2000. One newspaper, *Hurriyet*, published pictures of Velioglu meeting with officials in the Iranian capital, Tehran. Velioglu was reported to have an Iranian foreign staff officer identification card. Documents were cited, explaining the training Hezbollah received in Iran. It was also reported in the Turkish media that captured Hezbollah members revealed that they received training and support from an ethnic Turkish Sunni group based in Iran called the Jerusalem Warriors. The Jerusalem Warriors are on the U.S. Terrorist Exclusion List.

The uncovering of Hezbollah marked the first time the Turkish public witnessed violent Islamic movements similar to those in Egypt, Algeria, and Israel. The government of Turkey proceeded to recognize violent religious activism as an imminent challenge to its social order.

In 2003, Hezbollah members killed more than sixty people in attacks against two synagogues, a British bank, and the British Consulate in Istanbul. Those arrested are said to have had direct orders from al-Qaeda to carry out the attacks.

PHILOSOPHY AND TACTICS

The Hezbollah organization has named its enemies as those they consider to be infidels, or unbelievers of Islam, as well as those who do not share their convictions. Hezbollah operates with the philosophy that religious piety comes through torturing and killing its enemies. Such violent acts are condoned and required in the Hezbollah interpretation of the Islamic faith. Hezbollah has opposed every group that does not have the same viewpoints on Islam, as they believe their path is the true path.

KEY EVENTS

1980s: The group emerged as a reaction to the communist Kurdish Workers' Party (PKK) and to the Kurdish separatist movement.

1984: Hezbollah targeted members of pro-PKK political parties, newspaper workers, and leading Kurdish figures.

1997: An attack on the Ecumenical Patriarchate of Constantinople was one of the first incidents that gave Hezbollah widespread attention

2000: A Turkish police raid revealed that Hezbollah members had brutally murdered dozens of people and had videotaped some of the killings.

2000: Media reports in 2000 indicated that Iran's government has supported Hezbollah with funding and military training.

2003: Sixty people died in Hezbollah attacks on two synagogues, a British bank, and the British Consulate in Istanbul

---

The Hezbollah radicalism has ties to the idea of "Modern Kharijites." Kharijites created the first rebellion against rulers of the Islamic world, with an uncompromising set of Islamic principles. Kharijites divided the Islamic world, declaring a *jihad* (holy war) against all nonbelievers and those they accused of being apostate Muslims.

Hezbollah is known for its extreme violence and brutality. Activities of the group included torture, shootings, arson, beatings, and attacks with acid on women who are not dressed in an Islamic manner. These extreme tactics are used to purposely inflict pain on victims, and to persuade them of the validity of the Hezbollah cause.

Secrecy has been a trademark of Hezbollah as well. The group never tried excessively to get attention. Many times, the group carried out its planned activities without making claims for attacks.

A two-level process is employed by Hezbollah to reach its objective of developing a separate Islamic state. The first step is the invitation process to build up supporters. Then, when there are enough supporters, the group begins to deal with other organizations in the region. Those who choose not to join the struggle are targeted and killed. This approach has led to the deaths of Kurdish businessmen who support the secular government, as well as religious people who do not embrace the approach of violence. The group is not known to target people or structures of the Turkish government.

Hezbollah's ideology is not largely accepted in Turkey. Turkey has historically been composed of many different ethnic and cultural groups for centuries, and lies in the unique position between Europe and Asia. The Turkish government has attempted to incorporate different ways of thought, including Islamic voices, into its system. Hezbollah is not looking for a voice, but rather a system that is governed by the organization's Islamic philosophy.

Hezbollah is not considered an international terrorist organization, as it operates only inside Turkey. This is unlike the Lebanese Hezbollah, which has been active throughout the Middle East, Europe, Africa, North America, and South America. Another difference between the Lebanese and Turkish Hezbollah is that the group in Turkey operates in a very secretive manner, and does not have anything to do with everyday life in the community.

The Hezbollah members are generally economically and socially isolated from society. They typically come from lower income families, and many are not employed full-time. In general, the education level of Hezbollah members is low. Many members are Kurdish Sunni Muslims who are not supportive of the Kurdish separatist movement. Other Hezbollah groups throughout the Middle East are typically Shi'ite Muslims.

There are three tiers to the organizational structure of the Turkish Hezbollah organization. First is the leadership level. This is typically divided into two roles—spiritual leadership and political leadership. The spiritual leader gives support by providing religious motivation to all members. The political leader has all of the decision-making power, and can modify or change the directions of the group. Generally, these roles are held by two different individuals.

PRIMARY SOURCE
Turkish Hizballah

DESCRIPTION

Turkish Hizballah is a Kurdish Sunni Islamic terrorist organization that arose in the early 1980s in response to the Kurdistan Workers' Party (PKK)'s secularist approach of establishing an independent Kurdistan. Turkish Hizballah spent its first ten years fighting the PKK, accusing the group of atrocities against Muslims in southeastern Turkey, where Turkish Hizballah seeks to establish an independent Islamic state.

ACTIVITIES

Beginning in the mid–1990s, Turkish Hizballah, which is unrelated to Lebanese Hizballah, expanded its target base and modus operandi from killing PKK militants to conducting low-level bombings against liquor stores, bordellos, and other establishments the organization considered "anti-Islamic." In January 2000, Turkish security forces killed Huseyin Velioglu, the leader of Turkish Hizballah, in a shootout at a safe house in Istanbul. The incident sparked a year-long series of counterterrorist operations against the group that resulted in the detention of some 2,000 individuals; authorities arrested several hundred of those on criminal charges. At the same time, police recovered nearly seventy bodies of Turkish and Kurdish businessmen and journalists that Turkish Hizballah had tortured and brutally murdered during the mid-to-late 1990s. The group began targeting official Turkish interests in January 2001, when its operatives assassinated the Diyarbakir police chief in the group's most sophisticated operation to date. Turkish Hizballah did not conduct a major operation in 2003 or 2004 and probably is focusing on recruitment, fundraising, and reorganization.

STRENGTH

Possibly a few hundred members and several thousand supporters.

LOCATION/AREA OF OPERATION

Primarily the Diyarbakir region of southeastern Turkey.

EXTERNAL AID

It is widely believed that Turkey's security apparatus originally backed Turkish Hizballah to help the Turkish Government combat the PKK. Alternative views are that the Turkish Government turned a blind eye to Turkish Hizballah's activities because its primary targets were PKK members and supporters, or that the Government simply had to prioritize scarce resources and was unable to wage war on both groups simultaneously. Allegations of collusion have never been laid to rest, and the Government of Turkey continues to issue denials. Turkish Hizballah also is suspected of having ties with Iran, although there is not sufficient evidence to establish a link.

Source: U.S. Department of State. *Country Reports on Terrorism*. Washington, D.C., 2004.

The second level is the top council (Sura), a central committee made up of high-ranking political and military members. The council discusses important military and political options, and then makes decisions for the organization.

Finally, there are lower-level councils in Turkish cities and towns. These councils are divided into military and political branches. The leader of a council's military branch is responsible for carrying out the armed operations of the group. There are unit leaders and operation teams within each military wing.

The political wing carries out the recruitment of new members and the dissemination of Hezbollah ideology. Members in the political wing are responsible for the preparation, printing, and dissemination of propaganda materials. Much of the recruitment takes place in schools and colleges. Information is also distributed in mosques and around villages and neighborhoods.

OTHER PERSPECTIVES

The Turkish government has been labeled as supportive, or once supportive, of the Turkish Hezbollah. There is a widely accepted theory that the government viewed Hezbollah as a tool to counter the Kurdish separatist movement and the PKK when it first came into existence. Nearly all of Hezbollah's victims have been from rival Islamic groups, or were PKK supporters. Hezbollah has rarely attacked government forces, an indication of the government's current or former support for the organization.

Further evidence for collaboration came about when it was discovered in the mid 1990s that Hezbollah was using weapons secretly imported by a Turkish governor. Additionally, when the PKK called a truce in 1999, Turkish forces began targeting Hezbollah, as they were no longer needed to counter the PKK.

In 2000, Turkish President Suleyman Demirel denied that official support was ever given to Hezbollah. Other theories suggest that Hezbollah did not attack government targets, because the group wanted to avoid direct confrontation with the government and any attempts to stop the group's activities.

It has also been widely accepted that the government of Iran supported the Turkish Hezbollah with funding and ideological and military training. This is the same type of support given by Iran to the Lebanese Hezbollah. The Iranian government has denied supporting the Turkish Hezbollah.

Evidence of Velioglu holding meetings and working in Tehran also gives evidence to Hezbollah's relationship with Iran. However, Velioglu did disassociate himself with ideology in Iran, by speaking out against the revolutionary teachings of the Iranian Ayatollah Khomeini. Khomeini was also a Shi'ite Muslim.

SUMMARY

The Turkish Hezbollah is said to have an estimated 20,000 members. The group is responsible for over 1,000 attacks, and hundreds of deaths. In the beginning, the group primarily targeted Kurdish Nationalists who were fighting for a state independent of Turkey. The group grew larger, and began a broader struggle against what it considered anti-Islamic targets.

The events in 2000 were a blow for the group, with the death of their leader, Velioglu. Many other Hezbollah members were arrested in raids the same year. However, the group remains active, as evidenced by the 2003 bombings of synagogues and British offices in Istanbul, which killed sixty.

Many of the Hezbollah members who escaped to Iran after Veliogla's death are said to be aligned with Iranian Islamist groups such as Ansar al Islam. Other Hezbollah members are said to have formed ties with al-Qaeda.

SOURCES

Periodicals

Aras, Bulent, and Gokhan Bacik. "Hezbollah Horror: A National Shame." *The Middle East Quarterly*. June 2000: vol. 9, i. 2, p. 147.

Aydintasbas, Asli. "Murder on the Bosporus." *Middle East Quarterly*. June 2000: vol. 7, i. 2, p. 15.

Gorvett, Jon. "The Mystery of Turkish Hizballah." *Middle East Policy* March 2000.

Web sites

BBC News World Edition. "Turkey Charges 'Key Bomb Suspect.'" < http://news.bbc.co.uk/2/hi/europe/3333501.stm > (accessed October 5, 2005).

BBC News World Europe. "Turkish Hezbollah: 'No State Links.'" < http://news.bbc.co.uk/1/hi/world/europe/615785.stm > (accessed October 5, 2005).

Center for DefenseInformation. "In the Spotlight: Turkish Hezbollah." < http://www.cdi.org/program/document.cfm/ > (accessed October 5, 2005).

International Strategic Research Organization—Journal of Turkish Weekly. "Turkish Hizballah: A Case Study of Radical Terrorism." < http://www.turkishweekly.net/articles.php?id = 28 > (accessed October 5, 2005).

National Memorial Institute for the Prevention of Terrorism—Terrorism Knowledge Base. "Turkish Hezbollah." < http://www.tkb.org/KeyLeader.jsp?memID = 5922 > (accessed October 5, 2005).

Ulster Defense Association/ Ulster Freedom Fighters

OVERVIEW

The Ulster Defense Association (UDA) is the largest loyalist paramilitary group in Northern Ireland. It was formed in 1971 as an umbrella organization to unite vigilante groups in Protestant areas that gathered together as a response to Irish Republican Army (IRA) violence. At its peak, it claimed to have a membership of more than 40,000. Its small but ruthless military wing, the Ulster Freedom Fighters, emerged as one of the most brutal and violent paramilitary groups in the province's three-decades-long troubles.

LEADERS: Johnny Adair; Jackie McDonald

YEAR ESTABLISHED OR BECAME ACTIVE: 1971

ESTIMATED SIZE: 2,000–4,000

USUAL AREA OF OPERATION: Northern Ireland; Scotland

DECLARED AN ILLEGAL TERRORIST ORGANIZATION BY THE BRITISH GOVERNMENT IN 1991; U.S. TERRORIST EXCLUSION LIST DESIGNEE: the U.S. Department of State declared the UDA to be a terrorist organization in December 2001

HISTORY

Amid the rising tensions and violence of the early 1970s in Northern Ireland, the Ulster Defense Association was launched in September 1971 to amalgamate the rising number of Protestant vigilante groups, originally set up in response to rising IRA violence. These self-styled defense associations were growing in strength in areas such as Shankhill as loyalists became increasingly concerned about the army's inability to either defeat or even contain a resurgent IRA.

Modeled along military lines, the UDA's membership peaked within a year of its formation at 40,000. In these early stages, it seemingly

The leadership of the pro-British terrorist group Ulster Freedom Fighters announce on December 8, 1999, that they have appointed representatives to meet with the body established to oversee disarmament in Belfast, Northern Ireland. AP/Wide World Photos. Reproduced by permission.

showed few of the hallmarks of a conventional terrorist organization, and extolled the motto "Law Before Violence." In March 1972, with the prospect of the Northern Ireland Parliament at Stormont being dissolved and direct rule imposed from Westminster, the UDA were instrumental in leading street protests and instigating strikes. The protests, nevertheless, came to nothing and, on March 28, 1972, Stormont adjourned for the last time.

This was a profound blow for Northern Ireland's Protestants and unionists, who regarded Stormont as the principle bulwark against nationalists and republicans. With fellow unionist groups, the UDA arranged massive demonstrations on the streets of Belfast during the summer of 1972, when thousands of uniformed members marched through the city center.

One of the biggest standoffs between the UDA and the British Army took place on July 3, 1972, in Belfast. Eight thousand UDA members dressed in masks and many armed with cudgels sought to erect barriers between the Catholic Springfield area and Protestant Shankhill. When confronted by 250 British troops, the soldiers backed down.

Yet this organization was no benevolent champion of human rights; rather, it was operating in the shadows as a brutal paramilitary organization, which ruthlessly hunted down civilians. The year 1972 was the bloodiest year of the "Troubles," in which 479 people were killed by paramilitary organizations or by the police or army. Of those lives, the UDA claimed twenty-eight, including twenty-four civilians. Despite being a self-styled defender in the face of IRA violence, none of those members killed

LEADERSHIP

JOHNNY "MAD DOG" ADAIR

As with the majority of Northern Ireland's paramilitary organizations, the UDA is run by an inner council. While this may seem inherently democratic, in practice the bulk of power rests with the individual who can most skillfully build up and manipulate allegiances. It is the Machiavellian input of a man like Johnny Adair that threatens to bring the system crashing down. In part because he successfully opposed Adair, Jackie McDonald, a South Belfast Brigade Commander has emerged as the UDA's most powerful figure in recent years.

Even in exile, however, it is Adair who remains the most synonymous with the UDA/UFF and, on account of his unashamed publicity-seeking, remains the organization's most famous—and infamous—relic. As commander of the UFF's C Company, he attracted notoriety as a brutal hitman in West Belfast in the early 1990s, which was the highpoint of UFF violence when the group claimed the lives of nearly 90 people; Adair is alleged to have been behind 40 of those killings. In October 1993, in an attempt to kill Adair, the IRA bombed a fish and chip shop on the Shankhill Road, where a UDA meeting was due to take place. However, the bomb went off early, killing one of the bombers as well as nine Protestant civilians. The UFF retaliated with a random attack on a Catholic bar near Londonderry, which killed seven people who had no paramilitary connections.

Adair was subsequently imprisoned after boasting to undercover police officers of his activities, but was released under the terms of the Good Friday Agreement. This marked the onset of a period in which Adair became almost a 'celebrity' paramilitary. Short, bullet headed, and bristling with tattoos, he was a distinctive addition to news schedules, and was usually willing to speak to media.

Yet, his colleagues viewed his publicity seeking with disdain, likewise his reputation for drug dealing, which seemed to contradict those who claimed the UDA were moral protectors of Ulster's loyalist community. Moreover, his pursuit of an alliance with the LVF was viewed with intense suspicion. Combined, these factors would bring Adair into a murderous feud with his fellow UDA bosses and lead to the revoking of his release from prison. In October 2003, the *Observer* concluded a lengthy article about Adair's travails by asking: "When he is finally released from jail...Adair will face a stark choice. Does he go back to the Shankill and try one last throw of the dice? Or does he settle quietly away from Belfast, hoping he can avoid assassination and live in peace with his family?" Since his release in January 2005, Adair has lived in Bolton, and while few of his new neighbors would claim he is a peaceful addition to their area (he has been implicated in drug dealing and various petty crimes), it seems that, for now, his paramilitary career is over.

belonged to any other terrorist organization but the UDA.

A year later, in 1973, it confirmed its notoriety when its emergent military wing, the Ulster Freedom Fighters (UFF), brutally murdered the Social Democratic and Labour Party (SDLP) politician, Paddy Wilson, and his secretary. When their bludgeoned bodies were found in a quarry, the violenct act provoked shock and consternation across the province. Still, the UDA retained its legality, and in 1974, it led strikes against the power-sharing executive at

Stormont, which brought the Northern Irish Parliament to its knees.

Yet, this marked the end of the UDA as a political entity of any real significance. Despite setting up the New Ulster Political Group in 1978 and the Ulster Loyalist Democratic Party in 1981 (which advocated independence for Northern Ireland—anathema to many of the UDA's traditional constituency), politically the group failed to make anything but insignificant inroads in the decades that followed.

KEY EVENTS

1971: UDA formed as an umbrella organization for emergent Protestant vigilante groups.

1972: Involved in organizing protests at dissolution of the Stormont Executive; linked to twenty-eight deaths in the most bloody year of Northern Ireland's "Troubles."

1973: Onset of Ulster Freedom Fighters paramilitary activity, including murder of SDLP politician, Paddy Wilson.

1988: UDA Brigadier, Michael Stone, kills three during a grenade attack at an IRA funeral.

1994: UDA announces ceasefire and backs the subsequent peace process, including the Good Friday Agreement.

2002: In the midst of internal wrangling, and a bloody feud, Johnny Adair is expelled from party ranks.

For most of the 1980s, Northern Ireland's conflict was stuck in an unsavory stalemate: the IRA gained further notoriety with atrocities on the British mainland and in the province; and the loyalist groups—notably, the Ulster Volunteer Force UVF), the UDA, and its military wing the UFF—played their part with retaliatory killings in Ulster.

In December 1987, John McMichael, then-deputy leader of the UDA, was killed in a bomb attack carried out by the IRA, although it was alleged that he had been set up by fellow members of the UDA. This event marked the onset of a period of radicalization in the UDA and soon large quantities of arms were secured by the organization. There was an upsurge in assassinations of Catholics. Also, it would emerge during a subsequent British government inquiry that the UDA had gained access to a large number of security files on republicans and suspected members of Republican paramilitary groups, leading to renewed accusations of collusion with the British military forces.

One of the UDA's most notorious attacks came in 1988 when its member, Michael Stone, attacked mourners at an IRA funeral with hand grenades. The dramatic attack, which had been designed to kill the Sinn Fein leaders, Gerry Adams and Martin McGuinness, was captured live on TV; the attack killed three and injured more than fifty.

Even more heinous was a number of multiple killings in the early 1990s targeted at Catholic civilians. By then, the British government had belatedly outlawed the UDA as a terrorist organization.

Yet, when moves towards a peace agreement came in 1994, the UDA matched the IRA in calling a ceasefire, a cessation that would hold until January 1998 when the Loyalist Volunteer Force leader, Billy Wright, was murdered by republicans in the Maze Prison. In the wake of that killing, on January 4, 1998, UDA and UFF prisoners had voted by 2-to-1 to withdraw support from the peace process. Four days later, however, they were visited by the British Northern Ireland Secretary, Mo Mowlam, and persuaded to change their minds. Four months later, the UDA endorsed the Good Friday Agreement.

It was hoped that the agreement would bring an end to the UDA's terrorist activities. The retaliatory killing with republican groups did virtually end, but a new kind of conflict erupted, this time with its one-time loyalist counterparts, the Ulster Volunteer Force (UVF). The feud centered on the belief that elements in the UFF were siding with the Loyalist Volunteer Force (LVF), which had its own feud with the UVF. Bubbling underneath the surface was also infighting over the spoils of Belfast's drug trade, which had become the prime cause of many former paramilitaries in the post-Good Friday era.

That rift was healed by late 2000, but another opened in 2002 with Johnny Adair, the controversial commander of the UDA's "C Company," at the center. Adair, a charismatic maverick in the mold of the LVF's former leader, Billy Wright, had been part of an effort to forge closer ties with the LVF. Yet, sections within the UDA/UFF union opposed such movements, viewing them as an attempt by Adair to take over the leadership of the UDA by winning external support. An internal feud within the UDA began, with several killed and many others burned out of their homes.

PRIMARY SOURCE

Ulster Defense Association/Ulster Freedom Fighters (UDA/UFF)

DESCRIPTION

The Ulster Defense Association (UDA), the largest Loyalist paramilitary group in Northern Ireland, was formed in 1971 as an umbrella organization for Loyalist paramilitary groups such as the Ulster Freedom Fighters (UFF). Today, the UFF constitutes almost the entire UDA membership. The UDA/UFF declared a series of cease-fires between 1994 and 1998. In September 2001, the UDA/ UFF's Inner Council withdrew its support for Northern Ireland's Good Friday Agreement. The following month, after a series of murders, bombings, and street violence, the British Government ruled the UDA/UFF's cease-fire defunct. The dissolution of the organization's political wing, the Ulster Democratic Party, soon followed. In January 2002, however, the UDA created the Ulster Political Research Group to serve in a similar capacity. Designated under EO 13224 in December 2001.

ACTIVITIES

The UDA/UFF has evolved into a criminal organization deeply involved in drug trafficking and other moneymaking criminal activities through six largely independent "brigades." It has also been involved in murder, shootings, arson, and assaults. According to the International Monitoring Commission, "the UDA has the capacity to launch serious, if crude, attacks." Some UDA activities have been of a sectarian nature directed at the Catholic community, aimed at what are sometimes described as 'soft' targets, and often have taken place at the interface between the Protestant and Catholic communities, especially in Belfast. The organization continues to be involved in targeting individual Catholics and has undertaken attacks against retired and serving prison officers. The group has also been involved in a violent internecine war with other Loyalist paramilitary groups for the past several years. In February 2003, the UDA/UFF declared a twelve-month cease-fire, but refused to decommission its arsenal until Republican groups did likewise and emphasized its continued disagreement with the Good Friday accords. The cease-fire has been extended. Even though numerous attacks on Catholics were blamed on the group, the UDA/ UFF did not claim credit for any attacks and in August 2003 reiterated its intention to remain militarily inactive.

STRENGTH

Estimates vary from 2,000 to 5,000 members, with several hundred active in paramilitary operations.

LOCATION/AREA OF OPERATION

Northern Ireland.

EXTERNAL AID

Unknown.

Source: U.S. Department of State. *Country Reports on Terrorism*. Washington, D.C., 2004.

In September 2002, Adair was expelled from the UDA, and the movement nearly collapsed in the wake of his attempts to woo senior UDA members into a renegade Loyalist Freedom Fighters organization. These efforts floundered, in part, because Adair returned to prison in January 2003.

A month later, in February 2003, a UDA divisional leader and enemy of Adair's, John Gregg, was shot dead along with another UDA member. The killing saw about twenty Adair supporters exiled from Northern Ireland by UDA members seeking to avenge Gregg's death.

As of 2005, the UDA remains in dispute with Adair, who, following his release from prison, is currently living in exile in Bolton, England. The group declared a cessation of hostilities with the UVF in February 2003—to which it has largely stuck.

PHILOSOPHY AND TACTICS

As its name suggests, the Ulster Defense Association was originally formed to protect the Protestant community of Northern Ireland in the face of rising IRA insurgency and a rising lack of police control. As a loyalist group, it vigorously opposes closer integration with the Republic of Ireland or a weakening of ties with the rest of the United Kingdom.

Yet, despite its purportedly defensive outlook and its founding motto "Law Before Violence," it soon became involved in terrorist activity, killing Catholic civilians as reprisal for IRA murders and targeting loyalist rivals. The Ulster Freedom Fighters initially set out to wage war on the IRA, but found that attacks on IRA members merely saw savage reprisals on its own. In more than three decades of activity, the UDA/UFF is only credited with the deaths of three republican paramilitaries. It found it far easier to kill civilians.

The UDA has also been strongly linked to far-right extremist groups operating on the British mainland, notably Combat 18. Johnny Adair, in his youth, was allegedly a skinhead and member of the British National Party, a neo-Nazi leaning apparently shared by some of his contemporaries.

In its present incarnation, the UDA operates through six largely independent brigades, who extend their influence—to varying degrees—across Northern Ireland. The UDA has been observing a ceasefire since February 2003, but this is largely irrelevant as the group has existed over most of the last decade as a criminal gang. Its activities extend to drug dealing, extortion and racketeering, and, like a Mafia family, in some areas its influence is all pervasive.

OTHER PERSPECTIVES

"Having got rid of the Catholic enemy within the increasingly powerful loyalist gangs, the Ulster Defense Association, the Ulster Volunteer Force, the Loyalist Volunteer Force and others fight each other for control of the shebeens, the drug trade and the protection rackets," wrote John Lloyd, a British journalist who covered Northern Ireland during the Troubles, of the new post-Good Friday Agreement realities of life in the province. "These are spreading over to the mainland, and are very lucrative. A paramilitary drug lord can drive a Mercedes, wear Armani suits and take holidays in the Bahamas—a long way from singing 'The Sash My Father Wore' on the Shankill, though it is loyalism that provides the discipline and the recruits for his criminal rackets." Lloyd believes that the UDA, in common with most paramilitary groups in Northern Ireland, purposely cows the populations it controls ("informers are murdered, dissenters tortured and the awkward individuals forced out of their houses, or out of the province") to reap personal profit and maintain power. He describes their role as a "cancer" in Northern Ireland's communities, which deepens the population's "alienation from the political process, and makes them more cynical, more sectarian."

"How, you might wonder, could a half-psychopath, half-showman such as Johnny Adair ever become so powerful in Belfast?" asked the journalist, Jenny McCarthy in the *Daily Telegraph* in 2003. "The reasons are many," she explained. "The Shankill Road itself, once a thriving working-class Protestant community, has been slowly transformed by bad planning, neglect and the Troubles into an urban semi-wasteland. As the police force has retreated from 'difficult' areas—hampered by dwindling resources—the paramilitaries have intensified their grip. Yet both the Government and the media, in different ways, have long bolstered Adair's inherent belief that he is a Very Important Person. The Government has alternated between courting his approval and struggling to contain his worst excesses. Journalists, on the other hand, have been fascinated by Adair's crudely crowd-pleasing sense of humour. 'Mad Dog' introduces his son as 'Mad Pup,' and wears a T-shirt proclaiming 'Simply The Best.' The Adair mythology—he was said to have survived thirteen assassination attempts—was pumped up by his boastful joking. Yet this has helped to mask the raw ghastliness of what his paramilitary career has been all about: the promotion of sectarian hatred, terror and drugs."

SUMMARY

The Ulster Defense Association remains the largest and most influential loyalist paramilitary organization in Northern Ireland, although, as of 2005, it remains less a "protector" of the province's Protestant community and murderous sectarian threat to Northern Ireland's Catholics than a powerful and pervasive criminal gang. Meting out summary justice to maintain their control over the drugs trade and their own communities might not have been the UDA's founding intention, but in Northern Ireland's post-Good Friday Agreement era, it reflects the reality of many former paramilitaries who have no wish to enter politics.

SOURCES

Books

Edwards, Ruth Dudley. *The Faithful Tribe*. New York: Harper Collins, 2000.

Jordan, Hugh, and David Lister. *Mad Dog: The Rise and Fall of Johnny Adair*. Edinburgh: Mainstream, 2003.

McDonald, Henry, and Jim Cussack. *The UDA*. New York: Penguin, 2004.

Web sites

Andrew Mueller. "A Brush With Death." < http:// www.andrewmueller.net/ > (accessed October 3, 2005).

> *Guardian Unlimited*. "The Downfall of Mad Dog Adair." < http://books.guardian.co.uk/extracts/ > (accessed October 3, 2005).

SEE ALSO

Combat 18

Ulster Volunteer Force (UVF)

LEADER: David Ervine

USUAL AREA OF OPERATION: Northern Ireland

OVERVIEW

The Ulster Volunteer Force is the oldest and second largest loyalist paramilitary organization in Northern Ireland. It is committed to the maintenance of Ulster in the United Kingdom.

HISTORY

The Ulster Volunteer Force (UVF) first emerged as a paramilitary organization at the start of the twentieth century. In 1912, Sir Edward Carson, a Dublin-born Protestant and former Conservative MP, along with James Craig, leader of the Ulster Unionist Party, concerned at the impetus behind moves to grant home rule to Ireland, formed the UVF as a militia to oppose any such settlement. As home rule seemed to near, the UVF enjoyed incredible support among Ulster's Protestants. As many as 500,000 people signed the "Ulster Covenant"—a petition opposing an independent Ireland—and the UVF claimed up to 100,000 members. Two shipments, consisting of 20,000 rifles and four million rounds of ammunition, were smuggled into Larne from Germany in April 1914, but the outbreak of World War I four months later put the independence issue on hold. During that conflict, many UVF members signed up for the 36th (Ulster) Division of the

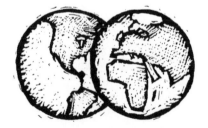

A "peace wall" in Ulster, Belfast, separates Catholic from Protestant neighborhoods. © *Abbas* / *Magnum Photos*

British Army, which would suffer horrendous losses in the Battle of the Somme. When peace came in 1918 and the Irish Free State emerged two years later—with Northern Ireland still part of the British union—many Ulster Protestants saw it as reward for their loyalty during the Great War. Even today, those who died on the Somme are immortalized in unionist lore.

The UVF thereafter disappeared from view for nearly half a century. It reincarnated in the summer of 1966, although it was a far cry from the mass movement that had preceded it. Formed by at most a dozen men in the pubs around the Shankhill Road district of Belfast, it was conceived to combat a practically non-existent IRA. Its principles were "serving Ulster," rather than fighting a religious war, although some Protestants would have regarded these principles indivisible.

The nascent UVF carried out a number of attacks that summer, claiming three lives, but these mostly seemed to be drunken escapades that had assumed a murderous complexion. Its first victim was a seventy-seven-year-old

Protestant widow killed in a fire at a Catholic bar the UVF had petrol bombed; the second was a Catholic man returning home from a pub heard singing "Up the republic! Up the rebels!"; the third, a Catholic barman who had dared stray into a pub on the Protestant side of Belfast's divide.

Most of Ulster's population treated such attacks with barely suppressed horror, but as the Republican civil rights movement grew and intensified its efforts to gain political recognition in the late 1960s, so too did the efforts of the UVF to curtail them. In winter 1969, the UVF bombed a number of water and electricity utilities to unsettle the government of the Northern Irish Prime Minister, Terence O'Neill, which had promised limited reforms in favor of Ulster's Catholics, and in the (initially correct) expectation that they would be blamed on the IRA.

Violence within Northern Ireland increased inexorably over the following three years, during which the UVF maintained a quiet, but occasionally deadly presence. However, on December 4, 1971, they fully announced their

An Ulster Volunteer Force band marches down the Crumlin Road, Belfast, on July 12, 2002. Thousands of Protestant marchers passed through Belfast on their way to a field outside the city area to commemorate the Protestant victory in the Battle of the Boyne in 1690. AP/Wide World Photos

arrival into Northern Ireland's emergent conflict when a bomb in the hallway of Belfast's McGurk's bar exploded without warning, destroying the entire building and killing 15 people, and injuring dozens more.

The following year, 1972—the most deadly of Northern Ireland's troubles—the UVF killed twenty-seven people, all civilians, in sectarian shootings and bombings. Nevertheless, it had been by far usurped as the preeminent loyalist party—in terms of ability to carry out acts of violence and above all in mainstream popularity—by the Ulster Defense Association (UDA), a populist movement that had emerged in 1971 in response to IRA attacks.

Although outlawed by the British government in 1966, the UVF's ban was lifted in 1974 in an attempt to engage the UVF in the political process. This failed miserably. On May 17, 1974, a series of bombs went off in Dublin and Monaghan, killing 33 people. These incidents would be shrouded in mystery for a number of years, leading to claims that the British intelligence unit MI5 was complicit in the bombings; in actuality, Irish Garda botched the investigation, and in 1993, the UVF admitted responsibility for the attacks.

Quickly, the UVF was marking a reputation as the most notorious of all of Northern Ireland's paramilitary organizations. This was secured in July 1975 with an attack on the Miami Showband, one of Ireland's most popular live bands. Returning from a performance in Banbridge, their minibus was flagged down by UVF men posing in British army uniforms. Band members were ordered to line up in a ditch while UVF paramilitaries attempted to plant a bomb inside the minibus, which they hoped would explode as the musicians headed home to Dublin. However, the bomb exploded prematurely, killing two of the UVF men, whereupon the remaining paramilitaries opened fire on the band, killing three of its members. Three months later, on a single day—October 2, 1975—the UVF was responsible for eight

LEADERSHIP

DAVID ERVINE

David Ervine is chief spokesman for the Progressive Union Party (PUP), which acts as the political wing of the UVF. A former UVF member who served a five-year jail sentence at the Maze Prison in the mid 1970s, having been found in possession of a bomb, Ervine is a Belfast City Councillor and Member of the Northern Ireland Assembly. Against the wishes of many Unionists—he has received death threats from both the IRA and his own community—he led the PUP and UVF to back the Good Friday Agreement in 1998. This seemingly marked the completion of Ervine's transition from killer to peacemaker, and he is one of the few unionist politicians to back the agreement. Speaking to a BBC documentary team a year after the Good Friday Agreement, he was asked about his paramilitary past: "Were you prepared to kill?" Irvine replied: "Without question ... totally. My decision and made by me and me alone."

sectarian civilian murders, as well as the deaths of four of its own (after a bomb exploded prematurely on the way to another mission). In total, thirteen bombs were detonated by the UVF on that day.

Worse came with the onset of killings by the so-called "Shankhill Butchers" faction of the UVF, who were notorious for torturing and disemboweling Catholics, purely on sectarian grounds. Many of the gang were jailed in a large-scale trial in 1979, in which eleven UVF members were sentenced on more than 100 charges, with sentences totaling more than 2,000 years.

The UVF was further weakened by the wide-scale British infiltration in the early 1980s, although it continued to carry out a string of attacks, mostly against civilians. It resurfaced towards the end of the decade with the

emergence of Billy Wright, dubbed "King Rat," one of the most controversial and violent individuals associated with Northern Ireland's Troubles. Wright has been linked with the murders of more than forty Catholics in the Portadown area of Ulster, most of whom were civilians and without connection to paramilitary activity. His notoriety brought him both minor fame and a loyal backing, but came at a time when the UVF was tentatively seeking to enter the peace process. Yet, Wright sought a more powerful role within the organization's leadership, ambitions, which, when stunted, would bring him into conflict with its hierarchy. After he broke a UVF ceasefire in 1996, he was expelled from the group and formed the rival Loyalist Volunteer Force (LVF), with which the UVF instantly assumed a deadly feud.

Despite backing the Good Friday Agreement of 1998, UVF violence since its 1994 ceasefire has centered more on fratricidal disputes than the sectarian killings that have characterized most of its history. In particular, it came into repeated conflict with the LVF—with whom it has also an historic grudge—and the Ulster Defense Association over the spoils of Northern Ireland's drugs, prostitution, and extortion rackets. In 2000, the LVF killed Richard Jameson, the UVF's alleged leader. Loyalist paramilitaries in the early twenty-first century have more in common with criminal gangs than paramilitary forces.

It has, nevertheless, returned to its sectarian roots on occasion, most usually around the time of the Orange Lodge's marching season. In September 2005, it was blamed for causing large-scale rioting and for firing upon police when a march was diverted from its usual route. Within days, the British Northern Ireland Secretary, Peter Hain, announced that the government no longer recognized its long-standing ceasefire.

PHILOSOPHY AND TACTICS

The Ulster Volunteer Force (UVF) is a loyalist paramilitary organization committed to the maintenance of the British union and to exorcise all possibility of a united Ireland.

During the height of the Troubles, the UVF carried out more than 400 killings, 80% of which were Catholic civilians. Like other loyalist

KEY EVENTS

1966: UVF forms as a loyalist paramilitary force, taking the name of Sir Edward Carson's old militia.

1969: Bombing of Belfast utilities contributes to the fall of the Northern Ireland government.

1971: Bombing of McGurk's Bar kills fifteen.

1974: Dublin and Monaghan bombings.

1975: Miami Showband massacre.

1970s: Emergence of Shankhill Butchers.

1994: UVF agrees to ceasefire as part of emergent peace process.

1996: Expulsion of Billy "King Rat" Wright for breaking the ceasefire; Wright forms the rival Loyalist Volunteer Force.

1998: UVF/PUP back the Good Friday Agreement.

2000: Murder of alleged UVF leader, Richard Jameson.

2005: Following severe rioting instigated by UVF members, British government refuses to acknowledge UVF ceasefire.

---

paramilitary groups, it found it easier to carry out sectarian killings against noncombatants than the Republican paramilitaries against which it had been established to defend. Most of its attack were shootings and bombings, although it is most notorious for its "Shankhill Butchers" faction, which carried out horrific knife attacks in the late 1970s. It agreed to a peace deal in 1994, which held until September 2005 when it was implicated in large-scale rioting following an Orange Lodge march.

As with all three main loyalist paramilitary groups, the end of the Troubles and sectarian murders have seen the reinvention of the UVF as a criminal gang. Notwithstanding its influence at the time of Orange Lodge marches, most of its violence is now directed at its own community and rival loyalist groups in defense of its criminal networks.

Over the years, the UVF has been accused of collusion with a myriad of ideologies. According to David Boulton, the original incarnation of the UVF in 1912 was an armed mobilization of Ulster's working class to protect the threatened economic interests of its bosses. As such, "It was Europe's first distinctly fascist movement." In the 1970s, they were accused by rivals of being communists. They have also been strongly linked to the far right on the British mainland, particularly the British National Party and Combat 18. At the same time, however, they have a long-standing alliance to the Progressive Unionist Party, which is politically orientated to the left.

OTHER PERSPECTIVES

In September 2005, the UVF orchestrated the worst rioting seen in Northern Ireland for years. At the root of it was an Orange Lodge march, which had been diverted, but the *Economist* believed that the reasons were more deep-seated: "In a rudimentary sense, the riots were ... and not about a march at all. Unionists enraged by the idea that their Republican opponents are getting an easy ride from politicians in London and Dublin talked of grievances unaddressed by the authorities, 'a cry of desperation,' said the Orange Order Grand Master ... Even if they were its victims, the poorer districts at first approved of the rioting. People told reporters that violence was the only way to get Mr Blair's attention: 'It's all concessions to the IRA—nationalists get everything they want,' one said.

"Poverty and the politics of victimhood are aggravated by a criminal feud between Ulster's loyalist paramilitaries. In a murky underworld, the Ulster Volunteer Force (UVF) has always been seen as more political than the larger Ulster Defence Association (UDA)—less steeped in "ordinary" criminality (a relative judgment, of course). In a depressing twist to today's violence, the UVF has been largely blamed for the rioting and for the four deaths in months of fighting with the splinter Loyalist Volunteer Force, a group that now appears entirely devoted to drug-dealing and gangsterism. These groups, recruited from Ulster's working-class Protestants, are divided from unionist politicians by social class and political rivalry. Their efforts a few years ago to form political parties, following the lead of Sinn Fein, collapsed amid rows about drug dealing and racketeering. For them, riots are just about the only way to make a noise."

The riots, which brought an end to British recognition of the UVF ceasefire, were the inevitable consequence of the British government's misplaced strategy for peace in the province, argued Jenny McCarthy in the *Daily Telegraph*. "The birth of the 'peace process' was the decision by the British Government to come to an arrangement with the IRA that would end the IRA's 'spectacular' bombing campaigns in England," she wrote. "As part of the pay-off, all IRA prisoners were released, and—to 'balance' this folly—the loyalist paramilitaries were let out of jail too. Thus a large group of people who had persistently shown the most heinous disregard for human life were unleashed once more, and returned to the welcoming embrace of the IRA, UVF and UDA: groups whose structures and aims remained fully intact. The RUC—the most effective opponent of the paramilitaries—was disbanded, and the media profile of Sinn Fein politicians boosted at every turn, as was that of the political representatives of the loyalist terrorists.

"Since then, the unspoken but insidious policy of the British Government in Northern Ireland has been 'don't upset the paramilitaries'. For who exactly were those masked men orchestrating the rioting in Northern Ireland last week, with the help of roving bands of disaffected teenage yobs? They were members of the Ulster Volunteer Force, who had stockpiled weapons for use against the police. These are the very gentlemen whom the late Mo Mowlam once described as 'the unsung heroes of the peace process.' They—like the IRA—have long been left virtually unchallenged by the authorities, free to pursue extortion, drug-pushing and intimidation in 'their' areas. The decision by the Northern Ireland Secretary, Peter Hain, to declare the UVF ceasefire at an end is the equivalent of sending a bunch of adult psychopaths to Super-nanny's naughty step."

SUMMARY

As with many former paramilitary groups, the UVF now exists primarily as a criminal gang, and has turned the sectarian bloodshed of yesteryear on its own community and rival gangs. However, its culpability in the September 2005 riots, which saw the British government end recognition of its longstanding ceasefire, shows that it still has the potential to engage in large-scale violence.

SOURCES

Books

Dill, Martin. *The Shankhill Butchers: A Case Study of Mass Murder*. London: Hutchinson, 1989.

McKittrick, David, and David McVeigh. *Making Sense of the Troubles*. London: Penguin, 2003.

Taylor, Peter. *Loyalists*. London: Bloomsbury, 2000.

SEE ALSO

Loyalist Volunteer Force

Ultras Sur

LEADER: Jose Luis Ochaita
YEAR ESTABLISHED OR BECAME ACTIVE: late 1980s
USUAL AREA OF OPERATION: Spain

OVERVIEW

Ultras Sur are a gang of right-wing football hooligans associated with Real Madrid, Europe's most successful club. Although they follow the Italian Ultra tradition and have been strongly associated with racist chanting and violence, football-related extremism in Spain is generally less prevalent than elsewhere in Europe, particularly Italy, where Ultra fans are longer established, and Eastern Europe, where football hooliganism has escalated dramatically since the fall of communism.

HISTORY

"Italy," the journalist and sociologist, Olivero Beha, once wrote, "is a Republic based on football." Nowhere else in Europe is the aphorism that the sport is more than a game truer than in a country where three daily broadsheet newspapers deal exclusively with football and where the ruling party (led by Silvio Berlusconi, Chairman of the country's second most successful club, AC Milan) takes its name—Forza Italia—from a football chant. At the vanguard of this national obsession are the Ultras, the most passionate section of each club's support.

The Italian term "ultra" is commonly translated to the English term "hooligan," but this

LEADERSHIP

JOSE LUIS OCHAITA

Jose Luis Ochaita is the leader of Real Madrid's Ultras Sur. Despite a long record of violence—he was arrested in 1998 in Germany for waving Nazi flags, and also banned from matches for three years for attacking a referee in Spain—he has been welcomed by both the Real Madrid players and hierarchy, which has drawn condemnation. In May 2005, following a game in which the Ultras Sur had been seen waving racist banners, Real Madrid's black full back, Roberto Carlos, caused consternation when he was seen giving Ochaita his shirt. Carlos apologized for the incident later, but stopped short of condemning Ultras Sur. He said: "I made a mistake of presenting the shirt at that moment. I wasn't aware of the controversial events that had occurred during the game."

ignores several important distinctions. Hooligan owes its name to a disreputable London-based Irish family from the end of the nineteenth century, and commonly denotes a violent mob; the term ultra, by contrast, is more all-embracing and has more overt political connotations (it has referred to the supporters of French kings; but also to post-1968 left-wing groups).

The term first came to be applied to football fans in the late 1960s and early 1970s. Post-war Italian society was politically polarized and sporting events were an extension of this schism, with supporters increasingly identifying their clubs with local political ideologies. In Milan, for instance, AC Milan represented the team of the working class (particularly the railway workers) and was considered left wing, whereas Internazionale was the team of the Milanese middle classes and considered a conservative club. Elsewhere, in Communist Emilio, Bologna, inevitably had left-wing supporters; while in Verona, which has a history of extreme right politics, its fans adopted the ideology of the city.

This assumed an organizational basis when representatives of the Italian Social Movement (Mussolini's neo-fascist political successors) were banned from Italy's streets and squares. Its members turned to leading and organizing fans groups as an alternative, and they would unfurl right-wing banners on the curved corner areas of a football stadium (also, traditionally, the cheap seats). Internazionale's Inter Boys and the Ultra of Lazio and Hellas Verona all owe their origins to the Italian Social Movement. Groups of left-wing fans from other clubs—such as Sampdoria, AC Milan, and Bologna—also organized their own ultra groups.

Although the Ultras proved just as adept at violence as their English rivals, they were different in many ways. They were more organized, carrying full membership activities and often operating with the support of the clubs they followed. This could extend to financial backing, free tickets, or simply toleration of some of their excesses. Their membership also extended to women, which set them apart from northern European hooligan gangs. Violence was not a prerequisite either, and many were concerned primarily with putting on a display of color and noise to show their allegiance. Napoli ultra, for instance, would enter their stadium in a mock funeral procession following a coffin covered by the rival team flag. This was a ritual developed from an English custom that dated back to the nineteenth century, although it did not necessarily denote violent intent.

There was also a certain deference shown to English football in general, and hooligans in particular. Many Italian clubs owed their origins to British workers in Italy in the late nineteenth century (several have the flag of St. George incorporated in their emblems); as well as being revered as the game's inventors, their hooligans were admired for being football's *bete noires* (black sheep). Many Ultra gangs adopted the dress code of the English football casual, designer clothing as opposed to the club's colors, although some gangs took this to an extreme. A section of the Lazio Ultras picked up the name of the Barbours because of their insistence of wearing a type of English waxed coat peculiar to the country's landed gentry.

Ultras could, and frequently did, engage in violence, however, which usually involved attacks on rival fans. The nature of their assaults was not as indiscriminate as in England, and the political tendency of a team colored not just rivalries but also provided the basis for alliances with fans from other clubs. For instance, the leftist Ultras of Bologna had a particularly heated rivalry with Hellas Verona's rightwing Ultras, but were also twinned with AC Milan's Ultras and would team up on match days against Verona Ultra—regardless of whether it was Bologna or AC Milan playing them—to attack its fans.

Part of English football hooliganism's reputation was exaggerated because of the actions of fans of its national team and club supporters following their teams in European competition. By contrast, Italian Ultra violence tended not to be associated with either. When thirty-nine Juventus fans died following a riot by Liverpool fans at Brussels' Heysel Stadium in 1985, they had barely been culpable in the fighting.

While the record of domestic football violence in Italy throughout the 1970s and 1980s is comparable to that within England, after 1990, when English football experienced a decline in hooliganism, Italian football violence continued to grow, with attacks becoming even better planned and assuming a nastier edge. Up to a dozen times a season, large-scale and well-orchestrated rioting would take place, with hundreds of incidents taking place on other occasions. On November 29, 1994, for instance, at a Brescia V Roma match, a pre-planned attack against police and Brescia Ultras was carried out by an alliance (which seemingly transcended traditional rivalries) of Roma and Lazio Ultras and neo-fascist ultra members from other Italian cities, using axes, knives, and other weapons. More widely publicized was the abandonment of the European Champions League match between AC Milan and Internazionale in 2005, after the AC Milan goalkeeper was hit on the head by a firework and Inter fans pelted the pitcher in an attempt to get the game cancelled and the score overturned.

Italian Ultras also became increasingly synonymous with the racism they extolled. This often expressed itself in the form of racist chanting against players not just of rival teams, but of their own teams, too. In 1996, Verona and Padova Ultras waged furious protests against their clubs, for signing black players for the following season. More seriously, the racism was carried outside the football stadiums and

brought to bear on Italy's immigrant communities. In June 1996, while celebrating their club's promotion to Serie A, a group of extreme-right Bologna hooligans—known as the Mods—violently attacked eight black immigrants. (Following the incident, the predominantly leftist Bolognese Ultra disowned the Mods, and even issued a press release condemning the attack.) Even more notoriously, following the assassination of the Serb warlord, Arkan, in 2000, Lazio's Ultras held up banners proclaiming their sympathy at his death.

While English football hooligans had served as an inspiration to certain supporters elsewhere in the 1970s and 1980s, since 1990, Italian Ultras have increasingly been the example followed by extremist fans in other countries. Across Eastern Europe, where football hooliganism virtually dominates, fan groups calling themselves Ultras carry out acts of extreme violence. Although their racism is even more pronounced than Italian Ultras, they often have more in common—both in terms of fan culture and because of their non-political nature and indiscriminate acts—with northern European skinheads.

In Spain, however, there has been a marked increase in the proliferation and notoriety of what could categorized Ultra groups by more than name alone. Although Spanish football shares many of the qualities of football in Italy—passionate fans, fierce local patriotism, an emphasis of loyalty towards club rather than international football—Ultra groups had been less prevalent, arguably because of the suppression of the Franco regime, up until the late 1980s. Fans of some teams, such as FC Barcelona, which are viewed as *de facto* representatives of the Catalan nation, could be seen as typifying some of the more positive aspects of Italian Ultras through their colorful flag waving, vociferous chanting, and so on, although they have seldom extolled similar violence or racism. Supporters of other Spanish teams have also shared such characteristics, but during the 1980s and 1990s, increasingly began to assume the political identities of their regions. Thus, sections of fans of Real Madrid, Valencia, and Espanyol (Barcelona's second club) became known for their right-wing posturing; while supporters of Athletico Bilbao, Deportivo La Coruna, and FC Barcelona have identified with the left.

cameras. Again, an apology was not forthcoming. It seems that racism has become the defining problem posed not just by Spain's Ultras, but by the Spanish football authorities, too.

KEY EVENTS

1960s: Creation of several far-right Italian Ultra groups by the Italian Social Movement; left-wing equivalents emerge at Bologna, AC Milan, and elsewhere.

1985: Heysel Stadium disaster.

1980s–1990s: Emergence of Ultra groups in Eastern Europe and Spain.

1994: Violent assault on Brescia fans and police by Ultras from Roma, Lazio, and other clubs.

2004: Spanish fans racially abusing black English players bring worldwide attention on Spanish racism problem.

2005: Internationale v. AC Milan match abandoned because of Inter fans rioting.

This has seldom teetered over into large-scale violence, but fans of so-called right-wing clubs have become notorious for their racist chanting, most notably Real Madrid's Ultras Sur. What is most shocking about this group is that it not only has formal ties to the club (as many Italian Ultras do to their own), but has its own offices in Madrid's Bernabéu Stadium in which they store pamphlets, drums, megaphones, and flags bearing General Franco's shield and other neo-Nazi symbols. After home matches, they have been known to organize hunts of blacks, prostitutes, tramps, gays, and supporters of other clubs. Among their favored chants is: "Six million Jews to the gas chambers."

The support given to Ultras Sur by Real Madrid itself is seen as part of a wider malaise within Spanish football. After a friendly match between Spain and England at the Bernabéu in November 2004 was dogged by racist chanting, the Spanish FA were slow in offering an unequivocal apology. Just weeks earlier, the Spainish national coach, Luis Aragones, had described Arsenal's French striker, Thierry Henry, as a "black shit" in front of national television

PHILOSOPHY AND TACTICS

Ultras Sur are a group of right-wing Real Madrid fans, who view the late fascist leader, General Franco, as their ideological leader. They are fiercely loyal to their team, and although often guilty of racist chanting, their prejudice does not usually extend to Real's own sizable contingent of black players. Although they have been accused of acts of violence, this is not on a scale comparable to that of Italian Ultras.

Elsewhere, Ultra groups are generally marked by a left- or right-wing political orientation. They are noted for their racism against opposition players and violence against fans of a rival allegiance—political or footballing—but they also represent some of football's most passionate and colorful fans who often have no liking for the darker elements of Ultra groups.

Ultras are more markedly organized than English football hooligans, and the violence propagated is less indiscriminate. Often, they have close ties to club administrations, and exist with either tacit or explicit support of the teams they represent.

OTHER PERSPECTIVES

Writing about the racist chanting in Madrid in the March 2005 issue of *Observer Sports Monthly*, the academic Martin Jacques argued that "Football is the faultline of racism in Europe. No other activity, be it cultural or political, commands the emotion, passion and allegiance, certainly of men, in the same way. Football is the cultural lingua franca of European men. Far from being some kind of hermetically sealed hobby on the periphery of society, a phenomenon only of interest to those who read the sports pages, football is an exemplar of society: it mirrors and gives expression to society's passions and prejudices in a way that politics, for example, is, for the most part, quite unable to do. Indeed, it is about the only activity in which men collectively and publicly express their own emotions. What happened in the Bernabéu exposed, in all its raw crudity, the prejudices that inform Spanish society. Official, polite society—parliament, the media and the rest—contains, channels, constrains and seeks to deny these prejudices. Football reveals them. Bernabéu was one of the most important political events in Europe in 2004, the largest mass racist demonstration in recent years."

Much of Spain was in a state of denial about the racist chanting, and some newspapers even blamed it on the British press for their earlier criticism of Luis Aragones' unsavory description of Thierry Henry. The reaction of *Marca*, a liberal daily, was more considered: "It is only the colour of the shirt that should count in a stadium or any sporting arena," proclaimed an editorial. "The monkey chants that were directed at England's black players last Wednesday oblige us to condemn them energetically, and invite all of us to make a profound reflection: Are we really racist?"

Nevertheless, it retained strong words for the English who, from the Prime Minister and head of the FA, down to ordinary football fans, had been universal in their condemnation. "As we admit our own errors and inappropriate attitudes, profoundly lamenting what happened and appealing that it may never happen again, English football has a part to play too," *Marca* claimed. "It should ask if it really has the moral authority to hand out lessons when its 'hooligans' continue to write some of the darkest pages in football history; when there have been similar episodes in its stadiums. The most coherent thing to do now would be to lead by example. England isn't exactly an example of 'fair play.' "

SUMMARY

The xenophobic abuse of England's black players by Spain fans in November 2004 highlighted not just the malaise of racism within Spanish football, but brought a focus its ultra groups—prior to this event, regarded as a far less malevolent force than "extremist" fans elsewhere in the world. Groups like Ultras Sur share many of the worst characteristics of the Italian Ultra groups they set out to imitate, but at the same time their abuses have not only gone unchecked, but have been carried out with the support of the clubs they claim to represent. Only when this approval dissipates will a decline in the extremist activities of Ultra groups be witnessed.

SOURCES

Books

Armstrong, Gary, and Richard Giulianotti. *Entering The Field: New Perspectives on World Football*. Oxford: Berg, 1997.

Ball, Phil. *Morbo: A History of Spanish Football*. London: WSC Books, 2003.

Brown, Adam (ed.). *Fanatics! Power, Identity and Fandom in FOOTBALL*. Oxford: Routledge, 1998.

Duke, Vic, and Liz Crolley. *Football, Nationality and the State*. New York: Longman, 1996.

Giulianotti, Richard, Norman Bonney and Mike Hepworth (eds.). *Football, Violence and Social Identity*. Oxford: Routledge, 1994.

United Liberation Front of Assam (ULFA)

OVERVIEW

The United Liberation Front of Assam (ULFA) is an extremist organization reportedly formed in 1979, in the northeastern Indian state of Assam. The group was thought to be formed by a few Assamese rebels with the purpose of forming a separate country of Assam, independent of Indian rule.

As of 2005, the ULFA still exists and continues with its same objectives. Since the early 1980s, the group has been reportedly involved in various terrorist operations in Assam and other northeastern states of India. The organization is also known as United Liberation Front of Asom.

HISTORY

The ULFA was reportedly formed on April 7, 1979, by a group of students belonging to the All Assam Students' Union—a union that was considered by many as anti-foreigner. Analysts state that ULFA was formed to promote an armed struggle against the government of India in order to create an independent country of Assam that would be ruled by socialists.

The group was relatively inactive until the mid 1980s. There were some reports of hiring during the early 1980s; however, no activities were carried

LEADER(S): Arabinda Rajkhowa, Paresh Baruah

YEAR ESTABLISHED OR BECAME ACTIVE: 1979

ESTIMATED SIZE: 3,000–4,000, including around a hundred women cadres

USUAL AREA OF OPERATION: India, primarily the northeastern state of Assam

A police officer examines a guitar as a part of a search operation in Gauhati, India, on April 2, 2005. The searches are a response to five bombings in the Assam province. AP/Wide World Photos

out during this period. In 1986, ULFA established associations with two other similar organizations in Assam and neighboring states—the Kachin Independence Army (KIA) and the Nationalist Socialist Council of Nagaland (NSCN). According to published reports, it was during this period that the group stepped up its fund-gathering activities. Significant funds were collected, reportedly through extortions from businesses and trading houses.

Anti-terrorism experts also maintain that the ULFA in the late 1980s had established strong links with the Assam Gana Parishad (AGP), the ruling party of Assam at the time. It is thought that leaders of the ULFA influenced many members of the AGP as well as the police force in Assam. Following such allegations in 1990, the Indian government banned ULFA and employed measures to counter the threat posed by the group. The state was also declared as a "troubled state" by the government.

After being banned by the government, the group started using violent tactics. Throughout the 1990s (and early 2000s), members of the ULFA claimed responsibility for numerous killings and kidnappings. The group is thought to mainly target state government buildings, security personnel, rail infrastructure, and politicians who opposed their ideologies.

In 1996, per published reports, the ULFA formed its own military wing, the Sanjukta Mukti Fouj (SMF). Anti-terrorism experts claim that this wing was formed specifically to plan and carry out terrorist activities against the government and security forces. During the 1990s, the organization is also thought to have set up training camps in neighboring countries such as Bhutan and Bangladesh. The total numbers of these training camps is reportedly in the thousands.

As of 2005, according to Indian intelligence reports, most leaders of ULFA are based in various cities in Bangladesh. Although since the

LEADERSHIP

ARABINDA RAJKHOWA

Arabinda Rajkhowa (also known as Rajiv Rajkonwar) is reportedly the chairman of the ULFA. He is also the co-founder of the group and has been the mastermind of several terrorist activities. Rajkhowa is allegedly based in Bangladesh and is also thought to have links with Inter-Services Intelligence (ISI), Pakistan's intelligence agency.

The United Liberation Front of Assam has many other prominent leaders. These include Paresh Baruah, Pradeep Gogoi, and Anup Chetia. According to published reports, both Pradeep Gogoi and Anup Chetia are in jail. Arabinda Rajkhowa and Paresh Baruah are the heads of the civil and military wings of ULFA.

early 2000s many ULFA militants have been reportedly arrested (or have surrendered), the group remains active and poses a major threat to the state government of Assam as well as the central Indian government.

PHILOSOPHY AND TACTICS

The United Liberation Front of Assam was formed with the aim of "liberating" Assam from India. Its leaders propose a socialist government to rule an independent country of Assam. The ULFA has adopted violent tactics in order to achieve its objectives. Since the early 1990s, several people have been killed and extensive damage has been caused to property as a result of the terrorist acts carried out by the group.

The operations of ULFA have been primarily aimed at government officials as well as security force personnel in Assam. The group claims that Assam can be liberated only through an armed struggle against the government of India. According to Indian intelligence reports,

KEY EVENTS

1990: ULFA is banned by the Indian government following increase in anti-terrorist activities; Assam is declared a "troubled state" and the president's rule is established.

1992: ULFA claims responsibility for killing ten security personnel from the Indian military.

1994: Pradeep Gogoi, Vice Chairman of ULFA, arrested.

1995–1996: More than thirty, including security force personnel, police officials, and local political leaders, killed by ULFA militants.

1996: Sanjukta Mukti Fouj (SMF), the military wing of ULFA, formed.

in the last two decades, ULFA militants have killed hundreds of security force personnel, and also many civilians as well as political leaders. Since the early 2000s, ULFA militants have reportedly targeted a number of public installations and civilian structures, causing significant damage to property as well as human life. Indian authorities allege that the group has also carried out a number of extortions and kidnappings in exchange for exorbitant ransoms.

In fact, as thought by the Indian government and monitor groups, extortion from businesses is the main source of funding for the ULFA. The group has also been charged with extensive drug trafficking from neighboring countries. Analysts state that the money generated from drug trafficking is used to buy arms and explosives. According to published reports, the organization also engages in legal business holdings in other countries, especially Bangladesh. These reports suggest that ULFA has a number of legal businesses in various cities of Bangladesh, another source of funding for the group.

The ULFA has a distinct civil and a military wing. The military wing, Sanjukta Mukti Fauj, is thought to be the unit responsible for

PRIMARY SOURCE
United Liberation Front of Assam (ULFA)

DESCRIPTION

Northeast India's most prominent insurgent group, ULFA—an ethnic secessionist organization in the Indian state of Assam, bordering Bangladesh and Bhutan—was founded on April 7, 1979 at Rang Ghar, during agitation organized by the state's powerful students' union. The group's objective is an independent Assam, reflected in its ideology of "Oikya, Biplab, Mukti" ("Unity, Revolution, Freedom"). ULFA enjoyed widespread support in upper Assam in its initial years, especially in 1985–1992. ULFA's kidnappings, killings and extortion led New Delhi to ban the group and start a military offensive against it in 1990, which forced it to go underground. ULFA began to lose popularity in the late 1990s after it increasingly targeted civilians, including a prominent NGO activist. It lost further support for its anti-Indian stand during the 1999 Kargil War.

ACTIVITIES

ULFA trains, finances, and equips cadres for a "liberation struggle" while extortion helps finance military training and weapons purchases. ULFA conducts hit and run operations on security forces in Assam, selective assassinations, and explosions in public places. During the 1980s–1990s, ULFA undertook a series of abductions and murders, particularly of businessmen. In 2000, ULFA assassinated an Assam state minister. In 2003, ULFA killed more than sixty "outsiders" in Assam, mainly residents of the bordering state of Bihar. Following the December 2003 Bhutanese Army's attack on ULFA camps in Bhutan, the group is believed to have suffered a setback. Some important ULFA functionaries surrendered in Assam, but incidents of violence, though of a lesser magnitude than in the past, continue. On August 14, one civilian was killed and eighteen others injured when ULFA militants triggered a grenade blast inside a cinema hall at Gauripur in Dhubri district. The next day, at an Indian Independence Day event, a bomb blast in Dhemaji killed an estimated thirteen people, including six children, and injured twenty-one.

STRENGTH

ULFA's earlier numbers (3,000 plus) dropped following the December 2003 attack on its camps in Bhutan. Total cadre strength now is estimated at 700.

LOCATION/AREA OF OPERATIONS

ULFA is active in the state of Assam, and its workers are believed to transit (and sometimes conduct operations in) parts of neighboring Arunachal Pradesh, Meghalaya and Nagaland. All ULFA camps in Bhutan are reportedly demolished. The group may have linkages with other ethnic insurgent groups active in neighboring states.

EXTERNAL AID

ULFA reportedly procures and trades in arms with other Northeast Indian groups, and receives aid from unknown external sources.

Source: U.S. Department of State. *Country Reports on Terrorism.* Washington, D.C., 2004.

---

organizing and performing terrorist activities. The organizational structure is reportedly divided into three categories: the Central unit, the Districts unit, and the Anachalik unit. The Central unit comprises of the central leadership of the group. The District unit is categorized into four subsections depending on the districts they target: the East District Zone, the West District Zone, the Central District Zone, and the South District Zone. Each zone is thought to have a president who reports to central leadership. Within the district units, the group is further divided into Anachalik units. These are comprised of the villages in a particular district. Reportedly, each anachalik unit also has a president.

According to Indian intelligence reports, the ULFA over the years has established associations with numerous militant groups in India (particularly in the northeastern states) and in those situated in neighboring countries such as Bangladesh and Bhutan. Training camps have allegedly been set up in these countries. The Indian government also claims that the ULFA has links with Pakistan's ISI, an agency that is accused of training ULFA militants in the past.

OTHER PERSPECTIVES

Indian government officials have often publicly condemned the terrorist activities of the ULFA. It has accused the ULFA of disrupting democratic elections in Assam. For instance, in 2001 during Assam state elections, various terrorist acts were reported. The Indian Ministry of Home Affairs issued a statement that read: "The Union Ministry of Home Affairs has taken a serious view of the recent incidents of violence perpetrated by the United Liberation Front of Assam (ULFA). The Ministry observes that the objective of these senseless killings of contesting candidates and political activists and workers by the ULFA is to vitiate the poll process for the general elections to the State Assembly in Assam. The Government of India is committed to ensure a free and fair poll in Assam."

The statement further read: "The ULFA is committing anti-democratic acts at the behest of the ISI [of Pakistan] and other foreign agencies inimical to India. Area dominance by the security forces in parts of Assam bordering Bhutan has been intensified. Having amassed ill-gotten money by extortions, the ULFA and NDFB are running camps in Bhutan by recruiting innocent youth of the State."

In 2004, world leaders supported the Indian government's measures of anti-terrorism in the northeastern region. After a series of blasts allegedly carried out by the ULFA in Assam in October 2004, the U.S. Ambassador to India, David C. Mulford, wrote to the Chief Minister of Assam, Tarun Gogoi, stating, "Should you find it helpful, the FBI would be pleased to provide technical support for your investigation."

SUMMARY

Since 1995, the Indian Security Force has reportedly arrested several hundred cadres of the ULFA. As thought by analysts and monitor groups, the terrorist activities have been reduced. Media reports indicate that both the Indian government and the ULFA leaders have taken some steps to hold talks in order to resolve their key issues. However, such talks have failed to stop terrorist activities in Assam.

Many ULFA militants have reportedly surrendered and are now assisting Indian security forces in counterterrorism operations in the region. As of 2005, the group still commands a sizeable strength and is thought to be a potent threat to peace initiatives in the state of Assam.

SOURCES

Web sites

Asia Times Online. "A New Dimension in India's Northeast Woes." < http://www.atimes.com/atimes/South_Asia/FJ23Df02.html > (accessed October 1, 2005).

Ministry of Home Affairs, Government of India. "Ministry of Home Affairs Reviews Security Scenario in Assam." < http://mha.nic.in/pr052001.htm > (accessed October 1, 2005).

MIPT Terrorism Knowledge Base. "Group Profile: United Liberation Front of Assam (ULFA)." < http://www.tkb.org/Group.jsp?groupID = 3686 > (accessed October 1, 2005).

South Asian Terrorism Portal. "United Liberation Front of Asom (ULFA)—Terrorist Group of Assam." < http://www.satp.org/satporgtp/countries/india/states/assam/terrorist_outfits/ulfa.htm > (accessed October 1, 2005).

United Patriots and Associates

LEADER: Ron Bass

USUAL AREA OF OPERATION: United States, mainly rural areas of the Midwest, and in the mountain regions of Idaho and Montana

OVERVIEW

The United Patriots is an extreme right-wing group that resists the involvement of the federal government in the lives of U.S. citizens. The group is part of a larger "Patriot" movement and is also called the United Patriots of America (UPA), or plainly Patriots.

HISTORY

The United Patriots are an extreme right-wing group found in the United States. This group encourages citizens to be prepared to take up arms to defend themselves against the federal government, which they say violates their constitutional rights.

The United Patriots are part of a larger Patriot movement that claims the United States is in an economic and social decline. The Patriot movement resists the federal government, claiming it is responsible for the country's problems of unemployment, crime, and loss of traditional religious values.

Patriot extremist groups are located primarily in the rural areas of the Midwest, and in the mountain regions of Idaho and Montana. A majority of members of the Patriot movement are middle- to lower-class Americans, with minimal education.

LEADERSHIP

RON BASS

Ron Bass is the founder and acting president of the United Patriots of America. He claims that the organization represents traditional mainstream America. Bass claims that the people represented by the United Patriots are the silent majority, whose opinions have not been heard by their government leaders. The goal, according to Bass, is to bring back representative government, and to educate people on how to do that.

Militias have been formed by Patriot groups throughout the United States. These militias are the military wing of the Patriot cause. Patriots legitimize the militias as a way to better ensure that their constitutional rights are not violated by the U.S. government. They say that without militias the federal government will not listen to their concerns.

The movement began to develop in the 1970s and 1980s in response to declining economic opportunities in rural areas. In Michigan, a state with a large number of Patriots, the automobile industry has experienced numerous cutbacks since 1980, when there were 600,000 jobs. By 1995, jobs in the automobile industry had dropped to 300,000. Many more job cuts came in the agriculture industry. Farm prices crashed in the 1980s, as a response to global recession. Land values decreased drastically, by as much as 66%. Leading up to the recession, the U.S. government gave a very positive outlook on the upcoming prospects of farming. The government predicted high returns in the 1980s, and farmers began expanding their production accordingly. These miscalculations by the government have fueled the Patriot movement.

The Patriot militia movement was fueled by the 1993 standoff in Waco, Texas, between the FBI and a cult called the Branch Davidian (which advocated resistance to the federal government). The FBI stormed the compound of the Branch Davidian, and eighty members of the cult were killed.

Patriot violence was most severe in the 1995 bombing of the federal building in Oklahoma City. The main perpetrators of that attack were members of Patriot militias. Other acts of violence have targeted federal government employees and U.S. police marshals.

PHILOSOPHY AND TACTICS

Patriots accuse the federal government of such things as violating constitutional rights of citizens, implementing immigration policies that are too liberal, not giving enough independence to individual states, and restricting land- and water-use practices. Patriot members resist U.S. involvement in globalization, and are against international treaties such as the North American Free Trade Agreement (NAFTA).

Patriots are nearly always aligned with pro-gun lobbies, including the National Rifle Association. Many Patriot militias look to neo-Nazi ways of teaching. Some Patriot militia members are former Ku Klux Klan members.

Patriots advocate the decentralization of government. They push for states to have more control of their own affairs, and for the federal government to be less involved. The Patriots want the federal laws to have less application at the state level. Most Patriots advocate the use of a state militia to ensure that their constitutional rights are being protected.

Patriot members also include anti-tax protestors, survivalists, and anti-environmentalists. Apocalyptic millenialists, including Christian zealots who believe the end times are near, have also been characteristic of those within the Patriot movement. These Apocalyptic millenialists believe society is facing the "mark of the beast" through supermarket bar codes, implantable computer chips, and designs for new currency. Patriot media often has racist undertones, with many Patriots having anti-Semitic or neo-Nazi beliefs.

The United Patriots speak out against immigrants, claiming they damage society by taking jobs and increasing the level of crime. They blame the U.S. government, claiming that they make it too easy for immigrants to come to the United States.

The common thread among the Patriots is a growing hate for government involvement in what they claim is their personal business. For example,

KEY EVENTS

1970s–1980s: Patriots movement developed following economic recessions.

1993: Standoff between FBI and the Branch Davidian in Waco, Texas.

1995: Patriot movement militia members carried out the bombing of the federal building in Oklahoma City, killing 168 people.

loggers feel violated by environmental laws. Ranchers are angry at what they label restrictive land-use and water-use policies. Those who find it hard to find gainful employment blame immigration and international trade agreements.

OTHER PERSPECTIVES

The Patriots have been described as a movement of undereducated middle-class Americans who have a nostalgic idea of what the United States used to be. They are said to be idealistic about a United States that does not need to work with the rest of the world, and that can survive on its own.

Many view the group as a violent organization that wants to create an alternative patriarchal society for white people. The national news media has discussed the "angry white male" segment of the anti-government community, associated with Patriot members. However, others point out that there are many non-racists involved with the United Patriots.

Some economists and social analysts explain that the Patriot movement is a result of the rich gaining more wealth, and the poor and middle class losing economic ground. An economist at New York University explains that nearly 40% of all assets in the United States (bonds, stocks, jewelry, etc.) is owned by 500,000 households. It is thought that as fewer people have access to such assets, the more they are going to join Patriot organizations.

SUMMARY

The Patriot movement developed in the 1970s and 1980s in rural areas around the United States that have faced economic recession and job losses. The Patriots claim the federal government is responsible for their problems. Armed militias have taken up the cause of the Patriots, and have carried out violent attacks against government officials. One of the most notorious was the attack on the federal building in Oklahoma City, resulting in the death of 168 people.

Patriot groups remain active in the United States. However, it is said that the Patriot movement reached its peak in 1996, following a crackdown on Patriot militias after the Oklahoma City bombing. A count in 2004 showed the number of Patriot groups had dropped to 152, from 171 in 2003. However, there are many other extremist groups that have formed in recent years, which might be comprised of former members of other Patriot groups.

SOURCES

Books

Abanes, Richard. *American Militias*. Downers Grove, IL: InterVarsity Press, 1996.

Cozic, Charles P., editor. *The Militia Movement*. Farmington Hills, MI: Greenhaven Press, 1997.

Periodicals

Ruiz, Albor. "No Room at Inn for This Flock." *New York Daily News*. February 24, 2004.

Web sites

Southern Poverty Law Center. "Anti-Semitism: 'Patriot' Publications Taking on Anti-Semitic Edge." < http://www.splcenter.org/intel/intelreport/article.jsp?aid = 68 > (accessed October 1, 2005).

Southern Poverty Law Center. "Hate Group Numbers Slightly Up in 2004." < http://www.splcenter.org/center/splcreport/article.jsp?aid = 135 > (accessed October 1, 2005).

SEE ALSO

Neo-Nazis

Ku Klux Klan

Vishwa Hindu Parishad (VHP)

ALTERNATE NAME: The World Hindu Council
LEADER: Praveen Togadia
YEAR ESTABLISHED OR BECAME ACTIVE: 1964
ESTIMATED SIZE: Thousands
USUAL AREA OF OPERATION: India; worldwide

OVERVIEW

The *Vishwa Hindu Parishad* (VHP), or World Hindu Council, is a Hindu extremist organization formed with the purpose of promoting Hinduism in India and the world. The VHP is an offshoot of another extremist Hindu organization—the *Rashtriya Svayamsevak Sangh* (RSS).

The group was reportedly formed in 1964. However, it is thought to have gained prominence only since the 1980s. The VHP, as of 2005, reportedly has thousands of members worldwide.

HISTORY

Members of the RSS (the parent organization of Vishwa Hindu Parishad) and prominent Hindu thinkers in India and abroad were reportedly invited to Mumbai (then Bombay) in India in August 1964. According to published reports, it was decided at the meeting that a new organization by the name of Vishwa Hindu Parishad would be formed and launched two years later, in 1966, at a world convention of Hindus.

Soon after its inception, the VHP turned its focus on the *Ramjanmbhoomi* (birthplace of Lord Ram) issue in Ayodhya, India. Hindu extremists allege that the place where Babri mosque is built in Ayodhya, in the western state of Uttar Pradesh, is the birthplace of Lord Ram

Members of Akhil Bharatiya Vidyarthi, the student faction of Bharatiya Janata Party (BJP), protest against Congress Party President Sonia Gandhi during a rally. The rally was aimed at undermining Gandhi's candidacy for prime minister of India because she was born in Italy. The poster reads "People of foreign origin go back." AP/Wide World Photos

(a revered Hindu God). Hindu fundamentalists, including the VHP, have been propagating the notion that the Babri mosque be "replaced" by a Hindu temple of Ram at the disputed site.

Throughout the 1980s and 1990s, the Vishwa Hindu Parishad reportedly expanded its member base garnering more support for the Ramjanmbhoomi and other issues. During the 1980s, the VHP also formed other organizations. As thought by most analysts, the most prominent was the formation of its youth wing—the *Bajrang Dal* (or Army of Lord Hanuman), in 1984. Experts state that the Bajrang Dal is more aggressive in its approach and tactics as compared to VHP. It is during the 1980s that the VHP formed an alliance with the *Bharitiya Janata Party* (BJP)—a national political party in India that has formed the Indian central government a few times since.

The VHP and its associate organizations stepped up the demands for demolition of the Babri mosque by the late 1980s. Analysts state that by the early 1990s, the Ram temple/Babri mosque dispute had become a national issue. Subsequently, on December 6, 1992, thousands of activists from VHP, BJP, and other similar organizations destroyed part of the Babri mosque structure. This incident caused widespread condemnation in India and around the world.

The aftermath of the Babri mosque demolition is thought by most to be one of the darkest periods in Indian history. Hindu-Muslim riots broke out in many parts of the country, especially Mumbai. Several thousand Hindus and Muslims were reportedly killed. The Indian government set up commissions to assess the role of BJP and VHP in inciting the Babri mosque demolition, and later the riots. Many VHP members were convicted. Sanctions were placed on the VHP, and many leaders were prevented from speaking at public rallies.

An Indian man gets ready to jump to his death as Hindu extremists call for the Babri mosque to be destroyed, 1990. © *Network Photographers | Alamy*

The situation calmed down in subsequent years. Reportedly, VHP still held extensive campaigns to promote its Ram Temple ideologies. In early 2002, the VHP allegedly heightened the tension once again after claiming that they wanted to perform a religious ceremony at the disputed site.

On February 27, 2002, more than 50 activists from the VHP were traveling from Ayodhya to the western state of Gujarat in a train. After reaching the city of Godhra (in Gujarat), the activists reportedly started shouting Hindu slogans that angered a mob of Muslims. The mob allegedly burnt the train, killing all the activists. This incident once again triggered Hindu-Muslim riots in Gujarat. According to news reports and Gujarat government figures, hundreds of Muslims and Hindus were killed in the riots.

PHILOSOPHY AND TACTICS

The Vishwa Hindu Parishad was formed by the RSS in 1964 to promote Hinduism and give Hindus a "sense of identity," as claimed by the group. According to analysts, at the time, leaders of the RSS felt the need to unite Hindus around the world in order to maintain and uphold Hindu values. The leaders claimed that other religions were more popular around the world because they were more organized and uniform as compared to Hinduism. The VHP is a non-political organization.

The VHP's main objective since the 1980s has been to build a temple for Lord Ram at the site where Babri mosque stands, in Ayodhya. To propagate its ideologies and garner more support for the temple, the VHP held peaceful demonstrations and rallies in various parts of the country. It also fought a legal battle in a bid to get the temple built. However, as analysts and reports suggest, by the late 1980s all measures failed. It is thought by most that these repeated failures led the VHP to adopt far more aggressive and violent tactics.

Reportedly, various leaders started holding demonstrations that were perceived to be anti-Muslim. In December 1992, leaders of the VHP

Activists of Hindu nationalist parties Shiv Sena and Vishwa Hindu Parishad stand on the train tracks in Bombay, India on September 26, 2002. The groups called a 24-hour strike in response to the killing of 32 people in a temple in Gandhinagar, India, on September 24, 2002. AP/Wide World Photos

allegedly led thousands of Hindu activists to the Babri mosque and destroyed part of the structure.

Many experts state that the transformation of VHPs tactics from peaceful demonstrations to hostile and forceful activities was due to a growing belief among its members (and followers) that the interests of Hindus were not being taken care of by the government. Many members of the group also alleged that religious leaders (of other religions such as Islam and Christianity) were promoting the conversion of Hindus to their religion in various parts of the country.

The tactics of the VHP have been reportedly violent ever since the Babri demolition. The group was banned by the government of India (the ban was, however, lifted in 1995), and leaders such as Praveen Togadia were barred from making public speeches. The Gujarat riots of 2002 are alleged to be instigated by leaders of the VHP.

The riots caused a massive furor in other parts of India. Political parties alleged that the Chief Minister of Gujarat, Narendra Modi, had been negligent in handling the situation and had supported the VHP in justifying the riots. As of 2005, most political parties and people of India hold Narendra Modi and VHP responsible for the 2002 Gujarat riots. The decades-long Ram temple–Babri mosque dispute still persists.

OTHER PERSPECTIVES

Indian government officials, leading anti-extremism analysts, as well as human rights workers have often condemned the actions of the VHP. According to a report by Amnesty International

LEADERSHIP

PRAVEEN TOGADIA

The VHP has had several prominent leaders throughout its period of existence. Since the mid 1990s, Praveen Togadia is thought to be one of the most vocal and controversial leaders of the organization. Praveen Togadia, a resident of the state of Gujarat, is a qualified oncologist. He owns hospitals in and around Ahmedabad, the commercial capital of Gujarat.

Togadia joined the VHP in the early 1990s, and ever since is known to be the foremost in propagating the radical Hindu ideologies of the group. According to published reports in the media, due to his inflammatory speeches, the government of India banned him from public speaking in the late 1990s. He has reportedly also been arrested numerous times on the charge of inciting Hindu people against Muslims.

As of 2005, Togadia serves as the International General Secretary of the VHP.

---

in 2004, the riots in Gujarat (in 2002) were mainly instigated by the VHP and BJP. The report stated, "More than 2,000 people had been killed in early 2002 in the wave of violence targeting the Muslim community. These killings followed an attack on a train in Godhra in February 2002 in which fifty-nine Hindus were killed by a mob. [Other] reports implicated police officers and members of Hindu nationalist groups, including the Vishwa Hindu Parishad (VHP) and the ruling BJP in the violence against Muslims."

However, the allegations that VHP was responsible for the riots have also been disputed. Justice Nanavati, who served as the Chief Justice of the Supreme Court of India, part of the Nanavati commission set up by the Supreme Court to investigate the riots, stated in an interview to a news agency (as reported in *Outlook India*), "Yes, there have been instances where people have said the Bajrang Dal and VHP

KEY EVENTS

1966: VHP launched at a world convention of Hindus, in Allahabad, India.

1984: VHP forms the Bajrang Dal—its youth wing.

1992: Many VHP activists, along with members of the BJP, succeed in destroying part of the Babri mosque structure. This incident is followed by widespread riots throughout India. VHP is subsequently banned by the Indian government.

2002: VHP activists are allegedly burnt to death by a Muslim mob in Godhra, Gujarat. Hindu-Muslim riots break out in Godhra and other parts of Gujarat. Thousands are reportedly killed.

---

workers at the local level instigated people to riot. But the complaints are primarily of a very general nature. There is no real evidence that has been brought to name individual Bajrang Dal or VHP leaders."

SUMMARY

The VHP claims to be the only organization (along with its parent entity—the RSS) in the world fighting for the rights of Hindus. Ever since its inception in the 1960s, the main focus of the VHP has been the construction of Ram temple at the Babri mosque site in Ayodhya.

Self-proclamations by leaders of the VHP state that all Indians who do not support their views are "traitors." The group's leaders claim that India as a country can move forward only when non-Hindus accept Hindu superiority. Reportedly, the group is viewed by many in India and around the world as a fundamentalist Hindu organization.

SOURCES

Web sites

BBC News. "Profile: The Vishwa Hindu Parishad." < http://news.bbc.co.uk/2/hi/south_asia/1860202.stm > (accessed October 3, 2005).

Outlook India.com. "Ltd Evidence against VHP, Bajrang Dal in Guj Riots." < http://outlookindia.com/pti_print.asp?id = 142748 > (accessed October 3, 2005).

Time Asia Magazine. "Hindu Backlash: Is India's Hindu Nationalist Government Taking Steps to Rein in Its Own Hardliners?" < http://www.time.com/time/asia/magazine/article/0,13673,501031027-524518,00.html > (accessed October 3, 2005).

U.S. Department of State. "International Religious Freedom Report 2004." < http://www.state.gov/g/drl/rls/irf/2004/35516.htm > (accessed October 3, 2005).

Volksfront

LEADER: Randall Lee Krager

USUAL AREA OF OPERATION: Arizona; California; Pennsylvania

OVERVIEW

Volksfront is a neo-Nazi extremist group based in the northwestern part of the United States. Many Volksfront members are skinheads with racist tendencies.

HISTORY

Volksfront is a radical neo-Nazi group with a history of race-driven assaults and murders. The group is headquartered in Portland, Oregon. It was founded in 1994 by Randall Lee Krager, an Oregon skinhead. Krager recruited members of violent skinhead groups in the Northwest, such as "Youth of Hitler" and "East Side White Pride." Many of the recruits had been involved in a White Aryan Resistance movement.

At the end of its first year in existence, Volksfront had started a white power rock group called Intimidation One. It was named after the hate crime law in Oregon and used extremely violent lyrics.

In 1996, a founding member of Volksfront, Troy Harlow, was jailed for a year after burning a cross in the yard of a black man. Harlow pleaded guilty to the charges of conspiring to deprive an African-American man of his constitutional rights.

LEADERSHIP

RANDALL LEE KRAGER

Randall Lee Krager, a skinhead from Oregon with a swastika tattooed on his neck, has a long history of involvement and interest in racially motivated violence. Authorities claim to have had 28 encounters with Krager in his late teen years. In 1989, at age fifteen, Krager got into trouble for a racially motivated attack on other teenagers in a park. At the age of sixteen, Krager attended the trial of a Southern California neo-Nazi, Tom Metzger, who Krager called a "cool guy."

Krager was put in jail in 1992 for violently attacking an African-American man. Upon his release in 1994, he established Volksfront. He was put in jail again in 1995 for 14 months, pleading guilty to first-degree intimidation of an anti-racist skinhead.

The police began to put pressure on Volksfront in 1998 for participating in and advocating the use of violence. At that point, the group seemed to disappear. They later said that the pressure from the police and government forced them to go underground.

For three years, the group was very quiet. But, it reemerged in 2001. The group claimed then that it had changed its stance on violence and was completely against it. Krager claimed that he came to this decision after spending a lot of time thinking while in prison.

In 2004, the group claimed on its web page that violence is discouraged in Volksfront. However, Volksfront says it recognizes that force must sometimes be used in order for the group to remain a free people.

The group grew in size between 2001 and 2003, increasing from fifty up to 100 serious members. It also added three new chapters, bringing the total number of chapters to eight. There are active units in Phoenix, Arizona, throughout California, and even east in Pennsylvania.

On June 1, 2003, Kurtis William Monschke, purportedly the group's leader for a Washington State chapter, was given a life sentence for his involvement in the beating death of a forty-two-year-old African-American man. During the trial, Volksfront spoke out against Monschke, saying he deserved the death penalty. This was accompanied by a reiteration that Volksfront was not in support of acts of violence.

PHILOSOPHY AND TACTICS

Volksfront has embraced different philosophies and used different tactics over the years. In its early beginnings in 1994, the group was a strong advocate for violence and intimidation against minorities, and those who sympathized with minorities. The group has always blamed racial and ethnic minorities, particularly blacks and Jews, for society's ills.

When it first formed, Volksfront produced a poster that illustrated the organization's agenda of using violence in the attack of minorities that the group believed to be the cause of crime and social disorder. The poster had the words "Take Back Your Streets," and showed a white skinhead beating three black men with a bat and boots. The black men were labeled "rapists," "muggers," and "drug dealers."

In more recent times, the group has followed a political ideology called the "Third Position" or "Third Way." By following this mindset, the group claims to put its support behind working-class whites, rejecting communism and capitalism, and strongly opposing non-white immigration. The group backs unions, particularly with activism in local construction unions.

The group also follows a racist version of *Asatrú*, a pagan religion in Scandinavia, that dates back to the Middle Ages.

Volksfront has created a number of alliances with different radical right groups. In 2004, it hosted Aryan Fest, a music event that featured white power rock bands. The event was attended by many people, and has helped Volksfront gain support throughout the far-right community.

Volksfront also sponsors a publication called *The Folk Tribune: The Independent Voice of the White Working Class*. The publication is

KEY EVENTS

1994: Volksfront was founded by nineteen-year-old Randall Krager, who recruits members from violent skinhead groups.

1998: Pressure by police caused Volksfront to cease its activities publicly.

2001: Volksfront remerged, claiming to be less supportive of violent attacks.

used to promote its ideas, and also to show support for the violent acts carried out by Volksfront members, and members of other organizations. The publication includes a "POW list," which features those members who have been put in prison. Authors of the POW list say even though Volksfront rejects violence, the group supports the POWs who committed violence in order to defend their people.

OTHER PERSPECTIVES

Analysts pose the question of whether or not the modern Volksfront is really a nonviolent movement, as the group claims to be. Volksfront has said violent acts are looked down upon by Volksfront, but they also created a database to track anti-racists, whom they call enemies. Security officials see this as a violent threat against anti-racists, which goes back to the early 1990s, when there was ongoing fighting between racist and non-racist skinheads.

The Southern Policy Law Center (SPLC) points out that Volksfront's publication continually promotes violence, and shows its support for people who have carried out violent attacks. Also, Volksfront promotes the rock band it created, Intimidation One, which advocates violence against anti-racists. Krager says Volksfront is disassociated with the band. However, Volksfront distributes the band's CDs and has them perform at Volksfront events.

In 2004, Volksfront requested to join Oregon's Coalition Against Hate Crimes (CAHC), an organization that includes representatives from government, law enforcement, and civil rights. Volksfront claimed they had contributions to make to CAHC. Their request was denied.

SUMMARY

Volksfront has been known for its violent attacks against racial and ethnic minorities, and their sympathizers. In more recent times, it is the group's rhetoric, intimidation, and support of the violent acts of others that have given the group attention.

Among the right-wing extremist groups in the United States, Volksfront is gaining a reputation as a leader. There have been some declines in other strong neo-Nazi groups, including Aryan Nations and National Alliance. These declines might explain the recent growth in Volksfront's membership and spread of activity. They have a very strong network in California, Oregon, Washington, and Arizona, with chapters as far east as Pennsylvania.

SOURCES

Periodicals

Feinstein, Adam. "People Will Not Take This Lying Down." *IPI Report*. February–March 1994: vol. 43

Web sites

Law Enforcement Agency Resource Network. "Volksfront." < http://www.adl.org/hate_symbols/groups_volksfront.asp > (accessed October 3, 2005).

Southern Poverty Law Center. "Two Faces of Volksfront: A Growing and Increasingly Important Neo-Nazi Group Claims It Opposes Any Kind of Political Violence. Could It Be True?" < http://www.splcenter.org/intel/intelreport/article.jsp?aid = 475 > (accessed October 3, 2005).

Southern Poverty Law Center. "Street Fighter: An Anti-racist Organizer's View of Skinheads." < http://www.splcenter.org/intel/intelreport/article.jsp?aid = 397 > (accessed October 3, 2005).

SEE ALSO

White Aryan Resistance

White Aryan Resistance (WAR)

LEADER: Tom Metzger

USUAL AREA OF OPERATION: United States

OVERVIEW

The White Aryan Resistance (WAR) is a neo-Nazi national-socialist organization that preaches racial discrimination and solidarity among the Anglo-Saxon segment of the population, especially among white blue-collar workers, as a means of racial survival of the white men. The anti-capitalistic doctrine of the organization is also known as "Third Force" or "Third Position," and based on the left-wing theories sponsored by Gregor Strasser, a German Nazi Party member, executed in 1934 by Hitler's order. The group also claims to be fighting against a Zionist-occupation government (ZOG) that purportedly controls the U.S. government, among others.

HISTORY

The White Aryan Resistance (WAR) is a white supremacist faction of the American neo-Nazi movement. WAR was founded in California by Tom Metzger in the early 1980s and promoted the formation of several racist-oriented skinhead gangs in California and throughout the United States. The organization gained visibility from 1984 on, when Tom Metzger inaugurated his cable television program, "Race and Reason." WAR accuses the U.S. government and the

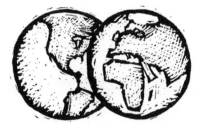

Tom Metzger, leader of the White Aryan Resistance group, appears outside the Kootenia County Justice building in Coeur d' Alene, Idaho, on Sept. 5, 2000, after meeting with Aryan Nation leader Richard Butler. AP/Wide World Photos

American political arena (as well as most of the press and televised media) of being under Zionist (e.g., pro-Israel Jewish political movement) control. WAR also promotes radio shows and distributes racist videotapes, lecturing about the neo-Nazism doctrine, other white supremacist movements, and skinheads. WAR aligns with two associated organizations, the Aryan Youth Movement (AYM) and the Aryan Women's League (AWL), which actively promote Tom Metzger ideas.

Tom Metzger's daughter, Lynn, who replaced her mother, is the head of the Aryan Women's League (AWL). According to Floyd Cochran, a former racist activist, AWL "is the largest women's organization within the organized hate movement." Still according to Cochran, WAR's leader, Tom Metzger is the founder of, and responsible for, "America's most violent skinhead organization." Led by John Metzger, Tom's son and Lynn's brother,

the Aryan Youth Movement (AYM) is the headquarters of the racist skinhead groups.

WAR suffered a major setback in October 1990, when skinheads Kenneth Mieske and Kyle Brewster from Oregon were convicted of the murder of Mulugeta Seraw, an Ethiopian immigrant, and Tom Metzger and his son, John, along with the White Aryan Resistance organization, were found guilty of conspiracy, substantial assistance, and encouragement of the defendants' actions against the victim. A total of $10,975,469.00, plus a yearly legal rate of 9% interest, was determined by the courts to be paid by the defendants for punitive and economic damages.

Another spokesman for WAR is Dennis Mahon, who became famous for being suspected of involvement with Timothy McVeigh in the Oklahoma federal building bombing, according to the British journal, "Guardian Unlimited." Although denying any participation in the bombing, Dennis Mahon stated to reporters that, "The bombing was a fine thing."

After the outcome of the Oregon trial in 1990, Tom Metzger has changed the White Aryan Resistance's tactics from frontal opposition to the system into what he defined as the "lone wolf lifestyle." The purpose is to promote the white separatism ideology through a subtler activism as a long-term strategy, whose ultimate goal is to overthrow the "super state" (e.g., the federal government and the Congress) through a future revolution, when such time is ripe. WAR intends to create small, independent white states throughout America.

PHILOSOPHY AND TACTICS

WAR's central premises are that racism is a matter of instinct underlying racial survival. The theory goes on claiming that "blue-eyed blonds and green-eyed redheads" were the dominant race throughout human history due to "thousands of years of pure hate racism." Furthermore, the white race is pictured as being the main target of an international Zionist conspiracy designed by the wealthy Jews of the world to dominate not only the governments, but also the world economic system, in search of an alleged Jewish supremacy. Such Zionist conspiracy would have infiltrated its agents at all levels of the American society,

Eddie Wilson, Jackson, Mississippi, police lieutenant, holds a Remington 700 hunting rifle. The rifle is one of seventeen firearms found in the apartment of accused sniper Larry Shoemake. AP/Wide World Photos

misleading the white younger generations into a state of passive alienation and manipulation by the social policies of racial integration and tolerance towards non-whites such as African Americans, Native Americans, Latinos, and Semites, in general. WAR denies the validity of equal rights based on the hypothetical existence of a natural racial hierarchy that, according to the WAR doctrine, would be determined by genetics. Genetics have supposedly endowed the white race with the best genes and talents, superior intellect, and higher moral qualities. The American government would therefore be at the service of the Zionists, and thus should not be recognized by Aryan activists as a legitimate institution. Actually, the movement refers to the American government and its institutions as "the enemy."

WAR claims that the white race can only survive by resisting the social integration with non-whites and by promoting racial segregation and the coalition of all white workers through the rekindling of racial hate. A fanatic zeal is encouraged as being a moral quality. For the time being, WAR recommends that its members become "lone wolves" as a form of resistance. Lone wolves should, according to Metzger, keep a low profile, working as very small cells or alone, trying to gain the respect and cooperation of other whites for the cause, while they infiltrate and take strategic positions in every level of the system—from the private to the public spheres. They should act as spies in their own surroundings, trust nobody, not even their peers and supporters, gathering any important background information about them, such as their military backgrounds, personal past history, relationships, etc. Lone wolves should act as eyes and ears for the white supremacist cause, by snooping into police communications, people's ideologies, civil records, etc., in order to avoid the infiltration of government agents among their cells. Lone wolves are also advised to develop an "economic support network with friendly businessmen," who share their racist feelings in

LEADERSHIP

TOM METZGER

When Tom Metzger founded WAR, he already had a history of racist activism, initiated in the early 1960s through his affiliation to the John Birch Society (JBS), an ultra right-wing political movement. After leaving JBS, he became an anti-tax activist for five years (1971–1975), refusing to pay income tax to the IRS (Internal Revenue Service). He joined the Ku Klux Klan (KKK) in 1975, and soon after, became the KKK Grand Dragon of the California Knights. In the same year, he entered the white supremacist movement known as New Christian Crusade Church, which he later repudiated. As a KKK Grand Dragon, in 1979 he organized a Klansmen platoon to hunt illegal Mexican immigrants near San Diego, California. In 1980, another KKK uniformed armed militia, created by Metzger, attacked a group of anti-Klan demonstrators in Oceanside, California, leaving seven people injured.

He embarked on three unsuccessful attempts to be elected for public offices: in 1978, for San Diego Supervisor; in 1980, for Representative of California's 43rd Congressional District; and in 1982, as a nominee to run for Senate by the Democratic Party. Before the 1982 campaign, he changed the name KKK California Knights to White American Political Association (WAPA). After losing the election for Senate, he changed WAPA's name to White American Resistance in 1983, and later, to White Aryan Resistance. The WAR newspaper, one of the propaganda tools used by the organization, is defined by Metzger as "the most racist newspaper on earth," and aims at promoting a coalition of white, Anglo-Saxon, blue-collar workers to make a racial revolution in the United States.

private without publicly expressing them. Another strong recommendation is that lone wolves should never talk to police officers, nor give any information under interrogation, whether in police precincts or in courts.

KEY EVENTS

1983: Metzger arrested for unlawful assembly and cross burning.

1992: Metzger arrested and deported from Canada where he and his son John were attempting to take part in a demonstration of the Heritage Front.

1990: WAR and its leadership was indicted and convicted at the Oregon trial.

Lone wolves should also maintain means of informing the public and spreading suspicion against government policies and against non-white groups, through the distribution of covert literature and forged black propaganda. WAR lone wolves are taught by Metzger how to recognize and approach those white individuals who are receptive to their doctrines, being advised as well to avoid discussing the cause with those already "infected" by liberal ideologies, including among their own relatives and friends. WAR expects that, once an extensive network is put together as result of long-term term and patient work, they will achieve an optimum momentum to start a racial revolution sometime in the future—"with surgical precision." WAR and other white supremacist groups are mutually supportive, such as the Aryan Nations, Stormfront.org, Creativity Movement, etc.

WAR response (through Metzger) to the September 11 al-Qaeda attacks was to blame the U.S. government and the intelligence agencies as being "idiots" and "incompetents," adding in a further communication that, "As far as the targets hit by the Islamic attackers, I do not consider the WTC a U.S. institution, but the headquarters of most that's wrong with our present masters... As far as the Pentagon, that is now the muscle headquarters for the Imperialist anti-white regime—I care nothing for its fate either."

In 2002, the White Aryan Resistance tried again to infiltrate the Immigration and Naturalization Service (INS) and the U.S./Mexico Border Patrol by distributing a

PRIMARY SOURCE

Chaos to Conspiracy: Racist Skinhead Violence Growing More Organized

To all appearances, the Independence Day murders of Daniel Shersty and Lin Newborn in the Las Vegas desert were far from typical Skinhead killings. This double murder had all the hallmarks of an execution.

Shersty and Newborn, well-known members of the Las Vegas Unity Skins who had had many run-ins with racist neo-Nazi skins, were not killed in some beer-fueled, Skinhead bar brawl. Friends say that the victims were deliberately lured to the desert by two white women affiliated with racist skins.

Shersty, a white 21-year-old stationed at an Air Force base, was shot dead next to his car. Newborn, a 25-year-old black man working at a tattoo parlor, was murdered some 200 yards away, apparently as he tried to flee.

A neo-Nazi Skinhead, John Butler, has been arrested in the murders, and authorities are investigating a possible greater conspiracy. Butler, 26, reportedly had connections with the larger neo-Nazi scene and Utah Skinhead leader Johnny Bangerter who once lived in Las Vegas. Officials believe that Shersty and Newborn were killed in a racist Skinhead plot to eliminate non-racist Skinhead critics.

Since the inception of the American racist Skinhead scene some 15 years ago, there has been a sea change in the nature of the crimes it produces. What began as a wave of spontaneous acts of violence—often erupting at the music shows that were once the prime venues of Skinheads—has escalated over the years, finally reaching the level of well-planned murders.

While there are many exceptions, the overall trend in Skinhead violence has been one of increasingly organized crime.

Originally, Skinhead violence usually occurred during encounters between racist and non-racist skins in the "mosh pits," areas just in front of musical stages where wild dancing and drinking often devolved into slugfests. By the late 1980s, however, there was an increasing number of killings, sometimes involving victims that racist Skinheads viewed as their enemies.

In Las Vegas, Skinheads involved in Satanism murdered a convenience store clerk. In Washington D.C., an 18-year-old skin beat a gay man to death with a baseball bat. In Denver, a Skinhead robbed a hair stylist and then shot him dead. In Pittsburgh, another racist skin murdered a social worker who worked with the blind.

communication to the lone wolves stating, "The Aryan Syndicate has been notified by insiders that the Immigration and Naturalization Service is looking for White Power People to help guard the borders. Apply today!"

OTHER PERSPECTIVES

The Anti Defamation League (ADL) is one of the centers that fight the hate propaganda by providing detailed information on hate groups, including the White Aryan Resistance, and by offering research resources for high school students. ADL reports that in June 2001, the National Conference for Community and Justice (NCCJ) for the

Arizona Region launched an educational campaign with the motto "Not in Our State" against hate group activists, especially Dennis Mahon and WAR. Mahon, who recently announced his plans to move to Kingman, Arizona, also sent the White Aryan Resistance journal to the community leaders of Gilbert. The response of NCCJ to WAR and its spokesman, Mahon, was the distribution of a petition to the public and to schools and the promotion of special educational activities to alert the public about WAR's intentions to spread racial hate in the region. The content of the petition said: "We, the citizens of the State of Arizona, affirm the basic value and dignity of all people, and thereby reject the promotion of hate and dehumanization of members of our community . . . There is no place for hate in our state." Schoolteachers,

In 1988, one of the first Skinhead murders connected to an organized hate group made headlines across the nation. Skinheads affiliated with White Aryan Resistance, a neo-Nazi group run by Tom Metzger that is based in California, beat an Ethiopian student in Portland, Ore., to death with a baseball bat.

Although the attack was triggered by a chance encounter on the streets, it showed the increasing influence of established hate groups on young, already violent street thugs. Southern Poverty Law Center attorneys sued the group and its leaders and won a $12.5 million verdict for the family of the victim.

In July 1993, the leader of the Fourth Reich Skinheads was a central figure in an unsuccessful plot to blow up the First African Methodist Episcopal Church in Los Angeles and spray its 8,500-member congregation with machine-gun fire. The plan also called for attacks on Rodney King, black celebrities and Jewish targets.

In the mid–1990s, racist Skinheads were involved in two major revolutionary racist groups. Three Skinheads were members of the deadly Kehoe gang—two of them falling victim to their own comrades-in-arms—and another three were convicted in connection with the bank-robbing, white supremacist Aryan Republican Army.

Late last year, Matthaus Jaehnig, a Denver Skinhead, led police on a wild car chase after being surprised while he burglarized a home. When he was cornered, Jaehnig was willing to do something no Skinhead had yet done in this country—murder a police officer. Jaehnig then committed suicide.

Investigators believe that Jaehnig may have been involved in a larger criminal enterprise, marketing hard drugs and trafficking in heavy weapons—like the machine gun he used in the murder.

Earlier this year, Skinhead Daniel Rick, 20, pleaded guilty to weapons charges in connection with a plot to blow up the Southern Poverty Law Center and murder its co-founder, Morris Dees. Police believe that he was involved in a ring that was selling fully automatic weapons to fund the cause of white supremacist revolution.

With the killing of Shersty and Newborn, these kinds of plots may have reached a new plateau—a successful assassination conspiracy aimed at furthering the Skinhead white supremacist agenda.

Source: Southern Poverty Law Center, 1998

Christian clergy leaders, Jewish leaders, community councils, and common citizens, throughout the state, signed the NCCJ petition. Another NCCJ communication stressed that "We cannot passively allow the Dennis Mahons of the world to target our young people when they are most impressionable."

Farhan Haq, in an article published by the "Albion Monitor," in June 1997, affirmed that the McVeigh conviction would not deter extremists. He also cited the White Aryan Resistance as one of the racist movements, and quoted Dennis Mahon's comments on the Oklahoma bombing: "I hate the federal government with a personal hatred.... I'm surprised that this hasn't happened all over the country."

According to Haq's analysis, McVeigh is seen as a martyr by the anti-government extremist groups, with more people seeking affiliation to the militias and to the white supremacist groups right after the bombing. However, the "Detroit Free Press," in an article by Judy L. Thomas, published several years later (April 2005), reported that antigovernment and hate groups are now weaker than before the Oklahoma bombing—at least those with a formal organizational structure, such as Aryan Nations, the Creativity Movement, and the White Knights. However, Thomas alerted that these movements are "testing new tools," new ways of gaining momentum again. The article informed that although most hate and antigovernment organizations were left in disarray in the last 10 years because of the intense alertness against domestic terrorism after the Oklahoma tragedy, and tougher anti-terror legislation, especially after the September 11 attacks, the danger is still out there. Particularly in a time when most of the intelligence resources of the country were shifted to fight international terrorism. The author cited as one of the examples a statement by WAR spokesman Dennis Mahon: "After the bomb went off in Oklahoma City, the White Knights completely collapsed . . . They shut down the post office . . . the hot line. They were scared to death. They just went down the hidey hole." Still quoting Mahon to exemplify the new tools in use by hate groups: " . . . I think it's just we all want to overthrow the government and get a state of our own. There's many ways to do that. It's called small cells and lone wolfism." The FBI recognizes that mobile, autonomous cells, or murderers acting alone, such as McVeigh, are much harder to detect.

Mark Potok, of the Southern Poverty Law Center, alerted to the dangers of the use of the Internet by the neo-Nazi groups, agreed with Les Back, of the Centre for Urban and Community Research at Goldsmiths College in London, who discussed the easy access by young people to learn how to make bombs on the web: "The real danger," he wrote, "is perhaps that in the information age isolated acts of racist terrorism may become a commonplace."

SUMMARY

The Internet, the elusive cyberspace, has become a pervasive tool for a myriad of terrorist groups, racist movements, and hate organizations, providing a network through which the several white supremacist movements can easily access each other, spread their propaganda, and attract new followers. The White Aryan Resistance was quick in perceiving how useful a tool the Internet can be. An ideological war between numbers of opposing groups is currently going on in the cyber-battlefield. Although different militia factions and other white supremacist organizations may eventually have their own rivalries and doctrinaire conflicts, as Les Back explains, they have found in the Internet "a common language of race and white solidarity." According to Back, the racist cyberspace has provided an ideal means to fostering racial separatism and the formation of "white fortresses" with a transnational impact. Skinhead racist groups for instance are reported in Brazil, Canada, England, Scotland, Germany, the Netherlands, and elsewhere. However, such global characteristics of cyberspace are also used by a growing number of humanistic and educational foundations, institutes, universities, and governmental agencies to inform the public about the criminal activities of extremist groups and the dangers posed by hate propaganda. Furthermore, they also address ethical issues such as human mutual respect through the appreciation of ethnic and cultural differences, and the essential oneness of all human beings.

SOURCES

Web sites

Albion Monitor. "McVeigh Conviction Won't Deter Extremists." < http://www.monitor.net/monitor/9706a/ mcvdeter.html > (accessed October 17, 2005).

Anti-Defamation League. "Still Howling." < http://www. adl.org/learn/extremism_in_america_updates/individuals/ tom_metzger/metzger_update_020801.htm > (accessed October 17, 2005).

Detroit Free Press. "Homegrown Hate: Ten years after Oklahoma City, anti-government and hate groups are weaker—but testing new tools." < http://www.freep. com/voices/sunday/ehate10e_20050410.htm > (accessed October 17, 2005).

San Francisco Chronicle (March 6, 2005). "A Web of White Power." < http://www.rickross.com/reference/ hate_groups/hategroups391.html > (accessed October 17, 2005).

UNESCO Courier. "White Fortresses in Cyberspace." < http://www.unesco.org/webworld/points_of_views/ back.shtml > (accessed October 17, 2005).

University of Wisconsin at Madison. "Tom Metzger and WAR." < http://slisweb.lis.wisc.edu/~jcherney/ osmond.html > (accessed October 17, 2005).

SEE ALSO

Ku Klux Klan

White Christian Soldiers

LEADER: John Richard Favorite

USUAL AREA OF OPERATION: United States

OVERVIEW

White Christian Soldiers (WCS) is a self-proclaimed, "nondenominational activist organization dedicated to the preventative maintenance of Christian society and culture in America and around the globe." Its national director, as well as founder, is John Richard Favorite. The group also has a political component, which calls itself the Theocratic Party of America. The Southern Poverty Law Center considers WCS an extremist hate group. WCS places a large emphasis on white supremacy and fundamentalist Christian rhetoric. The group seems to use its web site as a way to draw in potential members, and it is where its specific methodology is outlined.

HISTORY

WCS was founded, and is still headed, as of 2005, by John Richard Favorite. There is not much information provided on the web site, or elsewhere, about Favorite himself, besides a letter he has written to (potential) members. The group web site is a place where possible and current members can learn about the organization, read articles, and find other materials relevant to the group's goals. The group does not claim to be white supremacist or racist, or

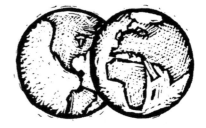

promoting of racial, religious, or cultural hatred. However, it can be contradictory in some cases, such as when the web site claims that white people should marry other white people and that possible candidates of the group should be able to trace their European ancestry to 75% accuracy, so that there will be strong bloodlines within the group. Although the group does not claim that its members should hate those that do not fit into this mold, their exclusion from the group certainly suggests that not everyone is eligible to be a part of the organization and that group members find these people flawed in some way.

PHILOSOPHY AND TACTICS

WCS hopes to bring American politics back to its roots, and focuses on Christianity as the foundation. It places much emphasis on keeping America contained, whether through cutting funding to other countries, not sending troops to aid countries in need of support, or not trading with countries with poor environmentally sound practices. It also seeks to protect those who are of European ancestry; one example is through ridding society of affirmative action programs. The group hopes to keep immigration into the United States open to all Christians, because "The entire reasoning behind the forming of America was to allow one place in the world where Christians could live together in harmony without any outside interference from those of other religions or races." However, the group is also opposed to illegal immigration and what they perceive to be an influx of non-Europeans.

The group also has a radical agenda for health care, stating that all of the population that is HIV positive should be placed in hospitals and should not come in contact with those that do not have the disease, and women should not be able to have an abortion, unless to save their lives, or in the case of rape or incest. The organization seeks to touch many different policies.

The WCS web site does not suggest much along the lines of tactical strategy, besides hinting at political change and suggesting that Favorite be added to political ballots. However, it does provide information regarding its prison ministries, and the organization is making an effort to recruit more followers through promoting membership of prisoners and their families. The reasons given for this program are to provide a support network for these prisoners and to help them overcome their positions, and "reenter society with a positive attitude, a spirit of evangelism and a new purpose of contribution, sharing and giving to the Christian American community in realizing their role as a Christian soldier in the Army of Christ." Its main tactical strategy of spreading the word of the organization seems to be to simply draw in members through the web site.

OTHER PERSPECTIVES

There is very little coverage of WCS from the perspective of others, as well as an extreme lack of information about the group, other than on its own web site. The group does have a listing on the Southern Poverty Law Center's web site as an active hate group in the United States, as of 2004. Although there is no further commentary about the group, the fact that it is listed as a hate group suggests that the Southern Poverty Law Center disagrees with the group's own interpretation of itself as not condoning hatred.

The only support that can be provided as of 2005 are those organizations listed on WCS's own web site, such as the International Network of Prison Ministries. This network is most likely in support of WCS because of WCS's own prison ministry.

SUMMARY

White Christian Soldiers is still operating as of 2005. Although not very well known, the group's web site provides an abundance of information, and this is most likely how it obtains new members. The web site also provides names of publications that the interested public can read, as well as a letter from John Richard Favorite, encouraging more people to get involved in the organization, including those in prison. It is still building its membership and is determined that the organization be successful.

SOURCES

Web sites

International Network of Prison Ministries. <http:// prisonministry.net/> (accessed October 3, 2005).

Southern Poverty Law Center Intelligence Project. "Active U.S. Hate Groups in 2004." <http:// www.splcenter.org/intel/map/> (accessed October 3, 2005).

White Revolution

LEADER: Billy Roper

YEAR ESTABLISHED OR BECAME ACTIVE: September 18, 2002

ESTIMATED SIZE: 1,000

USUAL AREA OF OPERATION: United States

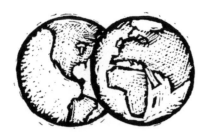

White Revolution is a neo-Nazi, white supremacist group that considers the white race best fitted to rule the other races. White Revolution was formed in West Virginia on September 18, 2002, by Billy Joe Roper II. It was soon moved to its present headquarters in Russellville, Arkansas. According to its Web site, its slogan is "The Only Solution," and its symbol is an upside down "V" painted in red (blood), black (earth), white (race), and gold (sun) used to represent ancient Greece, which, in Roper's opinion, is the cultural pinnacle of the white race.

One of the primary purposes of Roper's organization is to promote cooperation between right-wing extremist groups and to assemble into one coalition all such groups, especially those disgruntled with the white power movement. In his capacity, Roper hopes to act as the coordinator in organizing multi-group extremist events—a task that Roper feels is often too big for any one group to handle.

HISTORY

For two years beginning in 2000, Roper was successful in his job as deputy membership coordinator for the neo-Nazi organization, National Alliance, a leading white supremacist group

White supremacist Bill McDermott (right) joins his friends in saluting outside the city hall building in Dubuque, Iowa. William F. Campbell | Time Life Pictures | Getty Images

founded by William Pierce. Roper held a high-profile position as he gave press interviews, coordinated activities for its units, and built alliances with other extremist groups.

However, Roper was fired on September 16, 2002. According to the May 2004 article, "Hate Group Leaflets Turn Up in Metuchen," written by Bryan Sabella of the Edison, New Jersey, *Sentinel*, a power struggle between different factions occurred after the death of Pierce. Its new leader, Erich Gliebe, did not like that Roper set up coalitions with skinheads, who Gliebe and Pierce despised. Roper also promoted associations with other extremist groups, which National Alliance leaders frequently rejected.

Ramifications were noticed throughout the right-wing extremist community because Roper

was viewed as a likeable and effective communicator and problem-solver. According to the 2002 article, "A Group is Born," from the Southern Poverty Law Center (SPLC), Roper started White Revolution on September 18, 2002, with about 100 activists (among them nearly 30 former National Alliance members), thousands of supporters, and endorsements from many white supremacist leaders. According to the SPLC, Roper charged $10 per month for a membership, which included membership in various other extremist groups. The requirements included being age eighteen or above, drug-free, and heterosexual, having no non-white dependents, and being totally of white European ancestry.

In its first full year, White Revolution sponsored several rallies such as a pro-white

LEADERSHIP

BILLY ROPER

Born in 1972, Roper was a skinhead as a teenager. At that time, he claimed that three generations of his family had been members of the Ku Klux Klan. After receiving his Master's in History, Roper became a high-school history teacher. In 2000, Roper was employed with National Alliance, becoming its organizer under the job title of deputy membership coordinator. Often described as gregarious, articulate, dedicated, and hard-working, Roper found this job ideal as he quickly helped the organization become one of the largest, most popular, and best-run domestic neo-Nazi organizations in North America. However, his policies did not always match with the group's policies. He was fired in 2002 but quickly formed his own white supremacist group, White Revolution. As of 2005, Roper continues to be the founding leader of the successful and rapidly growing white supremacist organization.

demonstration in Montgomery, Alabama; a Remember the Alamo anti-immigration rally in San Antonio, Texas; anti-invasion demonstrations in Little Rock, Arkansas, and Chicago, Illinois; and a regional meeting in Fort Smith, Arkansas.

By 2004, Roper was actively speaking at various public extremist events. Roper spoke of his strong convictions such as opposing the 2004 Olympic Games in Athens, Greece, because it combined athletes of different races. One of the most successful events sponsored by White Revolution, according to the 2002 article, "Revolting in Arkansas," by the Southern Poverty Law Center, was a sixty-five-person rally at the Montgomery, Alabama, SPLC headquarters.

In 2005, White Revolution held joint events or co-sponsored rallies with such groups as Aryan Nations, the Creativity Movement,

factions of the Ku Klux Klan, National Socialist Movement, and White Aryan Resistance. That same year, former National Alliance attorney Victor Gerhard joined White Revolution after disagreeing with activities associated with his former organization. Gerhard also brought in his business, Condor Legion Ordinance—a racist paraphernalia business that is in direct competition with Resistance Records, a subsidiary of National Alliance.

PHILOSOPHY AND TACTICS

The philosophy of Roper, which he pursues through White Revolution, is to assure that the white race exists in the future. According to Chuck McCutcheon, the author of the July 2004 article, "Right-Wing Extremist Groups Becoming More Active After Post-9/11 Lull," Roper is not concerned with whether or not White Revolution continues to exist in the future. Rather, Roper is focused on the more important goal—that of assuring the continued existence of the white race. Roper considers that, at present, the U.S. government and other such governments are denying the white race the right to survive.

According to the Sabella article, Roper's ultimate goal is to combine all white supremacist groups under one organization. However, in the group's beginning stages, Roper admitted that his organization is simply expanding its membership roster as it competes for members with other whites-only groups.

The mission statement of White Revolution, taken from its web site, includes the admission that the white race is growing smaller both in the United States and throughout the world. As a result, Roper is against unregulated non-white immigration into the United States because—as he declares from projected demographic studies—such activities will result in whites becoming a minority by 2025. In order to regain control of the white fate, members of White Revolution hope to establish a government within the United States whose priority is the preservation of the white race.

As reported on its web site, Roper conjectures that the multimedia industry, government agencies, and other related organizations are controlled primarily by Jews, who intend to influence and control public opinions. As a

Hampshire, New Jersey, North Carolina, Ohio, Texas, and West Virginia.

KEY EVENTS

2000: Roper begins job as deputy membership coordinator for National Alliance.

2002: Roper is fired from his National Alliance job.

2002: White Revolution is founded by Billy Roper in West Virginia, and soon moved to Arkansas.

2004: White Revolution evolves in just two years as one of the most active right-wing extremist group in the United States

2005: Roper emerges as an effective leader who is attempting to unify various white separatists groups through White Revolution.

result, Roper and his White Revolution organization are anti-Semitic, along with being anti-Israel and anti-U.S. government.

As of 2005, leaders realize that because of the group's size, it is only able to educate and organize its members. Its long-term goal, however, is to eventually be large and strong enough to openly confront its enemies. Roper realizes that the group's best tactic is to act peacefully and legally by distributing written materials and using emails, its web site, videos, and other communications methods to publicize its positions. However, Roper suggests that violence may be necessary at some future point.

According to the November 24, 2004, article, "Police Say White Revolution Racist Flyers 'Not Illegal,'" from *The Monroe Courier* in Shelton, Connecticut, Roper is attempting to establish units in the eastern United States because, in his mind, its white citizens rebel quickly when freedoms are threatened. However, White Revolution membership in the mid-Atlantic and northeastern regions is still limited. It has been most active in the following sixteen states: Alabama, Arizona, Arkansas, California, Connecticut, Florida, Georgia, Illinois, Indiana, Massachusetts, New

OTHER PERSPECTIVES

Leaders of the Anti-Defamation League (ADL) stated that, during White Revolution's first two years of existence, it evolved from a small group in a rural area of Arkansas to the largest and most active extremist organization in the state.

Morris Dees, SPLC co-founder and its chief trial lawyer, once called Roper a person who has enough ambition to become the most influential neo-Nazi leader in the United States. Similarly, ADL member Mark Pitcavage stated that he seriously considers Roper a potential future leader for the white-supremacist movement. In an interview conducted by Pitcavage, Roper explained that his two-fold goal is to end the feuding between many extremist groups and to counter the influence of Jews, African Americans, and other minorities. Roper went on to say that whites have as much right to fight for their rights as other groups.

Shai Goldstein, a member of the New Jersey ADL chapter, said in the Sabella article that White Revolution philosophy is essentially the same as other white power groups: that world problems are caused by Jews and that the United States promotes the Jewish position through its businesses, governments, and general society.

As when he first started White Revolution, Roper remains well respected within the white power community, with members liking his outgoing and pleasant personality that many feel could strengthen their cause. In fact, Matt Bishop, a former member and leader of White Revolution, once compared Roper to a present-day Adolph Hitler because he is a charismatic and well-spoken leader with devotion to his cause and knowledgeable when dealing with the media. In *The Arkansas Times* article, "A Young Skinhead Makes a Conversion—Of Sorts" by David Koon, Bishop states that Roper is a type of leader who can likely succeed in joining together the different factions of the white power movement.

SUMMARY

White Revolution has been successful in its activities to unite the movement. With many influential leaders in prison, recently deceased, or aging, the charismatic Roper has been able to greatly influence many white supremacists.

In its first few years of operation, in order to bring cohesion to the white power movement, Roper has placed leaders of other organizations onto his board of directors and in other leadership positions. Although extremist groups do not traditionally have long lifetimes, Roper has so far successfully positioned White Revolution as the leading umbrella organization among the white power culture without threatening the authority of its leaders.

SOURCES

Periodicals

Koon, David. "A Young Skinhead Makes a Conversion—Of Sorts." *The Arkansas Times*. May 27, 2005.

McCutcheon, Chuck. "Right-Wing Extremist Groups Becoming More Active After Post 9/11 Lull." *Newhouse News Service*. July 13, 2004.

"Police Say White Revolution Racist Flyers 'Not Illegal.'" *Monroe Courier*. November 24, 2004.

Sabella, Bryan. "Hate Group Leaflets Turn Up in Metuchen: Community Leaders, Police Describe Distribution as Limited." *Sentinel*. May 12, 2004.

Web sites

Intelligence Report, Southern Poverty Law Center. "Revolting in Arkansas." < http://www.splcenter.org/intel/intelreport/article.jsp?pid = 214 > (assessed October 3, 2005).

Intelligence Report, Southern Poverty Law Center. "A Group Is Born: Billy Roper, a Fired National Alliance Official, Has Formed His Own Group Called White Revolution." < http://www.splcenter.org/intel/intelreport/article.jsp?sid = 53 > (accessed October 3, 2005).

Law Enforcement Agency Resource Network, Anti-Defamation League. "White Revolution/Billy Roper." < http://www.adl.org/learn/ext_us/w_revolution.asp?print = true > (assessed October 3, 2005).

SEE ALSO

National Alliance

Aryan Nations

Ku Klux Klan

White Aryan Resistance

Women for Aryan Unity

Established in 1990, Women for Aryan Unity (WAU) is an organization of women devoted to advancing white culture and promoting a pro-white racial agenda. Their motto, "securing our future one child at a time," expresses the group's primary goal: to focus on women's role with *Kirche, Küche, Kinder* (church, kitchen, children)—paralleling Hitler's message to women.

Women for Aryan Unity claims to have sixteen chapters in Europe, North America, South America, and Australia. They identify themselves as "racialists" and white supremacists.

LEADER: Christine Greenwood (reputed)

YEAR ESTABLISHED OR BECAME ACTIVE: 1990

ESTIMATED SIZE: Unknown

USUAL AREA OF OPERATION: Sixteen chapters in four continents: North America, South America, Europe, and Australia.

HISTORY

Women for Aryan Unity was founded in 1990 in Canada, though the group quickly spread into the United States as part of the white supremacist movement. The group, pagan in nature, was founded to encourage women to become more actively involved in the white supremacist movement. WAU members are often associated with other white power groups, ranging from the World Church of the Creator to the Hammerskin Nation.

The group promotes the idea that women must come to the aid of their pro-white men when "war" requires it and that women must

White supremacists and neo-Nazis watch a swastika burn at an annual racist group gathering known as NordicFest. © *Jonas Bendiksen / Magnum Photos*

KEY EVENTS

1990: WAU founded.

2002: Reputed leader of WAU, Christine Greenwood, is charged with possession of bomb-making materials; the charges are later dropped.

Christine Greenwood, an American, as one of the founders, while other sources claim that the WAU founder is Canadian.

PHILOSOPHY AND TACTICS

According to the Women for Aryan Unity mission statement on their web site, "At this time in the Movements [sic] history, when the great task of redefining a Woman's role in the cause is posed; of reinventing the concept of 'feminism' within the parameters of Race and Revolution, WAU can only be a group of equals, a staff of educators and disseminators, not hangers on, joiners, or pseudo-soldiers."

The focus on the role of motherhood dominates the group's writings. One e-zine produced by WAU, *Motherhood Tips*, sometimes reads like any parenting publication, with articles on bedtime issues, teething, homeschooling, gun safety and children, and more. Rarely does the group's pro-white agenda come through in these articles, except with the occasional reference to a white person being a part of "the beloved race."

Other publications include *Little Warriors* an e-zine devoted to the children of members of the group. The e-zine "focuses on activities that will get children out from in front of the television, and get their little minds working." These activities include directions for making homemade bubble soap and play dough, activities that speak to the group's focus on motherhood and home life. At no point does the group's

not be "squeamish" and must be ready to fight alongside (or instead of) men. A woman's role, therefore, is to focus on domestic life but also to be a survivalist. By focusing on home life, raising children within the pro-white movement, and supporting their men in the white supremacist movement, the group seeks to define the role of women in this movement. The group uses goddess imagery, including Greek, Norse, Roman, Slavic, and Aryan (Indo-European) mythology, as part of its philosophy in finding meaning behind white supremacy and a feminine perspective in the movement.

Women for Aryan Unity claims to have sixteen chapters on four continents, though their membership is concentrated in the United States and Europe. WAU is part of a wave of organizations designed to recruit women and children in the white supremacist movement.

Sources contradict each other concerning the founders of the group. Some sources name

LEADERSHIP

CHRISTINE GREENWOOD

Christine Greenwood is noted in some news reports as the reputed leader of Women for Aryan Unity. Other sources state that unnamed Canadian "odinists" started the organization. Greenwood is best known for her arrest in 2002 on charges of possession of bomb-making materials in California. She was released, the charges dropped, and little more is known about her.

pro-white message come through in *Little Warriors*.

In the group's print publications, the messages still contain a great deal of content on everyday life, addressing topics such as vegetarianism, the effects of television on children, and reviews of books and music. The sixth issue of the magazine *Morrigan Rising* includes these articles alongside topics such as "women's roles in the movement" and "introduction to *volksfront*"—articles that directly address white supremacists goals and ideas. The print publication *Instinct* focuses on survivalist tactics for members of WAU. The WAU states that the purpose of *Instinct* comes from the "dangers we face on a daily basis; especially being racialists. We as Women have to deal with the threat of rape and physical violence on a daily basis, most of our homelands are no longer safe for white women, so we hope to give you the helping hand you need in order to defend yourself. We will focus on many different aspects of survival via *Instinct*."

Membership involves a complicated, two-part process. Members are required to become an Associate Member first, and must "write for at least two WAU Publications, they must participate in our fundraising projects for Aryan Prisoners and our Aryan Family Clothing Program," must write to prisoners within the white supremacist movement, and must pay a

monthly membership fee. After six months to two years, the Associate Member obtains a sponsor (a chapter head) and then all WAU chapter heads in either the United States or Europe vote on the Associate Member's acceptance as a full member.

The group has stayed out of the headlines with one exception. On November 18, 2002, police arrested Christine Greenwood and charged her with possession of bomb-making materials. The Southern Poverty Law Center claims that Greenwood is the founder of Women for Aryan Unity, and is closely associated with other pro-white groups such as Blood and Honor, Aryan Nations, and the neo-Nazi World Church of the Creator. The charges against Greenwood were dropped. Greenwood was noted for her charitable efforts in forming an "Aryan Baby Drive" that provides racial supremacists with food and baby items if needed. The Women for Aryan Unity web site also sponsors a "Welcome to the World Little One" baby basket program, in which group members donate essential baby items for new parents. The program is in line with the pro-family, pro-motherhood ideals, and is labeled by WAU as "an initiative to secure the future of our Folk—one child at a time."

OTHER PERSPECTIVES

According to Kathleen Blee, a sociology professor at the University of Pittsburgh and the author of a Southern Poverty Law Center Intelligence Report on women in the white supremacist movement in the United States, many women are recruited into their organizations with an eye toward expanding membership; by including the woman, the man is more likely to remain a part of the group.

In addition, prospective female members often find the normalcy of group activities, such as homeschooling or e-zines such as *Motherhood Tips* and *Little Warriors* to be innocuous and comforting. In the search to be part of a community, Blee theorizes, women in movements such as Women for Aryan Unity do not necessarily identify with the racialist goals, but are searching for a community to join.

PRIMARY SOURCE

All In The Family: Women, Formerly the Helpmates of the Radical Right, Are Becoming Increasingly Outspoken as a Debate on Female Roles in the Movement Takes Shape

In the late 1960s, in the heyday of radical left-wing groups, a debate developed within the Weathermen about the role of revolutionary women, who had been largely confined to supporting their menfolk. Before it was over, the Weathermen were renamed the Weather Underground, and many of the group's women were taking up the gun.

Thirty years later, in a distant echo of that debate, women on the radical right—who a leading analyst says now comprise 25% of many groups and as many as half of new recruits—are increasingly re-examining their position in the world of white supremacy.

And while they are far from radical feminists, many are espousing a new female activism and even leadership—often to the dismay and anger of the men in their movement.

"For years, it seemed that a White woman's role in the Racial movement was to write lonely prisoners and stand behind their boyfriends without much of an opinion about anything," writes Lisa Turner, who began the "Women's Frontier" of the neo-Nazi World Church of the Creator (WCOTC) in May 1998.

"In the last year or so, we have seen a lot of changes in this area. Everyone is starting to realize that if we are going to overcome in this struggle we are going to have to do it together—Man and Woman—side by side!."

From California to Maryland, and abroad from Australia to Canada to Europe, the voices of "racialist" women are being heard increasingly in a variety of forums. In the past, these movement women have been Nazi "Aryan breeders," the Klan moms who stayed home sewing robes for their men, the secretaries and helpmates of neo-Nazi leaders, the transmitters of "Aryan" values to the next generation.

Now, some of these women are seeking new, expanded roles for themselves and their gender. And although most reject "feminism"—which is widely seen as a Jewish plot to destroy the white race—they are leading key efforts to build a viable movement.

While their men try to tear down the current society, these women are building up the culture they hope to replace it with.

"There is a vacuum of leadership, and one that our menfolk must honestly look within themselves to explain," writes Turner, who recruits via the Internet. "Leadership is a legitimate and necessary role . . . which women in the Church can fill."

WCOTC, which like almost all hate groups is led by a man, is only the most visible example

SUMMARY

Christine Greenwood's arrest brought the Women for Aryan Unity organization into the media spotlight for a brief time. The organization claims to be growing, with newest recruits in the United States and Europe. Because the group requires members to write for its publications, the 12 e-zines and magazines provide a vehicle for spreading the group's message. With no direct political agenda or call for action outside of domestic life, Women for Aryan Unity remains a fairly quiet, though steadily growing, part of the

white supremacist movement's attempt to reach more women.

SOURCES

Books

Blee, Kathleen M. *Inside Organized Racism: Women in the Hate Movement*. Los Angeles: University of California Press, 2003.

Web sites

Anti-defamation League. "Feminism Perverted: Extremist Women on the World Wide Web." < http://

of a concerted effort by the movement to reach out to women.

Forums for and about women, particularly on the Internet, are proliferating. They range from chat rooms featuring discussions about women's leadership capabilities to Skinhead Web sites with photographs of skimpily clad examples of Aryan female beauty to Internet advice columns for racist mothers on how to save money with homemade baby wipes.

FROM KITCHEN TO CROSS-BUILDING

On Stormfront, the Web's oldest hate site, a debate on the role of women in the movement has been raging for months. One man wrote to a woman who had posted an earlier message: "I'm sorry to inform you, but a woman's place is in the kitchen. ...[M]en are physically stronger, which makes us more valuable.... A real white racialist woman understands this."

A second woman, speaking to the first, replies: "Don't be discouraged. Neanderthal attitudes like this one are few in the movement. ... I do think we should support our men, but we do not necessarily have to stay in the kitchen to do it."

Women for Aryan Unity (WAU), a Web site run by a group of racist Odinist women in Canada, declares that "squeamish, bug fearing females" should "lose your forest phobias and start preparing for tomorrow" by acquiring survivalist, weapons and fighting skills.

A person identified as "Max Hammer" takes a similar view in a posting on the Web site: "Certain male elements who hold a rather Turkish attitude toward our feminine comrades should wise up and think Nordic, while certain female elements should cease behaving like mindless groupies and start doing political exercises instead."

Sigrdrifa Publications, a unit of WAU, publishes a quarterly magazine "100% produced" by "Proud Aryan Women" with a mix of features like "Women of History," "Aryan Recipes," "White Prisoner Sponsorship Program" and "Baby Bulletin."

It also maintains a Web site for women describing, among other things, "Aryan Beginnings for Children (ABC)," a "co-operative of racialists... organized to assist racially aware parents... in raising proud white children in today's society." ABC plans "White Heritage" coloring books and newsletters on children's developmental stages.

Source: Southern Poverty Law Center, 1999

www.adl.org/special_reports/extremist_women_on_web/feminism_intro.asp > (accessed October 1, 2005).

Southern Poverty Law Center. "The Other Half: Interview with Sociologist Kathleen M. Blee." < http://www.splcenter.org/intel/intelreport/article.jsp?aid = 134 > (accessed October 1, 2005).

SEE ALSO

World Church of the Creator

Blood and Honour

Aryan Nations

World Church of the Creator

ALTERNATE NAME: Creativity Movement
LEADERS: Ben Klassen, Matthew Hale
YEAR ESTABLISHED OR BECAME ACTIVE: 1973
ESTIMATED SIZE: Less than 500
USUAL AREA OF OPERATION: United States

OVERVIEW

The Creativity Movement was founded by Ben Klassen in 1973 with its original name, Church of the Creator. Klassen described the group's ideology as a replacement for "Judeo-democratic-Marxist" values, based upon the foundation of race. The group's foundational teachings are a list of sixteen "Commandments of Creativity," each of which deals with loyalty to, and proliferation of, the white race. The group denies the existence of the Holocaust, rejects interracial marriage, and works to promote the advancement of white individuals and institutions in all phases of life.

The group's name was changed in 1996 to World Church of the Creator and then again in 2003 to the Creativity Movement, in response to a copyright infringement suit. The Creativity Movement, under all its various names, has compiled a lengthy history of violence and bloodshed. Following the 2005 sentencing of leader Matthew Hale to forty years in prison, the movement appears to be in a state of disarray.

HISTORY

The Creativity Movement was founded in 1973 by Ben (Bernhardt) Klassen. In his writings, Klassen describes his religious and ethical pilgrimage from

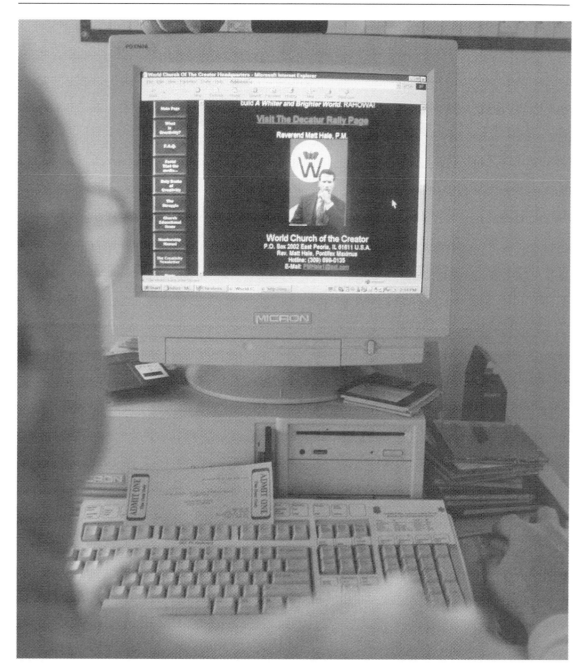

A Spokane, Washington intelligence officer uses the internet to track and monitior extremist groups' Web sites, such as the one headed by Rev. Matthew Hale, founder of the World Church of the Creator. AP/Wide *World Photos. Reproduced by permission.*

his parents' conservative beliefs to his own white-supremacist views. He discusses his experiences in politics and his eventual disillusionment with Christianity, concluding that the New Testament is in fact a book of suicidal teachings intended by Christ and his apostles, all of whom were Jewish, to lead to the eventual destruction of all non-Jews.

Klassen's beliefs were simple: any practice beneficial to whites is good, while any practice harmful to whites is evil. Klassen's simple creed resonated with white supremacists around the world, and he was able to attract several hundred "creators," as church members are known, to his movement. Klassen's inflammatory rhetoric

Rev. Matthew Hale, leader of the World Church of the Creator, delivers a message to fellow white supremicists on October 26, 2002, during a KKK rally held in downtown Fayetteville, West Virginia.
AP/Wide World Photos

inspired his followers to work toward his ultimate goal, what he described in his writings as, "a whiter, brighter world."

Klassen wrote that his movement was peaceful, stating that every step of his group's plan for a brighter future was legal and non-violent. Despite these public assertions, group members were repeatedly linked with acts of racial violence. In 1991, "creators" George and Barbara Loeb were charged with murdering an African-American military veteran in Neptune Beach, Florida. While the couple claimed they acted in self-defense, George Loeb was sentenced to life in prison. One year later, the victim's family successfully sued the Creativity Movement and was awarded $1 million.

Following the verdict, Klassen sold the group's headquarters and appointed Richard McCarty as the group's new leader. Soon thereafter, Klassen took his own life with an overdose of sleeping pills, calling his action an honorable choice, given that life no longer had any meaning for him. The group continued its activities,

including the firebombing of an NAACP office and other attempted attacks.

In 1996, Matthew Hale was appointed *Pontifex Maximus* (supreme leader) of the organization. Hale had a long history of violence and racism; at age 12, he had organized a group he called the Little Reich at his school. In 1991, Hale was arrested for allegedly threatening three African Americans with a gun and for obstruction of justice. In 1992, he attacked a mall security officer, for which he received thirty months probation and six months house arrest.

Upon taking over the movement, Hale added the word "world" to the group's name, emphasizing the group's ambition to spread its doctrine of white superiority across the planet. Hale was handsome and intelligent; in 1998, he graduated from Southern Illinois Law School and passed the state bar exam. However, the Illinois Bar refused to grant Hale a license to practice law, stating that his racial views made him unfit to practice law in Illinois.

LEADERSHIP

BEN KLASSEN

Born in 1918, Bernhardt (Ben) Klassen was a Polish immigrant. His early views of religion were shaped by his reading of *Mein Kempf* and other right-wing works. Following his involvement with the John Birch Society (which later repudiated his extremist views) and other political groups, he formed the Church of the Creator in 1973. Klassen led the group, which worked for the ascension of whites to world dominance, until he stepped down shortly before his suicide in 1993. At the time of his death, the group numbered several hundred.

Klassen's teachings are still held in high regard by the movement today. His contributions include books such as *The White Man's Bible* (1986), *Expanding Creativity* (1985), and *Nature's Eternal Religion* (1992). Klassen is also credited with popularizing the term "racial holy war," which his followers shorten to "RaHoWa" and continue to use as a rallying cry. Klassen consistently denied that his organization taught or condoned the use of violence for the achievement of its goals.

MATTHEW F. HALE

Following the death of founder Ben Klassen in 1993, the Church of the Creator found itself in disarray, although violence by its members continued. In 1996, Matthew Hale was named the group's new supreme leader. Hale directed the group's operations from an office in his father's home in Illinois, where he reportedly used an Israeli flag as a doormat. Hale was married for three months to Terra Herron, a 16-year-old member of the church. Despite completing law school and passing the Illinois Bar, he was refused a law license based on his moral beliefs.

Hale rose to national prominence following the Benjamin Smith shooting spree, when Hale appeared on national television defending the church's teachings of white superiority and hatred for other racial groups. Hale was entering a federal court building to answer charges of contempt of court when he was arrested and charged with conspiring to murder a federal judge. He was convicted and is currently incarcerated at a high-security federal penitentiary in Colorado.

Two days after Hale was denied his license, a church member named Benjamin Smith began a three-day shooting spree in which he randomly attacked minorities in Indiana and Illinois. Smith killed two people and wounded nine before killing himself. In television appearances after Smith's death, Hale said that his church did encourage hatred of anything that threatened his racial group. The group's membership grew slightly in the months following the killings.

The final chapters in the church's history were set in motion in 2000, when an Oregon Christian group operating under the name "Church of the Creator" filed a trademark infringement suit against Hale's organization. Hale and his followers received a favorable ruling in early 2002, allowing them to use the name. But in December, U.S. District Court Judge Joan Lefkow reversed the decision on appeal, awarding the use of the name to the Oregon group.

Following the ruling, Matthew Hale legally changed the group's name for the final time, trademarking the title "Creativity Movement." On January 8, 2003, Hale was arrested and charged with soliciting the murder of Judge Lefkow; Hale had been turned in by his security chief, who was in fact an FBI informant. Hale was convicted in April 2004, and sentenced to forty years in prison. Little has been heard from the group since Hale's imprisonment. The group's web site lists Matthew Hale and George Loeb as POW's.

PHILOSOPHY AND TACTICS

The Creativity Movement holds a white supremacist perspective, with the ultimate goal of creating a world populated solely by people of Western European ancestry. Members of the

KEY EVENTS

1973: Ben Klassen forms the Church of the Creator.

1991: Church member George Loeb is convicted of murdering an African-American veteran in Florida.

1992: The victim's family successfully sues the church for $1 million.

1993: Ben Klassen commits suicide.

1996: Matthew Hale is appointed the group's new leader, changes church name to World Church of the Creator.

2002: Judge Joan Lefkow rules against the church in a copyright infringement suit. In response, Hale legally changes the group's name to the Creativity Movement.

2004: Hale is sentenced to forty years in prison for soliciting the murder of Judge Lefkow.

---

group believe that a person's race is his highest defining trait and hence should be protected from contamination or dilution. In practice, they reject interracial marriage as well as social interactions among different racial groups. They also consider blacks and Jews to be inherently inferior to whites.

Church members are called "creators," and are encouraged to relocate to central Illinois where the church is headquartered. In keeping with founder Ben Klassen's philosophy, the church encourages members to practice "salubrious living," which refers to eating natural foods and avoiding chemical contaminants or intoxicants. In deference to the church's founding in 1973, members reject the Gregorian calendar in favor of one that begins in that year. With 1973 labeled "Inception of Creativity" (I.C.), 1974 becomes 1 A.C. The years prior are labeled P.C., making 1972 the year 1 P.C. The church celebrates several holidays, including the founder's birthday, and the last week of the year is dedicated to white racial pride and purity.

Church members are encouraged to disseminate their beliefs using a variety of methods. In some cases, members have been encouraged to employ call-in radio shows as a pulpit. Some creators have been taught to cold-call when recruiting, choosing numbers at random from the phone book, and claiming a wrong number was dialed if the person answering does not sound white. Creators are also taught that if national laws prohibit the distribution of hate literature, they are expected to ignore those laws.

Violence is a primary tool used by the organization. White supremacists distributing Creativity literature outside a rock concert in 1997 noticed an African-American man and his son nearby. Eleven of the group attacked the two, and several were convicted and sentenced for the crime under the stricter hate-crime sentencing guidelines. Group members also continue to use other forms of harassment, though in one recent case, the tactic apparently backfired. A May 2005 federal court ruling ordered the church to pay $450,000 in attorney's fees, in part because the court found compelling evidence that church members left threatening phone messages for opposing attorneys in an ongoing legal case.

Definitions of right and wrong are uniquely provided by the Creativity Movement's philosophy. Whereas most world religions look to an ethical code such as the Bible or the Quran for guidance, Klassen offered his own set of moral teachings, all tied to race. At its core is the belief that actions that benefit the white race are inherently right, and the greater the benefit, the more valuable the action. Conversely, actions that are detrimental to the white race are reprehensible and, in Klassen's doctrine, constitute sin.

Like many other religious thinkers, Klassen wrote from a position of dissatisfaction with American culture. However, he framed America's struggles as issues of race, blaming interracial marriage and a lack of racial identity among whites for the country's problems. He also taught that health and well-being can be achieved only when one experiences both love and hate. In the case of Klassen's church, this prescription was expressed in the group's powerful love of whites and its equally powerful hatred for non-whites.

Both Ben Klassen and Matthew Hale have taken seemingly contradictory public positions, openly advocating hatred for non-whites while

PRIMARY SOURCE

Pontifex Ex: The Trial that Sent neo-Nazi Matt Hale to Prison Also Revealed the Shabby Reality of His World Church of the Creator

When Matt Hale shambled into a small Chicago courtroom on April 6, commencing the first day of a trial that could land him in prison for life, nobody gasped audibly. But the first glimpse of Hale, David Duke's only serious rival for the title of America's most famous neo-Nazi, left looks of profound confusion on dozens of faces around the courtroom.

Looks that said: That can't possibly be him, can it?

But yes, this was him. This was the man who had spent more than a decade crafting a public image as the handsome, clean-cut, suit-and-tie-wearing boy genius of American neo-Nazism.

Now, for the most critical three weeks of his life, Hale had decided to eschew his Sunday best and come to court in an orange prison jumpsuit, carelessly unbuttoned at the top, a stretch of white T-shirt showing underneath.

Puzzled reporters later discovered that Hale had chosen his attire as a way of protesting his incarceration, of marking himself as a "political prisoner" for all the world to see. But since the judge reportedly refused to let Hale's attorney explain his appearance to the jury, the prison jumpsuit only served to mark him as a criminal.

It wasn't the first time Hale had left people scratching their heads. The reality of Matt Hale—like that of the neo-Nazi group he commanded—has never come close to the image. He made grandiose claims about the World Church of the Creator's membership, for instance, sometimes telling gullible reporters and supporters there were as many as 80,000—when the real number never reached one thousand.

But Hale exaggerated so expertly that even the normally sharp *New York Times* columnist

Nicholas Kristof fell for it, calling WCOTC the standard-bearer of "Hate, American Style."

Nothing mattered more than the personal image of Hale himself. A mere 25 years old in 1996, when he was crowned Pontifex Maximus (high priest) of an obscure, nearly moribund organization called "Church of the Creator," Hale quickly displayed a rare gift for attracting publicity.

Like Duke, he recognized that a presentable, well-spoken, youthful neo-Nazi leader would certainly have novelty on his side. Especially one who, like Hale, could boast about being a law student at a reputable university.

As he traveled the country, mingling with his fellow neo-Nazis at rallies and watering down his message of racial holy war ("RaHoWa") for small-town library audiences, Hale always made one thing perfectly clear: He was a cut above the herd.

To reinforce this illusion, Hale added "World" to the name of his group. He christened two upstairs rooms in his father's humble house in East Peoria, Ill., the "World Headquarters." Wherever he went, he made sure he was accompanied by his "elite security force," the White Berets. His thin, quavering voice spoke in measured, lofty tones.

When reporters from big magazines like *GQ* came calling, he might even break out his violin, emphasizing that he was not only a law student but—get this!—a classically trained musician, as well. For photos, he would often remove his glasses and clench his jaw, making his face look fuller, more dignified.

Source: Southern Poverty Law Center, 2004

---

carefully avoiding any suggestion of violence or other illegal activity. A church document, *The Creator Membership Manual*, states that members who commit crimes or incite others to do so

will be expelled from church membership, though Klassen's earliest writings admonish readers to see racial differences as a "fight" that whites must accept and win.

Writing in *The Little White Book*, Klassen outlined his plan to overcome what he described as tyranny against the white race. In opening the discussion, he declares his opposition to violence, but quickly moves to tactics such as boycotting Jewish-owned businesses, driving other races from society "just as Hitler did in Germany," and forcing these "parasites" to leave the United States. The final three of Klassen's eight points deal with weapons and violence, which would be held as a reserve plan should the non-violent approach fail to achieve the group's objectives.

The seeming contradiction between the group's non-violent claims and its hate-filled rhetoric may be partially resolved by considering the history of group members' actions and the church's response. For a relatively small group, the church's members have been linked to a disproportionately large number of violent attacks. From 1991 to 2003, church members were involved in the murder or attempted murder of fifteen people in the United States and abroad, as well as a planned series of terrorist bombings that police discovered and thwarted. In none of these cases, some of which involved church leaders, did the church or its representatives express regret or outrage at its members' actions.

OTHER PERSPECTIVES

Though the white-supremacist rhetoric of the World Church of the Creator is similar to other supremacist extremists, the group does not often partner with other groups. Members of the World Church of the Creator vehemently oppose the use of religious-based messages and ideology such as those used by the Christian Identity Movement. Despite its ideological discord with similar organizations, Hale and the World Church of the Creator received significant financial and other support from fellow supremacist organizations during Hale's trial.

SUMMARY

Founded in 1973, the Creativity Movement (formerly the Church of the Creator) is a white supremacist group committed to advancing whites and reducing or eliminating black, Jewish, and other non-white populations. Ben Klassen, the group's founder, believed that all of the meaningful contributions to human progress have been created solely by whites, and that whites are the rightful rulers of the Earth. His writings advocated non-violence, but frequently strayed into discussions of when violence might be used. He committed suicide in 1993.

The group's second significant leader, Matthew Hale, led the group beginning in 1996, and is currently in federal prison for soliciting the murder of a federal judge. Hale is the latest of several church members tried and convicted for acts of violence. Since his conviction, the group has drawn little attention and appears to be without direction. Some analysts suggest that the eventual emergence of a new charismatic leader will be required if the group is to survive.

SOURCES

Books

B'nai B'rith. Anti-defamation League. *The Church of the Creator: Creed of Hate*. New York: Anti-Defamation League, 1993.

Web sites

RAHOWA.com . " Klassen's Teachings." < http://www. rahowa.com > (accessed October 1, 2005).

Religious Tolerance.org . "The Creativity Movement." < http://www.religioustolerance.org/wcotc.htm > (accessed October 1, 2005).

SEE ALSO

Ku Klux Klan

Yahweh's Truth

LEADER: James P. Wickstrom

USUAL AREA OF OPERATION: Wisconsin

OVERVIEW

Yahweh's Truth (YT) is both a socio-religious group belonging to the Identity Movement (IM) and a radio broadcasted program led by a white supremacist known as Pastor James Wickstrom. The Two-Seedline Racial Covenant Identity, or Identity Movement (IM), claims that the Anglo-Saxon race descends directly from Adam and Eve, through the lineage of Seth. Therefore, YT and IM claim that the Anglo-Saxon race is the true Israelite people, whereas Jews would be the descendants of Cain, who, according to this theology, was begotten through the intercourse of Eve with Satan, the Serpent of Eden.

One of the branches of the Aryan Nations, led by Charles Juba, and some other white supremacist groups do sponsor the Yahweh's Truth doctrines and theories advocated by James Wickstrom. Through the interpretation of the biblical texts and apocryphal biblical literature, YT preaches that white American men and women should fight against government and its institutions, should oppose globalization policies, and prepare for a final armed conflict against the authorities and other racial opponents. The ultimate goal of YT and the Identity Movement as a whole is to overthrow the U.S. government through military conflict. Aryan Nations, Montana Freemen, Ku Klux Klan, the Church of Jesus Christ-Christian, Posse Comitatus, and some other neo-Nazi militia

LEADERSHIP

JAMES P. WICKSTROM

James Wickstrom, born in Michigan in 1942, joined the military service in 1964. After serving in Vietnam, he was discharged in 1966. His first contact with the Identity Movement and Posse Comitatus took place in the early 1970s through Thomas Stockheimer, who led the Wisconsin Posse Comitatus and was a Christian Identity's preacher. Together, they started a study group in Wickstrom's home, with approximately 45 other participants. The group was disrupted when Stockheimer was arrested in 1974 for assaulting an IRS employee in his own home. Two years later, Wickstrom moved to Schell City, Missouri, where he founded the Mission of Jesus the Christ Church in 1977. In 1978, he moved back to Wisconsin to form a chapter of the Posse Comitatus near Shawano County. This Posse chapter was named Constitutional Township of Tigerton Dells. Self-appointed as the "National Director of Counter Insurgency" of this separatist township, Wickstrom acted as judge and municipal authority as well as pastor.

Wickstrom started spreading both the Identity and Posse ideology to the farmers of the region and to the small town population nearby. According to Floyd Cohran, who grew up in a farm nearby, in times of deep economical crisis among small farmers, Wickstrom was preaching that Jews were to be blamed for their difficulties. In concert with federal authorities

and its disastrous policies, Jews wanted to take away their land. Therefore, not only the federal government was illegitimate, but they should organize militia groups to lynch IRS agents, Jews, and any other individuals who represented a hindrance to the sovereignty of the people. By 1980, Tigerton Dells had became a center for militia training. As the FBI discovered in 1985, they also had a large stock of illegal weapons, ammunition, and explosives. Under Wickstrom's advice, several farmers stopped paying their debts and taxes, and ended up actually losing their properties. Between 1981 and 1983, Wickstrom received a great deal of attention from the press, being interviewed by Larry King, Geraldo Rivera, and Phil Donahue. In 1983, he was arrested and convicted to serve thirteen months in jail for illegally forming the separatist Constitutional Township of Tigerton Dells. After his release, he continued to preach Christian Identity throughout the country as a self-proclaimed Aryan Nations' Chaplain. He was accused of planning to distribute counterfeit bills totaling $100,000 in 1988, but the trial was nullified. However, after Victor F. Rizzo, who was indicted for conspiracy to the purchase of counterfeit U.S. currency and the possession of unregistered firearms and silencers, acted as a witnessed against Wickstrom. Wickstrom was convicted in 1991 to serve thirty-eight months in federal prison.

groups are either directly associated with or can be considered different expressions of the Identity Movement. The Identity Movement is practically undistinguishable, for instance, from the Church of Jesus Christ–Christian, the Christian Identity, Kingdom Identity, or the Aryan Nations, besides being the cradle of Yahweh's Truth (YT). YT, along with the previously mentioned groups, is at the same time a political and religious movement aiming at the social and political destabilization of the United States in order to restore the white men's power

and self-determination through the formation of separated, independent townships.

HISTORY

The doctrines sponsored by Yahweh's Truth originated from the British Israelism movement of the nineteenth century, a racist theological doctrine born in England. These anti-Semitic ideas were brought to the United States at the turn of the nineteenth and twentieth centuries, where they gradually gave rise to several extremist racist organizations, such as the Ku Klux Klan, under the leadership of Wesley Swift, who in 1946 founded the Church of Jesus Christ–Christian in California. Yahweh's Truth is one among hundreds of modern spin-offs of the original group founded by Swift. These groups share a common socio-theological view about race supremacy (e.g., that of the Anglo-Saxon race) and claim that non-white races are inferior and impure, because they descend from those begotten through spurious intercourse between the fallen angels, which followed Lucifer, and women.

Yahweh's Truth seems to be a movement directly derived from the Posse Comitatus, which the law enforcement authorities dispersed in 1985 through the destruction of the Constitutional Township of Tigerton Dells (Wisconsin) and Wickstrom's arrest. The community, founded by Wickstrom, had declared its independence from the United States Federation and was fomenting racial violence and tax evasion among farmers throughout the Midwest. Posse Comitatus or Sheriff's Posse Comitatus (meaning, sheriff's power of the county) was a U.S.-based white supremacist group, founded in the beginnings of 1970 by William Potter Gale, Henry L. Beach, and other followers of the Christian Identity Movement. James Wickstrom, now leading Yahweh's Truth, became the most vocal Posse Comitatus leader in the early 1980s. Based on their particular interpretation of the Bible, Posse Comitatus claimed the existence of an international Zionist conspiracy that led to the Jewish control of Western governments, especially the United States, which would be under the control of a purportedly Zionist-occupation government (ZOG). Authorities considered Posse Comitatus and the Aryan Nations the two more violent supremacist groups operating in the United States. Several Posse members were indicted for murder, racial violence, death threats, tax evasion, and bank robberies, especially during the 1970s and the 1980s. The doctrines of Yahweh's Truth (YT), preached by Wickstrom, were also at the core of Posse ideology, with the sermons and lectures defending the formation of paramilitary groups, persecution and murdering of Jews, homosexuals, and communists, as well as tax evasion. Wickstrom continues to preach through YT those ideas, along with the Posse claims of the federal government's illegitimacy.

KEY EVENTS

1977: Wickstrom founded the Mission of Jesus the Christ Church.

1983: Wickstrom was arrested and convicted to serve thirteen months in jail for illegally forming the separatist Constitutional Township of Tigerton Dells.

1991: Wickstrom was convicted to serve thirty-eight months in federal prison.

After his release from prison, Wickstrom tried to revive Posse Comitatus in 2001 without much success, and started the Yahweh's Truth organization, first meeting in a borrowed location in Hampton Township, Michigan, and later spreading its propaganda through the Internet, radio shows, and cable television. The organization is maintained through donations and the selling of videotapes.

PHILOSOPHY AND TACTICS

Yahweh's Truth combines German Nazi theories about the supremacy of the Anglo-Saxon race and the racial inferiority of other non-white populations. Like the Nazis of the first half of the twentieth century, they dedicate an especial hatred against Jews, who are blamed for the moral and social corruption of modern societies and held as the authors of an international conspiracy to dominate the world. The modern international financial system, the international and American press, and TV news networks as well as the globalization process, according to Yahweh's Truth and other similar Christian Identity theorists, would all be strategies orchestrated by a purportedly invisible Jewish organization known as the Zionist-occupation government (ZOG), as part of such strategy for global domination. As far as the United States is concerned, ZOG would be the invisible power behind the American government and Congress, which resulted in their illegitimacy to represent the Anglo-Saxon American population.

U.S. domestic policies toward ethnic and multicultural diversity, respect, mutual understanding, and reciprocal tolerance are viewed as a means to weaken the Anglo-Saxon population by the ZOG and a menace to the white race survival. They believe that interracial marriages are not only immoral, but essentially a sin that, along with homosexuality, should be punished with death.

The alleged white Anglo-Saxon superiority and the moral validity of racial hatred is, according to YT, justified by the Bible. They believe that Lucifer, the fallen angel mentioned in the Book of Genesis, along with one-third of the angelic population were expelled from the Heavens and bound to the primordial Earth, where they assumed mortal human bodies and gave birth to a demonic race. The Serpent of Eden, who tempted Eve, would be Lucifer (e.g., Satan) himself, who sexually seduced Eve, thus begetting Eve's first born, Cain. Therefore, Cain would be the son of Satan and Eve, instead of Adam's, as taught by the three mainstream religions, Christianity, Judaism, and Islam. The YT and the Christian Identity Movement alike do claim that the Jewish population and other Semitic racial groups are descendants from Cain, whereas the Anglo-Saxon race descends from Seth, the third son of Eve and Adam, begotten after the murder of Abel by Cain. These are the central ideas sponsored by YT and the Christian Identity Movement, under the name the Two Seedlines doctrine.

YT and other Identity neo-Nazi groups, therefore, believe that the Anglo-Saxon race is the true, legitimate lineage of Adam and Eve, constituting the true Israelite people, who are destined to inherit the Earth at the end of time. Until then, they should wage a war against the satanic races in order to guarantee the white race's survival and to destroy the ZOG and its allies. The means to do so are twofold: to spread their own socio-theology and to prepare a paramilitary resistance. The Internet has become a very useful tool in accomplishing these objectives, using the neo-Nazi ideas as a common language to unite with other foreign white supremacist groups through the globe, including in countries such as Brazil, Argentina, South Africa, Germany, Austria, Poland, England, Canada, etc.

OTHER PERSPECTIVES

Communities throughout the United States are awakening to the dangers posed by hate groups and hate propaganda. Many law enforcement authorities and city councils are campaigning to make their citizens aware of the disruptive influence hate doctrines can cause, especially upon troubled adolescents. The Anti-Defamation League has suggested that citizens should be instructed to turn hate leaflets and other similar materials in to the local police, educators, religious authorities, and anti-racist organizations. The FBI Report on hate crimes for the period between 1991 and 2001 showed that hate crime incidents have more than doubled from 4,558 in 1991 to 9,730 in 2001. Anti-hate educational campaigns in schools and parental surveillance at home is essential to protect children from hate propaganda and to combat hate crimes, according to several experts.

The Southern Poverty Law Center (SPLC) points to the influence of Yahweh's Truth and Wickstrom's ideas over Terry Nichols, who was convicted with Timothy McVeigh in the Oklahoma federal building bombing. The SPLC also reports that Terry's brother, James Nichols, who was a Posse Comitatus activist in the 1980s and still has ties with Wickstrom, has pledged his life to a white supremacist religion, after his brother's conviction. In an interview with Michael Moore, during the filming of *Bowling for Columbine*, Nichols told Moore that, "They [the American people] will revolt with anger! Merciless anger! There will be blood running in the streets!" (when the American people realize that they are "enslaved"). SPLC asserted that Wickstrom is the most incendiary Identity preacher, and through his and other similar preaching as those sponsored by his Yahweh's Truth organization and the Identity movement, hatred from one generation infects the next.

SUMMARY

Domestic terrorism and hate crimes feed on racism and socio-religious sects that preach separatism and foster antigovernment feelings. Anti-white supremacist groups also add to the violence and extremist antisocial attitudes. The results are expressed in tragedies such as the Oklahoma bombing and the Columbine shootings, to name only two. Reporters, who interviewed Wickstrom on several different occasions, and law enforcement officials consider him one of the most vicious and insidious advocates of racial violence and antigovernment activism. In spite of Tigerton Dells' failure, several problems with the law and two convictions, the "Intelligence Report." (Winter 2002) written by Susan Buchanan, mentioned that he is now the Chaplain of the Aryan Nations' branch led by Charles Juba, where he will continue to preach his Yahweh's Truth doctrines.

SOURCES

Web sites

Anti-Defamation League. "Michigan Community Unites Against Hate." < http://www.adl.org/PresRele/Extremism_72/4255_72.asp > (accessed October 17, 2005).

Anti-Defamation League. "Border Disputes: Armed Vigilantes in Arizona." < http://www.adl.org/PresRele/Extremism_72/4255_72 > (accessed October 17, 2005).

Anti-Defamation League. "The Growing Cost of Combating Hate Crimes." < http://www.adl.org/learn/news/cost_of_hate.asp > (accessed October 17, 2005).

Anti-Defamation League. "FBI Hate Crime Statistics 1991–2002." < http://www.adl.org/99hatecrime/comp_f-bi.asp > (accessed October 17, 2005).

Anti-Defamation League. "How to Combat Hate Crime." < http://www.adl.org/blueprint.pdf > (accessed October 17, 2005).

The Bethune Institute for Anti-Fascist Studies. "Aryan Nations: Christian Identity and Fascist Terror." < http://bethuneinstitute.org/documents/cift.html > (accessed October 17, 2005).

Southern Poverty Law Center. "A Soldier's Ransom." < http://www.splcenter.org/intel/intelreport/article.jsp/ > (accessed October 17, 2005).

Southern Poverty Law Center. "Return of the Pastor." < http://www.splcenter.org/intel/intelreport/article.jsp/ > (accessed October 17, 2005).

UNESCO Courier. "White Fortresses in Cyberspace." < http://www.unesco.org/webworld/points_of_views/back.shtml > (accessed October 17, 2005).

U.S. Court of Appeals, Third Circuit. "U.S. v. Wickstrom, 893 F.2d 30 (3d Cir. 1989)." < http://www.cs.cmu.edu/afs/cs.cmu.edu/user/wbardwel/public/nfalist/us_v_wickstrom.txt > (accessed October 17, 2005).

SEE ALSO

Posse Comitatus

Aryan Nations

Zapatista Army of National Liberation

LEADER: Subcommandante Marcos, widely presumed to be Rafael Sebastian Guillén

YEAR ESTABLISHED OR BECAME ACTIVE: November 17, 1983

ESTIMATED SIZE: 5,000

USUAL AREA OF OPERATION: Chiapas, Mexico

OVERVIEW

The Zapatista National Liberation Army (*Ejército Zapatista de Liberación Nacional*, EZLN) began a rebellion against the Mexican government in the southern state of Chiapas on January 1, 1994. The organization is committed to fighting for the rights of indigenous and poor Mexicans. It is part of the global opposition to the North American Free Trade Agreement (NAFTA).

The designation of EZLN as a terrorist group is in dispute. The government of former Mexican President Ernesto Zedillo linked EZLN to the terrorist National Liberation Forces. Most Mexicans, including those in Congress and in the government of Chiapas, do not regard it as a terrorist force. Instead, they view EZLN fighters as irregular forces participating in a civil war. The U.S. government has occasionally described EZLN members as terrorists.

HISTORY

The rebellion in Chiapas has its roots in the agricultural history of centuries past. The state had been an isolated region in which the owners of large, underdeveloped estates made their incomes mostly from cattle, sugar, and grains that they produced with Indian labor conscripted from nearby villages. Trade in these products was

Subcomandante Marcos, leader of the Zapatista National Liberation Army (EZLN) in La Realidad, located in the Mexican state of Chiapas on May 18, 1999. AP/Wide World Photos. Reproduced by permission.

mostly contained within the state. In the 1890s, Chiapas suddenly became one of the most profitable agricultural regions in Mexico. Over the next century, it was the nation's largest source of coffee, providing approximately 40% of the annual harvest. It was also consistently one of the top Mexican states in the production of chocolate, sugar, bananas, corn, and beans.

To produce these agricultural products, labor was needed but there was a shortage of workers. The state government had advertised Chiapas land as an investment property to the Germans, Americans, Spaniards, English, and French while touting the area's abundance of plentiful, docile, hardworking, and underutilized Indian laborers. To make its claims true, the government had to get the Indian population to work on the plantations. Accordingly, it imposed new taxes to force Indians into debt and accompanied these taxes with widespread

arrests of indigenous tax-evaders at markets and their subsequent auction to labor contractors. When planters, labor contractors, and the government realized that as long as Indians had the capacity to feed themselves from their own lands they could avoid debts, they sought to reduce the landholdings of the indigenous people. Such actions would also force the Indians to come to markets where they could be captured and sold. From 1890 to 1910, the Chiapas government appropriated and sold most of the land that the indigenous people held. Police and army forces backed the actions of the government and the planters.

The government land policy was enormously effective. At the start of the 1970s, an estimated 80,000 indigenous men out of a total population of 100,000 males were moving around the state each year, from one harvest to another. Even agrarian reform, which came to Chiapas in the 1930s, failed to remedy this problem. Over time, the land that did return to indigenous hands failed to keep pace with population growth. The net effect was to keep indigenous people tied down. They had enough land to make it difficult for them to abandon their communities but not enough land to allow them to be self-sufficient.

As agriculture began to decline in profitability in the 1970s, large landowners in Chiapas stopped investing in their land and scaled back production. Some plantations were converted to cattle ranches. By the 1990s, most large landholders had abandoned the countryside altogether to be replaced by small landholders and communal holders. These new landowners did not need as much hired labor as the plantations that they replaced. Meanwhile, the population of Chiapas had dramatically increased. By 1990, it was estimated that more than 200,000 men were seeking work. Adding to the labor woes, about 80,000 adult Guatemalan Mayas had taken refuge in Chiapas, starting in the 1980s. The refugees were also looking for agricultural jobs, were competing with the native Mexicans, and were accepting less money to do the same work previously performed by Chiapas's Indians. Essentially, Chiapas's indigenous people, who for almost a century had been maneuvered into relying on seasonal, often migratory, labor to maintain themselves, suddenly found that they were no longer needed.

Mexican Army soldiers search Zapatista supporters at a security checkpoint in the Mexican state of Chiapas on May 7, 1999. AP/Wide World Photos. Reproduced by permission.

The EZLN was formed on November 17, 1983, by three mixed-race and three indigenous people. Meanwhile, tensions in Chiapas continued to build, but EZLN leaders did not believe that situations were right for an uprising. In 1992, when the indigenous people of Chiapas rioted to commemorate Columbus's 500-year anniversary of "discovering" the Americas, one of EZLN's leaders, Marcos, persuaded them to forgo the launching of a full-scale rebellion. Throughout 1993, there were rumors of the presence of guerillas in the mountains of Chiapas.

Many people familiar with Chiapas were not surprised that a rebellion began on January 1, 1994, inauguration day for NAFTA. Indians were increasingly frustrated by abuses to their dignity and rights. The new trade agreement paid no attention to the labor and environmental concerns of the indigenous people. The Zapatistas suddenly emerged from the jungle, seizing towns and clashing with security forces. About 150 people were killed before Mexican armed forces crushed the uprising. The remaining EZLN members retreated to a few villages in rural Chiapas, where the government has not pursued them.

Both sides, under pressure from both Mexican and international public opinion, agreed to a ceasefire. By February 1994, peace negotiations had begun. The Zapatistas claim that they have been in a defensive posture since February 1994. They expected that talks would yield results. Optimism was also high among the Mexican public that the Chiapas rebellion would push Mexico toward political reform quickly and without additional bloodshed. However, the peace negotiations stalled.

Meanwhile, the territory under EZLN control grew rapidly from December 1994 to February 1995. As local people joined the rebellion, thirty-eight municipalities became free, outside of government control. These municipalities also rejected government aid. At the same time, as the EZLN expanded its reach, the Mexican peso lost half its value. Middle-class Mexicans could not pay their bills and the poor lost much of their buying power. The economic crisis led to public anger and increased public support for the Zapatistas. The revolutionaries now seemed to speak for an ever-larger share of Mexicans.

An increasingly desperate Mexican government broke the ceasefire in February 1995, when

LEADERSHIP

SUBCOMMANDANTE MARCOS

Subcommandante Marcos, identified by the Mexican government as Rafael Sebastian Guillén, helped found the EZLN in 1983. Always clad in military fatigues and a black ski mask, the pipe-smoking revolutionary has become the group's primary spokesperson.

The fourth of eight children of a prosperous furniture store owner in the northern state of Tamaulipas, Guillén was born July 19, 1957. He earned degrees in philosophy and sociology from the National Autonomous University of Mexico (UNAM) before acquiring a Master's degree in Paris. He worked as a university lecturer in graphic design at UNAM before vanishing in 1984. Marcos is rumored to have trained with the insurgent Sandinista army in Nicaragua in 1987, under the name Jorge Narvaez. Known for being austere and highly cultured, Marcos reportedly has a son with Mexican journalist Gloria Munoz Ramirez.

The Chiapas uprising has made the revolutionary leader into a popular hero in the Chiapan highlands. Marcos has taken advantage of his popularity to co-author a novel, *Uncomfortable Dead*, with Mexican crime writer Paco Ignacio Taibo II. While Marcos occasionally comes out of hiding, he spends much of his time at his jungle base 800 kilometers from Mexico City. He has repeatedly denied that he plans to run for a Mexican political office.

it invaded Zapatista territory in an effort to capture the EZLN high command. They did not succeed, but in the weeks that followed, the army did retake large areas of EZLN-controlled land. In March, congressional representatives from Mexico's four largest political parties sought to halt the bloodshed. The political leaders formed the Commission of Conciliation and Pacification (COCOPA) to focus on discussions of Indian culture and Indian rights.

On February 16, 1996, the EZLN and the Mexican government signed the San Andrés Accords on Indigenous Culture and Rights that had been developed by COCOPA. The Accords were a package of constitutional amendments on autonomy for Mexico's Indians. Such political reform was the EZLN's one precondition for laying down arms. The EZLN went on a tour to promote congressional approval of the Accords. The Zapatistas were permitted to address Congress, and they drew about 100,000 people to a Mexico City rally. However, the Accords were gutted by conservative lawmakers before they were passed, causing the rebels to break off the peace dialogue. The gutting of the accords was protested by Indian groups across Mexico, many of whom pledged civil disobedience to pressure the Mexican Congress to reverse the changes.

While the truce has largely held, rightist paramilitary groups have been blamed for dozens of deaths in Chiapas. The situation in Chiapas has since disintegrated into an undeclared civil war between the indigenous poor and the mixed-race or white wealthy. The EZLN has never put down its arms, but most of the hundreds of deaths in fighting since 1994 have been blamed on the government-sponsored paramilitary forces. Many leftist non-governmental organizations have formed to aid the Zapatistas.

In June 2005, the EZLN put itself on Red Alert in anticipation of an attack from the Mexican government. Marcos cancelled all EZLN leaves and put the organization into a cell structure to enable it to withstand an assault. He also announced that the Zapatistas were moving toward politics and away from armed conflict. The EZLN embarked on a cross-country, pre-election tour aimed at uniting workers, students, and activists around a left-wing agenda. The new phase of Zapatista action aimed to make EZLN into a peaceful political force in Mexico, Latin America, and the rest of the world.

PHILOSOPHY AND TACTICS

The EZLN has had three major influences. The Zapatistas are named for Emilio Zapata, an early twentieth-century peasant leader who wanted to decentralize and reform the corrupt

KEY EVENTS

1983: The EZLN was formed.

1994: The EZLN went public.

2005: The EZLN went on Red Alert, anticipating an attack by the Mexican government.

Mexican government of the time. While building on the legacy of Zapata, EZLN also reflects the 1970s tradition of Latin American guerrillas. The guerrillas of the 1970s consisted of Marxist-Leninist ideologues who wanted to transform the world to create a dictatorship of the proletariat. The EZLN additionally drew on the increasing radicalization of the Catholic Church. The original Zapatistas—Marcos, Daniel, and Pedro—assumed biblical names to signal their support for liberation theology. Despite non-indigenous influences on the group, the EZLN is composed mostly of Chiapan Indians.

The political platform of the Zapatistas lists eleven goals: work, land, shelter, food, health, education, independence, liberty, democracy, justice, and peace. The EZLN focuses on anti-neo-liberalism, environmentalism, and, chiefly, indigenous rights. The EZLN regards the pitfalls of neo-liberalism as the principal global threat facing Mexicans. Neo-liberals in Mexico controlled the government and pushed a 1992 constitutional amendment that codified the end of land reform in Mexico and permitted the privatization of public lands. Such changes made it more difficult for Indians to possess enough land for subsistence. In 1992, Marcos wrote an article that called attention to the mounting ecological crisis in Chiapas and the horrific living standards endured by the indigenous people, who compose the majority of the state's population. He pointed out that more than 80% of highland residents suffered from malnutrition, and that Chiapas had the highest mortality rate in Mexico. For the

EZLN, the trampling of indigenous people came in the context of imperialist exploitation of Chiapas's rich natural resources, such as gas and oil.

The tactics of the Zapatistas rely very heavily on public relations. Except for minor skirmishes with government forces and right-wing death squads, armed conflict between the Mexican military and the Zapatistas ended on January 12, 1994. Unable to match Mexico militarily, they have compensated by trying to win the hearts and minds of the Mexican public. They operate a web site, speak often to the press, conduct occasional Zapatourists through Chiapas, write essays, and publish a magazine.

In their first published essay, "Declaration of the Lacandona Jungle," the Zapatistas lamented that their declaration of war was a method of last resort. The Zapatistas criticized the poor living standards of Chiapas's Indians as an attempt at genocide on the part of the Mexican government. They complained about the lack of democracy in Mexico, a country notorious for its history of political corruption. To EZLN, the inability of the poor to use the political process had made violence a necessity for survival.

In their magazine, *El Despertador Mexicano* (The Desperate Mexican), EZLN has called for fair wages for Mexican workers, agrarian reform, and equal rights for women. In Mexico's patriarchal society, the Zapatistas insist on women's right to become revolutionaries and to participate politically, to have access to basic health and education services as well as fair employment, and to control the number of children that they bear.

OTHER PERSPECTIVES

Most commentators agree that the Zapatistas are not stereotypical terrorists. Emilio Ulloa Perez, a federal deputy with the left-opposition Party of the Democratic Revolution (PRD) and a member of the congressional negotiating team for the peace dialogue with the EZLN, compared the Mexican activists with other agitators: "We can't put the guerrillas in the same category as groups in the Middle East, or the Balkans or the terrorist responsible for the Oklahoma bombing in the United States. In Mexico, we don't have guerrillas who put bombs in restaurants."

SUMMARY

The EZLN is a revolutionary organization for the media age. Since 1994, the Zapatista movement has been largely nonviolent. The group fights through the press and the Internet. While it has had success in attracting global attention to its message of indigenous rights and anti-capitalism, it has not had much luck in bettering the situation of the Indians in Chiapas. The EZLN has failed in its goal of becoming a political force.

SOURCES

Books

Ponce de León, Juana. *Our Word Is Our Weapon: Selected Writings of Subcomandante Marcos.* New York: Seven Stories Press, 2001.

Rochlin, James F. *Vanguard Revolutionaries in Latin America: Peru, Colombia, Mexico.* Boulder, CO: Lynne Rienner Publishers, 2003.

Ross, John. *Rebellion from the Roots: Indian Uprising in Chiapas.* Monroe, ME: Common Courage, 1995.

Rus, Jan, et al. *Mayan Lives, Mayan Utopias: The Indigenous Peoples of Chiapas and the Zapatista Rebellion.* Lanham, MD: Rowman & Littlefield, 2003.

Sources Consulted

BOOKS

Abanes, Richard. *American Militias*. Downers Grove, IL: InterVarsity Press, 1996.

Aburish, Said. *Arafat: From Defender to Dictator*. London and New York: Bloomsbury, 1998.

Abuza, Zachary. "The War on Terrorism in South East Asia." *Strategic Asia* (2003–2004): 321–364.

Africa, C., J. Christie, R. Mattes, M. Roefs, and H. Taylor. *Crime and Community Action: Pagad and the Cape Flats, 1996–1997*. Cape Town: Public Opinion Service, Institute for Democracy in South Africa, 1998.

Alexander, John K. *Samuel Adams: America's Revolutionary Politician*. Lanham, MD: Rowman & Littlefield, 2002.

American Nazi Party. *Official Stormtrooper's Manual*. Arlington, VA: American Nazi Party, 1962.

Anderson, Chris. *The Billy Boy: The Life and Times of Billy Wright*. Edinburgh: Mainstream, 2003.

Anderson, Sean, and Stephen Sloan. *Historical Dictionary of Terrorism, 2nd Edition*. Lanham, MD: Scarecrow Press, 2002.

Baird, Robert M., and Stuart E. Rosenbau, eds. *The Ethics of Abortion: Pro-Life vs. Pro-Choice*. Amhurst, NY: Prometheus Books, 2001.

Balasingham, Anton. *The Politics of Duplicity: Revisiting the Jaffna Talks*. Mitcham, England: Fairmax Publishing, 2000.

Ball, Phil. *Morbo: A History of Spanish Football*. London: WSC Books, 2003.

Barkun, Michael. *Religion and the Racist Right: The Origins of the Christian Identity Movement*. Chapel Hill, NC: The University of North Carolina Press, 1997.

Best, Steven, and Anthony J. Nocella (eds.). *Terrorists or Freedom Fighters: Reflections on the Liberation of Animals*. New York: Lantern Books, 2004.

Blee, Kathleen M. *Inside Organized Racism: Women in the Hate Movement*. Los Angeles: University of California Press, 2003.

B'nai B'rith. Anti-defamation League. *The Church of the Creator: Creed of Hate*. New York: Anti-Defamation League, 1993.

B'nai B'rith. *Extremism in America*. New York: Anti-Defamation League, 2002.

Brown, Adam (ed.). *Fanatics! Power, Identity and Fandom in FOOTBALL*. Oxford: Routledge, 1998.

Burke, Jason. *Al-Qaeda*. New York: Penguin, 2004.

Burnett, Christina Duffy, and Burke Marshall, editors. *Foreign in a Domestic Sense: Puerto Rico, American Expansion, and the Constitution*. Durham, NC: Duke University Press, 2001.

Byrnes, Rita M. "A Country Study: South Africa." *Library of Congress, Federal Research Division* May 1996.

Chapman, William. *Inside the Philippine Revolution*. New York: W.W. Norton, 1987.

Cleveland, William L. *A History of the Modern Middle East*. New York: Westview, 2000.

Combs, Cindy. *Terrorism in the Twenty-First Century*. Upper Saddle River, NJ: Prentice-Hall, 2000.

Conaghan, Catherine M. *Fujimori's Peru: Deception In The Public Sphere*. Pittsburgh: University of Pittsburgh Press, 2005.

Congressional Testimony. "Iran: Weapons Proliferations, Terrorism and Democracy." May 19, 2005.

Cook, David. *Understanding Jihad*. Berkeley: University of California Press, 2005.

Copeland, David A. *Debating the Issues in Colonial Newspapers: Primary Documents on Events of the Period*. Westport, CT: Greenwood Press, 2000.

Copesy, Nigel. *Contemporary British Fascism: The British National Party and the Quest for Legitimacy*. NY: Palgrave Macmillan, 2004.

Corbett, James. *England Expects*. London: Aurum, 2006.

Corpus, Victor N. *Silent War*. Zuezon City, Philippines: VNC Enterprises, 1989.

Courtemanche, Gils. *A Sunday at the Pool in Kigali*. Edinburgh: Canongate Books, 2004.

Cozic, Charles P., editor. *The Militia Movement*. Farmington Hills, MI: Greenhaven Press, 1997.

Cummings, Bruce. *Inventing the Axis: The Truth about North Korea, Syria and Iran*. New York: New Press, 2004.

Dailaire, Romeo. *Shake Hands With the Devil*. New York: Arrow, 1995.

Dawson, Henry B. *The Sons of Liberty in New York*. New York: Arno Press and the New York Times, 1969.

Deeb, Marius (ed.). *Syria's Terrorist War on Lebanon and the Peace Process*. New York: Macmillan, 2004.

Dill, Martin. *The Shankhill Butchers: A Case Study of Mass Murder*. London: Hutchinson, 1989.

Dixon, B. and L. Johns. *Gangs, PAGAD & the State: Vigilantism and Revenge Violence in the Western Cape*. Cape Town: Center for the Study of Violence and Reconciliation, 2001.

Dolgin, Jane. *Jewish Identity and the JDL*. Princeton: Princeton University Press, 1977.

Duke, Vic, and Liz Crolley. *Football, Nationality and the State*. New York: Longman, 1996.

Edwards, Ruth Dudley. *The Faithful Tribe*. New York: Harper Collins, 2000.

Ellingwood, Ken. *Hard Line: Life and Death on the U.S.-Mexican Border*. New York: Pantheon, 2004.

Evans, Richard J. *Lying about Hitler: History, Holocaust, and the David Irving Trial*. New York: Basic Books, 2002.

Farrell, William R. *Blood and Rage: The Story of the Japanese Red Army*. Lexington, MA: D.C. Heath, 1990.

Fisk, Robert. *Pity the Nation*. Oxford: Oxford Press, 2001.

Gardell, Mattias. *Gods of the Blood: The Pagan Revival and White Separatism*. NC: Duke University Press, 2003.

George, John, and Laird Wilcox. *American Extremists: Militias, Supremacists, Klansmen, Communists & Others*. NY: Prometheus Books, 1996.

Giulianotti, Richard, Norman Bonney and Mike Hepworth (eds.). *Football, Violence and Social Identity*. Oxford: Routledge, 1994.

Glenny, Misha. *The Balkans 1804—1999: Nationalism, War and the Great Powers*. London and New York: Granta, 2000.

Goritti, Gustavo. *The Shining Path: A History of the Millenarian War in Peru*. Durham, North Carolina: University of North Carolina Press, 1999.

Gourevitch, Philip. *We Wish to Inform You That Tomorrow We Will Be Killed With Our Families*. London: Picador, 2000.

Griffin, D. *Radical Common Law Movement and Paper Terrorism: The State Response*. National Conference of State, 2000.

Hellmann-Rajanayagam, Dagmar. *The Tamil Tigers: Armed Struggle for Identity*. Stuttgart: Franz Steiner Verlag, 1994.

Hitler's Apologists: The Anti-Semitic Propaganda of Holocaust Revisionism. New York: Anti-Defamation League, 1993.

Hoerder, Dirk. *Crowd Action in Revolutionary Massachusetts, 1765–1780*. New York: Academic Press, 1977.

Hutton, Joseph B. *The Subverters*. New York: Arlington House, 1972.

Ibrahim, Abdullah, editor. *Between Democracy and Terror: The Sierra Leone Civil War*. Dakar, Senegal: Council for the Development of Social Science Research in Africa, 2004.

Ignatieff, Michael. *Blood and Belonging: Journeys into the New Nationalism*. New York: Farrar, Straus and Giroux, 1995.

Jacquard, Roland. *In the Name of Osama bin Laden: Global Terrorism and the bin Laden Brotherhood, Revised and Updated Edition*. Durham, NC : Duke University Press, 2002.

Jakes, Dale, Connie Jakes, and Clint Richmond. *False Prophets: The Firsthand Account of a Husband-Wife Team Working for the FBI and Living in Deepest Cover with the Montana Freemen*. Allen Park, MI: Dove Books, 1998.

Jordan, Hugh, and David Lister. *Mad Dog: The Rise and Fall of Johnny Adair*. Edinburgh: Mainstream, 2003.

Kahane, Meir. *The Story of the Jewish Defense League*. Radnor, PA: Chilton Books, 1975.

Karpin, Michael, and Ina Friedmann. *Murder in the Name of God, the Plot to Kill Yitzhak Rabin*. New York: Granta, 1999.

Kepel, Gilles. *Jihad: The Trail of Political Islam*. Cambridge, MA: Belknap, 2003.

Kepel, Gilles. *Muslim Extremism in Egypt*. Los Angeles: University of California Press, 2003.

Khaled, Leila. *My People Shall Live: The Autobiography of a Revolutionary*. London: Hodder and Stoughton, 1973.

Kinzer, Stephen. *All the Shah's Men: An American Coup and the Roots of Middle East Terror*. Hoboken, NJ: John Wiley and Sons, 2004.

Leahy, Michael. *Against Liberation: Putting Animals in Perspective*. Oxford: Routledge, 1993.

Lee, Martin A. *The Beast Reawakens*. New York: Little, Brown, 1997.

Levitas, Daniel. *The Terrorist Next Door: The Militia Movement and the Radical Right*. New York: St. Martin's Press, 2002.

Lifton, Robert Jay. *Destroying the World to Save It: Aum Shinrikyo, Apocalyptic Violence, and the New Global Terrorism*. New York: Owl Books, 2000.

Lipstadt, Deborah E. *Denying the Holocaust: The Growing Assault on Truth and Memory*. New York: Plume (reprint edition), 1994.

Loader, B., and D. Thomas. *Cybercrime: Law, Security And Privacy in the Information Age*. New York: Routledge, 2000.

Lowles, Nick. *White Riot: The Rise and Violent Fall of Combat 18*. London: Milo Books, 2001.

Maier, Pauline. *From Resistance to Revolution: Colonial Radicals and the Development of American Opposition to Britain, 1765–1776*. New York: Knopf, 1972.

Malcolm, Noel. *Kosovo: A Short History*. New York: Macmillan, 1998.

Maloney, Ed. *Secret History of the IRA*. London: Penguin, 2003.

Marsden, Peter. *The Taliban: War and Religion in Afghanistan*. London: Zed Books, 2002.

Martin, Ian. *Self Determination in East Timor*, International Peace Academy Occasional Paper Series. Boulder, CO: Lynne Rienner Publishers, 2001.

Mason, Carol. *Killing for Life: The Apocalyptic Narrative of Pro-Life Politics*. Ithaca, NY: Cornell University Press, 2002.

Matthiessen, Peter. *In The Spirit of Crazy Horse*. New York: Viking Press, 1983.

McDonald, Henry, and Jim Cussack. *The UDA*. New York: Penguin, 2004.

McDonough, Frank. *Hitler and the Rise of the NSDAP*. London and New York: Pearson/Longman, 2003.

McKittrick, David, and David McVeigh. *Making Sense of the Troubles*. London: Penguin, 2003.

McTaggart, David. *Rainbow Warrior*. Munich: Goldmann, 2002.

Merkl, Peter H. and Leonard Weinberg, editors. *Right-wing Extremism in the Twenty-first Century*. London and Portland, OR: Frank Cass, 2003.

Mishal, Shaul, and Avraham Sela. *The Palestinian HAMAS: Vision, Violence and Co-Existence*. New York: Columbia University Press, 2000.

Moloney, Ed. *Secret History of the IRA*. London: Penguin, 2003.

Mooney, John, and Michael O'Toole. *Black Operations: The Secret War against the Real IRA*. County Meath, Ireland: Maverick House, 2003.

Moore, Robin. *The Hunt for bin Laden*. New York: Random House, Inc., 2003.

Morris, David B. *Earth Warrior: Overboard With Paul Watson and the Sea Shepherd Conservation Society*. Golden, Colorado: Fulcrum Publishing, 1995.

Mukarji, Apratim. *Sri Lanka: A Dangerous Interlude*. Chicago: New Dawn Press, 2005.

Murillo, Mario Alfonso, and Jesus Rey Avirama. *Colombia and the United States: War, Terrorism, and Destabilization*. New York: Seven Stories Press, 2003.

Murphy, Patrick, et al. *Football on Trial: Spectator Violence and Development in the Football World*. Oxford: Routledge, 1990.

Núñez Astrain, Luis. *The Basques: Their Struggle for Independence*. Cardiff: Welsh Academic Press, 1997.

Nantulya, Paul. "Exclusion, Identity and Armed Conflict: A Historical Survey of the Politics of Confrontation in Uganda with Specific Reference to the Independence Era."

Nusse, Andrea. *Muslim Palestine: Ideology of HAMAS*. London: Taylor & Francis, 1999.

Parenti, Michael. *To Kill a Nation: The Attack on Yugoslavia*. New York and London: Verso, 2001.

Parry, Richard Lloyd. *In a Time of Madness*. New York: Random House, 2005.

Pearce, Jenny. *Inside Colombia: Drugs, Democracy, and War*. New Brunswick, NJ: Rutgers University Press, 2004.

Ponce de León, Juana. *Our Word Is Our Weapon: Selected Writings of Subcomandante Marcos*. New York: Seven Stories Press, 2001.

Preston, Paul. *A Concise History of the Spanish Civil War*. New York: HarperCollins, 1996.

Quarles, Chester L. *Christian Identity: The Aryan American Bloodline Religion*. Jefferson, NC: McFarland & Company, 2004.

Rashid, Ahmed. *Jihad: The Rise of Militant Islam in Central Asia*. New Haven, CT: Yale University Press, 2002.

Rashid, Ahmed. *Taliban: Militant Islam, Oil and Fundamentalism in Central Asia*. New Haven: Yale University Press, 2001.

Reader, Ian. *Religious Violence in Contemporary Japan: Case of Aum Shinrikyo.* Honolulu: University of Hawaii Press, 2000.

Rochlin, James F. *Vanguard Revolutionaries in Latin America: Peru, Colombia, Mexico.* Boulder, CO: Lynne Rienner Publishers, 2003.

Rosenthal, David. *Racism on the Internet.* Geneva: World Conference Against Racism, Racial Discrimination, Xenophobia, and Related Intolerance, 2000.

Ross, John. *Rebellion from the Roots: Indian Uprising in Chiapas.* Monroe, ME: Common Courage, 1995.

Rus, Jan, et al. *Mayan Lives, Mayan Utopias: The Indigenous Peoples of Chiapas and the Zapatista Rebellion.* Lanham, MD: Rowman & Littlefield, 2003.

Ryan, Nick. *Homeland: Into a World of Hate.* Edinburgh, Scotland: Mainstream, 2004.

Safford, Frank, and Marco Palacios. *Colombia: Fragmented Land, Divided Society.* England: Oxford University Press, 2001.

Savigh, Yezid. *Armed Struggle and the Search for State: The Palestinian National Movement, 1949—1993.* England: Oxford University Press, 1999.

Scully, Matthew. *Dominion: The Power of Man, the Suffering of Animals, and the Call to Mercy.* New York: St. Martin's Press, 2002.

Seale, Patrick. *Abu Nidal: A Gun For Hire.* New York: Random House, 1992.

Seale, Patrick. *Assad of Syria: The Struggle for the Middle East.* Berkeley, CA: University of California Press, 1989.

Singer, Peter. *Animal Liberation, (3rd Edition).* New York: Harper Collins, 2002.

Sison, Jose Maria. *The Philippine Revolution: The Leader's View.* New York: Crane Russak, 1989.

Smith, Barbara. "Heaven or Hell?: Terrorism Hurts Revenue from Tourism." *The Economist* no. 350 (1999): 14–15.

Solinger, Rick (ed). *Abortion Wars: A Half Century of Struggle, 1950–2000.* Berkeley, CA: University of California Press, 2001.

Spielvogel, Jackson J. *Hitler and Nazi Germany.* Upper Saddle River, NJ: Prentice-Hall, 2001.

Sprinzak, Ehud. *Brother Against Brother: Violence and Extremism in Israeli Politics from Altalena to the Rabin Assassination.* New York: The Free Press, 1999.

Sprinzak, Ehud. *Kach and Meir Kahane: The Emergence of Jewish Quasi-Fascism.* New York: The American-Jewish Committee, 1985.

Stern, Kenneth S. *A Force upon the Plain: The American Militia Movement and the Politics of Hate.* New York: Simon and Schuster, 1995.

Strum, Philippa. *When the Nazis Came to Skokie; Freedom for Speech We Hate.* Lawrence, Kansas: University Press of Kansas, 2000.

Sykes, Andrew. *The Radical Right in Britain.* NY: Palgrave Macmillan, 2004.

Tarik, Judith Palmer. *Hizbollah:The Changing Face of Terrorism.* London: I B Tauris, 2004.

Taylor, Peter. *Loyalists.* London: Bloomsbury, 2000.

Taylor, Peter. *Loyalists: War and Peace in Northern Ireland.* New York: TV Books, 2004.

Taylor, Peter. *The Provos: The IRA and Sinn Fein.* London: Bloomsbury, 1998.

Tonge, Jonathan. *Northern Ireland: Conflict & Change.* New York: Longman, 2002.

Toolid, Kevin. *Rebel Hearts, Journeys in the Republican Movement.* NY: Picador, 1995.

Tsoukalas, Steven Malcolm. *The Nation of Islam; Understanding the Black Muslims.* Phillipsburg, New Jersey: P&R Publishing, 2001.

Tucker, Jonathan, editor. *Toxic Terror: Assessing Terrorist Use of Chemical and Biological Weapons (BCSIA Studies in International Security).* Cambridge, Massachusetts: MIT Press: Bantam, 2000.

Wade, Wyn C. *The Fiery Cross: The Ku Klux Klan in America.* Oxford, England: Oxford University Press, 1998.

Wallach, Janet. *Arafat: In the Eyes of the Beholder.* Amsterdam: Citadel, 2001.

Walvin, James. *Football and the Decline of Britain.* London and New York: Macmillan, 1986.

Wessinger, Catherine. *How the Millennium Comes Violently: From Jonestown to Heaven's Gate.* New York: Chatham House Publishers, 2000.

Weyler, Rex. *Greenpeace: How a Group of Ecologists, Journalists and Visionaries Changed the World.* New York: Rodale, 2004.

White, Paul J. *Primitive Rebels or Revolutionary Modernisers?* London and New York: Zed, 2000.

Woodworth, Paddy. *Dirty Wars, Clean Hands: ETA, the GAL, and Spanish Democracy.* Ireland: Cork University Press, 2001.

Wright, Richard T. *Environmental Science: Toward a Sustainable Future (9th edition).* NY: Prentice Hall, 2004.

X, Malcolm. *The Autobiography of Malcolm X (As Told to Alex Haley).* New York: Balantine Publishing Group, 1964.

PERIODICALS

Aras, Bulent, and Gokhan Bacik. "Hezbollah Horror: A National Shame." *The Middle East Quarterly* (June 2000) v9 i2 p147.

"As He Lay Dying." *The Village Voice* September 4–10, 2002.

Aydintasbas, Asli. "Murder on the Bosporus." *Middle East Quarterly* (June 2000) v7 i2 p15.

Aziz, A.A. "The Burden of Terrorism in Malaysia." *Prehospital Disaster Medicine* no. 18(2) (2003): 115–119.

Barsky, Yehudit. "Terrorism Briefing Islamic Jihad Movement in Palestine." *American Jewish Committee* July 18, 2002.

Brennan, Charlie. "Al-Fuqra Tied To Colorado Crimes: Leader Owned Land In Buena Vista; Followers Convicted In Bombing Of Krishna Temple." *The Rocky Mountain News* February 12, 2002.

Bridges, T. "Duke Brewed Hatred in a Potion of Lies." *Times-Picayune* (March 16, 2003: 7).

Calabres, Massimo. "My Tea with Arkan the Henchman." *Time* (April 12, 1999).

Carassave, Anthee. "Arrest Destroys Noble Image of Guerilla Group in Greece." *New York Times* (July 29, 2005).

"Central Europe's Skinheads: Nasty, Ubiquitous, and Unloved." *The Economist* (March 20, 1999).

Charney, Marc. "Word for Word / The Skinhead International; Some Music, It Turns Out, Inflames the Savage Breast." *The Economist* (July 2, 1995).

"Communist Terrorists Bomb Police Offices." *United Press International* May 6, 1985.

Daly, Sara. "The Algerian Salafist Group for Call and Combat: A Dossier." *The Jamestown Foundation* Volume 3, Issue 5 (March 11, 2005).

Davenport, Coral, M. "Elusive Terrorist Group Takes a Hit Finally." *Christian Science Monitor* July 5, 2005.

Desmond, Edward, W. "The Spirit of the Age Is in Favor of Equality, through Practice." *Time International* (April 13, 1992).

Dickey, Christopher, Mark Hosenball, and Michael Hirsh. "Looking for a Few Good Spies." *Newsweek* (February 14, 2005).

Feinstein, Adam. "People Will Not Take This Lying Down." *IPI Report* (February–March 1994, v.43).

"Fighters on the ropes." *Time International* (May 26), 2003 v161 i21 p46.

"Four Accused of Terror Group Links." *United Press International* (December 16, 1985).

"Germans Outlaw Neo-Nazi Group." *Evening Standard (London)* (February 24, 1995).

"Germany Bans Two Neo-Nazi Groups, Police Carry Out Raids." *Deutsche Press-Agentur* (February 24, 1995).

"Germany to Ask Court to Ban Neo-Nazi Party." *Agence France Presse* (September 15, 1993).

"Germany: Far Right Organization Banned." *U.S. News and World Report* (September 28, 2000).

Gorvett, Jon. "The Mystery of Turkish Hizballah." *Middle East Policy* March 2000.

Graham, Fred P. "Rockwell's Nazis Lost Without Him." *New York Times* (April 8, 1968, p. 21).

"Group Claims Bombings As Protest of U.S. Missiles." *United Press International* (October 4, 1984).

Haven, Paul and Katherine Shrader. "U.S., Pakistan Exploit Rifts within Factions of Al-Qaeda." *Ottawa Citizen* (May 11, 2005).

Hawthorne, Peter. "No Laughing Matter. A Shadowy Group of Racist Afrikaners Is Plotting to Bring Down the Government." *Time International* (October 21, 2001).

Henrard, Kristin. "Post-apartheid South Africa: Transformation and Reconciliation." *World Affairs* Vol. 6 No. 1 (July 1, 2003).

Hosenball, Mark. "Mixed Signals on MEK." *Newsweek* (April 11, 2005).

"IMU Controls Drug Traffic to Central Asia." *Pravada* (May 30, 2001).

"In Search of Uganda's Lost Youth." *Time International* v162 i4 p42, July 28, 2003.

"India: The Politics of Extremism." *The Economist* (October 2, 1999).

"India: Untouchable Bihar." *The Economist* June 24, 2000.

"Italian Northeast Seen as Fertile Recruitment Ground for Terrorism." *BBC* (March 24, 2002).

Ivaldi, Gilles. "Conservation, Revolution and Protest: A Case Study in the Political Cultures of the French National Front's Members and Sympathizers." *Electoral Studies* Vol. 15, No. 3, pp. MO-362, 1996.

Japan Economic Newswire. "Chukakuha Claims Series of Attacks." *Kyoto News International Inc* (November 1990).

Japan Economic Newswire. "Nineteen Activists Given Sentences over Airport Clash." *Kyoto News International Inc* (October 1989).

Japan Economic Newswire. "Radical Leader Held over Narita Threats." *Kyoto News International Inc* (September 1989).

"Jewish Cemetery Desecrated by Neo-Nazis in Eastern Germany." *United Press International* (September 8, 1993).

Karmon, Ely. "The Bombing of the U.S.S. Cole: An Analysis of the Principle Suspects." *International Policy Institute for Counter Terrorism* (October 24, 2000).

Kefner, John. "Lott, and Shadow of a Pro-White Group." *The New York Times* (January 14, 1999).

Kerr, Simon. "Yemen Cracks Down on Militants." *Middle East Journal* (December 1, 1999).

Kohen, Arnold S. "Making an Issue of East." *The Nation* (Feb 10, 1992) v254 n5 p162(2).

Koon, David. "A Young Skinhead Makes a Conversion—Of Sorts." *The Arkansas Times* (May 27, 2005).

Mahoney, Edmund. "A Rocket Attack, an FBI Revelation." *Hartford Courant* (November 12, 1999).

McCaffery, Jen. "Muslim Terrorists Convicted on Firearms Charges in the U.S." *The Roanoke Times* (December 1, 2001).

McCutcheon, Chuck. "Right-Wing Extremist Groups Becoming More Active After Post 9/11 Lull." *Newhouse News Service* (July 13, 2004).

McGregor, Andrew. "Strike First." *The World Today* (December 1, 2002).

Ojeda-Rios, Filberto. "The Boricua-Macheteros Popular Army, Origins, Program, and Struggle." *Latin American Perspectives* Issue 127, Vol. 29 No. 6 (2002): 104–116.

Ottey, Michael A.W. "Many Hondurans Say Guerillas, Not Gangs, Were Behind Massacre." *The Miami Herald* (December 29, 2004).

Perry, Alex. "Deadly Cargo." *Time Magazine* (October 14, 2002).

"Police Say White Revolution Racist Flyers 'Not Illegal.'" *Monroe Courier* (November 24, 2004).

Radmacher, D. "Most Whites in U.S. Not Exactly Oppressed, Earn More than Minorities." *The Charleston Gazette* (August 25, 2000: 4A).

Ruiz, Albor. "No Room at Inn for This Flock." *New York Daily News* (February 24, 2004).

Sabella, Bryan. "Hate Group Leaflets Turn Up in Metuchen: Community Leaders, Police Describe Distribution as Limited." *Sentinel.* May 12, 2004.

Sale, Richard. "Pakistan ISI Link to Pearl Kidnap Probed." *United Press International* (January 29, 2002).

Schanzer, Jonathan. "Lurking in Lebanon." *Washington Institute for Near East Policy.* June 4, 2003.

Schanzer, Jonathan. "Algeria's GSPC and America's War on Terror." *Washington Institute.* October 15, 2002.

Seper, Jerry, and Steve Miller. "Militant Muslims Seek Virginia Base." *The Washington Times* (July 1, 2002).

Sheean, Thomas. "Italy: Terror on the Right." *The New York Review of Books* Volume 27, Number 21 & 22, 1981.

Shepardson, David, Gary Heinlein, and Oralandar Brand-Williams. "White Supremacist Record Company in Oakland (Michigan) Raided in Tax-Fraud Probe." *The Detroit News.* April 11, 1997.

Southern Poverty Law Center. "A League of Their Own." *Intelligence Report* (Summer 2000).

Southern Poverty Law Center. "Against the Wall." *Intelligence Report* (Fall 2003).

Southern Poverty Law Center. "From Push to Shove." *Intelligence Report* (Fall 2002).

Staff writer. "Bigotry Racism Lingers." *The Charleston Gazette* (August 26, 2000: 4A).

Stanley, Alessandra. "Rome Journal; Agony Lingers, 20 Years After the Moro Killing." *New York Times* (May 9, 1998).

Suarez, Manny. "Possible Macheteros Office Contained FBI Information." *The San Juan Star* (April 5, 1984).

Taghavi, Seyed Mohammad Ali. "Fadaeeyan-i Islam: The Prototype of Islamic Hard-liners in Iran." *Middle Eastern Studies* (January 2004).

Tamayo, Juan O. "Attacks Put Puerto Rican Separatists Back in the Limelight." *The Miami Herald* (August 28, 1998).

"Terrorist Bombings Knock Out NATO Supply Lines." *United Press International* (December 12, 1984).

Thomas, Jo, and Ralph Blumenthal. "Rural Muslims Draw New, Unwanted Attention." *The New York Times* (January 3, 2002).

Thompson, Ginger. "Gunmen Kills 28 on Streets of Honduras; Street Gangs Blamed." *New York Times International* (December 25, 2004).

Trendle, Giles. "Splintered Loyalties, Shattered Lives." *Middle East.* February 1, 2003.

Turbiville, Graham H. Jr. "Naxalite Insurgency Draws Indian Concerns." *J.F.K. Special Warfare Center and School.* February 21, 2005.

Turner, Harry. "Macheteros Suspects May Face '79, '81 Raps." *The San Juan Star.* October 8, 1987.

"UGANDA: Museveni offers to Negotiate with LRA Rebels, Kampala." *IRIN News.* 16 April 2004.

"Uganda the Horror." *Smithsonian* v35 i11 p90 (February 2005).

"U.S. Senator Orrin Hatch (R-UT) holds hearing on Judiciary and FALN." *Wire Transcription Service.* October 10, 1999.

Wolin, Richard. "Mussolini's Ghost; Europe and the Specter of Fascism." *Tikkun* Vol. 9, No. 4, p.13, 1994.

"World: South Africa, The Wind Rises in Welkom in Defense of Apartheid." *Time* (May 28, 1990).

Wright, Lawrence. "The Man Behind Bin Laden: How an Egyptian Doctor Became a Master of Terror." *The New Yorker* (September 16, 2002).

WEB RESOURCES

ABC Asia Pacific. "Cause and Effect—Profiles of Terrorist Groups." < http://abcasiapacific.com/cause/network/sayyaf.htm > (accessed September 14, 2005).

Abortion facts.com. "U.S. Statistics." < http://www.abortionfacts.com/statistics/us_stats_ abortion.asp > (accessed October 16, 2005).

Activist Cash.com. "Norway to the USA: Stop Sea Shepherd." < http://www.activistcash.com/organization_overview.cfm/oid/347 > (accessed September 30, 2005).

Activist Cash.com. "People for the Ethical Treatment of Animals." < http://www.activistcash.com/organization_overview.cfm/oid/21 > (accessed October 19, 2005).

Activist.com. "Earth First!" <http://www.activistcash. com/organization_overview.cfm/oid/271> (accessed September 29, 2005).

Activist.com. "At ActivistCash.com, We Follow the Money—for You." <http://www.activistcash.com/ aboutUs.cfm> (accessed October 21, 2005).

ADL.org. "National Alliance." <http://www.adl.org/ learn/ext_us/N_Alliance.asp> (accessed October 15, 2005).

African National Congress. "I am Prepared to Die: Nelson Mandela's Statement." <http://www.anc.org. za/ancdocs/history/rivonia.html> (accessed October 11, 2005).

African Studies Quarterly. "Conventional Wisdom and Rwanda's Genocide." <http://web.africa.ufl.edu/asq/ v1/3/10.htm> (accessed October 12, 2005).

African Terrorism Bulletin. "Renewed Threat from Defeated Ugandan Rebel Group?" <http://www.iss. org.za/Pubs/Newsletters/Terrorism/0305.htm> (accessed September 22, 2005).

Albion Monitor. "McVeigh Conviction Won't Deter Extremists." <http://www.monitor.net/monitor/9706a/ mcvdeter.html> (accessed October 17, 2005).

American Civil Liberties Union. "Planned Parenthood of the Columbia/Willamette Inc. v American Coalition of Life Activists (1999 decision)." <http://www.aclu.org/ ReproductiveRights/ReproductiveRights.cfm?ID= 13583&c=227> (accessed October 21, 2005).

American Forces Information Service. "Tenent Briefs Senate on Terror Threats." <http://www.globalsecurity. org/intell/library/news/2004/intell-040224-afps01. htm> (accessed October 18, 2005).

American Religion.com. "The Identity Movement." <http://www.americanreligion.org/cultwtch/identity. html> (accessed September 29, 2005).

Amnesty International. "Colombia, A Laboratory of War: Repression and Violence in Arauca." <http:// web.amnesty.org/library/index/engamr230042004> (accessed October 21, 2005).

Amnesty International. "Report into al-Aqsa Intifada." <http://www.stoptorture.org.il/eng/images/uploaded/ publications/43.pdf> (accessed October 21, 2005).

Amnesty International. "Algeria: A Human Rights Crisis: Civilians Caught in a Spiral of Violence." <http:// web.amnesty.org/library/Index/ENGMDE280361997? open&of=ENG-313> (accessed July 28, 2005).

Amnesty International. "Colombia, A Laboratory of War: Repression and Violence in Arauca." <http:// web.amnesty.org/library/index/engamr230042004> (accessed September 30, 2005).

Amnesty International. "Colombia: Report 2005." <http://web.amnesty.org/report2005/col-summary- eng> (accessed September 30, 2005).

Amnesty International. "PERU: Summary of Amnesty Internationals concerns 1980–1995." <http://web. amnesty.org/library/Index/ENGAMR460041996?open &of=ENG-PER> (accessed October 5, 2005).

Andrew Mueller. "A Brush With Death." <http:// www.andrewmueller.net/scroll.lasso?ID=56&story= A%20BRUSH%20WITH%20DEATH_full_story> (accessed October 3, 2005).

Anti Terrorism Force Protection 1st Marine Aircraft Wing. "Chukakuh-ha." <http://www.1maw.usmc.mil/ ATFP/News/02-3.pdf#search='MiddleCore%20 Faction'> (accessed September 27, 2005).

Anti-Defamation League "Farrakhan Reaches Out to Anti-Semitic Black Panther Party." <http://www.adl. org/main_Anti_Semitism_Domestic/farrakhan_black_ panther_party.htm> (accessed October 18, 2005).

Anti-Defamation League. "Border Disputes: Armed Vigilantes in Arizona." <http://www.adl.org/PresRele/ Extremism_72/4255_72> (accessed October 17, 2005).

Anti-Defamation League. "Council of Conservative Citizens: December 21, 1998." <http://www.adl.org/ backgrounders/ccc.asp> (accessed October 23, 2005).

Anti-Defamation League. "Don Black: White Pride World Wide." <http://www.adl.org/poisoning_web/ black.asp> (accessed October 2, 2005).

Anti-Defamation League. "Extremism in America: Council of Conservative Citizens." <http://www. adl.org/learn/ext_us/CCCitizens.asp?xpicked=3 &item=12> (accessed October 23, 2005).

Anti-Defamation League. "FBI Hate Crime Statistics 1991–2002." <http://www.adl.org/99hatecrime/ comp_fbi.asp> (accessed October 17, 2005).

Anti-defamation League. "Feminism Perverted: Extremist Women on the World Wide Web." <http:// www.adl.org/special_reports/extremist_women_on_ web/feminism_intro.asp> (accessed October 1, 2005).

Anti-Defamation League. "How to Combat Hate Crime." <http://www.adl.org/blueprint.pdf> (accessed October 17, 2005).

Anti-Defamation League. "James 'Bo' Gritz." <http:// www.adl.org/learn/ext_us/gritz.asp?xpicked=2&item= 5> (accessed September 29, 2005).

Anti-Defamation League. "Michigan Community Unites Against Hate." <http://www.adl.org/PresRele/ Extremism_72/4255_72.asp> (accessed October 17, 2005).

Anti-Defamation League. "Muslims of the Americas: In Their Own Words." <http://www.adl.org/extremism/ moa/default.asp> (September 21, 2005).

Anti-Defamation League. "NAAWP." <http://www.adl. org/hate_symbols/groups_naawp.asp> (accessed October 18, 2005).

Anti-Defamation League. "Patriot Profiles #2: Patriot Purgatory: Bo Gritz and Almost Heaven." <http:// www.militia-watchdog.org/gritz.asp> (accessed September 29, 2005).

Anti-Defamation League. "Peter J. 'Pete' Peters." < http://www.adl.org/learn/ext_us/Peters.asp?LEARN_Cat = Extremism&LEARN_SubCat = Extremism_in_America&xpicked = 2&item = 8 > (accessed September 30, 2005).

Anti-Defamation League. "Still Howling." < http://www.adl.org/learn/extremism_in_america_updates/individuals/tom_metzger/metzger_update_020801.htm > (accessed October 17, 2005).

Anti-Defamation League. "The Growing Cost of Combating Hate Crimes." < http://www.adl.org/learn/news/cost_of_hate.asp > (accessed October 17, 2005).

Anti-Defamation League. "Ku Klux Klan." < http://www.adl.org/learn/ext_us/kkk.asp > (accessed October 18, 2005).

Anti-Defamation League. "Al-Fuqra: Holy Warriors of Terrorism." < http://www.adl.org/extremism/moa/al-fuqra.pdf > (September 21, 2005).

Apologetics Index. "Aum Shinrikyo." < http://www.apologeticsindex.org/a06.html > (accessed October 10, 2005).

Asia Times Online. "A New Dimension in India's Northeast Woes." < http://www.atimes.com/atimes/South_Asia/FJ23Df02.html > (accessed October 1, 2005).

Asia Times Online. "Goons or Terrorists? Bangladesh Decides." < http://www.atimes.com/atimes/South_Asia/GC10Df04.html > (accessed October 16, 2005).

Associated Press. "Hundreds of Villagers Killed in Algeria's Worst Massacre." < http://www.southcoasttoday.com/daily/08-97/08-30-97/a03wn016.htm > (accessed September 25, 2005).

Australian Broadcasting Corporation. "The Salafist Group for Call and Combat." < http://abcasiapacific.com/cause/network/salafist.htm > (accessed October 16, 2005).

BBC News Online. "Profile: Algeria's Salafist Group." < http://news.bbc.co.uk/1/hi/world/africa/3027621.stm > (accessed October 16, 2005).

BBC News Online. "Profile: Eugene Terreblanche." < http://news.bbc.co.uk/2/hi/africa/3797797.stm > (accessed October 10, 2005).

BBC News Online. "South Africa's Terreblanche Freed from Jail." < http://news.bbc.co.uk/2/hi/africa/3796467.stm > (accessed October 10, 2005).

BBC News UK Edition, British Broadcasting Corporation. "Profile: Turkey's Marxist DHKP-C." < http://news.bbc.co.uk/1/hi/world/europe/3591119.stm > (accessed October 19, 2005).

BBC News UK Edition. "Italy's Andreotti Cleared of Murder." < http://news.bbc.co.uk/1/hi/world/europe/3228917.stm > (accessed October 20, 2005).

BBC News UK Edition. "Profile: Jean-Marie Le Pen." < http://news.bbc.co.uk/1/hi/world/europe/3658399.stm > (accessed September 29, 2005).

BBC News World Edition "Victory for Timor Freedom Party." < http://news.bbc.co.uk/2/hi/asia-pacific/1526725.stm > (accessed October 1, 2005).

BBC News World Edition. "Italy's History of Terror." < http://news.bbc.co.uk/2/hi/europe/3372239.htm > (accessed October 20, 2005).

BBC News World Edition. "Profile: Uganda's LRA Rebels." < http://news.bbc.co.uk/1/hi/world/africa/3462901.stm > (accessed October 20, 2005).

BBC News World Edition. "Profile: Xanana Gusmao." < http://news.bbc.co.uk/1/hi/world/asia-pacific/342145.stm > (accessed October 1, 2005).

BBC News World Edition. "Timeline: East Timor." < http://news.bbc.co.uk/2/hi/asia-pacific/country_profiles/1504243.stm > (accessed October 1, 2005).

BBC News World Edition. "Turkey Charges 'Key Bomb Suspect.'" < http://news.bbc.co.uk/2/hi/europe/3333501.stm > (accessed October 5, 2005).

BBC News World Europe. "Turkish Hezbollah: 'No State Links.'" < http://news.bbc.co.uk/1/hi/world/europe/615785.stm > (accessed October 5, 2005).

BBC News, British Broadcasting Corporation. "Can UN Force Restore Peace?" < http://news.bbc.co.uk/1/hi/world/africa/742196.stm > (accessed October 3, 2005).

BBC News, South East Asia. "Profile: Bombay's Militant Voice." < http://news.bbc.co.uk/1/hi/world/south_asia/841488.stm > (accessed October 4, 2005).

BBC News, South East Asia. "Shiv Sena: Profile." < http://news.bbc.co.uk/1/hi/world/south_asia/3551067.stm > (accessed October 4, 2005).

BBC News. "Animal Rights, Terror Tactics." < http://news.bbc.co.uk/1/hi/uk/902751.stm > (accessed September 14, 2005).

BBC News. "Battling Online Hate." < http://news.bbc.co.uk/1/hi/world/americas/1516271.stm > (accessed October 2, 2005).

BBC News. "Cyber-racists 'Safe in US.'" < http://news.bbc.co.uk/1/hi/world/americas/645262.stm > (accessed October 2, 2005).

BBC News. "Egypt: The New Spectre of Terror." < http://news.bbc.co.uk/1/hi/world/analysis/32048.stm > (accessed September 21, 2005).

BBC News. "Loyalist Splinter Threat." < http://news.bbc.co.uk/hi/english/static/northern_ireland/understanding/themes/loyalist_splinter.stm/ > (accessed October 19, 2005).

BBC News. "Loyalists 'Aim to Create Peace Crisis.'" < http://news.bbc.co.uk/1/hi/events/northern_ireland/latest_news/276539.stm > (accessed October 19, 2005).

BBC News. "PAGAD: Vigilantes or Terrorists?" < http://news.bbc.co.uk/1/hi/world/africa/923701.stm > (accessed October 19, 2005).

BBC News. "Police Seize 'Red Brigades' Cache.'" < http://news.bbc.co.uk/go/pr/fr/-/2/hi/europe/3337809. stm > (accessed October 20, 2005).

BBC.co.uk "Paramilitaries: Loyalist Volunteer Force." < http://www.bbc.co.uk/history/war/troubles/factfiles/ lvf.shtml > (accessed October 14, 2005).

BBC.co.uk. "Adolf Hitler (1889–1945)." < http://www. bbc.co.uk/history/historic_figures/hitler_adolf.shtml > (assessed October 20, 2005).

BBC.com. "Full Circle for German Revolutionaries." < http://news.bbc.co.uk/1/hi/world/europe/1250944. stm > (accessed October 15, 2005).

BBC.com. "German Red Army Faction Disbands." < http://news.bbc.co.uk/1/hi/world/europe/80960.stm > (accessed October 15, 2005).

BBC.com. "Germany Recalls Its 'Autumn of Terror.'" < http://news.bbc.co.uk/1/hi/world/europe/2340095. stm > (accessed October 15, 2005).

BBC.com. "Jewish Bomb Plotter Jailed in US." < http:// news.bbc.co.uk/2/hi/americas/4273790.stm > (accessed October 15, 2005).

BBCNews.com. "Meeting Taleban's Foreign Fighters." < http://news.bbc.co.uk/1/hi/world/south_asia/ 1669996.stm > (accessed October 16, 2005).

BBCNews.com. "Profile: Mullah Mohammed Omar." < http://news.bbc.co.uk/2/hi/south_asia/1550419.stm > (accessed October 16, 2005).

Beat Witschi, CNN.com, and Time.com. "Who Is Abdullah Ocalan? (Ocalan: Key Moments of His Life)." < http://edition.cnn.com/SPECIALS/1999/ocalan/ stories/ocalan.profile/ > (accessed October 20, 2005).

Black Press USA. "Blacks and Jews Split—again—over Farrakhan (New Black Panther Party Will Attend MMM)." < http://freerepublic.com/focus/f-news/ 1404429/posts > (accessed October 18, 2005).

Bobby Seale's Homepage, Black Panther Party Founder. "From the Sixties ... to the Future." < http:// publicenemy-seale.com/ > (accessed October 18, 2005).

Boston.com. "Last of the Confederates." < http:// www.boston.com/news/globe/editorial_opinion/oped/ articles/2005/02/21/last_of_the_confederates/ > (accessed October 18, 2005).

Brickman. "The Involvement of Arafat, PA Senior Officials and Apparatuses in Terrorism against Israel, Corruption and Crime." < http://www.brickman. dircon.co.uk/naveh.html > (accessed October 21, 2005).

CAIN Web Service "Speech by Ruairi O'Bradaigh." < http://cain.ulst.ac.uk/issues/politics/docs/sf/rob 021186.htm > (accessed September 28, 2005).

Camera One Public Interest News and Culture. "Inaugural Protests Biggest Since Vietnam." < http://www. cameraone.org/inaguration.html > (accessed October 18, 2005).

Canadian National Security. "Mujahedine-e Khalq Organization." < http://www.psepc-sppcc.gc.ca/ national_security/counter-terrorism/Entities_e.asp# 38 > (accessed October 14, 2005).

Canadian Security Intelligence Service. "Perspectives: Trends in Terrorism." < http://www.csis-scrs.gc.ca/eng/ miscdocs/200001_e.html > (accessed October 19, 2005).

CBC Archives. "The Hijacking of Achille Lauro." < http://archives.cbc.ca/IDC-1-71-1153-6340-11/ that_was_then/conflict_war/achille_lauro > (accessed October 22, 2005).

CBS NEWS.com/U.S. "'Army of God' Anthrax Threats." < http://www.cbsnews.com/stories/2001/11/ 09/national/main317573.shtml > (accessed September 25, 2005).

Center for Contemporary Conflicts. "Libya's Return to the Fold?" < http://www.ccc.nps.navy.mil/si/2004/mar/ boucekMar04.asp > (accessed October 18, 2005).

Center for Defense Information. "In the Spotlight: The Salafist Group for Call and Combat." < http://www.cdi. org/terrorism/gspc-pr.cfm > (accessed October 16, 2005).

Center for Defense Information. "Harakat ul-Jihad-i-Islami." < http://www.cdi.org/program/document.cfm? DocumentID = 2374&from_page = ./index.cfm > (accessed October 20, 2005).

Center for Defense Information. "In the Spotlight: Alex Boncayao Brigade (ABB)." < http://www.cdi.org/ friendlyversion/printversion.cfm?documentID = 2052& from_page = ./program/document.cfm > (accessed September 15, 2005).

Center for Defense Information. "In the Spotlight: Al-Ittihad al-Islami (AIAI)." < http://www.cdi.org/ program/document.cfm?DocumentID = 3026&from_ page = ./index.cfm > (accessed September 21, 2005).

Center for Defense Information. "In the Spotlight: Asbat al-Ansar." < http://www.cdi.org/terrorism/asbat.cfm > (accessed October 15, 2005).

Center for Defense Information. "In the Spotlight: First of October Anti-Fascist Resistance Group." < http:// www.cdi.org/program/document.cfm?DocumentID = 2873&from_page = ./index.cfm > (accessed October 15, 2005).

Center for Defense Information. "In the Spotlight: IMU." < http://www.cdi.org/terrorism/imu.cfm > (accessed October 19, 2005).

Center for Defense Information. "In the Spotlight: Islamic Army of Aden." < http://www.cdi.org/program/ document.cfm?DocumentID = 2679&from_page = ./ index.cfm > (accessed October 16, 2005).

Center for Defense Information. "Palestine Islamic Jihad." < http://www.cdi.org/program/document.cfm? DocumentID = 1176&StartRow = 1&ListRows = 10& appendURL = &Orderby = D.DateLastUpdated% 20deSC&programID = 39&IssueID = 0&Issue = &Date_ From = &Date_To = &Keywords = PIJ&ContentType = &Author = &from_page = documents.cfm > (accessed October 20, 2005).

Center for Strategic and International Studies. "The Nexus Between Counterterrorism, Counterproliferation, and Maritime Security in Southeast Asia." < http:// www.csis.org/pacfor/issues/v04n04_ch3.cfm > (accessed October 11, 2005).

Center for Studies on New Religions. "Project Megiddo." < http://www.cesnur.org/testi/FBI_004.htm > (accessed September 30, 2005).

Center for the Defense of Free Enterprise. "Earth Liberation Front." < http://www.cdfe.org/elf.htm > (accessed October 21, 2005).

Center for the Defense of Free Enterprise. "Ecoterror Response Network." < http://www.cdfe.org/ern.htm > (accessed October 21, 2005).

Center for the Defense of Free Enterprise. "Ecoterrorism Top Stories." < http://www.cdfe.org/top_stories.htm > (accessed September 29, 2005).

Center for the Defense of Free Enterprise. "The Center View: Profiles in Ecoterror Advocacy." < http:// www.cdfe.org/rosebraughs%20degree.htm > (accessed October 21, 2005).

Christian Science Monitor. "A Band of Maoist Rebels Terrorizes an Indian Region." < http://www.csmonitor. com/2002/0813/p07s02-wosc.html > (accessed October 11, 2005).

CIA Government Factbook. "Tunisia." < http://www.cia. gov/cia/publications/factbook/geos/ts.html > (accessed October 15, 2005).

CNN World Edition Online. "Spanish Terror Suspects Arrested." < http://edition.cnn.com/2000/WORLD/ europe/11/09/france.grapo/ > (accessed October 15, 2005).

CNN.com/U.S. "Army of God Letters Support Accused Bomber Eric Rudolph." < http://archives.cnn.com/2002/ US/03/18/army.god.letters/index.html > (accessed September 25, 2005).

CNN.com/U.S. "Atlanta Olympic Bombing Suspect Arrested." < http://www.cnn.com/2003/US/05/31/ rudolph.main/ > (accessed September 25, 2005).

CNN.com/World. "South East Asia's Crackdown." < http://edition.cnn.com/2002/WORLD/asiapcf/ southeast/01/07/terror.factbox/ > (accessed October 11, 2005).

CNN.com. "India Launches Major Ground Assault in Kashmir; Talks Set with Pakistan." < http://edition. cnn.com/WORLD/asiapcf/9905/29/india.pakistan.02 > (accessed October 19, 2005).

CNN.com. "Islamic Group Suspected in Kenya Attacks." < http://cnnstudentnews.cnn.com/2002/WORLD/ africa/11/29/somali.group/ > (accessed September 21, 2005).

CNN.com. "Islamic Terrorists Slaughter Algerian Villagers." < http://edition.cnn.com/WORLD/9708/29/ algeria.new/ > (accessed September 25, 2005).

CNN.com. "Special Report, War Against Terror: Osama bin Laden." < http://www.cnn.com/SPECIALS/2001/ trade.center/binladen.section.html > (accessed September 22, 2005).

CNN. "The Death of Richard Klinghoffer." < http:// www.cnn.com/resources/video.almanac/1985/achille. lauro/klinghoffer.dead.45.mov > (accessed October 22, 2005).

Colombia Journal Online. "The Hypocrisy of the Peace Process." < http://www.colombiajournal.org/ colombia103.htm > (accessed September 30, 2005).

Colombia Report. "Good Terrorists, Bad Terrorists: How Washington Decides Who's Who." < http://www. colombiajournal.org/colombia62.htm > (accessed Octo 21, 2005).

Council on Foreign Relations. "Irish Loyalist Paramilitary Groups." < http://cfrterrorism.org/groups/uvf_print. html > (accessed October 19, 2005).

Council on Foreign Relations. "Kurdistan Workers' Party." < http://cfrterrorism.org/groups/kurdistan. html > (accessed October 20, 2005).

Council on Foreign Relations. "Terrorism: Questions and Answers: Mujahedine-e Khalq Organization." < http:// cfrterrorism.org/groups/mujahedeen.html > (accessed October 14, 2005).

Council on Foreign Relations. "Uzbekistan." < http:// cfrterrorism.org/coalition/uzbekistan.html > (accessed October 19, 2005).

Countercurrents.org. "Shiv Sena On The Threshold Of Disintegration." < http://www.countercurrents.org/ comm-ketkar011104.htm > (accessed October 4, 2005).

Dennis Roddy, Post-Gazette. "Jared Taylor, a Racist in the Guise of 'Expert,'" < http://www.post-gazette.com/ pg/05023/446341.stm > (accessed October 23, 2005).

Detroit Free Press. "Homegrown Hate: Ten years after Oklahoma City, anti-government and hate groups are weaker—but testing new tools." < http://www. freep.com/voices/sunday/ehate10e_20050410.htm > (accessed October 17, 2005).

Dogu Ergil, CNN/Time In-Depth Special, CNN.com, and Time.com. "The Kurdish Question after Ocalan." < http://www.cnn.com/SPECIALS/1999/ocalan/stories/ kurdish.question/ > (accessed October 20, 2005).

Domestic Terrorist Group Profiles—MILNET. "Sword and Arm of the Lord (SAL)." < http://www.milnet. com/domestic/data/sal.htm > (accessed October 3, 2005).

Dr. Charles A. Russell, Air University Review. "Transnational Terrorism." < http://www.airpower. maxwell.af.mil/airchronicles/aureview/1976/jan-feb/ russell.html > (accessed October 20, 2005).

Embassy of India, Washington D.C. "Profile of the Terrorist Group Involved in Hijacking of Indian Airlines Flight IC-814." < http://www.indianembassy. org/pic/PR_1999/December_99/PR_Dec_27_1999. html > (accessed October 19, 2005).

Embassy of the Philippines. "History of the Philippines." < http://www.philembassy.au.com/phi-hist.htm > (accessed October 21, 2005).

Enzo Di Matteo, NOW Magazine, NOW Communications. "A Racist No Longer: Ex-White Rights Fan Just Wants to be a Rock Star." < http://www.nowtoronto.com/issues/2001-01-25/news.html > (accessed October 15, 2005).

Ernie B. Esconde, The Manila Times. "A Former Rebel Town: A Case in Perspective." < http://www.manilatimes.net/national/2004/aug/11/yehey/prov/20040811pro12.html > (accessed October 21, 2005).

Eye on Hate, Seeking a Kinder and Gentler World. "Martyrs, Heroes, & Prisoners of War: The Order." < http://eyeonhate.com/pows/pows3.html > (accessed October 5, 2005).

FAS Intelligence Resource Program. "Islamic Army of Aden." < http://www.fas.org/irp/world/para/iaa.htm > (accessed October 16, 2005).

FAS Intelligence Resource Program. "Macheteros." < http://www.fas.org/irp/world/para/faln.htm > (accessed October 14, 2005).

FAS Intelligence Resource Program. "People's War Group (PWG)." < http://www.fas.org/irp/world/para/pwg.htm > (accessed October 11, 2005).

FAS Intelligence Resource Program. "Revolutionary Organization 17 November." < http://www.fas.org/irp/world/para/17_nov.htm > (accessed July 29, 2005).

Federal Bureau of Investigation "The Threat of Eco-Terrorism." < http://www.fbi.gov/congress/congress02/jarboe021202.htm > (accessed September 29, 2005).

Federal Bureau of Investigation. "Testimony of J. T. Caruso, Acting Assistant Director, Counter Terrorism Division, FBI." < http://www.fbi.gov/congress/congress01/caruso121801.htm > (accessed September 21, 2005).

Federal Bureau of Investigation. "Wanted Poster for al-Zawahiri." < http://www.fbi.gov/mostwant/terrorists/teralzawahiri.htm > (accessed October 10, 2005).

Federation of American Scientists. "Abu Sayyaf Group (ASG)." < http://www.fas.org/irp/world/para/asg.htm > (accessed September 14, 2005).

Federation of American Scientists. "Anti-Imperialist Territorial Nuclei (NTA)." < http://www.fas.org/irp/world/para/nta.htm > (accessed August 1, 2005).

Federation of American Scientists. "Harakat ul-Jihad-I-Islami/Bangladesh (HUJI-B) (Movement of Islamic Holy War)." < http://www.fas.org/irp/world/para/huji-b.htm > (accessed October 16, 2005).

Federation of American Scientists. "Patterns of Global Terrorism: 1992, Asia Overview." < http://www.fas.org/irp/threat/terror_92/asia.html > (accessed September 27, 2005).

Federation of American Scientists. "Revolutionary United Front (RUF)." < http://www.fas.org/main/home.jsp > (assessed October 3, 2005).

Flemish Republic. "Brussels: Europe's Hub of Terror." < http://www.flemishrepublic.org/extra.php?id = 1&jaargang = 1&nr = 1 > (accessed October 16, 2005).

Florida Center for Instructional Technology, University of South Florida. "Victims." < http://www.spartacus.schoolnet.co.uk/GERnazi.htm > (assessed October 20, 2005).

Foreign and Commonwealth Office. "Asbat al-Ansar." < http://www.fco.gov.uk/servlet/Front?pagename = OpenMarket/Xcelerate/ShowPage&c = Page&cid = 1049909003789 > (accessed October 15, 2005).

Foreign and Commonwealth Offices. "Islamic Movement of Uzbekistan." < http://www.fco.gov.uk/servlet/Front?pagename = OpenMarket/Xcelerate/ShowPage&c = Page&cid = 1049909003533 > (accessed October 19, 2005).

Foreign Policy Research Institute. "E-Notes: Terrorism in Colombia." < http://www.fpri.org/enotes/latin.20020121.posada.terrorismincolombia.html > (accessed September 30, 2005).

Fox News Channel. "ELF Suspected in California Eco-Terror." < http://www.foxnews.com/printer_friendly_story/0,3566,146927,00.html > (accessed October 21, 2005).

Fox News Channel. "Fire May Be Connected to 'Eco-Terrorism' Group." < http://www.foxnews.com/printer_friendly_story/0,3566,122902,00.html > (accessed October 21, 2005).

FOXNews.com—U.S. & World. "Abortion Doctor's Murderer Dies by Lethal Injection." < http://www.foxnews.com/story/0,2933,96286,00.html > (accessed September 25, 2005).

freebarghouti.org. "Supporters of Marwan Barghouti." < http://www.freebarghouti.org/index.html > (accessed October 21, 2005).

Frontline. "A Parochial Project." < http://www.flonnet.com/fl2010/stories/20030523004803200.htm > (accessed October 4, 2005).

Frontpagemag.com. "New Black Panther Mouthpiece." < http://www.frontpagemag.com/Articles/ReadArticle.asp?ID = 12053 > (accessed October 18, 2005).

Fur Commission USA. "In Their Own Words." < http://www.furcommission.com/debate/words6.htm?FACTNet > (accessed October 21, 2005).

GlobalSecurity.org. "Algerian Insurgency." < http://www.globalsecurity.org/military/world/war/algeria-90s.htm > (accessed October 16, 2005).

GlobalSecurity.org. "Kumpulan Mujahidin Malaysia." < http://www.globalsecurity.org/military/world/para/kmm.htm > (accessed October 11, 2005).

GlobalSecurity.org. "Alex Boncayao Brigade (ABB)." < http://www.globalsecurity.org/military/world/para/abb.htm > (accessed September 15, 2005).

GlobalSecurity.org. "Allied Democratic Forces: National Army for the Liberation of Uganda (NALU)." < http:// www.globalsecurity.org/military/world/para/adf.htm > (accessed September 22, 2005).

GlobalSecurity.org. "Jaish-e-Mohammed." < http:// www.globalsecurity.org/military/world/para/jem.htm > (accessed October 20, 2005).

GlobalSecurity.org. "Revolutionary United Front (RUF)." < http://www.globalsecurity.org/military/world/para/ruf.htm > (accessed October 3, 2005).

GlobalSecurity.org. "Sikh Terrorists." < http:// www.globalsecurity.org/military/world/para/sikh.htm > (accessed October 11, 2005).

Government of Sierra Leone. "Bio Data of The President of Sierra Leone." < http://www.statehouse-sl.org/ biodata.html > (accessed October 3, 2005).

Guardian Unlimited. "Interview with Simon Tindale: What Happened Next?" < http://observer.guardian.co. uk/magazine/story/0,,1118794,00.html > (accessed October 12, 2005).

Guardian Unlimited. "The Downfall of Mad Dog Adair." < http://books.guardian.co.uk/extracts/story/0,, 1055999,00.html > (accessed October 3, 2005).

Guardian Unlimited. "Who is Foday Sankoh?" < http:// www.guardian.co.uk/sierra/article/0,2763,221853, 00.html > (accessed October 3, 2005).

Guardian.com "$4.4m for Environmentalists Framed by FBI." < http://www.guardian.co.uk/print/0,3858, 4431940-103681,00.html > (accessed September 29, 2005).

Heidi Beirich and Bob Moser, Intelligence Report, Southern Poverty Law Center. "Communing with the Council." < http://www.splcenter.org/intel/intelreport/ article.jsp?pid = 804 > (accessed October 23, 2005).

Houston Chronicle.com. "Still True Today: 'The Republic of Texas' Is No More." < http://www.chron.com/ content/chronicle/editorial/97/05/01/brock.0-1.html > (accessed October 16, 2005).

Human Rights News. "Nepal: Government Forces, Maoist Rebels Target Civilians." < http://hrw.org/ english/docs/2004/10/07/nepal9452.htm > (accessed October 21, 2005).

Human Rights Watch Group. "Algeria: Human Rights Development." < http://www.hrw.org/worldreport99/ mideast/algeria.html > (accessed September 25, 2005).

Human Rights Watch. "Bosnia and Hercegovina Unfinished Business: The Return of Refugees and Displaced Persons to Bijeljin." < http://www.hrw.org/ reports/2000/bosnia/index.htm#TopOfPage > (accessed October 17, 2005).

Human Rights Watch. "Colombia and the "War." on Terror: Rhetoric and Reality." < http://hrw.org/english/ docs/2004/03/04/colomb7932.htm > (accessed October 21, 2005).

Human Rights Watch. "Egypt: Human Rights Background." < http://www.hrw.org/backgrounder/ mena/egypt-bck-1001.htm > (accessed September 21, 2005).

Human Rights Watch. "Human Rights Developments, India." < http://www.hrw.org/worldreport99/asia/ india.html > (accessed October 4, 2005).

Human Rights Watch. "Leave None to Tell the Story." < http://www.hrw.org/reports/1999/rwanda/ > (accessed October 12, 2005).

Human Rights Watch. "Peru." < http://hrw.org/english/ docs/2004/01/21/peru6988.htm > (accessed October 4, 2005).

Human Rights Watch. "War without Quarter: Colombia and International Humanitarian Law." < http:// www.hrw.org/reports98/colombia/ > (accessed October 21, 2005).

Institute for Security Studies. "Uganda." < http:// www.iss.co.za/AF/profiles/Uganda/SecInfo.html > (accessed September 22, 2005).

Institute for the Study of Academic Racism. "Council of Conservative Citizens." < http://www.ferris.edu/isar/ Institut/CCC/homepage.htm > (accessed October 23, 2005).

Institute for War and Peace Reporting. "New Danger from Ugandan Rebel Group?" < http://www.reliefweb. int/rw/RWB.NSF/db900SID/RMOI-6D53DW?Open Document > (accessed September 22, 2005).

Intelligence and Terrorism Information Center at the Center for Special Studies (C.S.S). "Profile of the Palestinian Islamic Jihad, Perpetrator of a Suicide Bombing Attack in Tel Aviv, February 25, 2005." < http://www.intelligence.org.il/eng/sib/3_05/pji.htm > (accessed October 20, 2005).

Intelligence Report, Southern Poverty Law Center. "A Group Is Born: Billy Roper, a Fired National Alliance Official, Has Formed His Own Group Called White Revolution." < http://www.splcenter.org/intel/ intelreport/article.jsp?sid = 53 > (accessed October 3, 2005).

Intelligence Report, Southern Poverty Law Center. "Resisting Arrest: Racist Resistance Records Isn't Slowing Down." < http://www.splcenter.org/intel/ intelreport/article.jsp?aid = 452 > (accessed October 15, 2005).

Intelligence Report, Southern Poverty Law Center. "Revolting in Arkansas." < http://www.splcenter.org/ intel/intelreport/article.jsp?pid = 214 > (assessed October 3, 2005).

Intelligence Resource Program, Federation of American Scientists. "Kurdistan Workers' Party (PKK)." < http:// www.fas.org/irp/world/para/pkk.htm > (accessed October 20, 2005).

International Crisis Group. "Jemaah Islamiyah In South East Asia: Damaged But Still Dangerous." < http://www.crisisgroup.org/library/documents/report_archive/A401104_26082003.pdf > (accessed October 14, 2005).

International Network of Prison Ministries. < http://prisonministry.net/ > (accessed October 3, 2005).

International Policy Institute for Counter-Terrorism. "Red Brigades." < http://www.ict.org.il/inter_ter/orgdet.cfm?orgid = 36 > (accessed October 20, 2005).

International Policy Institute for Counter-Terrorism. "Revolutionary Organization 17 November." < http://www.ict.org.il/organizations/orgattack.cfm?orgid = 38 > (accessed July 29, 2005).

International Policy Institute for Counter-Terrorism. "Revolutionary People's Liberation Party/Front Attacks: from 1988–the present." < http://www.ict.org.il/organizations/orgattack.cfm?orgid = 39 > (accessed October 19, 2005).

International Policy Institute for Counter-Terrorism. "The Red Brigades: Cooperation with the Palestinian Terrorist Organizations." < http://www.ict.org.il/articles/red_brigades-palestinians.htm > (accessed October 20, 2005).

International Policy of Counter-Terrorism. "Chukakuh-ha." < http://www.ict.org.il/inter_ter/orgdet.cfm?orgid = 9 > (accessed September 27, 2005).

International Relations Center. "Council of Conservative Citizens." < http://rightweb.irc-online.org/org/cofcc.php > (accessed October 23, 2005).

International Strategic Research Organization—Journal of Turkish Weekly. "Turkish Hizballah: A Case Study of Radical Terrorism." < http://www.turkishweekly.net/articles.php?id = 28 > (accessed October 5, 2005).

Islamic Republic of Iran Broadcasting. "Navab Safavi's Martyrdom." < http://www.irib.ir/occasions/Navab-e-Safavi/Navab-e-Safavi-En.htm > (accessed October 7, 2005).

Islamist Watch. "Jihad: The Absent Obligation." < http://www.islamistwatch.org/texts/faraj/obligation/oblig.html > (accessed October 10, 2005).

Jewish Telegraphic Agency. "Fears of Jewish Underground Rise." < http://www.jewishaz.com/jewishnews/020517/fears.shtml > (accessed October 15, 2005).

Jewish Virtual Library, The American-Israeli Cooperative Enterprise. "Holocaust Denial." < http://www.jewishvirtuallibrary.org/jsource/Holocaust/denial.html > (assessed October 20, 2005).

Jewish Virtual Library. "Rabbi Meir Kahane (1932–1990)." < http://www.jewishvirtuallibrary.org/jsource/biography/kahane.html > (accessed October 22, 2005).

Jonathan Marcus, BBC News, British Broadcasting Corporation. "Brutal Child Army Grows Up." < http://news.bbc.co.uk/1/hi/world/africa/743684.stm > (accessed October 3, 2005).

Kahane.org. "Shavuot and the Cultural War." < http://www.kahane.org/ > (accessed October 22, 2005).

Latin American Studies. "Los Macheteros." < http://www.latinamericanstudies.org/epb-macheteros.htm > (accessed October 14, 2005).

Law Enforcement Agency Resource Network, Anti-Defamation League. "White Revolution/Billy Roper." < http://www.adl.org/learn/ext_us/w_revolution.asp?print = true > (assessed October 3, 2005).

Law Enforcement Agency Resource Network. "Volksfront." < http://www.adl.org/hate_symbols/groups_volksfront.asp > (accessed October 3, 2005).

Major Rodney S. Azama, GlobalSecurity.org. "The Huks and the New People's Army: Comparing Two Postwar Filipino Insurgencies." < http://www.globalsecurity.org/military/library/report/1985/ARS.htm > (accessed October 21, 2005).

Mark Potok, Intelligence Report, Southern Poverty Law Center. "The Year in Hate: A Period of Realignment and Rebuilding Follows a Tumultuous Year on the American Radical Right." < http://www.splcenter.org/intel/intelreport/article.jsp?aid = 374&printable = 1 > (accessed October 15, 2005).

Martin Kramer on the Middle East. < http://www.martinkramer.org/pages/899526/index.htm > (accessed October 13, 2005).

Media Matters for America.org. "Who is Randall Terry?" < http://mediamatters.org/items/200503220001 > (accessed October 16, 2005).

Middle East Intelligence Bulletin. "Intelligence Briefs: Lebanon." < http://www.meib.org/articles/0110_lb.htm#lb1 > (accessed October 15, 2005).

Middle East Policy Council Journal. "Qadhafi's Libya and the Prospect of Islamic Succession." < http://www.mepc.org/public_asp/journal_vol7/0002_takeyh.asp > (accessed October 18, 2005).

Mike Doughney's Page. "People Eating Tasty Animals." < http://mtd.com/tasty/ > (accessed October 19, 2005).

Ministry for Safety and Security, South African Government. "Media Statement by Mr. Sydney Mufamadi, Minister for Safety and Security, Pretoria, 11 December 1996." < http://www.info.gov.za/speeches/1996/12170x86496.htm > (accessed October 19, 2005).

Ministry of External Affairs, India. "L.K. Advani's Speech after Terrorist Attack on Indian Parliament." < http://meaindia.nic.in/speech/2001/12/18spc01.htm > (accessed October 20, 2005).

Ministry of External Affairs, India. "Transcript of Press Conference by Shri Jaswant Singh, External Affairs and Defense Minister." < http://meaindia.nic.in/mediainteraction/2001/10/11mi01.htm > (accessed October 19, 2005).

Ministry of Home Affairs, Government of India. "Ministry of Home Affairs Reviews Security Scenario in Assam."

< http://mha.nic.in/pr052001.htm > (accessed October 1, 2005).

MIPT Terrorism Knowledge Base. "Republic of Texas (ROT)." < http://www.tkb.org/Group.jsp?groupID = 95 > (accessed October 16, 2005).

MIPT Terrorism Knowledge Base, National Memorial Institute for the Prevention of Terrorism (MIPT). "Anti-Imperialist Territorial Nuclei for the Construction of the Fighting Communist Party." < http://tkb.org/Group.jsp?groupID = 16 > (accessed August 1, 2005).

MIPT Terrorism Knowledge Base, National Memorial Institute for the Prevention of Terrorism. "DHKP-C." < http://www.tkb.org/Group.jsp?groupID = 38 > (accessed October 19, 2005).

MIPT Terrorism Knowledge Base, National Memorial Institute for the Prevention of Terrorism. "Group Profile: New People's Army (NPA)." < http://www.tkb.org/Group.jsp?groupID = 203 > (accessed October 21, 2005).

MIPT Terrorism Knowledge Base, National Memorial Institute for the Prevention of Terrorism. "Kurdistan Workers' Party." < http://www.tkb.org/Group.jsp?groupID = 63 > (accessed October 20, 2005).

MIPT Terrorism Knowledge Base, National Memorial Institute for the Prevention of Terrorism. "Revolutionary United Front (RUF)." < http://www.tkb.org/Group.jsp?groupID = 4247 > (accessed October 3, 2005).

MIPT Terrorism Knowledge Base, National Memorial Institute for the Prevention of Terrorism. "Terrorist Group Profile: Al-Fuqra." < http://www.tkb.org/Group.jsp?groupID = 3426 > (September 21, 2005).

MIPT Terrorism Knowledge Base. "African National Congress." < http://www.tkb.org/Group.jsp?groupID = 305 > (accessed October 11, 2005).

MIPT Terrorism Knowledge Base. "Alex Boncayao Brigade (ABB)." < http://www.tkb.org/Group.jsp?groupID = 3011 > (accessed September 15, 2005).

MIPT Terrorism Knowledge Base. "Basque Fatherland and Freedom." < http://www.tkb.org/Group.jsp?groupID = 31 > (accessed October 20, 2005).

MIPT Terrorism Knowledge Base. "Breton Revolutionary Army." < http://www.tkp.org/Group.jsp?groupID = 3548 > (accessed July 20 2005).

MIPT Terrorism Knowledge Base. "Group Profile—Covenant, Sword, and Arm of the Lord (CSA)." < http://www.tkb.org/Group.jsp?groupID = 3226 > (accessed October 3, 2005).

MIPT Terrorism Knowledge Base. "Group Profile: Red Army Faction." < http://www.tkb.org/Group.jsp?groupID = 163 > (accessed October 15, 2005).

MIPT Terrorism Knowledge Base. "Group Profile: United Liberation Front of Assam (ULFA)." < http://www.tkb.org/Group.jsp?groupID = 3686 > (accessed October 1, 2005).

MIPT Terrorism Knowledge Base. "Islamic Movement of Uzbekistan." < http://www.tkb.org/Group.jsp?groupID = 4075 > (accessed October 19, 2005).

MIPT Terrorism Knowledge Base. "Ku Klux Klan, Key Leader Profile: Berry, Jeff." < http://www.tkb.org/KeyLeader.jsp?memID = 109 > (accessed September 29, 2005).

MIPT Terrorism Knowledge Base. "Macheteros." < http://www.tkb.org/Group.jsp?groupID = 3227 > (accessed October 14, 2005).

MIPT Terrorism Knowledge Base. "Montana Freemen." < http://www.tkb.org/Group.jsp?groupID = 3406 > (accessed October 18, 2005).

MIPT Terrorism Knowledge Base. "Mujahedine-e Khalq Organization." < http://tkb.org/Group.jsp?groupID = 3632 > (accessed October 14, 2005).

MIPT Terrorism Knowledge Base. "National Army for the Liberation of Uganda (NALU)." < http://www.tkb.org/Group.jsp?groupID = 3515 > (accessed September 22, 2005).

MIPT Terrorism Knowledge Base. "Palestinian Islamic Jihad." < http://www.tkb.org/Group.jsp?groupID = 82 > (accessed October 20, 2005).

MIPT Terrorism Knowledge Base. "Salafist Group for Call and Combat." < http://www.tkb.org/Group.jsp?groupID = 3777 > (accessed October 16, 2005).

MIPT Terrorism Knowledge Base. "Terrorist Group Profile: Armed Forces of National Liberation." < http://www.tkb.org/Group.jsp?groupID = 3229 > (accessed October 18, 2005).

MIPT Terrorism Knowledge Base. "Terrorist Group Profile: Orange Volunteers (OV)." < http://www.tkb.org/Group.jsp?groupID = 79 > (accessed October 19, 2005).

MIPT Terrorism Knowledge Base. "The People's War Group (PWG)." < http://www.tkb.org/Group.jsp?groupID = 3658 > (accessed October 11, 2005).

MIPT Terrorism Knowledge Base. "Tunisian Combatant Group." < http://www.tkb.org/Group.jsp?groupID = 4346 > (accessed October 16, 2005).

MIPT Terrorism Knowledge Database. "The Libyan Islamic Fighting Group (LIFG)." < http://www.tkb.org/Group.jsp?groupID = 4400 > (October 18, 2005).

MIPT Terrorism Knowledge Database. "Revolutionary Organization 17 November." < http://www.tkb.org/Group.jsp?groupID = 101 > (accessed September 14, 2005).

MIPT Terrorism Knowledge Database. "First of October Antifascist Resistance Group." < http://www.tkb.org/Incident.jsp?incID = 13139 > (accessed October 15, 2005).

Monterey Institute of International Studies. "Islamic Movement of Uzbeckistan." < http://cns.miis.edu/research/wtc01/imu.htm > (accessed October 19, 2005).

MosNews.com. "Moscow Court Bans Russia's Radical National Bolshevik Party." < http://www.mosnews.com/ news/2005/06/29/nbpliquidated.shtml > (accessed October 15, 2005).

MSNBC.com. "Poll Finds Muslim Support for bin Laden Waning." < http://www.msnbc.msn.com/id/8569229/ > (accessed September 22, 2005).

MSNBC.com. "Time & Again—Wounded Knee—Siege of 1973." < http://msnbc.com/onair/msnbc/Timeand Again/archive/wknee/1973.asp > (accessed October 15, 2005).

MSNBC.com. "U.N. Seeks First Political Definition of Terrorism." < http://www.msnbc.msn.com/id/8676132/ > (accessed September 22, 2005).

MSNBC. "Former Spy to Testify about Cuban Support for Los Macheteros." < http://www.cubanet.org/ CNews/y99/dec99/30e3.htm > (accessed October 14, 2005).

National Commission on Terrorist Attacks upon the United States. "The Rise and Decline of Al Qaeda." < http://www.9-11commission.gov/hearings/hearing3/ witness_gunaratna.htm > (accessed October 20, 2005).

National Institute of Justice. "The American Terrorism Study: Patterns of Behavior, Investigation and Prosecution of American Terrorists." < http://www. ncjrs.org/pdffiles1/nij/grants/193420.pdf > (accessed October 18, 2005).

National Library of Medicine, National Institutes of Health. "The Story of NLM Historical Collections." < http://www.nlm.nih.gov/hmd/about/collection history.html > (accessed October 11, 2005).

National Memorial Institute for the Prevention of Terrorism—Terrorism Knowledge Base. "Chukakuha." < http://tkb.org/Group.jsp?groupID = 3578 > (accessed September 27, 2005).

National Memorial Institute for the Prevention of Terrorism—Terrorism Knowledge Base. "Cinchoneros Popular Liberation Movement." < http://www.tkb.org/ Group.jsp?groupID = 3987 > (accessed September 28, 2005).

National Memorial Institute for the Prevention of Terrorism—Terrorism Knowledge Base. "Turkish Hezbollah." < http://www.tkb.org/KeyLeader.jsp? memID = 5922 > (accessed October 5, 2005).

National Public Radio's Weekend Edition (audio clip). "FARC." < http://www.npr.org/templates/story/ story.php?storyId = 1127278 > (accessed September 30, 2005).

National Public Radio. "Afghanistan Takes Steps to Reconcile with Taliban Fighters." < http://www. npr.org/templates/story/story.php?storyId = 4469449 > (accessed October 16, 2005).

National Security Australia. "Islamic Army of Aden (IAA)." < http://www.nationalsecurity.gov.au/agd/ WWW/nationalsecurityHome.nsf/Page/Listing_of_ Terrorist_Organisations_terrorist_listing_Islamic_ Army_of_Aden_-_Listed_11_April_2003 > (accessed October 18, 2005).

NBC5i.com. "New Black Panther Party Emerges, Voices Demands." < http://www.nbc5i.com/news/3277640/ detail.html > (accessed October 18, 2005).

Nobel Prize. "José Ramos-Horta—Curriculum Vitae." < http://nobelprize.org/peace/laureates/1996/ramos- horta-cv.html > (accessed October 1, 2005).

Northern Ireland Office. "Homepage of the Decommissioning Commission." < http://www.nio.gov. uk/decommissioning > (accessed October 24, 2005).

Observer Sports Monthly. "Lost Lives That Saved A Sport." < http://football.guardian.co.uk/News_Story/ 0,1563,1448505,00.html > (accessed October 20, 2005).

Observer. "Equality in Death." < http://observer. guardian.co.uk/magazine/story/0,11913,1200794,00. html > (accessed October 21, 2005).

Office of the Press Secretary, Malacanang, Philippines. "President George W. Bush's Speech during the Joint Session of Congress." < http://www.ops.gov.ph/ pgwbvisit2003/speeches.htm > (accessed September 14, 2005).

Office of the Press Secretary, The White House. " President Bush Calls for New Palestinian Leadership." < http://www.whitehouse.gov/news/releases/2002/06/ 20020624-3.html > (accessed October 20, 2005).

Overseas Security Advisory Council (OSAC). "Anti-Imperialist Territorial Nuclei (NTA) a.k.a. Anti-Imperialist Territorial Units." < http://www. ds-osac.org/Groups/group.cfm?contentID = 1306 > (accessed September 25, 2005).

Overseas Security Advisory Council. "Asbat al-Ansar." < http://www.ds-osac.org/Groups/group.cfm?content ID = 1275 > (accessed October 15, 2005).

Overseas Security Advisory Council. "First of October Antifascist Resistance Group (GRAPO)." < http:// www.ds-osac.org/Groups/group.cfm?contentID = 1312 > (accessed October 15, 2005).

Overseas Security Advisory Council. "Revolutionary People's Liberation Party/Front (DHKP/C)." < http:// www.ds-osac.org/Groups/group.cfm?contentID = 1296 > (accessed October 19, 2005).

Overseas Security Advisory Council. "Tunisian Combatant Group." < http://www.ds-osac.org/Groups/ group.cfm?contentID = 1335 > (accessed October 16, 2005).

PBS.org. "Alcatraz Is Not an Island." < http://www. pbs.org/itvs/alcatrazisnotanisland/activism.html > (accessed October 15, 2005).

PBS.org. "Hostage Crisis." < http://www.pbs.org/ newshour/bb/latin_america/december96/peru_12– 19.html > (accessed October 5, 2005).

PBS.org. "Inside al-Qaeda." < http://www.pbs.org/ wgbh/pages/frontline/shows/network/alqaeda/ > (accessed September 22, 2005).

Peter C. Andersen's Sierra-Leone.org. "Footpaths to Democracy: Toward a New Sierra Leone." < http://www.sierra-leone.org/footpaths.html > (accessed October 3, 2005).

Public Broadcasting Service (PBS). "Profile: Abu Sayyaf." < http://www.pbs.org/newshour/terrorism/international/abu_sayyaf.html > (accessed September 14, 2005).

RAHOWA.com. " Klassen's Teachings." < http://www.rahowa.com > (accessed October 1, 2005).

ReasonOnline. "David Foreman vs. the Cornucopians." < http://www.reason.com/rb/rb082901.html > (accessed September 29, 2005).

Red Pepper Magazine. "Interview with Leila Khaled." < http://www.redpepper.org.uk/intarch/x-khaled.html > (accessed October 19, 2005).

Religious Tolerance.org. "Christian Identity Movement." < http://www.religioustolerance.org/cr_ident.htm > (accessed September 29, 2005).

Religious Tolerance.org. "How Christians View Non-Christian Religions." < http://www.religioustolerance.org/chr_othe2.htm > (accessed October 16, 2005).

Religious Tolerance.org. "The Creativity Movement."." < http://www.religioustolerance.org/wcotc.htm > (accessed October 1, 2005).

Resource Center of the Americas.org. "28 Killed in Bus Attack—Weekly News Update on the Americas #778." < http://www.americas.org/item_17213 > (accessed September 28, 2005).

Rick A Ross Institute. "Christian Identity." < http://www.rickross.com/groups/christian_identity.html > (accessed September 25, 2005).

Rod Usher, Time International, Time.com. "Nationalists Without a Nation." < http://www.time.com/time/daily/special/ocalan/nationalists.html > (accessed October 20, 2005).

Salon.com. "Brand New War for the Army of God? Parts 1 and 2." < http://www.salon.com/news/feature/2002/02/19/gays/index_np.html > (accessed September 25, 2005).

Salon.com. "The Angry Patriot " < http://www.salon.com/news/feature/2005/05/11/minuteman/ > (accessed October 23, 2005).

San Francisco Chronicle (March 6, 2005). "A Web of White Power." < http://www.rickross.com/reference/hate_groups/hategroups391.html > (accessed October 17, 2005).

SAPRA India. "Indian Airlines Plane Hijack: Background Articles." < http://www.subcontinent.com/sapra/terrorism/harkat > (accessed October 19, 2005).

Seattle Weekly. "Violence and Protest." < http://www.seattleweekly.com/features/0315/news-dawdy.php > (accessed October 21, 2005).

SHAC. "News Index." < http://www.shac.net/ > (accessed October 22, 2005).

Slate.com. "The Republic of Texas." < http://www.slate.com/id/1057 > (accessed October 16, 2005).

South Asia Analysis Group. "ABU SAYYAF: The Cause for the Return of U.S. Troops to Philippines?" < http://www.saag.org/papers5/paper417.html > (accessed September 14, 2005).

South Asia Analysis Group. "Bangladeshi & Jihadi Terrorism, An Update." < http://www.saag.org/papers9/paper887.html > (accessed October 16, 2005).

South Asia Analysis Group. "Paper No. 376 Jaish-e-Mohammed." < http://saag.org/papers4/papers376.html > (accessed October 20, 2005).

South Asia Analysis Group. "Students Islamic Movement of India (SIMI)." < http://www.saag.org/papers9/paper825.html > (accessed October 21, 2005).

South Asia Terrorism Portal. "Harakat ul-Jihad-i-Islami." < http://www.satp.org/satporgtp/countries/india/states/jandk/terrorist_outfits/HuJI.htm > (accessed October 20, 2005).

South Asia Terrorism Portal. "Jaish-e-Mohammed Mujahideen e Tanzim." < http://www.satp.org/satporgtp/countries/india/states/jandk/terrorist_outfits/jaish_e_Mohammed_mujahideen_e_tanzeem.htm > (accessed October 20, 2005).

South Asia Terrorism Portal. "Jamaat ul-Fuqra." < http://www.satp.org/satporgtp/countries/pakistan/terroristoutfits/jamaat-ul-fuqra.htm > (September 21, 2005).

South Asia Terrorism Portal. "The People's War Group (PWG)." < http://www.satp.org/satporgtp/countries/india/terroristoutfits/pwg.htm > (accessed October 11, 2005).

South Asian Terrorism Portal. "Sipah-e-Sahaba Pakistan, Terrorist Group of Pakistan." < http://www.satp.org/satporgtp/countries/pakistan/terroristoutfits/ssp.htm > (accessed October 1, 2005).

South Asian Terrorism Portal. "Students Islamic Movement of India (SIMI)." < http://www.satp.org/satporgtp/countries/india/terroristoutfits/simi.htm > (accessed October 21, 2005).

South Asian Terrorism Portal. "United Liberation Front of Asom (ULFA)—Terrorist Group of Assam." < http://www.satp.org/satporgtp/countries/india/states/assam/terrorist_outfits/ulfa.htm > (accessed October 1, 2005).

Southern Poverty Law Center. "A Soldier's Ransom." < http://www.splcenter.org/intel/intelreport/article.jsp?aid = 71&printable = 1 > (accessed October 17, 2005).

Southern Poverty Law Center. "Active U.S. Hate Groups in 2004." < http://www.splcenter.org/intel/map/hate.jsp?T = 22&m = 3 > (accessed September 28, 2005).

Southern Poverty Law Center. "Anti-Abortion Violence: Two Decades of Arson, Bombs, and Murder." < http://www.splcenter.org/intel/intelreport/article.jsp?aid = 411 > (accessed October 21, 2005).

Southern Poverty Law Center. "Anti-Semitism: 'Patriot' Publications Taking on Anti-Semitic Edge." < http://www.splcenter.org/intel/intelreport/article.jsp?aid = 68 > (accessed October 1, 2005).

Southern Poverty Law Center. "Appeasing the Beast." < http://www.splcenter.org/intel/intelreport/article.jsp?aid = 66 > (accessed September 25, 2005).

Southern Poverty Law Center. "False Patriots." < http://www.splcenter.org/intel/intelreport/article.jsp?pid = 366 > (accessed October 18, 2005).

Southern Poverty Law Center. "Hate and Hypocrisy: What Is Behind the Rare-but-recurring Phenomenon of Jewish Anti-Semites?" < http://www.splcenter.org/intel/intelreport/article.jsp?aid = 73 > (accessed October 21, 2005).

Southern Poverty Law Center. "Hate Group Numbers Slightly Up in 2004." < http://www.splcenter.org/center/splcreport/article.jsp?aid = 135 > (accessed October 1, 2005).

Southern Poverty Law Center. "Intelligence Report: Anti-Immigration Groups." < http://www.splcenter.org/intel/intelreport/article.jsp?sid = 175 > (accessed September 24, 2005).

Southern Poverty Law Center. "Return of the Pastor." < http://www.splcenter.org/intel/intelreport/article.jsp?aid = 507&printable = 1 > (accessed October 17, 2005).

Southern Poverty Law Center. "Sharks in the Mainstream." < http://www.splcenter.org/intel/intelreport/article.jsp?aid = 360 > (accessed October 23, 2005).

Southern Poverty Law Center. "Street Fighter: An Anti-racist Organizer's View of Skinheads." < http://www.splcenter.org/intel/intelreport/article.jsp?aid = 397 > (accessed October 3, 2005).

Southern Poverty Law Center. "The Neo-Confederates." < http://www.splcenter.org/intel/intelreport/article.jsp?pid = 461 > (accessed October 23, 2005).

Southern Poverty Law Center. "The Other Half: Interview with Sociologist Kathleen M. Blee." < http://www.splcenter.org/intel/intelreport/article.jsp?aid = 134 > (accessed October 1, 2005).

Southern Poverty Law Center. "Two Faces of Volksfront: A Growing and Increasingly Important Neo-Nazi Group Claims It Opposes Any Kind of Political Violence. Could It Be True?" < http://www.splcenter.org/intel/intelreport/article.jsp?aid = 475 > (accessed October 3, 2005).

Spartacus Educational. "Nazi Party (NSDAP)" < http://www.spartacus.schoolnet.co.uk/GERnazi.htm > (assessed October 20, 2005).

Steven Alan Hassan's Freedom of Mind Center. "About Kerry Noble." < http://www.freedomofmind.com/resourcecenter/articles/noble.htm > (accessed October 3, 2005).

Suzanne Kelly, Time Interactive, CNN.com. "Ocalan Trial Casts Light on Turkey's Human Rights Record." < http://cnn.com/SPECIALS/1999/ocalan/stories/turkey.human.rights/ > (accessed October 20, 2005).

Tamil Tigers. "Southern Journalists on Goodwill Mission to Trincomalee." < http://www.tamilnet.com > (accessed October 10, 2005).

Terrorism Knowledge Base. "Kumpulan Mujahidin Malaysia." < http://www.tkb.org/Group.jsp?groupID = 4401 > (accessed October 11, 2005).

The Anti-Defamation League. "Fighting Anti-Semitism, Bigotry and Extremism." < http://www.adl.org/ > (accessed October 13, 2005).

The Anti-Defamation League. "Institute for Historical Review (IHR): Outlet for Denial Propaganda" < http://www.adl.org/holocaust/ihr.asp > (accessed October 15, 2005).

The Anti-Defamation League. "Neo-Nazi Hate Music, A Guide." < http://www.adl.org/main_Extremism/hate_music_in_the_21st_century.htm?Multi_page_sections = sHeading_1 > (accessed September 26, 2005).

The Avalon Project, Yale University. "Program of the National Socialist German Workers' Party." < http://www.yale.edu/lawweb/avalon/imt/nsdappro.htm > (assessed October 20, 2005).

The Bethune Institute for Anti-Fascist Studies. "Aryan Nations: Christian Identity and Fascist Terror." < http://bethuneinstitute.org/documents/cift.html > (accessed October 17, 2005).

The Center for Consumer Freedom. "GRRR ... PETA Pitches Violence to Kids." < http://www. consumerfreedom.com/news_detail.cfm/headline/1904 > (accessed October 19, 2005).

The Dr. Huey P. Newton Foundation. "There is No New Black Panther Party: An Open Letter from the Dr. Huey P. Newton Foundation." < http://www.blackpanther.org/newsalert.htm > (accessed October 18, 2005).

The Fox News Channel. "FBI: Radical-activist Groups Are Major Threat." < http://www.foxnews.com/printer_friendly_story/0,3566,161825,00.html > (accessed October 21, 2005).

The Guardian. "Breton Separatists on Trial for Attacks." < http://www.guardian.co.uk/france/story/o.html > (accessed July 20, 2005).

The Guardian. "Ulster Braced for Week of Orange Unrest." < http://www.guardian.co.uk/uk_news/story/0,,339130,00.html > (accessed October 19, 2005).

The High North News. "Sea Shepherd Conservation Society." < http://www.highnorth.no/Library/Movements/Sea_Shepherd/st-se-sh.htm > (accessed September 30, 2005).

The Institute of Cetacean Research. "Sea Shepherd's Violent History." < http://www.icrwhale.org/eng/history.pdf > (accessed September 30, 2005).

The Jamestown Foundation. "The Libyan Islamic Fighting Group (LIFG)." < http://www.jamestown.org/publications_details.php?volume_id = 411&issue_

id = 3275&article_id = 2369477 > (accessed October 18, 2005).

The Jerusalem Quarterly. "Gush Emunim; The Tip of the Iceberg." < http://www.geocities.com/alabasters_archive/gush_iceberg.html > (accessed October 18, 2005).

The Mackenzie Institute. "Babbar Khalsa Banned at Last." < http://www.mackenzieinstitute.com/2003/terror060403.htm > (accessed October 11, 2005).

The Manila Times Internet Edition SPECIAL REPORT. "Struggle Continues for Rebels." < http://www.manilatimes.net/others/special/2003/dec/26/20031226 spe1.html > (accessed September 15, 2005).

The Media Monitors Network. "Gush Emunim; The Twilight of Zionism?" < http://www.mediamonitors.net/cantarow1.html > (accessed October 18, 2005).

The Middle East Forum. "Tablighi Jamaat: Jihad's Stealthy Legions." < http://www.meforum.org/article/686 > (accessed October 20, 2005).

The National Post. "Al-Qaeda Targets Gaddafi." < http://209.157.64.200/focus/f-news/1046103/posts > (accessed October 18, 2005).

The Nizkor Project. "Paranoia as Patriotism: Far-Right Influences on the Militia Movement. Covenant, Sword, and Arm of the Lord." < http://www.nizkor.org/hweb/orgs/american/adl/paranoia-as-patriotism/covenant.html > (accessed October 3, 2005).

The Ontario Institute for Studies in Education of the University of Toronto (OISE/UT). "History of Education: Selected Moments of the 20th Century." < http://fcis.oise.utoronto.ca/~daniel_schugurensky/assignment1/1994stretz.html > (accessed September 24, 2005).

The Open University, British Broadcasting Corporation (BBC). "Adolf Hitler Timeline." < http://www.open2.net/oulecture2005/hitler_timeline.html > (assessed October 20, 2005).

The Pittsburgh Channel. "Group Claims Credit For Irvine, Pa., Lab Fire; < http://www.thepittsburgh channel.com/team4/1775308/detail.html > (accessed October 21, 2005).

The Somaliland Times. "Terrorists Use Somalia As Hub." < http://www.somalilandtimes.net/2003/63/6304.htm > (accessed September 21, 2005).

The Southern Poverty Law Center. "Intelligence Project; Monitoring Hate and Extremist Activity." < http://www.splcenter.org/intel/intpro.jsp > (accessed September 25, 2005).

The Spokesman-Review.com. "Our Cops Doing a Lot More Than Just Wingin' It." < http://www. spokes manreview.com/news-story.asp?date = 011204&ID = s1470404 > (accessed September 28, 2005).

The Spokesman-Review.com. "Pischner Up against White Supremacist Foe." < http://www.spokesmanreview.com/pf.asp?date = 102100&ID = s868919 > (July 31, 2005).

The St. Petersburg Times. "Ban on National Bolshevik Party Overturned by Court." < http://www.sptimes.ru/story/483 > (accessed October 15, 2005).

The Time 100 (The Most Important People of the Century), Time, Inc. "Adolf Hitler." < http://www.time.com/time/time100/leaders/profile/hitler.htm > (assessed October 20, 2005).

The Tribune. "Organisation Had Links with Laden." < http://www.tribuneindia.com/2001/20010929/main2.htm > (accessed October 21, 2005).

The Turkish Times. "PKK and DHKP-C in U.S. Terrorism Report." < http://www.theturkishtimes.com/archive/02/06_01/ > (accessed October 19, 2005).

The Turkish Times. "Shaping a Common Security Agenda for Southeast Europe: New Approaches and Shared Responsibilities." < http://www.anticorruption.bg/eng/news/artShow.php?id = 1112 > (accessed October 19, 2005).

The U.S. Embassy at Manila. "U.S., Philippine Presidents Announce Boost to Bilateral Ties." < http://usembassy.state.gov/posts/rp1/wwwhr006.html > (accessed September 14, 2005).

The University of Arizona Press "Coyotes and Town Dogs: Earth First! and the Environmental Movement." < http://www.uapress.arizona.edu/books/bid1417.htm > (accessed September 29, 2005).

Thomas Sanction, Time.com. "A Terrorist's Bitter End." < http://www.time.com/time/daily/special/ocalan/bitterend.html > (accessed October 20, 2005).

Time Magazine Europe. "From Quaint to Bloodthirsty." < http://www.time.com/time/Europe/magazine/2000.0501/burgerbomb.html > (accessed July 20, 2005).

Time Magazine. "Habash: 'Israel Will Fall.'" < http://www.time.com/time/archive/preview/0,10987,945844,00.html > (accessed October 19, 2005).

Time.com. "All You Need Is Hate: White-power Music Is Thriving Abroad—And Also in the U.S." < http://www.time.com/time/musicgoesglobal/na/mnoise.html > (accessed October 15, 2005).

Time.com. "Loathing Abe Lincoln." < http://www.time.com/time/nation/article/0,8599,1077193,00.html > (accessed October 18, 2005).

Time.com. "Primer: The Taliban and Afghanistan." < http://www.time.com/time/nation/article/0,8599,175372,00.html > (accessed October 16, 2005).

Time: Asia. "Untangling the Web." < http://www.time.com/time/asia/news/magazine/0,9754,197713,00.html > (accessed October 11, 2005).

TimeAsia.com. "Asia's Own Osama." < http://www.time.com/time/asia/features/malay_terror/hambali.html > (accessed October 14, 2005).

Tribung Pinoy. "A Brief History of the Philippines from a Filipino Perspective." < http://www.tribo.org/history/history3.html > (accessed October 21, 2005).

Truth and Reconciliation Commission (in Spanish). "Final Report." < http://www.cverdad.org.pe/ifinal/index. php > (accessed October 4, 2005).

U.S. Court of Appeals for the Ninth Circuit. "Planned Parenthood of the Columbia/Willamette Inc. v American Coalition of Life Activists (2002 decision)." < http://www.ca9.uscourts.gov/ca9/newopinions.nsf/ 0F569EF00290007188256BC0005876E6/$file/9935320 ebcorrected.pdf?openelement > (accessed October 21, 2005).

U.S. Court of Appeals, Third Circuit. "U.S. v. Wickstrom, 893 F.2d 30 (3d Cir. 1989)." < http://www. cs.cmu.edu/afs/cs.cmu.edu/user/wbardwel/public/ nfalist/us_v_wickstrom.txt > (accessed October 17, 2005).

U.S. Department of Justice. "Eight Montana Skinheads Sentenced for Civil Rights Crimes." < http://www. usdoj.gov/opa/pr/2002/March/02_crt_114.htm > (accessed October 4, 2005).

U.S. Department of State. "Country Reports on Terrorism, 2004." < http://library.nps.navy.mil/home/ tgp/mek.htm > (accessed October 14, 2005).

U.S. Department of State. "Patterns of Global Terrorism, 2003, April 2004." < http://www.state.gov/documents/ organization/31947.pdf > (accessed October 11, 2005).

U.S. Department of State. "Remarks Secretary of State Condoleezza Rice To the National Conference of Editorial Writers." < http://www.ncew.org/member_ services/State%20Department%20Briefing/C%20 Rices%20Comments.pdf > (accessed October 4, 2005).

U.S. State Department. "Patterns of Global Terrorism." < http://www.state.gov/s/ct/rls/pgtrpt/2003/31638. htm > (accessed October 15, 2005).

U.S. State Department. "Patterns of Global Terrorism." < http://www.state.gov/s/ct/rls/pgtrpt/2003/31638. htm > (accessed October 16, 2005).

UMN.edu. "The Earth Liberation Front and Environmental Terrorism." < http://www.is.wayne.edu/ mrichmon/earth_liberation_front.htm > (accessed October 21, 2005).

United Nations. "Conflict Diamonds: Sanctions and War." < http://www.un.org/peace/africa/Diamond. html > (accessed October 3, 2005).

University of Wisconsin at Madison. "Tom Metzger and WAR." < http://slisweb.lis.wisc.edu/~jcherney/osmond. html > (accessed October 17, 2005).

US Memorial to Beirut Dead. "History: U.S. Embassy Bombing." < http://www.beirut—memorial.org/history/ embassy.html > (accessed October 13, 2005).

Uterecht University. "Genealogies of Islamic Radicalism in Post-Suharto Indonesia." < http://www.let.uu. nl/~martin.vanbruinessen/personal/publications/ genealogies_islamic_radicalism.htm > (accessed October 14, 2005).

Glossary

A COMPENDIUM OF ACRONYMS
AND TERMS FOUND IN THIS BOOK

A

17 November Organization: Revolutionary Organization 17 November (17 November).

AAIA: Aden-Abyan Islamic Army (AAIA).

ABB: Alex Boncayao Brigade (ABB).

ADF: Allied Democratic Forces (ADF).

Agent provocateur: An operative or agent who infiltrates a group or organization with the purpose of inciting its members to self-destructive acts.

AIAI: Al-Ittihad al-Islami (AIAI).

AIIB: Anti-Imperialist International Brigade (AIIB).

Air marshal: United States air marshals are the first police force of the federal government created solely to protect against air terrorism.

Aleph: Aum Supreme Truth (Aum) Aum Shinrikyo, Aleph.

ALIR: Army for the Liberation of Rwanda (ALIR).

Al-Qaeda: Responsible for the September 11, 2001, terrorist attacks upon the United States, Al-Qaeda (also known as Al-Qaida) was established by Osama bin Ladin (also spelled Usama Bin Ladin or Osama bin Laden) in the late 1980s to bring together Arabs who fought in Afghanistan against the Soviet Union. Al-Qaeda helped finance, recruit, transport, and train Sunni Islamic extremists for the Afghan resistance. Al-Qaeda's current goal is to establish a pan-Islamic Caliphate throughout the world and has declared the United States to be an enemy to be attacked by terrorist actions.

ANSIR: FBI Awareness of National Security Issues and Response Program.

Anthrax: Anthrax refers to a disease that is caused by the bacterium *Bacillus anthracis*. The bacterium can enter the body via a wound in the skin (cutaneous anthrax), via contaminated food or liquid (gastrointestinal anthrax), or can be inhaled (inhalation anthrax). Potentially fatal, anthrax has been developed for use as a biological weapon.

APF: Alliance of Palestinian Forces (APF).

Aryan: As used by white supremacist groups, the term Aryan refers to whites of Northern European descent who are supposedly a superior "master race."

ASG: Abu Sayyaf Group (ASG).

Assassination: A sudden, usually unexpected act of murder committed for impersonal reasons, typically with a political or military leader as its target.

Asset: Agents, sympathizers, or supporters that intelligence agencies can exploit to complete mission objectives.

ATF: In accordance with the Homeland Security Act of 2002, on January 24, 2003, the Bureau of Alcohol, Tobacco, and Firearms (ATF or BATF) was transferred from the Department of the Treasury to the Department of Justice. There it became the Bureau of Alcohol, Tobacco, Firearms, and Explosives, but retained the initials ATF.

AUC: United Self-Defense Forces/Group of Colombia (AUC).

Aum Shinrikyo, Aleph: Aum Supreme Truth (Aum) Aum Shinrikyo, Aleph.

B

Bacillus anthracis: The bacterium that causes anthrax.

Ballistic fingerprint: A ballistic fingerprint is the unique pattern of markings left by a specific firearm on ammunition as it is discharged.

Barrel (of oil): The traditional unit of measure by which crude oil is bought and sold on the world market. One barrel of oil is equivalent to 159 liters (42 U.S. gallons).

BCIS: U.S. Department of Homeland Security, Bureau of Citizenship and Immigration Services.

Biocontainment laboratories: A biocontainment laboratory is a laboratory that has been designed to lessen or completely prevent the escape of microorganisms.

Biodetectors: Biodetectors are analytical devices that combine the precision and selectivity of biological systems with the processing power of microelectronics.

Biological warfare: As defined by The United Nations, the use of any living organism (e.g. bacterium, virus) or an infective component (e.g., toxin), to cause disease or death in humans, animals, or plants. In contrast to bioterrorism, biological warfare is defined as the "state-sanctioned" use of biological weapons on an opposing military force or civilian population. Biological weapons include pathogenic viruses, bacteria, and biological toxins.

Biological weaponization: Putting a pathogen in a form or suspension to make it an effective military weapon.

Biometrics: An automated technique measuring physical characteristics (such as fingerprints, hand geometry, iris, retina, or facial features) of an individual for the purpose of identification or authentication of that individual.

Bioterrorism: Bioterrorism is the use of a biological weapon against a civilian or military population by a government, organization, or individual. As with any form of terrorism, its purposes include the undermining of morale, creating chaos, or achieving political goals. Biological weapons use microorganisms and toxins to produce disease and death in humans, livestock, and crops.

Black September: aka/see: Abu Nidal organization (ANO).

Blackmail: The threat to expose an individual's illegal or immoral acts if the individual does not comply with specific demands.

Bomb-grade nuclear materials: Uranium or plutonium that has been refined to the point that it can be used as fuel for a nuclear weapon.

Botulinum toxin: Botulinum toxin is among the most poisonous substances known. The toxin, which can be ingested or inhaled, disrupts transmission of nerve impulses to muscles. It is naturally produced by the bacterium *Clostridium botulinum*. Certain strains of *C. baratii* and *C. butyricum* can also be capable of producing the toxin. Botulinum toxin can be used as a biological weapon.

Brainwashing: An attempt to tear down an individual's former beliefs and replace them with new ones through an intense psychological and sometimes physical process.

C

CDC: CDC is an acronym for Centers for Disease Control and Prevention. Headquartered in Atlanta, Georgia, the CDC is one of the foremost public health institutions in the United States and in the world. The CDC serves United States national security by monitoring the incidence of infectious disease in the U.S. (and around the world), and through the development and implementation of disease control procedures.

CDIS: Counter Drug Intelligence System.

Cell: Most fundamental or basic unit of a network (e.g. terrorist network).

CFF: Cambodian Freedom Fighters (CFF).

Chemical warfare: Chemical warfare involves the aggressive use of bulk chemicals that cause death or grave injury. These chemicals are different from the lethal chemical compounds that are part of infectious bacteria or viruses.

Chlorine gas: Lung irritant generally mixed with phosgene when used as a chemical weapon.

CIA: United States Central Intelligence Agency.

CIRA: Continuity Irish Republican Army (CIRA).

CNC: Crime and Narcotics Center [CNC], United States.

Cold War: The Cold War was an ideological, political, economic, and military conflict primarily between the United States, United Kingdom and Western allies against the Union of Soviet Socialist Republics (U.S.S.R.) and Soviet dominated Eastern bloc nations that began in the aftermath of World War II and ended in 1989. From the outset, the Cold War was inextricably linked with the development of the atomic bomb and its use as military deterrent.

Counterintelligence: In the context of national security, the process of protecting national assets and secrets from covert threats, especially enemy spying.

D

DEA: Drug Enforcement Administration.

DHKP: Revolutionary People's Liberation Party/Front (DHKP/C).

Dirty Bomb: A conventional bomb packed with usually low-level radioactive debris. It cannot cause a massive nuclear chain reaction and explosion, but the conventional explosives in the bomb can spread the waste over a wide area, contaminating it.

DNA: Deoxyribonucleic Acid. The molecular composition of genetic material that is, in part, made up of nitrogenous bases that form a genetic code.

DNA fingerprinting: DNA fingerprinting is the term applied to a range of techniques that are used to show similarities and dissimilarities between the DNA present in different individuals.

DNA profile: Evaluation of an individual's DNA to establish a unique pattern of markers that can be used for identification purposes.

E

E-bomb: An e-bomb, or electronic bomb, is a non-explosive artillery shell or missile that sends out an electromagnetic pulse (EMP) of enormous power, capable of permanently disabling mechanical and electronic systems.

ELA: Revolutionary People's Struggle (ELA).

Electromagnetic pulse (EMP): A short burst of high-intensity electromagnetic energy (such as radio waves). An EMP can induce electrical currents in metal objects and damage or destroy electrical or electronic equipment, including computers, radios, and electrical grids.

ELN: National Liberation Army (ELN)-Colombia.

ETA: Basque Fatherland and Liberty (ETA).

EU: European Union.

EURATOM: European Atomic Energy Community.

Executive order: A guideline issued by the President of the United States, directed toward a particular issue, and possessing the status of a de facto law. Unlike presidential directives, executive orders are unclassified.

F

FARC: Revolutionary Armed Forces of Colombia (FARC).

Fatwa: A legal opinion or ruling issued by an Islamic scholar.

FBI: United States Federal Bureau of Investigation.

FBIS: CIA, Foreign Broadcast Information Service.

Fingerprints: Fingerprints are the patterns on the inside and the tips of fingers. The ridges of skin, also known as friction ridges, together with the valleys between them form unique patterns on the fingers. Fingerprint analysis is a biometric technique comparing scanned image of prints with a database of fingerprints.

FOIA: Freedom of Information Act. Sometimes known as the Freedom of Information-

Privacy Acts, a term referring to 1967 (FOIA) and 1974 (Privacy Act) statutes and their amendments, which greatly restrict government agencies' authority to collect information on individuals, and to withhold that information.

Forensic science: Forensic science is a multidisciplinary subject used for examining crime scenes and gathering evidence to be used in prosecution of offenders in a court of law. Forensic science techniques are also used to examine compliance with international agreements regarding weapons of mass destruction.

G

GAO: United States General Accounting Office.

GIA: Armed Islamic Group (GIA).

Globalization: The integration of economies and markets worldwide.

GRAPO: First of October Antifascist Resistance Group (GRAPO).

GSPC: Salafist Group for Call and Combat (GSPC).

GSS: Israeli General Security Service.

Guerilla warfare: In the modern era, guerilla warfare refers to armed resistance by paramilitary or irregular groups toward an occupying force. Guerilla warfare also describes a set of tactics employed by smaller forces against larger, better equipped, and better supplied forces.

H

Habeas Corpus: U.S. Constitutional right to avoid unlawful detention or imprisonment. Taken from the Latin phrase "You have the body."

Hacktivism: The use of computer hacking in the service of political activism.

HAMAS: Islamic Resistance Movement (HAMAS).

High-altitude electromagnetic pulse: Any nuclear explosion 25 miles (40 km) or higher above the ground produces a high-altitude electromagnetic pulse (HEMP), a short-lived, overlapping series of intense radio waves that blanket a large swath of ground. These radio waves can induce electrical currents in metallic objects and so cause damage to electrical and electronic equipment, including electrical power grids, telephone networks, radios, and computers.

HUJI: Harakat ul-Jihad-I-Islami (HUJI).

HUJI-B: Harakat ul-Jihad-I-Islami/Bangladesh (HUJI-B).

HUM: Harakat ul-Mujahidin (HUM) (Movement of Holy Warriors).

I

IAA: Islamic Army of Aden (IAA).

IAEA: International Atomic Energy Agency.

IBIS: The Interagency Border Inspection System (IBIS) is a database of names and other identifying information used to deter and append suspects—including suspected terrorists—as they attempt to pass through international border crossing checkpoints.

Identity theft: An identity thief typically may obtain access to a victim's social security number, driver's license information, bank account numbers, credit card numbers, etc. with the intent to opens accounts in the victim's name and make purchases or perform other transactions.

IG: Al-Gama'a al-Islamiyya (Islamic Group, IG).

Illegal immigrant: Someone who has entered into a country illegally.

IMF: International Monetary Fund.

IMU: Islamic Movement of Uzbekistan (IMU).

Infectious diseases: Infectious diseases are those diseases that are caused by microorganisms such as bacteria and viruses, many of which are spread from person to person. An intermittent host, or vector, aids the spread of some infectious diseases.

INL: International Narcotics and Law Enforcement Affairs (INL), United States Bureau for.

INS: As of March 1, 2003, the newly created United States Department of Homeland Security (DHS) absorbed the former Immigration and Naturalization Service (INS). All INS border patrol agents and investigators—along with agents from the U.S. Customs Service and Transportation Security Administration—were placed under the direction of the DHS Directorate of Border and Transportation Security (BTS). Responsibility for U.S. border security and the enforcement of immigration laws was transferred to BTS. Former INS immigration service functions are scheduled to be placed under the direction of the DHS Bureau of Citizenship and Immigration Services. Under the DHS reorganization plan, the INS formally ceases to exist on the date the last of its functions are transferred.

Intelligence: In the context of national security, information about the enemy or potential enemies. Also the act of gathering such information, through spying and other means.

Intelligence Community (IC): The group of U.S. government agencies that are collectively responsible for intelligence activities, including the CIA, NSA, FBI, military intelligence branches, and other federal government agencies.

INTERPOL: International Criminal Police Organization.

Intifada: Literally, "shaking off," a term applied to the Palestinian uprising against Israel's occupation of the West Bank and Gaza.

IRA: Irish Republican Army (IRA).

Isotope: A form of a chemical element distinguished by the number of neutrons in its nucleus. E.g., ^{233}U and ^{235}U are two isotopes of uranium; both have 92 protons, but ^{233}U has 141 neutrons and ^{235}U has 143 neutrons.

IT: Information technology, a term that encompasses computers and related materials, machines, and processes.

IW (Indications and warnings): Intelligence that relates to time-sensitive information involving potential threats.

J

JEM: Jaish-e-Mohammed (JEM) (Army of Mohammed).

JI: Jemaah Islamiya (JI).

Jihad: In Islam: A holy struggle or war.

JUI-F: Jamiat Ulema-I-Islam Fazlur Rehman faction (JUI-F).

L

LRA: Lord's Resistance Army (LRA).

LT: Lashkar-e-Tayyiba (LT) (Army of the Righteous).

LTTE: Liberation Tigers of Tamil Eelam (LTTE).

LVF: Loyalist Volunteer Force (LVF).

M

MKO: Mujahedin-e Khalq Organization (MKO).

Money laundering: Disguising the origins of money by transferring it through other organizations. Money laundering usually involves taking money gained through criminal activity and passing it through the hands of one or more legitimate businesses so it will then appear to have been generated legally.

MRTA: Tupac Amaru Revolutionary Movement (MRTA).

N

NACIC: National Counter Intelligence Center.

NALU: National Army for the Liberation of Uganda (NALU).

Narcoterrorism: Terrorism undertaken by groups directly or indirectly involved in producing, transporting, or distributing illegal drugs.

NCR: National Council of Resistance (NCR).

Network: A group of individuals or cells (subgroups) engaged in specific operations (e.g., espionage or terrorist operations).

NLA: The National Liberation Army of Iran (NLA).

NPA: New People's Army (NPA).

NSA: The United States National Security Agency. The NSA is the leading cryptologic organization in the United States intelligence community, responsible for code-making, code-breaking, and monitoring communications systems.

NTA: Anti-Imperialist Territorial Nuclei (NTA).

Nuclear weapons: Nuclear weapons are devices that utilize the processes of nuclear fission and/or fusion to release nuclear energy in the form of a very powerful explosion.

O

OPEC: Organization of Petroleum Exporting Countries, a cartel (group) of oil-producing nations that controls much of the world's petroleum production.

OV: Orange Volunteers (OV).

P

PAGAD: People Against Gangsterism and Drugs (PAGAD).

PATRIOT Act: The Patriot Act, or Uniting and Strengthening America by Providing Appropriate Tools Required to Intercept and Obstruct Terrorism Act (Public Law 107-56), was signed into law on October 26, 2001, in the wake of terrorist attacks on the World Trade Center and Pentagon. The law grants law enforcement and intelligence agencies more power to detain and question suspects for longer periods of time, and increases their ability to conduct surveillance operations.

PFLP: Popular Front for the Liberation of Palestine (PFLP).

PFLP-GC: Popular Front for the Liberation of Palestine-General Command (PFLP-GC).

PIJ: Palestine Islamic Jihad (PIJ).

PIRA: Provisional Irish Republican Army (PIRA).

PLO: Palestine Liberation Organization (PLO).

PKK: Kurdistan Workers' Party (PKK).

PLF: Palestine Liberation Front (PLF).

PMOI: People's Mujahidin of Iran (PMOI).

POG: Hizballah (Party of God).

Profiling: The process of developing descriptions of the traits and characteristics of unknown offenders in specific criminal cases. Also, targeting someone for particular attention because they bear a resemblance ("fit the profile"), real or imagined, of a criminal or terrorist. For example, giving special scrutiny to people who appear to be of Middle Eastern background.

Propaganda: Propaganda is a form of communication that attempts to influence the behavior of people by affecting their perceptions, attitudes and opinions.

R

Ricin: Ricin is a highly toxic protein that is derived from the bean of the castor plant (*Ricinus communis*). The toxin causes cell death by inactivating ribosomes, which are responsible for protein synthesis. Ricin can be produced in a liquid, crystal or powdered forms and it can be inhaled, ingested, or injected. It causes fever, cough, weakness, abdominal pain, vomiting, diarrhea and dehydration and death. There is no cure for Ricin poisoning.

Ring: A group or network.

RIRA: Real IRA (RIRA).

RJO: Revolutionary Justice Organization.

RN: Revolutionary Nuclei.

RN group (Greece): Revolutionary Nuclei.

Rogue state: A nation that harbors terrorists and/or poses a serious security threat to its neighbors.

RPA: Revolutionary Proletarian Army (RPA).

RUF: Revolutionary United Front (RUF).

S

Sarin gas: Sarin gas (O-Isopropyl methylphosphonofluoridate), also called GB, is a dangerous and toxic chemical. It belongs to a class of chemical weapons known as nerve agents, all of which are organophosphates. The G nerve agents, including tabun, sarin and soman, are all extremely toxic, but not very persistent in the environment. Pure sarin is a colorless and odorless gas, is extremely volatile, and can spread quickly through the air.

Sendero Luminoso: Sendero Luminoso (Shining Path, or SL).

Shin Bet: The Israeli intelligence agency.

Shin Beth: Israeli counterintelligence service.

Shining Path: Sendero Luminoso (Shining Path, or SL).

SL: Sendero Luminoso (Shining Path, or SL).

Supreme truth: Aum Supreme Truth (Aum) Aum Shinrikyo, Aleph.

T–W

Terrorism: Terrorism is the systematic belief in the political, religious, or ideological efficacy of producing fear by attacking—or threatening to attack—unsuspecting or defenseless populations, usually civilians, and usually by surprise.

TIFG: Tunisian Islamic Fighting Group.

UDA/UVF: Ulster Defense Association/Ulster Freedom Fighters (UDA/UVF).

Vigilante: A private citizen who is acting to detect and/or punish violations of the law. These violations may be real or only perceived, and the tactics used by vigilantes may include violence, intimidation, and other tactics that are themselves illegal.

Virus: Viruses are essentially nonliving repositories of nucleic acid that require the presence of a living prokaryotic or eukaryotic cell for the replication of the nucleic acid. There are a number of different viruses that challenge the human immune system and that may produce disease in humans. In common, a virus is a small, infectious agent that consists of a core of genetic material (either deoxyribonucleic acid [DNA] or ribonucleic acid [RNA]) surrounded by a shell of protein.

VOA: Voice of America.

Weapons of mass destruction: Weapons of mass destruction are weapons that cause a high loss of life within a short time span. Nuclear, chemical, and biological weapons are classified as weapons of mass destruction.

Weapons-grade material: Weapon-grade (or "bomb-grade") uranium or plutonium is any alloy or oxide compound that contains enough of certain isotopes of these elements to serve as the active ingredient in a nuclear weapon.

White supremacy: The concept that people of European, especially northern European, descent are inherently superior to other peoples.

WHO: World Health Organization.

WMD: Weapons of mass destruction.

World Islamic Front for Jihad: A group absorbed by Al-Qaeda (also known as Al-Qaida).

Index

Page references appearing after "1:" are in volume 1. Page numbers after "2:" are in volume 2. Bold page numbers indicate an entry on the extremist group in question. Italicized page numbers indicate a reference to an illustration.

17 November Organization (17N), 1:**1–6**, *2*, 2:728, 729, 730

A

ABB (Alex Boncayao Brigade), 1:**94–98**, *95, 96*
Abbas, Abdul. *See* Abbas, Abu
Abbas, Abu, 2:615–19, 641
Abbas, Mahmoud, 1:44–45, 297, 2:609, 613
Abbas, Mohammed. *See* Abbas, Abu
Abbas al-Musawi, Sayyid, 1:358
ABC (Aryan Beginnings for Children), 2:895
Abdel Rahman, Omar, 1:50–51, 56, *56*, 59, 61
Abdelaziz, Abbi, 2:744
Abdelouadoud, Abu Mossab, 2:742
Abdennabi, Khaled, 1:384, 385, 386, 2:514, 516, 517
Abductions. *See* Kidnappings
Abdul-Al, Abdul-Salam, 1:78–79
Able Danger counterterrorism unit, 1:88
Abortion protest groups. *See* Pro-life groups

Abou Abderrahmane Amine. *See* Zitouni, Djamel
Abrahamiam, Ervand, 2:524
Abrahams, Moeneeb, 2:627
Absentionism from Irish parliament, 1:250, 377
Abu Nidal, 1:7–14, 2:611
Abu Nidal Organization (ANO), 1:**7–14**, 2:641, 645
  airport attacks, 1:*8, 11*
  Fatah and, 1:295
  Munich victims, 1:*10*
  training camp, 1:*9*
Abu Sayyaf Group (ASG), 1:**15–23**
  bodies of victims, 1:*16, 18*
  Harakat ul-Mujahidin and, 1:352
  members, 1:*19*
  wanted poster, 1:*17*
Achille Lauro cruise ship hijacking, 2:614, 616, 617, 618
Achilles, Leonard, 2:627
Acholi peoples, 2:483, 484, 486
Acid attacks, 2:838
ACLA (American Coalition of Life Activists), 1:**108–14**, 2:696, 797–98
ACLU (American Civil Liberties Union), 2:507
  Ku Klux Klan and, 1:450
  neo-Nazi defenders, 2:565
  Posse Comitatus rights supporter, 2:658
Action Directe (AD), 1:372, 2:676
Actionaid, 1:102
ActivistCash.com web site, 1:273
AD. *See* Action Directe

Adair, Johnny "Mad Dog," 1:239, 2:493, 843, 844, 845, 846
Adams, Gerry, 1:252, 377, 379, 380, 2:663–64, 667, 668, 844
Adams, Samuel, 2:788, 789, 790
Aden Islamic Army. *See* Muhammed's Army
ADF (Allied Democratic Forces), 1:**99–103**
Admiral Duncan pub bombing, 1:*238*, 239
Adolat, 1:389, 390, 391
Advani, L.K., 1:398, 399
Advocates for Life Ministries, 1:110, 2:691
AFDL (Alliance of Democratic Forces for the Liberation of Zaire), 1:161
Afghan Northern Alliance, 2:811, 823
Afghani, Sajjad, 1:340
Afghanistan
  Afghan Northern Alliance, 2:811, 823
  Al-Qaeda hideouts, 1:*87*
  Harakat ul-Jihad-I-Islami, 1:339–43, *340*
  Islamic Movement of Uzbekistan, 1:390
  Jaish-e-Mohammed, 1:395–96, 397, 399
  Jemaah Islamiyah, 1:409
  Taliban, 2:810–15
  U.S. attacks, 1:85
  See also Soviet Union-Afghanistan conflict

J

Ja'am Combattante Tunisienne. *See* Tunisian Combatant Group
Ja'Arie, Jihad, 1:42
Jabbar, Abdul, 1:399
Jabotinsky, Ze'ev, 1:416
Jackal, Carlos, 1:404
Jackson, Ed, 1:448
Jackson, Rev. Jesse, 2:531, 570
Jaehnig, Matthaus, 2:881
Jaish Adan al Islami. *See* Muhammed's Army
Jaish-e-Mohammed (JEM), 1:**394–400**, *395, 396*, 2:467, 474
    Al-Fuqra and, 1:52
    Harakat ul-Jihad-I-Islami and, 1:341, 399
    Harakat ul-Jihad-I-Islami/ Bangladesh and, 1:347
    Harakat ul-Mujahidin and, 1:352, 353, 395, 397, 399
    Lashkar-e-Tayyiba and, 2:472
    Sipah-e-Sahaba and, 2:778
Jamaat al Islamiya. *See* Al-Gama'a al-Islamiyya
Jama'at al-Nur, 1:184
Jamaat ud-Dawa. *See* Markaz-ud-Dawa-wal-Irshad (MDI)
Jamaat ul-Faqra. *See* Al-Fuqra
Jamaat ul-Furqaan (JUF), 1:396, 399
Jamaat ul-Mujahidin (JUM), 1:340
Jamaat-ul-Ulema-e-Islami, Fazlur Rehman faction (JUI-F)
    Harakat ul-Jihad-I-Islami and, 1:342
    Harakat ul-Mujahidin and, 1:352
    Jaish-e-Mohammed and, 1:399
Jamaat-ul-Ulema-e-Islami (JUI)
    Harakat ul-Jihad-I-Islami and, 1:339–40, 342
    Harakat ul-Mujahidin and, 1:352
    Jaish-e-Mohammed and, 1:397, 399
Jamat-e-Islam (JeL), 2:778
Jamat-Ulema-e-Islam, 2:778
James, Heather, 2:792–93, 794
Jameson, Richard, 2:491, 851
Jamiat al-Jihad, 1:383, 2:515
Jamiat Ansar-ul-Afghaneen, 1:341
Jamiat-ul-Ansar (JUA). *See* Harakat ul-Mujahidin
Jammu and Kashmir region. *See* Kashmir region
Janjalani, Abdurajak Abubakar, 1:16, 19, 20
Janjalani, Khadaffy Abubakar, 1:*19,* 20
Japan
    Aum Supreme Truth, 1:186–93
    Chukakuha, 1:230–33

Japanese Red Army, 1:401–7
Japanese Communist League, 1:401
Japanese Embassy hostages taking, Peru, 1996, 2:828, *829, 830,* 831–34
Japanese Red Army (JRA), 1:**401–7,** *402, 403,* 2:647
Jarboe, James F., 1:280
Jaysh Adan. *See* Muhammed's Army
Jaysh adan-Abiyan al-Islami. *See* Muhammed's Army
JBS (John Birch Society), 2:594, 596
    Klassen, Ben and, 2:899
    Metzger, Tom, and, 2:879
JDL. *See* Jewish Defense League
Jehadi activists, 2:466
Jeish-e-Mahammed. *See* Jaish-e-Mohammed
JeL (Jamat-e-Islam), 2:778
JEM. *See* Jaish-e-Mohammed
Jemaah Islamiyah (JI), 1:**408–14,** *409, 410,* 454, 455, 456
Jerusalem Warriors, 2:837
Jewish Defense League (JDL), 1:**415–21,** *416, 417, 418, 419*
    American Border Patrol and, 1:106
    Jewish Underground and, 1:427, 428, 430
    Kach and, 1:432, 434, 435
Jewish Direct Action, 1:427
Jewish Fighting Organization (Eyal), 1:**422–26,** *423, 424,* 427
Jewish Fighting Union, 1:427
Jewish settlements. *See* Israeli settlements
Jewish Underground, 1:**427–30,** *428, 429*
Jews, activism against. *See* Anti-Semitism
Jhangvi, Haq Nawaz, 1:398
Jhangvi, Maulana Haq Nawaz, 2:466, 775, 776, 777
JI. *See* Jemaah Islamiyah
JIB (Jihad Movement of Bangladesh), 1:346
Jibril, Ahmad, 2:614, 615, 639, 641, 642, 645
Jihad Group. *See* Al-Jihad
Jihad Movement of Bangladesh (JIB), 1:346
Jilani Hashemi, Sheikh Mubarik Ali. *See* Hashemi, Mubarik Ali Jilani
John Birch Society (JBS), 2:594, 596
    Klassen, Ben, and, 2:899
    Metzger, Tom, and, 2:879
Jonas, Kevin, 1:137, 2:795–96, 798
Jordan
    Al-Qaeda, 1:91

"Black September" incident of 1970, 1:294–95
    Fatah and, 1:291–93, 294
Jordan, Colin, 1:123
Journal of Historical Review, 1:364, 366
Journalist targets (Hezbollah), 1:357, 360–61
Joyu, Fumihiro, 1:190, 192
JRA. *See* Japanese Red Army
JUA (Jamiat-ul-Ansar). *See* Harakat ul-Mujahidin
Juan Carlos, King of Spain, 1:196, 198, 299
Juba, Charles, 2:903, 907
JUF (Jamaat ul-Furqaan), 1:396, 399
JUI. *See* Jamaat-ul-Ulema-e-Islami
JUI-F. *See* Jamaat-ul-Ulema-e-Islami, Fazlur Rehman faction
JUM (Jamaat ul-Mujahidin), 1:340
Jung, Rudolf, 2:555
Justus Ranch, 1:304–5, 307, 308

K

Kabanda, Abdullah Yusef, 1:100, 101
Kabanda, Rogers, 1:103
Kabbah, Alhaji Ahmad Tejan, 2:734, 735, 738
Kabila, Laurent, 1:161
Kach, 1:**431–36,** *433*
    hate graffiti, 1:*432*
    Jewish Defense League and, 1:417, 418, 420
Kachin Independence Army (KIA), 2:860
Kaddoumi, Farouk, 1:295
KADEK (Kurdistan Freedom and Democracy Congress). *See* Kurdistan Workers' Party
Kadirgamar, Lakshman, 2:818–19
Kagame, Paul, 1:161
Kahane, Binyamin, 1:434, 435
Kahane, Meir
    Jewish Defense League and, 1:415–16, 417, 418, *418,* 420, 421
    Jewish Underground and, 1:428, 430
    Kach and, 1:432, 433–34, 435, 436
    memorial, 1:*429*
Kahane Chai, 1:434
Kahane Movement, 1:435
Kahl, Gordon, 2:654, 655, 656
Kanther, Manfred, 1:316
Kanu, Abu, 2:733, 734, 738
Karameh refugee camp battle of 1968, 1:292–93
Karatas, Dursun, 2:702, 703, *703,* 706